Storage Management in Data Centers

Volker Herminghaus • Albrecht Scriba
Authors

Storage Management in Data Centers

Understanding, Exploiting, Tuning, and Troubleshooting Veritas Storage Foundation

Volker Herminghaus
Nieder-Olm
Germany
v.herminghaus@anykey-dcs.de

Dr. Albrecht Scriba
Mainz
Germany
albrecht@albrecht-scriba.de

ISBN   978-3-642-09867-3   e-ISBN   978-3-540-85023-6

DOI 10.1007/978-3-540-85023-6

Cover design: KuenkelLopka GmbH Heidelberg,

Printed on acid-free paper

springer.com

For my wife and children, who taught me what really counts.

Volker Herminghaus

Dedicated to my wife and children.

Dr. Albrecht Scriba

This book is designed to meet the needs of UNIX architects and administrators working in data centers. While it will be useful for the computer science student or the newcomer who has been attracted to volume management by Symantec's release of a free version of its Volume Manager software its focus is on the data center. Most data center applications nowadays handle amounts of data that had been unconceivable at the time when the most commonly used storage media - the hard disk - was developed. As a consequence, the design of the hard disk simply cannot match the requirements posed by current applications. Its physical attributes and limits need to be overcome by additional layers of hardware or software. These layers, if properly designed and thoughtfully applied, convert a set of physical disks to a supply of storage space whose properties better match application requirements. Instead of physical disks with their physical limitations, logical entities known as volumes are now commonly used. These volumes can be fault tolerant, accelerated to the limits, replicated to remote locations, and made almost infinitely large. Additionally, volumes can even be reshaped and their features changed while they are in use, enabling the data center administrator to adapt to changing requirements without suffering an application downtime.

The technical term for this is software or hardware layer is "volume management".

Veritas Volume Manager® is the most widely used software for volume management. It is used in data centers all over the world and has proven to be stable and deliver high performance under most circumstances. While there are other volume management software products on the market (e.g. AIX LVM, Sun microsystems' SunVM, or several Linux LVMs), most of them suffer from one or more limitations that hamper their widespread deployment. They are either limited to the manufacturer's operating system or they have less to offer than the Veritas product. In most cases, both is true at the same time. This has led to Veritas Volume Manager, or VxVM in short, being the most widely deployed product on the market, which in turn led to most administrators learning at least the basic skills required for its administration.

However, mastering the basic skills is something quite different from fully understanding a product and making full use of the available power. In data center operations it is imperative that the operators know precisely how things are supposed to work, rather than apply the skills of "experimental computer science". Even today's personal computers are too complex for any kind of experimental approach to solving a problem or finding a solution. This is much more true in data centers, where the motto must be: "If you do not know it, then learn it or leave it, but don't fumble it".

In my time as both an independent data center consultant and an independent trainer for the Veritas product suite I have tried to educate people enough so that they would at least realize what is possible if they could harness VxVM to its full extent. Staying in close contact with my clients, it dawned on me that what they need is a written guide they can rely on when they actually try some of the more advanced features. If you are responsible for a mission critical application then the last thing you want is to incur a downtime. And with only some diffuse background knowledge and elementary skills left over from the last VxVM training, most of you would rather stick to established procedures than try something new.

My first attempt at writing down what I knew was a training companion book called "Veritas Storage Foundation" published by Springer in 2006 (ISBN: 3-540-34610-4) and endorsed by Switzerland's biggest Symantec partner, Infoniqa SQL AG (www.sql.ch) as their official training material. This book had been written together with Albrecht Scriba, one of the most respected Veritas trainers in Europe. It covered Veritas Volume Manager (VxVM) and Veritas Cluster Server (VCS) and was received very well by the administrators. However, its drawback was that it was written in German, our native tongue, so its distribution was severely limited by the language barrier. Having been approached numerous times by international colleagues I decided to take the next step and write a new, English book that concentrates on VxVM and the Veritas File System (VxFS), again with Albrecht acting as the co-author for some of the toughest chapters. It is not a training companion like the first one but uses a more classical approach. There are many walkthroughs to make you understand what you can do, how you can do it and what exactly is going on inside VxVM and VxFS so you can understand it and repeat it step by step on your own systems. It also holds a large section on troubleshooting that points out how problems can be found and fixed.

So here is your guide that helps you understand - in detail - the principles and the problems of mass storage, volume management, and file systems and how to manage them. It also tries to correct some common misconceptions about storage and UNIX, and highlights the most limiting factors in today's data center environments: anachronistic thinking and the sluggish speed of light!

About the Authors

Volker Herminghaus

Born in the stone ages (1963) and raised in a family full of physicists, he studied mechanical engineering and computer science in Darmstadt, Germany. Took some really deep looks at the kernel of AT&T UNIX System V Release 3.2 for his thesis and has been claiming to know what he's talking about since then.

He started computing on a Commodore 64 and switched to Atari ST as it became available, then finally to NeXTSTEP. Deeply enamoured with its elegance and power he has since stuck to descendants of this operating system (MacOS X) for his own use. Professionally, he has been working on Solaris and other UNIX variants as a consultant since the early 1990s. He has just co-founded his second data center consulting company: the **anykey-dcs**.

Dr. Albrecht Scriba

Albrecht studied mathematics and religious science in Mainz until 1998 (including thesis and State doctorate). Being familiar with ancient languages like Aramaic as well as computer programming he hacked the Atari ST's Signum! program in assembler to optimize printing of those languages' fonts. Albrecht has long been working as a Consultant and as a Trainer for Veritas/Symantec. He left Symantec in 2008 and is now working for anykey-dcs, Symantec and other companies as a free lancer. Fallen in love with Unix since his very first encounter, his motto is: "Never type a command twice, write a program for it!"

ACKNOWLEDGEMENTS

A book like this is not created out of thin air. It takes a lot of work, energy, resources, and determination to keep going all the way to the publication. Many people have helped us finish this task and have thus contributed to the successful completion of this book. The first round of thanks goes to the contact persons at Springer: Hermann Engesser and Gabriele Fischer, for providing a perfect office into which to throw all the unstructured suggestions, ideas, questions, and draft versions of this book. But most of all, for saying "YES" before we could even finish our sentence asking if they would like to publish our second book. That immediate and unquestioning positive reply provided the motivation required to kick off the project.

The second round goes to our wives and kids, who always suffer most when fathers decide to dedicate the better part of two years to sitting down late at night hacking, experimenting, and writing.

The third round goes to all the people that gave us gems of background information on storage management: Of these, Ron Karr and particularly Oleg Kiselev, two of the inventors of Veritas Volume Manager and extremely smart people, provided the most insight into VxVM's design ideas and implementation as well as a broad overview about modern storage systems in general.

Sun Microsystems' benchmarking center in Langen, Germany, allowed us to access their powerful Sun servers tied to high-end storage in order to run a multitude of tests and simulations. Special thanks go to all involved at Sun for their efficient, competent and friendly support: Kirsten Prahst, Rüdiger Frenk (who also maintains the only complete Sun hardware museum in the world), and Peter Hausdorf.

A final round of thanks goes to the many hundreds of people who have participated in our trainings or been our consulting clients. They never failed to come up with new questions, setups or problems that kept our brains busy.

This book was edited in Adobe InDesign Creative Suite 3 on an Apple MacBook Pro running Mac OSX. All graphics were created with ease and great joy using OmniGraffle Professional.

ACKNOWLEDGMENTS

TABLE OF CONTENTS

CHAPTER 1: DISK AND STORAGE SYSTEM BASICS

by Volker Herminghaus

1.1 OVERVIEW

1.1.1 STORAGE HARDWARE SITUATION AND OUTLOOK

Disk media are the entities that all persistent user data is eventually stored on. Because the surface of a disk medium can be permanently magnetized, disks can store information across reboots and power failures, when data residing in the computer's internal volatile memory is lost. Disks can not be replaced by any amount of volatile memory. After all, where would you put all that data after a shutdown? But a transition is slowly getting under way: A few months before work on this book was begun, Apple Inc. released a notebook computer that did not have a disk drive but used flash memory instead. EMC, a vendor of mass storage systems, announced a storage array that used flash. These events marked the beginning of a trend away from moving macroscopic mechanical spindles for storing data - an incredibly arcane concept when compared to light-based fibre-channel communications and memory cells holding only a few dozen electrons per bit.

However, flash is still much more expensive than disk storage, and even with prices falling and some problematic properties of flash being alleviated, disk based storage systems will be here for a long time. They will eventually be found at the back end of the storage chain, similar to tape reels in the times of the old mainframe computers. Disk

V. Herminghaus and A. Sriba, *Storage Management in Data Centers,*
DOI: 10.1007/978-3-540-85023-6_1, © Springer-Verlag Berlin Heidelberg 2009

storage will still need to be managed, and volume management software will still do that job. Emphasis will likely be shifting from performance towards reliability, as more people become aware of the fact that with the amount of data processed today, data errors will be a frequent problem very soon. Error rates looked extremely low a few years ago, but when multi-terabyte databases are processed at high speed around the clock, the seemingly low probability for errors that slip through all error checking and prevention mechanisms soon turns to certainty.

Rock Bottom Basics of Hard Disks

You probably know most of this already, but a little walk-through still makes sense because a lot of the terminology introduced here will be used in later chapters. You can skip this if you are very familiar with the interior of hard disks.

A hard disk consists of one or more flat, round platters covered with magnetic material and fixed to a spindle rotating at around 5,000 to 15,000 rpm. At an extremely short distance (about 20nm or 1/30th the wavelength of visible light!) above the platters there are one or more arms ("actuators") moving perpendicular to the rotation if the disks. These arms carry (usually) one tiny solenoid called the read/write head that serves two purposes: When a current is sent through it, then it creates a magnetic field that permanently magnetizes the surface of the disk platter. This is called the write cycle. In the read cycle, no current is sent to the solenoid and the magnetic field rushing along below it induces a tiny current which is then caught by appropriate circuitry and ultimately converted to a binary value, 0 or 1. This bit is shifted into a register while the next bit is read. When a full byte is assembled, the byte is put into a buffer while the next byte is read and so on.

Current 1TB 3.25" disks have bit densities of more than 100 GBit per square inch.

Data on a disk is organized in blocks (also called sectors), and a sector or block is the smallest addressable entity in disk input/output (or I/O). That means that a disk will always transfer whole blocks to the host computer. The length of a block is usually 512 bytes, although some disks use 1024 byte blocks. Each block is protected by a checksum that is written behind its usable contents and is not accessible at the user level. Because of the layout of the disk data hard disks are so-called **"block addressed devices"**. I.e. it is not possible to directly change a certain byte or bit on a disk, but the whole sector must be read from the host, modified, and written back. This alone makes access to a disk very different from access to random access memory (RAM).

Furthermore disk data is organized into tracks (all sectors on a surface that are located at the same distance from the center) and cylinders (the same track each across all platters). Fortunately, both of these can be considered irrelevant today; they are mere remnants of past physical qualities and are merely emulated for backwards compatibility. A disk is now simply a device that can read and write blocks of data, linearly addressed by the block number.

From here on we will use the term **"extent"** to specify a stretch of magnetic storage that starts at a certain block number and is a given number of blocks long. It is the most convenient data structure when discussing block addressed devices.

1.1.2   Physical Limits

Whenever one has to deal with physical entities one has to deal with the limits of same. In contrast to objects of the virtual world, physical objects are rigid, inflexible, error-prone and generally undesirable. The purpose of a great amount of software in data centers is mostly to replace all physical objects with virtual counterparts, which can then be used instead of the physical entities. Physical disks are among the most limiting entities nowadays, because they are still dominated by mechanical access methods. This is extremely arcane in comparison to almost all other computer system's components, which are based on electrical or optical components.

Let us look at the limiting physical qualities of physical hard disks:

Performance

Imagine the mechanical overhead that a disk read or write incurs. First of all, the arm assembly carrying the read/write heads has to be moved to the correct cylinder and the correct read/write head is electronically selected. Moving the actuators takes several milliseconds, roughly between 1ms for a close track to 10ms for one that is far away. Next, it must settle on the track (i.e. stop vibrating from the sudden rapid movement). Then the disk electronics must wait for the appropriate sector to actually fly by under the read/write head. This takes, on average, half a disk rotation (the probability for the sector being "close" vs. being "far" is 50%).

Very clever algorithms in the disk's on board controller, like tagged command queuing and elevator sorting try to minimize the effects of the mechanical nature of the device, but after all there remains an average latency of about 5 ms even for very good disks. That means that on average, we can get no more than 200 independent operations per second to or from a disk device. Also, just for comparison, or a bit of data travelling inside a computer would have travelled 1000 km in the same time that the disk read/write moved those 5 mm!

Reliability

If a hard disk fails your data is likely lost forever. Occasionally you may only have a faulty on-board controller which you might replace but more likely the mechanical or magnetic parts have suffered damage. Basically, if you are using hard disks without some kind of redundancy layer on top of it, your only hope is a really good backup system.

Size and Performance per Size

Size is less of a problem now than it used to be, but no matter how many disks you have attached to your system, storing a file that is larger than your disks will simply fail. Now of course you can get Terabyte-sized hard disks, but they are still limited to around 200 I/Os per second. It is hard to imagine a TB in an enterprise database idling around at no more than 200 accesses per second While that sounds reasonable to the average home computer user, data centers handle thousands of users per server concurrently. The real performance measure we need is not size. It is not performance, as measured in transactions per second. It is performance per size! How many transactions per second can be done per GB of data-

3

base, is the question. A TB of data is never just sitting around except maybe as a database export file destined for a backup device. This kind of file is read and written sequentially so there is less of a bottleneck. But for general-purpose, especially for database volumes, the most important question is how many TX/s/GB can the volume deliver to the database. Due to the exponential increase in hard disk size, the ratio of performance per GigaByte has dropped to abysmal levels in recent years.

Flexibility

To put it shortly: disks are not flexible. You cannot change their size nor their speed nor their reliability. The only flexible thing about hard disks is the wire that attaches it to the computer.

Manageability

Managing a disk that is directly attached to a server means physically going there and plugging or unplugging it from the server or power supply. No remote management is usually possible.

MOORE'S LAW AND THE PROBLEM WITH MECHANICS

Hard disks became anachronistic in the 1980's when computers started outpacing disks by a bigger margin every year. Unfortunately they are still anachronistic today and we are stuck with them. A well-known fact known as "Moore's law" states that the density of microelectronics doubles every 18 months (or gains a factor of ten every five years). This is basically true for hard disks as well. However, while in computers denser structures on chips increase their processing speed, for disks the increasing density led merely to three things:

1) Increased processing speed in the on board controller of the disk (which never was much of a problem anyway)
2) Increased speed of sequential read/write operations because more data is packed onto each track and is read in the same revolution. This is an advantage only in large sequential transfers, which are not typical for data center usage (databases)
3) Increased capacity of the disk, meaning more accesses per second are directed to the same hard disk

What Moore's law of exponential growth did not help was the rotational speed of the platters, which is limited by the centrifugal force exerted on the platters, and the speed at which the read/write heads are moved by the actuator. The latter is limited by the amount of heat that is generated and must be dissipated from the device. There were efforts to put several actuators into the same housing as well as several read-write heads per platter onto each actuator but for various reasons they all failed in the long run. So in the end Moore's law ran away generating gigantic amounts of storage space, bandwidth and processing power while leaving the hard disks' transactions per second sadly behind, forever tied to their mechanical internals. That is still the situation we are facing today.

It is also the reason why hard disks destined for private or SOHO use are usually larger than "server-grade" disks. It just does not make a bit of sense putting 1 TB onto a single spindle with one actuator if you want multi-user access on the database that resides on it. But it does make sense to have a few TB on your desktop to use for streaming media and backing up your data. Both are highly sequential types of access, and definitely not multi-user so they can be satisfied with a single, large disk.

Consider the following data points. In 1988, the typical hard disk was 20 MB, cost US$ 1000.- transferred 0.5 MB/s and allowed about 20 random access operations per second. Twenty years later, in 2008, disks are ten times faster and ten times cheaper: 200 random access operations per second at around US$ 100.-. That sounds like a big improvement, but bandwidth has increased even more: 50 MB/s or 100 MB/s are easily reached; an improvement by a factor of one or two hundred! But now take a deep breath and look at the size of the disk: Its capacity has increased from 20 MB to one TeraByte. That is a factor of 50,000 (fifty-thousand)! That means that even though disk mechanics are now ten times faster than they used to be, a very large database based on modern disks is five thousand times slower (measured in accesses per second) than the same database based on old disks. It is also half a million times cheaper.

The point is that you must never base your volume or LUN requirements on size alone, but always mostly on the number of physical disks you need in order to handle the load. Size is irrelevant. Size is basically free. Disks cost money, but it's the physical disks heads that you need in order to perform actual work. Ignore your storage array sales representatives when they talk about capacity in terms of size. They are fooling you. You get much more space per physical disk than you can put to reasonable use. The last type of disk that could efficiently handle enterprise database traffic was the 9 GB 10.000 RPM disk. Current disks only deliver about 1/100th the performance per GB as those 9 GB ones did.

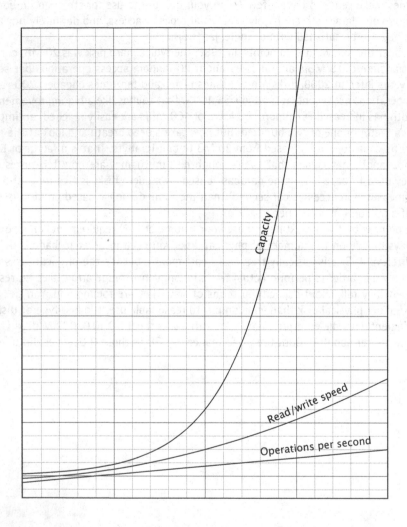

Figure 1-1: Non-quantitative graph showing how Moore's law only applies to disk capacity, while bandwidth and particularly operations per second are left behind. The X axis shows the years, while the Y axis shows the criterion that the curves are labelled with. Note that for the most importance today, namely TX/sec/GB, the capacity (which grows exponentially) is in the denominator, leading to exceedingly poor random read performance!

1.1.3 Trying to Fix the Problems - and Failing!

A number of approaches have been executed trying to get rid of or at least abate the problems caused by the mechanical heritage of physical hard disk drives. They have been successful in the past, sometimes yielding surprising performance benefits at their times and in their area of application. However, all the while Moore's law has been stomping on and on, grinding away any improvement that even the smartest software engineers came up with. Moore's law being exponential in nature has long since destroyed all attempts by storage providers to keep their disk drives' image as a fast, convenient and reliable storage medium. Let us have a look at the various attempts in a little more detail.

RAID Software

In order to alleviate the performance and reliability problems the University of California in Berkeley in the 1980s developed a software solution that allowed to group disks together and distribute and/or multiplex I/Os across all members of the group. They called the software RAID, for Redundant Array of Inexpensive Disks. This was later changed to Redundant Array of Independent Disks by people who wanted to make money off the concept and did not like the term "Inexpensive".

RAID introduced the idea of inserting a virtual device called a "volume" between the application (usually a file system) and the physical disks, thus making it possible to circumvent the restrictions and limits of physical disks to a certain degree. There were different approaches to circumvent the various limitations, each with its own merits and drawbacks. They were called RAID levels. You have probably heard about RAID software and what it does, so this will only be a short introduction into the various RAID levels in use today.

1) **RAID-0 concat** concatenates disks so that when one disk fills up the next one in the chain is used. The capacity of the volume equals the sum of the capacities of the individual disks, and the disks can vary in size. Due to the way most modern file systems are organized, losing any one of the disks means that the volume is no longer usable although one may get lucky occasionally trying to restore that one important file before giving up the volume.

Figure 1-2:   A RAID level 0 (concat) volume's block numbers are counted from beginning to end of the first disk, then skip to the next disk. In effect, storage on all disks is appended in a linear fashion. Disks of different sizes and types can be mixed freely.

2) **RAID-0 stripe** interleaves disks with what is called the striping factor, stripe width or **stripe size.** The volume's address space is logically chopped into extents the size of

the stripe width. These are then mapped to the individual **columns** of the stripe set, one column usually consisting of one disk. The first extent is mapped to the beginning of the first column, the second extent to the beginning of the second column and so on, up to the number of columns in the stripe set. The next extents are then mapped behind the first extent on the first column, then the second, and so on. The size of the volume is equal to the size of the smallest disk multiplied by the number of disks in the stripe set.

Figure 1–3:   A RAID level 0 (stripe) volume's block numbers are combined into chunks of blocks. The number of blocks in a chunk is called the stripe unit size, or stripe size. Each chunk maps to a disk linearly before mapping skips to the chunk in the next so-called "column". A column could be a single disk, a slice (or partition) of a disk, or any concatenation of such. All columns are neces- sarily the same size. The disks underlying each column must be on separate physical spindles for performance reasons.

3) **RAID–1 mirror** writes data to more than one disk. Each block is written to all disks in the mirror (usually two). Data that is flagged to be flushed to disk synchronously must be persistently written to all members of the mirror set before control is returned to the writing process, while normal, buffered I/O may leave the mirror in an inconsis- tent state for a while. **Note that this is not a problem** because buffered I/O does not guarantee data persistence to the user anyway!

Figure 1–4:   A RAID level 1 volume's blocks map to more than one disk. Writes are flushed to all members, while reads are generally read in a round-robin fashion for load balancing. Some low-end RAID solutions try to increase speed by issuing read requests to all members and only processing the first one. While that optimizes single-threaded performance, multi-threaded performance is lost because disk queues become longer and disks are overloaded with unnecessary redundant traffic.

4) **RAID-4 parity** maps extents in the same way that a normal stripe does. But RAID-4 adds an extra column for a special checksum extents created by combining the values of all corresponding extents of the data columns using the lossless exclusive-OR (XOR) operator. Thus, if any of the disks in the stripe set fails, the data for each extent can be recovered by reading the extents from all the remaining disks including the parity disk and recombining them with another exclusive-OR operation. Of course, these operations take time and there are many problems including write consistency and performance especially in degraded mode (when a disk has failed) or with multi-user access. I will not go into great detail about the many performance penalties incurred when doing RAID-4 in software. In short, doing it in hardware is OK, in software it is close to a nightmare.

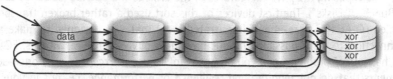

Figure 1-5: A RAID level 4 volume's blocks map onto the backing store in the same way as a common RAID level 0 stripe, except that one column is excluded from data I/O. Instead, whenever a row of the stripe is changed, RAID-4's special write policy generates an extra block containing a checksum over all data blocks in that row, and writes it to the excluded column. The checksum is based on the lossless bitwise exclusive-OR (or XOR) operation the result of which is 0 if the sum of all input bits is even, and 1 if it is uneven. Therefore, the checksum is also called the **parity**.

5) **RAID-5 distributed parity** is similar to RAID-4 but distributes the parity blocks across all columns thus improving RAID-4's performance problem when handling multi-threaded writes. Multi-threaded writes used to be one of the worst flaws of RAID-4 because they overloaded the dedicated parity-disk.

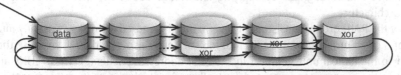

Figure 1-6: A RAID level 5 volume maps its blocks like a RAID level 4 volume, but parity distribution requires skipping parity blocks during reads and writes. The checksum itself is calculated in the same way as with RAID level 4.

1.1.4 SAN-Attached Hard Disks

In order to increase performance and manageability the second step the industry took was to introduce a fibre-channel based network for storage devices called a SAN (storage area network). Devices were thus accessible from more than one server and could be managed by programming the SAN switches accordingly. SANs introduced a whole set of problems into the administrator's world, many of which still are not solved. Attaching the disks to a SAN did not help the performance very much, although vendors like to boast about their multi-Gigabit/s connections. Unfortunately the speed of the channel is not the problem, as will become obvious later (beginning on page 214). But I have yet to meet a sales representative that is willing to understand the problem **and** advise the customers appropriately.

Initially SAN disks were packaged in boxes with little if any internal intelligence or caching, thus exposing the physical features of the disks to the outside (so called JBODs, for "Just a Bunch Of Disks"). The first devices of this sort used a rather broken transport protocol called FC-AL (for fibre-channel arbitrated loop) that was designed to make a cheap fibre connection to disks possible without having to buy expensive switches. FC-AL had and still has lots of problems and you do not want to use it except in very price-sensitive environments that do not require good resilience or performance. I.e. not in your typical data center.

1.1.5 Storage Arrays and LUNs

The third step in the scramble to alleviate the problems introduced by the hard disk's mechanical legacy was to bundle groups of disks together into a chassis with relatively large amounts of battery-backed RAM. These assemblies are manufactured and sold by many vendors, e.g. HP, Hitachi, IBM, Sun microsystems, EMC and are called **storage arrays**, **cache machines**, **SAN boxes** or similar. Layout and feature set of all of these devices is similar: They consist of one or more chassis holding the disk units and a central control unit containing back-end controllers that connect to the disks, front-end controllers that connect to the SAN. They may employ interconnects that connect to another box of the same vendor for remote replication or mirroring, and they usually have a large battery-backed RAM as a read- and write-buffer and lots of CPUs that control access from and to disks (back end) and hosts (front end). The disks are grouped into internal RAID groups of some sort (often some variant of RAID-4). In this step, care is usually taken to achieve a good load balance and throughput by applying knowledge about the internals of the storage array's architecture.

Now the RAID group, consisting of several multi-hundred GB disks, is usually much too large for a given problem so it is split into logical units (also called LUNs because they correspond to the logical unit numbers in the SCSI addressing scheme). These LUNs are then mapped to the appropriate front-end controllers via which the host can access them as if they were physical hard disks. To the host computer, there is no obvious difference between a LUN and a physical hard disk.

Usually more than one path is provided by the storage array by mapping the same LUN to more than one front-end controller. The host runs some variant of multi-pathing software at the driver level to make use of this redundancy. The paths are either used one at a time and only switched when a path fails. This is called an active-passive configuration. Alternatively, the paths can be used in a round-robin manner for load balancing. This configuration is called active-active.

The storage arrays use advanced algorithms to do both read-ahead and write-behind caching, they allow LUNs of various sizes, remote copying, instant snapshots and a lot more. That is why storage array vendors often claim no software volume management is necessary if the customer uses their box.

However, as usual, things are much more complicated than what the sales reps say.

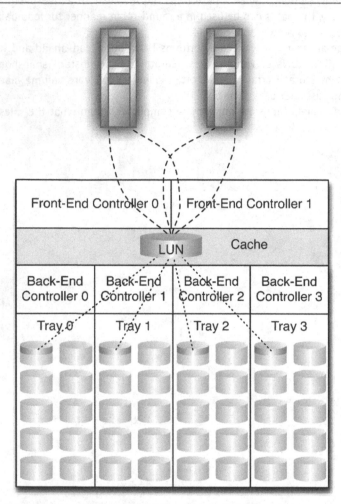

Figure 1-7: A storage array's architecture in principle: Physical disks reside in trays, each of which is controlled by a back-end controller. Slices of these physical disks are combined via RAID logic and create a virtual object inside the storage array called a LUN (Logical Unit Number, from the SCSI addressing parlance). The LUN is mapped onto one or more front end controllers (or "service processors"), from which they can be accessed by the host machines. Each connection from a host to a LUN via a front end controller is called a path. If a host accesses the same LUN via more than one path then multipathing software is required in order to coordinate access and to make use of the extra redundancy. The RAID level used inside the storage array is often a variant of RAID-5.

What LUNs Can Do

- **They can** take lot of writes per second and acknowledge them to the host OS very rapidly, then flush them to disk asynchronously when load permits. This is possible because their RAM is battery-backed. As soon as the data is in the storage array's cache RAM, it can be considered safely written. In case of a power failure the array logic will use battery power to flush the data to the disk drives.
- **They can** deliver pretty high throughput in sequential I/O, both read and write, due to their smart read-ahead and write-behind caching.
- **They can** balance I/O automatically if you let them - they observe usage patterns and move data if necessary to enable more rapid access
- **They can** replicate data to a remote site, but this is only useful in special cases, like short distances or flat file systems.

What LUNs Cannot Do

- **They cannot** offer you the flexibility of storage objects that a software volume management offers. This is due to several reasons:

  1) Most organizations will not allow a UNIX administrator to log into the storage array. Usually someone from the SAN group makes the storage objects (LUNs) for the UNIX admins and that's it.

  2) The granularity of the storage array's external objects is, of course, the LUN. Freeing up bit of space from one volume by reducing its size, then moving the freed space to another volume works on the server, not in the storage array.

  3) Backing up your volume configuration every night and being able to restore it on a per-volume basis and thus recover from all kinds of outages is easy in VxVM. I know of no way to do this in any storage array.

- **They cannot** increase **scattered read** (also known as random read) performance by giving you "cache hits". The myth about cache hits was introduced a long time ago, when storage arrays were sold mainly to the IBM mainframe market. It had some validity in those days but it does not any more. Unfortunately it has not disappeared since. The mainframes of that time used 31-bit addressing (yes, 31 **is** indeed a prime number. Remember we are talking about IBM mainframes here...). So all they could address directly was 2 GB of RAM. Storage arrays have been more free in implementing their internals and they used block addressing, so they could address 32-bit times 512 byte blocks. Having a lot of RAM in the mass storage system made some sense in those days, especially when the disks were smaller than they are now. Total RAM would be, say, 64 GB, and total disk capacity maybe one TB, which yielded about a 6% cache rate (see picture). Together with the OS's limited address space there was actually a pretty good chance for cache hits, especially because the storage array was often dedicated to a single mainframe. Nowadays however servers use 64-bit addressing. They tend to have much more RAM than they used to, easily going into the hundreds of GBs. What's more, many servers usually share a single storage array. And the disks inside the storage array are much larger. All these factors together distort the magnitudes enough to make the cache completely irrelevant for scattered reads. And even if we were lucky and the desired block actually was in the storage array's cache, then it is almost guaranteed to be in the server's cache anyway. Because the amount of cache that the storage array allocates **per server** is usually much smaller than that server's file system buffer cache. So you can safely forget about speeding up random read access using storage arrays. The only thing the cache does effectively is read ahead and write behind and thus speed up sequential read and all write transfers.

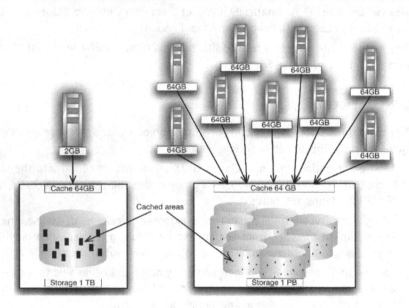

Figure 1-8:   While ten years ago storage arrays may have offered some cache hits due to the ratios of OS memory, number of machines per storage array, and cache/disk inside the storage array (left), today a cache hit for a scattered read is almost like winning the lottery (right).

- **They cannot** replicate online database traffic across great distances. Replication means storing an consistent copy of the data in a remote location for disaster recovery. It is different from a mirror in that updates to the replica may be delayed somewhat while updates to a mirror must not be. In addition, the replica is not accessible to the user at the remote site until - usually while testing or after a disaster - the direction of replication has been reversed. While some storage array vendors will claim that their hardware replicates databases quickly and consistently across great distances, this is not true. They may not know they are not telling the truth, but the simple fact is that physics makes it impossible. If you are interested in why the speed of light is too slow, and why 4 GBit/second are not helpful when it comes to long distances, read the discussion about light speed and protocols in the chapter about dual data centers (page 214). The conclusion is that in order to replicate database traffic quickly and consistently the replicating agent needs information about the write sequence that only the operating system has. Therefore it is not possible to achieve this goal with a purely external solution but you need a special device driver. Veritas Volume Manager comes with a built-in solution for replication that is both fast and consistent. It is called VVR, or Veritas Volume Replicator. Unfortunately there is no free lunch and VxVM-based replication is not easy to learn or administer.

1.1.6 COMMON PROBLEMS

SCATTERED READ LATENCY

All the technological advances of the last thirty years have failed to fix one basic yet crucial problem: access to a random data block generally incurs a relatively long latency consisting of positioning the actuator and waiting for the right sector to fly by. In fact, the problem got worse and worse. It is still getting worse with every new generation of hard disks. You need to understand what exactly the problem is so that you can make smart decisions about the layout of your storage. Let us look at the problem, at how bad it already is and why it keeps getting worse.

When RAID was conceived the usual hard disks were a few dozen megabyte in size, let's say 20MB. A typical disk of that era had a rotational speed of 3600rpm, a data transfer rate of half an MB per second and an a seek time of about 60ms. It used an interleaving factor of 3 to 5 because the interface between disk controller and host computer could not transfer the data at the full speed of the rotating platter. so you had to read the same track several times in order to transfer all of it to or from the computer. Let's look at a sample data transfer from one of these disks:

1) Position the actuator - 35ms
2) Wait for head to settle down - 7ms
3) Wait for first sector under read/write head - 8ms
4) Read track four times to gather all the sectors, and transfer - 70ms

That's a total of 120ms. You could do eight of these large I/Os in a second, or twice as many if you only read one sector per I/O. Now what can we do today? In 2008 hard disks have much faster access times: a good average value is 6ms; ten times faster than in the days of the first RAID concepts. The also boast transfer speeds beyond 50MB/second, that is one hundred times the bandwidth we used to have. They also store one terabyte instead of 20MB. A database of 1GB that migrated from fifty old 20MB disks with their 60ms latency to fifty of today's 6ms hard disks would be ten times faster in random access, and a hundred times faster in sequential access! It could accommodate ten or twenty times more users than the old setup, depending on the I/O mix! It even turns out it would be about twenty times cheaper even with the same number of disks because hard disk prices have dropped a lot since the 1980s.

So what is the problem?

The problem is that, while access times have improved by a factor of ten, and bandwidth has improved by a factor of one hundred, size has increased by a factor of 50,000 (fifty thousand, from 20MB to 1000 GB)! So nobody is going to put that 1GB database on fifty individual spindles because that would waste fifty terabyte minus 1 GB of hard disk space. Try explaining to procurement why you need 50 disks and only use 0.002% of their space. Well, let us be fair: you may not need the tenfold performance increase; you may just stick with the performance you used to have, so you can actually use ten times as much space: 0.02%! Try explaining that. Good luck!

The problem is that disks have so incredibly much space that you are tempted to use it, but because the mechanics basically haven't changed since 1980 you cannot use it for data that is accessed in a random fashion.

Yet people do it and that is what causes many of today's performance bottlenecks. How come most people do not recognize the problem? It is hard to say, but one thing is probably that benchmarking is often done the wrong way. Many times people benchmark only the "classic worst case" scenario, namely: scattered write I/O. This kind of I/O is the worst case for **physical** hard disks because not only does a write access incur the seek latency and write time, but the disk controller also has to verify that the data was properly written, which means that another revolution of the disk has to be waited for. A **physical** hard disk in a data center should never acknowledge a write I/O as soon as it has received the data from the host computer and put it into its cache (write back mode, the default on many personal computer systems). The data is only safe when it is actually persisted onto backing store, i.e. on its magnetic media, and that is when the I/O can be safely acknowledged to the host (write through).

The second worst case is scattered read I/O, but why measure the second worst if you can measure the worst case, right? Wrong!

A storage array buffers all writes, both scattered and sequential, and acknowledge them to the host as soon as the data is in its cache. It does write back instead of write through, and in the case of the storage array, that is OK. Remember that the storage array has internal batteries that keep the array running in case of a power failure. Additionally, data in their cache is usually organized with enough metadata so that even when the storage array CPU fails it will replay the data from its cache onto the backing store when control is regained by the CPU.

So if scattered write performance is measured on LUNs the result is hugely distorted due to the storage array's caching effects. The write benchmark merely measures the speed of the channel and the controller, which is fair by itself because he storage array will actually deliver that performance in real life, too. But what people tend to forget is that what used to be the second worst case is now by far the worst case: scattered reads.

Another weak point in benchmarking today is that benchmarks (and optimization runs) are usually run on a single machine, while in fact the storage array is (or will be) connected to dozens if not hundreds of machines, each of which will put some load on the array. Because a combined benchmark is normally impossible due to logistical limitations (who could afford to shut down the whole data center just for benchmarking?) people limit themselves to benchmarking a single machine. But the results of such benchmarks are usually invalid because they do not replicate the real world in any significant way.

1.1.7 PHYSICAL DISKS VS. LUNS

ADVANTAGE LUN

Being the more recent and modern type of storage, LUNs have a number of advantages over physical disks. In particular there are the following advantages to LUNs:

- **Write Performance**: Storage arrays are at an the advantage when it comes to writing (both random and sequential) because of their write behind caching strategy. Because the storage array is built to survive power outages and other mishaps, a data block received from the host can be acknowledged as soon as it arrives at the storage array. There is no need to wait until the data has been persisted to magnetic storage. The storage array's cache memory is already persistent, and disks are just the backing store into which the cache contents are flushed for long-term storage. Because the storage array acknowledges received blocks immediately, the time waiting for the mechanical components of the disks is saved.

- **Sequential Read Performance**: Sequential (or "streaming") reads are also served very well by storage arrays because due to their vast caches they read ahead many more data blocks than an individual disk with its limited memory could. When the prefetched data is subsequently requested by the host the storage array can deliver it much more rapidly than a disk could. This is not because the storage array has more powerful CPUs. In fact, its I/O controllers are industry standard components. It is purely because the storage array has read so far ahead that no actual disk head movement needs to be done and thus the crucial bottleneck is mostly avoided when doing sequential I/O.

- **Reliability**: LUNs are almost always based on some kind of redundant internal construct. In many cases, some variant of RAID-5 is used. As a result, read/write errors from head crashes, power supply or even logic board failures on disk spindles, simply do not happen. LUNs are like disks that cannot break - unless the SAN admin inadvertently breaks them by misconfiguration. You may still lose part or all of your connectivity to the storage array, and you may still lose a LUN due to administrator error. But having defective sectors on a LUN is next to impossible.

- **Management**: Apart from performance and reliability they also have an advantage when it comes to (remote) management. Most large storage arrays include fibre-channel switch hardware that is integrated with the array logic to facilitate easier zoning, masking and mapping of LUNs to hosts. While this could also be done using external SAN switches and fibre-channel JBODs it is generally easier to use the integrated approach.

ADVANTAGE DISK

What, using physical disks has advantages over using LUNs? Yes, it does, and probably more than you would think possible:

- **Lower latency**: While writes and sequential reads are usually better served by a storage array, the additional overhead created by talking to the front-end controller which puts the request into a queue from whence it is passed to the appropriate back-end controller which then talks to the disk, and the whole way back introduces significant extra latency. This aggravates the scattered read latency problem, which is already the ultimate bottleneck in today's storage systems.

- **Transparency and Dedication**: When you encounter a performance problem on a database the classical approach is to consult your sysadmin tools to find out which disk gets the most I/O and then balance it using the appropriate tools When you do this, then if you are running from physical hard disks you can be rather confident to get the expected result. But if you are running on a storage array chances are very high that you are not alone on the array, or on the physical spindles inside it. What appears to your sysadmin tools as a spindle is in fact a complicated construct comprised of several spindles, each of which may be part of more such constructs (see picture page 12). These are likely in use by some other machines in your data center that you may not even be aware of. It is a frequent complaint that storage arrays give relatively good average performance but can suffer unpredictable and severe performance degradations occasionally. This is often because some other machines peak at that time because they are doing disk-intensive tasks, like database imports, full table scans, export or backups, taking away all the IOPS (I/Os Per Second) which you thought were exclusively yours.

- **Price**: JBODs are typically much cheaper per GB than storage arrays. This is not only because JBODs need less components, but also because the target market for storage arrays is mostly medium-sized to large enterprises who are expected to put their most mission-critical data onto storage arrays. Therefore, the array vendors must offer thorough, worldwide support on a 365/24 basis. They must also test their equipment very thoroughly to exclude bugs as much as possible, and work together with server, HBA and SAN hardware makers on interoperability issues. All this consumes a lot of financial resources which must be recovered by the higher equipment price.

Other features like snapshots, redundancy etc. can all be done in software with physical hard disks and Volume Manager. There is just one special thing that cannot easily be done in software, and that is creating an incremental snapshot of a volume (a snapshot based on the differences from the original) and moving it to another host for offhost processing. This is logically impossible for a host based approach because both hosts would need to have read and write access to the volume, and only one of them would maintain the snapshot. This would not work without a lock manager and a modified file system. Veritas has actually implemented that with a product called a "Volume Server" but that product is not widely used and it may never be.

1.2 DISK ADDRESSING AND LAYOUT

BLOCKS AND EXTENTS

Every object that the host system sees as a disk, i.e. a LUN, a physical disk inside a JBOD, or a single disk (e.g. the boot disk) must be addressable in the same way or else there would be different code paths for different media types. Both developing and debugging for the programmer as well as administration and fault analysis for the administrator would be unnecessarily complicated by this. Fortunately, it is a universal truth that LUNs, JBODs and physical disks are indeed addressed in the same way and share the same layout.

As discussed before, disks are basically addressed as a one-dimensional address space segmented into blocks of BLKSIZE bytes (usually 512, sometimes 1024). The tracks and cylinders do not actually play a role any more except to shoot yourself in the foot if you mess them up. They are purely legacy information. In former times this information was used to optimize disk access, but it is irrelevant today. The SCSI device driver expects every hard disk to report them and so they diligently do, but the actual physical layout of the disk uses a variable amount of sectors per track (outside cylinders are longer so they can hold more sectors than inside cylinders), and the number of cylinders and even heads is emulated by the disk's firmware. Only when mirroring boot disks the cylinder information plays a little role, because the Solaris VTOC entries are required to start on cylinder boundaries.

In order to illustrate disk addressing we will use several variations of the following graphical element for the disk address space, in which each of the little rectangles stands for one disk block or sector:

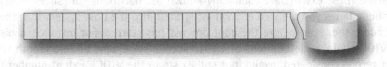

Figure 1-9:   A disk is addressed as a sequence of blocks or sectors of the same length, usually 512 bytes (1024 bytes on some HP-UX machines)

The next step up from disk blocks towards something more usable is the **extent**. An extent is a data structure which is widely used in both Volume Manager and File System. Once you get used to extents you begin to wonder why everybody does not use them since they are such a useful abstraction. What is an extent? An extent is a contiguous range of blocks starting somewhere at a given block number and stretching over a number of blocks. Veritas File System uses only powers of two for extent sizes, but VxVM uses a less stringent definition of extent: an extent in VxVM is simply a sequence of disk blocks defined by a starting block and a number of blocks (or a beginning and a length, if you prefer that notion).

A partition (another word for "slice") can also be seen as an extent. It starts at an offset (given as a block number) and extends across a number of disk blocks. An extent is anything that is given as an offset and a length. The disk itself is an extent, beginning at block zero and extending across the whole disk. A file could – almost – be an extent if the file system was smart enough to recognize what it is doing and allocate contiguous storage space. It is not really an extent, even if it is contiguously allocated, because it is not block-addressed but byte-addressed, i.e. it could end anywhere inside a disk block. By the way, VxFS actually does a very good job at allocating blocks contiguously, as does UFS, the common UNIX file system. Current implementations of UFS are derived from BSD's Fast File System (FFS); the original UFS from AT&T was very poor at allocating contiguously.

VTOC, Partition Table, Volume Label

At some fixed location on whatever the operating system identifies as a disk (i.e. a real hard disk or LUN) there needs to be some meta information that describes that medium. Such metadata include the length of the medium and the location of some critical extents like boot code or root file system etc. In principle it would be possible to derive much of the required metadata via I/O control system calls (ioctls) from the device driver (e.g. the length and blocksize of the device could be determined this way). However it makes a lot of sense to do this only once, then store the results along with other metadata in some fixed location on the device so it can be read and written without hassle.

In Solaris and several other operating systems, the extent that holds the metadata starts at block zero and has a length of one block. In other words, block number zero holds the metadata for the device. The Solaris name for the metadata extent is VTOC, which stands for Volume Table Of Contents. Other names from other operating system parlances are "partition table" or "volume label".

That metadata contains additional information about the usable extents residing on the medium. These extents are commonly known as "partitions" or "slices". They start at cylinder boundaries and are well enough integrated into the host system that they can be directly addressed, even before the boot process has started. For instance, a disk with a Solaris VTOC contains descriptions of eight extents. An extent of zero length that starts at offset zero is considered invalid (but still exists in the VTOC). Extent number two is by default initialized as an extent that contains the whole disk and is called the "backup slice". (A long time ago, when Moore's Law was not yet applicable to hard disks and you could actually buy the same type of hard disk for a few years, system administrators liked to make backups of their system disks by copying data from the "backup slice" onto tape. Note that the backup slice also contained the metadata extent (block zero) so when a disk was terminally broken one could install a new disk, copy the backup from tape to the new disk device's backup slice and thus recover both metadata (VTOC, slices, boot code) as well as user data of all file systems in one step. Hence the term "backup slice".)

Figure 1-10:   The Solaris VTOC (black) is located in a one-block extent starting
                at offset zero. It points to up to eight extents (on SPARC systems)
                which are also called slices or partitions. Slice 2 is an extent that
                covers the whole disk.

In Solaris, the extents known as slices or partitions carry a tag in the VTOC that is used
to identify the partition's purpose. For instance, there is a special tag for the swap slice
which is used by the Solaris installation program to find an extent into which a "mini-root"
file system can be written without possibly overwriting important user data.

BOOT CODE

The boot code, also called boot block, is (again, in Solaris systems) located in an extent that
is 15 blocks in size and starts at an offset of 1 block from the root slice. Why is there an
offset of 1 block? It is there simply in case the root slice starts at cylinder zero of the disk.
In that case, if the boot code actually started at block zero it would overwrite the VTOC
(which is located at block zero of the disk) and render it useless. So to accommodate for
this special case, block zero of every extent on a Solaris disk is unused by any higher-level
code.

The boot code contained in these fifteen blocks is smart enough to read UFS file system
structures and load the kernel from its subdirectory path in e.g. /kernel/sparcv9/.... There
will be more on booting and the boot process later in the discussion of making a third boot
disk mirror for maintenance purposes.

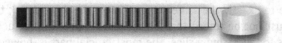

Figure 1-11:   The boot code (grey) on a Solaris disk resides in an extent that
                starts at offset one from any slice and is 15 blocks long. This
                slice is tagged as the boot or root slice, which contains the root
                file system.

Similar to the gap left for the VTOC "just in case" the slice happens to start on cylinder
zero of the disk there is another gap that the file system leaves for the boot code "just in
case" it happens to be located on the root partition: The first sector, block zero, is skipped
because we do not want to overwrite the VTOC. The following fifteen blocks, block 1-15,

are also skipped by the file system in order to prevent overwriting the boot block if this slice happens to be the root slice that contains the boot code.

In summary, a Solaris slice or partition may start at any cylinder boundary but the file systems that reside in it will always skip the first 16 blocks "just in case" they happen to be on the root slice so they will not overwrite the VTOC or boot code. This is why the super block for a Solaris file system always resides at block 16 instead of block 0 of a slice. The same holds true even for database using raw devices: their access methods also skip the first 16 blocks for the same reason.

Figure 1-12:   The superblock, the entry point for a file system, is contained in an extent that starts at offset 16 and has a length of one block.

SLICES OR PARTITIONS

Slices, also called partitions, are container extents into which a file system or a database writes and from which it retrieves data that was previously written. They are discussed here because of the implications they have for volume management. A volume is, after all, a logical construct that ultimately serves as a backing store for a file system or a database raw device. To paraphrase: a volume is an extent that must act as an **exact equivalent** to a slice under all conditions. If a volume would behave in even a slightly different way from a partition the file system or database accessing the volume could run into situations it is not prepared for, and crash.

What is the most critical nature of a disk extent that must be emulated by its logical equivalent, the volume? Well, of course it must be able to store data in a persistent way. It must also adhere to exactly the same semantics on the driver level; the file system or data base driver must not be forced to use a different paradigm for accessing a volume than the one it uses for accessing a slice. The most crucial part is, however, that under all circumstances the virtual equivalent of a slice – the volume – must deliver one and only one set of data contents for any specific block until that block's contents are changed by that same device driver. It is not at all obvious that this is always the case. For instance, consider a volume that is a three-way mirror. If during an update to this mirror the host loses power, then because not all extents are written at exactly the same time you may have up to three different contents of any data block that was being written to when the outage occurred. Which one is "the right copy"? Should the write be transactional so that this cannot happen? Should we always refer to a "MASTER" copy, a preferred mirror side that is always up-to-date? Then what if the disk holding that mirror fails?

These questions will be answered beginning on page 132 and you will be surprised at how sophisticated the problem, yet how simple the solution is.

1.3 PATHS AND PATH REDUNDANCY

A disk is not worth much if there is no way to access it. In order to access a disk there must be one or more I/O paths to it that the operating system can use. Over the course of time many types of paths have been developed. The ones most commonly used in data centers will be discussed here. They are: SCSI, fibre-channel (FC) and iSCSI. Two of these, FC and iSCSI, are network protocols, while SCSI is point-to-point and has been abandoned in most data centers by now. The SCSI protocol is still discussed here because its command set is the foundation for most block-addressed storage today. The SCSI heritage turns out to become a big problem occasionally, as we will later see.

SCSI AND SCSI ADDRESSING

We will not go into the historical details about how Alan Shugart invented SCSI as a network protocol for hard disk access. There are better sources for that kind of information. But it is important to know the naming conventions and some protocol intricacies in order to understand the later chapters, especially latency concerns and system deadlocks.

First of all SCSI is a stateful protocol that uses commands sent from the initiator (usually the host computer) to initiate data block transfers between the initiator and the target. A transaction consists roughly of the following steps (for a data read): first the initiator selects the target which the target acknowledges. The initiator then sends the command, e.g. a read command, which is again acknowledged. The target can then choose to decouple from the initiator and fetch the data. When the target has retrieved the data from its storage medium it reconnects to the initiator who then fetches the data from the target and ultimately deselects the target.

How is the target addressed?

The target address used to be an integer number between 0-7, later 0-15, that was put onto the three (later four) address lines of the parallel SCSI interface. The operating systems had internal logic to translate names like /dev/sd4, /dev/sd5c etc. to the appropriate counterparts on the SCSI bus, in this case SCSI-ID 4 and SCSI-ID 5 slice 3 (the c in sd5c) etc. Later, when multi-instance devices appeared and systems with several controllers became more common this naming scheme became very inconvenient and had to be extended by what has become known as the LUN address.

The SCSI LUN

Imagine a device that houses more than one actual media. A good example is a CD-ROM changer. Such a device consists of just one controlling unit and therefor occupies just one SCSI target. But it is able to address more than one logical device, namely the individual CDs in the slots that the changer provides. In order to address such multi-instance devices an extension to the SCSI protocol was provided called a "Logical Unit Number". Does that sound familiar? It is the term we use when talking about virtual hard disks acquired from a storage array, the LUNs. Remember that storage arrays are multi-instance devices, too. They consist basically of a control unit with a mass-storage back end and can deliver multiple instances of block-addressed storage, so it makes sense to apply the same addressing scheme to them as with other multiple-instance devices. Initially there was a maximum of

16 LUNs due to limitations of the number of wires on the parallel SCSI bus. That limitation does not exist any more with serial interfaces (the limit was due to the number of address lines on the parallel SCSI cable) so it is up to the device driver how many LUNs it can address. Usually 256 LUNs per target is the limit.

Modern UNIX Device Naming Convention

Using names like /dev/sd4 or /dev/hdisk5 does not work very well when hundreds of disks need to be addressed. First of all it clutters the /dev directory. Then, all the names may change when a disk is added or removed and the system is reinitialized. That makes it very hard to keep the file system tree organized in a system with frequent device changes. So a more clever naming scheme was conceived, which identifies a device by the various entities on the path to that device: Controller or host-bus-adapter (HBA), Endpoint (Target), Disk (or LUN), and Slice. Typically, a path to a disk block device would be /dev/dsk/c#t#d#s#, with the # standing for the corresponding object number. The controller is the operating system's internal controller number that has been enumerated upon boot by the hardware integration layer. The endpoint or target number is the SCSI-ID in case of JBODs or – in case of a storage array – the fibre-channel port in the array to which the controller is connected. The disk number is the port-specific number of the array-internal volume. Each port of a storage array gets a number of array-internal volumes (the "LUN" in the storage array picture on page 12) for each connecting host bus adapter. That internal number is passed on the SCSI bus to the host and turns into the disk number in the device tree.

To prevent clutter in the /dev directory, the device nodes are put into separate subdirectories for block and raw addressing called /dev/dsk and /dev/rdsk. A device name like /dev/dsk/c4t9d2s0 identifies the block device for controller 4 -> target 9 -> disk 2 -> slice 0, and /dev/rdsk/c8t15d7s2 identifies the raw device for the whole disk on controller 8 -> target 15 -> disk 7 (remember that slice 2 addresses the whole disk in Solaris).

When disks are added or removed on one controller or target, this does no longer change the names of all the other entities on different controllers or targets. This naming scheme is very convenient since it is immediately obvious which disks are connected to a certain controller (c4) or a certain storage array port (t9). There are other naming conventions but they will not be used in this book.

FIBRE-CHANNEL

Fibre-channel is currently the most widely used interface for disks in data centers. Fortunately, switched fibre-channel fabrics have displaced the previous, rather unreliable and slow FC-AL (Fibre-Channel Arbitrated Loop) architectures. The physical layers of fibre-channel are not too interesting in this context and are not covered in this book; there are many good books that explain FC very well (I very much recommend Tom Clark's "Designing Storage Area Networks"). But what you need to know are the following facts:

-   Fibre-channel can use both copper or light as the physical transport medium. Copper is used for short distances only (usually inside the machine or array) while several variants of glass fibre are used for cheap medium-range connections (multi-mode) or more expensive long-range connections (mono-mode). It is quite common to multiplex several light connections onto a single physical channel to increase bandwidth without increasing cost at the same rate. This is done by a technique called [D]WDM for [Dense] Wavelength Division Multiplexing. This type of multiplexing means no more than using lasers of different wavelengths (i.e. colors) in parallel on the same fibre.

- Fibre-channel uses a variant of the SCSI protocol command set called FC-3 (for Fibre-Channel based on SCSI-3). In fact, the standard SCSI protocol driver is used on top of the FC host bus adapter (HBA) driver. This can cause great problems as you will see toward the end of this chapter.

- Fibre-Channel is a network architecture. It was originally designed to replace ethernet for high-end applications but that failed due to the high cost of recabling, and because Ethernet developed very quickly to Gigabit versions. Fibre-Channel works with multiple initiators, multiple targets, switches and routers. It also has the usual set of network problems like missing or wrong routes, nodes that fail to answer or answer late, buffer overflows etc.

iSCSI

This protocol is gaining momentum because it allows to use a storage area network to be installed over an existing ethernet infrastructure. The expenses for fibre-channel components are saved, and administration is simplified. Similar to FC, iSCSI uses the existing SCSI protocol driver on top of the TCP driver to directly address iSCSI devices as block devices. (This is in contrast to NFS where the server does not serve data blocks but file semantics. NFS and other file servers are outside the scope of this book.)

MULTIPATHING

No matter which protocol is used it is always a good idea to have redundant paths to the disks. SCSI, Ethernet and FC connectors are not perfect and they can only withstand a very limited amount of force. In addition, especially in the case of network based storage it is always possible that an intermediate node loses power or crashes. If there was no path redundancy you would lose disk connectivity immediately and the data would no longer be accessible. If you were lucky, then you would lose only one side of each mirrored volume, but you would have to resynchronize all mirrored volumes after such an event. All this can be prevented by having redundant paths. But there are more reasons for having path redundancy:

- You can switch one of the paths off and upgrade the firmware on your HBA or on the storage array's controller to which this path is connected. After the upgrade is successful, you switch the path back on and repeat the procedure with the other path. This enables online upgrades with no downtime.

- The load is distributed across more than one controller so that peak loads do not run into a bottleneck.

Multipathing drivers come in a variety of flavors. Some are provided by the operating system vendor, like Sun microsystems' MPXIO driver. Others are provided by the storage vendor, like EMC's PowerPath driver. And some come with the volume management software, like Veritas' Dynamic Multi Pathing (DMP). There are two places in the driver stack where they fit in: below the SCSI protocol driver or above it.

Sun vHCI Driver

The vHCI (virtual Host Controller Interface) driver that implements Sun's MPXIO is an example for a nexus driver. A nexus driver is a driver that is part of a driver chain, i.e. one driver accessing or being accessed by another driver. In this case it operates between the SCSI protocol driver and the HBA (host bus adapter or pHCI, for physical Host Controller Interface) driver. The SCSI driver therefore only sees a single path which never seems to fail because the software driver below uses two or more redundant paths to do the I/O. That makes it easier for software that sits on top of the SCSI protocol because that software will rarely have to deal with path errors. It also makes it easier for system administrators to identify multipathed devices because each device only appears once in the device tree, only has one device node etc. More about the vHCI device driver can be found here: http://www.patentstorm.us/patents/6904477-description.html and, of course, later in this book. Here is a somewhat simplistic graphical depiction of where the vHCI driver resides in the driver hierarchy of a system running Veritas Volume Manager:

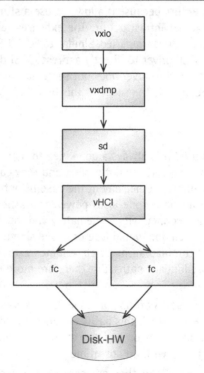

Figure 1-13:   The Sun vHCI driver is located below the sd driver. The operating
system only offers the DMP driver a single path to each disk

Veritas DMP Driver

The Veritas DMP driver is a layered driver that sits on top of the SCSI protocol and bundles several standard SCSI paths to one redundant path. The /dev directory keeps the device nodes for all SCSI devices after DMP is installed, but a /dev/dmp directory is added, which contains meta-nodes for devices accessed via the redundant paths. This has the advantage of making online installation and deinstallation of the driver possible because devices can still be accessed via their original device nodes. But this can be both positive and negative for the system administrator because common operating system commands and utilities continue to work on the original, individual paths, while Volume Manager and its tools use the redundant paths. For instance the Solaris format command may display two or four times as many disks as are actually connected to the system if they are connected via two controllers or two controllers and two switches, respectively. This can be confusing to the uninitiated. The following graphic illustrates where DMP resides:

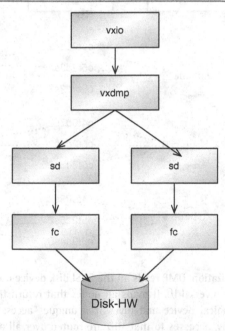

Figure 1-14:   The Veritas DMP driver is located above the sd driver. The operating system offers the DMP driver several paths to each disk

How Does the DMP Driver Work?

This is obviously not a discussion of actual DMP implementation details, but one can get a good idea of how DMP works by using the following simplified description:

Whenever a device discovery is started (e.g. upon system boot or when the administrator asks VxVM to scan for new disks) DMP reads the disk's unique ID (UID) from all devices in /dev/rdsk/c*t*d*s2, i.e. from all disk devices that are known to the system (CD-ROMs etc. are skipped). It then builds a list of all UIDs and adds to each UID all paths via which that particular UID was found. This is called building the DMP device tree. The result of this is that each disk device is mapped to all paths that reach that particular device.

During operation DMP issues I/Os for a certain UID in a round-robin fashion across all its paths. If a path encounters an error it is marked bad and henceforth skipped for I/Os. In order to regain that path when it comes back online a kernel thread called restored reads the list of bad paths from the dmp driver at a configurable interval (default: 300 seconds). It then issues a small read-I/O to test if the path has come back online. If it has, then that path is reactivated in DMP and taken off the bad path list and thus returns to normal operation.

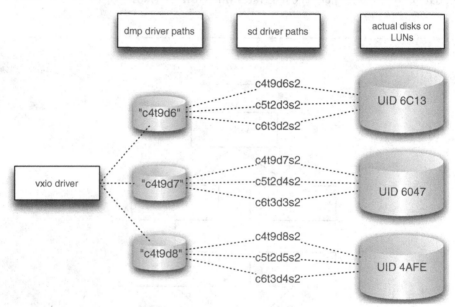

Figure 1-15:   Upon initialization, DMP reads all the SCSI disk device nodes and finds their universal ID. It maps all nodes that return the same UID to a logical device and gives it a unique "access name". Subsequently, accesses to that UID are routed over all available paths that originally returned the same UID. The standard sd driver remains functional, but is unaware of the fact that many of its paths are actually the same device.

EMC Powerpath

Powerpath is a commercial product which is sold by EMC's strong sales force. It resides on the same layer as the dmp driver, i.e. on top of the sd driver. But it does something that should be considered at least problematic: Besides routing I/O to the powerpath drivers it also intercepts calls to the normal sd drivers underlying powerpath, and reroutes them via powerpath's internal logic to any of the paths via which the desired target can be reached. It therefore interferes with the operating system's own drivers as well as with other multipathing drivers.

Using Powerpath and DMP Together

Powerpath **cannot** be used in conjunction with DMP without a major hassle or risking data loss under certain circumstances. If a path fails, DMP and powerpath will not typically recognize the failure at the exact same point in time, so write I/Os that are pending via DMP may be rerouted via powerpath to a path that has already been found faulted by DMP, or vice versa. The result is that those I/Os may never be flushed to persistent storage and/or DMP may never find out about this and notify the vxio driver (which could then signal the application to retry the I/O). The result is occasional data loss in case of path failure.

Because powerpath does not seem to solve any problems that DMP hasn't solved we strongly advise against using them both at the same time. The illustration depicting the combination of DMP and powerpath hopefully speaks for itself:

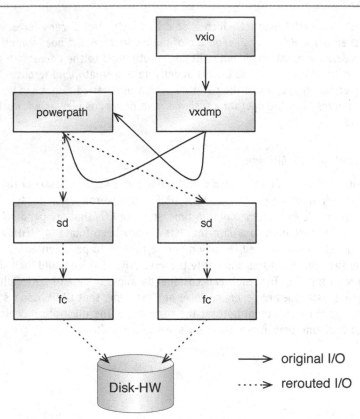

Figure 1-16:   The EMC powerpath driver is located at the same level as the DMP driver. The operating system offers the DMP driver several paths to each disk, but usage of these paths is caught and redirected by powerpath

1.4   THE TROUBLE WITH NETWORKED DISK ACCESS

PROCESS SLEEP BEHAVIOR

Using networks as a transport medium for SCSI-addressed devices is - from a technical perspective - not a particularly good idea. The reason is a hierarchy of limitations and intricacies of the UNIX kernel, and of networked systems in general, which may cause disastrous results under some circumstances. The most common of these circumstances is an overloaded machine on a poorly performing SAN. Let us look at the individual points whose combination may cause a machine to hang or panic if you use a SAN:

The first problem is that the UNIX device driver model works in the following way (roughly; the details are much more complicated):

A process that requests an input or output operation will go to sleep and will receive a wakeup call when the I/O request is ready to be served. For instance, a process that reads from a terminal, like an interactive UNIX shell or command interpreter, will go to sleep when the read system call is made. It will wake up when the user has completed his input by pressing the carriage return key or, if the process uses the terminal in raw mode in order to interpret the cursor and other special keys, upon any keypress. Since it is not clear when or if the user will actually create any input (he may have gone to lunch) the device driver sleeps in an interruptible way. That means that if the user decides to stop the program, leave the session, turn off his terminal etc., the process will be interrupted or terminated in a controlled way by the kernel jumping into the process' signal handler code, where exception processing can be handled by the user process. The drivers for devices that typically exhibit indefinite or at least long response times, and especially the application that use these drivers (in this case, anything that uses the terminal, like the shell etc.) take great care to avoid blocking system resources, i.e. they will typically not lock any data structures or allocate a lot of kernel memory and so on. After all, these valuable resources could be blocked for a long time.

Slow Devices vs. Fast Devices

Networks, too, are considered slow devices, just like terminals or serial lines. Due to the intricacies of network architectures, all sorts of delays are possible and must be reckoned with. Router reboots, slow or unresponsive nodes, network congestion and so on can all cause delays. This is represented by the typical timeout values for networks being in the minute range (usually between 1 and 10 minutes). Of course, network based device drivers and applications will use kernel resources sparingly and avoid locking any data structures while waiting for their data to arrive or their timeouts to occur.

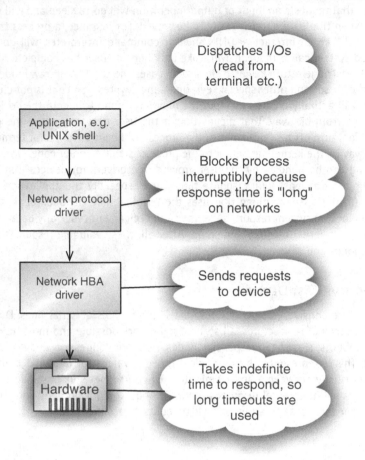

Figure 1-17: Drivers for devices which are known to exhibit potentially slow
response times sleep interruptibly. They also typically do not
require a lot of resources, and the applications that use them will
not keep important data structures locked while they do I/O.

The opposite example is a SCSI disk driver. The classic SCSI driver issues an I/O request
to a disk that is attached via a parallel data cable to a hard disk drive. The driver expects
the I/O to be served in a very short period of time, since the SCSI command and data
exchange protocol is fairly quick. For that reason it need not be interruptible, which sim-
plifies the context switch and thus improves performance. The device driver and especially
the applications that use it – the file system or database – can also keep some kernel data
structures or code regions locked, or keep large buffers allocated – the I/O response is due
in very short order anyway, so there is no need to go through the trouble of making the
system call interruptible.

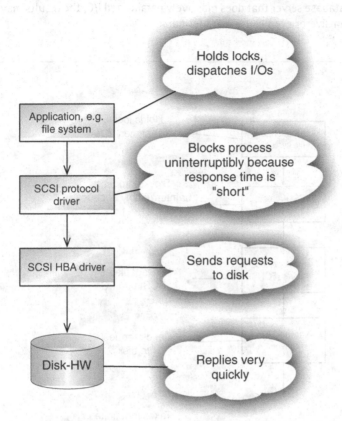

Figure 1-18:   Drivers for devices which are considered to respond quickly will
allocate resources much more aggressively, since the response is
due in very short order anyway. The I/O is made uninterruptible
for performance and other reasons.

THE PROBLEM OF MIXING SLOW AND FAST DEVICES

The problem of mixing fast and slow devices in the same nexus hierarchy is the following:
Remember that the SCSI protocol driver sits on top of the HBA driver, i.e. a device driver
for a quick device calls the device driver for a networked, or very slow, device. What happens is that the SCSI driver, depending on how well it is written and how much it sacrifices
reliability to performance, might allocate or lock quite a lot of kernel resources while it is
doing its presumably quick I/O. But then it calls the networked device driver to actually
serve the physical I/O. Everything works out if the device responds quickly, which it usually does, but if the SAN infrastructure experiences problems because of congestion, not
enough buffer credits, network reconfiguration, slow disk response due to scattered read
latency or otherwise (see page 4), all the resources allocated by either of the device drivers

33

will remain allocated for a long time. This is not a problem by itself, but if this happens on a heavily loaded database server that does massively parallelized I/O, the results may render the system unresponsive or even cause a kernel panic.

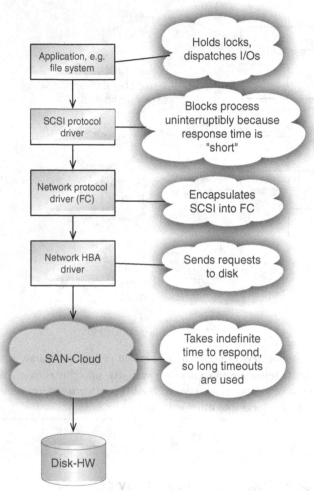

Figure 1-19: Layered device drivers become a big problem if the upper layers expect a rapid response, but the lower layers do not deliver as rapidly. Locks, memory, and process contexts get stuck for an extended time, eventually leading to deadlock situations.

Why Systems Hang – the Deadlock Situation

Because now another problem becomes visible: deadlock avoidance algorithms are not perfect. Deadlock avoidance belongs to a class of problems known to mathematicians and computer scientists as NP problems. NP is an abbreviation of non-polynomial [time] and refers to a complexity class whose problems cannot be solved in a time that is a mere polynomial function of the problem's complexity. What that means is that while a simple case of an NP problem could be solved relatively quickly, as the problem grows larger the time required to find the optimal solution grows at a much faster rate than the problem size. And very quickly the time becomes so long that the optimal solution to the problem cannot be guaranteed to be found any more in any reasonable time.

Travelling Salesman Problem

You may be familiar with one example of this class of problems, the travelling salesman problem. Imagine a salesman (and by this and all other similar occurrences of "man" in the text I mean "man" in the sense of "human"; please forgive me for sacrificing political correctness for legibility) who needs to visit his clients at several places and is looking for the best route to visit them all. If there is just one client, the problem is easily solved: drive to the client, and drive back. If there are two clients the problem is still easy. With five clients, there may be several orders and routes that look good, and it will be quite hard to figure out which is the best one. But now imagine a thousand clients and the poor salesman needs to find the **best** route. The problem would likely be unsolvable in any reasonable time.

Finding a Practical Solution

On the other hand, exactly this problem - the problem of finding the best route through several points - is addressed very effectively on a daily basis by cheap electronic devices called GPS navigation systems. Is that not a contradiction? No, actually it is not. The solution that these devices offer is not generally **optimal**. It is merely **very good** and can therefore be calculated in a rather short time. So the programmers of navigation system devices are trading off precision for speed. Finding the **optimal** route would still take forever, and that would not be useful. So they do try to **approach** the optimal solution but then stick with just a **very good** one to make it practically useful.

Deadlock Avoidance Problem

Operating systems programmers face the same dilemma when trying to avoid deadlock situations. If one process or kernel thread holds resource A locked and then requires resource B, but another process or thread holds resource B and needs resource A, they get into what is called a deadlock, i.e. they are both stuck until either one releases his lock to the other one. Of course, operating systems programmers have for decades been able to handle deadlocks by implementing deadlock avoidance strategies into their kernels. But unfortunately, deadlock avoidance is also a member of the NP problem class. What that means is that while there are algorithms that work under all circumstances to resolve any deadlock situation, those algorithms my take literally forever and are therefore never implemented in any OS. As is the case with navigation systems however, there are very practical algorithms that avoid deadlocks under **almost** all circumstances which are deemed reasonable and that have a very short runtime. Only the really pathological cases are not covered by these algorithms. This kind of algorithm is now found in all modern operating systems.

Identifying Pathological Cases

What are the pathological cases I mentioned? They are cases in which a large amount of processes or kernel threads exist, and many locks are held for a long time.

As the number of CPU cores per system grows and I/O parallelism especially in databases increases in order to make use of these cores, the number of processes and threads that an operating system has to deal with threatens to grow out of bounds of what the practical deadlock avoidance algorithms can handle.

If in addition to the large number of threads that hold locks in an uninterruptible context, the underlying network does not function perfectly, then a deadlocked system becomes a very likely result. This was actually the reason for many of the outages that we analyzed during the past five years, and the frequency of such events seems to increase.

You need to be aware that large systems doing massively parallel I/O to a SAN will tend to deadlock when the SAN response time increases. The result will be an unresponsive system that will eventually either call a system panic and dump its core to the dump device, or one that will have to be manually revived by causing an NMI (non maskable interrupt) on the console and rebooting it.

Keep this in mind for later chapters, where we will deal with latency and the problem sets that arise from it. We will see that light speed is not fast enough in many common cases, which in the end leads to what looks like an unresponsive SAN. Under these circumstances systems will suffer similar deadlock crashes even if the SAN is actually in perfect working condition. This has indeed become a major problem in many data centers, because storage is typically bought by size rather than the more appropriate "transactions per second per gigabyte" metric. Additionally, SANs are still considered to be very fast, and people tend to overload their machines.

More on this in the chapter on dual data centers, page 213.

1.4.1 SUMMARY

This chapter provided an overview of disk hardware and its development through the last twenty or so years. It showed what Moore's Law is and how it makes the speedy hard disks of yesteryear turn into really slow devices if proper care is not taken to balance the amount of IOPS (I/Os per second) against the number of physical hard disk spindles available. It introduces the most important, yet largely unknown, measure required for storage systems today: TX/sec/GB, or performance per gigabyte. Particular emphasis was put on the unsolvable problem of scattered reads, which cannot be tackled with any conventional approach no matter what the storage vendors may try to argue. The chapter also gave an overview of RAID software and RAID hardware-assisted systems, also known as "storage arrays", and where either storage arrays or disks have an advantage over the other.

In addition you got an insight into the basic data structure of "extent", into how addressing both logical and physical disk blocks work and how the data is laid out on a disk.

We further delved into the device drivers used to talk to disks, SAN basics and UNIX device driver specifics that may sound complicated but the knowledge of which is mandatory in order to understand and fix problems should they arise. You should now also be familiar with one of the main reasons for deadlocked systems and why these situations are almost inevitable unless your SAN is working perfectly – and sometimes even then.

CHAPTER 2: EXPLORING VXVM

by Volker Herminghaus

2.1 GETTING STARTED

Getting started with the actual Veritas Volume Manager product is easiest if you first gain an overview of the concepts behind Veritas Volume Manager (or VxVM in short), what virtual objects it uses and how they act together to form a complete volume management layer. After the extensive problem introduction in the previous chapter let us gain some insight into what VxVM does and how it does it. You will be intrigued by how straightforward and clear the design, yet how powerful and extensible the resulting architecture is.

In the following walkthrough you will encounter several commands which are not generally useful for everyday work. This is because they tend to be rather low-level commands which have long since been superseded by much more convenient commands that take much less parameters, preparation and time than the ones used in this chapter. We still like to use the inconvenient ones because they make it much clearer what exactly happens inside VxVM. But there is no need to learn those commands any more. Whenever low-level commands are used they are marked appropriately by using a slanted fixed-width fond like this: *vxlowlevel command you need not remember*. Normally the common higher-level commands are discussed close to the low level ones. They are set in a straight fixed-width font like this: `vxhighlevel command you should remember`.

2.1.1 HELLO, VOLUME!

Let us create the VxVM equivalent of Kernighan & Ritchie's famous "Hello, World!" C-language program: A thoroughly explained walk through of VxVM's essential data structures and virtual objects. By the end of the chapter you will know a fair amount about volume management in general and VxVM's virtual objects in particular. You will actually know more than most UNIX administrators that just use VxVM on a daily basis without ever wondering what is going on behind the scenes.

2.1.2 VXDISKSETUP: TURNING DISKS INTO VM DISKS

Since VxVM must eventually store volume data on a magnetic surface there must be a way of integrating disks or LUNs into the VxVM object hierarchy, to take storage media away from operating system control and pass them over to VxVM control. And of course there is. Using a simple command - `vxdisksetup` <diskname> - you reserve a disk for VxVM use. Since a disk treated with this command is now virtualized by an additional software layer it has gained some rather handy features. For instance, you can now use software commands - *vxdisk online* and *vxdisk offline* - to switch the disk on and off; something that is not possible using just operating system commands.

Of course these commands do not actually make the disk stop rotating or keep the controller from responding; they merely simulate turning the disk on and off to the other virtualized layers above. But as long as you do not break the paradigm and stay inside the virtualized layers, this is for all practical purposes identical to actually switching the disk on and off.

WHAT DOES VXDISKSETUP DO?

It first checks the disk's physical properties, like size, type of storage array it resides on (if it is a LUN) and the device paths that DMP provides to the disk. It then uses the knowledge just gained to define an internal data structure called an access record through which it can do read and write I/O from and to the disk via DMP. The process of creating the access record is implemented by the command *vxdisk define*, which is called from inside the `vxdisksetup` script. The access record created by *vxdisk define* also contains flags like the physical and virtual online or offline state of the disk, the list of paths to the disk along with their state, possibly information about the location of the disk (the "site" variable), and the disk's universal device ID (UDID). Remember that all these variables are just software data which are used inside VxVM to represent a physical disk as accurately as possible while extending its abilities by things like reservation, software on/off or software failed/ OK state. (More information about disk flags is provided in the **miscellaneous** chapter beginning on page 479.)

Next on the list of things that `vxdisksetup` needs to do, at least in the great majority of cases, is to reserve some private space on the disk medium in where it can persistently store all the information pertaining to the disk. For instance, if VxVM set the "failing" flag for a disk because an unrecoverable read error occurred on some user data, you would like this state information to be persistent across reboots. No offense intended, but only

Windows users try to fix problems by rebooting. In UNIX and other serious operating systems rebooting a system should not normally change a lot, except maybe enable a kernel level patch or driver configuration change to become relevant.

SLICED FORMAT

VxVM, or more specifically the vxdisksetup command, reserves space for its private use by allocating a (normal) slice on the disk and marking it as a "Private Region" of VxVM by giving it the reserved tag 15 in the Solaris VTOC. That slice is a perfectly normal slice which can be inspected using Solaris' format or prtvtoc commands. The tags are not usually interpreted by the operating system; anyone could theoretically use any tag for their partitions. There are conventions, however, that can make life easier. For instance, if a slice has tag 3 this marks it as a swap device, and the Solaris install program will use it as a destination for its mini-root file system during install. There are also tags for "root", "boot", "home" and several others.

The "Private Region" used to be the smallest number of cylinders that would yield at least 1MB, although that has changed several times in recent releases. In any cae, its size is no longer relevant since the advent of the new CDS disk layout which has superseded the classic format and which will be discussed later.

The vxdisksetup command, after reserving the private region, then reserves the rest of the disk by allocating another slice and marking it as the "Public Region" (tag 14). To an administrator, and to all UNIX tools that handle disks, the disk now looks like its space is completely used up; there is no free space on it that is available for the operating system after vxdisksetup is run.

The disk format generated by vxdisksetup as described above is called the "sliced" format, because private and public regions reside in visibly separate slices of the disk. Because it relies on the Solaris VTOC, such a disk can only be used on platforms which are compatible with Solaris VTOCs, namely Solaris and Linux. It is no longer generally useful since the advent of the new, universally compatible format called CDS (Cross-platform Data Sharing, discussed below) and only discussed here for reasons of conceptual clarity.

To initialize a disk as a sliced disk use the following command:

```
# vxdisksetup -i c#t#d# format=sliced
```

CDS FORMAT

In more modern versions of VxVM the whole disk is marked as a "Private Region" by vxdisksetup, which has led to some confusion among users. The usual reason for this confusion is the (wrong) assumption that the private region held **only** metadata, while the public region held **only** user data. While this was true with the original sliced format, the whole truth seems to be that a disk that is under VxVM control needs two things in order to coexist with the operating system: First, a way of telling VxVM that it is valid for VxVM. That is achieved by using the special VxVM tag number 15 for the Private Region, and of course by initializing the Private Region with a valid data structure. And second, a way of telling the rest of the system to keep their hands off the disk because it's under VxVM control now. The latter is achieved by marking the whole disk as allocated through the allocation of a single slice covering the whole disk. Previously these two things were done by the Private Region slice serving the first purpose and the Public Region slice serving the second purpose. A close look revealed that both could be served at the same time by just allocating the whole disk to one huge Private Region, thus telling VxVM that the disk is destined for VxVM and telling everybody else that the disk is fully allocated at the same time. (The Private Region holds all the metadata VxVM needs for allocation of virtual objects on the disk; VxVM never actually required the Public Region slice for that purpose.) This is what is done in the current default layout, called CDS for Cross-platform Data Sharing. CDS formatted disks can be freely moved between Solaris, Linux, AIX and HP-UX as long as they are all running VxVM 4.0 or above.

The last step that `vxdisksetup` does is initialize the Private Region with reasonable values. It does so only if it has been passed the `-i` command line switch, i.e. if the command was not just `vxdisksetup <diskname>` but `vxdisksetup -i <diskname>` instead. Initializing the private region is done by the *vxdisk init* command which again is called from inside the `vxdisksetup` script, so you never need to call it manually. To initialize a disk for VxVM as a CDS disk use one of the following commands:

```
# vxdisksetup -i c#d#t#          # cds is the default format since 4.0
```

   or

```
# vxdisksetup -i c#t#d# format=cds      # if default has been changed
```

It is also possible to encapsulate a disk that already contains file systems (either from the operating system's addressing scheme or from other volume management products) by a process called encapsulation. This process is extensively handled in its own chapter beginning on page 319.

So now, after initializing the disk, we are ready to go one step further up the hierarchy: Grouping disks together to build a base for creating volumes.

2.1.3   Disk Groups: Putting VM Disks into Virtual Storage Boxes

Any software that implements RAID functionality will have to use more than one physical disk if it tries to do anything useful. Trying to break the limits of physical disks while constraining oneself to a single disk does really not make any sense. So VxVM never works on individual disks when creating virtual objects of a higher level. Instead, the least thing that VxVM needs is a collection of disks that can be addressed as a container for virtual objects like volumes. This collection is called a **disk group** or DG. You may think of a disk group as a virtual box of disk media, which can be attached to and detached from hosts by using software commands, effectively moving storage between servers.

Of course it is debatable if we actually need to collect disks together into DGs in order to handle them. Why not just use all the disks connected to our system, and allocate from all of them? The answer has to do with highly-available systems or clusters: In order to have a highly available service we need to virtualize not just the mass storage layer but also the server itself. I.e. we need more than one physical instance of a server and then map these multiple instances of server hardware onto one or more logical server instances, called "Logical Hosts" or "Service Groups". These service groups work on data that is alternatively, sometimes even concurrently, accessed by any of the hosts of the cluster. In order to allow a controlled failover of a service group from one physical host to another the data is encapsulated into individual groups of disks. Each service group contains (typically) one disk group that holds all the storage resources required by the service. If a service group fails on one host, the service group's resources are stopped on that host and then started on another host. This means that access to the disk group is disabled on the host on which the service has failed, and enabled on the spare host. If the disks were not organized into disk groups then it would be hard to pass control over just part of the storage (i.e. the storage required by one service group) to another host. Therefore the use of disk groups does indeed make a lot of sense. Disk groups are created by the vxdg init command. Because disk groups are made to move between systems they must be completely self-describing, i.e. **all the information about the disk group resides inside the disk group itself**. Otherwise it would be hard to move the disk group from one system to another without having to transfer some description file along with it. Because all information about a disk group is contained inside the disk group, a disk group must always contain at least one disk. It is not possible to have a disk group without a disk, so you must pass at least one disk on the command line when you create a disk group.

Here is an example that creates a disk group named mydg from three disks: c0t2d0, c0t3d0, and c0t4d0:

```
# vxdg init mydg mydg01=c0t2d0 mydg02=c0t3d0 mydg03=c0t4d0
```

Now after having created a disk group containing several individual virtual disks we can look at what parts of the storage are unused by asking VxVM to report the free extents. This is done by using the low-level command *vxdg free*. Since there may be many disk groups in use by our system VxVM always requires that we pass it the name of the disk group with the command. So the correct command is actually *vxdg -g mydg free* (the -g flag obviously stands for "group"). The result is a list of extents, one per disk, which are free for user data.

```
# vxdisk -g mydg free
DISK       DEVICE      TAG       OFFSET    LENGTH     FLAGS
mydg01     c0t2d0s2    c0t2d0    0         17909696   -
mydg02     c0t3d0s2    c0t3d0    0         17702192   -
mydg03     c0t4d0s2    c0t4d0    0         17679776   -
```

The free extents (remember: offset and length, both given in 512-byte blocks) are printed in boldface. Each disk has a single free extent starting at block 0 and covering all the free space available to VxVM.

Disk groups are covered in their own chapter beginning on page 71.

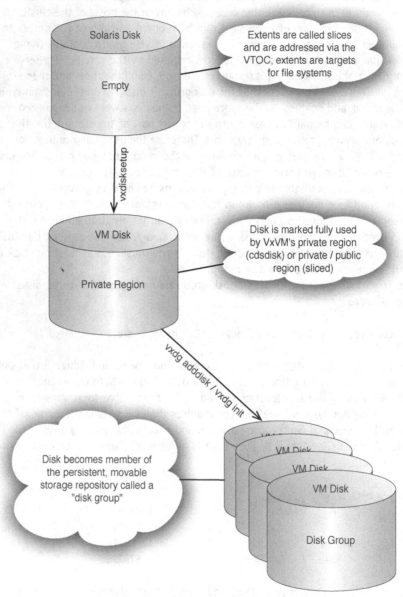

Figure 2-1:   Initializing a disk for VxVM creates a so-called VM disk, which is
               marked "completely full" for the operating system (but not for
               VxVM). It can then be added to a disk group using the appropri-
               ate command, and subsequently used as persistent backing store
               for virtual volumes.

We have now virtualized our physical hard disks to serve as a VxVM-addressable backing store for our storage objects The next step is to allocate space from this backing store. We used to allocate space by defining a partition (or slice) in the VTOC of a hard disk. However, the limitations of the VTOC format would not let us define more than 8 slices per disk. After all, the VTOC is only a single 512-byte block that cannot hold much information. There just isn't enough space available in the VTOC for allocating little extents and mixing them together in some fancy way to get a mirrored or striped volume. Remember the VTOC is plain Solaris' equivalent of the VxVM private region, but much too small to hold enough information for any serious kind of virtualization. It was never designed for doing that.

So how do we go about allocating an extent from a VxVM disk? There are two ways to do it. One is a low-level command called *vxmake* which is used to create almost any kind of VxVM object. The other one is a high-level command called vxassist that creates, allocates and connects all the objects required for the task that you give it (for instance, creating a four-way striped mirror in one go).

If you don't want to learn about the internal objects now, you can skip to page 53 at the end of this chapter, where we show the easy way to create volumes. But do come back to this part eventually if you need to understand VxVM!

2.2   THE HARD WAY: A LOW-LEVEL WALKTHROUGH

2.2.1   SUBDISKS: EXTENTS FOR PERSISTENT BACKING STORE

You're still reading? Good! In order for *vxmake* to create the right object we need to pass it the object type first. The object type we want is an extent, i.e. part of a disk. In VxVM terminology this is called a **subdisk or sd**. The *vxmake* command needs to know which type of object to create (sd), which disk group to use (mydg), what the name of the subdisk to create (mydg01-01), the disk to allocate storage from (mydg01), and the extent information, i.e. offset and length (offset 4000, length 2 GB). We have chosen an offset of 4000 for no specific reason; it just looks nicer than an offset of 0.

The low-level command that is actually run looks something like this:

```
# vxmake -g mydg sd mydg01-01 disk=mydg01 len=2g offset=4000
```

This will allocate from VxVM's virtual disk mydg an extent of 2GB length beginning at offset 4000 blocks from the beginning of the virtual disk's public region (wherever that is; VxVM keeps track of it so we do not actually care) and note its existence under the name "mydg01-01" in the Private Region. After the extent has been allocated, VxVM makes sure no other extent will use blocks from the extent we just allocated; any attempts to do so will fail. We can then check vxdg free again and see that the extent we just allocated is extracted from the free storage pool and is no longer available.

```
# vxdg -g mydg free
DISK        DEVICE      TAG         OFFSET      LENGTH      FLAGS
mydg01      c0t2d0s2    c0t2d0      0           4000        -
```

```
mydg01          c0t2d0s2        c0t2d0        4198304      13711392   -
mydg02          c0t3d0s2        c0t3d0        0            17702192   -
mydg03          c0t4d0s2        c0t4d0        0            17679776   -
```

As you see, the disk mydg01 now lists two free extents: one from 0 to 4000, the other one starting at 2 GB behind 4000 and extending all the way to the end of the public region.

We can also use a print command – vxprint – to check and see that the object was indeed allocated. The command for this is vxprint -g mydg.

```
# vxprint -g mydg
TY NAME          ASSOC         KSTATE     LENGTH    PLOFFS    STATE     TUTIL0    PUTIL0
dg mydg          mydg          -          -         -         -         -         -

dm mydg01        c0t2d0s2      -          17909696  -         -         -         -
dm mydg02        c0t3d0s2      -          17702192  -         -         -         -
dm mydg03        c0t4d0s2      -          17679776  -         -         -         -

sd mydg01-01     -             ENABLED    4194304   -         -         -         -
```

The length of the subdisk (in the last line of output) is shown as 4194304 blocks of 512 bytes, which is exactly 2 GB, as you can verify like this:

```
# echo 4194304/1024/1024/2 | bc -l
2.0000000000
```

2.2.2 PLEXES: MAPPING VIRTUAL EXTENTS TO PHYSICAL EXTENTS

The next layer up in the virtual storage hierarchy is a data structure that implements concatenation, striping or striping with parity. In order to do so it maintains an internal mapping table which maps its address space to appropriate extents on VxVM subdisks. In doing so this virtual layer is able to implement some of the RAID levels. For instance, concatenation is implemented by mapping individual subdisks sequentially into the plex's address space. The virtual object that implements this behavior is called the **plex** (plex is a latin suffix meaning "-fold", as in twofold, manifold). The plex's address space is identical to the address space of a virtual volume, i.e. it is block-addressed, starts at an offset of zero and extends contiguously and typically without holes (although there can be "sparse" plexes) to the end. In that respect it is similar to a partition, which also exposes a single, linear, block-addressed space to the layer above it (usually the file system or raw device layer).

Concatenation is not the only type of mapping that the plex object can implement. It can also do striping and striping with parity (RAID-5). These layout types are implemented by mapping several subdisks into the address space in an interleaved manner. In the simple case they all start at a plex-offset of zero and extend all the way to the end of the plex. The plex's access methods implement skipping from column to column appropriately, and generating the parity checksum in the case of a RAID-5 plex.

In a more complicated case, several subdisks will have to be concatenated inside one or more column(s) so they will start at their respective offsets inside the plex, rather than at offset zero. In the case of a striped layout the mapping of plex addresses to subdisk addresses is done via internal logic of the plex. The plex methods know the layout of the plex as well as the number of columns and the stripe size. With this information the plex is able to calculate the correct physical extent on a subdisk for any given logical extent in a plex, and issue the I/Os to the SCSI driver appropriately.

This is how a plex is created with a low-level command:

```
# vxmake -g mydg plex myvol-01

# vxprint -g mydg
```

TY	NAME	ASSOC	KSTATE	LENGTH	PLOFFS	STATE	TUTIL0	PUTIL0
dg	mydg	mydg	-	-	-	-	-	-
dm	mydg01	c0t2d0s2	-	17909696	-	-	-	-
dm	mydg02	c0t3d0s2	-	17702192	-	-	-	-
dm	mydg03	c0t4d0s2	-	17679776	-	-	-	-
sd	mydg01-01	-	ENABLED	4194304	-	-	-	-
pl	myvol-01	-	DISABLED	0	-	-	-	-

Note that no disk is specified. The plex actually does not have any backing store now; it is just like an empty balloon that needs to be filled before use. As you can see in the last line of output above, where the plex is displayed, its length is zero.

So now we created this virtual object called a plex, and we had created another virtual object before called a subdisk, which can be used as backing store for plexes. Let us bring the two together, or **associate** them, using another low-level command. This is the *vxsd assoc* command (*sd* obviously stands for subdisk, *assoc* stands for associate):

```
# vxsd -g mydg assoc myvol-01 mydg01-01
# vxprint -g mydg
```

TY	NAME	ASSOC	KSTATE	LENGTH	PLOFFS	STATE	TUTIL0	PUTIL0
dg	mydg	mydg	-	-	-	-	-	-
dm	mydg01	c0t2d0s2	-	17909696	-	-	-	-
dm	mydg02	c0t3d0s2	-	17702192	-	-	-	-
dm	mydg03	c0t4d0s2	-	17679776	-	-	-	-
pl	myvol-01	-	DISABLED	4194304	-	-	-	-
sd	mydg01-01	myvol-01	ENABLED	4194304	0	-	-	-

Now the plex and subdisk belong together and the plex' size has grown from zero to the size of the subdisk it contains. There is a slightly easier way of creating a plex with subdisks that works by specifying the *sd=<sd-list>* parameter on the *vxmake* command line.

Two more low-level commands for creating plexes are provided as samples here: The first one will create a concat plex containing just the subdisk that was allocated above, the second one will create a three-column striped plex with a stripe size of 1MB (2048 blocks) out of three subdisks which we have not created here (so the command would actually fail if you typed it in without creating the subdisks first. It is meant as a sample for the command syntax):

```
vxmake -g mydg plex myvol-01 sd=mydg01-01
vxmake -g mydg plex myvol-02 sd=mydg02-01,mydg03-01,mydg4-01 \
       layout=stripe ncol=3 stripewidth=2048
```

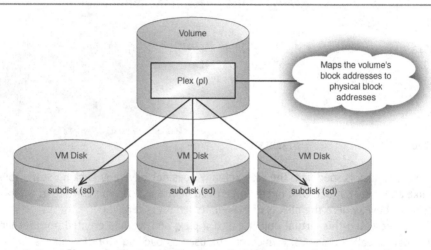

Figure 2-2:   Plexes do the translation work. Each plex maps the contents of the whole volume onto persistent storage (i.e. subdisk). Having more than one plex in a volume therefore is equivalent to mirroring. Up to 31 plexes can be in a volume.

2.2.3   VOLUMES: VIRTUAL PARTITIONS FOR ANY PURPOSE

So now we have virtualized disks, disk groups, subdisks, and plexes. Can we finally put a file system onto something now? Actually we can not. While a subdisk object is by its nature very much the same as a partition, namely an extent of blocks on a magnetic disk, it does not provide a device driver node in the /dev directory onto which we could issue an mkfs or newfs command, let alone mount it into the file system tree. Even the plex object, with its clever logic able to distribute I/Os across several disks in a number of ways (concat, stripe, RAID-5) does not provide us with a device driver node. So how are we going to use the raw, plain magnetic storage (subdisk) or the cleverly organized magnetic storage (plex)? The answer is simple: we need another object type to build on top of the plex. Why does VxVM not just use the plex and provide a device driver so we can write into a plex? The reason is that a plex, being just a mapping layer for redirecting virtual extents to physical extents, contains only one single instance of the address space, not several instances. In other words, it does not provide a mirroring functionality. Because Volume Manager needs to implement mirroring, too, there must be a container object that can hold a number of plexes. In order to implement mirroring VxVM puts several plexes into a single container called a volume. This container object (volume) implements a device driver node in side the /dev directory hierarchy, and thus lets the file system driver address the volume. The volume will multiplex write I/Os to all plexes inside the volume, and satisfy read I/Os from any one of the plexes in the container using each plex's individual mapping function to address the correct pieces of backing store for each plex. In other words, the volume object is the type of virtual object that offers the device driver that we can write into and read out of. Without a volume around it, a plex is just a cleverly mapped, yet inaccessible stretch of blocks. The volume objects implements the UNIX device node that we need to access the plex or plexes which ultimately offer the mapped backing store for the volume.

A volume object is created by e.g. the following low-level command:

 # vxmake -g mydg vol myvol usetype=fsgen len=2g

Ignore the parameter *usetype=fsgen* for now; it is used to tell VxVM the intended purpose of the new volume and is syntactically required for the command. Let's see what we get:

```
# vxprint -g mydg
TY NAME          ASSOC        KSTATE    LENGTH    PLOFFS  STATE   TUTIL0  PUTIL0
dg mydg          mydg         -         -         -       -       -       -

dm mydg01        c0t2d0s2     -         17909696  -       -       -       -
dm mydg02        c0t3d0s2     -         17702192  -       -       -       -
dm mydg03        c0t4d0s2     -         17679776  -       -       -       -

pl myvol-01      -            DISABLED  4194304   -       -       -       -
sd mydg01-01     myvol-01     ENABLED   4194304   0       -       -       -

v  myvol         fsgen        DISABLED  4194304   -       EMPTY   -       -
```

Again, the new object is not yet connected to any other objects. It is a standalone, empty volume object with no plex inside it. Now let us put the plex into the volume. Again, the volume is just an empty data structure or virtual object that bears some flags and other information, like the information that it is 2 GB in size (we specified *len=2g*, just like we did with the subdisk). The operation that puts a plex into a volume is called **attaching** a plex. A plex attach operation has the effect of copying the volume data onto the plex, overwriting the plex's previous contents. Of course this only happens if the volume already holds data (i.e. if there already is at least one plex in the volume), which is not the case here. So in our case nothing will be copied when we issue the plex attach command, but the volume will subsequently contain the data that is stored in the plex's blocks:

 # vxplex att myvol myvol-01

OK, so now the subdisk is inside the plex so that the plex has backing store to do its I/O to. And the plex is attached to a volume so that the volume can take actual I/O requests from the device driver interface (which only the volume provides). Where is the device driver that corresponds to our precious, hand-made volume? Let us look into the /dev directory!

In the /dev directory you find the usual subdirectories for buffered (dsk) and unbuffered (rdsk) disk access. Buffered is also referred to as "block I/O" and unbuffered as "raw" or "character I/O".

What's new in the /dev directory since we installed VxVM is a new directory /dev/vx, with vx being short for Veritas. Inside /dev/vx you will find dsk and rdsk directories, just like the ones we saw in /dev. The difference is, the /dev/*dsk directories contain device drivers to physical devices, so you will find the usual c#t#d#s# or similar device names inside of them. Opposed to the physical view offered by /dev/*dsk. the /dev/vx/*dsk directories offer a view of the virtualized storage. So in these directories we obviously do not need to cope with clunky controller names, but we get the elegant ones that we chose for our virtual objects, nicely arranged in a hierarchical order. What we see is the device node with VxVM's major number (in this case: 270) and the volume's minor number (31000):

```
# ls -l /dev/vx/dsk/mydg
total 0
brw-------   1 root    root    270, 31000 Nov  3 14:38 myvol
```

In general, the device paths result from the prefix /dev/vx/*dsk, followed by a directory that carries the name of the disk group (mydg) followed by the device driver that carries the name of the volume (myvol).

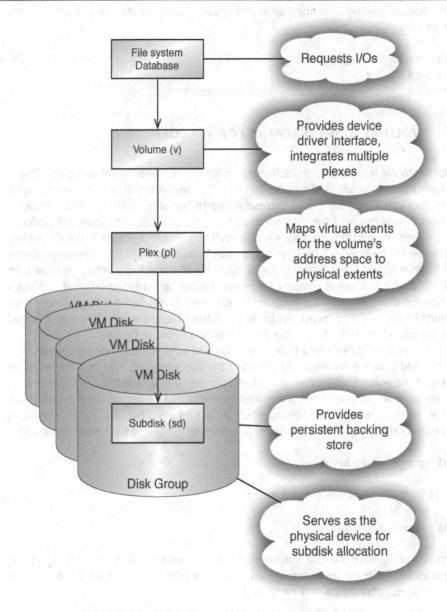

Figure 2-3:   The hierarchy of virtual storage objects in VxVM.

So now we will try putting a file system on the volume. That should work just like on any partition, because as you should remember VxVM must strictly adhere to emulating a partition's behavior towards the higher level drivers. If a volume behaved in any way differently from a partition then the file system or database or whatever else it is that uses the volume might get unexpected results and panic the machine. That is why VxVM undertakes great efforts to maintain behavioral consistency with a partition.

Yet when we now try to actually do anything useful with our manually created volume we get an error:

```
# newfs /dev/vx/rdsk/mydg/myvol
Are you sure ...? y
/dev/vx/rdsk/mydg/myvol: no such device or address
```

2.2.4   VOLUME START: PREPARE FOR TAKEOFF

Why doesn't VxVM let us access our self-made volume? The reason is actually quite simple: The volume needs to be checked for consistency before use. After all, a partition only holds a single data container: the extent corresponding to the slice itself. A volume however might hold several copies of the data, up to 32 to be exact. What if these are not perfectly identical? Then the partition paradigm would really be broken, because if the file system gets different contents every time it reads the same extent., this will cause major problems. For that reason VxVM needs to check the consistency of the volume before you can start using it. Of course it does not compare the whole volume contents but rather it employs a clever concept of states and state transitions with which it can derive if the volume's contents **must** be OK or if they **might not** be. In the latter case, the volume's contents indeed need to be resynchronised, while in the former nothing needs to be done.

It would be a rather silly idea if VxVM checked the volume's consistency permanently, or if it checked before every single I/O. We want the checking done exactly once; when we begin using the volume, and never thereafter until we give up control of the volume by deporting the disk group for some other host to use it. That other machine is out of our control so we must re-check the volume when we get it back. Checking and thus enabling the volume is called "starting" the volume. It is done by executing the simple command:

```
# vxvol -g mydg start myvol
```

or, to start all volumes in the disk group:

```
# vxvol -g mydg startall
```

Now we really have a virtual volume that can be used for everything that a partition can be used for: Buffered file system I/O, unbuffered or "raw" database I/O, creation of file systems, ufsdump/ufsrestore and everything else.

```
# newfs /dev/vx/rdsk/mydg/myvol
/dev/vx/rdsk/mydg/myvol:  4194304 sectors in 2048 cylinders of 32 tracks, 64 sectors
        2048.0MB in 47 cyl groups (44 c/g, 44.00MB/g, 11008 i/g)
super-block backups (for fsck -F ufs -o b=#) at:
 32, 90208, 180384, 270560, 360736, 450912, 541088, 631264, 721440, 811616,
 3334496, 3424672, 3514848, 3605024, 3695200, 3785376, 3875552, 3965728,
 4055904, 4146080,
```

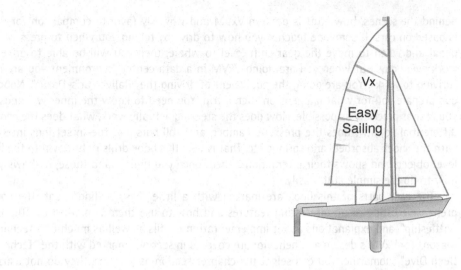

2.3 THE EASY WAY: VXASSIST

If the above sounded complicated to you then please remember that the low-level commands are there just for you to understand the basic data structures and virtual objects. You never actually create them in the way described above. The real way of creating volumes, together with all the virtual objects they contain (plexes and subdisks) is to use a single, high-level command named vxassist. This command will do all the smart thinking and hard working for you and present you with a volume that is ready to go and looks exactly like you specified it (unless you did not bother to specify a lot, in which case vxassist will choose reasonable defaults). Once you have a disk group with a few disk in it, all of the above could have been done by this very simple command:

```
vxassist -g mydg make myvol 2g
```

And the striped volume (which we did not even finish due to lack of subdisks) would have been created, including allocation of subdisks, creation of plex, and starting of the volume, by this command:

```
vxassist -g mydg make myvol2 layout=stripe ncol=3 stripewidth=2048
```

2.3.1 SUMMARY

This chapter contained a hard-core walkthrough of VxVM's basic virtual objects and how they connect together to form a virtualized container for you to use instead of a simple hard disk or LUN partition. Do not be intimidated by the complexity of what you just read; using VxVM is normally quite simple, as you could see from the last paragraph. Getting up to speed in VxVM is fairly straightforward and easy. But if you are working in a data center you are probably not served well by a simple guide to VxVM. You need to understand what's behind the scenes, how stuff is done in VxVM and why. My favorite comparison for that is based on cars: If someone teaches you how to drive by telling you when to press which pedal and when to move the gear shift level to where, then you will be able to drive to work every day. But when you are doing VxVM in a data center environment you are not "driving to work". You are doing the equivalent of driving the "Rallye Paris-Dakar". Nobody can prepare you for what happens on such a trip. You need to know the inner workings of your car as precisely as possible. How does the steering actually work, what does the center differential do, how does tire pressure, camber, anti-roll bars and toe-in settings interact with the shock absorbers and springs etc. That is why this book drills right down to the low level objects and shows their interactions. Then, once you understand those, it shows you how to do the simple stuff easily.

The easy parts of this book are marked with a little "Easy Sailing" boat. The comprehensive listing of all interesting features and how to use them is marked by "The Full Battleship", and explanations about implementation details as well as much of a technical reasons for VxVM's design and behavior are covered in sections marked with the "Technical Deep Dive" submarine. You can select the chapter section as you like, they do not usually depend on each other.

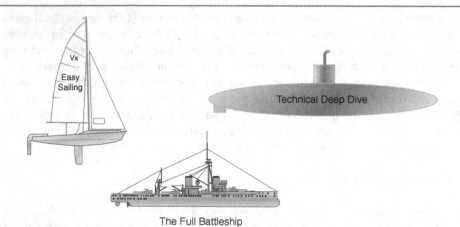

The Full Battleship

Figure 2-4:   The vessels that will guide you through this book, and what they stand for: Easy Sailing, The Full Battleship, and the Technical Deep Dive

CHAPTER 3: INCORPORATING DISKS INTO VXVM

by Volker Herminghaus

In the previous chapter you gained an overview over what the concept behind Veritas Volume Manager (or VxVM) is, what storage objects are used and how they act together to form a complete volume management layer. So now, after the extensive problem introduction in chapter one and the in-depth look at VxVM objects from chapter two, let us get some actual work done. We will start with a machine that is already running VxVM, go through all steps necessary to incorporate a new disk into a VxVM disk group and discuss what is going on as well as alternative ways to do it.

V. Herminghaus and A. Sriba, *Storage Management in Data Centers*,
DOI: 10.1007/978-3-540-85023-6_3, © Springer-Verlag Berlin Heidelberg 2009

3.1 Solaris Disk Handling

3.1.1 Getting a New Disk into Solaris

Once VxVM has been successfully installed and configured the command `vxdisk list` shows all disks attached to the system and known to VxVM. Attaching a new disk (or LUN, remember the two are the same to VxVM) to a Solaris machine does not make that device visible to the operating system. What is necessary in order for the OS to see a new disk? First of all the OS needs a device driver which it can use to physically "talk" to the HBA (host bus adapter) to which the disk is attached. We will assume for now that the HBA driver is already installed. The machine obviously also needs a SCSI protocol driver to use on top of the HBA driver so it can talk SCSI protocol with the disk. The SCSI driver is always installed, otherwise we would not have been able to boot from a SCSI disk. Theoretically, if you boot from a network or other non-SCSI device you could actually be missing the SCSI driver, but unless something really weird happened the SCSI driver would be automatically loaded by the kernel as soon as it is required. So let us pretend we have both the HBA and the SCSI protocol driver installed in the system already.

Now we physically connect a new disk device (or zone a new LUN) to the system. Does this make Solaris recognize the new device? Of course it does not. Even a reboot will go no step towards making the disk visible, unless we supply the reconfigure-flag (`reboot -- -r`) or create a file named /reconfigure before booting in order to make Solaris actually look for new devices. But we do not need to actually reboot; this would be quite an insult to the operating system, so to speak. What the OS (Solaris 9; 10 skips the first step) does when it boots in reconfigure mode is execute the command `luxadm -e create_fabric_device` to re-acquire FC targets that were previously configured by the admin using `cfgadm` and whose WWPNs (World Wide Port Names) the `cfgadm` command stored in /etc/cfg/fp/fabric_WWN_map. After these `luxadm` commands it eventually calls the command `devfsadm`. This command instructs the device file system configuration daemon process to inquire all devices on all controllers and check for new devices as well as ones that have been lost. For the new devices it will then create device nodes in /dev and /devices so that the device will be accessible via the UNIX file system tree.

This is when VxVM first gets a chance to see the device. Unless a valid device file exists Volume Manager cannot access the disk, nor can it somehow miraculously see things that the OS does not see or fix things that the OS cannot fix. VxVM, like any other product, first requires that the OS be capable of physical access to the device.

3.1.2   You Don't Format with "format"

Now that the OS sees the disk device we can almost switch to purely using VxVM commands so that we can finally get rid of all that physical disk legacy. But first, one more thing needs to be done by operating system means, and that is to format the disk, i.e. to put a valid Solaris label (or VTOC) on it so that the higher software layers can not just read and write individual blocks of the disk, but can actually get some reasonable meta information about it, like its size, number and locations of partitions etc. Why can that not be done without a valid label? The reason is actually very simple: When devfsadm finds a new disk and creates its device node it does not create just one device file but eight; one for each slice. Now imagine your new LUN is a re-used one from some antique, crufty operating system that stores some arcane partition table in block zero of the disk. We get this new LUN into our system, devfsadm creates eight device files so we can access each of the Solaris slices that can be registered in the VTOC block. But alas, there is not a single usable partition on this former Windows (or other) disk. All we can see is illegible stuff in an unintelligible format. At the byte offsets where we expect a 32-bit block number specifying the offset for partition three, for instance, there might even be a negative value! What would newfs do when we tried to create a file system on such a partition? It might actually skip backwards and overwrite important data unless the programmers took extra caution to prevent this.

This is why every disk or LUN that is to be used in Solaris must always carry a valid VTOC. You use the format command to write a valid VTOC (which is called "labelling" in the format program). You can also actually issue a SCSI "format" instruction to a disk from the Solaris format command, but this is almost never done since all modern disks come pre-formatted. All they need is a valid Solaris VTOC. The same is essentially true for other operating systems as well, since they all need some kind of fixed entry point into the disk's or LUN's internal data structures, and this fixed entry point must be initialized before the medium can be used.

3.1.3   Finding New Disks in VxVM

So now that the LUN or disk is working, the OS sees it, and the LUN is even labeled correctly so the OS does not stumble over some leftover from the previous user. When will VxVM see this new disk? How do we even know if VxVM sees the disk?

Well, the last one is easy. The command vxdisk list shows all disks that VxVM knows, one per line, with their access records to the left and their status to the right. Here's an example:

```
# vxdisk list
DEVICE       TYPE          DISK        GROUP       STATUS
c0t0d0s2     auto:none     -           -           online invalid
c0t10d0s2    auto:none     -           -           online invalid
```

Apparently in this case, VxVM only sees two disks: Their access records are c0t0d0 (which happens to be the boot disk) and c0t10d0. Will it see new disks if we reboot? Yes, but that would be very Windows-like, and not very friendly towards the 14,786 users connected to the online banking system that we are currently working on. All we need to do is tell VxVM to go check for new disks. The right command for this is

```
# vxdisk scandisks
```

This command could even be further limited to look for just specific new disks, controllers and the like, but the given form is the most useful one since it is rare that someone wants to make VxVM see some of the new disks but not all etc. In these cases, man vxdisk does a much better job at explaining what command to issue than this book could.

Many of our readers will be surprised because they may be familiar with a different command to make VxVM scan for new disks. This command is

```
# vxdctl enable
```

This command (vxdctl stands for Veritas daemon control – it controls the Veritas Configuration Daemon vxconfigd) does indeed find new disks (and has done so in all recent releases), but it also does a lot more. It actually does a physical I/O to each disk to check whether the disk is still accessible. If the disk was previously uninitialized it may or may not try to re-read the VTOC in order to find a valid Private Region. It may then decide to read or not to read the Private Region to find out if it is valid or if it has become invalid etc. It also rebuilds the DMP tree and does a lot of other things. Unfortunately what exactly it does differs from version to version, so I would like to suggest you start out with vxdisk scandisks and only use the vxdctl enable command if the new disks do not pop up right away. Let's try integrating my newly attached disk, which we expect to be c0t11d0:

```
# vxdisk list
DEVICE       TYPE          DISK        GROUP       STATUS
c0t0d0s2     auto:none     -           -           online invalid
c0t10d0s2    auto:none     -           -           online invalid
```

It's not there, because the OS has not created the device node yet.

```
# devfsadm      # make all necessary device nodes
# vxdisk list
DEVICE       TYPE          DISK        GROUP       STATUS
c0t0d0s2     auto:none     -           -           online invalid
c0t10d0s2    auto:none     -           -           online invalid
```

It's there, but VxVM's cache does not know it needs to be refreshed. All display commands for VxVM objects read from cached data, as mass storage access could slow the machine or process down.

```
# vxdisk scandisks        # refresh VxVM's cache
# vxdisk list
DEVICE      TYPE        DISK      GROUP       STATUS
c0t0d0s2    auto:none   -         -           online invalid
c0t10d0s2   auto:none   -         -           online invalid
c0t11d0s2   auto:none   -         -           online invalid
```

Here we are!

3.1.4   What if My New Disk is Not Found?

If vxdisk scandisks and vxdctl enable both fail to yield the desired result then there are several further steps you can take in order to make VxVM recognize disk changes. Note that recognition of new LUNs is normally painless, but recognition of disks that had their VTOC changed, or that had their Private Region overwritten or restored (something we like to do in VxVM trouble shooting courses) may require further measures. These may also need to be taken if for instance you get new LUNs that actually have valid Private Regions but that stem from outdated disk groups which had been freed (or worse: deleted on raw disk level) from another server before.

These further measures are, in the order they should be tried:

```
# vxdisk scandisks # tells vxconfigd to scan for new disks
# vxdctl enable # tells vxconfigd to scan a lot of things for a lot of changes
# vxconfigd -k # kills and restarts the configuration daemon
# vxconfigd -k -r reset # additionally resets most of the VxVM drivers'
                        # internal data structures
# reboot # resets all of VxVM's internal data structures
```

The last command is usually a no-no and is only necessary if you encounter a bug in DMP or VxVM or if you are running Cluster Volume Manager, which is much more difficult to handle in special situations than plain VxVM.

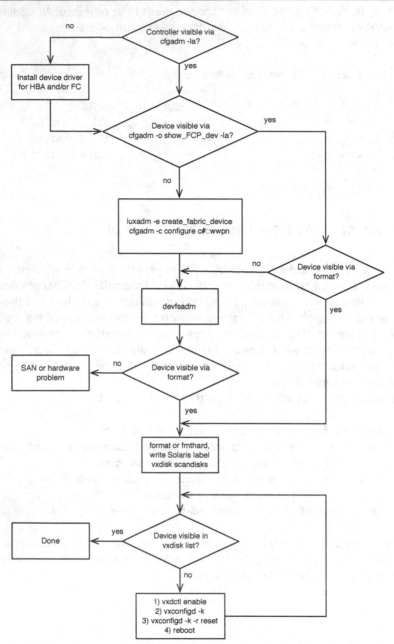

Figure 3-1:   Flow chart outlining incorporation of new LUNs into Solaris and
              VxVM

3.1.5   Leaving Physics Behind – Welcome to VxVM!

Now that the new disk is a fully valid member of the Solaris (or other OS) crowd we can finally incorporate it into VxVM, thus virtualizing it and leaving device physics behind (at least to the degree possible). Virtualizing a disk is done by one simple command:

```
# vxdisksetup -i <accessname>
# vxdisksetup -i c4t9d3
```

The -i flag will initialize the Private Region of the disk. If the disk had already been initialized before and need not be re-initialized you can omit the -i flag. For instance, in the Solaris OS, calling vxdisksetup without -i will just install the Private (and Public) partitions in the VTOC without initializing the Private Region.

There is one specialty with the accessname that Solaris admins sometimes do not get right at the first try: The access name does not include the slice number (slice 2) of the "whole disk" slice. It is merely a path like c4t9d3 rather than c4t9d3s2 The reason for this is VxVM's cross-platform interoperability: Other OSes simply do may not have slice addressing. For example, both HP-UX and AIX have a logical volume management incorporated into the kernel, so slices look really outdated to them. Since the command syntax is supposed to vary as little as possible between the different UNIX dialects only the common denominator – the standard addressing by controller, target, and disk – is used.

After treating the disk or LUN with vxdisksetup -i it now has a valid Private Region and can be incorporated into one and only one disk group. From now on it will be easy for many chapters until we get to the really hard stuff. The part where light speed is too slow for us. The part where buffer credits take a big toll on WAN performance. The part where disks fail and need to be replaced. But all of that is still a long way to go. Now it is just simply stuff that works, so let us look forward to it! You can skip the rest of the chapter and proceed with page 71 if you want. In the rest of this chapter we will only delve more deeply into VxVM disk formats and into what else can be done with the vxdisk command.

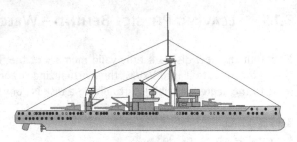

The Full Battleship

3.2   VxVM DISK HANDLING

3.2.1   VxVM DISK FORMATS

What we saw in the example above was this output:

```
# vxdisk list
DEVICE          TYPE            DISK            GROUP           STATUS
c0t0d0s2        auto:none       -               -               online invalid
c0t10d0s2       auto:none       -               -               online invalid
```

The disks' type is `auto:none`, and their status is `online` and `invalid`. What do these values mean? While the access record should be obvious the type and status are not, so let's take a little diversion to find out more about those.

A type of `auto` means that VxVM has received the disk from the operating system by inquiring the disk device list. Old operating systems sometimes could not do this, so you had to define your own disk access records. But this is no longer necessary on any current hardware, so your devices should always be shown as "auto". The sub-type behind `auto:` refers to the initialization scheme or "format" that was used to incorporate the LUN into VxVM. For instance, `none` means that the disk does not have a Private Region. The subtype `sliced` means that Private and Public Region are located on different slices of the disk, and `cdsdisk` means that the whole disk is tagged as a Private Region. In our case, neither disk has a Private Region and both have been auto-discovered so they are both of type `auto:none`.

The status column shows two values: `online` and `invalid`. The first one refers to the operating status of this disk. A disk is `online` only if the OS can access it and the disk has not been offlined in software by the `vxdisk offline` command. This is how the software ON/OFF switch works:

```
# vxdisk offline c0t10d0
# vxdisk list
DEVICE          TYPE            DISK            GROUP           STATUS
c0t0d0s2        auto:none       -               -               online invalid
```

```
c0t10d0s2   auto          -             -              offline
# vxdisk online c0t10d0
# vxdisk list
DEVICE      TYPE          DISK         GROUP          STATUS
c0t0d0s2    auto:none     -             -             online invalid
c0t10d0s2   auto:none     -             -             online invalid
```

What does the `invalid` status refer to? It refers not to the general status but instead to the VxVM-only status. For instance, `invalid` means that a valid Private Region could not be found on this disk. If we create a Private Region by initializing the disk using `vxdisksetup -i`, then the invalid flag will go away, and the format will change (in this case, to `cdsdisk`):

```
# vxdisksetup -i c0t10d0
# vxdisk list
DEVICE      TYPE          DISK         GROUP          STATUS
c0t0d0s2    auto:none     -             -             online invalid
c0t10d0s2   auto:cdsdisk  -             -             online
```

3.2.2 CDSDISK AND SLICED

As you can see the invalid status has disappeared because a valid Private Region was found. The type and format of `auto:cdsdisk` expresses that the Private and Public Region do not reside in separate slices but the most modern disk format is used. CDS stands for Cross-platform Data Sharing. A CDS-disk is a disk that has been initialized by the `vxdisksetup` command with a Private Region spanning all of the disk. But there is more to it: The `vxdisksetup` command also created compatibility volume labels for all the major UNIX-based operating systems so that the disk can be used interchangeably between Solaris, Linux, AIX, and HP-UX. This is achieved by writing a Solaris-compatible VTOC at block zero (where Solaris expects its VTOC), and in addition writing an AIX-compatible volume label at the offset where AIX expects its volume label, and putting a third, HP-UX compatible volume label at the place where HP-UX expects its volume label. Linux compatibility comes for free because Linux can read Solaris VTOCs and will use it when it sees one. It was only possible to implement the CDS format because fortunately, these three volume labels do not reside in overlapping blocks. Windows, for example, uses block zero as the master boot record. This overlaps with the Solaris VTOC block and because the two formats are mutually incompatible the Windows version of VxVM will not recognize a CDS disk and cannot share disk groups with UNIX operating systems.

We can also initialize a disk with different formats than CDS. Before VxVM 4.0 the default format was `sliced`. To compare a sliced disk with a CDS disk let us initialize one of each and compare their VTOCs. First, a look at the CDS disk:

```
# vxdisksetup -i c0t10d0
# vxdisk list
DEVICE      TYPE          DISK         GROUP          STATUS
```

```
c0t10d0s2    auto:cdsdisk    -              -            online
# vxdisksetup -i c0t10d0 format=sliced
# vxdisk list
DEVICE       TYPE            DISK         GROUP          STATUS
c0t10d0s2    auto:sliced     -            -              online

# prtvtoc /dev/rdsk/c0t10d0s2
* /dev/rdsk/c0t10d0s2 partition map
*
* Dimensions:
*     512 bytes/sector
*     133 sectors/track
*      27 tracks/cylinder
*    3591 sectors/cylinder
*    4926 cylinders
*    4924 accessible cylinders
*
* Flags:
*   1: unmountable
*  10: read-only
*
*                         First     Sector    Last
* Partition  Tag  Flags   Sector    Count     Sector  Mount Directory
      2       5    01          0  17682084  17682083
      7      15    01          0  17682084  17682083
```

Note that partition 7 is identical to partition 2 in size and position – they both cover the whole disk. Only the tag is different: 5 (backup) for slice 2, and 15 (VxVM Private Region) for slice 7.

Let's see how much space is left for VxVM. In order to do that, we must put the disk into a DG and then check the DG for free extents:

```
# vxdg init adg adg01=c0t10d0
# vxdg -g adg free
DISK         DEVICE          TAG          OFFSET       LENGTH      FLAGS
adg01        c0t10d0s2       c0t10d0      0            17616288    -
```

OK, there are 17616288 blocks free on the CDS disk for VxVM. Now let's compare that to the sliced layout on the same disk.

```
# vxdg destroy adg
# vxdisksetup -i c0t11d0 format=sliced
# vxdisk list
DEVICE       TYPE            DISK         GROUP          STATUS
c0t10d0s2    auto:sliced     -            -              online
# prtvtoc /dev/rdsk/c0t10d0s2
* /dev/rdsk/c0t10d0s2 partition map
```

```
*
* Dimensions:
*     512 bytes/sector
*     133 sectors/track
*      27 tracks/cylinder
*    3591 sectors/cylinder
*    4926 cylinders
*    4924 accessible cylinders
*
* Flags:
*    1: unmountable
*   10: read-only
*
* Unallocated space:
*      First      Sector    Last
*      Sector     Count     Sector
*         0       3591      3590
*
*                          First     Sector     Last
* Partition  Tag  Flags   Sector     Count      Sector    Mount Directory
      2       5    01          0    17682084    17682083
      3      15    01       3591       68229       71819
      4      14    01      71820    17610264    17682083
```

We see that cylinder zero is left unallocated; the Private Region starts at sector 3591 which is exactly one cylinder offset from zero (see the "Dimensions" section at the beginning of the output as well as the "Unallocated space" section in the middle). The Private Region itself resides on slice 3 and has tag 15, while the Public Region resides on slice 4 and has tag 14 (the identifier tag for Public Region).

```
# vxdg init adg adg01=c0t11d0
VxVM vxdg ERROR V-5-1-6478 Device c0t10d0s2 cannot be added to a CDS disk group
```

Oops. The default format for disk groups is CDS. Only DGs that have the CDS flag can be cross-imported between platforms. In order for that to work, all the disks in such a DG must have the CDS layout. If we want to use sliced disks to create a DG, then we must turn the CDS flag for the disk group off by specifying cds=off when creating the DG.

```
# vxdg init adg adg01=c0t11d0 cds=off
# vxdg -g adg free
DISK        DEVICE       TAG       OFFSET    LENGTH     FLAGS
adg01       c0t10d0s2    c0t10d0   0         17610256   -
```

In this case we are left with 17610256 free blocks for VxVM. Due to the empty cylinder and varying internal size of the Private Region the free block count differs between CDS and sliced layout.

3.2.3 How to Mix CDS and Sliced Disks in a Disk Group?

Since the advent of the cdsdisk format there has been a lot of confusion about what to use when and how to mix sliced disks and cdsdisks in the same disk group. The concept is – as always – rather straightforward. But this has been obfuscated by lack of understanding of the concepts and by the confusing names: Disk media can be of CDS format, and disk groups can have a CDS flag set. They sound the same, but they are not the same. So let us clear this up and reveal its simplicity:

Idea: If disk metadata (VTOC, label) were cross-platform readable then because VxVM is also cross-platform, a VxVM disk group could be used cross-platform.

Implementation: VxVM for HP-UX knows how to write a HP-UX compatible label, VxVM for AIX knows how to write an AIX compatible label, VxVM for Solaris knows how to write a Solaris compatible label. Combine this cross-platform know-how and have vxdisksetup write all three label types on every disk.

Problem: If there is a legacy disk of sliced format in a disk group then this disk will not be cross-platform readable and accordingly, the disk group can not be imported on other platforms. Do we want VxVM to find out after importing 999 of 1000 disks in a disk group that the 1000th disk is sliced and the disk group cannot be imported? No, we don't. We want to know before trying to import a DG if the import is going to fail anyway.

Solution: Create an extra flag in the disk group data structure that can be set to ON if and only if all disks in the disk group are cross-platform shareable. Make this value the default for DG creation so that the DG's functionality is automatically enhanced by the CDS feature. If the users do not want CDS to work they can (or must) switch it off be setting the CDS flag to OFF for the DG like this:

```
# vxdg -g mydg set cds=off
```

Limitation: Whenever a sliced disk is added to a disk group that disk group's CDS flag must first be reset to OFF. Likewise, when creating a new DG from sliced disks the flag must be reset in the disk group creation process by specifying cds=off.

Unfortunately, the latter is not done automatically by VxVM.

Note that a Solaris **boot disk is always sliced** because the OS needs to find a partition with the root tag to boot from. So the CDS format cannot be used for the boot disk.

If a disk is initialized with a sliced layout then enough space is reserved to be able to convert it into a cdsdisk later. That is why you saw the first cylinder unallocated from the sliced disk in the example before. Conversion to cdsdisk layout is done by the utility /usr/lib/vxvm/bin/vxcdsconvert.

3.2.4 Other Disk Formats

In addition to cdsdisk and sliced there are two more formats: none and simple. The none format is actually not a real format, i.e. you cannot specify it to vxdisksetup -i. It is displayed if no Private Region can be found on the disk.

The simple format can be specified to vxdisksetup and yields a VTOC that looks similar to that of a cdsdisk, i.e. it has Private and Public Region together in one single, large slice. The difference is that the slice is not slice 7 as for a cdsdisk, but slice 3, and the first cylinder is again unallocated in case a later conversion to cdsdisk is desired. A simple disk also does not hold the AIX and HP/UX compatibility labels.

Come to think of it: why would anyone ever use a sliced disk layout except for a boot disk, where it is required to use individual slices? Keeping Private and Public Regions separate in a way that is visible to the operating system and user is not optimal and seems unnecessary. Use cdsdisk whenever possible!

3.2.5 ENCAPSULATION OVERVIEW – INTEGRATING LEGACY DATA

The vxdisksetup command alters the partition table in a rather radical way: all previous data partitions are wiped off the disk unless one of them is currently mounted! If we do not want to copy the data from our partition-based file system to a new volume-based one, how do we get the data under VxVM control?

The answer is encapsulation. This is a different way of bringing a LUN or disk under VxVM control. The idea is to have VxVM find some free space on the disk where it can put its Private Region (which is only a few MB in size), and find one (for simple layout) or two (for sliced layout) free slots in the VTOC in order to store the pointers to the Private Region and Public Region. Then, the encapsulation process reads the information about existing extents (i.e. partitions or slices) from the VTOC and maps them into VxVM subdisk objects (which are, as you know, nothing but extents). It then writes them into the disk group's Private Region database. Additionally, so that the user can access the subdisks, each subdisk is put into a straight concat plex which is then put into a normal volume object. All this is done by one simple command: vxencap. The names for the virtual objects are appropriately chosen by the encapsulation command if they can be derived from their partition tags: rootvol, swapvol etc. or they are simply derived from the controller paths that were used to mount them.

To sum up, encapsulation consists of the following steps:

1) Allocate free space for the Private Region
2) Allocate free VTOC slots for Public and Private Region
3) Map existing slices to subdisks and associate them with plexes and volumes
4) Remove all slices from the VTOC that are not required during the boot phase
5) Modify /etc/vfstab to update slice mounts to mounts of the new volumes
6) Demand a reboot from the user if the root disk has been encapsulated, or wait for the user to reboot if a data disk has been encapsulated.

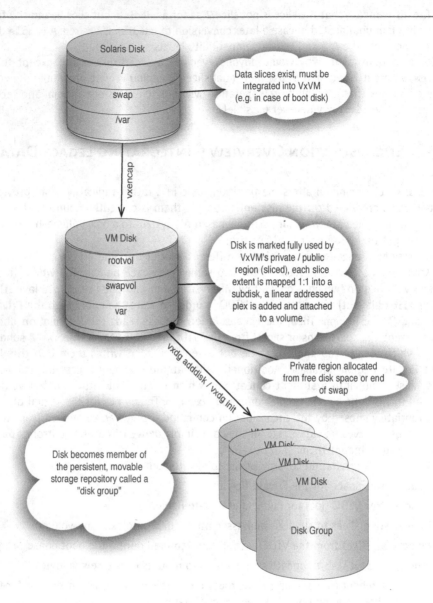

Figure 3-2:   Encapsulating a disk creates volumes from existing partitions by allocating subdisks that line up exactly with the original location of the slices, associating these subdisks with plex objects and attaching them to volume objects.

After the reboot you can mount the new volumes at the same place where you used to have the slices mounted. Because they are no longer bound to their slice legacy you can now do cool stuff with the volumes, like change their layout, mirror them, resize them or move them to somewhere else. Of course this does not work well with those volumes that are required by the boot process because their VTOC entries must not be deleted and therefore these volumes are stuck to legacy behavior. There are ways around this but they are what hackers describe as **non-trivial**.

Encapsulation of a disk is performed by issuing the vxencap command and passing it the right parameters: accessname, target DG and – if applicable – a flag to create the target DG and its format. Here are two examples, the first one for a standard disk, the second one for the root disk:

```
# vxencap -g mydg mydg02=c0t2d0  # mydg exists, so add this disk to it
# vxencap -g bootdg -f sliced -c rootdisk=c0t0d0 # -c: create new "bootdg"
```

Read more about encapsulation in Albrecht Scriba's dedicated chapter beginning on page 319, which should leave no question about encapsulation unanswered. It takes you on a tour so low-level that it will show you how to encapsulate a whole disk manually, without using the vxencap command! It will show you precisely and in detail how VxVM's volume management works, how it addresses its storage and how one can incorporate data from any other volume management software provided the basic addressing schemes are compatible (i.e. no bit-slicing or content-addressing or similarly weird stuff is involved).

3.2.6   SUMMARY

You should now know much more than you ever wanted to know about initializing disks for VxVM. If you are still hungry for more, please read the man pages for vxdisk and vxdisksetup. There is a lot more to vxdisk than what is written here, but this book was intended not to become more than twice the weight of a 2008 notebook computer...

CHAPTER 4: DISK GROUPS

by Volker Herminghaus

4.1 OVERVIEW

In the previous chapter we discussed how disks or LUNs get incorporated into VxVM. That was admittedly a complicated chapter. From here on it is relatively straightforward, at least until you reach the technical deep dive section. Veritas had some very bright developers when they designed VxVM, and it shows. Some of the concepts are not easy to grasp because of the genius behind them. But once you understand them and get the hang of them, you will never want anything else. Guaranteed.

4.1.1 WHAT IS A DISK GROUP?

How would a single disk be useful in the RAID context? If we used individual disks, we would still be limited to a certain limited and fixed size, to a certain limited and fixed number of IOPS, to zero redundancy and so on. It does not make any sense to work with individual disks if you are running a volume management software. The least you need is a number of disks working together to overcome the physical limitations of individual disks. Preferably working together in such a way that control over the whole "disk group" (as we will call it from here on) can be easily transferred from one host to another in order to enable easy and reliable failover for cluster configurations. This is **exactly** what Veritas implemented with their VxVM disk groups, no less, no more.

To put it quite shortly: A DG is to a SAN what a partition is to a disk: it splices the available storage into separate items for independent use. When laying out disk groups

V. Herminghaus and A. Sriba, *Storage Management in Data Centers*,

DOI: 10.1007/978-3-540-85023-6_4, © Springer-Verlag Berlin Heidelberg 2009

care must be taken to balance the amount of independence against space constraints. As an analogy: you could layout your root disk with just one file system and keep all of /var, /usr, /home and /opt in the root (/) file system. The advantage is that very little space is lost to boundary effects: All directories share the same free disk blocks. Whereas if root (/), /var, /usr, /home and /opt are all separate file systems it would be possible for an application that is creating a lot of e.g. log data to let the /var file system run out of space while /usr still has a lot of free space left. What a waste! On the other hand, if all of the root disk was in a single file system, then the application that used to fill up just the /var file system may eventually fill up the whole, unified file system, eventually rendering the system unusable.

The same principle applies to DGs: You place a few disks into a DG destined for a database, a few others into a DG for a web server, and again others are used in a separate DG for your mirrored boot disks. How many DG should you create? This question is easily answered once you think of what kind of software VxVM is. Its purpose is to serve as a basis for high-availability cluster environments. An HA cluster uses multiple servers connected together and attached to shared storage to run a service on one server. In case of failure, another server automatically takes control and starts running the service. In order to do so it first has to take control over the storage, which it does by reserving the set of disks that are required in order to run the service. That set of disks is what is called a disk group in VxVM terminology. In the case outlined above, the cluster software would have one service for the database and another, independent service for the web server. Each service stores its data on the volumes contained in one disk group. When the host running the web server fails, the other server takes control of the web server DG by a process called importing the DG

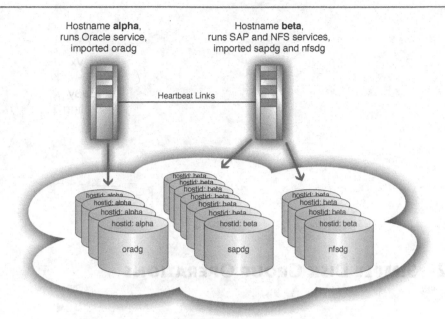

Figure 4-1:   Disk groups are designed with high-availability clusters in mind. A disk group contains all storage resources for a certain service group and is dynamically imported and deported by the cluster software. During import the hostname of the importing host is written into the private region database of the disks in the disk group to prevent concurrent imports by other hosts.

Basically .you would use one DG for your boot environment (although that is not mandatory) and a DG for every service which the machine is running and which might eventually be taken over by or migrate to another host. Migration would be done by simply issuing a command to relinquish control of the disk group (called deporting) on this host and another command to gain control over the DG on the target host (importing).

As a rule of thumb: If you are absolutely sure that you will never ever move data between hosts then you might stick with just one DG. In a cluster, use one DG per service group. If you want to make sure that I/O from one application does not affect another application then it is a good idea to use DGs to separate them, too.

4.2 SIMPLE DISK GROUP OPERATIONS

CREATING AND DISPLAYING A DISK GROUP

The command for DG operations is called vxdg. It takes a command word and one or several disk group names and will then work on these objects. To create a DG you pass the init command word to vxdg, followed by the name of the DG you want created as well as at least on disk medium that will become part of the DG. For example, to create a DG consisting of just one disk, you could type the following:

```
# vxdg init mydg c0t2d0
```

This command will create a new disk group, make disk c0t2d0 a member of it and flush this metadata to the Private Region of c0t2d0.

```
# vxdisk list
DEVICE       TYPE          DISK      GROUP        STATUS
c0t0d0s2     auto:none     -         -            online invalid
c0t2d0s2     auto:cdsdisk  c0t2d0    mydg         online
c0t10d0s2    auto:cdsdisk  -         -            online
c0t11d0s2    auto:cdsdisk  -         -            online
```

As you can see c0t2d0 now carries the name mydg in the GROUP columns of the vxdisk list output. The DISK column of c0t2d0 says c0t2d0, which is redundant with the access name. The disk name was initialized with the access name because we didn't supply a different name. Having the access name as the disk name can be annoying because eventually the access name may change (e.g. because you attach the disk to a different controller). So when we add the next disk to the DG we will take care to supply a name for it.

ADDING DISKS TO AND REMOVING DISKS FROM A DISK GROUP

Adding a disk to a DG is done by supplying the adddisk command word to vxdg. We also need to tell vxdg which DG we mean by specifying the switch -g <DG-name>.

```
# vxdg -g mydg adddisk mydg02=c0t10d0
# vxdisk list
DEVICE        TYPE          DISK          GROUP         STATUS
c0t0d0s2      auto:none     -             -             online invalid
c0t2d0s2      auto:cdsdisk  c0t2d0        mydg          online
c0t10d0s2     auto:cdsdisk  mydg02        mydg          online
c0t11d0s2     auto:cdsdisk  -             -             online
```

Looking at the DISK column we find the name mydg02 that we supplied. The suggested naming convention when naming disks is to use the DG-name followed by a two-digit counter. We started at 02 because we know that we are going to change the first disk to mydg01 later on. How can we do that? There are several possibilities. For instance we could remove the disk from the DG again, then put it back in and supply the right name at that time. Removing disks from a DG is done by supplying the rmdisk command word to vxdg.

```
# vxdg -g mydg rmdisk c0t2d0
# vxdisk list
DEVICE        TYPE          DISK          GROUP         STATUS
c0t0d0s2      auto:none     -             -             online invalid
c0t2d0s2      auto:cdsdisk  -             -             online
c0t10d0s2     auto:cdsdisk  mydg02        mydg          online
c0t11d0s2     auto:cdsdisk  -             -             online
```

```
# vxdg -g mydg adddisk mydg01=c0t2d0
# vxdisk list
DEVICE        TYPE          DISK          GROUP         STATUS
c0t0d0s2      auto:none     -             -             online invalid
c0t2d0s2      auto:cdsdisk  mydg01        mydg          online
c0t10d0s2     auto:cdsdisk  mydg02        mydg          online
c0t11d0s2     auto:cdsdisk  -             -             online
```

Now we add a third disk:

```
# vxdg -g mydg adddisk c0t11d0
# vxdisk list
DEVICE        TYPE          DISK          GROUP         STATUS
c0t0d0s2      auto:none     -             -             online invalid
c0t2d0s2      auto:cdsdisk  mydg01        mydg          online
c0t10d0s2     auto:cdsdisk  mydg02        mydg          online
c0t11d0s2     auto:cdsdisk  c0t11d0       mydg          online
```

Oops, looks like we forgot to specify a name again! Let's fix this without removing the disk this time.

RENAMING VIRTUAL OBJECTS

The command vxedit can rename almost any VxVM object at any time. Exceptions are disk group names (which can only be renamed during the import or deport process) and objects in DGs that are not currently imported (because that is when we have no control over them).

```
# vxedit -g mydg rename c0t11d0 mydg03
# vxdisk list
DEVICE       TYPE         DISK         GROUP        STATUS
c0t0d0s2     auto:none    -            -            online invalid
c0t2d0s2     auto:cdsdisk mydg01       mydg         online
c0t10d0s2    auto:cdsdisk mydg02       mydg         online
c0t11d0s2    auto:cdsdisk mydg03       mydg         online
```

Now let's look at where the disk group appears in our UNIX file system, particularly in the /dev/vx directory structure:

```
# ls -ld /dev/vx/*dsk
drwxr-xr-x  4 root     root        512 May 14 16:57 /dev/vx/dsk
drwxr-xr-x  4 root     root        512 May 14 16:57 /dev/vx/rdsk
# ls -l /dev/vx/dsk
total 2
drwxr-xr-x  2 root     root        512 May 14 16:57 mydg
```

DEPORTING AND IMPORTING DISK GROUPS

What happens when we relinquish control over the DG by a process called **deporting**? We pass the deport command word to vxdg and see what happens, then import the DG again and check again:

```
# vxdg deport mydg
# ls -l /dev/vx/dsk
total 0
# vxdg import mydg
# ls -l /dev/vx/dsk
total 2
drwxr-xr-x  2 root     root        512 May 14 16:57 mydg
```

Obviously when a DG is imported it is represented in the file system of the computer as a directory bearing the DG's name located in /dev/vx/dsk and /dev/vx/rdsk. Deporting the DG also removed the file system representation of the DG by removing these two directories. Thus, the objects in the DG can no longer be accessed. Whichever host imports the DG gets the appropriate directory created in /dev/vx/dsk and /dev/vx/rdsk and can access the DG objects.

You can get a listing of all DGs currently imported on a system by issuing the command:

```
# vxdg list
NAME            STATE           ID
mydg            enabled,cds     1210795596.81.infra0
```

What you see here is the name of our disk group (mydg), its state (enabled and cds) and the internal ID by which VxVM addresses it. This ID is generated by the timestamp (number of seconds since the UNIX epoch – January 01, 1970, 00:00:00 UTC), a short random number and the hostname of the machine that created the DG. All of this together makes it highly unlikely that two IDs are ever the same except in the case of a hardware copy from a storage array (which can indeed be a problem, but at least VxVM 5.0 is prepared for such cases).

What we know as the name of the DG is merely the human-readable representation for us poor mortals. Internally, VxVM uses unique IDs for all objects and sometimes we can make use of them, too, e.g. for reviving disk groups that had been accidentally destroyed.

DESTROYING DISK GROUPS

Speaking about destroying, we haven't destroyed a DG yet, so let's do it:

```
# vxdg destroy mydg
# vxdg list
NAME            STATE           ID
```

OK, all gone. Let's see what disks we have...

```
# vxdisk list
DEVICE      TYPE            DISK        GROUP       STATUS
c0t0d0s2    auto:none       -           -           online invalid
c0t2d0s2    auto:cdsdisk    -           -           online
c0t10d0s2   auto:cdsdisk    -           -           online
c0t11d0s2   auto:cdsdisk    -           -           online
```

Now we create the whole DG with all three disks in one single command:

```
# vxdg init mydg mydg01=c0t2d0 mydg02=c0t10d0 mydg03=c0t11d0
# vxdisk list
DEVICE      TYPE            DISK        GROUP       STATUS
c0t0d0s2    auto:none       -           -           online invalid
c0t2d0s2    auto:cdsdisk    mydg01      mydg        online
c0t10d0s2   auto:cdsdisk    mydg02      mydg        online
c0t11d0s2   auto:cdsdisk    mydg03      mydg        online

# vxdg list
NAME            STATE           ID
```

```
mydg        enabled,cds         1210802401.96.infra0
```

Just as a side note: If you are really smart then you can use `perl` to find out exactly what day it was when this example disk group was created. Remember the DG ID holds the number of seconds since the UNIX epoch? This is the command you need:

```
# perl -e 'print scalar localtime (1210802401),"\n"'
Thu May 15 00:00:01 2008
```

Nice, isn't it? OK, since creating a DG with multiple disks in a single step was so easy (you can do this when adding disks, too: just supply multiple `name=<accessname>` pairs), let's try removing multiple disks. Does that work, too?

```
# vxdg -g mydg rmdisk mydg01 mydg02 mydg03
VxVM vxdg ERROR V-5-1-10127 disassociating disk-media mydg03:
     Cannot remove last disk in disk group
# vxdisk list
DEVICE       TYPE           DISK        GROUP       STATUS
c0t0d0s2     auto:none      -           -           online invalid
c0t2d0s2     auto:cdsdisk   mydg01      mydg        online
c0t10d0s2    auto:cdsdisk   mydg02      mydg        online
c0t11d0s2    auto:cdsdisk   mydg03      mydg        online
```

What do we learn from this? First of all, actions in VxVM are transactional, i.e. they either work or not; they do not start and then break off leaving garbage behind. We also learn that specifying multiple arguments to rmdisk is valid syntax, since the command was obviously preparing to remove the third of the three disks when it failed. So it should be possible to at least remove the two others in one go:

```
# vxdg -g mydg rmdisk mydg01 mydg02
# vxdisk list
DEVICE       TYPE           DISK        GROUP       STATUS
c0t0d0s2     auto:none      -           -           online invalid
c0t2d0s2     auto:cdsdisk   -           -           online
c0t10d0s2    auto:cdsdisk   -           -           online
c0t11d0s2    auto:cdsdisk   mydg03      mydg        online
```

That looks good. Now let's try to get rid of the last disk:

```
# vxdg -g mydg rmdisk mydg03
VxVM vxdg ERROR V-5-1-10127 disassociating disk-media mydg03:
     Cannot remove last disk in disk group
```

We get the same error message. And it should indeed be obvious why VxVM must give us that error message. Remember that all data about a disk group is exclusively stored inside the DG itself! In other words, when you remove the last disk from a DG then there is no space left where VxVM can store information about this DG, like its name, state, flags, volumes etc. There is no storage medium to hold this information. In other words, the DG cannot exist without at least one member to hold the information about the DG. So removing the last disk from a DG is equivalent to destroying the DG, and this action should not be implicitly executed by VxVM for convenience, because it could potentially destroy important information. Maybe you just wanted to replace the old disks in the DG with new ones but you wanted to keep the complicated structure of its virtual objects. So you just remove the old disks from the DG and plan to insert the new ones in the next step. Only to find out that the DG was implicitly deleted when you removed the old disks, so that when you try to add the new ones VxVM informs you that there is no such DG. That is surely not desirable, so VxVM will always ask you to explicitly destroy a DG if that is what you really want. So let's do it:

```
# vxdg destroy mydg
# vxdisk list
DEVICE          TYPE            DISK            GROUP           STATUS
c0t0d0s2        auto:none       -               -               online invalid
c0t2d0s2        auto:cdsdisk    -               -               online
c0t10d0s2       auto:cdsdisk    -               -               online
c0t11d0s2       auto:cdsdisk    -               -               online
# vxdg list
NAME            STATE           ID
# ls -l /dev/vx/dsk
total 0
```

As we can see, nothing is left of our disk group after destroying it. In the technical deep dive section at the end of the chapter you will learn how to revive an accidentally destroyed DG!

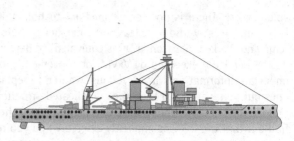

The Full Battleship

4.3 ADVANCED DISK GROUP OPERATIONS

In addition to creating and destroying, importing and deporting, and adding and removing disks from DGs there are more actions and options that we should get into. They are not normally necessary for day-to-day operations, but may come in handy now and then, so let's go through them one by one:

STARTING ALL VOLUMES IN A DG

When a DG is imported its volumes are not started. Starting a volume needs to be done before access is allowed because VxVM needs to check the volume's status and consistency in order to guarantee data integrity. You can start volumes individually or you can start all volumes in a DG at once. This is done by executing one of the following commands, respectively:

```
# vxvol -g <DGname> start volname
# vxvol -g <DGname> startall
```

LISTING DGs THAT ARE NOT IMPORTED

You can see the names of DGs even if they are not imported on your machine. You use the command vxdisk -o alldgs list for that. It will (kind of) do a physical I/O to each non-imported disk and read its DG name from the Private Region. The name is then displayed in parentheses in the normal output format.

```
# vxdisk list # three DGs are imported
DEVICE       TYPE          DISK         GROUP      STATUS
c0t2d0s2     auto:cdsdisk  firstdg01    firstdg    online
c0t10d0s2    auto:cdsdisk  seconddg01   seconddg   online
c0t11d0s2    auto:cdsdisk  thirddg01    thirddg    online
# vxdg deport firstdg seconddg # two are going away
# vxdisk list # How are we going to import them if we forgot their names?
DEVICE       TYPE          DISK         GROUP      STATUS
c0t2d0s2     auto:cdsdisk  -            -          online
c0t10d0s2    auto:cdsdisk  -            -          online
```

```
c0t11d0s2    auto:cdsdisk    thirddg01    thirddg      online
# vxdisk -o alldgs list # That's how: Here are the names!
DEVICE       TYPE            DISK         GROUP        STATUS
c0t2d0s2     auto:cdsdisk    -            (firstdg)    online
c0t10d0s2    auto:cdsdisk    -            (seconddg)   online
c0t11d0s2    auto:cdsdisk    thirddg01    thirddg      online
```

4.3.1   OPTIONS FOR IMPORTING OR DEPORTING A DG

A DG is normally imported by the vxdg import <DG> command. In some cases it may be necessary to supply additional options to the vxdg command to modify its behavior. The following options are available:

FORCED IMPORT IF DISKS ARE MISSING

If an import fails because not all of the disk in the DG can be accessed, then you can use the -f flag (forced import) to import the DG regardless. The default is for vxdg import to refuse import of a DG if not all of its disks can be accessed. The rationale behind that is that if you were to import such a DG and start its volumes, then if a redundant plex is located on a missing disk that plex would be marked STALE and would have to be resynchronised when the disk later comes online. Since it could happen that one of two storage boxes that hold a DG's disks is unavailable (powered off or disconnected) when we import the DG we do not want that to cause a full resynchronisation of potentially large amounts of data. Therefore, the import of such a DG must be manually forced by the administrator.

```
# vxdg -f import mydg
```

FORCED IMPORT OF A DG THAT IS IMPORTED SOMEWHERE ELSE

If an import fails because the DG is already marked as imported by another host then **if and only if we are really sure that the DG is not actually imported by another host** we can specify the -c flag (clear hostid) to undo the other host's reservation. A host that imports a DG will write its hostname into the Private Region of the DG's disks and thus mark the DG as imported. The VxVM running on another host trying to import the DG will see that the DG is imported and normally refuse the import. This is a reservation technique based on goodwill and cooperation. However, it is just as good as any hard reservation technique, for instance using SCSI-2 reservation commands. The reason for it being just as good is that in any reservation technique that is designed as a basis for automated failover there **must** be a way to break the reservation in software. Otherwise no automated failover would be possible if the host that holds the reservation crashes. Even the most elaborate reservation scheme, using SCSI-3 PGR (persistent group reservation) can break the reservation in software. Of course, care must be taken not to break the reservation lightly or out of convenience. I have once been called to a customer that was having problems with data consistency and crashes, and saw them routinely checking the "Clear Hostid" button in VxVM's GUI. When I asked why they were doing that they replied: "because if we don't then sometimes the import doesn't work". They were obviously unaware that their data became corrupted exactly because of what they were doing!

If you want to know more about the hostid field and about "who writes what where when" then read the technical deep dive section of this chapter beginning at page 89.

```
# vxdg -C import mydg
```

RENAMING A DG

Changing the name of a DG is not as easy for VxVM as changing any other object. You may remember that the `vxedit rename` command can be used to alter the name of almost any virtual object. disk groups are different because they are also connected to the physical layer: their names appear as directory names in /dev/vx/*dsk. So if `vxedit` did change the name of the DG object it would also have to change the name of the DG's directory in /dev/vx/*dsk. But this directory is not under VxVM control but under the administrator's control, so we might not have the permissions required to rename the directory. In addition, existing mount points to volumes inside this directory may become confused if part of the path changes while the volume is still mounted. You see that renaming a DG that is already imported is difficult to do right. On the other hand, we need to have the DG imported before we can make any changes to it. If we did not import the DG then we did not reserve it and any other host might change the DG's name also.

The solution to this is that renaming can be done while importing or deporting a DG. In order to do so, we supply the -n flag (new name), followed by the new name, to vxdg. Depending on whether or not the DG is already imported, use either of the following to change the name of the DG from old_dg to new_dg:

```
# vxdg -n new_dg import old_dg
# vxdg -n new_dg deport old_dg
```

TEMPORARY CHANGES TO A DG

Some changes to a DG can be made only temporarily. These are importing a DG and renaming a DG upon import. If you supply the -t flag (temporary) when importing a DG then two things will be different from a normal import: A DG name change will not be persistent, i.e. the name will only be temporarily changed and will revert to the original when the DG is imported, or even when the system crashes. This is done by simply omitting to write the new name to the Private Regions of the DG's disks. The new name resides in memory only and will be forgotten when as the DG is no longer imported.

One more thing happens: Upon normal import a DG is flagged as both "imported" and "autoimport" and the hostid field is filled with the host's system name. If the host was to crash and restart, then when VxVM comes up the DGs are scanned to find ones that bear the right hostid and are flagged autoimport. Those DGs are then automatically imported by vxconfigd. The reason for this is to provide similar behavior for DGs as for plain disks, which do not need to be explicitly prepared for use like DGs. Basically, a DG that was imported before a reboot will automatically appear imported again after the reboot. Temporarily importing a DG will flag the DG noautoimport, which makes the system ignore the DG when it reboots. This is the way that cluster software is supposed to import DGs.

Because when crashed system comes back up, then another node may forcefully import the DG while the rebooting host's VxVM is autoimporting the DG simultaneously, leading to a race condition.

```
# vxdg -t import mydg
# vxdg -t -n new_dg import old_dg # temporarily rename a DG
```

Deporting a DG to a specific host

If you want to deport a DG so that it can only be imported by a specific host then you can do so by specifying the -h flag (host) followed by the name of the target host to the vxdg deport command. This functionality is rarely needed so we will no go into great detail here. What happens when you do this is that VxVM writes the new target host name into the hostid field of the DG when it deports the DG. Any host that then tries to import the DG will find that the DG appears to be already imported and refuse to import the DG unless the import is forced using the -C (clear hostid) flag. See the technical deep dive section for more info on the hostid field.

```
# vxdg -h targethost deport mydg
```

4.3.2   Disk Group Operations for Off-Host Processing

Splitting a Disk Group in Two

If you use so-called snapshots, or point-in-time copies, of volumes for backups and you do not want you production host to do the backing up of the snapshot contents itself, then you may want to give the snaphshot to a backup media server which can then read the data on the snapshot and copy it to backup media. This is called off-host processing. Off-host processing is not limited to making backups. It can also be used to optimize a file system, or for creating test data from a live production database. More will have to be said about snapshots in a later chapter before you can fully understand what is going on in this context (because we need to cover volumes first), but because this is the disk group chapter we will cover it here, and you can come back later from the snapshot chapter.

For now, just imagine that we have a disk group consisting of two disks: mydg01 and mydg02. We can split the DG by specifying which disks (or other virtual objects) we want to split out of the DG, and supplying a name for the new DG. This is called DG split and is executed by using the vxdg split command. The syntax is vxdg split <sourceDG> <destinationDG> <object>:

```
# vxdisk list
DEVICE        TYPE          DISK       GROUP      STATUS
c0t2d0s2      auto:cdsdisk  -          -          online
c0t10d0s2     auto:cdsdisk  mydg01     mydg       online
c0t11d0s2     auto:cdsdisk  mydg02     mydg       online
# vxdg split mydg newdg mydg02
# vxdisk list
```

```
DEVICE          TYPE              DISK        GROUP        STATUS
c0t2d0s2        auto:cdsdisk      -           -            online
c0t10d0s2       auto:cdsdisk      mydg01      mydg         online
c0t11d0s2       auto:cdsdisk      mydg02      newdg        online
# vxdg list
NAME            STATE             ID
mydg            enabled,cds           1210850191.114.infra0
newdg           enabled,cds           1210850431.115.infra0
```

Note that while the DG name has changed for c0t11d0, its disk name is unchanged. It is still mydg02. We could change that using e.g. vxedit -g newdg rename mydg02 newdg01, but in most cases the DGs are rejoined after off-host processing, so it is not normally done.

JOINING TWO DISK GROUPS TOGETHER

To join two DGs together (typically after off-host processing) just specify them to the vxdg join command. The syntax is vxdg join <sourceDG> <destinationDG>. For example, to join the two DGs that were split in the section above, you would use the following command:

```
# vxdg join newdg mydg
# vxdisk list
DEVICE          TYPE              DISK        GROUP        STATUS
c0t2d0s2        auto:cdsdisk      -           -            online
c0t10d0s2       auto:cdsdisk      mydg01      mydg         online
c0t11d0s2       auto:cdsdisk      mydg02      mydg         online
```

MOVING OBJECTS BETWEEN DISK GROUPS

You can also move objects, like disks or volumes, between two existing DGs by using the vxdg move command. The syntax is vxdg move <sourceDG> <destinationDG> <object>:

```
# vxdisk list
DEVICE          TYPE              DISK        GROUP        STATUS
c0t2d0s2        auto:cdsdisk      otherdg01   otherdg      online
c0t10d0s2       auto:cdsdisk      mydg01      mydg         online
c0t11d0s2       auto:cdsdisk      mydg02      mydg         online
# vxdg move mydg otherdg mydg01
# vxdisk list
DEVICE          TYPE              DISK        GROUP        STATUS
c0t2d0s2        auto:cdsdisk      otherdg01   otherdg      online
c0t10d0s2       auto:cdsdisk      mydg01      otherdg      online
c0t11d0s2       auto:cdsdisk      mydg02      mydg         online
```

4.3.3 MISCELLANEOUS DISK GROUP OPERATIONS

SETTING, INQUIRING, AND RESETTING THE DEFAULT-DG

Having to specify a -g flag every time we issue a command can become rather unnerving. Pre-4.0 versions of VxVM used to require the existence of a DG with the name rootdg. This DG was intended for use with the host's internal disks, where deporting would not make any sense anyway. Without the rootdg VxVM would not be able to import any other disk group. In other words, where there was VxVM, there was also a rootdg. This made it a rather convenient default location for all kinds of objects. It was the default disk group for all actions. If you did not specify a DG for a command then VxVM would try to find a DG that contained all of the named objects, starting with the rootdg. Once it found a match it would use this DG and create, delete or modify the objects as requested. This made it very easy for beginners to work with VxVM.

Unfortunately it also made it rather easy for administrators to do horrible mistakes, like unwillingly delete an important volume whose name was not unique. Veritas therefore decided to prefer safety over convenience and not have VxVM search for the specified virtual objects automatically any more, but always require the user to explicitly name the DG. Because the default rootdg is no longer a requirement we can now set and check the default-DG as we like, using the following commands:

```
# vxdctl defaultdg mydg # to set the default-DG to mydg
# vxdg defaultdg # to inquire the current default
mydg
```

We now no longer need to pass the disk group name for every command. However, this is a global setting that is valid for the whole machine. It is entered into VxVM's boot info file, /etc/vx/volboot, where VxVM keeps important information so it can find its own identity (the hostid that it writes to the DGs is in here, too), the root disk etc. BTW: **never** alter this file manually. **Never!** It is created by the vxdctl init command and is formatted in a special way. If you mess with it your system may become unbootable!

If you just want to override a system-wide default DG, or set a default DG just for one session, or if every user wants their own default, then you can export a shell variable named VXVM_DEFAULTDG and set it to the desired disk group name. You can double-check if you used the correct variable name by first setting it to a nonexistent DG name and checking for an error message when you try to create an object. If you get an error message, then it was indeed the right name and you can then use command line repetition to set the same variable to the correct DG name.

```
# export VXVM_DEFAULTDG=wrongdg
# vxassist make testvol 100m
VxVM vxassist ERROR V-5-1-607 Diskgroup wrongdg not found
```

ENCLOSURE-BASED AND OS-BASED NAMING

If you use SAN disks then VxVM will by default use what are called enclosure-based names. Their access names are derived not from the physical paths by which the disk can be reached, but from the type and instance of the storage array they reside in. Depending on the type of storage you use you may see access names such as the ones below (which are admittedly simulated for lack of big storage array hardware). The first one is a JBOD disk, the second one is disk number 8 from IBM shark storage array number 0, and the third is disk number 4 from EMC Symmetrix number 1:

```
# vxdisk list
DEVICE         TYPE          DISK      GROUP      STATUS
Disk_0         auto:cdsdisk  -         -          online
IBM_SHARK0_8 auto:cdsdisk    -         -          online
EMC1_4         auto:cdsdisk  -         -          online
```

If you prefer the controller paths as access names then you can instruct VxVM to switch the naming scheme to either ebn (enclosure based naming) or osn (OS based naming). The change is immediate and only requires you to run the following command:

```
# /usr/sbin/vxddladm set namingscheme=ebn # for enclosure based names
# /usr/sbin/vxddladm set namingscheme=osn # for OS based names
```

Be aware that neither OS-based names nor enclosure-based names are guaranteed to be identical across hosts! Never write scripts that use access names together with any kind of force-option, as this may inadvertently destroy data. Don't forget that the words "it used to work" do not mean "it always works"!

In version 5.0 of VxVM a new namingscheme was introduced: gdn, which stands for Global Device Naming. It was meant to be a way of naming disks the same on all hosts accessing the disks. This is not currently possible unless a private region is put on the disk to hold the access name information. So gdn sounded like a nice idea, but cycling through several iterations of ebn, osn, and gdn shows that the gdn device names change all the time, even when we stay on the same host. Look at the following example of what happens when you switch between gdn and any other naming scheme:

```
# vxdisk list
DEVICE         TYPE          DISK      GROUP      STATUS
d_1            auto:cdsdisk  mydg01    mydg       online
d_2            auto:cdsdisk  mydg03    mydg       online
d_3            auto:cdsdisk  mydg02    mydg       online
# vxddladm set namingscheme=osn
# vxdisk list
DEVICE         TYPE          DISK      GROUP      STATUS
c0t2d0s2       auto:cdsdisk  mydg01    mydg       online
c0t10d0s2      auto:cdsdisk  mydg02    mydg       online
c0t11d0s2      auto:cdsdisk  mydg03    mydg       online
# vxddladm set namingscheme=gdn
```

```
# vxdisk list
DEVICE         TYPE            DISK         GROUP         STATUS
d_4            auto:cdsdisk    mydg01       mydg          online
d_5            auto:cdsdisk    mydg03       mydg          online
d_6            auto:cdsdisk    mydg02       mydg          online
# vxddladm set namingscheme=ebn
# vxdisk list
DEVICE         TYPE            DISK         GROUP         STATUS
Disk_1         auto:cdsdisk    mydg01       mydg          online
Disk_2         auto:cdsdisk    mydg03       mydg          online
Disk_3         auto:cdsdisk    mydg02       mydg          online
# vxddladm set namingscheme=gdn
# vxdisk list
DEVICE         TYPE            DISK         GROUP         STATUS
d_7            auto:cdsdisk    mydg01       mydg          online
d_8            auto:cdsdisk    mydg03       mydg          online
d_9            auto:cdsdisk    mydg02       mydg          online
```

As you see the gdn names change every time. It may just be a bug in this version, but I suggest it's better not to speak any more about gdn in order to protect the incompetent.

Listing Disks with their OS Native Access Names

If you use enclosure-based names then you may occasionally want to see their actual controller paths. There are two ways to do that without having to reset the naming scheme for the whole VxVM installation. The first is to do vxdisk list <accessname> and check the multipathing info in the last few lines. The second is much better but less commonly used because not everybody knows it:

```
# vxdisk -e list
DEVICE        TYPE     DISK       GROUP        STATUS      OS_NATIVE_NAME
Disk_0        auto     -          -            online      c0t2d0s2
IBM_SHARK0_8  auto     -          -            online      c0t10d0s2
EMC1_4        auto     -          -            online      c0t11d0s2
```

4.3.4 SUMMARY

In this section you learned about disk groups: what the reasoning is behind them, how they are created and destroyed as well as deported and imported. You saw how to add disks to a DG and how to take disks away from a DG. We explained where the meta data of a DG must be stored (100% of it inside the DG itself!) and why this is the case. You know where a DG object is represented in the UNIX file system and that it will appear on import and disappear on deport.

If you want to know more, feel free to take the technical deep dive in the next section. If you want to get on to the next chapter, skip over the deep dive and come back later for more. It's worth it.

Technical Deep Dive

4.4 DISK GROUP IMPLEMENTATION DETAILS

In the UNIX implementations of VxVM there is exactly one type of disk group. In the Windows implementation of VxVM there are no less than five types of disk groups, and none of them really seems to improve on the UNIX type of disk group (the five DG types are: basic, primary dynamic, secondary dynamic with no protection, secondary dynamic with SCSI reservation protection, and secondary dynamic for cluster, i.e. with a quorum acquisition scheme). This illustrates quite nicely how thoroughly a way of thinking or the environment of an operating system can influence software design. The UNIX VxVM disk group object fulfills all the needs for reliable enterprise computing. The Windows versions makes things much more complicated with its five different types of disk groups and adds nothing noteworthy to the UNIX VxVM's disk group functionality. You will see how easily a perfect disk group object can be constructed in the following paragraphs.

First of all we need to remember that a disk group's functions include moving the whole DG from one host to another. This rules out once and for all storing any information about a DG in the local file system. Why is that? It is simply because if there was (meta) data about the disk group stored in the local file system, then after the host that holds the disk group becomes unavailable (e.g. due to crash or power failure) the disk group could not be easily transferred to the failover host because the meta data cannot be extracted from the failed host's file system. Alternatively, the DG metadata could be stored in some kind of repository on all of the hosts that could potentially gain access to it

So where does VxVM store all the meta information about a disk group? It stores it inside the disk group itself. All of it. Is that hard to do? Well, not really: there is the Private Region which is destined for VxVM meta data, so there is room for the disk group meta data. Plus there are access methods inside VxVM to read and write the Private Region so it can't be too hard. What we would like to know is the concrete data structures that get written onto a disk when it joins a disk group. Or more precisely: the data structures that get written to **all of the disks** in the disk group when a new disk joins.

REPRESENTATION OF DISK GROUPS IN THE PRIVATE REGION

In order to understand exactly how a disk group works let's have a look at what changes in the Private Region when we use one. To look at the most prominent information of a disk group we use the `vxdisk list <accessname>` command, which will reveal quite a lot. Let's pick our disk c0t2d0 and look at it before it has been treated by vxdisksetup:

```
# vxdisk list c0t2d0
Device:    c0t2d0s2
devicetag: c0t2d0
type:      auto
info:      format=none
```

```
flags:      online ready private autoconfig invalid
pubpaths:   block=/dev/vx/dmp/c0t2d0s2 char=/dev/vx/rdmp/c0t2d0s2
guid:       -
udid:       IBM%5FDNES-309170Y%5FDISKS%5FAJF18581%20%20%20%20%20%20%20%20
site:       -
Multipathing information:
numpaths:   1
c0t2d0s2        state=enabled
```

This is what VxVM knows about the disk without even initializing it. For instance, look at the flags section: The disk is flagged as online (this same online status turns up in the common vxdisk list output). It is also marked as autoconfig (which corresponds to the auto:... type in vxdisk list, and because it has no Private Region it is flagged as invalid (just like the invalid status in vxdisk list). Note also the multipathing information in the last three lines. This is where you see the actual number and details of the controller paths used by DMP to access the device. Now let's compare this to what the disk looks like once it is initialized with a Private Region (for our referential convenience the output was numbered by piping it through cat -n):

```
# vxdisksetup -i c0t2d0
# vxdisk list c0t2d0 | cat -n
 1  Device:     c0t2d0s2
 2  devicetag:  c0t2d0
 3  type:       auto
 4  hostid:
 5  disk:       name= id=1210805068.106.infra0
 6  group:      name= id=
 7  info:       format=cdsdisk,privoffset=256,pubslice=2,privslice=2
 8  flags:      online ready private autoconfig autoimport
 9  pubpaths:   block=/dev/vx/dmp/c0t2d0s2 char=/dev/vx/rdmp/c0t2d0s2
10  guid:       {4dfc8d52-1dd2-11b2-8dfa-080020c28592}
11  udid:       IBM%5FDNES-309170Y%5FDISKS%5FAJF18581%20%20%20%20%20%20%20%20
12  site:       -
13  version:    3.1
14  iosize:     min=512 (bytes) max=2048 (blocks)
15  public:     slice=2 offset=65792 len=17846208 disk_offset=0
16  private:    slice=2 offset=256 len=65536 disk_offset=0
17  update:     time=1210805069 seqno=0.2
18  ssb:        actual_seqno=0.0
19  headers:    0 240
20  configs:    count=1 len=48144
21  logs:       count=1 len=7296
22  Defined regions:
23   config   priv 000048-000239[000192]: copy=01 offset=000000 disabled
24   config   priv 000256-048207[047952]: copy=01 offset=000192 disabled
25   log      priv 048208-055503[007296]: copy=01 offset=000000 disabled
26   lockrgn  priv 055504-055647[000144]: part=00 offset=000000
```

```
27  Multipathing information:
28  numpaths:    1
29  c0t2d0s2          state=enabled
```

OK, that is clearly too much information. Let us just go through the most important lines and see what we can make of them:

- Line 4 shows an empty hostid. This means the disks is available to all systems because it is not dedicated to a single host or cluster.
- Line 5 shows a disk ID (but no human readable disk name yet). Like the disk group ID, the disk ID also contains the number of seconds since the UNIX epoch.
- Line 6 shows that there is no disk group name or ID (no wonder; the disk in not a DG member yet)
- Line 7 shows the format (cdsdisk) as well as Public Region offset and slices for Pub/Priv
- Line 8 shows a new flag, autoimport, which will be explained shortly
- Line 12 lists a site, which is uninitialized. This is actually a highly interesting feature that you can use in stretched dual data centers to optimize performance by defining the location of the disks as well as the location of the servers and have them read from the physically closest mirrors. We will not go into further detail on that here, but now you know where to look for optimization in case of stretched clusters.
- Line 17 lists the timestamp of the last change to the disk's configuration. If you know perl well then you can find out that it has gotten rather late by now (the computer's time zone is Germany, which is UTC plus 1 hour).

LOW-LEVEL OBSERVATIONS OF DISK GROUP BEHAVIOR

Now let us reduce the output to the most interesting lines and only check those while we go through creating, importing, deporting, renaming and destroying a disk group. We do so by using egrep with an extended search pattern:

```
# vxdisk list c0t2d0 | egrep '^hostid: |^disk: |^group: |^flags: '
hostid:
disk:      name= id=1210805068.106.infra0
group:     name= id=
flags:     online ready private autoconfig autoimport
```

OK, now we create a disk group from this disk and check to see what has changed:

```
# vxdg init mydg mydg01=c0t2d0
# vxdisk list c0t2d0 | egrep '^hostid: |^disk: |^group: |^flags: '
hostid:    infra0
disk:      name=mydg01 id=1210805068.106.infra0
group:     name=mydg id=1210806514.110.infra0
flags:     online ready private autoconfig autoimport imported
```

OK, that makes a lot of sense, actually: The `hostid` field now holds our system name (`infra0`), the disk name is filled in with the name we provided (`mydg01`), the disk group information (line 3: `group`) is updated with name and a newly generated ID (oh my gosh it's late. Look at the time stamp in the disk group ID!). And there is one more flag that says the DG is currently imported. We just created the DG, and since we know that only the server that has imported the DG can alter its contents it makes a lot of sense that VxVM automatically keeps a newly created DG imported.

OK, what happens when we deport the DG from our host, thus relinquishing control of it and freeing the DG for anyone on the SAN to take it?

```
# vxdg deport mydg
# vxdisk list c0t2d0 | egrep '^hostid: |^disk: |^group: |^flags: '
hostid:
disk:      name= id=1210805068.106.infra0
group:     name=mydg id=1210806514.110.infra0
flags:     online ready private autoconfig
```

What we see is that the `hostid` is returned to an empty field, which means that the disk (or rather: the disk group) is no longer reserved by our host. The `imported` flag has gone away, which is rather obvious since the disk group is indeed not imported any more. The disk's ID has survived but its readable name has disappeared (which is also OK because whoever has imported the disk group by now might have changed the disk's name using `vxedit rename`). And the disk group's ID and name have survived. The reason for this is not immediately obvious. But consider that the disk group will eventually be re-imported by our host by passing its name to the `vxdg import` command. If the DG name was lost upon deporting we would have a hard time importing the DG back. Let's re-import the DG back onto our system and see if we get exactly the same output as we got before we deported it:

```
# vxdg import mydg
# vxdisk list c0t2d0 | egrep '^hostid: |^disk: |^group: |^flags: |^update'
hostid:    infra0
disk:      name=mydg01 id=1210805068.106.infra0
group:     name=mydg id=1210806514.110.infra0
flags:     online ready private autoconfig autoimport imported
update:    time=1210807801 seqno=0.11
```

Yes, everything is exactly the same as before: our host as written its name into the hostid field to prevent other VxVM-based systems from trying to import the DG, the disk name is back, and the DG is marked as imported again. Only the `update` time stamp shows the author that it really is time to continue writing this book tomorrow ;)

IDENTIFYING FREE EXTENTS IN A DG

You normally do not care about where the individual free extents in a DG are, because you do not allocate extents for volumes yourself using vxmake. Instead, you use vxassist as a high-level command to help you gather space for your volume. Therefore you would

normally ask vxassist how large a volume you can make given the required layout constraints.

But if you still want to check for individual free extents, out of fun or interest, you can
do so by issuing the `vxdg free` command:

```
# vxdg -g mydg free
GROUP       DISK        DEVICE     TAG       OFFSET    LENGTH      FLAGS
mydg        mydg01      c0t2d0s2   c0t2d0    0         17846208    -
```

SETTING AND INQUIRING PRIVATE REGION REDUNDANCY

Normally VxVM will not write to all Private Regions in a DG. It will only activate the first
five disks in any DG and store the Private Region data on those If the disk group is spread
across more than one controller, then the default value is six: three on each controller. They
are called the config disks because they hold the configuration database. The configuration
database is the database of all user-initiated changes to a DG. For instance, when a volume
is created, modified, or deleted this is written into the configuration database of all config
disks. The configuration database (or config-DB) hold much more information than just disk
and volume information. It contains everything that VxVM knows about the DG.

There is another database, which is called the log-DB. The log-DB holds information
about configuration changes that happened without user initiation. E.g. if a disk fails then
the VxVM kernel will detach all plexes that have subdisks on the failed disk. This is effectively a change of the VxVM configuration, yet it was not user-initiated.

You can check which disks are config disks and which are log disks with the `vxdg list`
command if you supply the disk group names as parameters:

```
# vxdg list mydg | cat -n
 1  Group:      mydg
 2  dgid:       1210850191.114.infra0
 3  import-id:  1024.113
 4  flags:      cds
 5  version:    140
 6  alignment:  8192 (bytes)
 7  ssb:              on
 8  detach-policy: global
 9  dg-fail-policy: dgdisable
10  copies:     nconfig=default nlog=default
11  config:     seqno=0.1066 permlen=48144 free=48137 templen=3 loglen=7296
12  config disk c0t2d0s2 copy 1 len=48144 state=clean online
13  config disk c0t10d0s2 copy 1 len=48144 state=clean online
14  config disk c0t11d0s2 copy 1 len=48144 state=clean online
15  log disk c0t2d0s2 copy 1 len=7296
16  log disk c0t10d0s2 copy 1 len=7296
17  log disk c0t11d0s2 copy 1 len=7296
```

Looking at the output you can see in line 10 that the number of copies for the config
and log databases are at their default value. Lines 12-14 list the config disks, 15-17 list the

log disks. Now let's change the number of configs and logs to 1 and 2, respectively. This is a tricky command line as you will see. It seems that the developers didn't really think deeply about how to implement it:

```
# vxedit set nconfig=1 mydg # fails because -g <DG> is missing
VxVM vxedit ERROR V-5-1-5455 Operation requires a disk group
# vxedit -g mydg set nconfig=1 # fails because no DG passed as a parameter
VxVM vxedit ERROR V-5-1-1670 must specify record names or a search pattern
# vxedit -g mydg set nconfig=1 mydg # works (ugly and redundant syntax)
# vxedit -g mydg set nconfig=2 mydg # same with the log disks
# vxdg list mydg | cat -n
 1  Group:     mydg
 2  dgid:      1210850191.114.infra0
 3  import-id: 1024.113
 4  flags:     cds
 5  version:   140
 6  alignment: 8192 (bytes)
 7  ssb:  on
 8  detach-policy: global
 9  dg-fail-policy: dgdisable
10  copies:    nconfig=1 nlog=2
11  config:    seqno=0.1071 permlen=48144 free=48137 templen=3 loglen=7296
12  config disk c0t2d0s2 copy 1 len=48144 state=clean online
13  config disk c0t10d0s2 copy 1 len=48144 disabled
14  config disk c0t11d0s2 copy 1 len=48144 disabled
15  log disk c0t2d0s2 copy 1 len=7296 disabled
16  log disk c0t10d0s2 copy 1 len=7296
17  log disk c0t11d0s2 copy 1 len=7296
```

We can see in line 10 that the number of config copies is now one and the number of log copies is two. lines 13 and 14 list the former config disks as disabled, and line 15 shows that one of the former log disks is now disabled. We can set the number of config or log copies to any value greater than zero. There are also the special values `default` and `all`, with their obvious meaning.

RESURRECTING AN ACCIDENTALLY DESTROYED DG

If we accidentally destroyed a DG and want it back, then here is a neat and undocumented trick: We cannot pass the name of the DG to the vxdg import command any more. That name is gone. It was invalidated when the DG was destroyed. But we can specify the old disk group's ID. All we need is find it. And it's actually easy to find: just use `vxdisk list <accessname>` on any of the disks that were in the DG, and the DG-ID will be listed in line 6 of the output:

```
# vxdisk -o alldgs list # DG is completely gone
DEVICE       TYPE         DISK         GROUP        STATUS
c0t2d0s2     auto:cdsdisk -            -            online
```

```
c0t10d0s2    auto:cdsdisk    -              -              online
c0t11d0s2    auto:cdsdisk    -              -              online

# vxdisk list c0t11d0 | grep ^group
group:      name= id=1210864274.146.infra0
# vxdg import 1210864274.146.infra0 # Just use DG-ID instead of DG name
# vxdisk list # The DG is back, and all volumes with it!
DEVICE       TYPE            DISK           GROUP          STATUS
c0t2d0s2     auto:cdsdisk    mydg01         mydg           online
c0t10d0s2    auto:cdsdisk    mydg02         mydg           online
c0t11d0s2    auto:cdsdisk    mydg03         mydg           online
```

IMPORTING MULTIPLE DGS OF THE SAME NAME

Because VxVM does not keep any information about deported DGs it is possible to create several DGs of the same name by deporting the first DG before creating the next one. For instance, we will create three independent DGs, all of the same name (adg, which stands for "a disk group").

```
# vxdg init adg adg01=c0t2d0
# vxdisk list
DEVICE       TYPE            DISK           GROUP          STATUS
c0t2d0s2     auto:cdsdisk    adg01          adg            online
c0t10d0s2    auto:cdsdisk    -              -              online
c0t11d0s2    auto:cdsdisk    -              -              online
# vxdg deport adg
# vxdg init adg adg01=c0t10d0
# vxdisk list
DEVICE       TYPE            DISK           GROUP          STATUS
c0t2d0s2     auto:cdsdisk    -              -              online
c0t10d0s2    auto:cdsdisk    adg01          adg            online
c0t11d0s2    auto:cdsdisk    -              -              online
# vxdg deport adg
# vxdg init adg adg01=c0t11d0
# vxdisk list
DEVICE       TYPE            DISK           GROUP          STATUS
c0t2d0s2     auto:cdsdisk    -              -              online
c0t10d0s2    auto:cdsdisk    -              -              online
c0t11d0s2    auto:cdsdisk    adg01          adg            online
```

Now let's make sure the other adg DGs are still there. We use the command **vxdisk -o alldgs list** to show all DGs, even the ones that are not currently imported.

```
# vxdisk -o alldgs list
DEVICE       TYPE            DISK           GROUP          STATUS
c0t2d0s2     auto:cdsdisk    -              (adg)          online
c0t10d0s2    auto:cdsdisk    -              (adg)          online
```

```
c0t11d0s2   auto:cdsdisk   adg01      adg         online
```

Now how do we import another `adg`? When we try vxdg import adg we get an error saying it is already imported:

```
# vxdg import adg
VxVM vxdg ERROR V-5-1-10978 Disk group adg: import failed:
Disk group exists and is imported
```

If we try deporting our adg and then importing another adg it fails because VxVM keeps timestamps on each DG and **vxdg import** favors the most recent DG. so it will always re-import the last `adg` we had. But remember the trick for reviving an accidentally destroyed DG? We can import and DG using its ID instead of its name. so let's find the ID of the adg that resides on c0t10d0 (the second one):

```
# vxdisk list c0t10d0|grep ^group
group:    name=adg id=1210858812.122.infra0
# vxdg import 1210858812.122.infra0
VxVM vxdg ERROR V-5-1-10978 Disk group 1210858812.122.infra0: import failed:
Disk group exists and is imported
```

OK, it doesn't work without changing the name because then we would have two DGs with the same name imported at the same time. But we can temporarily rename the new `adg`:

```
# vxdg -t -n xdg import 1210858812.122.infra0
# vxdisk list
DEVICE      TYPE          DISK       GROUP       STATUS
c0t2d0s2    auto:cdsdisk  -          -           online
c0t10d0s2   auto:cdsdisk  adg01      xdg         online
c0t11d0s2   auto:cdsdisk  adg01      adg         online
```

And the third one, too:

```
# vxdisk list c0t2d0|grep ^group
group:    name=adg id=1210858684.120.infra0
# vxdg -t -n ydg import 1210858684.120.infra0
# vxdisk list
DEVICE      TYPE          DISK       GROUP       STATUS
c0t2d0s2    auto:cdsdisk  adg01      ydg         online
c0t10d0s2   auto:cdsdisk  adg01      xdg         online
c0t11d0s2   auto:cdsdisk  adg01      adg         online
```

So now we have three DGs with identical names imported under alias, but as soon as we deport them, because we supplied the -t flag their names will revert to their original names. Note that VxVM does not complain about duplicate disk names. They are in separate name spaces (each DG has its own name space, i.e. its own subdirectory in

/etc/vx/*dsk).

4.4.1 MAJOR AND MINOR NUMBERS FOR VOLUMES AND PARTITIONS

Let's look at the volume. First, check what the volume looks like in the file system:

```
# ls -l /dev/vx/*dsk/adg/simplevol
brw-------  1 root    root    270, 62000 May 16 21:15 /dev/vx/dsk/adg/
simplevol
crw-------  1 root    root    270, 62000 May 16 21:16 /dev/vx/rdsk/adg/
simplevol
```

OK, we see a block" and a "character" device. Compare these to normal disk partitions:

```
# ls -lL /dev/*dsk/c0t10d0s2
brw-r-----  1 root    sys     32, 74 May 17 01:48 /dev/dsk/c0t10d0s2
crw-r-----  1 root    sys     32, 74 May 17 01:48 /dev/rdsk/c0t10d0s2
```

As you know, ls outputs the major and minor number instead of the file size when it displays device files. So the major number for the volume is 270, while the major number for a normal partition is 32. What do these major numbers correspond to?

```
# egrep " 32$| 270$" /etc/name_to_major
sd 32
vxio 270
```

As we can see partition I/O is done by the sd (SCSI disk, major number 32) driver, while volume I/O is passed to the vxio driver (major number 270).

CHANGING THE MINOR NUMBERS FOR VOLUME DEVICES

The minor number identifies the instance that the driver has to deal with. it is different for each device but identical for character or block device of the same instance. Each DG carries a base minor number that serves as the bottom value for device minor numbers for the volumes that reside in the DG. The base minor number is generated randomly along with the DG in a way that it does not conflict with any existing volume minor numbers. It is stored as the variable base_minor, which you can inquire using vxprint -F with the appropriate variable names (there will be more about this specific flag in a later section):

```
# vxprint -g adg -F %name,%base_minor
adg,62000 # base_minor of the DG adg
adg01,-
adg02,-
(...)
```

But of course it can always happen that we import a DG from another host, or that we create a new DG while some of our other DGs are deported, and thus VxVM does not know that the base minor number it picks may result in a conflict.

If a DG is imported that has the same minor numbers as the volumes in a DG that is already imported, then a warning is output and the volumes are automatically adjusted to non-conflicting values. However, the DG is not permanently changed. But we can also manually reminor the DG permanently. This is done by the vxdg reminor command:

```
# vxdg reminor adg 10000
# ls -l /dev/vx/*dsk/adg/simplevol
brw-------   1 root      root      270, 10000 May 17 01:57 /dev/vx/dsk/adg/
simplevol
crw-------   1 root      root      270, 10000 May 17 01:57 /dev/vx/rdsk/adg/
simplevol
```

As you can see, the minor number has changed from 62000 to 10000.

Why Change the Base Minor Number on a DG?

The base_minor will, as we said before, adjust itself in case of a conflict. However, there is an important case where this is not a good idea: If you are running an NFS server, then the clients identify the files on the NFS server by the NFS handle, which is a cookie comprised of several values. Among these values are the major and minor number of the device and the inode number of the file. If a failover occurs in a highly available NFS environment, and the failover host changes the minor numbers of the volumes that it takes control of, then the clients' NFS handles will become stale and cannot be used any more. NFS failover will not be transparent any more (which it would otherwise be).

In this case it would indeed be advisable to reminor the DG permanently in order to avoid future problems. Of course you should also make sure the **major** numbers are identical. This can be done by editing the /etc/name_to_major files to make the major numbers for vxdmp and vxio match on all cluster machines, or by using the haremajor script supplied with Veritas Cluster Server.

Another Kind of Volume Manager

CHAPTER 5: VOLUMES

by Volker Herminghaus

5.1 OVERVIEW

In the previous chapter you learned a lot about disk groups, or DGs. But DGs are mere containers for the truly interesting virtual objects, namely volumes. In this chapter we will concentrate on volumes: how they are created, modified, and removed. How you put a file system on them and use them for productive work. How they behave on disk, path or host failures. How I/O to a mirrored volume is handled and how consistency is always guaranteed. What internal virtual objects a volume consists of and how you can inspect and understand them, and much more.

5.1.1 WHAT IS A VOLUME?

A VxVM volume is a modern replacement for a slice or partition. It serves as a container for file system or raw data and allows I/O operations to proceed without being volume-aware, i.e. the software layers above the volume need not be changed in order to work with volumes. Volume I/O is completely transparent unless extra effort is undergone to find out the exact nature of the device. So for all purposes a volume can replace a Solaris or Linux partition, an AIX volume or an HP-UX volume (especially since HP's internal volume management is based on an old version of Veritas Volume Manager). Be aware that a VxVM volume is **not** the virtualized equivalent of a **hard disk**, however! If it was, then it could have a VTOC in block zero and you could partition it or use `vxdisksetup` or `vxencap` on it. That wouldn't make too much sense, would it? Instead of emulating a hard disk it emulates

V. Herminghaus and A. Sriba, *Storage Management in Data Centers,*
DOI: 10.1007/978-3-540-85023-6_5, © Springer-Verlag Berlin Heidelberg 2009

a partition. And what is a partition? A partition is a block-addressable extent that stores data persistently, nothing else. So it should be something relatively easy to emulate.

But there is one crucial feature of a partition that is not so easy to emulate in a volume management software, and that is the following: A partition, since it holds just one copy of the data, will always deliver the same data for any given extent unless you update the data. In a redundant volume, let's say a three-way mirror, this is not at all easy to emulate. Of course you write data to all three mirrors when a write is issued to the volume. But will they all succeed? What if there are hundreds of I/Os outstanding on each of the mirrors and then the host crashes. After a reboot, how can we be sure that all mirror sides are identical? Is there a preferred mirror side that gets written first and holds the most recent data? No, there isn't! Does VxVM copy one mirror side over all the others? No, it doesn't! Does VxVM compare the mirror sides? No, it doesn't! Does VxVM break the partition paradigm and actually deliver different data on consecutive reads of the same extents? No, it doesn't. Well, how does VxVM the guarantee conformance to the critical partition paradigm: to give exactly the same data for the same extent unless the extent is updated?

The answer to this question has to do with quantum physics and Schrödinger's cat (really!). This answer, and much more, will be discussed in detail in the sections that follow. But first, some simple stuff.

Vx
Easy
Sailing

5.2 SIMPLE VOLUME OPERATIONS

5.2.1 CREATING, USING AND DISPLAYING A VOLUME

All common volume operations are done via one simple, unified command. This command is called **vxassist**. In very early versions of VxVM volumes were created by allocating extents from disks in a disk group, associating them with plexes, and putting them into volume objects. But that was much too complicated and cumbersome to be useful. So the command **vxassist** was created, which did all the magic of allocating virtual objects, calculating disk and plex offsets, mapping everything together and starting the volume. In fact, you can still watch part of what **vxassist** does internally when you pass the -v switch to the command. You can then see what other tools are called by **vxassist** internally. Although the allocation commands are usually not displayed because allocations are done by calls to the vxvm allocation library. Let us start by creating a DG out of six disks. Let's call the DG "**adg**" for "a disk group". Then, let's create a simple volume "**avol**" (for "a volume") in our DG using the **vxassist** command. We'll put a file system on the volume and mount the file system. Keep in mind what you learned in chapter 2 (Exploring VxVM) that the device driver for VxVM resides in /dev/vx/*dsk/<DGname>/<Volname>:

```
# vxdisk list # check what we have: six VxVM disks in cdsdisk format
DEVICE       TYPE          DISK       GROUP       STATUS
c0t2d0s2     auto:cdsdisk  -          -           online
c0t3d0s2     auto:cdsdisk  -          -           online
c0t4d0s2     auto:cdsdisk  -          -           online
c0t10d0s2    auto:cdsdisk  -          -           online
c0t11d0s2    auto:cdsdisk  -          -           online
c0t12d0s2    auto:cdsdisk  -          -           online
# vxdg init adg adg01=c0t2d0 adg02=c0t3d0 adg03=c0t4d0 (...) # make a DG
```

```
# export VXVM_DEFAULTDG=adg # Set our default DG for this session
# vxassist make simplevol 1g # Create a volume of exactly 1 GB
# newfs /dev/vx/rdsk/adg/simplevol # Make a UFS file system on the volume
newfs: construct a new file system /dev/vx/rdsk/adg/simplevol: (y/n)? y
/dev/vx/rdsk/adg/simplevol:    2097152 sectors in 1024 cylinders of 32 tracks,
64 sectors
         1024.0MB in 32 cyl groups (32 c/g, 32.00MB/g, 15872 i/g)
super-block backups (for fsck -F ufs -o b=#) at:
 32, 65632, 131232, 196832, 262432, 328032, 393632, 459232, 524832, 590432,
 1443232, 1508832, 1574432, 1640032, 1705632, 1771232, 1836832, 1902432,
 1968032, 2033632,
# mount /dev/vx/dsk/adg/simplevol /mnt # Mount the file system (FS)
# df -h /mnt # Check the FS: 1MB used, 903MB free
Filesystem   size used  avail capacity  Mounted on /dev/vx/dsk/adg/simplevol
             961M  1.0M  903M   1%      /mnt

# cp -r /kernel/* /mnt/. # Put some data on the volume
# df -h /mnt # Check the FS: 89MB used, 815MB free
Filesystem   size used  avail capacity  Mounted on /dev/vx/dsk/adg/simplevol
             961M  89M   815M   10%     /mnt
# ls /mnt
crypto      drv      exec     ipp       lost+found  misc      strmod
dacf        dtrace   fs       kmdb      mac         sched     sys
```

OK, the volume seems to work just like a normal partition. Now let's look at the volume. First, check what the volume looks like in the file system tree, i.e. what attributes the device file has:

```
# ls -l /dev/vx/*dsk/adg/simplevol
brw-------   1 root root  270, 62000 May 16 21:15 /dev/vx/dsk/adg/simplevol
crw-------   1 root root  270, 62000 May 16 21:16 /dev/vx/rdsk/adg/simplevol
```

OK, we see a block and a character device. Compare these to normal disk partitions:

```
# ls -lL /dev/*dsk/c0t10d0s2
brw-r-----   1 root     sys       32, 74 May 17 01:48 /dev/dsk/c0t10d0s2
crw-r-----   1 root     sys       32, 74 May 17 01:48 /dev/rdsk/c0t10d0s2
```

They look just the same except the volume is not group readable by **sys** and has different major and minor numbers. We actually cannot see a lot about the volume in the file system representation of a volume. We cannot see what virtual objects it consists of, or what state they are in. Why can't we see that in the file system? Because, as was stressed before, the volume has to look exactly the same as a partition to the rest of the system, so there is simply no file system interface to look into the details of the volume. Can we derive much about the internals of a **partition** by looking at the disk **partition** device node? No, we cannot. With volumes it is just the same. The device node is not the right place to look in order to find more information about the storage object.

What we need to do is ask VxVM to show us what it knows about the volume. There is a command for that purpose: it is called **vxprint** and normally takes the DG as a parameter (it does **not** respect the default-DG). It shows all virtual objects residing in the DG, or all virtual objects from all DGs if no DG is specified.

```
# vxprint -g adg
TY NAME         ASSOC       KSTATE   LENGTH  PLOFFS STATE    TUTIL0  PUTIL0
dg adg          adg         -        -       -      -        -       -

dm adg01        c0t2d0s2    -        17846208 -     -        -       -
dm adg02        c0t3d0s2    -        17702192 -     -        -       -
dm adg03        c0t4d0s2    -        17616288 -     -        -       -
dm adg04        c0t10d0s2   -        17616288 -     -        -       -
dm adg05        c0t11d0s2   -        8315008 -      -        -       -
dm adg06        c0t12d0s2   -        35771008 -     -        -       -

v  simplevol    fsgen       ENABLED  2097152 -      ACTIVE   -       -
pl simplevol-01 simplevol   ENABLED  2097152 -      ACTIVE   -       -
sd adg01-01     simplevol-01 ENABLED 2097152 0      -        -       -
```

The output of the vxprint command is easy to parse if you know what to look for, so let's go through it in this Easy Sailing part. If you are bored, you can skip to The Full Battleship part beginning on page 120.

5.2.2 USEFUL VXPRINT FLAGS EXPLAINED

In the later parts of this book we will use several more flags to make the output more palatable to the reader. These flags are:

- -t to display each line in its individual format, with a header at the beginning of each disk group record explaining what the meaning of each column of output is for the given object
- -q to suppress the header information (once you get used to the output format you don't need the headers any more, and they take away a whole lot of space)
- -h to hierarchically list all objects below the specified ones (i.e. if you specify volumes it will also list the plexes and subdisks contained inside the volumes)
- -v to display the volumes and, due to the -h flag above, all records associated with them. If we did not specify -v, or if we used -r (related) instead of -h, then the output would also list the disk group and disk media information, which we like to suppress here in order to save valuable page space.

Basically, the output consists of several sections: a header section, a disk group section, a Disk Media section, and a Volume section. The header section in the example above consists of only a single line listing Type, Association, KernelState, Length, PlexOffset, User State, and TemporaryUtility and PermanentUtility fields. The header section will be expanded in the next command to show much more detail.

The DG section is right below the header and starts with the abbreviation for disk group, "dg". As you can see, it is associated to itself and has neither state nor other information to display. The Disk Media section is below that and has lines starting with the abbreviation for Disk Media, "dm". It shows what access names are associated with our VxVM disk names, and their length. Everything else that appears in the header line is inapplicable, which is indicated by a dash ("-").

The last part is the most interesting: It shows three objects: The volume (simplevol, in the line beginning with a "v" for volume), a plex called simplevol-01, its line beginning with "pl" for plex. It is associated with the volume, as you can see from looking at the ASSOC column of the plex record. And finally a record beginning with "sd" for subdisk and listing the attributes of the subdisk adg01-01. The name implies that it is the first subdisk that was allocated from the disk medium adg01. This subdisk is associated with the plex avol-01. Again, you can check this by looking at the value in its ASSOC column. The vxprint command knows the association hierarchy and arranges the objects accordingly: The volume at the top level, then the plex, then the subdisk.

All of these objects have kernel state (KSTATE) information (ENABLED) etc., but still many of the fields are inapplicable in this output format.

To improve on the output format, we suggest you use the -r and -t flags for vxprint. This will use an individual format and show individual headers for each object type and thus pack much more useful information into the lines. Later, when you are familiar with the output format, you can add the -q flag, which will suppress the large block of headers at the beginning.

Now that we have seen all we wanted to see by using vxprint let's get rid of the volume to create some new ones. There are several ways to do remove a volume: one is using vxassist remove volume <volname> and one is using the more low-level vxedit -rf rm <volnames> command. The vxedit command actually has several advantages: it involves less typing, it can remove more than one volume at a time, and is can remove volumes regardless of their status, while vxassist tends to have problems removing volumes that are somehow mangled, have associated snapshots, don't have all plexes enabled and such. Here are the two alternative commands, choose for yourself:

```
# vxassist remove volume simplevol
# vxedit -rf rm simplevol
```

You may wonder what the -rf flags do that we pass to vxedit. The short explanation is that vxedit will simple remove any virtual object you pass it. But if that object has associated subobjects, then vxedit will need to recurse into the subtree and remove all the associated objects recursively, from bottom to top. That is the reason for supplying the -r flag, because that will enable recursive deletion. If the volume is currently started (i.e. it is ENABLED and ACTIVE) then vxedit also requires the use of the -f flag (force). You can omit the -f flag if the volume is stopped.

If you tried the commands you will have noticed you get an error message:

```
VxVM vxedit ERROR V-5-1-1242 Volume simplevol is opened, cannot remove
```

This is because the volume is still mounted. Once you unmount it you can delete the volume. Rest assured that VxVM keeps you from deleting objects that are currently in active use, just like the `format` command prohibits you from deleting a currently mounted partition. by telling you: "`Cannot label disk while it has mounted partitions`".

So we unmount the volume and delete it:

```
# umount /mnt
# vxedit -rf rm simplevol
```

This time it works! Now you know how to create, use, inspect, and remove volumes from a disk group. Time for some more interesting topics.

5.2.3 STARTING AND STOPPING VOLUMES

VxVM's STATE MACHINE

When a volume becomes available to the system (via creation or via DG import) the system does not know if the contents of the volume can or cannot be trusted. For instance, a volume on a DG that was deported and is now imported might have had write errors while it was imported by another host. Or the other host could have crashed while it was writing to a redundant volume etc. It is obvious that some kind of check needs to be done before we can trust the volume's integrity.

This is analogous to what the `mount()` system call needs to do when a user wants to mount a file system: can the contents of the file system be trusted? Was the file system properly unmounted, thus flushing all buffers and leaving it in a proper state? Or had the system crashed and left the file system in an inconsistent state? In classical UNIX, the `mount()` and `umount()` system calls use a single bit, the **dirty flag**, which is persisted in the file system's superblock, to remember the state of the file system. When a file system is mounted, the dirty flag is inspected and, if it is clean, the file system is mounted and the dirty flag set to `dirty`. When the file system is unmounted, the dirty flag is reset to `clean`. If a system crashes, then the dirty flag is, of course, not reset and remains dirty. So the next time a user tries to mount the file system, the `mount()` system call inspects the dirty flag and finds it `dirty`. In that case, the file system is not mounted by a file system check (`fsck`) is requested.

The same kind of check must be done by volume manager, albeit on a lower level, to ensure that a mirrored volume is internally consistent. This check does by no means imply reading and comparing all mirrors, just like mounting a file system does not always require a file system check (`fsck`). That would be very wasteful. Instead, VxVM maintains state information in the configuration database that get changed when certain events happen. For instance, when a volume is written to the first time after opening it, a bit in the configuration database is set that flags the fact that the device is now potentially out of sync. When the volume is closed (which can only be done after all I/O has been flushed to all mirrors) this bit is reset. This can be directly compared to . There is more state information like this. For instance, a plex that has encountered unrecoverable I/O errors to one of its subdisk is marked DISABLED so that no further read (or write) traffic for the plex is generated. Then, when the subdisk is repaired, the plex state is set to STALE, indicating that the data inside the plex is not current.

When you want to use a volume then all this state information needs to be checked to find out if I/O to the volume is possible and reasonable, or if e.g. the mirrors are out of sync. This process needs to be done only once, at the beginning. Whatever happens while the volume is online and undergoing I/O will be caught by VxVM and lead to appropriate reactions. But the initial state must be checked before using the volume. Exactly that is done by the `vxvol start` command. It is a volume sanity check followed by allowing I/O if the volume is sane. It does so by setting the volume's state to ACTIVE and its kernel state to ENABLED.

So what does `vxvol stop` do? Functionally it does nothing but set the ENABLED flag off so that further user access is impossible. It is neither necessary nor required by VxVM to stop your volumes before deporting a DG. It does make some maintenance commands easier that otherwise require an extra option flag to force an action in order to work on a started volume, but that's about it. You don't normally stop any volumes, nor do you normally need to.

There is much more about the state machine in the troubleshooting sections of this book beginning on page 349.

5.3 VOLUME LAYOUTS AND RAID LEVELS

In this section you will learn how to specify the various RAID levels for VxVM volumes. The first thing you will learn is that VxVM does not actually use RAID levels numbered 0 through 5. Instead, it uses what would properly be called volume features: The striping feature, the mirroring feature, the XOR-parity feature, the concatenation feature, the logging feature and so on. You will see that these features can be added to make up almost any reasonable volume type. Not all combinations are possible, but then again, not all are reasonable either, and what's possible should make you a pretty happy administrator indeed.

5.3.1 VOLUME FEATURES SUPPORTED BY VxVM

CONCATENATION

This is the simplest layout of all the RAID levels. Originally called RAID-0, it was intended to connect disks together to overcome the size limitation. By concatenating disks, the capacity of the resulting volume was equivalent to the sum of the capacities of the individual disks. Disks could be of different sizes.

Of course, VxVM will not concatenate **disks** to form a larger virtual disk, like the original RAID concept did. Instead, it will concatenate **subdisks** (extents on physical disks) by mapping them into a plex at different plex offsets (which turns up as PLOFFS in vxprint), resulting in a contiguous virtual address space that can grow to almost unlimited size. There is no need to specify anything particular on the command line for VxVM to enable concatenation. The concat volume layout is the default layout unless the `/etc/default/vxassist` file forces a different layout. VxVM will concatenate as necessary, provided there is enough space left that has the required storage attributes. We will say a little more on storage attributes later.

Synopsis and sample command to create a volume with the concatenation feature:

```
# vxassist -g <DGname> make <volname> <size> [layout=concat]
# vxassist -g adg make avol 1g
# vxprint -htv -g adg
```

```
v  avol         -              ENABLED ACTIVE  2097152 SELECT   -        fsgen
pl avol-01      avol           ENABLED ACTIVE  2097152 CONCAT   -        RW
sd adg01-01     avol-01        adg01   0       2097152 0        c0t2d0   ENA
```

The first line starts with the letter v. This means it is a line describing the volume virtual object. The next line starts with the string pl, which means that this line describes a plex virtual object. The third line describes a subdisk, which can be identified by the string sd at the beginning of the line. The second columns of each line describes the virtual object's name. And the third column of each line of the output identifies what other virtual object the given object is associated to. The volume, as we can see, is not associated to anything; its third column contains a dash (–). The plex, however (whose name is avol-01), is associated to an object called avol, which happens to be the volume that the plex resides in. And the subdisk (adg01-01) is associated with the plex avol-01. We emphasized these words to make you find the relevant information more quickly.

Note that the sizes in column six of volume, plex, and subdisk are identical to what we specified, but are given in blocks of half a kilobyte each. So in order to find the amount of megabytes we have to divide by 2 and then by 1024, or just simply by 2048:

```
# bc -l
2097152/2048
1024.0000000000 # Exactly what we wanted: 1024 MB equals 1.0 GB!
```

Other information you will find useful to know is the following:

The word SELECT in column 7 of the volume line means the read policy. This could be SELECT, ROUND, and PREFER. More information on volume read policies can be found later in this chapter. In the same column of the plex line you will see the word CONCAT. This designates the layout of the plex (there is actually no such thing as a volume layout - a plex has all the layout; the volume just has one or more plexes, turning it into a mirrored or unmirrored volume).

In column four and five the virtual objects plex and volume display a kernel state and a (user) state. A state of ENABLED means that I/O to the object is possible, while DISABLED means no I/O is possible to the object at all. There is also a third kernel state, namely DETACHED, which means that user I/O is not possible but kernel I/O is possible. This is needed for internal resynchronisation or RAID-5 initialization mechanisms and not of general interest here.

If we stop the volume, or before the volume is started after importing the disk group, the kernel states will be disabled and I/O will not be possible:
```
# vxvol stop avol # stop the volume
```

```
# vxprint -qhtvgadg # look what's changed
v  avol          -            DISABLED CLEAN   2097152  SELECT    -        fsgen
pl avol-01       avol         DISABLED CLEAN   2097152  CONCAT    -        RW
sd adg01-01      avol-01      adg01    0       2097152  0         c0t2d0   ENA
```

```
# newfs /dev/vx/dsk/adg/avol # trying to use the volume fails
/dev/vx/rdsk/adg/avol: No such device or address
# vxvol start avol # start the volume again
# vxprint -qhtvgadg # DISABLED has become ENABLED; CLEAN has become ACTIVE
v  avol          -            ENABLED  ACTIVE  2097152  SELECT    -        fsgen
pl avol-01       avol         ENABLED  ACTIVE  2097152  CONCAT    -        RW
sd adg01-01      avol-01      adg01    0       2097152  0         c0t2d0   ENA
# newfs /dev/vx/dsk/adg/avol # using the volume now works
newfs: construct a new file system /dev/vx/rdsk/adg/avol: (y/n)? y
/dev/vx/rdsk/adg/avol:  2097152 sectors in 1024 cylinders of 32 tracks, 64 sec-
tors
        1024.0MB in 32 cyl groups (32 c/g, 32.00MB/g, 15872 i/g)
super-block backups (for fsck -F ufs -o b=#) at:
 32, 65632, 131232, 196832, 262432, 328032, 393632, 459232, 524832, 590432,
 1443232, 1508832, 1574432, 1640032, 1705632, 1771232, 1836832, 1902432,
 1968032, 2033632,
```

STRIPING

Striping originated as RAID-0, just like the concat layout. To prevent misunderstandings: the RAID levels were more specifically called **RAID-0 concat** and **RAID-0 stripe**, respectively. The RAID levels have been discussed in chapter 1 on page 7-9 to some extent, but let's reiterate the basics here.

A striped volume distributes its contents in a regular pattern over its subdisks. The intention of striping originally was to alleviate the long wait times that occurred on large read/write I/Os to slow disks. These disks' controllers or the HBAs were so slow that the disks were often formatted with an interleaving factor because data could not be transferred at full speed to the host. Striping is a little complicated to explain in words, but it may be okay if we use a somewhat creative analogy here:

Imagine you had ten salamis, and you want to make salami sandwiches. The salamis are your separate disk spindles and the sandwiches are your volumes. Then if you make a concat volume, you slice up the first salami and put the slices on the sandwiches until the first salami is gone, then you take the second salami and so on. If you were VxVM, by the way, then you would try cutting each salami at exactly the right angle so that a single slice covers the whole sandwich, while IBM's AIX LVM would cut the salamis into lots of tiny slices and then cover the sandwich with them but that's not the issue here.

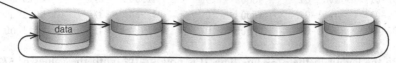

Figure 5-1:   Striping is reminiscent of making a salami sub. Data is mapped
               in identically sized slices, one slice at a time, across multiple
               "columns". The size of a data slice is called stripe size, stripe unit
               size, stripe width, or similar. There is no generally accepted term
               for the size of one "layer of salami", i.e. the size of a slice times
               the number of columns.

When you are striping then you are taking tiny slices from each salami and putting them on your sandwiches in a row, so that the slice from salami two follows salami one, salami three follows salami two, salami 4 follows salami three, and so on, until your last salami's slice is followed by a slice from salami one again. The number of salamis you are using is the number of columns, while the size of the individual slices is called the stripe width or stripesize. This ensured the taste is about average even if all your salamis are different, and that all salamis are used more or less evenly regardless of which way you bite the sandwich.

The default stripesize for VxVM is 64 KBytes (which BTW is far too small - 1MB would be a lot better but it is probably best not to stripe at all nowadays).

Striping has become much more common recently due to the advent of storage arrays that stripe internally, and of both system administrators and database administrators becoming more familiar with the concepts. However, most of them have forgotten Moore's law and the problem of mechanics, and therefore get most of their decisions wrong when it comes to storage layout.

Striping may be one of the most misused features of all RAID systems, so please make sure you know what you are doing by reading and fully understanding the appropriate discussion on volume formats beginning on page 137. The short version is this: Striping was great 20 years ago. Striping is often a bad idea today when you are using JBOD disks (because Moore's Law has been working against you for 20 years or so). Striping may still improve your individual performance if your data are on a storage array, but it will invariably do so at the cost of reducing the performance for everybody else who is using the same storage array. Read more about that later this chapter where we compare volume formats.

Here is the synopsis and a sample command to create a volume with the striping feature:

```
# vxassist -g <DGname> make <volname> <size> layout=stripe [ncol=<x>] …
# vxassist -g adg make avol 1g layout=stripe ncol=5 stripewidth=2048
# vxprint -qhtvgadg
v  avol        -                ENABLED  ACTIVE  2097152  SELECT   avol-01  fsgen
pl avol-01     avol             ENABLED  ACTIVE  2099200  STRIPE   5/2048   RW
sd adg01-01    avol-01          adg01    0       419840   0/0      c0t2d0   ENA
```

109

```
sd adg02-01      avol-01      adg02    0    419840   1/0    c0t3d0   ENA
sd adg03-01      avol-01      adg03    0    419840   2/0    c0t4d0   ENA
sd adg04-01      avol-01      adg04    0    419840   3/0    c0t10d0  ENA
sd adg05-01      avol-01      adg05    0    419840   4/0    c0t11d0  ENA
```

Note the layout in the plex line (line 2) is now STRIPE, with the values of 5/2048 for the number of columns and the stripe width. Below the STRIPE, you can see which column each subdisk belongs to, e.g. 3/0 means the subdisk belongs to column three and it mapped into the striped plex at offset 0.

MIRRORING

Mirroring originated as RAID-level 1 and was the first layout that created redundant volumes. As always, in contrast to the original RAID concepts, VxVM will never mirror a physical disk onto another physical disk. Instead it will allocate subdisks for two plexes and put two plexes into a volume, resulting in the data to be written into each plex and thus being redundant. Mirroring can be done by specifying the "mirror" attribute to the layout subcommand in vxassist. It can also be added after the fact by issuing vxassist mirror <volname> with an already created volume. Mirroring can be done with up to 32 mirrors and mirrors can be added and removed transparently while the volume is online and undergoing I/O. The VxVM allocation library will automatically arrange storage allocation such that no two mirrors ever share the same disk, as that would reduce both performance and redundancy of the volume. If you want more than simple redundancy (that would be equivalent to a number of two mirrors) you can specify a different number of mirrors using the nmirror subcommand.

Synopses and sample commands to create a volume with the mirroring feature:

```
# vxassist -g <DGname> make <volname> <size> layout=mirror [nmirror=<x>]
# vxassist -g adg make avol 1g layout=mirror [nmirror=3]

# vxassist -g <DGname> make <volname> <size> nmirror=<x>
# vxassist -g adg make avol 1g nmirror=3
vxprint -qhtvgadg
v  avol         -            ENABLED  ACTIVE  2097152  SELECT  -       fsgen
pl avol-01      avol         ENABLED  ACTIVE  2097152  CONCAT  -       RW
sd adg01-01     avol-01      adg01    0       2097152  0       c0t2d0  ENA
pl avol-02      avol         ENABLED  ACTIVE  2097152  CONCAT  -       RW
sd adg02-01     avol-02      adg02    0       2097152  0       c0t3d0  ENA
pl avol-03      avol         ENABLED  ACTIVE  2097152  CONCAT  -       RW
sd adg03-01     avol-03      adg03    0       2097152  0       c0t4d0  ENA
```

In this output all plex lines were emphasized in order for you to understand the volume structure more easily. Since each data plex is a container for the whole volume's contents, with three plexes you have three containers and accordingly a three-way mirror. Not that the layout of each plex is CONCAT, because inside the plexes there is neither striping nor RAID-5.

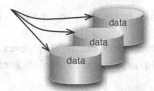

Figure 5-2:   Mirroring means more than instance of the data is stored in the volume. One instance of the data is stored in each data plex. Each data plex is either striped or concatenated (RAID-5 plexes in a mirror are not supported, although that could be forced with a little trickery). In this picture, each row constitutes one concat plex in a three-way mirror. This is what the above vxprint sample output displays: three plexes, each plex has a CONCAT layout, each plex has a single subdisk mapped inside it.

RAID-5

RAID-5 is actually nothing but a stripe, but with a special extra column that holds a lossless checksum of all data columns. The extra columns is called the parity column, because each bit in this columns holds information about the parity of the sum of the corresponding bits in all data column. If any of the data columns fails, then VxVM can use the parity columns to regenerate the original data on the failed column by combining all data plus parity using an XOR operation. The details of this are discussed in The Full Battleship. Suffice it to say that a parity-protected stripe can lose one column and still work, no matter how many columns there are. Loss of a second disk, however, will result in loss of volume integrity and therefore loss of data. The predecessor to RAID-5, RAID-4, used a dedicated column (or disk) for parity, which led to a bottleneck on multi-threaded writes. RAID-5 overcomes this bottleneck by distributing the parity information across all columns on a stripesize-by-stripesize basis.

RAID-5 is a feature that you will not want to use any more once you know how it needs to be done in a host-based system. No matter which way you look at it, RAID-5 will be slow on small writes. It will be unreliable after a single disk failure. And it will be slowed down after a disk failure and made more unreliable because of that failure in addition to being extra slow. It also needs one disk more than you think it needs, because running RAID-5 in software without a transaction log is irresponsible, so it loses part of the price advantage it has against mirroring. In short, we can almost guarantee that after you read the part of volume layouts you will never even think about deploying RAID-5 in an enterprise. It can still make a lot of sense in SOHO or university environments where cost needs to be as low as possible and uptime is not the most critical factor. But you will not deploy it in a financial institution if you like your job there.

The number of columns that is given on the command line does include the parity column but not the additional log plex that is highly recommended for RAID-5 and that is automatically added unless you prohibit it. So you need at least one more disk than the columns specification (one per column plus one for the log, which must not reside on any of the columns.

Synopsis and sample command to create a volume with the concatenation feature:

```
# vxassist -g <DGname> make <volname> <size> layout=raid[5] [ncol=<x>] …
# vxassist -g adg make avol 1g layout=raid5 ncol=5 stripesize=256k
# vxprint -qhtvgadg
```

v	avol	-	ENABLED	ACTIVE	2097152	RAID	-	raid5
pl	avol-01	avol	ENABLED	ACTIVE	2097152	RAID	5/512	RW
sd	adg01-01	avol-01	adg01	0	524288	0/0	c0t2d0	ENA
sd	adg02-01	avol-01	adg02	0	524288	1/0	c0t3d0	ENA
sd	adg03-01	avol-01	adg03	0	524288	2/0	c0t4d0	ENA
sd	adg04-01	avol-01	adg04	0	524288	3/0	c0t10d0	ENA
sd	adg05-01	avol-01	adg05	0	524288	4/0	c0t11d0	ENA
pl	avol-02	avol	ENABLED	LOG	76800	CONCAT	-	RW
sd	adg06-01	avol-02	adg06	0	76800	0	c0t12d0	ENA

You will notice that there are two plexes here. But this does not mean that the volume is mirrored. Only one of the plexes is marked ACTIVE, while the other one is marked LOG. This means that the plex does not contain user data, but log data, which is just a very small amount compared to the volume size. Only data plexes count for redundancy, not log plexes!

But you will notice a few more things: The volume's read policy (column seven of the first line) is neither SELECT, ROUND, or PREFER, but a new policy: RAID. And this is the same as the data plex's layout. Apart from that, the data plex looks just like a standard five-column stripe.

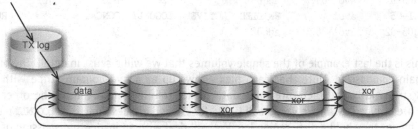

Figure 5-3:   This is what the above vxprint sample output displays. The plex
                marked RAID in the vxprint output consists of five columns,
                four of which are actually available as net capacity for user data.
                One fifth is lost to the distributed parity information which is
                spread across all columns in left-symmetric layout (simplified
                to just three clusters marked "XOR"). The second plex, which
                is marked LOG in the vxprint output is actually a small concat
                plex. But it does not hold a copy of the volume data. Instead, the
                RAID-5 write method uses it to store the five most recent write
                transactions to the volume. This makes recovery faster and the
                volume more reliable in special cases..

COMBINING VOLUME FEATURES

Using VxVM it is really easy to combine volume features. For the basic layout parameters,
just pass them in a comma-separated list on the command line. Other variables, like the
number of mirrors, logs, or columns, can be passed as key/value pairs similar to what we've
already been doing when naming disk media (e.g. adg01=c0t2d0). We will discuss a large
number of such parameters in The Full Battleship of this chapter.

Synopsis and sample command to create a volume with combined features:

```
# vxassist -g <DGname> make <volname> <size> [layout=<feature0>,<feature1>,…]
# vxassist -g adg make avol 100m layout=stripe,mirror,log nlog=2 nmirror=3
# # vxprint -qhtvgadg
```

v	avol	-	ENABLED	ACTIVE	204800	SELECT	-		fsgen
pl	avol-01	avol	ENABLED	ACTIVE	204800	STRIPE	2/128	RW	
sd	adg01-01	avol-01	adg01	0	102400	0/0	c0t2d0	ENA	
sd	adg02-01	avol-01	adg02	0	102400	1/0	c0t3d0	ENA	
pl	avol-02	avol	ENABLED	ACTIVE	204800	STRIPE	2/128	RW	
sd	adg03-01	avol-02	adg03	528	102400	0/0	c0t4d0	ENA	
sd	adg04-01	avol-02	adg04	0	102400	1/0	c0t10d0	ENA	
pl	avol-03	avol	ENABLED	ACTIVE	204800	STRIPE	2/128	RW	
sd	adg05-01	avol-03	adg05	528	102400	0/0	c0t11d0	ENA	
sd	adg06-01	avol-03	adg06	0	102400	1/0	c0t12d0	ENA	

pl avol-04	avol	ENABLED	ACTIVE	LOGONLY	CONCAT	-		RW
sd adg05-02	avol-04	adg05	0	528	LOG	c0t11d0	ENA
pl avol-05	avol	ENABLED	ACTIVE	LOGONLY	CONCAT	-		RW
sd adg03-02	avol-05	adg03	0	528	LOG	c0t4d0	ENA

This is the last example of the simple volumes that we will discuss in detail. The plexes are again emphasized. Note that each plex shows up as a two-column stripe with 128 blocks stripewidth, and there are three data plexes total (the first three). The other two plexes are of type CONCAT, are very small (528 blocks), and are designated as LOGONLY plexes, which means they hold a dirty region log. We will deal with an in-depth discussion of logs in a later chapter.

Figure 5-4:   The volume from the above vxprint sample output looks like this picture. It consists of three plexes, each marked as STRIPE in the vxprint output. Each of these corresponds to one of the rows in the right hand part of this picture The last two plexes, marked LOGONLY in the vxprint output, constitute a tiny, mirrored bitmap called the Dirty Region Log, or DRL. The DRL is used to improve startup behavior after system crashes and is discussed in the log chapter (chapter 7).

5.4 VOLUME MAINTENANCE

ADDING A MIRROR

Adding a mirror is easy with VxVM: just tell vxassist to mirror the volume. This will create another plex and attach it to the volume. The plex attach action will initialize the new plex with the volume's contents. If you specify a number of mirrors/plexes to add, that number of plexes will be added to the volume. It does not matter whether the volume was already mirrored or not, or if it is a concatenated or striped volume. RAID-5 volumes can not be mirrored this way, at least not in a single vxassist command.

Synopsis and sample command to add a mirror to a volume

```
# vxassist -g <DGname> mirror <volname> [nmirror=<x>]
# vxassist -g adg mirror avol nmirror=3 # will add three mirrors
```

REMOVING A MIRROR

Removing a mirror is almost as simple as adding one. It just requires passing an extra command word to vxassist, namely remove mirror instead of mirror. You can also specify a number if mirrors to the remove command, but this will not work as expected: while when adding mirrors the nmirror=<x> parameter specifies the number of new mirrors to add, in the case of removing it specifies how many mirrors are to remain!

Synopsis and sample command to remove a mirror from a volume

```
# vxassist -g <DGname> remove mirror <volname> [nmirror=<x>]
# vxassist -g adg remove mirror avol nmirror=3 # will leave three mirrors
```

ADDING A LOG

Just like mirrors, you can add a log to a volume by simply passing the right parameter to vxassist. The keywords here are addlog, nlog=<x>, and logtype={dco|drl}. The nlog parameter defines the number of logs to add to the volume, and the logtype parameter defines whether it is going to be a DRL (dirty region log) or DCO (data change object)

We have not discussed what each type of log is or does. There are various kinds of logs., and they are discussed in chapter 7 beginning on page 173. Because this book is also recommended for looking up frequent procedures we chose to put the part about managing logs here where it belongs, and explain it later to those readers who prefer to read the book as a technical training guide.

Synopsis and sample command to add a log to a volume

```
# vxassist -g <DGname> addlog <volname> [nlog=<x>] [logtype={dco|drl}
# vxassist -g adg addlog avol nlog=2 # will add two log plexes
```

REMOVING A LOG

Like a mirror, a log can be removed by specifying remove log instead of addlog to the vxassist command. And as in the case of the mirror, if you also pass a number of logs, then this number does not specify the number of logs to be removed, but the number of logs to remain in the volume
!
Synopsis and sample command to remove a log from a volume

```
# vxassist -g <DGname> remove log <volname> [nlog=<x>] [logtype={dco|drl}
# vxassist -g adg remove log avol logtype=dco # will remove one DCO log
```

Growing a Volume with a File System

Growing a volume that has a ufs or vxfs file system on it requires two steps: first, the data container (i.e. the volume) must be resized so it can hold the desired larger amount of file system blocks. After this is done, the file system also needs to be resized to make use of the increased container size. It would not make a lot of sense to grow the container but have the file system still report the same old size. The superblock needs to be updated to reflect the new size, and in the case of ufs, new cylinder groups must be created and initialized. In the case of vxfs, the newly gained free space must be incorporated into the free extent list so that it can subsequently be allocated for files. There are convenient commands to grow a ufs or vxfs file system, so none of this has to be done manually.

The command to grow a volume that has a file system on it is one layer above vxassist. It is a tool that calls vxassist to resize the volume and then for vxfs calls fsadm (file system administration) or for ufs calls /usr/lib/fs/ufs/mkfs -G (the -G flag is undocumented) to grow the file system. The name of the tool is vxresize and it takes the volume name (and the ubiquitous -g <DG>) and a VxVM size specification. Alternatively, you can specify a size increment by prepending the number with a plus (+) sign. For ufs it does not make any difference whether the file system is mounted or not. You can do it offline as well as online. For vxfs however, the file system needs to be mounted. Why is that the case? Well, because of the rather simple file system structure and limited capabilities of ufs there exists a simple standalone command that can modify a ufs's internal data structures without risk. On the other hand, the vxfs file system is highly sophisticated and complex. While in a ufs file system the file system metadata (like free block bitmap, inode table etc.) is static and its locations are fixed, vxfs allocates all file system metadata dynamically, as files (yes, vxfs metadata are files, too. Read all about it in the "point-in-time copies" (page 233) and "file system" (page 434) chapters). In order to allocate metadata for managing the extra volume space the file system driver must be used for that volume, so that (meta data) files can be modified. This means that the volume needs to be mounted.

Synopsis and sample command to grow a volume and its file system

```
# vxresize -g <DGname> <volname> <[+]size>
# vxresize -g adg avol +2g # enlarge avol plus file system BY 2g
# vxresize -g adg avol 20g # enlarge avol plus file system TO 20g
```

Growing a Volume Without a File System

Growing a volume without a file system, e.g. before putting a new FS onto it or if you are using database raw device access, can be done with a vxassist command. There are two subcommands to vxassist for growing: growby and growto, whose meanings should be immediately obvious. For growby you supply an increment, while for growto you supply the final size of the volume.

Notable fact: As soon as the command is executing it is safe to use the full new size of the volume. In the case of a redundant volume VxVM will still resynchronize the new extents, but that should not stop you from feeling comfortable using the new space. It is just as safe and redundant as the rest of the volume. If you find this hard to believe, look up RDWRBACK synchronisation in the index and read all about this interesting fact.

Synopsis and sample command to grow a volume without file system

```
# vxassist -g <DGname> grow[by|to] <volname> <size>
# vxassist -g adg growby avol +2g # enlarge avol BY 2g
# vxassist -g adg growto avol 30g # enlarge avol TO 30g
```

SHRINKING A VOLUME WITH A FILE SYSTEM

Shrinking a volume with a file system on it only works with vxfs, not with ufs. The action is in principle the same as for growing, but in reverse order and of course direction. First, the file system is told to shrink to the desired size using fsadm -b. Next, the volume is shrunk using the appropriate vxassist shrinkto or vxassist shrinkby command. This vxassist command must be run with the -f flag (force) because shrinking a container that contains a file system could result in loss of data. Of course vxresize is again the tool of choice, as it will do both in a single step with less fuss.

Synopsis and sample command to shrink a volume and its file system

```
# vxresize -g <DGname> <volname> <[-]size>
# vxresize -g adg avol -2g # shrink avol plus file system BY 2g
# vxresize -g adg avol 10g # shrink avol plus file system TO 10g
```

SHRINKING A VOLUME WITHOUT A FILE SYSTEM

Shrinking just the volume is easy: just issue the appropriate vxassist shrinkto or vxassist shrinkby command. You must use the -f option to force the operation, however. This is because all volumes created by vxassist are of usage type fsgen, which stands for **file system generic**. This is how VxVM finds out that it is meant for a file system and that it's not, for example, the root disk's swap volume which would not need to be resynchronised if re-opened after a crash etc.

In other words, VxVM will have to assume that you are using the volume for a file system and it wants you to think twice before you truncate the container that hold it. Of course, if you really know what you're doing then adding -f should not be a big extra effort. And if you really **don't** know what you're doing, then you are doomed anyway if they let you play with VxVM. No offense intended :)

Synopsis and sample command to shrink a volume without file system

```
# vxassist -g <DGname> shrink[by|to] <volname> <size>
# vxassist -g adg shrinkby avol 2g # shrink avol BY 2g
# vxassist -g adg shrinkto avol 10g # shrink avol TO 10g
```

GROWING OR SHRINKING JUST THE FILE SYSTEM

For ufs there is the command /usr/sbin/growfs, which is a shell script that calls /usr/lib/fs/ufs/mkfs -G to grow the file system. You can call the latter directly or use growfs as you like. Shrinking a ufs file system is not possible, but if necessary then you can first convert it to a vxfs using /opt/VRTSvxfs/sbin/vxfsconvert, linked to by /opt/VRTS/bin/vxfsconvert, and then shrink the vxfs file system in the way outlined below. The latter may not work well in older versions of VxVM because an important data structure for vxfs gets placed way back towards the end of the volume from where it unfortunately cannot be relocated. So it is sometimes not possible to shrink the volume significantly. It is probably the best to try it out with the software you are actually running.

For vxfs there is the tool /opt/VRTSvxfs/sbin/fsadm, linked to by /opt/VRTS/bin/fsadm, which can resize a vxfs file system in both directions: It is called with the –b flag and either the new size or the relative change as shown in the example below:

```
# vxassist make avol 1g
# mkfs -Fvxfs /dev/vx/rdsk/adg/avol
    version 7 layout
    2097152 sectors, 1048576 blocks of size 1024, log size 16384 blocks
    largefiles supported
# mkdir /vxfs
# mount /dev/vx/dsk/adg/avol /vxfs
mount: /dev/vx/dsk/adg/avol is not this fstype # Oops, need to specify vxfs!
# mount -F vxfs /dev/vx/dsk/adg/avol /vxfs # That's better!
# df -h /vxfs
Filesystem             size   used  avail capacity  Mounted on
/dev/vx/dsk/adg/avol   1.0G   17M   944M    2%      /vxfs # 1 Gig!
# vxresize avol +1g # Enlarges volume and then file system, too
# vxprint -v avol
TY NAME        ASSOC     KSTATE    LENGTH   PLOFFS   STATE    TUTILO  PUTILO
v  avol        fsgen     ENABLED   4194304  -        ACTIVE   -       -
```

Remember that VXVM sizes are always blocks if not otherwise given. So the above 4194304 blocks are exactly 2GB, not 4GB (Solaris disk blocks are 1/2KB each).

```
# df -h /vxfs
Filesystem             size   used  avail capacity  Mounted on
/dev/vx/dsk/adg/avol   2.0G   18M   1.9G    1%      /vxfs # 2 Gig!
# fsadm -b 1g /vxfs # We will have a 1G file system on a 2G volume!
UX:vxfs fsadm: INFO: V-3-23586: /dev/vx/rdsk/adg/avol is currently 4194304 sectors - size will be reduced
# fsadm -b +1g /vxfs # Back to 2G! Just to try out all the ways...
UX:vxfs fsadm: INFO: V-3-25942: /dev/vx/rdsk/adg/avol size increased from 2097152 sectors to 4194304 sectors
# fsadm -b -512m /vxfs # Down to 1.5G!
UX:vxfs fsadm: INFO: V-3-23586: /dev/vx/rdsk/adg/avol is currently 4194304 sectors - size will be reduced
```

```
# df -h /vxfs
Filesystem           size  used  avail capacity  Mounted on
/dev/vx/dsk/adg/avol 1.5G  17M   944M    2%      /vxfs # 1.5 Gig!
# vxprint -v avol
TY NAME      ASSOC   KSTATE   LENGTH   PLOFFS   STATE    TUTIL0  PUTIL0
v  avol      fsgen   ENABLED  4194304  -        ACTIVE   -       -
# vxassist -f shrinkto avol 1g+512m # Cool way of specifying volume size!!
# vxprint -v avol
TY NAME      ASSOC   KSTATE   LENGTH   PLOFFS   STATE    TUTIL0  PUTIL0
v  avol      fsgen   ENABLED  3145728  -        ACTIVE   -       -
# df -h /vxfs # File system is unchanged by vxassist shrink!
Filesystem           size  used  avail capacity  Mounted on
/dev/vx/dsk/adg/avol 1.5G  17M   1.4G    2%      /vxfs
```

DISADVANTAGES OF USING VXRESIZE OVER VXASSIST AND FSADM

There are two slight disadvantages to using vxresize instead of issuing separate commands for vxassist and fsadm yourself: One is limited storage allocation. The vxassist command can be made to allocate very specific storage classes in a very fine-grained way. For instance, you can tell it to stripe across enclosures and mirror across controllers, to use only certain controllers or trays, or to exempt any of these objects and more. The vxresize command, while it ultimately calls vxassist itself, is not able to parse all of this storage allocation information. It is limited to a small subset of storage allocation. So while you can always use vxresize to shrink a volume you should use it for growing a volume only if you do not care where your subdisks will reside in the end. If you do, then it is better to use the combination of vxassist and fsadm instead.

If you wonder what vxresize does if the file system and volume sizes differ at the beginning, e.g. because someone messed with vxassist or fsadm, then the comforting answer is: it fixes the situation by making them both the same size. In other words, you can use vxassist to allocate storage with more control over the allocation. You can do so even if you forgot how to change the file system size, because instead of subsequently calling fsadm you can follow up with vxresize, which will then just adapt the file system if the volume already has the right size.

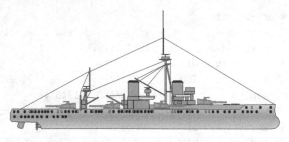

The Full Battleship

5.5 TUNING VXASSIST BEHAVIOR

It is sometimes desired to specify what parts of the storage equipment we want vxassist to use when allocating volume space. There are several keywords to vxassist that we can use on the command line to make vxassist do exactly what we want. In particular, you can control which disks or LUNs you want to use, which enclosures (storage arrays), which trays inside the storage array, and which controllers. You can also negate any of these criteria. You can specify whether to mirror across controllers, trays, or enclosures. And you can specify allocation of volume logs just like allocation of data plexes. The secret to this fine tuning lies in a few variables that can be passed to vxassist and that control its behavior. Let's go through them one at a time:

5.5.1 STORAGE ATTRIBUTES – SPECIFYING ALLOCATION STRATEGIES

Allocation can be modified by specifying the alloc=... variable on the vxassist command line. alloc= must be followed by a single shell-word containing a list of all entities which we want to allow vxassist to allocate from. The shell word can consist of just a single disk name, a comma-separated list of disk names, or a quoted string of space-separated disk names.

Synopsis and sample of a vxassist command with storage specification:

```
# vxassist make <volname> <size> [layout=<volume features>] [alloc=<disklist>]
# vxassist make avol 1g layout=stripe alloc=adg03,adg04,adg05
```

The latter can also be written without the "alloc=" keyword as shown below. This is a short form and you are free to use it, but it helps to remember that logically we are supplying an **allocation** information. Why does that help? Because later, when we **remove** objects instead of **creating** them we can also pass such allocation information. However, this will lead to those disks passed on the command line to be **excluded** from deletion, rather than **specified** for deletion. This is more understandable when you are aware that what you pass to vxassist is a list of storage objects where virtual objects are to **reside** on (i.e. allocated) rather than just a list of disks to "do something" with. That said, the following command line is equivalent to the previous one:

```
# vxassist make avol 1g layout=stripe adg03 adg04 adg05
```

Will specifying a storage allocation enforce VxVM to use all the specified disks? I.e. if you tell **vxassist** to create some small volume, but pass it ten LUNs as a storage allocation, will it then magically allocate one tenth of the storage from each of the LUNs passed on the command line?

No, it won't.

The storage allocation limits VxVM's normal allocation strategy to the given subset of all available storage. If the DG contains ten empty LUNs of ten GB each and you create a concat volume of 20GB, then VxVM will use exactly two LUNs out of the available ten to create the volume. If you give it a storage allocation of five disks, it will pick any two of the five that you passed. If you pass exactly two LUNs, it will of course pick those two. If you pass it only one LUN, the command will fail because not enough storage can be found in the storage allocation you gave.

ADDING AND REMOVING A MIRROR ON A SPECIFIC DISK

Just like you can control the storage allocation when creating a volume you can also control storage allocation when creating any other virtual object, e.g. another data plex, or a log plex (more about log plexes later). It works the same way. To add a mirror to a volume using specific disks you specify them on the vxassist command line:

Synopsis and samples of a **vxassist** command with storage specification:

```
# vxassist mirror <volname> [alloc=<disklist>]
# vxassist mirror avol alloc=adg00,adg01,adg02
# vxassist mirror avol adg00 adg01 adg02
```

Or you could specify to mirror across enclosures by this command:

```
# vxassist mirror avol mirror=enclr
```

To remove a mirror that resides on a certain disk you can also use storage allocation, but you need to revert the logic. Remember what we said above: Since it is an allocation that means we specify the LUNs that will **contain** objects after the command has finished. To remove a mirror from a specific disk, you need to use the negation operator "!" in front of the storage object.

Synopsis and samples of a **vxassist remove mirror** command with storage specification:

```
# vxassist remove mirror <volname> [alloc=!<disk>]
# vxassist remove mirror avol alloc=!adg00
# vxassist remove mirror avol !adg00
# vxassist remove mirror avol \!adg00 # If bash or a csh-variant is used
```

If you are using a csh-derived shell like bash, zsh, tcsh, or csh, then the command will most likely fail with a cryptic "event not found" error message. This is because these shells use the bang-operator ("!") to recall previous command lines, and unless you used a command line that started with the name of the disk (adg00 in this case) the shell will complain. The solution is to Use A Real Shell™ (/bin/ksh) or to escape the bang operator with a backslash or use single- or double-quotes around the storage allocation.

ADDING AND REMOVING A LOG ON A SPECIFIC DISK

Of course you can also use storage allocation with any other object, for creation as well as for deletion (see above). For instance, logs can be put onto a specific LUN using the same approach when adding them after the volume has been already created.

Synopsis and samples of a vxassist addlog command with storage specification:

```
# vxassist addlog <volname> [alloc=<disklist>]
# vxassist addlog avol alloc=adg02
# vxassist addlog avol adg02
```

And again the same is true for removal of specific logs.

Synopsis and samples of a vxassist remove log command with storage specification:

```
# vxassist remove log <volname> [alloc=!<disklist>]
# vxassist remove log avol alloc=!adg02
# vxassist remove log avol !adg02
# vxassist remove log avol "!adg02"        # For bash users
```

There is also a possibility to specify storage allocation for data plexes and log plexes in the same command, but this makes use of the rather complicated suboption -o ordered of vxassist. It is rarely used and probably not very useful for you, so here is just one example that creates a mirrored volume with data plexes on adg01 and adg02, plus a dirty region log on adg04:

```
# vxassist -o ordered make avol 1g layout=mirror,log alloc=adg01,adg02
logdisk=adg04
```

MORE STORAGE ALLOCATION VARIABLES

As we said before there are even more things that you can specify to direct storage allocation. You can set or exclude controllers, enclosures, trays, and targets. The following example shows how to mirror an existing volume avol using only LUNs that are attached to controllers c4 and c9, will exclude target c4t56 but specifically allow LUN c4t56d9:

```
# vxassist mirror avol ctlr:c4,c9 alloc=!c4t56,c4t56d9
```

To find out all about the possible criteria to allocation ask vxassist for an up-to-date explanation pertaining to the version you are running:

```
# vxassist help alloc
Allocation attributes for vxassist:
Usage: vxassist keyword operands ... [!]alloc-attr ...
   or: vxassist keyword operands ... wantalloc=mirror-attr[,attr[,...]]


 disk                Specify the named disk in the disk group.
 dm:disk             Specify the named disk in the disk group.
 da:device           Specify a disk, by disk device (e.g., da:c0t2d0).
 ctlr:controller     Specify a controller (e.g., ctlr:c1).
 target:SCSI-target  Specify a SCSI target (e.g., target:c0t2).
 ctype:driver-type   Specify a disk controller type (e.g., ctype:emd).
 ctype:ssa           Specify SPARCserver Array controllers.
 driver:driver-type  Specify a disk driver type (e.g., driver:sd).

NOTE: wantalloc indicates desired, but not required, restrictions.
NOTE: !alloc-attr requests that the specified storage should NOT be used.
NOTE: for allocation attributes of the form attr:value, value can be „same"
      to indicate that allocations should use disks with the same value for
      the attribute (e.g., ctlr:same requests use of the same controller).
```

SPECIFYING THE NUMBER OF DATA PLEXES (MIRRORS)

There is a simple parameter that you can pass to vxassist that lets you adjust the number of data plexes that our volume will have. The parameter is called nmirror and is used in a similar way to alloc, layout etc. You just specify the number to vxassist. For instance:

```
# vxassist make avol 1g layout=mirror nmirror=2
```

will create a 2-way mirror. A five-way mirror can be created by this command:

```
# vxassist make avol 1g layout=mirror nmirror=5
```

Up to 32 data plexes can reside in any volume. But remember that for reasons of both performance and redundancy no disk may ever be used for two different data plexes of the same volume, nor for two different columns of a stripe. So if you really were to create e.g. 10-way stripe across 5 columns, then your DG would have to have 10 times 5 equals free space available on fifty different disks. Otherwise you get the famous error message:

```
VxVM vxassist ERROR V-5-1-435 Cannot allocate space for <XXXXXXXXX> block volume
```

This error message usually comes from lack of independent disks rather than actual lack of **space**.

SPECIFYING THE NUMBER OF LOG PLEXES

The number of dirty region log (DRL) plexes or data change object (DCO) log volumes is defined using the `nlog` variable, just like the `nmirror` variable defines the number of data plexes:

```
# vxassist make avol 1g layout=mirror,log nmirror=4 nlog=3
```

SPECIFYING THE NUMBER OF STRIPE COLUMNS

The number of stripe columns is set using the `ncol` variable. If you do not explicitly set the number of columns then `vxassist` will calculate and use a default number based on the number of disks in the DG. If the volume is not mirrored then the number of columns will be at most half the number of disks in the DG (so the volume can later be mirrored). If it is mirrored then it will be calculated to fit onto the free disks in the DG. The actual number of columns will be between a minimum and a maximum value which you can inquire using the command `vxassist help showattrs`:

```
# vxassist help showattrs
#Attributes:
layout=nomirror,nostripe,nomirror-stripe,nostripe-mirror,nostripe-mirror-
col,nostripe-mirror-sd,
noconcat-mirror,nomirror-concat,span,nocontig,raid5log,noregionlog,diskalign,no
storage
mirrors=2 columns=0 regionlogs=1 raid5logs=1 dcmlogs=0 dcologs 0
autogrow=no destroy=no sync=no
min_columns=2 max_columns=8 # The default range for the "ncol" value
regionloglen=0 regionlogmaplen=0 raid5loglen=0 dcmloglen=0 logtype=region
stripe_stripeunitsize=128 raid5_stripeunitsize=32
stripe-mirror-col-trigger-pt=2097152 stripe-mirror-col-split-trigger-pt=2097152
usetype=fsgen diskgroup= comment="" fstype=
sal_user=
user=0 group=0 mode=0600
probe_granularity=2048
mirrorgroups (in the end)
alloc=
wantalloc=vendor:confine
mirror=
wantmirror=
mirrorconfine=
wantmirrorconfine=protection
stripe=
wantstripe=
```

```
tmpalloc=
```

Let us not get into too much detail about these variables. Suffice it to say you can change these defaults by entering them into the file /etc/defaults/vxassist.

SPECIFYING THE STRIPESIZE

The size of a stripe unit, i.e. the number of blocks after which vxio jumps to the next column in a stripe, can be set using a large number of keywords. You can find them all by using the UNIX command strings -a on the vxassist executable and then pick the one you like best. Being a lazy UNIX person I prefer the shortest form, stwid:

```
# strings -a /opt/VRTS/bin/vxassist | egrep "^st.*wid"
stwid
stwidth
st_width
stripewidth
stripe_width
stripeunitwidth
stripe_stwid
stripe_stwidth
stripe_st_width
stripe_stripeunitwidth
```

So let's first find out what the default stripesize is, and then make a striped volume with a reasonably large stripesize (we discussed the doubtful merits of small stripesizes before)

```
# vxassist help showattrs | grep stripe_
stripe_stripeunitsize=128 raid5_stripeunitsize=32 # 128 blocks is way too small!
# vxassist make avol 1g layout=stripe ncol=6 stwid=2048 # 1MB is reasonable
```

Actually you can leave the layout keyword away in many cases. It's just a way of specifying some features with their default values. E.g. if you want to create a two-way mirrored stripe with one dirty region log and the default number of columns then you might specify it using this vxassist command line:

```
# vxassist make avol 1g layout=mirror,log,stripe
```

But if you need something special, like three-way mirroring, two logs, and four columns, then instead of writing

```
# vxassist make avol 1g layout=mirror,log,stripe nmirror=3 nlog=2 ncol=4
```

it is easier to just specify the individual features like this:

```
# vxassist make avol 1g nmirror=3 nlog=2 ncol=4
```

Likewise, if you want a volume with a striped layout with the default number of columns and a stripesize of 2048 blocks you could write:

```
# vxassist make avol 1g layout=stripe stwid=2048
```

or you could just make vxassist imply that you want a stripe by issuing this command:

```
# vxassist make avol 1g stwid=2048
```

Specifying a stripesize is sufficient because there is no other way for vxassist to satisfy your request for a certain stripesize but to create a striped layout.

5.5.2 SKIPPING INITIAL MIRROR SYNCHRONISATION

When a volume is created manually then the first state that this volume will have is the EMPTY state. The EMPTY state means that VxVM has no idea about the validity of the data inside the plexes. They might be valid (e.g. if you were a very clever person) or they might be totally uninitialized (which is the more normal case). It may be a bad thing to use uninitialized data, so a volume that has an EMPTY state cannot be started without extra precautions. These precautions being to check if the volume is redundant. If it is not, it can indeed be started. But if it is indeed redundant, then all the plexes will first be synchronised so they all hold the same data. But while this precautionary measure is extremely safe it is not optimal, because it is usually unnecessary. We will learn both why it can be skipped and how to skip it a few lines from here.

The vxassist command will always try to give you a reliable, working volume. So vxassist will by default create the volume, then for redundant volumes start it by initiating a synchronisation process for the volume. The volume can be used immediately, but in the background a kernel thread will continue synchronisation until all of the volume is synchronised.

You can modify this behavior simply by passing a different initial state to the vxassist command. For instance, you can tell it to make the volume ACTIVE immediately, without synchronisation:

```
# vxassist make avol 1g nmirror=3 init=active
```

This will create a three-way mirror of 1GB without doing any synchronisation. You could also choose to zero out all data on the plexes, which is a faster way to start a new RAID_5 volume (because the parity of a stripe containing just zeros is also zero, the parity information need not be calculated if you initialize with zero) . The initial state to pass to vxassist in this case is zero:

```
# vxassist make avol 1g nmirror=3 init=zero
```

This will successfully create a three-way mirror of 1GB without doing any synchronisation. You can use `zero` initialization with all layout types. It is not limited to RAID-5 or mirrored volumes; you can even use it to initialize a concat volume.

Of course you can also specify that `vxassist` not initialize your volume at all, but leave it in an `EMPTY` state. In this case, you pass `none` instead of `zero` or `active` to `vxassist`:

```
# vxassist make avol 1g [nmirror=x] [ncol=y] init=none
```

There is much more on synchronisation mechanisms starting on page 380 in the troubleshooting chapter.

5.5.3   CHANGING THE LAYOUT OF A VOLUME

Changing a volume's layout on the fly, while user I/O is active on it, is probably one of the coolest demonstrations that can be done with VxVM. Unfortunately many users do not trust the relayout feature and would rather not use it in production environments. Whatever their reasons may be – they might just not believe such a thing is possible – in all but the most exceptional cases relayouting a volume works really well. It can be interrupted (even by a system failure, e.g. panic or power loss) and will automatically restart upon volume start. It can even be stopped before it is done, and reversed to restore the original layout. All this is possible while the volume is active and undergoing user-I/O! But while the relayout engine in the back end is a truly remarkable feature (although parts of its implementation could be improved) the parameter processing for the `vxassist relayout` command is rather poorly implemented. For instance, even in versions of VxVM that used to search through all DGs to find the specified object, relayout was the one command that would not do it and instead required specification of the DG. Then, if your target layout features striping, the number of columns is not initialized from the default as it is when creating a volume. The `ncol` parameter appears to be uninitialized, so it is in many cases too large for the DG and the command fails. If the target layout features mirroring, the result will always be a layered volume even if you explicitly specified a non-layered layout. This is particularly ridiculous because the same command (`vxassist`) can then be used to convert the result to what you really wanted (a non-layered volume; you will learn more about layered and non-layered volumes soon). And while relayout can actually generate any kind of volume features it will refuse to work unless the internal layout of a plex actually changes. For instance, if you covert from a `concat` to a `mirror` and vice versa, relayout will complain that this is not a relayout operation (the mapping inside the plex does not change, but a plex is merely added or taken away). It will then try to convert the volume between layered and non-layered, which will also fail because this is not what was requested. So the command ultimately fails.

But if you relayout from concat to some other plex mapping, like `stripe` or RAID-5, and then use `vxassist relayout` to create your desired layout (mirrored concat), it will work just fine.

To sum it up: `vxassist relayout` is powerful, but very picky. But anyway, it is indeed a nice feature, especially when you finally learned to master it. So let's begin with a concat volume:

```
# vxassist make avol 1g [layout=concat]  # create our base volume
# vxassist relayout avol layout=stripe ncol=4 stwid=2048 # takes some time
```

(avol is now a striped volume!)

```
# vxassist relayout avol layout=stripe ncol=2 stwid=1024
```

(avol is now just 2 columns wide, with 1024 blocks stripesize)

```
# vxassist relayout avol layout=mirror,concat
```

(avol is now a mirrored layered volume; a concat-mirror)

```
# vxassist relayout avol layout=raid,nolog ncol=4 stwid=128
```

... and so on. Depending a little on the hardware it takes roughly one minute per GB of volume size, just like synchronizations and other low-level VxVM I/O. Such I/O is always throttled to pause for several milliseconds between I/Os in order not to overload the machine. There is actually no way to make that pause disappear. You can only increase it. You can also increase the size of the individual I/Os but in all the tests that we did over the years with several versions of VxVM it never did speed up the volume operations. Your mileage may vary.

VXRELAYOUT START / REVERSE / STATUS

While a relayout process is running you can inquire its status, pause it, restart it, or reverse it. And while it is running in reverse, you can do the same again, practically jumping to and fro between two layouts. Not that it makes a lot of sense, but it really is a cool demo, at least to those who still have to manually allocate partitions for use with Solstice Disk Suite (SunVM) or some Linux LVM.

Synopsis and example of the command syntax for handling relayout tasks:

```
# vxrelayout status <volname>
# vxrelayout status avol
# vxassist make avol 1g layout=concat
# vxprint -q -ht -gadg avol # -q to suppress headers, -ht for nicer output
v  avol         -            ENABLED  ACTIVE  2097152  SELECT   -       fsgen
pl avol-01      avol         ENABLED  ACTIVE  2097152  CONCAT   -       RW
sd adg01-01     avol-01      adg01    0       2097152  0        c0t2d0  ENA
# vxassist relayout avol ncol=3 stwid=2048 &
[1]     21756
# vxtask list
TASKID  PTID TYPE/STATE    PCT    PROGRESS
   220        RELAYOUT/R 10.05% 0/4194304/419431 RELAYOUT avol adg
# vxrelayout status avol
 CONCAT --> STRIPED,  columns=3,  stwidth=2048
```

```
Relayout running, 15.00% completed.
# vxtask abort 220 # The relayout task can only be found using "vxtask list"
VxVM vxrelayout INFO V-5-1-2288 Aborting readloop (task 220)
VxVM vxrelayout INFO V-5-1-2291 Attempting to cleanup ...
VxVM vxassist ERROR V-5-1-2302 Cannot complete relayout operation
[1] + Done(7)                       vxassist relayout avol ncol=3 stwid=2048 &
 # vxrelayout status avol
CONCAT --> STRIPED, columns=3, stwidth=2048
Relayout stopped, 20.00% completed.
# vxrelayout start avol & # restart the relayout process
# vxrelayout status avol # and see how it's coming along
 CONCAT --> STRIPED, columns=3, stwidth=2048
 Relayout running, 25.00% completed.
# vxtask list
TASKID PTID TYPE/STATE   PCT    PROGRESS
   224          RELAYOUT/R 44.67% 0/3985408/1780288 RELAYOUT avol adg
# vxtask abort 224       # abort the poor relayout yet again
VxVM vxrelayout INFO V-5-1-2288 Aborting readloop (task 224)
VxVM vxrelayout INFO V-5-1-2291 Attempting to cleanup ...
[1] + Done(7)                       vxrelayout start avol
# vxrelayout reverse avol # reverse the relayout process, go back to original
# vxrelayout status avol # and see how it's coming along
 STRIPED, columns=3, stwidth=2048 --> CONCAT # going back to original layout
 Relayout running, 80.08% completed.
```

If you want to sleep really bad tonight, then you can try to parse the output of **vxprint -rt** for a volume that is currently undergoing a relayout operation. But be warned: it is not a pretty sight!

Technical Deep Dive

5.6 Methods of Synchronisation

Whenever there is more than one data plex (container for one instance of the volume's data) in a volume then there is at least a theoretical possibility that the contents of the plexes differ. They may differ for any several reasons, some of which are more, some less likely. Let's look at some of the more unlikely ones first:

- Bit rot, i.e. the unintentional flipping of bits on the medium, can be considered unlikely, although it does indeed happen occasionally. Disks are typically very well protected against this using Reed-Solomon code error checking.

- The probability for a bad data transfer for current disks is about 1x10-14 or one in 100,000 billion. This sounds like an extremely low probability, but let's see how quickly this would happen if you were to stream data from a disk 24 hours a day at a little over 60 MB/sec: 60 MB per second is 60 times 1024 times 1024 times 8 bits per second, or 503,316,480 bits. Let's round off all those numbers. 500,000,000 times the number of seconds per day (86400) is 43,200,000,000,000 or 4.32x10E13 bits/day. In other words it takes less than three days for an unrecoverable error to reach the host if the disk is on full blast. Fortunately for us while the error may not be recoverable but it still is detectable, so our host will just do a retry of the read request and everything should be fine. Similarly, if the disk writes a block and finds that it did not verify, then it will retry the write/verify cycle until the block has been correctly written, and/or it will revector the block to somewhere else.

- Someone using dd or so to write on the raw device that a subdisk resides on is also rather unlikely, although there are companies where this statement is debatable.

So if all those reasons are so unlikely, then what are the **likely** reasons for different contents in plexes of the same volume? The likely reasons are:

- The volume has not been initialized yet (this is very likely; it happens with every redundant volume we ever created).

- A new plex is just being added to the volume and therefore has not been initialized yet (this happens every time we add a mirror).

- A system failure has interrupted one or several writes to the volume (this happens whenever power is lost, the machine panics, or other rather low-level errors occur).

All of these cases are handled except for someone accessing the raw device below a subdisk. There is nothing that keeps anybody from doing this, and it's very hard to tell it happened. The first two (unlikely) cases are handled by hardware and OS mechanisms, the case of the raw device access using dd or some other tool would wreak havoc even if it was a partition and not a volume. The other three, the more regular cases, are handled very elegantly within the VxVM state machine.

There is one case left and that is if someone mounts a partition instead of a volume from an encapsulated and mirrored boot disk read-write. That is the one case where the administrator must be really careful about. That is and must remain a no-no until this chapter as well as the troubleshooting part is fully understood. Because you will learn how to modify VxVM's object states to make the VxVM state machine work for you.

Let us now return to the three cases that we admitted are relatively frequent: uninitialized volumes, uninitialized plexes, and plexes with open writes.

5.6.1 ATOMIC COPY

Whenever a new data plex is attached to a volume that already has a valid data plex, the new plex is first of all set to write-only mode. Being in write-only mode sounds utterly useless at first (after all, what would you do with data that you can write, but not read)? But in fact it is a very clever way to make sure that the volume can remain online while the plex is being synchronised. Being in write-only mode the new plex actually receives both synchronisation data from an existing plex and actual user-I/O. It is, from a writing standpoint, already active. If it was not active in write-only mode, then we would either have to stop I/O to the volume while the synchronisation is taking place. This would force us to take the volume offline. Or we would have to remember all the extents that have been written to since the synchronisation started, and resynchronize them later. But then while we are resynchronizing the changes, new changes may come in. We would be caught in a circle with an unknown end.

We will now start with an unmirrored concat volume and watch as a new plex is being attached. You can observe the write-only flag (WO) in the output of vxprint:

```
# vxassist make avol 1g # Create our well-known 1 GB concat volume
# vxprint -q -htv -g adg # Look at it: volume, plex, subdisk, nothing fancy
v  avol          -            ENABLED  ACTIVE    2097152  SELECT   -      fsgen
pl avol-01       avol         ENABLED  ACTIVE    2097152  CONCAT   -      RW
sd adg01-01      avol-01      adg01    0         2097152  0        c0t2d0 ENA
# vxassist mirror avol & # Allocate a new plex and attach it in background
# vxprint -qhtvgadg # Look at the volume. See the WO mode to the right!
v  avol          -            ENABLED  ACTIVE    2097152  SELECT   -      fsgen
pl avol-01       avol         ENABLED  ACTIVE    2097152  CONCAT   -      RW
sd adg01-01      avol-01      adg01    0         2097152  0        c0t2d0 ENA
pl avol-02       avol         ENABLED  TEMPRMSD  2097152  CONCAT   -      WO
sd adg02-01      avol-02      adg02    0         2097152  0        c0t3d0 ENA
# vxtask list # This command shows all VxVM kernel threads
TASKID  PTID TYPE/STATE   PCT    PROGRESS
   160          ATCOPY/R 09.86% 0/2097152/206848 PLXATT avol avol-02 adg
```

Look at the output of the vxtask list command above. From left to right you see: the task ID, which you can use to vxtask abort, vxtask pause, or vxtask resume the thread. The next field would be the parent task ID, but since this is not a compound action consisting of several sub actions it is empty. Next is type and state of the thread. The type is interesting: it is shown as ATCOPY, with a state of R. We will get back to that type very soon, but let's jump ahead for now. The R stands for running, which is what the task is doing (the status P means paused, and K means killing the thread). The percentage is how much of the task has already been accomplished, and progress is basically the same, but given not in percent but as a tuple of "first block / last block / current block". The rest of the line is interesting because it actually tells us what action is happening: PLXATT avol avol-02 adg means that a plex is being **attached** to volume avol, the plex's name is avol-02 and the activity happens in the disk group adg.

And what does ATCOPY stand for? It stands for atomic copy, because that is exactly what is going on here. The new plex is receiving the data in a single, atomic operation. If the process was stopped it would have to start from scratch again. An ATCOPY is a complete copy from one plex into one or several other plexes. This is what it looks like when you add two mirrors at once (to bvol in this case). You see that two plexes, bvol-02 and bvol-03, are being added in the same operation, i.e. the data is only read once and then written twice:

```
# vxassist -g bdg mirror bvol nmirror=2 &
# vxtask list
TASKID  PTID TYPE/STATE    PCT    PROGRESS
   170       ATCOPY/R 03.52% 0/2097152/73728 PLXATT bvol bvol-02 bvol-03 bdg
```

Coming back to our mirror operation on avol we see that the vxtask is done and that the volume has reached its final layout: two data plexes. And now both of them are read-write. In other words, after the plex has been fully initialized the WO flag is reset to RW (read-write) and thus the plex can start satisfying read requests, too, instead of being limited to just receiving synchronisation data plus all current write I/Os.

```
# vxprint -qhtvgadg
v  avol          -         ENABLED  ACTIVE   2097152  SELECT    -         fsgen
pl avol-01       avol      ENABLED  ACTIVE   2097152  CONCAT    -         RW
sd adg01-01      avol-01   adg01    0        2097152  0         c0t2d0    ENA
pl avol-02       avol      ENABLED  ACTIVE   2097152  CONCAT    -         RW
sd adg02-01      avol-02   adg02    0        2097152  0         c0t3d0    ENA
```

5.6.2 Read–Writeback, Schrödinger's Cat, and Quantum Physics

Atomic copy was really easy to understand, so let's switch to something intellectually more challenging. This may be one of the hardest parts to understand for anyone learning VxVM. It usually takes two or three attempts for anyone trying to understand it until "enlightenment" is reached, but it is worth the trouble, if just for the nice sizzling feeling when you finally begin to grasp the idea and the beauty of the concept. The train of thought required for its understanding is basically the same as that required for understanding the very basics of quantum physics: That the state of any object (especially a very tiny object like an elementary particle (electron, proton, photon, etc.) is undefined until somebody measures it! An object is in limbo until you look. This is a very unusual thought for most people. After all, we like to think that everything exists whether somebody is looking or not. But it turned out that it is just not so (in Physics), because it has been proven over and over again using hundreds of (rather complicated) experiments.

The theory of quantum physics sounded so wrong to many physicists in the early years of the twentieth century that a Mr. Schrödinger created a thought experiment for the purpose of demonstrating just how absurd the whole quantum theory was. We will need it for analogy later, so let's look at the thought experiment. it is called Schrödinger's cat paradox and it goes like this:

A cat (as a placeholder for any macroscopic object that you can touch and see directly) is put into a sealed container. The container also holds a technical apparatus that consists of

- A hammer
- A vial of poison (the poor cat is probably lucky it's just a thought experiment)
- An extremely tiny bit of radioactive material
- An amplifying device that will cause the hammer to hit the vial if a radioactive decay happens.

The amount of radioactive material is so small that the probability for a decay happening in one day is fifty percent. The theory (which, along with the theory of relativity, is now one of the best proven theories in physics) says the following:

If the decay happens then the hammer will hit the vial, break it, ad the cat will die from poisoning immediately

If no decay happens, then the cat will stay alive (assuming it has been fed etc.)

As long as we haven't measured if the decay has happened, the cat is: what?

Well: Quantum theory says that unless we have measured its actual state the cat is neither dead nor alive, but it is actually both, in an interleaved state. That is because the state of any elementary particle (like the particle sent off by the decay that triggers the deadly contraption) is undefined until it is actually measured. Therefore the state of the whole system internal to the box must be undefined. In other words the cat is both alive and dead at the same time, and only when we open the box will we find that it is still meowing or has actually been dead for some time. All the time before we looked the cat was both alive and dead.

Just in case that got you interested in the topic: There are many very good books on the topic and I am not qualified to try and summarize them; you'll just have to believe it for now, or get one of those books:

Now sit back and relax, free your mind and get ready to enter the world of **reliable uncertainty**.

Suppose we had a volume that contained more than one plex, i.e. it is a redundant, possibly multi-way mirrored volume. How is that volume written? It is written in the following way: If a write I/O is done for a file that was opened with the O_SYNC option then the write is completed after all plexes have been physically updated. That means the data has been persisted to all mirrors. Only then is control passed back to the caller. In this case, there is no uncertainty about the mirror contents, because the application only undertakes the next step in its processing when the write has completed to all mirrors. Keep this in mind: O_SYNC traffic is always written to all mirrors synchronously. There is therefore never a consistency problem with data that has been written with the O_SYNC flag set. All critical data, like file system meta data, database transaction logs etc. is written this way.

Resynchronizing Volumes

Now comes the hard part: Data that is written without the O_SYNC option is not flushed to all mirrors synchronously, but is flushed when the OS finds is suitable. For this reason, it is typical for an active mirror to have differing contents with respect to the most recent asynchronous write I/Os. So far, so good. Now our system crashes and reboots. Some questions immediately pop up:

1. Can the volume be used right away or do we need to synchronize first?
2. Where is the most current data?
3. How do we go about synchronizing the mirror contents?

The first question can be safely answered with "use it right away". Making software for highly available computers would not b very helpful if after a crash we stopped everything until we repaired our own data structures and kept the user volumes from doing useful work. So: all volumes are available immediately for read and write. This leads us to question 2, which takes the most effort to answer and to understand. I'll try to make it short: we do not care where the most current data is! There, it's out! What will you think of VxVM now that you know we don't care about your precious data? Is VxVM unreliable and useless?

It is most certainly not. Quite the opposite, actually. VxVM takes its job very seriously, and it never works less reliably than a simple partition would. But the fact is that its developers had an unusually clear view of exactly what is or is not required for a volume management to work right. You see, if VxVM was trying to save the most recent data, then it would make a lot of fuss and gain close to nothing, as we will see. Let's look at some alternative approaches that a normal programmer might implement:

Silly Approach #1

We always write to the first plex in the volume first, and only after data is persisted to that plex do we write the other plexes. This way, when the system comes back up after a crash, we know that this plex has the good data and we can use it to copy the good data over the stale data in all the other plexes. During that time the volume is only available read-only, because any updates would bring the plexes out of sync again. Once the process has finished, we can then enable the volume for read-write use.

This approach is often suggested when we ask Joe Sysadmin how they would think a volume management might tackle the problem. They never get it right, and they usually don't even understand the right answer, so don't feel bad if you don't get it the first time, OK? The problem with silly approach number 1 is that if we ask Joe Sysadmin what the volume management would have to do when a disk in the "good" plex has failed and this event has triggered a reboot (this is not a double fault so we need to catch it!), they fail to find an answer. Eventually they will say something like: Well in **that** case we'll just have to pick any one plex and use that as the source. To which my inevitable answer is "well, if picking any plex in **that** case is good enough, why shouldn't it be good enough in **any** case? The point being that if there are circumstances under which you need to fall back to a perceived "inferior" solution then it is better to get that solution right and use is exclusively than to have different ways of doing things depending on the circumstances. We might end up producing a lot of code paths that are hardly ever taken and contain bugs that are very hard to find.

So how do we get it right?

Silly Approach #2

We keep a log bitmap that tracks every I/O to every plex. Before a write I/O is flushed to a plex a bit in the log is set for the corresponding volume region that is written to. When the next plex is written the bitmap for that plex is set etc. When the system comes back online after a crash, we can just inspect the bitmaps to find which data plex holds the most current data.

True, but what effort are we going through? We need a synchronous write to a bitmap for every asynchronous I/O to every plex! This is outrageously expensive!

Well, says the silly developer, it may be expensive but isn't it worth the expense?

The very clear answer is: It is not. Look at what you gain: **nothing**! At least nothing worth mentioning. Remember that valuable data is written with the O_SYNC flag, and is persisted to all plexes before the write completes and returns to the user. That means that we are doing the logging, leaving a volume read-only, writing to a special plex first etc. just for the worthless asynchronous data! Our duty as a volume management product is simply to behave like a partition, and asynchronous writes to a partition are not guaranteed to persist either. Asynchronous writes are kept in the file system buffer cache until the OS decides to eventually flush them to disk. So trying to catch "the best" of those flushes is just utterly useless! Considering the overhead involved with any of the silly approaches their required CPU time and I/O capacity would be much better invested in just flushing the file system buffer cache more often!

Catching the most recent data on a mirrored volume is roughly equivalent to delaying the crash by some fractions of a second. What good is that? The valuable data is on disk anyway, and the asynchronous data is not valuable, so why save it?

VxVM's Approach

Having (hopefully) understood that it is worthless to try and save the "newest" data on a crashed mirror we arrive at question 3: How do we actually resynchronize a mirror?

This is a process that consists of several actions:

- Creating a "dirty region" bitmap in memory that marks those regions that need to be resynchronised (the "dirty" regions)
- Initializing the dirty region bitmap so that everything is marked dirty (i.e. needs resynchronisation)
- Starting the volume in a special Read-Writeback access mode (RDWRBACK)
- Spawning a kernel thread that reads the whole volume contents
- Resetting the access mode to normal once the thread has finished reading the volume

The secret to the resynchronisation process is the RDWRBACK mode. What happens in this mode?

WRITING IN RDWRBACK MODE – NOTHING SPECIAL

In RDWRBACK mode a write is handled almost normally: data is written to all plexes. The difference is that if all plexes have confirmed that the data has been persisted to disk then the corresponding bit in the dirty region bitmap is reset.

READING IN RDWRBACK MODE – VERY SPECIAL!

This is the interesting part: Remember that VxVM only has to make the volume look exactly like a partition just so the file system driver does not get confused and crash? Good! Now what does a partition **never** do that a mirrored volume **might** do? A partition never returns different contents for the same block when it is read more than once. That's the crucial part! That, and no more than that, is what VxVM must deliver! And how does it do it? It's actually very simple. Before a block (or region or extent) is read it is read the dirty region bitmap is inspected to see if that particular block of the volume is already in sync or not. If it is in sync, then the read proceeds normally. If the bitmap indicates the region is dirty, however, then the read is processed using the normal, round-robin pattern that is the default for all volume manager volumes. But then, **once the block is read its contents are not delivered to the user right away. Before the user sees it, the block is first copied to the appropriate location on all the other plexes.** Only after this copying is the block passed to the user process. Its contents are thus guaranteed never to vary between consecutive reads. The next read my indeed be satisfied by another plex, but that plex will contain exactly the same data, because that data has previously been copied to all the other plexes.

Of course, after the data has been copied to the other plexes the corresponding bits in the dirty region bitmap are reset to indicate that this particular portion need not be resynchronised over and over again.

This behavior is exactly analogous to Schrödinger's cat experiment. We do not know which version of the data we will be getting until we ask for it. Until then, all versions of the data – new, old, corrupt – are equally valid choices because they are exactly what could have resided on a partition after a crash, too. But once we do read a block, we commit the data that we read to be **THE ONE AND ONLY** data, and all other possibilities are immediately eliminated.

In principle we could live with this behavior forever. But it would be extra overhead having to check the dirty region bitmap on each read I/O just in case there still was some piece of the volume left out of sync. We could even crash and re-crash all the time while resynchronizing without changing anything in terms of volume reliability. We would just get the dirty region bitmap reset every time we crash, causing some extra I/O, but there would be no problem at all with data consistency.

But in order to make sure the resynchronisation process is finite so we can eventually get rid of checking the dirty region bitmap for every read I/O volume manager starts a kernel thread that reads the volume's dirty regions from beginning to end, throwing the results away. Because the volume is in RDWRBACK mode this means that all the dirty regions will have been read and their dirty region bits reset when the thread terminates and therefore the volume access mode can safely be reset to normal.

We know this is pretty tough stuff to understand, but we hope you made it. If you didn't get it the first time, sleep over it and try it again tomorrow. It's worth it for everyone who enjoys a beautiful software design.

5.7 VOLUME FEATURES IN DETAIL

5.7.1 CONCAT

A volume of concat layout is much better than you may think. You will now learn why that is the case.

First of all, let's again look at the data transfer rate of a disk. A disk as well as a LUN in the year 2008/2009 transfers on the order of 50-100MB/sec. It does so very effectively when it is streaming the data sequentially across the channel. As soon as the head needs to move, however, we are again limited to about 100-200 transactions/sec. If those transactions were reads (which can not be buffered by the storage array's large cache), then we would accordingly be limited to let's say 200 reads per second. Say the size of the data to be read is 8KB, which it is in many databases. Then we are limited to 200 times 8KB, or1600KB or roughly 1.5MB/sec. This is about one percent of the sequential transfer rate. On top of that, non-sequential data transfers create a lot more work for the CPUs and the storage array front end controllers, which have to keep track of many more I/O requests than in the case of a large sequential I/O.

But: Do we have any chance to keep scattered reads from happening? We hardly ever do, as this is dictated by the application. We could try to influence the application developers, and they might even listen, but other than that, our I/O subsystem will just have to satisfy whatever request comes.

So why do we even read this chapter, if we cannot keep scattered reads from happening? Well, what we do have is a chance not to make things **worse**! We'll show you how to avoid this:

Never stripe volumes with a small stripesize across a large number of disks.
When in doubt, use concat instead.

A concat layout will not introduce additional CPU load and seek traffic to sequential I/Os. Striping does that by splitting a single I/O into several smaller ones, which then need to be serviced by the I/O subsystem. Read more about this in the next part.

5.7.2 STRIPE

Unlike you probably think striping will typically **not** improve random I/O. It will also tend to **slow down** sequential I/O. There is a myth about how striping makes volumes faster, but that myth is based on very old data from times when it was true. On today's hardware it will generally tend to make things worse instead of improving them because of a number of reasons. First of all, striping was invented for load balancing and for parallelizing I/O, which both sound like A Good Thing™. Even when striping was invented, there was noticeable extra CPU load and a noticeable increase in volume latency. But those negative effects were offset by the advantage of being able to do multiple I/Os in parallel, so the overall effect of striping was perceived as positive.

But due to Moore's law and the problem with mechanics the numbers shifted over time by factors between 10 and 20,000, so what we are left with today is just the increased latency and increased CPU load, while the effect of increased parallelity is negligible. Look at the following example:

STRIPING ON EARLY DISK DRIVES

In the days of the old disks, when you did a sequential I/O to a single disk, the disk controller initially had to wait for the first sector to fly by, then it started reading and transferring sector by sector to the host (we'll leave out the possible interleaving factor for simplification). Reading the sectors may have taken a few revolutions, so let's say the I/O took the following times: half a rotation (on average) to wait for the initial sector, plus (say) four rotations for the data transfer, because there were relatively few sectors on each track. In total, this would be 4.5 rotations.

Doing the same I/O and a volume that was striped across eight disks would exhibit a totally different behavior: On the plus side, the number of rotations (once the right sector was under the read/write head) would sink by a factor of eight. So instead of four rotations there would only be half a rotation for the transfer. All I/Os was parallelized, and this was obviously faster than before.

On the minus side, however, there was an increased latency in waiting for the first sector. This was because now we did not have to wait for **one** first sector but for eight different ones. And the chance for one of those sectors being relatively far away from the read/write head was eight times higher than before. So the rotational latency would increase. Let us say for the sake of simplicity that the rotational latency increased from an average of 0.5 to an average of (close to) one. Then the whole transfer would take one rotation for the latency plus half a rotation for the parallel transfers, or 1.5 rotations total.

Obviously, that was a huge advantage.

And then Moore's Law came into play.

STRIPING ON CURRENT DISKS AND LUNS

The amount of data on a track multiplied by factors of several thousands, while due to the limitations of the mechanical systems on a disk the rotational speed merely doubled or tripled (from 3,600-5,000rpm to 7,200-15,000rpm). So what does a striped I/O look like today?

A data transfer that would be satisfied from a single disk (or concat volume) would take half a rotation (average) to wait for the first sector, and then only a few degrees, maybe one tenth of a rotation, for the data transfer. The sum is 0.6 rotations. Stripe this across eight disks and you double the average initial latency to almost one rotation, and then divide the tiny part that actually transfers data (one tenth of a rotation) by eight. The total is one rotation plus 1/80th or so, which is negligible.

Congratulations, you just increased the latency, loaded your CPU with seven extra I/O setups (each of which take about as long as a 64K block transfer), loaded the storage array's front-end and back-end controllers with extra I/Os, trashed the read-ahead cache in the storage array, and put extra seeks onto everybody else's LUNs (which use the same physical disks that your LUNs use). Your array vendor will gladly offer you an upgrade to a more expensive machine!

I think we agree that striping is not a good idea for sequentially accessed volumes. How about random I/O?

If you think about it you will find that random I/O across the whole volume is not helped by striping at all. Random I/O, by definition, is distributed across a large volume area, and whether you stripe your volume or concat it does not make any difference in the distribution of I/Os that hit each disk. So striping brings no advantage for random I/O either. To sum it up, striping brings a disadvantage to sequential I/O, and no advantage to random I/O.

Your DBA may demand an 8KB stripe size for the database volumes because (as many DBAs think) this improves database performance by distribution of I/O requests across all LUNs. Such a DBA is probably not aware that random I/O is distributed across the storage anyway, and those nice large sequential I/Os will be hacked into minced meat by the time they reach the storage array

Having said that, there are still (a few) reasons pro striping. For instance, if your volume was not evenly filled with data but the data only occupied the first part of the volume, then it would indeed be better to stripe the volume in order to distribute some of the I/O to other physical disks. Keep in mind, however, that modern file systems already try to distribute their allocations across all the available space. The old ufs file system uses cylinder groups for that purpose, vxfs allocates across the whole volume also, but without the need for cylinder groups. If you are using data base raw device I/O that is one case where such a usage pattern would be conceivable.

Another reason may be controller or path saturation in the host or in the storage array, which could be alleviated by striping.

Whatever your reasons are to stripe your volumes, be aware of the following basic facts:

- The more columns a stripe has the more the volume's latency will increase
- The more columns a stripe has the more the probability for fault increases. If any column fails the whole volume is unusable.
- The smaller the stripe size the more extra I/Os you create because I/Os span more than one column and must be sliced into more than one physical I/O
- The worst case is a small stripe size and a misaligned data file on top. Imagine an 8KB stripe size and 8KB I/O happening on it, but at an offset of 4KB. Every single I/O will have to be sliced in two and handled separately.

If you do not have dedicated physical disks for yourself, then the more you stripe, the more you impact everybody else's performance.

5.7.3   MIRROR

Redundancy is not an option, it is a necessity. Data needs to be redundant in order to be reliably accessible. The main question is where to put the redundancy: in the storage array or in the host. If you use redundant LUNs then in many cases they will be some implementation of parity-stripe, i.e. RAID-4 or RAID-5. There is not much to say against this concept, as long as the implementation is done in hardware, with predictive error analysis and automatic reporting, and with a large enough write buffer. All of this is usually the case with the large storage vendors. In many cases you can also use mirrored LUNs internally, but this often is not much better than the internal parity stripes. If you use host based mirroring anyway, e.g. because you are mirroring between two or more data centers, then you may decide to use non-redundant LUNs. There is no Right Way™ to do it, so I will just give you some help for your decision for or against host-based mirroring.

HOST–BASED MIRRORING VS. STORAGE–BASED MIRRORING

Storage-based redundancy has several advantages and few disadvantages, but please weigh the arguments yourself.

Arguments pro storage-based mirroring are:

- You only transfer that data once across the channel; the storage array's CPUs take care of creating the redundancy.
- Storage-based redundancy exposes you less to media errors. Basically, your disks never seem to fail.
- You needn't check your volumes for disabled plexes as frequently and thoroughly as you would with non-redundant storage.
- You don't generally need to deal with recovery from media errors in VxVM.
- VxVM won't need to deal with failures to write to Private Regions.

And the arguments pro host-based mirroring are:

- System administrators can manage redundancy according to demand. Mirrors can be added and removed, even low-level repairs can be done because the system administrator has access to all the basic data structures from VxVM. Of course, that requires quite a lot of expertise.
- Host-based mirroring can be cheaper in those cases where remote mirroring is employed. If your system mirrors data to a remote data center then using mirrored storage in both data centers would effectively constitute a four-way mirror, which costs a lot more than a simple, two-way mirror. While remote mirroring can be done inside the storage array, too, it typically has issues with latency and I do not generally advise it. You won't believe how slow the speed of light is when used with those synchronous replication/mirroring protocols! On the other hand, if one of your data centers fails and all you have is host-based mirroring, then be aware that for the whole time between failure and full resynchronisation you will have no redundancy at all. This may or may not be acceptable to your company.

To sum it up: storage-based mirroring helps everywhere and just hurts your wallet. Host-based mirroring can be a nice addition if you mirror between locations, which cannot usually be done efficiently by storage-based (remote) mirroring.

VxVM MIRROR READ POLICY

If you decided to use host-based mirroring then it is good to know what exactly VxVM does when it writes to or read from a mirrored volume. Here's what it does:

Write I/O: Asynchronous

If data is written to a mirror without the O_SYNC flag set (i.e. normal user file system I/O), then the write is scheduled for all plexes and control is immediately returned to the user process. The actual I/O operations are initiated as the queue is being processed, and they will typically complete out-of-sync. So if there are asynchronous I/Os on a mirror, then even if the user process that initiated the write has regained control it is not sure if the data has been persisted onto all plexes, onto some plexes, or even onto any plex. This sounds alarming, but it is in fact identical to the behavior of a partition. The SCSI driver will acknowledge an asynchronous I/O to a partition before the SCSI I/O has actually completed. Even if the user process has regained control (i.e. the system call has returned) it is not sure whether or not the data has been flushed to disk. This is not normally a problem because normal file I/O is not considered critical. If critical data are written, like database entries or file system meta data, then those data are written synchronously (see below).

Write I/O: Synchronous

A write that carries the O_SYNC flag or that is executed on a raw device or a mount point that has been mounted with the -o directio option will not return to the initiating process before all plexes have been successfully written to. I.e. if the user process regains control after writing synchronous data then it is guaranteed that all instances of the data on all plexes are identical. This is important because synchronous I/O is typically generated by applications that require some kind of guaranteed behavior. When a synchronous write returns and data has not actually been persisted then this breaks the software's writing paradigm and will eventually lead to unpredictable results.

Read I/O

A read from a mirrored volume is satisfied from any one of the active plexes, i.e. those plexes that contain valid data (those that have failed in the meantime are flagged accordingly and not used any more). There are two ways that VxVM uses to read from a mirror: One is called "Round Robin" (rdpol=round). This means that reads are satisfied from one plex after the other until all plexes have been used, and then the first plex is used again. This is done in order to balance the load between the individual LUNs or disks. The other one is called "Preferred Plex", and the preferred plex is named and associated with the volume. This means that all reads are satisfied from that preferred plex (because it has faster storage, because that storage is located closer to the host and thus has lower latency, etc.).

By default, volumes have a read-policy called "Select", which means no more than VxVM will select the most appropriate read policy between "Round Robin" and "Preferred Plex" by examining the volume layout. If the volume consists of plexes with identical layout, then the "Round Robin" policy is used. If one plex has a larger number of stripe columns than the others then that the read policy will be "Preferred Plex" for the plex with the highest number of columns. To set the read policy to "Preferred Plex" manually, or back to "Round Robin" or "Select", use the vxvol rdpol command:

```
# vxvol rdpol prefer avol avol-02
# vxvol rdpol round avol
```

```
# vxvol rdpol select avol
```

5.7.4   RAID-4 and RAID-5

These RAID-Levels sound good, because they combine the classic stripe load distribution scheme with volume redundancy. But that comes at a price. In general, RAID-4 and RAID-5 stripes suffer on small writes. You will soon see why. Their redundancy is also severely limited, and in summary, using software implementations of RAID-4 or RAID-5 for enterprise systems does not usually make much sense. Veritas Volume Manager does not implement RAID-4, but RAID-5 is offered (see The Full Battleship). Since this is the Technical Deep Dive section, let's look at how RAID-4 and RAID-5 are implemented. We will need to look at four major areas: Parity calculation and distribution, read/write behavior, degraded mode (i.e. after a single media has failed) and recovery behavior.

Parity Calculation

Parity calculation is a very clever scheme to quickly recover lost data. This is how the principle works: Take any number of bits, i.e. ones and zeros, and note if the amount of ones in that set of bits is an even or an uneven number. E.g. the bit pattern

1 0 1 0 1 1 0 1

consists of three zeros and five ones. Five is an uneven number so we note that the parity of this bit pattern is uneven. We do this by setting its parity bit to one. The resulting extended bit pattern (the bit pattern including the parity bit) will thus have even parity.

1 0 1 0 1 1 0 1 1

Now if any of the bits in the original pattern were to get lost we could use the parity information to calculate what the original bit had been by just doing the parity check again. If the parity of the current bit set (including the parity bit, but not including the bit that was lost – we cannot access it) is even, then the original bit must have been zero. If the parity is uneven, then the original bit must have been one. Of course, if we lost another bit, then all would be lost and we would have no chance of recovering the lost bits.

This parity scheme is how RAID-4 and RAID-5, which are therefore called parity stripes, are implemented. The individual bits in out bit set represent the columns of the parity stripes. The parity bit represents the additional parity column of the parity stripe volume. Of course addressing and counting every single bit in every block of the stripe on every write would be extremely slow. Instead of actually counting the individual bits, the CPU's XOR operation is used, which can be applied to whole words rather than bits. The XOR operation combines two values bitwise such that the resulting bit is equal to one if exactly one of the input values was equal to one. If they are both zero, the resulting bit is zero, and if they are both one, the resulting bit is also zero. In other words, XOR flags differences in the input values. In effect, this yields exactly the parity information. So what happens in a parity stripe is that the blocks on each stripe are combined using blockwise XOR and the resulting block, that contains the parity information for the whole stripe, is then written to the separate column in the RAID-4 implementation.

It quickly becomes obvious when one thinks about the problem for a while that the parity column will be overloaded with I/O as soon as several processes write to the RAID-4 volume. Each write needs to flush the corresponding parity information to the dedicated parity column, so while user data my be distributed to different disks, each write also puts load on the parity column. This is why in the next iteration, RAID-5, the parity was no longer put onto a dedicated column, but rather distributed across all columns. The technical term for the distribution, in case you are interested in obscure and useless tidbits, is "left-symmetric layout".

READ BEHAVIOR

Read behavior for RAID-4 is identical to a common stripe, read behavior for RAID-5 is a little bit different because the parity information is distributed and thus one more column is effectively working for user I/O. Hence, RAID-5 read performance tends to be a little better than a standard stripe, because it uses one column more than a normal stripe of the same size.

WRITE BEHAVIOR

Write behavior is indeed very interesting for parity stripes. We are rather sure that after reading this, you will quickly forget about parity stripes and use different layouts from then on.

Full–Stripe Write

In the best case, a full stripe is written. This is a relatively quick and easy process: The parity information is calculated from all the data buffers, the data is flushed onto the data columns for that volume region, and the parity information is written onto the parity column for that volume region (remember that the parity column is not constant with RAID-5). This is a little work for the CPU as well as an extra I/O for the parity column, but one extra I/O is certainly less than twice the I/Os, as we would have to do if the volume was a mirrored one. However, consider what happens when the write is interrupted because of a system fault (panic, power loss etc.). The parity information would not match the data any more. If you imagine a case where the system panics because of an error in the SAN that makes the system lose a disk in a funny way, then VxVM would have to reconstruct the data on the missing column using outdated parity information. If this happens to an area that holds important meta data then the meta data that is calculated by XORing the remaining columns with the parity column software will be seriously corrupt. It will be random data. Not just old data, but random! You don't want random data on your superblock, do you?

How do we solve the problem? We solve it by adding another protection mechanism called a transaction log. The transaction log is located on a different LUN from the data and parity column. It represents a circular buffer that holds (in the case of VxVM) the last five writes to the parity stripe. That means that all write I/O is effectively done twice: first to the transaction log, then to the actual data and parity columns.

Storage arrays will store the transaction log in non-volatile memory instead of on disk, which makes such hardware implementations much faster. They can also use special hardware for parity calculation, which again speeds up the hardware implementations vs software implementations.

In any case, storage array or VxVM, if the volume is started after a crash, all transactions from the transaction log are reapplied to the parity stripe in the order they appear in the log, in order to ensure consistency between data and parity and also to have the most current data available.

Most–Stripe Write

If most, but not all columns are written then if we just write the data the parity will be out of sync with the data because the new data is not represented in the parity. If we write data plus the newly calculated parity of the data the problem is not solved because then the remaining old data is not represented in the parity. What we need to do is actually read the remaining old data columns, the ones that will not be overwritten, then calculate the parity using that old data plus the new data that is to be written, and then write the new data and new parity. Of course, since we write via the transaction log, what actually happens if we do a most-stripe write is this:

1) Read remaining columns
2) Calculate new parity
3) Write new data plus new parity to transaction log
4) Write new data plus new parity to their respective columns

Doesn't sound quick, does it? Now look what we have to do when we write just a small number of columns

Few–Stripe Write

In this case it would be suboptimal to read all the remaining columns from the volume; there could be many. Instead, we read the columns that we are going to overwrite, plus the parity column. Then, we XOR the old data out of the parity data, XOR the new data into the parity, write the transaction log and finally the volume. It looks like this:

1) Read columns that will be overwritten
2) Read parity column
3) XOR old data with parity to extract old data's parity
4) XOR new data with parity to insert new data's parity
5) Write new data plus new parity to transaction log
6) Write new data plus new parity to their respective columns

Doesn't sound efficient either, does it? Wait until you see degraded mode!

Degraded Mode Read/Write Behavior

When one of the columns in a parity stripe fails the volume is switched to degraded mode. This means several things:

- The volume is no longer redundant
- Reads from existing data columns are satisfied in the normal way
- Writes to the volume proceed in the normal way
- Reads from the failed data columns are satisfied by reconstructing the missing data.

Reconstruct-read, as it is called, is performed by using all the other columns plus the parity information to calculate what had originally been on the column that is no longer accessible. What does that mean for the volume's performance and reliability? It means that when, for instance, in a 10-column RAID-5 volume one disk fails, then for 10% of the read I/Os (the ones that would read from to the missing disk), nine columns must be read instead of just one, i.e. the number of disk accesses caused by reads practically doubles. Additionally, the XOR calculations must be performed by the CPU. Imagine a RAID-5 volume that is suffering from lots of scattered reads (the worst case today, as we proved near the beginning of this book). If one of the disks overheats, e.g. because a fan in the tray is broken, then all the other disks will have to deliver twice the amount of reads! This will not only slow down the performance even more, but it will also lead to more heat, increasing the probability for another failure. But now we are no longer redundant, so if the next disk fails the volume will become inaccessible!

Recovery Behavior

As soon as a column has failed in a parity stripe we must restore redundancy in order to keep up reliability. Unfortunately, what that means is that the replacement for the failed disk must be initialized with exactly the data that was lost. No problem in principle, since we can always reconstruct that data using the parity column plus all the remaining data columns. But if you read the last paragraph then you know that by now the number of read-I/Os to the remaining disks has already doubled, and now we're forcing even more I/O onto the system by systematically requesting all the data in the lost column – even the empty blocks since we are reconstructing on the raw device level! Keep in mind that for every extent whose data we want to reconstruct we have to read the corresponding extents on all the other data columns plus the parity column, and then calculate the original data and write it to the extent! This is an enormous strain on the I/O subsystem as well as the CPU. It therefore takes a long time, during which we are very slow and very vulnerable to further failures.

It is for these reasons that I do not recommend using parity stripes for enterprise applications; at least not software implementations of parity stripes. Hardware implementations are better because they do not require physical writes to a transaction log (which is in battery-backed memory), they do predictive failure analysis pretty well and they usually have hardware-assisted parity calculation engines to reduce the CPU load

5.7.5   MIRROR-CONCAT

This is actually exactly the same as a plain mirror. Concatenation is the default layout, and even a volume with just a single, tiny subdisk is called a concat volume. This is similar to the cat command in UNIX, which is called that way because it **can** concatenate several files, but you still cat a file even if it's just a single one.

5.7.6   MIRROR-STRIPE

A mirror-stripe layout combines striping with mirroring. It is equivalent to the combined RAID level RAID-01. The basic plex layout of the volume is stripe, and another striped plex is attached to the volume. This has the advantage of adding mirror-like redundancy to the stripe, which is much better than a parity-stripe. If any of the disks in plex 1 fails then plex 2 still has the complete set of data. Further disk failures in the plex 1 stripe do not affect the volume because plex 1 is detached as soon as the first failure is detected. If another disk failure occurs in plex 2, the volume will be unavailable because plex 2 is also detached due to the disk failure.

Read/write I/O is performed according to the same read policy as a mirror (round robin/select/preferred plex), and of course data is always striped across all columns as it is in a stripe.

There is a much better layout called stripe-mirror, or RAID-10, which instead of mirroring stripes will create individual mirrors and then stripe across them. This is called a layered volume and is covered in the chapter on layered volumes.

5.7.7   MIXED LAYOUTS

It is possible in all UNIX versions of VxVM to have a different layout in every plex. It is not possible in the Windows implementations, but that operating system has more serious limitations to worry about than VxVM limits anyway.

You cannot create mixed layout volumes with a single vxassist command, but once you have a volume you can just add plexes to it using vxassist mirror, and specify any kind of layout you want. Actually, adding a RAID-5 plex to a volume or adding another plex to a RAID-5 volume is not a straightforward task with vxassist either (it requires using layered volumes, but it does work). Once you have the multi-layout volume you can use it just like any other volume, but some features will not work any more. These are:

- Snapshots
- Fast mirror resynchronisation
- Relayout
- Resize

For these reasons you may want to stick with standard layouts. They are more thoroughly supported. But it sure is good to know that there is no hard limit inside VxVM that enforces identical layouts for all data plexes.

5.8 RELAYOUT IN DETAIL

The relayout feature of VxVM is pretty fascinating to watch in action, and you may wonder what is going on inside. We can tell you some of it, but we did not write the code, and the actual behavior varies with source and destination layouts, so please pardon if sometimes the details may seem a little odd. In order to understand this explanation it is absolutely necessary that you have a good understanding of what a layered volume is, so please make sure you have read the chapter on layering and layered volumes.

What happens when you relayout a volume is this:

- First of all the volume to relayout is being layered and pushed down several layers (depending on the exact parameters, typically to layers three or four). This allows VxVM to still access the volume from both user and kernel perspective, while at the same time enabling very thorough rearrangement of plexes and subdisks inside the volume.

- The next thing that vxassist does is look at the size of the volume to find the right size for a mirrored internal temporary buffer subvolume that the relayout process uses to copy data from the source subvolume to the destination subvolume. This buffer is then created as just a normal, mirrored volume, which is then layered and stuffed deep down into the volume that is about to undergo relayout. We will find usually it in layer three or four, and if you look at the output of vxtask list right after you start the relayout process then you will find a subvolume that is being synchronised using the RDWRBACK synchronisation method. This is the synchronisation of the internal buffer subvolume.

- If the volume to relayout is very small (i.e. smaller than 50MB) then it creates a buffer subvolume that is the same size as the volume. If the volume is between 50MB and 1GB then it will create a 50MB buffer subvolume, and if the volume is larger than 1GB it will create a 1GB buffer subvolume. Actually the 50MB value is outdated now, but it used to be true. With Storage Foundation 5.0 the value seems to be more dynamically allocated and generally be slightly more than 10% of the source volume's size.

- The next thing that happens – after persisting the intended relayout operation in the private region – is that the relayout kernel thread fills the buffer volume with data from the beginning of the source subvolume. Let us assume the extent of the buffer subvolume is 50MB. It then maps the buffer subvolume into the first 50MB of the source subvolume and unmaps the first 50MB of the source subvolume to free the subdisks. Now it allocates and maps the first 50MB of the destination subvolume in the correct destination layout and begins to copy the data from the buffer to the destination subvolume. Remember that all those subvolumes are contained in what the user uninterruptedly sees as the original data volume. They are just pushed way down several layers.

- Once the buffer subvolume's contents have been copied the first 50MB of the user volume are remapped to point to the new, destination volume. So from now on accesses to the first 50MB extent will be directed to the target subvolume, and accesses to the rest will be directed to the source volume.

- Now the circle repeats with the next 50MB, then the next, and so on, until the whole source subvolume is copied onto the target subvolume.

- Then, the buffer subvolume as well as the rest of the source subvolume are freed, the target subvolume is unlayered and the relayout intent removed from the Private Region. Relayout is finished.

What actually happens is much more complicated than that. You will see up to seven subvolumes involved in a relayout process, not all of which can be easily explained, but this is the rough idea of it.

Since we are in the Technical Deep Dive section anyway, here is a short walk-through of a relayout:

```
# vxprint -qrtL -g adg # -q: no headers, -rt: more info, -L: separate layers
v  avol        -            ENABLED ACTIVE  4194304  SELECT   -        fsgen
pl avol-01     avol         ENABLED ACTIVE  4194304  CONCAT   -        RW
sd adg01-01    avol-01      adg01    0       4194304  0        c0t2d0   ENA
# vxassist relayout avol  ncol=4 & # Start the relayout process
[1]    21976
# vxtask list # Let's look at the temporary buffer volume
TASKID PTID TYPE/STATE   PCT   PROGRESS
    241       RDWRBACK/R 16.12% 0/419328/67584 VOLSTART avol-T01 adg
# bc -l # Let's see how large the buffer subvolume "avol-T01" is
419328/2048
204.7500000000  # 204.75 MB, around 10% of the volume size
# vxtask list # Let's see if the actual relayout has started yet.
TASKID PTID TYPE/STATE    PCT   PROGRESS
    243       RELAYOUT/R 00.05% 0/8388608/4096 RELAYOUT avol adg
# vxrelayout status avol
 CONCAT --> STRIPED, columns=4, stwidth=128
 Relayout running,  0.00% completed.
# vxtask list
TASKID PTID TYPE/STATE    PCT   PROGRESS
    243       RELAYOUT/R 02.25% 0/8388608/188416 RELAYOUT avol adg
# vxprint -qrtL -g adg # Look at those six subvolumes in layers 2 and 3!
[...]
v  avol         -            ENABLED ACTIVE  4194304  SELECT   -        fsgen
pl avol-tp01    avol         ENABLED ACTIVE  4194304  CONCAT   -        RW

sv avol-ts01    avol-tp01    avol-I01 2      4194304  0        3/5      ENA
v2 avol-I01     -            ENABLED ACTIVE  4194304  ROUND    -
relayout
p2 avol-Ip01    avol-I01     ENABLED(SPARSE) SRC 4194304 CONCAT -       RW

sv avol-Is01    avol-Ip01    avol-S01 1      2936320  1257984  1/1      ENA
v3 avol-S01     -            ENABLED ACTIVE  2936320  SELECT   -        fsgen
p3 avol-01      avol-S01     ENABLED ACTIVE  2936320  CONCAT   -        RW
s3 adg01-01     avol-01      adg01    1257984 2936320  0        c0t2d0   ENA
p2 avol-Ip02    avol-I01     ENABLED(SPARSE) TMP 1677312 CONCAT -       WO
```

```
sv avol-Is02    avol-Ip02    avol-T01 1      419328    1257984  2/2        ENA
v3 avol-T01     -            ENABLED  ACTIVE  419328    SELECT   -          fsgen
p3 avol-T01-01  avol-T01     ENABLED  ACTIVE  419328    CONCAT   -          RW
s3 adg02-01     avol-T01-01  adg02    0       419328    0        c0t3d0     ENA
p3 avol-T01-02  avol-T01     ENABLED  ACTIVE  419328    CONCAT   -          RW
s3 adg03-01     avol-T01-02  adg03    0       419328    0        c0t4d0     ENA
p2 avol-Ip03    avol-I01     DISABLED UNUSED  4194304   CONCAT   -          RW


sv avol-Is03    avol-Ip03    avol-U01 1            4194304    0         0/1      DIS
v3 avol-U01     -            DISABLED EMPTY        4194304    SELECT    -        fsgen
p3 avol-Up01    avol-U01     DISABLED(SPARSE) ACTIVE 5031552  STRIPE 4/128      RW
s3 adg01-02     avol-Up01    adg01    314496      943488    0/314496  c0t2d0    ENA
s3 adg04-01     avol-Up01    adg04    314496      734080    1/314496  c0t10d0   ENA
s3 adg05-01     avol-Up01    adg05    314496      734080    2/314496  c0t11d0   ENA
s3 adg06-01     avol-Up01    adg06    314496      734080    3/314496  c0t12d0   ENA
p2 avol-Ip04    avol-I01     DISABLED(SPARSE) WOD 0  CONCAT   -         WO


sv avol-Is04    avol-Ip04    avol-W01 0       0         0        1/1        ENA
v3 avol-W01     -            ENABLED  ACTIVE  0         SELECT   -          fsgen
p3 avol-Wp01    avol-W01     ENABLED  ACTIVE  0         STRIPE   4/128      RW
p2 avol-Ip05    avol-I01     ENABLED(SPARSE) DST 1257984 CONCAT  -         RW


sv avol-Is05    avol-Ip05    avol-D01 1       1257984   0        1/1        ENA
v3 avol-D01     -            ENABLED  ACTIVE  1257984   SELECT   avol-Dp01
fsgen
p3 avol-Dp01    avol-D01     ENABLED  ACTIVE  1257984   STRIPE   4/128      RW
s3 adg01-03     avol-Dp01    adg01    0       314496    0/0      c0t2d0     ENA
s3 adg04-02     avol-Dp01    adg04    0       314496    1/0      c0t10d0    ENA
s3 adg05-02     avol-Dp01    adg05    0       314496    2/0      c0t11d0    ENA
s3 adg06-02     avol-Dp01    adg06    0       314496    3/0      c0t12d0    ENA
```

We'll let some time pass here to give the relayout process some time to proceed with doing its work. Look at the highlighted output. What you can identify are the source sub-volume (SRC), a temporary subvolume (TMP), an unused subvolume (UNUSED), a write-only and write-on-demand subvolume (WO, WOD), and the destination subvolume (DST).

```
# vxrelayout status avol
 CONCAT --> STRIPED, columns=4, stwidth=128
 Relayout running, 69.98% completed.
# vxprint -qrtLgadg # Subvolume sizes have changed!
[...]
v  avol        -            ENABLED  ACTIVE  4194304   SELECT   -          fsgen
pl avol-tp01   avol         ENABLED  ACTIVE  4194304   CONCAT   -          RW


sv avol-ts01   avol-tp01    avol-I01 2       4194304   0        4/5        ENA
v2 avol-I01    -            ENABLED  ACTIVE  4194304   ROUND    -
```

```
relayout
p2 avol-Ip01     avol-I01     ENABLED(SPARSE) SRC 4194304 CONCAT    -       RW

sv avol-Is01     avol-Ip01    avol-S01 1      839680   3354624   1/1     ENA
v3 avol-S01      -            ENABLED ACTIVE  839680   SELECT    -       fsgen
p3 avol-01       avol-S01     ENABLED ACTIVE  839680   CONCAT    -       RW
s3 adg01-01      avol-01      adg01   3354624  839680   0         c0t2d0  ENA
p2 avol-Ip02     avol-I01     ENABLED(SPARSE) TMP 3354624 CONCAT  -       RW

sv avol-Is02     avol-Ip02    avol-T01 1      419328   2935296   2/2     ENA
v3 avol-T01      -            ENABLED ACTIVE  419328   SELECT    -       fsgen
p3 avol-T01-01   avol-T01     ENABLED ACTIVE  419328   CONCAT    -       RW
s3 adg02-01      avol-T01-01  adg02   0        419328   0         c0t3d0  ENA
p3 avol-T01-02   avol-T01     ENABLED ACTIVE  419328   CONCAT    -       RW
s3 adg03-01      avol-T01-02  adg03   0        419328   0         c0t4d0  ENA
p2 avol-Ip03     avol-I01     DISABLED UNUSED 4194304  CONCAT    -       RW

sv avol-Is03     avol-Ip03    avol-U01 1      4194304  0         0/1     DIS
v3 avol-U01      -            DISABLED EMPTY  4194304  SELECT    -       fsgen
p3 avol-Up01     avol-U01     DISABLED(SPARSE) ACTIVE 13418112 STRIPE 4/128 RW
s3 adg01-02      avol-Up01    adg01   838656   2515968  0/838656  c0t2d0  ENA
s3 adg04-01      avol-Up01    adg04   838656   209920   1/838656  c0t10d0 ENA
s3 adg05-01      avol-Up01    adg05   838656   209920   2/838656  c0t11d0 ENA
s3 adg06-01      avol-Up01    adg06   838656   209920   3/838656  c0t12d0 ENA
p2 avol-Ip04     avol-I01     ENABLED(SPARSE) WOD 3354624 CONCAT  -       WO

sv avol-Is04     avol-Ip04    avol-W01 1      419328   2935296   1/1     ENA
v3 avol-W01      -            ENABLED ACTIVE  419328   SELECT    avol-Wp01
fsgen
p3 avol-Wp01     avol-W01     ENABLED ACTIVE  419328   STRIPE    4/128   RW
s3 adg01-05      avol-Wp01    adg01   733824   104832   0/0       c0t2d0  ENA
s3 adg04-03      avol-Wp01    adg04   733824   104832   1/0       c0t10d0 ENA
s3 adg05-03      avol-Wp01    adg05   733824   104832   2/0       c0t11d0 ENA
s3 adg06-03      avol-Wp01    adg06   733824   104832   3/0       c0t12d0 ENA
p2 avol-Ip05     avol-I01     ENABLED(SPARSE) DST 2935296 CONCAT  -       RW

sv avol-Is05     avol-Ip05    avol-D01 1      2935296  0         1/1     ENA
v3 avol-D01      -            ENABLED ACTIVE  2935296  SELECT    avol-Dp01
fsgen
p3 avol-Dp01     avol-D01     ENABLED ACTIVE  2935296  STRIPE    4/128   RW
s3 adg01-03      avol-Dp01    adg01   0        733824   0/0       c0t2d0  ENA
s3 adg04-02      avol-Dp01    adg04   0        733824   1/0       c0t10d0 ENA
s3 adg05-02      avol-Dp01    adg05   0        733824   2/0       c0t11d0 ENA
s3 adg06-02      avol-Dp01    adg06   0        733824   3/0       c0t12d0 ENA
[1] + Done                   vxassist relayout avol  ncol=4 &
# vxprint -qrtLgadg
[...]
```

```
v  avol        -           ENABLED  ACTIVE  4194304  SELECT  avol-01  fsgen
pl avol-01     avol        ENABLED  ACTIVE  4194304  STRIPE  4/128    RW
sd adg01-03    avol-01     adg01    0       1048576  0/0     c0t2d0   ENA
sd adg04-02    avol-01     adg04    0       1048576  1/0     c0t10d0  ENA
sd adg05-02    avol-01     adg05    0       1048576  2/0     c0t11d0  ENA
sd adg06-02    avol-01     adg06    0       1048576  3/0     c0t12d0  ENA
```

The relayout has successfully completed, and the volume now has the desired target layout of stripe with four columns.

We hope this has enlightened you about several things:

1) You can trust VxVM's relayout feature. It is not magic, but actually understandable with reasonable effort.

2) Relayout would be really hard to do manually, if you had to allocate your own storage objects.

3) It actually works online, with no downtime to the application.

4) It is crash-proof and can be restarted and reversed at will.

CHAPTER 6: LAYERED VOLUMES

by Volker Herminghaus

6.1 OVERVIEW

In the previous chapter you learned about volumes and the merits of the various volume layouts. You learned how easy it is to specify storage allocations and other features. The relayout feature was discussed, and we made an advance mention of the term **layered volume**. This chapter will talk about what at first looks like just two more volume layouts: `concat-mirror` and `stripe-mirror`. In the more technical sections, especially the technical deep dive, you will see what the idea behind these so-called **layered volumes** is, and how it enables such features as relayout and RAID-5 mirroring.

6.1.1 WHY USE LAYERED VOLUMES?

The VxVM volume layouts that we have discussed so far all work pretty well and cover the needs of most administrators. But everything can be improved, and so volume layouts were improved, too. If we take a deep look we will find that **in the case of a disk failure**, there are a few minor issues with, for instance, a mirrored stripe. It is in this case, and only in this case, that something can be gained from using a layered volume layout instead of a standard volume layout. As long as all disks are OK, there is no noticeable advantage to either layout except for improved readability and simplicity on the part of the non-layered layouts.

In order to understand what can be improved, we need to know how a conventional layout volume behaves in case of a disk failure. Look at the layout of a conventional mir-

V. Herminghaus and A. Sriba, *Storage Management in Data Centers*,
DOI: 10.1007/978-3-540-85023-6_6, © Springer-Verlag Berlin Heidelberg 2009

rored stripe, i.e. a volume that was created with the layout specifier `mirror-stripe`:

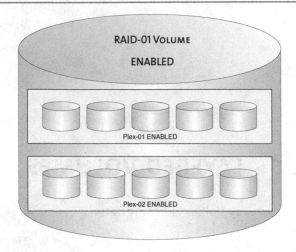

Figure 6-1:   A RAID-01 volume in normal operation. Both plexes are enabled,
                    the volume is enabled and active.

You see that the volume consists of two data plexes, i.e. two containers for identical volume data. Now the normal behavior of this volume when undergoing read-I/O is the following: The `select` volume read policy uses the round read method to read all plexes in a round-robin fashion. The specific details of this read method vary from array to array as the DDL (dynamic device layer) uses libraries that are specifically tuned for each storage type. But in general, first major read I/O will be satisfied from one plex, the next major read I/O will be satisfied from the next plex, and so on. In effect, this reduces the number of I/Os on each LUN and thus the queue length on the LUNs. Performance is gained by this act of load balancing, especially for the infamous **scattered read** I/O type.

But consider what happens when any one of the LUNs or disks fails: The whole plex will be detached.

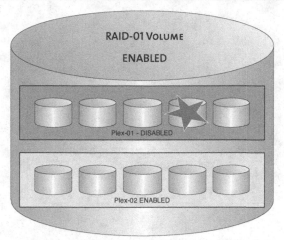

Figure 6-2: A RAID-01 volume after a single disk has failed. One plex has been disabled, the volume is still enabled and active.

This means that even if only one out of the, say, five LUNs making up a striped plex fails, all five disks will stop doing any work for us! They will just idle; nobody asks them for data any more. And that is for good reason, because the plex is now detached and its data is becoming rapidly out of sync with the active plex. You don't want stale data, do you?

This is the first problem that will be solved by layered volumes.

Now consider a second disk failing. The probability of the other plex being affected is fifty percent (actually it is a little higher, since the failed disk cannot fail again). That means the other plex is now detached, too, and the volume has become unusable. We might have valid data on four out of five columns of one plex, and also have valid data on some other four out of five columns of the other plex, but still the volume is unusable. Does that make any sense?

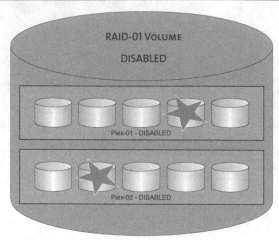

Figure 6-3:   A RAID-01 volume after a second disk has failed, on the other plex. Both plexes have been disabled, the volume is disabled.

Well, it does, because that is how VxVM was designed, and the way it was designed (and BTW the way most high-availability software was designed) is to compensate for any **one** fault, but not for double-faults. Why do we not compensate for two faults? Because compensating for just one fault alone requires a lot of design the software, architecting the solution, and operating it. There are dozens of possible single points of failure that we need to guard against. If you had to plan for double faults, that would be not two times dozens, but dozens times dozens! It is simply too complex to even try. Therefore it has been almost universally agreed that a double-fault is nothing that a high-availability solution needs to worry about. Not because it cannot happen, but because it would be impossible to catch reliably anyway.

Losing a second disk without losing the volume was, although this feature did not have to be implemented for "official" reasons, the second problem that was solved with layered volumes.

Going back to our single-fault situation, however, we find another thing that does not work as well as it could: Imagine if you replace the failed disk, and that was one out of five disks that made up the detached plex. What needs to be done? Volume manager needs to resynchronize the whole plex! Remember that as soon as the plex was detached due to the disk failure, no more read or write I/O was performed to it. So at the very minimum all those regions that have been written to must now be copied to the fixed plex before it can be read again. But wait! So far we have not learned of any way to track where changes have been made, which regions have been written to. That means that indeed we must resynchronize the whole plex. Five times as much as would have been necessary if we had kept those other four disks in sync. But that was impossible because they belong to the same plex, and VxVM cannot detach just part of a plex, but only a whole plex.

So, to sum it up, there are three things wrong with volumes **in case of a disk failure**:

1) Load balancing is lost due to the whole plex being detached.

2) For the same reason, the whole plex needs to be resynchronised after disk repair.

3) While the plex is detached, failure of any disk in the other plex renders the volume unusable (if we only have two plexes – we could have more than two and the volume would still be online, of course).

More information on disk and plex failures and how to cope with them can be found in the troubleshooting chapter beginning on page 349.

OK, let's get started and make some layered volumes and look at them in the Easy Sailing chapter!

6.2 Introducing Layered Volumes

The idea of layering comes from the following fact, that eventually hit the designers of VxVM:

In conventional volumes, space is allocated from physical disks. Physical disks have some limitations as to their size and reliability etc. So the subdisks that reside on those physical disks share their limitations.

Why can we not use volumes – instead of physical disks or LUNs - as the basis for subdisks? If we could use volumes instead of disks as the basis for subdisk allocation, then the subdisks could be made redundant or arbitrarily sized on their own, freeing us from some limitations such as the ones we see when a failed disks leads to a whole detached plex.

If the subdisks were allocated from – usually redundant – volumes, then a failing disk would not make the subdisk fail (it is redundant and therefore survives a single failure). Instead, the subdisk would continue to run fine, and the volume would be unaffected. Only one layer deeper, inside the volume that the subdisk was allocated from, would the corresponding plex be detached. The subvolume would be degraded because the plex that contains the failed disk is no longer active. But the subvolume itself as well as the volume that builds on top of it would be unaffected. See the following graphics and compare them to the ones about the RAID-01 volume.

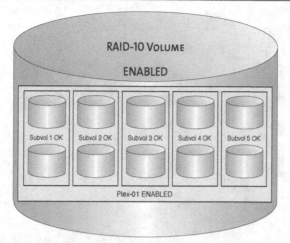

Figure 6-4:   A volume in RAID-10 layout. Note how the user data is structured in exactly the same way as in the case of RAID-01. Only the metadata is rearranged to group the subdisks differently, yielding higher resilience.

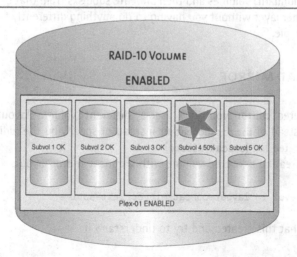

Figure 6-5:   A volume in RAID-10 layout after a single disk has failed. The volume is only slightly degraded, as load balancing still takes place on most of it. Also, recovery would only require resynchronisation of a small portion of the total volume. The unaffected parts are still updated and need not be synchronized after replacing the failed disk (only the mirrored subvolume need to be resynchronised).

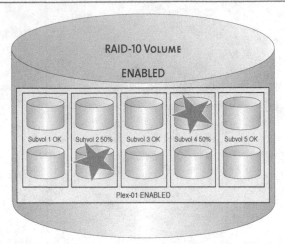

Figure 6-6: A volume in RAID-10 layout after another disk failure. The volume is still accessible. In fact, it could bear three more disk failures, provided they all happen to different columns.

Being so clearly superior to RAID-01, the concept of layering (RAID-10) was added to VxVM. Layering is implemented transparently, which means that vxassist will build for you a base layer of (redundant) volumes and then allocate subdisks from that base layer to form a volume on a higher layer without you having to do anything differently from before. Let's try it, it's really simple.

6.2.1 CONCAT-MIRROR

To create a layered mirror you just use a different volume layout specification: concat-mirror instead of mirror-concat or instead of specifying the individual attribute as a comma-separated list (concat,mirror).

Synopsis for creating a layered volume with a concat-mirror layout:

```
# vxassist make avol 1g layout=concat-mirror init=active
```

But look at what this created and try to understand it:

```
# vxprint -qvhtgadg
v   avol                    -               ENABLED  ACTIVE   2097152  SELECT    -         fsgen
pl  avol-03       avol                      ENABLED  ACTIVE   2097152  CONCAT    -         RW
sv  avol-S01      avol-03      avol-L01  1            2097152  0         2/2       ENA

v   avol-L01                -               ENABLED  ACTIVE   2097152  SELECT    -         fsgen
pl  avol-P01      avol-L01                  ENABLED  ACTIVE   2097152  CONCAT    -         RW
sd  adg01-03      avol-P01     adg01        204800   2097152  0         c0t2d0    ENA
```

```
pl avol-P02      avol-L01      ENABLED   ACTIVE   2097152  CONCAT    -        RW
sd adg02-03      avol-P02      adg02     204800   2097152  0         c0t3d0   ENA
```

That is the one major drawback: a layered volume consists of more objects and there-fore its layout is harder to understand by looking at the output of vxprint. It looks like two volumes were created (which is true). If you look closely at the highlighted words in the third line of output you will see that it is not a subdisk (sd), but a subvolume (sv), i.e. a subdisk that is based on a volume instead of a disk. You will also see where the sub-volume was allocated from: avol-L01. And if you look at the next line you see that the second volume that was created is actually called avol-L01. In other words, the vxassist command created a mirrored volume, then used that volume as the basis for allocating a subdisk for another volume. That is why this is called a layered volume: one volume lies on top of the other.

We will give you some help in understanding the layout very soon; it's actually not as complicated as it first looks.

6.2.2 STRIPE-MIRROR

Creating a layered striped mirror is just as easy as creating a layered concat mirror. Of course the layout parameter is different: stripe-mirror instead of mirror-stripe or mirror,stripe.

Synopsis for creating a layered volume with a stripe-mirror layout:

```
# vxassist make avol 1g layout=stripe-mirror init=active
# vxprint -qvhtgadg
v  avol           -             ENABLED   ACTIVE   2097152  SELECT    avol-03  fsgen
pl avol-03        avol          ENABLED   ACTIVE   2097408  STRIPE    3/128    RW
sv avol-S01       avol-03       avol-L01  1        699136   0/0       2/2      ENA
sv avol-S02       avol-03       avol-L02  1        699136   1/0       2/2      ENA
sv avol-S03       avol-03       avol-L03  1        699136   2/0       2/2      ENA

v  avol-L01       -             ENABLED   ACTIVE   699136   SELECT    -        fsgen
pl avol-P01       avol-L01      ENABLED   ACTIVE   699136   CONCAT    -        RW
sd adg01-03       avol-P01      adg01     204800   699136   0         c0t2d0   ENA
pl avol-P02       avol-L01      ENABLED   ACTIVE   699136   CONCAT    -        RW
sd adg04-03       avol-P02      adg04     204800   699136   0         c0t10d0  ENA

v  avol-L02       -             ENABLED   ACTIVE   699136   SELECT    -        fsgen
pl avol-P03       avol-L02      ENABLED   ACTIVE   699136   CONCAT    -        RW
sd adg02-03       avol-P03      adg02     204800   699136   0         c0t3d0   ENA
pl avol-P04       avol-L02      ENABLED   ACTIVE   699136   CONCAT    -        RW
sd adg05-03       avol-P04      adg05     204800   699136   0         c0t11d0  ENA

v  avol-L03       -             ENABLED   ACTIVE   699136   SELECT    -        fsgen
pl avol-P05       avol-L03      ENABLED   ACTIVE   699136   CONCAT    -        RW
sd adg03-03       avol-P05      adg03     204800   699136   0         c0t4d0   ENA
```

```
pl avol-P06      avol-L03      ENABLED ACTIVE   699136  CONCAT    -         RW
sd adg06-03      avol-P06      adg06   204800   699136  0         c0t12d0   ENA
```

6.2.3   UNDERSTANDING VXPRINT OUTPUT FOR LAYERED VOLUMES

So far, so good. We have just created our first layered volumes. Now how could we more easily understand the vxprint output for a layered volume? It's actually not so hard. Once you know the basics the secrets reveal themselves.

Let's use three different output formats for vxprint to try and combine understanding of the volume layout with readability in your day-to-day job. The highlighted parts are what you need to inspect more closely; they contain the layout of the volume and the layout of the subvolume. The other parts are redundant because they show only the layouts of the other subvolumes.. When created with vxassist, all subvolumes share the same layout so they do not need further attention unless a volume has a problem.

Now here are the formats:

1. Easy but maybe too easy, and confusing us with extra volumes: vxprint -ht

```
# vxprint -ht -g adg
<...>
v  avol         -             ENABLED ACTIVE   2097152 SELECT    avol-03   fsgen
pl avol-03      avol          ENABLED ACTIVE   2097408 STRIPE    3/128     RW
sv avol-S01     avol-03       avol-L01 1       699136  0/0       2/2       ENA
sv avol-S02     avol-03       avol-L02 1       699136  1/0       2/2       ENA
sv avol-S03     avol-03       avol-L03 1       699136  2/0       2/2       ENA

v  avol-L01     -             ENABLED ACTIVE   699136  SELECT    -         fsgen
pl avol-P01     avol-L01      ENABLED ACTIVE   699136  CONCAT    -         RW
sd adg01-03     avol-P01      adg01   204800   699136  0         c0t2d0    ENA
pl avol-P02     avol-L01      ENABLED ACTIVE   699136  CONCAT    -         RW
sd adg04-03     avol-P02      adg04   204800   699136  0         c0t10d0   ENA

v  avol-L02     -             ENABLED ACTIVE   699136  SELECT    -         fsgen
pl avol-P03     avol-L02      ENABLED ACTIVE   699136  CONCAT    -         RW
sd adg02-03     avol-P03      adg02   204800   699136  0         c0t3d0    ENA
pl avol-P04     avol-L02      ENABLED ACTIVE   699136  CONCAT    -         RW
sd adg05-03     avol-P04      adg05   204800   699136  0         c0t11d0   ENA

v  avol-L03     -             ENABLED ACTIVE   699136  SELECT    -         fsgen
pl avol-P05     avol-L03      ENABLED ACTIVE   699136  CONCAT    -         RW
sd adg03-03     avol-P05      adg03   204800   699136  0         c0t4d0    ENA
pl avol-P06     avol-L03      ENABLED ACTIVE   699136  CONCAT    -         RW
sd adg06-03     avol-P06      adg06   204800   699136  0         c0t12d0   ENA
```

The output of this command consists of several parts, separated by blank lines. First you see the high-level volume with its solitary plex and the subdisks. But as showed in the initial example they are now based not on disks but on volumes and are therefore called not subdisks but subvolumes (they are listed as type sv). OK, so subvolumes are in the plex instead of subdisks. Where are the volumes that the subdisks were allocated from? They are right below the volume, listed as normal volumes (which they are **not**, in fact. They do not have a device driver in /dev/vx/*dsk/... to write to them). If we want to look at the top layer volume's layout we inspect the plex line of that volume. In the layout column it will either say STRIPE or CONCAT meaning it will be either a stripe-mirror or concat-mirror, respectively. Next, to find out if the base volumes are mirrored once, twice, or more often, we will look at the layout of one of them (their layout is always identical if they were created with vxassist). If we see a base volume with two data plexes, that's simple mirroring. If the base volume shows three data plexes, that means the layered volume is a three-way mirror etc. It's actually very simple. The main problem with this output format is that it is not immediately obvious where the individual subvolumes belong in the layered volume. Besides, they look just like normal volumes. A shell script might confuse them with normal volumes and try to start them, create snapshots from them etc., which would fail because they really are not independent volumes but subvolumes belonging to a higher level virtual object.

   2. Compact but certainly not easy: vxprint -rt

```
# vxprint -rt -g adg
<...>
v  avol         -              ENABLED  ACTIVE  2097152  SELECT   avol-03   fsgen
pl avol-03      avol           ENABLED  ACTIVE  2097408  STRIPE   3/128     RW
sv avol-S01     avol-03        avol-L01 1       699136   0/0      2/2       ENA
v2 avol-L01     -              ENABLED  ACTIVE  699136   SELECT   -         fsgen
p2 avol-P01     avol-L01       ENABLED  ACTIVE  699136   CONCAT   -         RW
s2 adg01-03     avol-P01       adg01    204800  699136   0        c0t2d0    ENA
p2 avol-P02     avol-L01       ENABLED  ACTIVE  699136   CONCAT   -         RW
s2 adg04-03     avol-P02       adg04    204800  699136   0        c0t10d0   ENA
sv avol-S02     avol-03        avol-L02 1       699136   1/0      2/2       ENA
v2 avol-L02     -              ENABLED  ACTIVE  699136   SELECT   -         fsgen
p2 avol-P03     avol-L02       ENABLED  ACTIVE  699136   CONCAT   -         RW
s2 adg02-03     avol-P03       adg02    204800  699136   0        c0t3d0    ENA
p2 avol-P04     avol-L02       ENABLED  ACTIVE  699136   CONCAT   -         RW
s2 adg05-03     avol-P04       adg05    204800  699136   0        c0t11d0   ENA
sv avol-S03     avol-03        avol-L03 1       699136   2/0      2/2       ENA
v2 avol-L03     -              ENABLED  ACTIVE  699136   SELECT   -         fsgen
p2 avol-P05     avol-L03       ENABLED  ACTIVE  699136   CONCAT   -         RW
s2 adg03-03     avol-P05       adg03    204800  699136   0        c0t4d0    ENA
p2 avol-P06     avol-L03       ENABLED  ACTIVE  699136   CONCAT   -         RW
s2 adg06-03     avol-P06       adg06    204800  699136   0        c0t12d0   ENA
```

This output format is for the experienced administrator who has seen a lot of layered volumes already and can parse them almost instantly. What you see is an apparently unstructured lot of output lines with no helpful separation at all. But in exchange for the separation you get some more valuable information: the subvolumes are now listed with their layer number in the type field: a volume on layer 2 (i.e. one down from the top layer, the regular base layer) will not be shown as a v but as a v2; a volume on layer 2. Likewise, a plex inside such a volume will not be a p1 object but a p2 object, and a subdisk not an sd object but an s2 object. That makes this output format better palatable for scripts and long-time VxVM hackers, who prefer it for its concise look.

3. Less compact and relatively easy: vxprint -rtL

```
# vxprint -rtL -g adg
<...>
v   avol         -              ENABLED  ACTIVE  2097152  SELECT  avol-03   fsgen
pl  avol-03      avol           ENABLED  ACTIVE  2097408  STRIPE  3/128     RW

sv  avol-S01     avol-03        avol-L01 1       699136   0/0     2/2       ENA
v2  avol-L01     -              ENABLED  ACTIVE  699136   SELECT  -         fsgen
p2  avol-P01     avol-L01       ENABLED  ACTIVE  699136   CONCAT  -         RW
s2  adg01-03     avol-P01       adg01    204800  699136   0       c0t2d0    ENA
p2  avol-P02     avol-L01       ENABLED  ACTIVE  699136   CONCAT  -         RW
s2  adg04-03     avol-P02       adg04    204800  699136   0       c0t10d0   ENA

sv  avol-S02     avol-03        avol-L02 1       699136   1/0     2/2       ENA
v2  avol-L02     -              ENABLED  ACTIVE  699136   SELECT  -         fsgen
p2  avol-P03     avol-L02       ENABLED  ACTIVE  699136   CONCAT  -         RW
s2  adg02-03     avol-P03       adg02    204800  699136   0       c0t3d0    ENA
p2  avol-P04     avol-L02       ENABLED  ACTIVE  699136   CONCAT  -         RW
s2  adg05-03     avol-P04       adg05    204800  699136   0       c0t11d0   ENA

sv  avol-S03     avol-03        avol-L03 1       699136   2/0     2/2       ENA
v2  avol-L03     -              ENABLED  ACTIVE  699136   SELECT  -         fsgen
p2  avol-P05     avol-L03       ENABLED  ACTIVE  699136   CONCAT  -         RW
s2  adg03-03     avol-P05       adg03    204800  699136   0       c0t4d0    ENA
p2  avol-P06     avol-L03       ENABLED  ACTIVE  699136   CONCAT  -         RW
s2  adg06-03     avol-P06       adg06    204800  699136   0       c0t12d0   ENA
```

The last output format may be the one best suited to sophisticated newcomers. It looks just like the previous, more demanding format, but inserts blank lines between the subvolumes so it is easier to parse to the untrained eye. You may even want to stick with this output format forever.

Technical Deep Dive

6.3 Understanding Layered Volumes

6.3.1 Manually Creating a Layered Volume

As always we would like to walk you through the individual virtual objects for this topic. We will now create a layered volume, a three-column stripe-mirror of 300MB to be exact, all by ourselves using only our bare hands and a UNIX shell! Actually we will use vxassist, too, but only for the first steps.

```
# export VXVM_DEFAULTDG=adg
# cd /dev/vx/dsk/adg
# ls -l
total 0
# vxprint -qvrtg adg
<nothing>
```

We start with an empty disk group. First we create some mirrored and therefore redundant volumes that we can later use to allocate subdisks from.

```
# vxassist make col0vol 100m layout=mirror init=active
# vxassist make col1vol 100m layout=mirror init=active
# vxassist make col2vol 100m layout=mirror init=active
```

Now let's try to allocate a subdisk from the volumes:

```
# vxmake sd col0sd disk=col0vol offset=0 len=100m
VxVM vxmake ERROR V-5-1-10127 creating subdisk col0sd:
        Volume does not have the storage attribute
```

OK, that doesn't seem to work. Volume manager tells us the volume "does not have the storage attribute", i.e. it is not storage that is usable for VxVM. Why is that? Easy, check this out:

```
# ls -l                      .
total 0
brw-------  1 root     root    270, 3000 Jun  8 01:42 col0vol
brw-------  1 root     root    270, 3001 Jun  8 01:42 col1vol
brw-------  1 root     root    270, 3002 Jun  8 01:42 col2vol
```

If the device nodes are visible, they could be used for file system, database and raw device access. Do we really want to use these publicly accessible devices as parts of a volume? Certainly not, since there would be no protection against somebody unknowingly writing to the devices, thus wrecking the contents of the aggregate volume. Besides, if the subvolumes keep existing as a separate entity we could start and stop it individually etc. In short, it would be a real mess trying to coordinate or rather separate accesses to the volume as a standalone entity or as part of a layered volume. That is why VxVM says the volume "does not have the storage attribute". For VxVM, this volume is not storage like disk or LUN space. It is a virtual object that exists purely for the user's benefit. There would be nothing to stop VxVM from using a volume as the basis for storage allocation, because volumes so closely resemble actual disks (well, partitions, but in for the purpose of alloca-tion it is really the same). But it refuses to do so because the user might use a different access path to the same data: the volume device driver in /dev/vx/*dsk/<DG>/<Volume>. So a volume needs to be explicitly turned into "storage" first.

How **do** we turn a volume into storage that can be used by VxVM for internal alloca-tion? There's a VxVM attribute that we can set to do so. It is called the `layered` attribute. If we set it to on, the volume will magically be turned into storage usable by VxVM:

```
# vxedit set layered=on col0vol
# ls -l
    total 0
brw------- 1 root     root      270, 3001 Jun  8 01:42 col1vol
brw------- 1 root     root      270, 3002 Jun  8 01:42 col2vol
```

Aha! The volume on which we set the `layered` attribute to on has had its device driver removed! With this trick VxVM is now able to allocate subdisks from this volume just like it would from a physical disk. There is no longer any danger of uncoordinated parallel access any more, since the volume is no longer accessible by the user. So let's try allocating a subdisk again on col0vol:

```
# vxmake sd col0sd disk=col0vol offset=0 len=100m
# vxprint -qrtg adg
<...>
```

SD NAME	PLEX	DISK	DISKOFFS	LENGTH	[COL/]OFF	DEVICE	MODE
<...>							
sd col0sd	-	col0vol	0	204800	-	-	ENA
v2 col0vol	-	ENABLED	ACTIVE	204800	SELECT	-	fsgen
p2 col0vol-01	col0vol	ENABLED	ACTIVE	204800	CONCAT	-	RW
s2 adg01-01	col0vol-01	adg01	0	204800	0	c0t2d0	ENA
p2 col0vol-02	col0vol	ENABLED	ACTIVE	204800	CONCAT	-	RW
s2 adg02-01	col0vol-02	adg02	0	204800	0	c0t3d0	ENA
<...>							

This actually seems to work! Look at how the objects are defined: The type in the left most column show that the first element is an sd record, i.e. a subdisk. In column four of the subdisk, where there used to be names like adg01, adg02 etc., there is the name of the volume: col0vol! That is actually rather obvious and straightforward when you think of it.

Of course, for our convenience the actual volume is appended to the subdisk line as a v2 record (volume on layer 2, with plexes being p2 and subdisks being s2), so that the internal layout characteristics of the subvolume can be easily determined (number of mirrors and logs etc.).

To finish manufacturing a layered volume we need to repeat the above process accordingly with the other volumes:

```
# vxedit set layered=on col1vol col2vol
# ls -l
total 0
# vxmake sd col1sd disk=col1vol offset=0 len=100m
# vxmake sd col2sd disk=col2vol offset=0 len=100m
# vxprint -qrtg adg
<...>
sd col0sd       -              col0vol    0      204800   -        -      ENA
v2 col0vol      -              ENABLED ACTIVE 204800   SELECT   -      fsgen
p2 col0vol-01   col0vol        ENABLED ACTIVE 204800   CONCAT   -      RW
s2 adg01-01     col0vol-01     adg01      0      204800   0        c0t2d0 ENA
p2 col0vol-02   col0vol        ENABLED ACTIVE 204800   CONCAT   -      RW
s2 adg02-01     col0vol-02     adg02      0      204800   0        c0t3d0 ENA

sd col1sd       -              col1vol    0      204800   -        -      ENA
v2 col1vol      -              ENABLED ACTIVE 204800   SELECT   -      fsgen
p2 col1vol-01   col1vol        ENABLED ACTIVE 204800   CONCAT   -      RW
s2 adg03-01     col1vol-01     adg03      0      204800   0        c0t4d0 ENA
p2 col1vol-02   col1vol        ENABLED ACTIVE 204800   CONCAT   -      RW
s2 adg04-01     col1vol-02     adg04      0      204800   0        c0t10d0 ENA

sd col2sd       -              col2vol    0      204800   -        -      ENA
v2 col2vol      -              ENABLED ACTIVE 204800   SELECT   -      fsgen
p2 col2vol-01   col2vol        ENABLED ACTIVE 204800   CONCAT   -      RW
s2 adg05-01     col2vol-01     adg05      0      204800   0        c0t11d0 ENA
p2 col2vol-02   col2vol        ENABLED ACTIVE 204800   CONCAT   -      RW
s2 adg06-01     col2vol-02     adg06      0      204800   0        c0t12d0 ENA
```

So we got all three of our subdisks together. All we need to do now is actually make a stripe from them. That's not so hard, just put them into a plex together, and throw the plex into a volume, then wrap a volume around it with the appropriate usage type (fsgen for file system generic). Creating a striped plex manually using vxmake requires the use of both the ncol and the stwidth parameter, so we'll pick something reasonable like ncol=3 and 1 MB stripesize.

```
# vxmake plex manualvol-01 layout=stripe ncol=3 \
        sd=col0sd,col1sd,col2sd stwidth=1m
# vxprint -qrtg adg
<...>
pl manualvol-01 -              DISABLED -      614400   STRIPE   3/2048 RW
sv col0sd       manualvol      col0vol    1      204800   0/0      2/2    ENA
```

```
v2 col0vol      -            ENABLED ACTIVE 204800 SELECT   -       fsgen
p2 col0vol-01   col0vol      ENABLED ACTIVE 204800 CONCAT   -       RW
s2 adg01-01     col0vol-01   adg01   0      204800 0        c0t2d0  ENA
p2 col0vol-02   col0vol      ENABLED ACTIVE 204800 CONCAT   -       RW
s2 adg02-01     col0vol-02   adg02   0      204800 0        c0t3d0  ENA
sv col1sd       manualvol    col1vol 1      204800 1/0      2/2     ENA
v2 col1vol      -            ENABLED ACTIVE 204800 SELECT   -       fsgen
p2 col1vol-01   col1vol      ENABLED ACTIVE 204800 CONCAT   -       RW
s2 adg03-01     col1vol-01   adg03   0      204800 0        c0t4d0  ENA
p2 col1vol-02   col1vol      ENABLED ACTIVE 204800 CONCAT   -       RW
s2 adg04-01     col1vol-02   adg04   0      204800 0        c0t10d0 ENA
sv col2sd       manualvol    col2vol 1      204800 2/0      2/2     ENA
v2 col2vol      -            ENABLED ACTIVE 204800 SELECT   -       fsgen
p2 col2vol-01   col2vol      ENABLED ACTIVE 204800 CONCAT   -       RW
s2 adg05-01     col2vol-01   adg05   0      204800 0        c0t11d0 ENA
p2 col2vol-02   col2vol      ENABLED ACTIVE 204800 CONCAT   -       RW
s2 adg06-01     col2vol-02   adg06   0      204800 0        c0t12d0 ENA
```

Note how the subdisk virtual objects (sd) have turned into subvolume virtual objects (sv) to denote that their base storage is not a disk, but a volume.

```
# vxmake vol manualvol usetype=fsgen plex=manualvol-01
# vxprint -qrtg adg
<...>
v  manualvol    -            DISABLED EMPTY 614400 ROUND    -       fsgen
pl manualvol-01 manualvol    DISABLED EMPTY 614400 STRIPE   3/2048  RW
sv col0sd       manualvol-01 col0vol 1      204800 0/0      2/2     ENA
v2 col0vol      -            ENABLED ACTIVE 204800 SELECT   -       fsgen
p2 col0vol-01   col0vol      ENABLED ACTIVE 204800 CONCAT   -       RW
s2 adg01-01     col0vol-01   adg01   0      204800 0        c0t2d0  ENA
p2 col0vol-02   col0vol      ENABLED ACTIVE 204800 CONCAT   -       RW
s2 adg02-01     col0vol-02   adg02   0      204800 0        c0t3d0  ENA
sv col1sd       manualvol-01 col1vol 1      204800 1/0      2/2     ENA
v2 col1vol      -            ENABLED ACTIVE 204800 SELECT   -       fsgen
p2 col1vol-01   col1vol      ENABLED ACTIVE 204800 CONCAT   -       RW
s2 adg03-01     col1vol-01   adg03   0      204800 0        c0t4d0  ENA
p2 col1vol-02   col1vol      ENABLED ACTIVE 204800 CONCAT   -       RW
s2 adg04-01     col1vol-02   adg04   0      204800 0        c0t10d0 ENA
sv col2sd       manualvol-01 col2vol 1      204800 2/0      2/2     ENA
v2 col2vol      -            ENABLED ACTIVE 204800 SELECT   -       fsgen
p2 col2vol-01   col2vol      ENABLED ACTIVE 204800 CONCAT   -       RW
s2 adg05-01     col2vol-01   adg05   0      204800 0        c0t11d0 ENA
p2 col2vol-02   col2vol      ENABLED ACTIVE 204800 CONCAT   -       RW
s2 adg06-01     col2vol-02   adg06   0      204800 0        c0t12d0 ENA
```

All we have left to do is to start the volume now:

```
# vxvol start manualvol
VxVM vxvol INFO V-5-1-12459 Volume col0vol of diskgroup adg is already started
VxVM vxvol INFO V-5-1-12459 Volume col1vol of diskgroup adg is already started
VxVM vxvol INFO V-5-1-12459 Volume col2vol of diskgroup adg is already started
```

Ignore the INFO messages; VxVM just tells us that it did not need to start the internal volumes because they were running already (the **vxassist make** command started them automatically). When we check the volume now, we find a perfectly good layered volume ready to serve us:

```
# vxprint -qrtg adg
<...>
```

v	manualvol	-	ENABLED	ACTIVE	614400	ROUND	-	fsgen
pl	manualvol-01	manualvol	ENABLED	ACTIVE	614400	STRIPE	3/2048	RW
sv	col0sd	manualvol-01	col0vol	1	204800	0/0	2/2	ENA
v2	col0vol	-	ENABLED	ACTIVE	204800	SELECT	-	fsgen
p2	col0vol-01	col0vol	ENABLED	ACTIVE	204800	CONCAT	-	RW
s2	adg01-01	col0vol-01	adg01	0	204800	0	c0t2d0	ENA
p2	col0vol-02	col0vol	ENABLED	ACTIVE	204800	CONCAT	-	RW
s2	adg02-01	col0vol-02	adg02	0	204800	0	c0t3d0	ENA
sv	col1sd	manualvol-01	col1vol	1	204800	1/0	2/2	ENA
v2	col1vol	-	ENABLED	ACTIVE	204800	SELECT	-	fsgen
p2	col1vol-01	col1vol	ENABLED	ACTIVE	204800	CONCAT	-	RW
s2	adg03-01	col1vol-01	adg03	0	204800	0	c0t4d0	ENA
p2	col1vol-02	col1vol	ENABLED	ACTIVE	204800	CONCAT	-	RW
s2	adg04-01	col1vol-02	adg04	0	204800	0	c0t10d0	ENA
sv	col2sd	manualvol-01	col2vol	1	204800	2/0	2/2	ENA
v2	col2vol	-	ENABLED	ACTIVE	204800	SELECT	-	fsgen
p2	col2vol-01	col2vol	ENABLED	ACTIVE	204800	CONCAT	-	RW
s2	adg05-01	col2vol-01	adg05	0	204800	0	c0t11d0	ENA
p2	col2vol-02	col2vol	ENABLED	ACTIVE	204800	CONCAT	-	RW
s2	adg06-01	col2vol-02	adg06	0	204800	0	c0t12d0	ENA

6.3.2 MIRRORING RAID-5 VOLUMES

We certainly are not great fans of software RAID-5, but we are fans of using whatever possibilities a software offers us, even if it is just to double-check if we got everything right so far. So let's try and trick VxVM into doing something it does not normally do: mirroring a RAID-5 plex. Look what happens normally when you try to do that (we use the nolog keyword here purely because it makes parsing the vxprint output a little easier. We also use init=zero to speed up synchronisation of parity data):

```
# vxassist make raid5vol 100m layout=raid,nolog ncol=3 init=zero
# vxprint -qrtg adg
```

v	raid5vol	-	ENABLED	ACTIVE	204800	RAID	-	raid5

```
pl raid5vol-01  raid5vol       ENABLED ACTIVE   204800   RAID     3/32      RW
sd adg01-01     raid5vol-01  adg01     0        102400   0/0      c0t2d0    ENA
sd adg02-01     raid5vol-01  adg02     0        102400   1/0      c0t3d0    ENA
sd adg03-01     raid5vol-01  adg03     0        102400   2/0      c0t4d0    ENA
# vxassist mirror raid5vol
VxVM vxassist ERROR V-5-1-344 avol: RAID-5 volumes cannot be mirrored
```

Well, we're not going to believe that. But we have to hide the fact that the layout is RAID-5 from VxVM. So we set the "storage attribute", allocate a subdisk from what has now become VxVM-usable storage, wrap a plex and a volume around it and end up with a layered RAID-5 volume.

```
# vxedit set layered=on raid5vol
# vxmake sd raid5sd disk=raid5vol len=100m offset=0
# vxprint -rtqgadg
<...>
sd raid5sd      -            raid5vol 0        204800   -        -         ENA
v2 raid5vol     -            ENABLED ACTIVE   204800   RAID     -         raid5
p2 raid5vol-01  raid5vol     ENABLED ACTIVE   204800   RAID     3/32      RW
s2 adg01-01     raid5vol-01  adg01     0        102400   0/0      c0t2d0    ENA
s2 adg02-01     raid5vol-01  adg02     0        102400   1/0      c0t3d0    ENA
s2 adg03-01     raid5vol-01  adg03     0        102400   2/0      c0t4d0    ENA
# vxmake plex layraid5vol-01 sd=raid5sd
# vxmake vol layraid5vol usetype=fsgen plex=layraid5vol-01
# vxvol start layraid5vol
# vxprint -rtqgadg
<...>
v  layraid5vol  -            ENABLED ACTIVE   204800   ROUND    -         fsgen
pl layraid5vol-01 layraid5vol ENABLED ACTIVE   204800   CONCAT   -         RW
sv raid5sd      layraid5vol-01 raid5vol 1       204800   0        1/1       ENA
v2 raid5vol     -            ENABLED ACTIVE   204800   RAID     -         raid5
p2 raid5vol-01  raid5vol     ENABLED ACTIVE   204800   RAID     3/32      RW
s2 adg01-01     raid5vol-01  adg01     0        102400   0/0      c0t2d0    ENA
s2 adg02-01     raid5vol-01  adg02     0        102400   1/0      c0t3d0    ENA
s2 adg03-01     raid5vol-01  adg03     0        102400   2/0      c0t4d0    ENA
```

Here we are, the proud owners of a layered RAID-5 volume. Now we can mirror it easily because VxVM does not check the conditions inside layered storage the same as it does otherwise.

```
# vxassist mirror layraid5vol
# vxprint -rtqgadg
<...>
v  layraid5vol  -            ENABLED ACTIVE   204800   ROUND    -         fsgen
pl layraid5vol-01 layraid5vol ENABLED ACTIVE   204800   CONCAT   -         RW
sv raid5sd      layraid5vol-01 raid5vol 1       204800   0        2/2       ENA
v2 raid5vol     -            ENABLED ACTIVE   204800   RAID     -         raid5
```

```
p2 raid5vol-01    raid5vol         ENABLED  ACTIVE  204800  RAID    3/32    RW
s2 adg01-01       raid5vol-01      adg01    0       102400  0/0     c0t2d0  ENA
s2 adg02-01       raid5vol-01      adg02    0       102400  1/0     c0t3d0  ENA
s2 adg03-01       raid5vol-01      adg03    0       102400  2/0     c0t4d0  ENA
p2 layraid5vol-P01 raid5vol        ENABLED  LOG     205056  STRIPE  3/128   RW
s2 adg04-01       layraid5vol-P01 adg04 0           68352   0/0     c0t10d0 ENA
s2 adg05-01       layraid5vol-P01 adg05 0           68352   1/0     c0t11d0 ENA
s2 adg06-01       layraid5vol-P01 adg06 0           68352   2/0     c0t12d0 ENA
```

The new plex even has the same number of columns! But it's a stripe, not a parity-stripe, therefore the subdisks in the second plex are smaller (they don't need to hold the additional parity data).

With a little more work we could, of course, have built another RAID-5 volume, layered that one, too, and put it into the volume to create a pure RAID-5 to RAID-5 mirror, but we are sure that with the knowledge you just gained you are able to do it yourself if you are so inclined.

CHAPTER 7: LOGS

by Volker Herminghaus

7.1 OVERVIEW

Using Veritas Volume Manager will make your data accessible, fast, and reliable. But as we said before there is nothing that cannot be improved. Consider the case where a mirrored volume is open while a system crash occurs. Because the plexes may not have been updated at identical times (this is optimistic - it would be a great coincidence if they actually **had** been updated at the same time) they probably contain different data in at least some volume regions. This would break the definition of volume management behavior: that a volume shall behave exactly the same as a partition. While a partition will always deliver the same data for the same blocks unless you change the blocks, a mirror with non-synchronous contents may not. This could cause the file system or database to crash, resulting in system panic or database corruption.

As another example of optimization potential consider a plex in a mirrored volume that is disabled because of a trivial, transient error, such as a disk that was switched off or otherwise unreachable when the volume was started. Most of the contents of the disk are probably identical to the contents of the other plex(es), but after the disk is back online VxVM will nevertheless have to resynchronize the whole volume because it simply did not keep track of which regions is changed in the remaining active plexes.

The same problem turns up when a plex was detached from a volume on purpose, in order to create a snapshot from the volume. Such so-called point-in-time copies, or PITCs, are often used for creating consistent backups that represent a specific point in time rather than the usually unrecoverable mess that a backup made from an active file system would create. Snapshots must be resynchronised before they are reused, and it would be nice if

V. Herminghaus and A. Sriba, *Storage Management in Data Centers*,
DOI: 10.1007/978-3-540-85023-6_7, © Springer-Verlag Berlin Heidelberg 2009

we could just resynchronize those portions of the volume that have actually changed (on the snapshot or the volume) since the snapshot was broken off.

7.1.1 WHAT IS A LOG?

In order to resolve these and other problems the designers of VxVM came up with the clever idea of multi-column bitmaps that reside in separate, so-called LOG plexes. Each bit in the bitmap corresponds to a region (extent) of the volume and tracks one aspect of its state. For instance, whether it is currently undergoing write I/O or if it has undergone write I/O since a plex was disabled or detached. I.e. whether the contents of the plexes in the region are guaranteed to be synchronous or not relative to some other plex.

Logs are usually contained in a volume or they reside in a separate volume that is connected to its data volume by a pointer called a "Data Change Object", or dco. There are various logs for the diverse applications drafted above, and there is a quite modern log, the "dco version 20" that combines the most interesting features into a single data structure. We will discuss the creation of this very modern log in the "Easy Sailing" chapter. This log is easy to use and very powerful, but the vxprint output of a volume with such a log attached can be quite confusing. Apart from this, understanding the logged volume's behavior in case of special situations like crashes or mirror-splits is difficult without some serious work at the basis. Therefore, in the "The Full Battleship" we discuss the various other (older) types of logs, which for the most part are subsets of the dco 20 log, so you understand what each log is meant for and what it does. In the "Technical Deep Dive" you will be shown what exactly happens inside VxVM when the logs are used and how they are used during recovery or resynchronisation. On the basis of this, you will be able to predict recovery and resynchronisation behavior for volumes containing or not containing a log of any given type. Some more information about logs can be found in the chapter on point-in-time copies (chapter 9) on page 238.

7.1.2 SIMPLE LOG OPERATIONS

The simplest way to prepare your volume for all possible havoc is the following command, issued on an existing volume (in this case our favorite, short-named avol):

```
# vxsnap prepare avol
```

Having done that, the volume is prepared for fast recovery after a system crash as well as for fast resynchronisation after a plex becomes disabled (due to I/O failure, for example), or detached (typically for a snapshot or point-in-time copy).

The difficult thing here is understanding the output of vxprint. Look at the volume before and after the command:

```
# vxassist make avol 1g layout=mirror init=active
# vxprint -qrtg adg
[...]
v  avol       -         ENABLED  ACTIVE  2097152  SELECT  -       fsgen
pl avol-01    avol      ENABLED  ACTIVE  2097152  CONCAT  -       RW
sd adg01-01   avol-01   adg01    0       2097152  0       c0t2d0  ENA
pl avol-02    avol      ENABLED  ACTIVE  2097152  CONCAT  -       RW
sd adg02-01   avol-02   adg02    0       2097152  0       c0t3d0  ENA

# vxsnap prepare avol
# vxprint -qrtg adg
[...]
v  avol       -         ENABLED  ACTIVE  2097152  SELECT  -       fsgen
pl avol-01    avol      ENABLED  ACTIVE  2097152  CONCAT  -       RW
sd adg01-01   avol-01   adg01    0       2097152  0       c0t2d0  ENA
pl avol-02    avol      ENABLED  ACTIVE  2097152  CONCAT  -       RW
sd adg02-01   avol-02   adg02    0       2097152  0       c0t3d0  ENA
```

```
dc avol_dco      avol          avol_dcl
v  avol_dcl      -             ENABLED  ACTIVE   544      SELECT    -       gen
pl avol_dcl-01   avol_dcl      ENABLED  ACTIVE   544      CONCAT    -       RW
sd adg03-01      avol_dcl-01   adg03    0        544      0         c0t4d0  ENA
pl avol_dcl-02   avol_dcl      ENABLED  ACTIVE   544      CONCAT    -       RW
sd adg04-01      avol_dcl-02   adg04    0        544      0         c0t10d0 ENA
```

Strange, isn't it? But when you parse the output top to bottom you will find just two volumes that stick together. So let's use `vxprint -rtL` to separate them for readability.

```
# vxprint -qrtLg adg
[...]
v  avol         -             ENABLED  ACTIVE   2097152  SELECT    -       fsgen
pl avol-01      avol          ENABLED  ACTIVE   2097152  CONCAT    -       RW
sd adg01-01     avol-01       adg01    0        2097152  0         c0t2d0  ENA
pl avol-02      avol          ENABLED  ACTIVE   2097152  CONCAT    -       RW
sd adg02-01     avol-02       adg02    0        2097152  0         c0t3d0  ENA
dc avol_dco     avol          avol_dcl

v  avol_dcl     -             ENABLED  ACTIVE   544      SELECT    -       gen
pl avol_dcl-01  avol_dcl      ENABLED  ACTIVE   544      CONCAT    -       RW
sd adg03-01     avol_dcl-01   adg03    0        544      0         c0t4d0  ENA
pl avol_dcl-02  avol_dcl      ENABLED  ACTIVE   544      CONCAT    -       RW
sd adg04-01     avol_dcl-02   adg04    0        544      0         c0t10d0 ENA
```

Using this output format it becomes clear that the original volume has simply received a new type of object, the DCO (data change object called `avol_dco`), which was appended to it at the bottom. In addition, a new, redundant volume was created which is of minimal size. The small size results from the fact that only a bitmap is stored in the volume, and no data. That volume is the DCL (data change log), and the DCO is a pointer connected to the original volume that points to its associated DCL as can be verified by looking at the ASSOC column of the dc object: `avol_dco` is associated with `avol_dcl`.

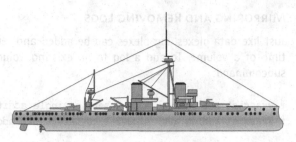

The Full Battleship

7.2 LOG MAINTENANCE

CREATING AND DISPLAYING A VOLUME WITH A LOG

All logs are created equal! At least in so far as logs of any kind are created using a variant of the same vxassist command. You can add a log specification to any layout by appending ",log" to the layout parameter. For instance, to create a mirrored volume with a DRL (or dirty region log) you would replace the common syntax:

```
# vxassist make avol 1g layout=mirror init=active
```

with:

```
# vxassist make avol 1g layout=mirror,log init=active
```

DRL is the default logtype for all volumes except RAID-5, where the only possible value is a raid5log. Displaying the new volume with vxprint will show that the volume has three plexes instead of two, which might lead to the assumption that the volume is now equipped with three mirrors. But closer examination will reveal that the third plex is actually not a data plex having the same size as the volume, but actually a plex which in place of the plex size is marked LOGONLY, and which only contains a very tiny subdisk. That subdisk holds a bitmap for initializing the dirty region map for RDWRBACK-synchronisation when a redundant volume is restarted after a system crash. Look at the output and find the log:

```
# vxprint -qrtg adg
v  avol       -          ENABLED  ACTIVE  2097152  SELECT   -        fsgen
pl avol-01    avol       ENABLED  ACTIVE  2097152  CONCAT   -        RW
sd adg01-01   avol-01    adg01    0       2097152  0        c0t2d0   ENA
pl avol-02    avol       ENABLED  ACTIVE  2097152  CONCAT   -        RW
sd adg02-01   avol-02    adg02    0       2097152  0        c0t3d0   ENA
pl avol-03    avol       ENABLED  ACTIVE  LOGONLY  CONCAT   -        RW
sd adg05-01   avol-03    adg05    0       528      LOG      c0t11d0  ENA
```

MIRRORING AND REMOVING LOGS

Just like data plexes, log plexes can be added and removed at any time during the lifetime of a volume. To add a log to an existing volume, use vxassist with the addlog subcommand:

```
# vxassist addlog avol # to insert a single additional log plex
# vxassist addlog avol nlog=2 # to insert two additional log plexes
```

This will add one or several DRL log plexes to any volume with a stripe or concat plex layout, and a raid5log to a volume with RAID-5 layout.

To remove a log plex from a volume use vxassist with the remove log subcommand, or just use the low-level command vxplex -o rm dis <plexname> (which can be used to remove any kind of plex - data or log).

```
# vxassist remove log avol # to remove a single log plex
# vxassist remove log avol nlog=2 # to remove all log plexes except two(!)
```

The latter command is somewhat confusing. When adding logs, nlog=… specifies the number of logs to add, but when removing logs, nlog=… does not specify the number of logs to remove, but the number of logs to leave attached to the volume. This is the same behavior as with adding and removing mirrors (which is actually obvious, since both are just plexes, albeit of different types).

USING OTHER THAN THE DEFAULT LOG TYPES

You may not want to use the default log type. The default is raid5log for RAID-5 volumes, DRL for all others. But those give you just logs that speed up recovery of a volume that crashed while active. To enable speedy resynchronisation of a volume with plexes that have been temporarily detached of disabled, e.g. because of loss of connectivity to a disk or storage array, or because a point-in-time copy was created and chopped off the volume, a different kind of log is required: a DCL (data change log). While a DCL is not just another plex in the volumes but actually a separate volume connected to the data volume by a special object called a DCO (data change object), it is still created by the same vxassist command syntax, just with an additional flag to specify the logtype. (BTW: The reason for the DCL residing in another volume has to do with more freedom in storage allocation for the log. There is no other magic reason about it.)

```
# vxassist make avol 1g layout=mirror,log logtype=dco # create volume with DCL
        # you can use "init=active" if you want, but we omitted it
        # (and may continue to do so) simply because of page space constraints.
```

ADDING AND REMOVING DCL PLEXES TO/FROM EXISTING VOLUMES

Adding and removing DCL/DCO logs to or from a volume is just as simple as adding and removing DRLs. But obviously we must specify the non-default log type of dco as the logtype using the logtype=dco parameter just as we do when creating a volume with a non-standard log. After all, how is VxVM supposed to know what kind of log we have in mind while we are typing the command? The following examples add and remove DCLs to and from a volume:

```
# vxassist addlog avol logtype=dco [nlog=X] # add X DCL(s) to a volume
# vxassist remove log avol logtype=dco [nlog=X] # remove all but X DCLs
# vxplex -o rm dis <plexname(s)> # removes the given plex(es) from DCL
```

The last command, the one that disassociated a plex (vxplex dis) and then removes it using the option rm (-o rm) is the most universal of all plex removal commands. It can remove any kind of plex: log, data, dco, sparse plex etc. in any state: enabled, disabled, iofail, recover etc. It is highly recommended to get used to the syntax for this command because it is so much more universal than the specific vxassist commands.

Technical Deep Dive

7.3 DETAILS ABOUT LOGS

7.3.1 DRL (DIRTY REGION LOG)

PURPOSE OF DRL

DRL logging serves exactly one purpose: to shorten the resynchronisation process of a mirrored volume that was open when VxVM's control over the volume was forcefully removed (e.g. by a system crash or by loss of access to the disk group due to I/O or path error). VxVM keeps a flag in the private region that tracks if the volume has received a write since it was opened. If that flag is set when a volume is started, then the implementation of VxVM (rightfully) demands the volume must be synchronised before use. This synchronisation is done via a RDWRBACK task as discussed in chapter 5, page 136.

Let's reiterate the process of RDWRBACK synchronisation shortly in draft form:

It begins with VxVM setting the access mode of the volume to RDWRBACK. The volume then becomes immediately accessible for reading as well as writing. In RDWRBACK access mode a write to a volume is done identically to the normal access mode. A read, however, is read from any of the volume's plexes according to its read policy (not read mode). The result of the read is not passed to the user right away, but instead it is first persisted (i.e. synchronously written) to all other plexes at the same offset. This makes sure the user will never get different data for the same block, thereby preserving the partition semantics.

When the volume is set to RDWRBACK access mode VxVM also allocates a bitmap representing the CLEAN/DIRTY state of every region of the volume (the region size that each bit represents may vary, but is roughly in the megabyte range). This bit is called the dirty region map (this is **not** the dirty region log!). Because it is unknown which regions actually are out of sync VxVM must assume the worst case, i.e. the case where every region is dirty, and will accordingly initialise all bits of the dirty region map to DIRTY.

When a region has been written to in the volume, the corresponding bit in the dirty region map is set to CLEAN because after the write the region is known to be in sync with the other plexes. Likewise, if a region has been read while in RDWRBACK mode it is known that the region must now be in sync, and therefore the region's bit is set to CLEAN.

As long as the volume is in RDWRBACK access mode the bitmap must be checked for every read or write operation, because it must be established if the I/O target region must be synchronised during the read and the bit reset, or if the write I/O must be followed by clearing the region's bit in the dirty region map.

Checking the bitmap for every I/O takes CPU time and induces latency, so it is desirable to eventually get rid of the dirty region map altogether. In order to do so, the volume must first be fully synchronised. For this purpose VxVM spawns a kernel thread for every volume undergoing RDWRBACK synchronisation. This thread simply reads all the dirty regions of the volume and throws the results away. The (desired) side effect of doing so is that because the volume is in RDWRBACK access mode, its contents will be completely synchronised after the thread has finished. Therefore, the last thing the thread does is set the access mode to normal before it finishes.

This thread is what you see in the output of vxtask list.

The whole idea of a dirty region log is to be able to initialise not all the regions of the dirty region map with DIRTY flag bits, but just those that might actually **be** dirty. In that case, the kernel thread will be finished in a very short time because it will only synchronize a few hundred regions, which takes only a few seconds. This way, most of the time the resynchronisation will be completed upon boot even before the application actually starts using the volume, yielding in no performance impact whatsoever.

IMPLEMENTATION OF DRL

DRL is implemented as a persistent bitmap (i.e. one that resides on disk), either in its own LOGONLY plex inside the volume, or as an additional column in a multi-column bitmap in a version 20 DRL. The theory for DRL access goes like this: Whenever a volume containing a DRL is written, then first of all the bit of the DRL that corresponds to the region must be set so that in case of a crash, the volume "remembers" that this region may be out of sync. This DRL write I/O must of course be synchronous, as we cannot allow the user data of one plex to reach the disk before the DRL I/O. This would leave a "write hole", where the plex is already out of sync, but the DRL does not yet reflect this. If the system crashed at that time, the partition semantics would be broken which is of course unacceptable.

In any case, only after the corresponding bit in the DRL (all plexes of it) is set, the write I/O is unblocked and allowed to continue. After completion of the write on all plexes, the bit can be reset to clean because the region is now once again synchronous.

If you looked at the DRL as a big panel full of lights - one light for each bit - the DRL would literally look like one of those "blinkenlights" panels from very old science fiction movies. The bits are constantly changing, but relatively few are on at any one time.

As is usual with a product such as VxVM there are a few things that are implemented differently from what the average programmer would do. One of these is the fact that there are actually two bitmaps in the DRL: one that is used during user I/O (the one discussed above). This is called the "active bitmap". And one that is used during recovery, which is called the "recovery bitmap". The latter contains only CLEAN bits during normal operation. When a recovery situation is encountered, VxVM combines the bits from the active bitmap with the bits in the recovery bitmap using the binary OR operation, i.e. it adds the bits from the active bitmap to the recovery bitmap. After that, the active bitmap is reset to CLEAN and recovery is started. In the unlikely event of another crash during the short period of recovery no information is lost, and no extra synchronisation overhead is encountered! VxVM will simply OR the new DIRTY bits into the recovery map and continue the (very short) synchronisation process.

PERFORMANCE IMPLICATIONS OF DRL

While common sense tells us that the write performance of a volume must suffer tremendously when a DRL is present, it is in fact not so. How can that be? The secret to this is the following:

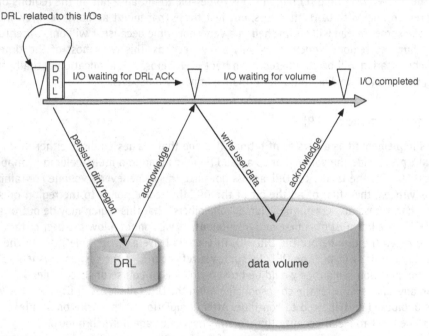

Figure 7-1:   A DRL introduces significant latency into volume I/O only on single, individual writes. A write I/O must first wait until its related I/O to the DRL has completed before it can start writing to the volume. In that case, performance is normally not an issue.

While a single I/O must indeed first be prepared by persisting the corresponding DIRTY bit into the DRL, this overhead diminishes, even virtually disappears, when a long queue of I/O requests is processed. In that case, the first I/Os are analyzed and the corresponding bits in the DRL identified and set. The DRL is persisted and, while VxVM waits for completion of the DLR I/O, the next I/Os are already analyzed, their bits set in the DRL and the DRL I/O is sent to the HBA. As soon as the first DRL write completes the I/Os corresponding to that instance of the DRL are unblocked and sent to the HBA, too. While that user data is written, more write I/Os are accumulated in the queue, inspected, and the corresponding DRL bits are set. By the time the first user data I/Os come back completed, the second DRL write is returned from the controller so the second batch of user data I/Os unblocks. Also, the third DRL is sent to the controller, unblocking more user data I/Os.

In effect, DRL write I/Os are simply inserted into the (usually long) I/O queue so that in general no process has to wait for DRL write completion unless the machine does only single, sparse write I/Os, in which case the performance is not usually limited by I/O anyway. Trying to make a graphical representation of this complicated matter has proven to be challenging. The picture we came up with does not look simple at all. But it is actually not much more than multiple instances of the former picture interleaved into one, as you will see upon closer inspection.

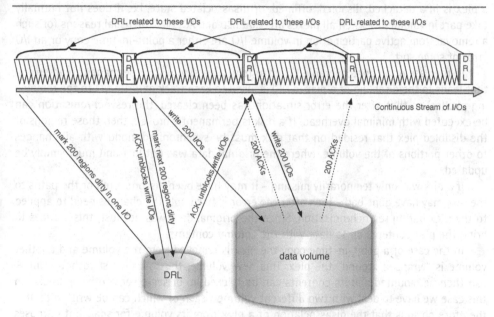

Figure 7-2:   When write I/Os are hammering on the LUNs DRLs are interspersed into the I/O queue. As soon as a DRL write (to all DRL plexes, of course) has been acknowledges from the storage the corresponding user data write I/Os are unblocked and can proceed. As those user data acknowledgements are collected from the HBA driver, the corresponding bits in the DRL become eligible to be reset. For performance reason, they are not reset immediately. Instead the number of "dirty" bits in the DRL is throttled at 200.

One can estimate that DRL adds roughly about 5% of I/Os to the write I/O stream. This has to do with the fact that VxVM throttles the amount of DIRTY bits in a DRL to a maximum of 200. I.e. VxVM does not reset DIRTY bits right away as soon as they are eligible for it, but waits until the threshold of 200 DIRTY bits is reached, then cleans the ones whose I/Os have been returned as "completed" by the disk controllers on all plexes.

In other words, DRL operation inserts small write I/Os into the I/O stream each of which may unblock dozens to hundreds of user data write I/Os and introduce only minimal extra latency except for the pathological, but normally uncritical, case of an almost empty write I/O stream.

7.3.2   DCL/DCO (Data Change Log / Data Change Object)

Purpose of DCL

A DCL is meant for keeping track of changes that occur to a volume during the time that a plex is in a detached, disabled, offlined, or disassociated state, i.e. it does not normally take part in volume I/O when all plexes are ENABLED and ACTIVE. The usual reasons for such a removal from active participation in volume I/O are either a point-in-time copy or an I/O error of some sort.

In the case of an unrecoverable I/O error (e.g. a missing disk or permanent read errors) that leads to the disabling of a plex, a DCL is used to keep track of write I/O to the remaining plex(es) so that after the error situation has been cleared, the resynchronisation can be executed with minimal overhead. If a disk is permanently broken, then those regions of the disabled plex that resided on that disk must be synchronised along with all changes to other portions of the volume, where the original data was not lost and must simply be updated.

If a disk was only temporarily missing - it may have been disconnected or the paths to the disk may have gone bad - then after the error is fixed only the changes need to applied to the plex during resynchronisation. Since the original data was not lost, this suffices to bring the plex contents up to date with the volume contents.

In the case of a point-in-time copy the plex is removed from the volume and another volume is "wrapped around" the plex. This new volume, the so-called snapshot-volume, can then be mounted and its contents can be backed up or serve some other purpose. In this case we have to deal with two different volumes, each of which can be written to. It is therefore obvious that the disassociation of a plex from its volume for snapshot purposes requires a DCL plex to be disassociated along with the data plex. If this is satisfied, then VxVM will keep track of changes not only in the original volume but also in the snapshot volume. Remember the snapshot volume can be used read-write.

Resynchronisation speed of snapshots is important because such point-in-time copies are often reused at regular intervals, typically for daily backups, and so their contents must be resynchronised frequently. Resynchronizing just the differences to the previous contents usually saves a great deal of time and I/Os. As a rule of thumb, it is unusual for a database to change more than five percent of its contents er day. Accordingly, resynchronisation would take twenty times longer without DRL than it would with DCL.

Because the creation of the correct amount, type and location of DCLs for all the purposes listed above and the correct modifications to the VxVM objects when snapshotting a volume are not trivial there is a new command that will create DCLs for you in such a way that they automatically do the The Right Thing™. And because the most complicated case is the case of the snapshot volume, the command is called vxsnap. Here's what you do to create a DCL that just works:

```
# vxsnap -g <DG> prepare <Volume>
```

(We are actually cheating a little here, but for you benefit. The command we just used, vxsnap prepare, will not create a pure DCL, but a DCL with a DRL included in a so-called multi-column bitmap. For the sake of the argument, we'll just pretend for the rest of the chapter that vxsnap prepare simply added a standard DCL. Creating standard DCL logs is done via vxassist addlog logtype=dco, but there is a lot of extra stuff you would have to think about in order to make it work right with snapshots, so let's just stick with the syntax we just used.)

We looked at the objects created by this command in the Easy Sailing section before, but let's parse it more thoroughly this time. We'll start with a new, mirrored volume avol, and we'll use the -L flag in addition to the normal flags to vxprint in order to separate the volumes so they are easier to read.

```
# vxassist -g adg make avol 1g nmirror=3 init=active
# vxprint -qrtLg adg
[...]
v  avol          -            ENABLED  ACTIVE  2097152  SELECT   -       fsgen
pl avol-01       avol         ENABLED  ACTIVE  2097152  CONCAT   -       RW
sd adg01-01      avol-01      adg01    0       2097152  0        c0t2d0  ENA
pl avol-02       avol         ENABLED  ACTIVE  2097152  CONCAT   -       RW
sd adg02-01      avol-02      adg02    0       2097152  0        c0t3d0  ENA
pl avol-03       avol         ENABLED  ACTIVE  2097152  CONCAT   -       RW
sd adg03-01      avol-03      adg03    0       2097152  0        c0t4d0  ENA

# vxsnap prepare avol
# vxprint -qrtLg adg
v  avol          -            ENABLED  ACTIVE  2097152  SELECT   -       fsgen
pl avol-01       avol         ENABLED  ACTIVE  2097152  CONCAT   -       RW
sd adg01-01      avol-01      adg01    0       2097152  0        c0t2d0  ENA
pl avol-02       avol         ENABLED  ACTIVE  2097152  CONCAT   -       RW
sd adg02-01      avol-02      adg02    0       2097152  0        c0t3d0  ENA
pl avol-03       avol         ENABLED  ACTIVE  2097152  CONCAT   -       RW
sd adg03-01      avol-03      adg03    0       2097152  0        c0t4d0  ENA
dc avol_dco      avol                  avol_dcl

v  avol_dcl      -            ENABLED  ACTIVE  544      SELECT   -       gen
pl avol_dcl-01   avol_dcl     ENABLED  ACTIVE  544      CONCAT   -       RW
sd adg04-01      avol_dcl-01  adg04    0       544      0        c0t10d0 ENA
pl avol_dcl-02   avol_dcl     ENABLED  ACTIVE  544      CONCAT   -       RW
sd adg05-01      avol_dcl-02  adg05    0       544      0        c0t11d0 ENA
```

As you can see, an additional volume was created, with as many plexes as the original volume. This new volume is the DCL volume, which is obvious from its size (very small, just big enough for a bitmap), and its name, avol_dcl. But another object has been created as well: if you look at the end of the original volume, there is now a new, as of yet unknown object called avol_dco. Its type (first column) is given as dc, and the name stands for "avol's data change object". This object points to the DCL and thus connects the two volumes.

To jump ahead to the chapter about snapshots, let's look at what happens when we actually add another plex in preparation for a snapshot action:

```
# vxsnap addmir avol
# vxprint -qrtLg adg
[...]
v  avol         -          ENABLED  ACTIVE    2097152 SELECT   -        fsgen
pl avol-01      avol       ENABLED  ACTIVE    2097152 CONCAT   -        RW
sd adg01-01     avol-01    adg01    0         2097152 0        c0t2d0   ENA
pl avol-02      avol       ENABLED  ACTIVE    2097152 CONCAT   -        RW
sd adg02-01     avol-02    adg02    0         2097152 0        c0t3d0   ENA
pl avol-03      avol       ENABLED  ACTIVE    2097152 CONCAT   -        RW
sd adg03-01     avol-03    adg03    0         2097152 0        c0t4d0   ENA
pl avol-04      avol       ENABLED  SNAPDONE  2097152 CONCAT   -        WO
sd adg06-01     avol-04    adg06    0         2097152 0        c0t12d0  ENA
dc avol_dco     avol       avol_dcl

v  avol_dcl     -          ENABLED  ACTIVE    544     SELECT   -        gen
pl avol_dcl-01  avol_dcl   ENABLED  ACTIVE    544     CONCAT   -        RW
sd adg04-01     avol_dcl-01 adg04   0         544     0        c0t10d0  ENA
pl avol_dcl-02  avol_dcl   ENABLED  ACTIVE    544     CONCAT   -        RW
sd adg05-01     avol_dcl-02 adg05   0         544     0        c0t11d0  ENA
pl avol_dcl-03  avol_dcl   DISABLED DCOSNP    544     CONCAT   -        RW
sd adg06-02     avol_dcl-03 adg06   2097152   544     0        c0t12d0  ENA
```

Another plex has been added to avol, and another plex has been added to avol_dcl as well. This plex is disabled because it currently has no meaning. The extra data plex is not used for reading anyway. To understand why this is the case, check out its state in the right most column: WO means Write-Only. This plex will only become RW (Read-Write) when it is put into its own, snapshot volume. As long as it is just a part of a data volume, ut not an actual mirror, it is kept in WO state. That means there is no way VxVM would write to just the snapshot plex but not the mirror, and so the DCL need not be active. Sounds difficult? Well, it is, but you can trust us on this.

Now let's look at what happens when a snapshot is actually created using a command with a very arcane-looking syntax (this syntax is actually necessary in order to create snap-shots of multiple volumes at exactly the same point in time, but it sure does look ugly):

```
# vxsnap make source=avol/new=SNAP-avol/plex=avol-04
# vxprint -qrtLg adg
v  SNAP-avol      -           ENABLED  ACTIVE  2097152 ROUND    -        fsgen
pl avol-04        SNAP-avol   ENABLED  ACTIVE  2097152 CONCAT   -        RW
sd adg06-01       avol-04     adg06    0       2097152 0        c0t12d0  ENA
dc SNAP-avol_dco  SNAP-avol   SNAP-avol_dcl

v  SNAP-avol_dcl  -           ENABLED  ACTIVE  544     ROUND    -        gen
pl avol_dcl-03    SNAP-avol_dcl ENABLED ACTIVE 544     CONCAT   -        RW
sd adg06-02       avol_dcl-03 adg06    2097152 544     0        c0t12d0  ENA
sp avol_snp       SNAP-avol   SNAP-avol_dco
```

```
v  avol          -            ENABLED  ACTIVE  2097152  SELECT   -        fsgen
pl avol-01       avol         ENABLED  ACTIVE  2097152  CONCAT   -        RW
sd adg01-01      avol-01      adg01    0       2097152  0        c0t2d0   ENA
pl avol-02       avol         ENABLED  ACTIVE  2097152  CONCAT   -        RW
sd adg02-01      avol-02      adg02    0       2097152  0        c0t3d0   ENA
pl avol-03       avol         ENABLED  ACTIVE  2097152  CONCAT   -        RW
sd adg03-01      avol-03      adg03    0       2097152  0        c0t4d0   ENA
dc avol_dco      avol         avol_dcl

v  avol_dcl      -            ENABLED  ACTIVE  544      SELECT   -        gen
pl avol_dcl-01   avol_dcl     ENABLED  ACTIVE  544      CONCAT   -        RW
sd adg04-01      avol_dcl-01  adg04    0       544      0        c0t10d0  ENA
pl avol_dcl-02   avol_dcl     ENABLED  ACTIVE  544      CONCAT   -        RW
sd adg05-01      avol_dcl-02  adg05    0       544      0        c0t11d0  ENA
sp SNAP-avol_snp avol         avol_dco
```

The extra DCL plex that had been created by the vxsnap addmir command has moved - along with the extra plex created by the same command - into the new volume with the name SNAP-avol. There it serves the purpose of keeping track of changes that VxVM does to the snapshot volume. It does so on any machine - you can use this snapshot on a different host. Check the chapter about snapshots to learn more about how this is done.

In addition to the movement of the data plex and DCL plex into the newly created SNAP-avol volume VxVM also created an "sp" object for each of the two volumes concerned, and appended that object to the volumes. An sp object is a "snapshot pointer". It connects the snapshot children to their snapshot parents, so that VxVM can find the way home to the original volume when you want to resynchronize a snapshot with its parent.

IMPLEMENTATION OF DCL

The DCL has been implemented as a bitmap with user-definable region-size, i.e. the size of the volume region each bit stands for can be adjusted according to the expected behavior of the application that uses the volume. If you used a very large region size, then you would create only few I/Os to the DCL but on the other hand, the log would fill up rather quickly with DIRTY flags if a lot of random writes occur. This would not make resynchronisation very much faster. If you used a very small region size, then most write I/Os would also create a write to the DCL if it is active (i.e. a plex has been deactivated from participating in the volume traffic). This would have an adverse affect on write performance, while on the other hand optimize resynchronisation to its maximum.

You can find much more detailed information about DCL/DCO in the chapter about point-in-time copies beginning on page 233.

PERFORMANCE IMPLICATIONS OF DCL

After the previous paragraphs it should be obvious that there are no performance implications for a volume that has a DCL attached during normal operation. Only if a plex has been split off from the volume or somehow disabled or stopped will a DCL be written to. In these cases the minimal extra I/O incurred by writing the DCL's bitmap is more than made up for by the I/O saved during the following resynchronisation cycle. One should therefore not hesitate to add DCLs to mirrored volumes unless one is afraid of the extra complexity in parsing vxprint output, or in the case that single plex deactivation is extremely unlikely or the volumes are so small that resynchronisation is not an issue (as a rule of thumb, resynchronisation speed, because it is throttled by VxVM, is usually around one or a few GB per minute, and the amount of throttling can only be increased, not reduced, by the user).

7.3.3   RAID5LOG

PURPOSE OF A RAID5LOG

Although we like to remind you that doing RAID-5 in software is not generally a good idea, for the sake of completion we will take a short look at the log for this type of volume. Why is a log for RAID-5 volumes necessary? In order to find out why a RAID-5 log is absolutely critical to have (and therefore created by default when you make a RAID-5 volume using the vxassist command) as well as what it should contain it is sufficient to look at a simple worst-case scenario: When a disk failure during a full-stripe write to a RAID-5 volume leads to a system panic!

When that happens, and the system comes back up and starts VxVM, then VxVM finds that one of the RAID-5 volume's columns is missing due to the faulted disks. It will allow user I/O on the volume, because the volume's RAID-5 plex has built-in redundancy.

But that is not enough!

Because there is a possibility that a write had been interrupted by the crash the parity data is not really reliable. Why is that? Consider a RAID-5 stripe consisting of 5 columns (including parity). A write is done that covers the whole stripe, but only columns zero and one are actually written, while a funky response from the failing disk for column two causes the system to crash and thus columns two and three as well as the parity column are not written because the system crashes before it can commit the writes. The volume is now in an unreliable state, because when data is read from the failed column VxVM must reconstruct the data by – remember? – reading all the remaining columns plus the parity column, and then XORing the data to extract what was originally stored on the failed column.

Unfortunately the reconstruction is done using mixed old and new data: some columns have already been updated, some have not, and the parity data does not correspond to this mixed state: the old parity data is valid only in combination with the old data; the new parity data is valid only in combination with the new data, but neither is valid with a mixture of old and new data! The whole calculation yields nonsensical data as a result. This nonsense will likely cause the operating system to panic, which is of course not desirable but you deserve it if you use software RAID-5 (we told you so ;=).

In addition to the very undesirable behavior of possibly causing an operating system panic, VxVM must also recalculate all the parity data once the failed disk has been replaced, because old and new data could have been mixed at any place; there is no record of it.

So to protect you from this unattractive scenario (if you still want to use RAID-5, that is), use the default VxVM behavior and let VxVM create a raid5log for you when you make a RAID-5 volume.

IMPLEMENTATION OF RAID5LOG?

A raid5log must reside on a disk that is not part of the RAID-5 plex (otherwise the problem would still be there if **that** disk were to fail). It is organized as a circular buffer that contains enough space for several full stripe writes (five of them the last time we looked). It works much like a file system intent log: Any write to the volume is done by first writing the data to the raid5log. Behind the data some information is written that marks the data as valid (because we do not want to replay interrupted transactions onto the volume). After the write to the raid5log has been completed, the written data is considered safe and will (eventually) be persisted to the actual RAID-5 volume. There is no big hurry to do so unless there are many writes hitting the volume and the log would overflow.

If the system crashes (with or without a disk fault), then VxVM will replay the raid5log data to the volume upon volume start. The raid5log contains enough data to identify which data goes where, which data is valid, and the order in which the individual writes must be replayed. So using a raid5log we end up with two advantages:

1) there is no need to recalculate all of the parity information

2) the volume will actually work – because it contains valid data – and not cause the operating system to panic over and over again.

CHAPTER 8: DUAL DATA CENTERS

by Volker Herminghaus

Since the attacks of September 11, 2001, many companies have started to move their data to two or more data centers located a few kilometers away from each other to account for possible threats by terrorists, warfare, natural disaster etc. General awareness has risen to the fact that a whole data center could fail. Surveys taken toward the end of the last century and valid until today have shown that more than 90% of all companies that suffered a total data loss did not survive the following years. They could neither reach, inform, nor bill their customers, who then walked away to the competition. The risk of not surviving a major blow to the informational infrastructure has shown to be so high as to warrant the expense of running a second, redundant data center just for availability purposes.

This chapter does not contain any Easy Sailing part. That it because dual data center setups simply are **not** easy.

8.1 VOLUME MANAGEMENT IN DUAL DATA CENTERS

It is obvious that in order to ensure operability in case of a disaster all data must be copied to the remote data center and be as up-to-data as possible. There are three basic ways to do this:

1) **Offline snapshotting** - copy a mirror to the remote site at regular intervals, e.g. every night

2) **Online replication** - use one of several host or array-based replication techniques

3) **Online mirroring** - use standard mirroring across geographically close data centers

While the first one, **offline snapshotting** is viable, it takes a great deal of coordina-

V. Herminghaus and A. Sriba, *Storage Management in Data Centers*,
DOI: 10.1007/978-3-540-85023-6_8, © Springer-Verlag Berlin Heidelberg 2009

tion of the hundreds, maybe thousands of different volumes that many companies use. For instance, you would have to create snapshots or other point-in-time copies of the data every night. This could be done either by VxVM-based snapshot volumes which are then split into new disk groups and taken over by the remote host to import in case of a disaster. These snapshots would have to reside in the remote site (we will call that the disaster recovery site, or DR site, from now on). Alternatively, the storage arrays could replicate point-in-time copies of their LUNs to the remote site. If bandwidth between main site and DR site is limited and the complexity of the data center is not too high, offline snapshotting is a possibility which is relatively cheap in terms of hardware. But obviously, the data at the remote site my be somewhat stale so you will need extensive roll-forward mechanisms in place to bring the data up to date in case of a actual failure or switch. If you plan this setup properly, then you get a cheap and quick backup solution for free: the most recent snapshot constitutes a backup which can be used to restore the most recent saved state of a volume or application without resorting to slow tape backups.

Online replication is relatively widely used. Unfortunately many data centers use a storage array-based approach, which is almost guaranteed to either fail or be incredibly slow if the distance between the sites exceeds a few kilometers. The latter is true no matter what the array vendors will say! There are physical constants (like the speed of light, for instance - you may have heard of that one ;-), that preclude efficient replication of database traffic to a remote site unless the operating system handles at least part of the replication. Therefore, all purely storage array-based replication methods can do either of two things: They will be **either correct or fast**, but never both at the same time, unless they employ a device driver for the operating system (which they usually do not). Read more about online replication and its limits as well as how to do it right (in software) in the section beginning on page 213.

Online mirroring is a very good way to keep your data safe in case of a disaster. But it only works with sufficient performance across relatively short distances. While a setup over 3 or 5 kilometers is well feasible, latency starts to kick in pretty badly when 10 kilometers or more are reached. This can slow down your volume performance significantly. And again, there is not much that you can do about it: it's all physics and it's natural constants, especially the speed of light. It may be surprising, but you can trust us: light speed is much too slow for efficient computing over great distances! We will go into more detail later, in the discussion of protocols and wire speed beginning on page 213.

8.1.1   GROWING A MIRRORED VOLUME ACROSS SITES

With data centers that are online mirrored across sites there begun to appear a deficiency of VxVM. Volume sizes are usually not static, and volumes are frequently resized to make room for the ever-growing databases. When **growing volumes across sites** or even just across enclosures at a single site, an important distinction between man and machine becomes obvious: Computers do not think along with their human operators. They just do whatever the operator tells them.

While any human in his right mind would not spend a second thinking about crossing mirror sides in the middle of a volume, there is no reason why a computer might not choose to do this. Unless, of course, the operator tells it to do it right, namely extend the mirror on site A with space from site A, and extend the mirror at site B using space allocated from site B.

But what if there is no way of telling the computer, or rather VxVM, what we want? This is exactly the reason for many misconfigured volumes and some outages: There used to be no way of telling VxVM to allocate storage in an enclosure-specific way **when resizing**. There were all kinds of ways of specifying allocation, even very fine-grained allocation, when **creating** a volume, but not when **growing** one. We will look at the current state of the VxVM art (as of 5.0MP1 Solaris) and find some workarounds for existing volumes on older VxVMs as well as show you how it is done correctly in later versions of VxVM..

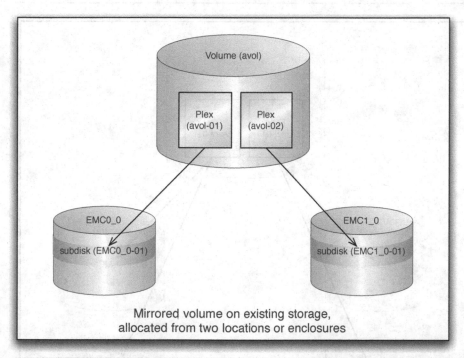

Mirrored volume on existing storage,
allocated from two locations or enclosures

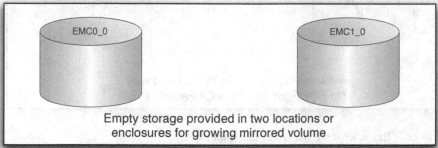

Empty storage provided in two locations or
enclosures for growing mirrored volume

Figure 8-1:   Growing a volume that is mirrored across two enclosures (or data
                centers) can be tricky, as you will see in the next pictures.

THE PROBLEM OF CROSS-SITE PLEXES

If you are using VxVM across data centers you may already have experienced one of the main issues concerning storage for dual data center setups, which is this: If you are using online mirroring, and you want to grow a mirrored volume, then unfortunately there is a good chance that the plexes of the volume will be grown using storage from the wrong, i.e. the "other", remote data center. A plex which begins in data center A will be extended by storage from data center B and vice versa. If any of the data centers fails, then because each plex has subdisks in each data center, both plexes will be disabled and thus the volume will be inaccessible. This is **not** high availability computing!

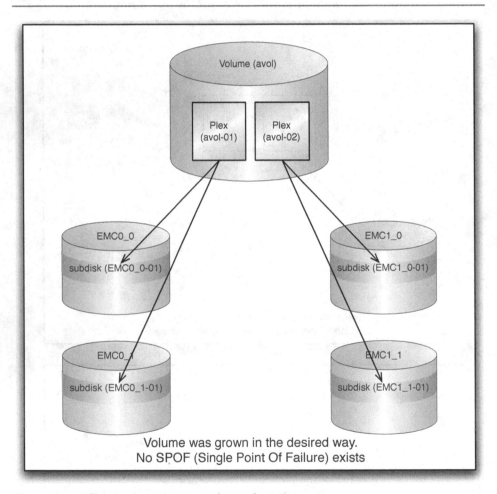

Figure 8-2:   This is what we want, and sometimes get.

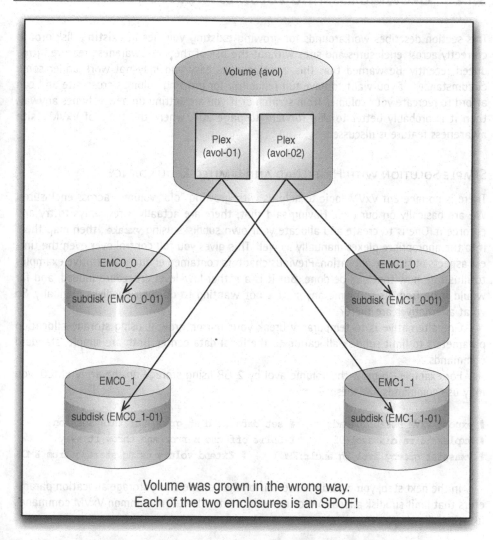

Volume was grown in the wrong way.
Each of the two enclosures is an SPOF!

Figure 8-3: But often we end up with this result, which is highly undesirable! Failure of one of the sites (or enclosures) will cause both plexes to be disabled and render the volume inaccessible.

So how do we grow a volume which is allocated across data centers (or across two enclosures)? The answer is that it is not easy if the volumes already exist, but VxVM does have support for creating new volumes which respect locality and will always deliver the correct result. We will first cover the case of existing volumes. Later in this chapter, on page 204, we will explain how to create new volumes that respect locality.

8.1.2 GROWING EXISTING VOLUMES ACROSS SITES

This section describes workarounds for growing **existing** volumes in **existing** disk groups correctly across enclosures and sites without the use of the site-awareness feature introduced recently. Be warned that this is not always easy and may not work under some circumstances. If you want to have full reliability for growing volumes cross-site and can afford to recreate your volumes from scratch or if you are setting up new volumes anyway, then it is probably better to skip forward to page 204, where the topic of VxVM's **site awareness** feature is discussed.

SIMPLE SOLUTION WITH HIGH LOAD AND LIMITED REDUNDANCY

There is no inherent VxVM logic to help us with growing "old" volumes across enclosures. We are basically on our own. Having said that, there are actually a few ways to try and enforce it. One is to create and allocate your own subdisks using vxmake., then map them into the appropriate plexes manually as well. This gives you full control over even the tiniest aspects of storage allocation. Previous chapters contained enough descriptive examples to illustrate how that can be done. But it is a rather low-level procedure indeed, and far would it be from us to blame anyone for not wanting to do their subdisks manually. So what alternatives are there?

One alternative is to temporarily break your mirror, grow it using storage allocation parameters to limit subdisk allocation to the local data center. Both are simple, standard commands.

For example, to grow the volume avol by 2 GB using storage on the array EMC0, you may use commands like these:

```
# export VXVM_DEFAULTDG=adg      # set default disk group for this session
# vxplex -o rm dis avol-02       # Split off the mirror and throw it away
# vxassist growby avol 2g enclr:EMC0     # Extend volume using storage from EMC0
```

In the next step, you would then re-mirror the volume using storage allocation parameters that limit subdisk allocation to the remote site, also using common VxVM commands like the following:

```
# vxassist mirror avol enclr:EMC1      # mirror volume to EMC1 storage
```

But that leaves your volume unmirrored for a while, and it introduces a large quantity of extraneous I/O. Mostly due to the heavy I/O caused by re-mirroring, and due to the lack of redundancy during the process it is not a generally accepted solution.

MORE COMPLICATION SOLUTION, LOW LOAD, FULL REDUNDANCY

A very viable way of making sure the volume remains mirrored across enclosures when growing it is tricking VxVM's storage allocation into doing the correct thing. In order to do that we first have to know what VxVM's basic procedure for allocating storage is.

How VxVM Allocates Storage

1) In the first step VxVM limits the number of disks to match whatever storage allocation you passed on the `vxassist` command line. For instance, if you specified `ctlr:c3,c5` then it will limit itself to use only targets that can be reached over controllers 3 or 5. If you specified `enclr:HDS9500_0` it will only use LUNs from that enclosure etc.

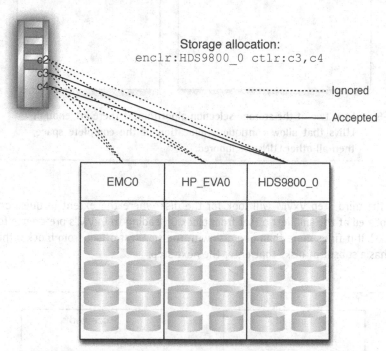

Storage allocation:
`enclr:HDS9800_0 ctlr:c3,c4`

.... Ignored

———————————— Accepted

Figure 8-4: Step one of the storage selection algorithm employed by VxVM: Only LUNs or disks that match all criteria given in the storage allocation are accepted, the rest is ignored. In this case, all those disks which are visible via controllers c3 or c4 on enclosure HDS9800_0 are accepted, while the rest is ignored.

2) In the second step VxVM searches for disks that allow the required extent to be allocated in one piece rather than concatenated. If it finds any, then it limits further searches to that subset of the disks. If it does not find any, then it just uses concatenation of smaller subdisks, but we have not further investigated into VxVM's behavior for that case.

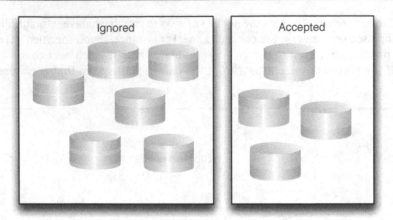

Figure 8-5:   Step two of the storage selection algorithm: If there are enough LUNs that allow contiguous allocation of the complete space, then all other LUNs are ignored.

3) In the third step VxVM will look for the disk where the extent in question can be allocated at the smallest offset from block 0 (leading to VxVM's preference for empty disks). If it finds more than one disk with the smallest offset from block 0 then again it has a subset of disks that enter the next step.

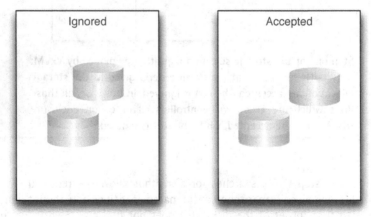

Figure 8-6:   Step three of the storage selection algorithm: LUNs that have enough contiguous free space at the lowest block offset from block zero are preferred (empty disks are typically preferred as a result). The other LUNs, which are ignored here, would be accepted if more space was needed. In the given case, the two LUNs to the right suffice so the other ones are ignored.

4) In the last step VxVM allocates "top to bottom" from the remaining subset of disks by sorting the accessnames of the disks (correctly distinguishing between alphabetical and numerical parts of the accessname) in ascending order and preferring the resulting disks in that order.

5) When a volume is extended, VxVM allocates storage plex by plex. It sorts the plex names in alphanumerically ascending order and begins with the first plex of the result, i.e. typically the plex that has a name like <volname-01>, then proceeds with <volname-02> and so on.

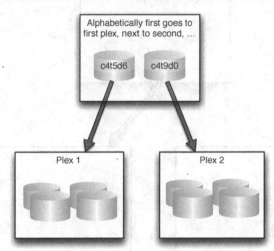

Figure 8-7:   Steps four and five of the storage selection algorithm: The LUNs are ordered alphanumerically and assigned to the plexes in ascending order.

Tricking VxVM's Allocation Strategy

If we find that VxVM uses disks on the wrong enclosure for the plexes then all we need to do is put a volume on the disks that it allocates first (in the current implementation the ones for the first plex). This volume needs to be large enough that the offset of the free extent to be used for extending the plex is at least one block larger than the offset on the disks intended for the other plex.

For example, if you are using two new, empty LUNs to extend a mirrored concat volume across enclosures, then because the free extents start at block 0 on both LUNs it would be sufficient to create a volume of length 1 block (only 512 bytes!) on the LUN that you want VxVM to allocate to the second data plex. Because VxVM will prefer the LUN that has the offset of 0 blocks it will allocate this LUN to the first plex, then use whatever is left for the second plex (which will happen to be our second disk; the one with the micro-volume on it). After successful extension you can then throw the micro-volume away.

In the more complicated case of adding, say, ten LUNs to either plex (total twenty) you can force creation of little subdisks by creating a 10-column stripe of minimal size on the disks that you want to allocate to the second plex, and nothing on the disks that you want to allocate to the first plex. This will make VxVM prefer the empty disks for the first plex and defer usage of the other disks (the ones with the tiny striped volume on them) until space for the second plex is allocated.

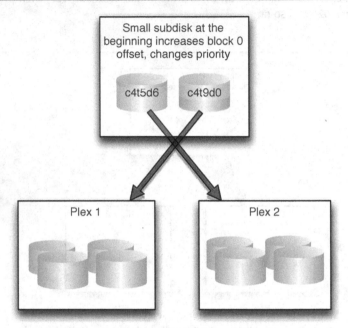

Figure 8-8:   Tricking VxVM's allocation strategy into doing the desired thing can be done by adding a tiny volume to the LUN that would be allocated to the first plex. This makes VxVM defer allocation from the LUN; the other one is used first, effectively swapping the allocation.

Do not worry about the minimal volumes taking up space. Even if you had to throw 10 MB at the problem (which in general you do not), that would be nothing compared to an outage due to cross-allocation, right? If you do not want to use this scheme because your LUNs are not always empty or it would be too much of a hassle, then the authors are sorry but cannot help you any further except point you to the end of the section, where a slightly oversized solution is presented. But if you refuse to use this scheme because you think that having a "hole" in your disk where there is no subdisk for a volume is unacceptable for any reason then be assured that there is no technical reason why you should not "waste" 1MB or so per LUN to tweak VxVM to do your stuff right. I.e there is no reasonable complaint against this procedure (but admittedly several unreasonable ones, which we choose to disregard – life is hard enough without unreasonable demands).

VOLUME LAYOUTS: STRIPE-MIRROR-SD VS. STRIPE-MIRROR-COL

If you are using volumes that are striped via VxVM, then there is a solution that you might not be aware of. Most admins will use the layered volume type of "stripe-mirror" for striped, redundant volumes across enclosures. But that is indeed not the optimal layout in terms of redundancy, as it does in fact allow the crossing of enclosure boundaries inside a single column. For instance, it might happen that you create a stripe-mirror using LUNs from the Bern and Zurich data centers, but inside a single column, both Bern and Zurich LUNs will be used in both plexes. This causes an undesired, unacceptable and often undetected single point of failure. The reason that this is allowed to happen is that VxVM maps the layout specification of stripe-mirror to the more specific layout of stripe-mirror-col, which means a stripe-mirror that mirrors its sub-entities by column, i.e. mirroring is done column by column. This bad point about this layout is that its requirements are satisfied even if both plexes in a column contain LUNs from the same enclosure! What you probably want to do is mirror at the subdisk level, i.e. have each subdisk mirrored on its own. That could mean you are ending up having more sub-volumes in your layered volume, but they will be mirrored piece by piece. A column can no longer have plexes containing storage from more than one enclosure, since that would imply more than one subdisk in the plex, which is forbidden in this layout. If this sounds good to you, then you are invited to try the layout specification stripe-mirror-sd, which stands for stripe-mirror on a subdisk level. Note that you can also relayout or convert you existing volumes to stripe-mirror-sd. In the case of a conversion, i.e. if your previous layout is stripe-mirror, it takes only a very short time and does no I/O to the public region; only the private region database is altered.

As it always seems to be the case, however, even this layout is not without drawbacks: while it works fine for storage systems that consist only of same-sized LUNs, and where each LUN is used for only one volume, it does not universally work for any kind of storage. This is due to the way that storage allocation works in the stripe-mirror-sd layout: It creates a subvolume over the **greatest** of the available subdisks rather than the **smallest**. While this behavior does limit the creation of a possibly excessive number of subvolumes, it unfortunately does not prevent creation of a single point of failure. Look at the following example, where we try to salvage a volume. The volume has acquired a single point of failure by a vxassist growby command and we try to undo the SPOF problem by converting it to the stripe-mirror-sd layout. We start from scratch, with eight LUNs, four each from the bern and Zurich site. They are marked by using appropriate disk names:

```
# vxdisk list # We got four disks from each site: bern and zurich
DEVICE        TYPE          DISK         GROUP        STATUS
[...]
c0t2d0s2      auto:cdsdisk  bern01       adg          online
c0t3d0s2      auto:cdsdisk  zurich01     adg          online
c0t4d0s2      auto:cdsdisk  zurich02     adg          online
c0t10d0s2     auto:cdsdisk  bern02       adg          online
c0t11d0s2     auto:cdsdisk  bern03       adg          online
c0t12d0s2     auto:cdsdisk  zurich03     adg          online
c0t13d0s2     auto:cdsdisk  bern04       adg          online
c0t14d0s2     auto:cdsdisk  zurich04     adg          online
```

We create a volume on the disks using a standard `vxassist make` command with a standard layout. But first, we check how large we can make the volume on half the disks.

```
# vxassist maxsize layout=stripe-mirror ncol=2 alloc=bern01,bern02,\
  zurich01,zurich02
Maximum volume size: 35358720 (17265Mb)
# vxassist make r10vol 17265m layout=stripe-mirror alloc=bern01,bern02,\
  zurich01,zurich02 init=active
# vxprint -qrtLg adg
[...]
v  r10vol        -                ENABLED ACTIVE  35358720 SELECT   r10vol-03
fsgen
pl r10vol-03     r10vol           ENABLED ACTIVE  35358720 STRIPE   2/128     RW

sv r10vol-S01    r10vol-03        r10vol-L01 1     17679360 0/0      2/2       ENA
v2 r10vol-L01    -                ENABLED ACTIVE  17679360 SELECT   -         fsgen
p2 r10vol-P01    r10vol-L01       ENABLED ACTIVE  17679360 CONCAT   -         RW
s2 bern01-02     r10vol-P01       bern01   0       17679360 0        c0t2d0    ENA
p2 r10vol-P02    r10vol-L01       ENABLED ACTIVE  17679360 CONCAT   -         RW
s2 zurich02-02   r10vol-P02       zurich02 0       17679360 0        c0t4d0    ENA

sv r10vol-S02    r10vol-03        r10vol-L02 1     17679360 1/0      2/2       ENA
v2 r10vol-L02    -                ENABLED ACTIVE  17679360 SELECT   -         fsgen
p2 r10vol-P03    r10vol-L02       ENABLED ACTIVE  17679360 CONCAT   -         RW
s2 zurich01-02   r10vol-P03       zurich01 0       17679360 0        c0t3d0    ENA
p2 r10vol-P04    r10vol-L02       ENABLED ACTIVE  17679360 CONCAT   -         RW
s2 bern02-02     r10vol-P04       bern02   0       17679360 0        c0t10d0   ENA
```

The volume looks fine. Even if the first plex is not always on the same side in all subvolumes (the plexes using LUNs from Bern have been emphasized), this does not harm resiliency at all; it is a purely cosmetic matter.

Now we grow the volume using only the extra LUNs that are still free.

```
# vxassist growby r10vol 1g alloc=bern03,bern04,zurich03,zurich04
# vxprint -qrtLg adg # and see what happens:
[...]
r10vol        -                ENABLED ACTIVE  37455872 SELECT   r10vol-03 fsgen
pl r10vol-03     r10vol           ENABLED ACTIVE  37455872 STRIPE   2/128     RW

sv r10vol-S01    r10vol-03        r10vol-L01 1     18727936 0/0      2/2       ENA
v2 r10vol-L01    -                ENABLED ACTIVE  18727936 SELECT   -         fsgen
p2 r10vol-P01    r10vol-L01       ENABLED ACTIVE  18727936 CONCAT   -         RW
s2 bern01-02     r10vol-P01       bern01   0       17679360 0        c0t2d0    ENA
s2 bern03-02     r10vol-P01       bern03   0       1048576  17679360 c0t11d0   ENA
p2 r10vol-P02    r10vol-L01       ENABLED ACTIVE  18727936 CONCAT   -         RW
s2 zurich02-02   r10vol-P02       zurich02 0       17679360 0        c0t4d0    ENA
s2 bern04-02     r10vol-P02       bern04   0       1048576  17679360 c0t13d0   ENA
```

```
sv r10vol-S02   r10vol-03    r10vol-L02 1      18727936 1/0       2/2      ENA
v2 r10vol-L02   -            ENABLED ACTIVE    18727936 SELECT    -        fsgen
p2 r10vol-P03   r10vol-L02   ENABLED ACTIVE    18727936 CONCAT    -        RW
s2 zurich01-02  r10vol-P03   zurich01 0        17679360 0         c0t3d0   ENA
s2 zurich03-02  r10vol-P03   zurich03 0        1048576  17679360  c0t12d0  ENA
p2 r10vol-P04   r10vol-L02   ENABLED ACTIVE    18727936 CONCAT    -        RW
s2 bern02-02    r10vol-P04   bern02   0        17679360 0         c0t10d0  ENA
s2 zurich04-02  r10vol-P04   zurich04 0        1048576  17679360  c0t14d0  ENA
```

As you can see in the highlighted parts above, a something bad has happened: some of the plexes are using storage from both locations, leading to SPOF susceptibility. We try to remedy the situation by mirroring each individual subdisk. This is done by converting the volume to a layout of stripe-mirror-sd.

```
# vxassist convert r10vol layout=stripe-mirror-sd # Takes only one second...
# vxprint -qrtLg adg
[...]
# vxassist convert r10vol layout=stripe-mirror-sd
# vxprint -qrtLg adg
v  r10vol        -            ENABLED ACTIVE    37455872 SELECT    r10vol-01
fsgen
pl r10vol-01    r10vol       ENABLED ACTIVE    37455872 STRIPE    2/128    RW

sv r10vol-S03   r10vol-01    r10vol-L03 1      17679360 0/0       2/2      ENA
v2 r10vol-L03   -            ENABLED ACTIVE    17679360 SELECT    -        fsgen
p2 r10vol-P05   r10vol-L03   ENABLED ACTIVE    17679360 CONCAT    -        RW
s2 bern01-01    r10vol-P05   bern01   0        17679360 0         c0t2d0   ENA
p2 r10vol-P06   r10vol-L03   ENABLED ACTIVE    17679360 CONCAT    -        RW
s2 zurich02-01  r10vol-P06   zurich02 0        17679360 0         c0t4d0   ENA

sv r10vol-S04   r10vol-01    r10vol-L04 1      1048576  0/17679360 2/2     ENA
v2 r10vol-L04   -            ENABLED ACTIVE    1048576  SELECT    -        fsgen
p2 r10vol-P07   r10vol-L04   ENABLED ACTIVE    1048576  CONCAT    -        RW
s2 bern03-01    r10vol-P07   bern03   0        1048576  0         c0t11d0  ENA
p2 r10vol-P08   r10vol-L04   ENABLED ACTIVE    1048576  CONCAT    -        RW
s2 bern04-01    r10vol-P08   bern04   0        1048576  0         c0t13d0  ENA

sv r10vol-S05   r10vol-01    r10vol-L05 1      17679360 1/0       2/2      ENA
v2 r10vol-L05   -            ENABLED ACTIVE    17679360 SELECT    -        fsgen
p2 r10vol-P09   r10vol-L05   ENABLED ACTIVE    17679360 CONCAT    -        RW
s2 zurich01-01  r10vol-P09   zurich01 0        17679360 0         c0t3d0   ENA
p2 r10vol-P10   r10vol-L05   ENABLED ACTIVE    17679360 CONCAT    -        RW
s2 bern02-01    r10vol-P10   bern02   0        17679360 0         c0t10d0  ENA

sv r10vol-S06   r10vol-01    r10vol-L06 1      1048576  1/17679360 2/2     ENA
v2 r10vol-L06   -            ENABLED ACTIVE    1048576  SELECT    -        fsgen
```

```
p2 r10vol-P11   r10vol-L06   ENABLED  ACTIVE   1048576  CONCAT   -         RW
s2 zurich03-01  r10vol-P11   zurich03 0        1048576  0        c0t12d0   ENA
p2 r10vol-P12   r10vol-L06   ENABLED  ACTIVE   1048576  CONCAT   -         RW
s2 zurich04-01  r10vol-P12   zurich04 0        1048576  0        c0t14d0   ENA
```

As you can see, now all plexes are rearranged in such a way that no single plex holds storage from both locations. But they are rearranged in a way that there still is a SPOF: Two of the subvolumes are mirrored inside a location! So this is not a general solution, but if you know what you're doing, and if you carefully inspect the volume after growing it you may get lucky.

8.1.3   MIRRORING SITE-AWARE VOLUMES ACROSS SITES

SITE AWARENESS: A SOLUTION FOR NEW DISK GROUPS AND VOLUMES

With VxVM 5.0 there is a new feature called "site awareness". This feature was created expressly with dual or even multiple data centers in mind. To reduce read latency and WAN traffic when reading from a mirror you can, with VxVM 5.0, define which site the host and the LUNs are located in. Then, if you set the appropriate read policy for the volumes, VxVM will only read from the local storage by preferring those LUNs that bear the same name tag as the host. It will also use automatic cross-site mirroring if you tell the disk group which sites there are, and VxVM 5.0 will even extend the mirrors correctly in that case! The downside is that as of SF5.0MP1 **existing** volume do not profit from this new capabilities, so unless you are setting up a new system or you are willing to accept some serious downtime, it may be better to stick with the workarounds mentioned before.

Note: the day after the last version of this book was finished and sent off to the press we were exposed to a newer release of SF: 5.0MP3 (Linux). In this version, the procedures discussed below do seem to work even with existing volumes. Due to the lack of testing time, however, this cannot be guaranteed. The book was delayed enough to integrate this extra paragraph but not enough to change the structure of this whole chapter.

Having said that, this is how site awareness is set up on the physical level

```
# vxdctl set site=<sitename>     # set the site for this server
# vxdctl list                    # check the site for this server
# vxdisk settag <accessname> site=<sitename>     # set the site for a disk
# vxdisk listtag      # check the site for all disks
# vxdg addsite <firstsite>
# vxdg addsite <secondsite>
```

A disk group that is prepared in the way outlined above will have different defaults than usual: it will, by default, mirror all new volumes across all sites added to the disk group using `vxdg addsite <sitename>`. Growing a mirror that was created in a disk group like this will automatically grow such that each plex remains confined to its site.

While the above sounds very good, VxVM will also add dirty region logs to all newly created volumes. To reiterate: DRLs are logs that remember which regions are currently undergoing write-I/O and must be resynchronised using RDWRBACK after a crash. It therefore speeds up crash recovery. Adding a DRL may not be the ideal solution since you may want to use vxsnap prepare instead, which creates a combined DRL and DCO log to cover all possible resynchronisation events: Plex resynchronisation using RDWRBACK and plex resynchronisation using ATCOPY. If you want to use the combined DRL/DCO log, specify layout=mirror,nolog to vxassist when you create the volume, then use vxsnap prepare to add the DRL/DCO log (DCO version 20). Specifying the nolog attribute keeps VxVM from creating the DRL that is unnecessary f you want to use vxsnap.

While site awareness is not the same as enclosure-awareness, it can still be used to keep the plexes confined to their enclosures. In order for that to work we need to define a "site" for each enclosure, and make VxVM handle each enclosure as an individual site. There is a little downside to that because VxVM will only read from the "local" site, but you can set the volume read policy to round (vxvol rdpol round $VOLNAME) to allow round-robin access. The other downside is that if your volumes span multiple enclosures at each site, then this procedure does not work because you would have to specify multiple enclosures acting as "locations" for your host, too.

That said, let's look at the following walkthrough of a disk group containing ten LUNs being set up for automatic site awareness, and subsequent growing of a volume in this disk group.

The general setup here is that there are two data centers, and we wish to mirror across these. The data centers are located in KEL (which stands for Kelsterbach; the location of a large data center in Germany) and FRA (Frankfurt, a location about 30km away from Kelsterbach, and home of many data centers for banks).

First we want to inform VxVM that our machine is located in KEL., then check if it was set successfully:

```
# vxdctl set site=KEL
# vxdctl list
Volboot file
version: 3/1
seqno:   0.9
cluster protocol version: 70
[...]
siteid:  KEL   # OK, looks good. The site info is persisted in /etc/vx/volboot
```

The following are our disks (with the boot disks omitted because they do not play a role here and just take up space)

```
# vxdisk list
DEVICE        TYPE           DISK       GROUP       STATUS
[...]
c1t1d0s2      auto:cdsdisk   adg00      adg         online
c1t1d1s2      auto:cdsdisk   adg01      adg         online
c1t1d2s2      auto:cdsdisk   adg02      adg         online
c1t1d3s2      auto:cdsdisk   adg03      adg         online
c1t1d4s2      auto:cdsdisk   adg04      adg         online
```

```
c1t1d5s2      auto:cdsdisk     adg05       adg        online
c1t1d6s2      auto:cdsdisk     adg06       adg        online
c1t1d7s2      auto:cdsdisk     adg07       adg        online
c1t1d8s2      auto:cdsdisk     adg08       adg        online
c1t1d9s2      auto:cdsdisk     adg09       adg        online
```

Let's check if this disk group knows anything about sites at all. Remember the `vxprint -m` command outputs every single bit of persistent information about a disk group, so we'll use it and `grep` for "site".

```
# vxprint -m -g adg | grep site
        siteconsistent=off # Aha! Interesting, but turned off...
     site=    # All the disks have a site tag, but it's empty
     site=
     site=
     site=
     site=
     site=
     site=
     site=
     site=
```

In the next step we will identify which disks reside in which location. If you are emulating sites for the sake of keeping your volumes confined to an enclosure, then you need to make sure not to mix up disks here. If you do, then VxVM will be forced to consistently allocate storage from the wrong disks, and we can certainly live without that.
This is the general syntax of the appropriate vxdisk command to set the location tag on a disk:

```
# vxdisk -g adg settag c1t1d0s2 site=FRA
```

But we do not want to type so much, and loops scale much better than repeating individual commands, so we'll put it all in a loop:

```
# for disk in 0 1 2 3 4; do vxdisk settag c1t1d${disk}s2 site=FRA; done
# vxdisk listtag
DEVICE          NAME                      VALUE
c1t1d0s2        site                      FRA
c1t1d1s2        site                      FRA
c1t1d2s2        site                      FRA
c1t1d3s2        site                      FRA
c1t1d4s2        site                      FRA
[...]
```

As you can see above the first five disks are now flagged with site **FRA**. Now we'll flag the other ones with **KEL**.

```
# for disk in 5 6 7 8 9; do vxdisk settag c1t1d${disk}s2 site=KEL; done
# vxdisk listtag
DEVICE          NAME                        VALUE
c1t1d0s2        site                        FRA
c1t1d1s2        site                        FRA
c1t1d2s2        site                        FRA
c1t1d3s2        site                        FRA
c1t1d4s2        site                        FRA
c1t1d5s2        site                        KEL
c1t1d6s2        site                        KEL
c1t1d7s2        site                        KEL
c1t1d8s2        site                        KEL
c1t1d9s2        site                        KEL
# vxprint -m -g adg | grep site
        siteconsistent=off
        site=FRA
        site=FRA
        site=FRA
        site=FRA
        site=FRA
        site=KEL
        site=KEL
        site=KEL
        site=KEL
        site=KEL
```

All the disks are flagged with their appropriate site. Let's have a look at the default volume parameters that VxVM is going to use when creating a new volume now:

```
# vxassist -g adg help showattrs
#Attributes:
layout=nomirror,nostripe,nomirror-stripe,nostripe-mirror,nostripe-mirror-
col,nostripe-mirror-sd,noconcat-mirror,nomirror-concat,span,nocontig,raid5log,no
regionlog,diskalign,nostorage
 mirrors=2 columns=0 regionlogs=1 raid5logs=1 dcmlogs=0 dcologs 0
[...]
```

Looks like it is not going to mirror, and not going to add a log to the volumes. Note that this will change quite dramatically as we tell the disk group about sites:

```
# vxdg -g adg addsite FRA          # We add a site to the disk group
# vxassist -g adg help showattrs
#Attributes:
 layout=mirror,nostripe,nomirror-stripe,nostripe-mirror,nostripe-mirror-
col,nostripe-mirror-sd,noconcat-mirror,nomirror-concat,span,nocontig,raid5log,-
regionlog,diskalign,nostorage
```

```
 mirrors=1 columns=0 regionlogs=1 raid5logs=1 dcmlogs=1 dcologs 1
[...]
```

Already, VxVM's default has changed to mirroring by default (albeit with only one plex, so it is not really mirroring). But it also now defaults to adding a DRL (see emphasized type above). Note that wile in the last line above it does say "regionlogs=1 [...] dcmlogs=1 dcologs=1" that does not mean these logs are added by default. Only a DRL (dirty region log) is added, and that is because the "regionlog" attribute (emphasized in the second line) is set. The line containing the DCM and DCO parameters just specifies the number of logs to use if logging is requested. It does not actually specify whether or not logging is default; that is done in the first part, where it says layout=mirror, [...], regionlog, [...] etc.

If we add the second site, the setup is complete:

```
# vxdg -g adg addsite KEL
# vxassist -g adg help showattrs
#Attributes:
 layout=mirror,nostripe,nomirror-stripe,nostripe-mirror,nostripe-mirror-
col,nostripe-mirror-sd,noconcat-mirror,nomirror-concat,span,nocontig,raid5log,-
regionlog,diskalign,nostorage
 mirrors=2 columns=0 regionlogs=2 raid5logs=2 dcmlogs=2 dcologs 2
[...]
```

As you can see the layout has not changed at all; mirror and regionlog are the only positive settings in the default layout line. But the number of elements has changed in the second line: mirrors=2 and all the count of all the logs is two also. That means that now VxVM will mirror (with two plexes), and add two DRLs unless we specify otherwise:

```
# vxprint -m -g adg | grep site
        siteconsistent=off
site FRA
site KEL
        site=FRA
        site=FRA
        site=FRA
        site=FRA
        site=FRA
        site=KEL
        site=KEL
        site=KEL
        site=KEL
        site=KEL
```

Note the two additional lines in the output that specify the FRA and KEL sites. These are from the disk group record, which now knows about the two sites because we added them to the disk group. Let's create a volume with the (new) default layout and see what we get:

```
# vxassist make avol 100m
# vxprint -qrtg adg
[...]
sr FRA          ACTIVE   # Site records now show up - one per site
sr KEL          ACTIVE   # They are part of the disk group
[...]
v  avol         -              ENABLED ACTIVE 204800  SITEREAD  -         fsgen
pl avol-01      avol           ENABLED ACTIVE 204800  CONCAT    -         RW
sd adg00-01     avol-01  adg00 528     204800  0        c1t1d0   ENA
pl avol-02      avol           ENABLED ACTIVE 204800  CONCAT    -         RW
sd adg05-01     avol-02  adg05 528     204800  0        c1t1d5   ENA
pl avol-03      avol           ENABLED ACTIVE LOGONLY CONCAT    -         RW
sd adg00-02     avol-03  adg00 0       528     LOG      c1t1d0   ENA
pl avol-04      avol           ENABLED ACTIVE LOGONLY CONCAT    -         RW
sd adg05-02     avol-04  adg05 0       528     LOG      c1t1d5   ENA
```

The volume consists of two data plexes – one at each site (adg00 is in FRA and adg05 is in KEL) – and two LOGONLY plexes, i.e. DRLs, on the same disks as the data plexes. Now look at what site-specific information is added to the volume:

```
# vxprint -m -g adg | grep site
        siteconsistent=off
site FRA
site KEL
        site=FRA
        site=FRA
        site=FRA
        site=FRA
        site=FRA
        site=KEL
        site=KEL
        site=KEL
        site=KEL
        site=KEL
        site=FRA
        site=KEL
        site=FRA
        site=KEL
        siteconsistent=on
        allsites=on
```

Apparently the volume inherits the siteconsistent attribute from the disk group, but for the volume it is set to on, while it remains off on the disk group itself. The volume also has another attribute, allsites, which is set to on. The disk group does not know such a attribute. So far the volume has been very small – a mere 100 MegaBytes – because this was just for demonstrating the principle. But when we grow the volume beyond the boundaries of our 50GB-LUNs, we see that VxVM stops using its more primitive, or at least site-agnostic, allocation strategy and switch to site-aware allocation:

```
# vxassist -b growby avol 100g
# vxprint -qrtg adg
[...]
sr FRA          ACTIVE    # Site records now show up - one per site
sr KEL          ACTIVE    # They are part of the disk group
[...]
v  avol         -         ENABLED  SYNC    209920000 SITEREAD  -        fsgen
pl avol-01      avol      ENABLED  ACTIVE  209920000 CONCAT    -        RW
sd adg00-01     avol-01   adg00    528     122107120 0         c1t1d0   ENA
sd adg01-01     avol-01   adg01    0       87812880 122107120  c1t1d1   ENA
pl avol-02      avol      ENABLED  ACTIVE  209920000 CONCAT    -        RW
sd adg05-01     avol-02   adg05    528     122107120 0         c1t1d5   ENA
sd adg06-01     avol-02   adg06    0       87812880 122107120  c1t1d6   ENA
pl avol-03      avol      ENABLED  ACTIVE  LOGONLY   CONCAT    -        RW
sd adg00-02     avol-03   adg00    0       528       LOG       c1t1d0   ENA
pl avol-04      avol      ENABLED  ACTIVE  LOGONLY   CONCAT    -        RW
sd adg05-02     avol-04   adg05    0       528       LOG       c1t1d5   ENA
```

So this is finally a working procedure of volume-growth where all plexes remain confined to their respective enclosures (emulated by defining them as sites).

ADDITIONAL SITE–SPECIFIC COMMANDS

There are more subcommand to vxdg for handling sites than just vxdg addsite. Anything that can be added can also be removed again, so there is vxdg rmsite, too. While this was obvious, there are two more commands that are designed to temporarily detach and then reattach a site. these are named accordingly (see below). Detaching a site disables all devices in the disk group that carry the tag of the given site. These devices then carry a new flag: detached. Reattaching the site removes the detached flag from the disks in the disk group that carry the appropriate site tag. Those volumes that were in use in the meantime must then be resynchronised by stopping and restarting them, or online by issuing the command vxrecover. Detaching a site can be useful in case of scheduled maintenance on an enclosure, path, or actual site. Here is the synopsis for the appropriate vxdg commands:

```
vxdg [-g diskgroup] [-o addmirror] addsite site
vxdg [-g diskgroup] [-o rmmirror] rmsite site
vxdg [-g diskgroup] [-f] detachsite site
vxdg [-g diskgroup] [-o overridessb] reattachsite site
```


USING SNAPSHOTS WITH SITES

If we wish to create snapshots of a volume that has been created with the default layout of a site-aware disk group (mirroring with DRL), then we need to prepare the volume first by adding a DCO version 20 log to it (see more about this in the chapter about snapshots).

Unfortunately, we get an error message when we actually try that because the volume still has the DRL attached:

```
# vxsnap prepare avol
VxVM vxassist ERROR V-5-1-8807 volume avol has DRL log attached. Prepare disal-
lowed.
```

In this case we need to remove the DRL before we can prepare it for snapshotting. So we could do:

```
# vxassist remove log avol nlogs=0      # Removes logs until 0 logs are left
# vxsnap prepare avol
[...]
# [vxedit -rf rm avol]   # Get rid of the volume for the next exercise
```

Instead of removing the DRL after volume creation we could deviate from the default layout when we create the volume. From an empty disk group, the whole process of creating a volume cross-site and then snapshotting it is done like this:

```
# vxassist make avol 100m layout=mirror,nolog
# vxsnap prepare avol
# vxsnap addmir avol alloc=site:FRA
# vxprint -qrtg adg
[...]
sr FRA          ACTIVE  # Site records now show up - one per site
sr KEL          ACTIVE  # They are part of the disk group
[...]
v  avol         -               ENABLED ACTIVE  204800  SITEREAD  -       fsgen
pl avol-01      avol            ENABLED ACTIVE  204800  CONCAT    -       RW
sd adg00-01     avol-01         adg00   0       204800  0         c1t1d0  ENA
pl avol-02      avol            ENABLED ACTIVE  204800  CONCAT    -       RW
sd adg05-01     avol-02         adg05   0       204800  0         c1t1d5  ENA
pl avol-03      avol            ENABLED SNAPDONE 204800 CONCAT    -       WO
sd adg02-01     avol-03         adg02   0       204800  0         c1t1d2  ENA
dc avol_dco     avol            avol_dcl
v  avol_dcl     -               ENABLED ACTIVE  544     SITEREAD  -       gen
pl avol_dcl-01  avol_dcl        ENABLED ACTIVE  544     CONCAT    -       RW
sd adg06-01     avol_dcl-01     adg06   0       544     0         c1t1d6  ENA
pl avol_dcl-02  avol_dcl        ENABLED ACTIVE  544     CONCAT    -       RW
sd adg01-01     avol_dcl-02     adg01   0       544     0         c1t1d1  ENA
pl avol_dcl-03  avol_dcl        DISABLED DCOSNP 544     CONCAT    -       RW
sd adg03-01     avol_dcl-03     adg03   0       544     0         c1t1d3  ENA
```

Note that VxVM used disks from the specified location (FRA) both the disk for the plex that is in state SNAPDONE (i.e. the one destined to become the snapshot volume) and the disk for the currently disabled DCO plex that is in state DCOSNP (the plex that is destined to become the DCO volume for the snapshot volume). So now the rest is standard snapshot

syntax as it has been covered extensively in the appropriate chapter. For completeness, it
is included here without comment:

```
# vxsnap make source=avol/new=snap_avol/plex=avol-03
# vxprint -qrtg adg
[...]
sr FRA          ACTIVE  # Site records now show up - one per site
sr KEL          ACTIVE  # They are part of the disk group
[...]
v  avol         -             ENABLED ACTIVE  204800  SITEREAD  -       fsgen
pl avol-01      avol          ENABLED ACTIVE  204800  CONCAT    -       RW
sd adg00-01     avol-01       adg00   0       204800  0         c1t1d0  ENA
pl avol-02      avol          ENABLED ACTIVE  204800  CONCAT    -       RW
sd adg05-01     avol-02       adg05   0       204800  0         c1t1d5  ENA
dc avol_dco     avol          avol_dcl
v  avol_dcl     -             ENABLED ACTIVE  544     SITEREAD  -       gen
pl avol_dcl-01  avol_dcl      ENABLED ACTIVE  544     CONCAT    -       RW
sd adg06-01     avol_dcl-01   adg06   0       544     0         c1t1d6  ENA
pl avol_dcl-02  avol_dcl      ENABLED ACTIVE  544     CONCAT    -       RW
sd adg01-01     avol_dcl-02   adg01   0       544     0         c1t1d1  ENA
sp snap_avol_snp avol         avol_dco

v  snap_avol    -             ENABLED ACTIVE  204800  ROUND     -       fsgen
pl avol-03      snap_avol     ENABLED ACTIVE  204800  CONCAT    -       RW
sd adg02-01     avol-03       adg02   0       204800  0         c1t1d2  ENA
dc snap_avol_dco snap_avol    snap_avol_dcl
v  snap_avol_dcl -            ENABLED ACTIVE  544     ROUND     -       gen
pl avol_dcl-03  snap_avol_dcl ENABLED ACTIVE  544     CONCAT    -       RW
sd adg03-01     avol_dcl-03   adg03   0       544     0         c1t1d3  ENA
sp avol_snp     snap_avol     snap_avol_dco
```

8.1.4 SUMMARY

While there still is no real solution to growing **existing** mirrors across enclosures or sites
we hope to have given a viable approach for most cases, i.e. the ones where new, empty
LUNs are provided for the purpose of extending the existing volume. The best solution is to
create new disk groups and build new volumes inside the new disk groups because in that
case, VxVM can actually be made aware of what you are trying to achieve and will assist
you rather than stand in your way.

But because this approach cannot always be used, resorting to the workaround for the time
being is often preferred. By using or knowledge of the internal storage allocation scheme
of VxVM we can still outmaneuver the VxVM allocator to use the disks the way we want,
and make it allocate in a way that leaves no SPOFs.

8.2 REPLICATION ACROSS DATA CENTERS

When the distance between the data centers exceeds a threshold, then latency becomes a dominant problem. Write I/Os that require synchronous acknowledgement from the storage array have to wait for a longer time before they return. Read I/Os incur the extra delay of having to travel several kilometers before they reach the destination host. This can make remote mirroring no longer viable in many cases, because of the many cases where immediate acknowledgement from the storage array is required.

8.2.1 REPLICATION VS. MIRRORING

When a volume is mirrored then all write I/Os are sent to all mirrors immediately, while read I/Os are satisfied from one of the mirrors, usually in a round-robin fashion. In VxVM 5.0 you can define the site for your own host as well as for your disks so that VxVM can prefer reading locally, but it will still write to all mirrors instantaneously. Mirrored volumes are considered to be consistent in all regular situations, and all sides are usually treated exactly equally.

If the distance between location becomes too great, or if bandwidth between the locations is too limited, then updating the remote mirror may take too long to guarantee trouble-free and high-performance operation. In these cases replication can be a good option.

Replication can be described as a time-lagged mirroring, with the remote side being allowed to become out of sync until it catches up. Because of this, and because of the general issues with bandwidth in WANs the remote site is write-only and accordingly, no read I/O can be serviced by the replica site to replicating host.

In case of a disaster that destroys the active host (or even data center) or renders it unusable a host at the remote site is employed to take over the replicated data (which has been read-only for that host so far). The remote hosts talks to the array, has the array turn around the direction of replication, or put it in failover (standalone) mode, in which this side of the replication couple becomes read-write. The remote host then proceeds to import and use the disk groups in the remote location just as the failed host used to with its set of the data (which has now turned read-only, or is unreachable).

Replication, if done correctly, can indeed bridge greater distances than mirroring can. But the ultimate barrier that both schemes face is their suitability to great distances of the low level block transfer protocol employed.

It is important to understand that the speed of light, although it is generally considered extremely fast, is a very real barrier to remote mirroring and remote replication. In order to understand the parameters and what they lead to, we need to become familiar with some of the fundamentals of physics. Don't worry, there will be no difficult mathematics involved, it is all relatively simple.

8.2.2 The Speed of Light and Latency

The speed of light is almost 300 thousand kilometers per second. This sure sounds comfortably fast for all applications except maybe interstellar travel, doesn't it?

Actually it is much too slow for computing across several kilometers of distance, unless great care is taken in using the right protocols. Why is light speed to slow for us?

Why the Speed of Light is Too Slow

The problem about light speed is that while 300,000 kilometers per second may seem like a whole lot, a gigahertz is also a whole lot. In order to find out how far a bit travels when it is transmitted via a 1 gigahertz link, we need to divide the 300,000 kilometers by the amount of cycles per second for one gigahertz. This gives the simple formula

```
300,000,000 (metres per second) : 1,000,000,000 (1 gigahertz) = 0.3
```

which yields the surprising result that a bit is only 0,3 metres (one foot) long at 1 gigahertz.

Efficiency: Why Wire Speeds are Mostly Irrelevant

The length of 1 foot per bit at 1 gigahertz is valid only in vacuum. In a fibre cable we need to divide this further by the refractive index of the medium, which is roughly 3/2, so actually a bit that runs along a 1 gigahertz fibre channel link is only about 20 centimeters (cm) long! At 2 gigahertz it would be only 10 cm, at 4 GHz it's 5 cm and so on. So basically with increasing transmission frequency the packet that we are transmitting is just getting smaller, but it isn't actually transferred any faster over the fibre. The first bit of a packet reaches its endpoint just as quickly at 1 GHz as it does at 4 GHz and as it would at 1 terahertz. The only speed advantage of using higher GHz on FC is that because the bits are shorter the **end** of the packet is reached earlier, and that more packets can be put on the fibre because a packet occupies a shorter range of the cable. Being able to put more packets onto the fibre per second is very important for increasing **total** bandwidth, especially in local SANs. But if the length of a packet is small relative to the distance over which the packet has to be transmitted, and especially if only one packet can be transferred at a time, then it really **does not make any difference** whether we are using 1 GHz or 4GHz fibre channel, or even just 100MHz Ethernet. Let us look at an example:

Using fibre channel arbitrated loop (a self-organizing topology and protocol from the early days of fibre channel) we transmit data to a remote site 25 kilometers away. Naturally, data is organized into blocks. In an arbitrated loop these blocks are usually transmitted in single transfers. Each transfer involves waiting for a token to come by, setting a flag in the token that says we would like to transfer data (requesting the bus), sending it off to the next station, which repeats the same, unaltered token unless it wants to send data itself (but we will assume the best case: that other node wants to send any data). After one whole round trip the token reappears at our host and it still contains our original request so we now know that our data transfer has been permitted by all participating nodes. We now put the data packet (which has been waiting the whole time for the token to come back) onto the channel where it, too, makes a round trip: to the receiver and back. Once it is back the loop is freed for the next packet transfer etc.

How high is the efficiency of this transfer?

Well, that depends on how long the data packet is. Data packets in fibre channel are limited to 2112 bytes, which are 8 x 2112 bits which is equivalent to 8 x 2112 x 0,2 metres or roughly 3380 metres.

There is only one packet of ~3.4 km on a transport medium. The total distance travelled is (remember the token has to travel a full round trip before the data round-trip) four times the distance between sender and receiver (which we said was 25 km). So the total distance travelled for the transfer (without any overhead, of which there can actually be quite a lot) is 100km. 3,4 km of these 100 km are used for data. The efficiency is immediately obvious: it is merely 3.4%, because only 3.4 km out of 100km are used.

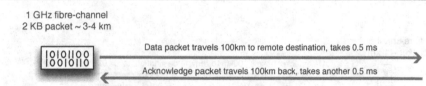

1 GHz fibre-channel
2 KB packet ~ 3-4 km

Data packet travels 100km to remote destination, takes 0.5 ms

Acknowledge packet travels 100km back, takes another 0.5 ms

Figure 8-9: There is practically no influence of wire speed on synchronous replication, as the total transfer time is dominated by the distance if that is more than a few times the packet size. At wire-speeds of about 200,000 km/sec, a block takes one millisecond to travel to a location 100 km away, and back. That is a very long time. It is in the range of hard disk access times, and we know that they are the limiting factor today!

If you used 4GHz then you would have four times the theoretical bandwidth but because the bulk of the delay is not caused by the length of the packet but by the (unchanged) distance it does not really improve the situation at all. We get four times higher bandwidth but in turn we also get almost four times lower efficiency. The packet is not 3.4 km now, but only a quarter of that: 0.85 km. But the distance is still 100km. so we end up with 0.85% efficiency on the 4 GHz fibre channel.

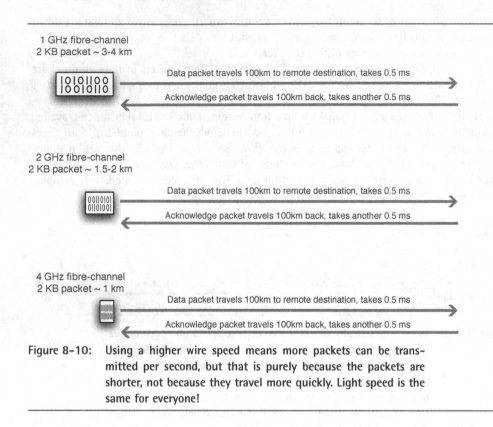

Figure 8-10:   Using a higher wire speed means more packets can be transmitted per second, but that is purely because the packets are
shorter, not because they travel more quickly. Light speed is the
same for everyone!

Of course the distance is actually 100 km **plus 3.4 km** in the first case and 100 km **plus 0.85 km** in the second case, but that would have complicated the formula and the small total difference is not worth the trouble.

WHY PROTOCOLS MAKE ALL THE DIFFERENCE

The low efficiency comes almost solely from the fact that in the example given above there is only a single packet on the wire at one time. This is dictated by the protocol we chose. For instance, switched fabric fibre channel architectures do allow multiple packets under way at any time, as long as the buffer credits do not run out.

If we had used a switched fabric in the above example the numbers would look much more friendly. The sending host would initiate block transfers without having to send a token out and wait for it to return first. And it would not have to stop transmitting new blocks until either of the following conditions occur:

- Two fabric nodes run out of buffer credits
- The host application's protocol requires it to wait for an acknowledgement of some sort.
- The host runs out of data to send.

So in the case of 1 GHz transport medium we could just line up packet after packet and will the whole distance with data. Obviously, with a higher medium speed (like 4 GHz) because of the shorter length of each packet we could actually fit in four times as many packets as we could with 1 GHz without losing efficiency.

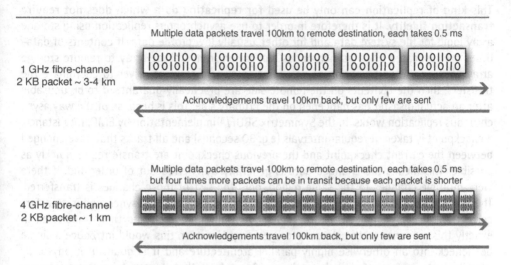

Figure 8-11: Higher frequencies help only in putting more data packets on the wire at the same time. the actual travel time is unchanged. In order to get any kind of performance out of long-distance replication it is mandatory to use asynchronous protocols which do not require immediate acknowledgement from the remote storage. But asynchronous replication cannot be done by the storage array alone and still be consistent: the operating system **must** be involved (see below).

Obviously it all depends on which protocol you choose and how you configure the basic transport parameters (like buffer credits, which we will discuss in detail in the technical deep dive section)

8.2.3 REPLICATION USING STORAGE ARRAY LOGIC

Most storage array manufacturers offer some way of replicating data in a synchronous or asynchronous way. Many times they will offer the synchronous variant for short ranges and the asynchronous variant for long range. When asked, they may occasionally agree that asynchronous replication will not create a consistent, usable copy at the remote side, but typically the importance of this is down played enough that it is ultimately used and goes into production. When disaster strikes, and only 70% of the applications at the remote site actually come up this is often hailed as a great success rather than the utter failure that it actually is. Let us look a little deeper into the two variants of replication: synchronous and asynchronous, and discuss their relative merits.

ASYNCHRONOUS REPLICATION USING STORAGE ARRAY LOGIC

This kind of replication can only be used for replicating data which does not require transaction fidelity. It is therefore in order to use asynchronous replication using storage array logic for file system data and for other, usually low profile data. If contents of databases are replicated using asynchronous replication from storage array to remote storage array without the participation of an operating system resident driver to coordinate the transfers, then the contents on the remote side are practically guaranteed to be unusable after an actual disaster has happened on the primary side. This is because of the way asynchronous replication works. In the Symmetrix SRDF/A implementation by EMC, for instance, a checkpoint is taken at regular intervals (e.g. 30 seconds) and all tracks that have changed between the current checkpoint and the previous checkpoint are transferred as quickly as possible. This means the changed data is generally transferred out of order and, if there were multiple changes to the same region, only the last of those changes is transferred. The only conceivable way in which storage arrays might handle asynchronous transfers correctly is if every single write I/O was sequentially numbered and then transferred in exactly this sequence to the remote storage array. However, this would introduce a single bottleneck into an otherwise highly parallel architecture and it is doubtful if any array vendors have implemented such a scheme. Apart from that, transmission error recovery would be a big challenge.

So generally speaking, in asynchronous mode, the storage array's internal logic simply has no means of knowing which blocks belong together to form a single, atomic transaction. So there is a high probability of transactions being literally ripped apart: one part is transferred while the other one is not transferred until the next checkpoint, which may be 30 seconds away.

This obviously leads to problems with transactional data, so you cannot use asynchronous storage array-based replication with transactional data. It will turn out to be unusable once the remote host tries to start the database after a disaster.

Note that **the corruption never happens if the direction of replication is voluntarily switched during the usual disaster recovery (DR) tests**. In these tests the operators are of course unwilling to actually simulate a hard shut down of the storage array because those are usually shared with many other, often productive, servers. So they just shut down the LUNs in software, or induce a replication direction switch using command line or GUI tools of the storage array. But you **must** be aware that this is not really a DR test! It may serve a vendor very well as a demonstration that their array works great, but it will not help you in case of an actual disaster. It is pure smoke-screening! If an array actually fails and you were using asynchronous replication then your transactional data **will be** broken!

SYNCHRONOUS REPLICATION USING STORAGE ARRAY LOGIC

There is a "nice try" kind of approach of the array vendors to do replication of transactional data right, which is called synchronous replication, but it is extremely sensitive to latency induced by distance. Basically, every single block must be acknowledged from the remote site before the next block can be sent, i.e. there can only be one block under way at any one time per transfer channel. That is why often several channels are used between storage arrays; that allows for some degree of concurrency (although it does not help consistency).

The reason why this has to be is not at all easy to understand. We will try to give you a coherent explanation, but the matter is rather complex. For this reason, we will just pick a single example of a transaction that will fail using a storage array, and allow ourselves to deduct from this example that they are flawed in principle **even if they tried to maintain write order** (which normally they don't).

Imagine the following setup:

- A storage array that replicates each individual write in the same write order, but does not wait for acknowledgements, but instead keeps grinding along;
- Host A: a database machine running some kind of financial database application that is connected (of course) to a network of other machines interacting with host A;
- Host B: the remote replica machine for host A;
- Host X: a machine interacting remotely via an outside network with host A, feeding financial transactions to host A.

The problem is **write order fidelity**, as you will see in the following example:

Host X has just fed a large financial transaction to host A that changed, let's say, first block 5000 and then block 6000 in a volume. Host A has processed the transaction locally, and has committed it to replicated storage. The storage system is busily replicating the data (synchronously) to the remote site(s), but is not waiting for he acknowledgement for block 5000 before sending block 6000. When the remote site acknowledges the receipt of both blocks, that data is deemed secure and host A acknowledges the successful transaction to host X. This means that e.g. some large amount of money has just been received or sent away, or that some large amount of stock has just been bought or sold.

Host A is now receiving the next transaction, which changes first block 7000 and then block 6000 of the same volume. It commits the transaction to local storage, and the storage array begins replicating the two blocks over to the remote site, but does not wait for individual acknowledgements before transferring each following block. It sends block 7000 on its way and block 6000 immediately thereafter. Block 7000 is not acknowledged because of a bad checksum or some other trivial error. Block 6000, however, is successfully transferred. After successful transfer of block 6000, the data center is destroyed by a disaster. Because it is not integrated into the operating system, the storage array's replication mechanism has no means of knowing that the changes to block 5000 and 6000 belong together, as well as the changes to block 6000 and 7000. For this reason, the remote storage array will indeed use the overwritten block 6000 in conjunction with the previously acknowledged block 5000 when host B comes up to take over after host A's catastrophic failure. But obviously this would lead to trouble! There is a full, possibly very important or very expensive transaction, that is half covered by a newer transaction, which has not yet completed and which may be rolled back, or may be reissued on the remote host, leading to write I/O on possibly quite different portions of the volume. The result is that the transaction is either not done at all (although it had been acknowledged to the business partner), or executed twice (although only one execution had been requested). Additionally, the database will have trouble starting up and running because of logical inconsistencies in the table spaced. In any case, there is a principal problem with the fact that a storage array has no intrinsic knowledge about which individual block writes belong to the same I/O operation, while an operating system-resident device driver does have this intrinsic knowledge. To illustrate the point: if you think the above is a very constructed example that is unlikely to happen in the real world, then think again: When there are several thousand write I/Os outstanding on a storage array the probability for such a scenario becomes several thousand times more likely! Also, please keep in mind that a disaster recovery solution only ever gets to do its work in such extraordinary situations, and it better work really well then. To emphasize the degree to which a user of current storage-array based replication is exposed, please ponder at least the following points:

Using anything but a flat concat volume will completely destroy the connection between you storage array's view of the data and your operating system's view of the data. For instance, a write I/O to a striped volume looks to the storage array like several completely independent write I/Os, each going to a different LUN (actually just columns of the same striped volume and therefore likely to be highly interdependent). A mirrored stripe is not any better, it is even worse because now there are two times the number of I/Os, whose interdependence is unclear.

Remembering Moore's law and current throughput numbers, you can estimate the number of outstanding I/O operations at any time. This number is typically a high one, not a low one. It is also increasing year over year. It is not at all unusual, but in fact very likely, that in the case of an actual disaster many transactions are indeed corrupted and/or rendered unusable **after** they have already been acknowledged to your business partners. This could lead to serious risks to the business. It is important to know that when picking the replication method. We know it is much easier to pass the job on to the SAN department, who claim to know what they are doing, and to ignore the risk because it's no longer one's own bailiwick. But it may not be such a good idea after all if the survival of your company is at stake.

8.2.4 Replication Using Kernel Mode Logic

If we were to use an operating system based solution then the information about coherency or interdependency of data blocks in not yet lost. Replication therefore has a chance to actually work, and indeed work both quickly and reliably. There is a very well working solution embedded in VxVM which is called VVR (Veritas Volume Replicator). This feature is already part of VxVM; it is activated by purchasing the appropriate license and adding the license key to the system.

Overview of VVR

VVR works by replicating volume changes (i.e. write I/O) via a normal IP connection to a similar volume on the remote hosts. A remote disk group must be imported on the remote host, and its volumes must be started, but they must not be mounted because the volume's data can change at the block level due to the data being replicated from the active site. A multitude of destination hosts is allowed, although using just one destination host is the usual setup. The IP address of the source and destination, along with some other meta-info like replication type etc. is contained in a data structure called an RLINK, which stands for **remote link**. The RLINK is created in the disk group that contains the volumes which are to be replicated. It also contains other global replication information pertaining to the disk group, such as the type of synchronisation and type of error handling, the state of the connection and such.

The actual data that must be replicated are not held in the RLINK itself (there is no persistent memory in an RLINK), but rather in a separate log volume, called the SRL (for Serial Replication Log) which is attached to the original volume. a similar log volume is attached to the remote, recipient volume. Any write-I/O is first persisted to the log volume, and a descriptor with information about the size and type of I/O is stored along with the data. While the data is being persisted to the log it is also transmitted to the recipient host(s), where it is likewise stored to the log volume. Once the data is written to the log it cannot be lost and is therefore considered safe. It will be written to the actual volume as soon as possible, but if anything happened in the meantime, the log will simply be replayed (both locally and remotely) and therefore it does not really matter so much whether the data is in the log volume or in the data volume.

The log volume is organized as a circular buffer: In the event of an extended downtime of the IP connection, or in case the bandwidth is overused for an extended time, the buffer will eventually fill up so it must be sized intelligently. But even in the event of a log volume filling up VVR will still remember all of the initial I/Os and replay them in order, while using a persistent log bitmap to remember the regions that have changed since the time that the log volume filled up.

It is in this final, exceptional state that VVR behaves only as well as a storage array replication mechanism: it forgets about write order and write coherence and block interdependency and just flags regions to replay later, when bandwidth is available again.

In the regular state VVR behaves much better that storage array based replication because it transmits and replays each I/O as a single entity, maintaining what is called write order fidelity. No matter if the I/O was small or huge it will always be replicated atomically, either in total or not at all. It will also be transmitted in the correct order, and in the case of subsequent writes to the same block, all writes are transmitted instead of just the most recent one. That is what all storage array based replication mechanisms fail to do correctly, because they have no chance of knowing about the write order in which the host has issued the I/Os. All they know about is independent blocks.

ASYNCHRONOUS REPLICATION USING VVR

When VVR is set up for a disk group with an RLINK indicating **asynchronous** replication, then all write I/O is acknowledged to the host as soon as the data is persisted to the local log. Loss of data is now considered impossible (SRL logs are usually mirrored) unless a disaster destroys the site. Data is always replicated as quickly as possible via the network, but the latency incurred from waiting for a remote machine to reply to a replicated I/O is saved. Because the SRL log is sequential, the local log write I/O is therefore usually even faster (and therefore subsequent I/Os may be dispatched more rapidly) than in the case of actually writing to the data volume, although with today's storage arrays the difference is diminishing. If disaster strikes, the remote site may not have received all transactions that have been locally acknowledged, but at least the database table space is not corrupt and all transactions are either complete or do not exist at all, rather than being ripped apart because a storage array knows nothing about the interdependence of blocks.

Synchronous Replication Using VVR

When VVR is set up for a disk group with an RLINK indicating **synchronous** replication, then all write I/O is acknowledged to the host only when the data is acknowledged by the remote host. Loss of data is now considered impossible even if a disaster destroys the site, as it is unlikely that the remote site fails at the same time. The latency from waiting for a remote machine to reply to the replicated I/O is incurred. But because VVR transmits all write I/Os transactionally and guarantees write order fidelity, there is no general need to wait for an acknowledgement of the first block before transmitting the next, the way that storage arrays need to in the synchronous transfer case. VVR can instead put as many transactions on the wire as possible and saturate the remote connection, provided the database and the application that drives it is sufficiently parallelized.

Technical Deep Dive

8.3 ESTIMATING REPLICATION SPEED

In order to calculate the maximum speed of a synchronous replication process over any significant distance it is important to first gain some understanding of the physical principles that underlie the process as well as a little more about transactions and storage arrays. We have learned above that storage array replication has no means of knowing which I/Os (from the storage array's perspective) belong together, so the array must transfer all blocks strictly in order or it will break the transaction paradigm (and you do **not** want that)! Now here comes another stepping stone to high-speed synchronous storage array replication: There is the possibility that the transfer of a block is unsuccessful and must be repeated, i.e. a block that had been sent before must be sent again because there was some kind of error happening on the way.

If it were the case that a storage array which synchronously replicates its LUNs replicated write I/Os – in the correct order because they would be useless otherwise – at full speed without waiting for an acknowledgement from the remote storage array, then the following might happen:

A block that had been transmitted towards the beginning turns out to have a bad checksum, so it must be resent by the originating storage array, The recipient storage array accordingly sends a message to the active storage array requesting a retransmission of said block. However, before that request is fulfilled, disaster strikes and the request is lost. The recipient site is now stuck with a stream of transactional data which may already have been persisted to disk, but of which a part is missing! This is a completely inacceptable situation! It has falsified our data; the database might not start up, or in could be corrupt in such a way that some large financial transaction was undone or repeated.

It would be theoretically possible to implement a protocol on the storage array level that kept track of not only write sequence, but also transmission state, and that would persist only those blocks to the remote site that have been successfully received, and persist them in the right order. Then, when a block must be retransmitted, the protocol on the recipient would no longer continue persisting data to disk until the block has been successfully resent, and then it would persist all of the blocks it has received so far – again, in the right order. But that protocol is loaded with overhead and it is not immediately clear what cleanup procedures would be necessary in the case of multiple transmission and retransmission errors etc. In short, as far as we know no array vendor has so far come up with a protocol that actually works synchronously without having to wait for acknowledgement from the remote site before sending the next block for the same LUN or LUN group.

We can therefore safely assume that a storage array will only put one write I/O per LUN and per connection on the wire at any one time.

Given this background, one may ask what the latency and the resulting bandwidth my turn out to be. The answer to this question is usually quite devastating, at least when replication is done across distances that are worthwhile, i.e. in the range of tens or hundreds of kilometers or more. This is where the speed of light really becomes an unexpected bottleneck, and you will see – in a few simple calculations – why this is the case.

Basic Physical Constants and Laws

The speed of light is just a little below 300 000 km/sec in vacuum. In a glass fibre the speed must be adjusted by the refractive index of the medium, yielding about two-thirds that, or 200 000 km/sec. While this sounds like a lot, hundreds of thousands of kilometers every second, keep in mind how many cycles a processor running at a measly 1 GHz goes through in a second: 1 billion! So on one hand there is light passing us at two hundred million metres per second through a fibre link, while the processor works so fast that it executes several cycles for each metre of the passing stream of light.

This comparison may seem a little weird at first, but you will understand why we chose it: It has enabled us to make a useful comparison between cycle speed and distance! If you consider an optical light module (OLM, or GBIC) that modulates its bit stream at one GHz onto the laser light for transfer to a remote site, then it will actually create bits that have a length of one-fifth of a metre. This is because at one GHz there are five cycles executed (i.e. five bits processed) while light is travelling one metre. So in effect, one can say that a bit in a fibre-channel has a length of 20cm.

Now comes the surprising and depressing part: if at one GHz a bit is 20cm, then a byte is eight times that (160cm), and a fibre-channel packet is 2112 times the length of a byte. One byte at 1.6 metres times 2112 bytes per fibre-channel packet is just shy of 3.4 km.

If you are using a synchronous storage array replication protocol and your remote site happens to be 34 km away, and you remember the fact that a packet must first be acknowledged before its successor can be sent (see The Full Battleship above for an explanation of this) then that means that a packet must in effect travel twice the 34 km (once forth, once back as an ACK), and the data is only 3.4 km long. This means your theoretical maximum speed is 3.4 km divided by 68 km, which is exactly 5% of the burst transfer rate.

And increasing the channel speed does not help either: It does not make the packet cross the distance any faster, it just shortens the length of the packet. So while the burst speed goes up, your efficiency drops by almost exactly the same amount!

There is no way to speed this up but to use a protocol that does not need to wait for acknowledgement, and such a protocol is inherently instable when implemented only inside storage arrays because they do not know about write order and block interdependence.

However, there is a workaround that alleviates the situation to some extent. It does not go all the way to deliver a perfect solution, but it at least abates some of the worst problems: the use of so-called Buffer-to-Buffer Credits, or more shortly Buffer Credits.

Buffer Credits vs. TCP–type Sliding Windows

We have outlined above that acknowledging every single packet on the application layer is not an option when crossing large distances. But large distances are a requirement for many data centers, so there must be a way to bridge them more efficiently. That is what the system of using buffer credits has been developed for. It is a little like TCP/IP's sliding window protocol, but is both more efficient and more error-prone than that. We will refer to the TCP sliding window occasionally for comparison, so let's reiterate shortly what it does: At the initiation of a connection the participants negotiate how many packets will be allowed to be sent without waiting for acknowledgement from the recipient. The number of packets is called the size of the sliding window. A solid value would be 64, for instance. During communication the sender numbers the packets and sends them away until the sliding window is exhausted. Normally the recipient will acknowledge packets as they arrive. But for performance reasons (all this must be handled in software inside the TCP stack) the recipient batches the acknowledgements, so that the sender will see, for example, an ACK after (let's say) every ten packets. The ACK packet contains the sequence number of the last packet that was received, so that the sender, in turn, can now send up to the sliding window size above that packet sequence number.

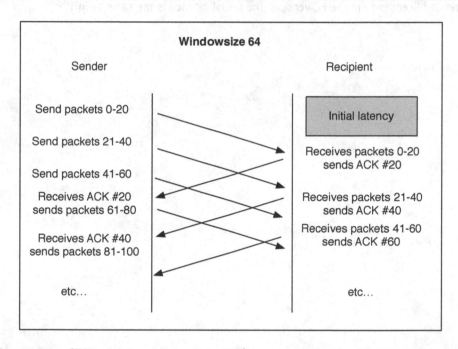

Figure 8-12:   Sliding windows as used in TCP/IP are endpoint-to-endpoint
protocol features. They are slower than node-to-node protocol
features, but provide reliable end-to-end communication.

This protocol is very efficient for large transfers, because once it has overcome its initial latency the data can be transmitted at close to wire speed. The braking factor here is the protocol processing overhead, which may be OK in end-to-end communication, but would be prohibitive to have inside the switching nodes of a SAN fabric. Too much state to keep track of, too much processing and interpreting sequence numbers in ACK packets etc.

Fibre-channel uses a more simplistic approach, because it must be implemented in hardware. In the FC approach, every block is acknowledged, but because it must be done as rapidly as possible (the ports need to be freed to handle "real" data) the acknowledgement only signals reception of "one block". No sequence number is transmitted in the ACK; that would require inspection of the packet contents, which would cause too much overhead.

Acknowledgements are called R_RDY for "receiver ready" in FC.

In order to enable the sender to put a number of packets on the wire at once, the ports of a fabric are given so-called buffer credits. The remaining buffer credits are decremented every time a packet is sent, and incremented every time an ACK is received. So a sender can send as many packets as he own buffer credits; eight buffer credits is a typical number today. Going back to our calculation above, this correlates to a stretch of eight times 3.4km at one GHz. But because the ACK must travel the same distance, the actual distance must be halved. So we end up at roughly 14km distance that could be traversed at full speed with eight buffer credits. Longer distances require more buffer credits and sometimes extended licenses from the FC vendors. The initial latency is the same as in TCP.

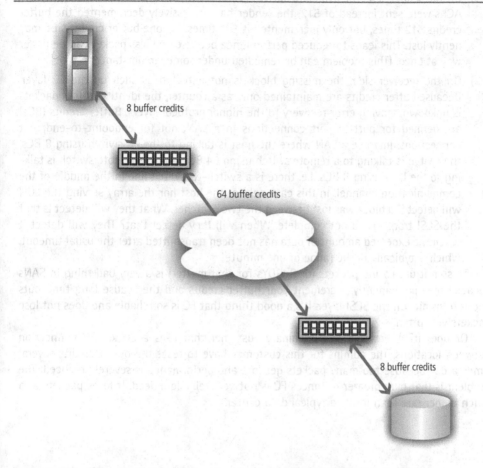

8 buffer credits

64 buffer credits

8 buffer credits

Figure 8-13: This picture shows a wide-area connection between host and disk. The connection consists of several legs: host HBA to SAN switch, SAN switch to remote SAN switch, and remote SAN switch to storage array port. Buffer credits are assigned port-to-port rather than endpoint-to-endpoint. They can be implemented with very little overhead, but do not offer good protection because the endpoints are not notified when credits are lost between two intermediate ports.

With this fine protocol, what can go wrong? Actually, a lot can go wrong! For instance, let's look at a SCSI I/O transmitted over an FC link. The total transfer is supposed to be 1 MB, which will be appropriately split into 512 packets of 2 KB each. Within any infrastructure there is a certain probability that individual packets get lost. That probability is normally very low, so that we do not generally need to think about it. But let's, for the sake of the argument, assume that one of the 512 packets gets lost and is therefore not acknowledged to the sender. The result is two-fold:

1) On the sender side, the available buffer credits are reduced by one. Because only 511 ACKs were sent instead of 512, the sender has successively decremented the buffer credits 512 times, but only incremented it 511 times. I.e. one buffer credit is permanently lost. This leads to reduced performance because one less packet can be under way at once. (This problem can be remedied under some circumstances)

2) On the receiver side, the missing block is not detected as such by the FC layer. Because buffer credits are maintained only as a counter, the identity of lost packets is unknown, leaving error recovery to the higher protocol layers. Buffer credits (BCs) are defined for port-to-port connections in a SAN, not for endpoint-to-endpoint connections. Imagine a SAN where the host is talking to the FC switch using 8 BCs, the switch is talking to a remote switch using 64 BCs, and the remote switch is talking to the LUN using 8 BCs. I.e. there is a switch-to-switch line in the middle of the communication channel. In this case neither the host nor the array serving the LUN will detect if a block was lost between the two switches. What they will detect is that the SCSI transfer did not complete. When will they detect that? They will detect it when the expected amount of data has not been transmitted after the usual timeout, which is typically in the range of one minute!

To sum it up: Losing packets (or R_RDYs for that matter) is a very bad thing in SANs because they permanently decrement your buffer credits and they cause long time-outs and retransmits on the SCSI layer. It's a good thing that FC is so reliable and does not lose packets very often.

Or does it? There is a non-imaginary customer that uses a 30 km FC connection between locations. The admins for this customer have to reset the buffer credits several times a day because too many packets get lost and performance is severely reduced. The problem is that over greater distances FC is not very reliable indeed. It loses packets at a much higher rate than inside a typical data center.

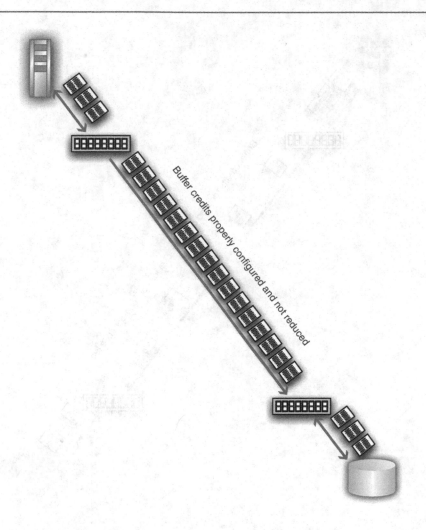

Buffer credits properly configured and not reduced

Figure 8-14:   If buffer credits are configured for the appropriate number of
packets that fit onto each leg, then bandwidth can be saturated.

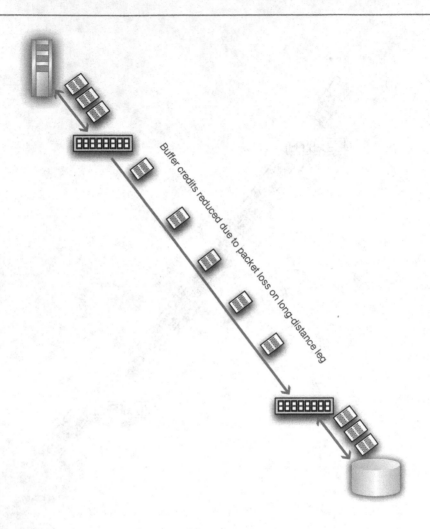

Figure 8-15: If buffer credits are lost in an intermediate leg, the endpoints will not notice. Bandwidth on the leg that is affected by the reduced buffer credit count is reduced because less packets can be put onto the wire before buffer credits are exhausted.

We hinted towards a remedy for permanently losing buffer credits above. The FC standard actually has a credit recovery mechanism for lost R_RDYs and lost frames. But both ports on the link must support that standard before it can be enabled. The protocol for lost buffer credit recovery consists of special primitive frames that are sent after every n-th packet. The number of packets between two primitives is a fixed power of two that can be set between 2^0 and 2^{15}. If a port receives such a primitive frame it checks if the appropriate number of R_RDYs (or packets) have been sent, and if not, transmits them or simply increases its own buffer credits accordingly. It thus fixes the first part of the problem: the persistence of decreased buffer credits. It does not fix the SCSI timeout problem. And the first part is also not fixed unless compatible components are deployed, which (as you can see from the example customer) is not always the case. The worst problem may be the one that occurs when such special frame gets lost (low probability, but possibly high impact); we have not investigated any further into this matter yet.

More on buffer credits and buffer credit extenders for long-distance traffic can be found in several US patents, one of the more readable ones is 7352701. It can be accessed from many public patent access sites, e.g. here (check out the date of issue: it is not a joke):

```
http://www.patentstorm.us/patents/7352701/description.html
```

CHAPTER 9: POINT IN TIME COPIES (SNAPSHOTS)

by Dr. Albrecht Scriba

9.1 OVERVIEW

Several tasks, like backups or lengthy data analysis jobs, require a frozen image of the application data while the application remains online and produces new data. For instance, reporting needs a stable state of information to generate coherent and usable data. A data copy must be sent to a testing data center with a specified time stamp. Or, as another example, you could wish to create backup images that require a reduced amount of recovery complexity after a restore operation (see notes below).

9.1.1 TYPES OF SNAPSHOTS

Veritas Storage Foundation provides several techniques to create a "frozen image" copy (also called "snapshot" or "point in time copy") of the current data set with different concepts, advantages, and disadvantages. Some techniques create the snapshot on the raw device, i.e. the volume layer, working with all data structures stored on the device: ufs, vxfs or other file systems, mounted or unmounted, tablespaces on the raw device itself, and so on. These can be referred to as volume-based snapshots.

V. Herminghaus and A. Sriba, *Storage Management in Data Centers*,
DOI: 10.1007/978-3-540-85023-6_9, © Springer-Verlag Berlin Heidelberg 2009

On the other side, the Veritas File System contains two mechanisms to create a file system based snapshot. These are file system-based snapshots, and the correct term in the Veritas world is "storage checkpoint".

Another way to classify snapshot procedures is by the expression pair physical – logical. A **physical** snapshot not only looks like a complete snapshot of all data, it is actually a complete copy of the data set. The advantage of a physical snapshot is its capability to be exported to another host without losing its snapshot function. I/O to the snapshot accesses only the snapshot device, the still running application based on the original device does not suffer performance degradation from snapshot I/O. On the other hand, as a disadvantage, the physical snapshot requires storage for a complete copy, and it takes remarkable time to synchronize its data from the original when created or refreshed.

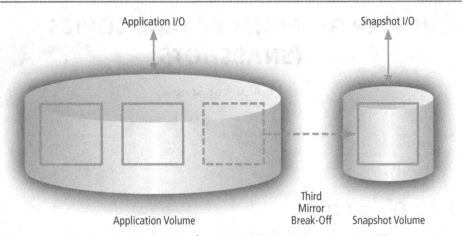

Figure 9-1: Physical raw device volume snapshot ("Third Mirror Break-Off")

A **logical** snapshot must simulate a complete snapshot, it only looks like, but it is not a complete frozen data copy. The underlying technique always combines two ways of accessing data through the snapshot. Data still unchanged since the creation of the snapshot are read from the original device, the snapshot device only points to the corresponding regions of the original device. In other words: An unchanged data set physically exists only once, but is accessed by both the original device and the snapshot. If the application wants to modify its data, the logical snapshot needs to store the original version of the data to be modified, before the new data set can be written to the application device (this is called "copy on first write", sometimes "copy before write" or "copy on write"). Apparently, the logical snapshot needs physical storage as well, but only in an amount sufficient to store the originals of application data modified since the creation and until the planned destruction of the snapshot. A logical snapshot therefore serves much better for temporarily limited tasks, such as backups or data transfers to another location. Furthermore, the concept of pointers to the original data set when creating a logical snapshot ensures, that the snapshot is available immediately. Note as a disadvantage of a logical snapshot its ongoing binding to the original device, snapshot I/Os are in many cases I/Os actually on the original device degrading application performance, and its physical export to a different host for offhost processing is impossible.

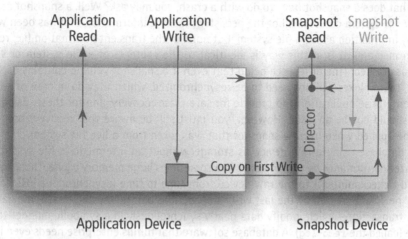

Figure 9-2:   Logical Snapshot

9.1.2   CONSISTENCY PROBLEMS FOR SNAPSHOTS

If as the snapshot is taken while the application is running on the original device or file system, the snapshot does not provide a consistent copy from the application's point of view. This is because the snapshot, if it is taken from a live application's file system, is not fully consistent on its own, but only in combination with the application's internal state and the file system's buffer cache. But neither application state nor buffer cache become part of the snapshot. So we would need to either quiesce the application and unmount the file system, which is not usually desired), or use some magic to fix some or all of the inconsistencies of the snapshot later.

Two examples will illustrate the point:

If an application is based on a mounted file system, the file system state flag in the main super block is "active", signifying that the file system is not "clean" due to data blocks in the file system cache that have not yet been flushed to persistent storage. If the file system is not cleanly unmounted (e.g. the system crashes), the "active" state forces a file system check, otherwise the mount system call will refuse to mount the file system. A raw device snapshot taken from a mounted file system contains a raw copy of all device data, so its main super block carries the "active" flag. A file system based snapshot, on the other side, could perform an (automated) file system check on the snapshot data set after having created it, because this technique is aware of the existence of the file system. That is the "magic" we talked about above. But nevertheless, even with a checked snapshot file system, you only get a "clean" file system data set, not necessarily a clean application data set,

235

because application write I/Os storing application transactions could consist of several file system I/Os to different files. A file system snapshot does not know about the application's internal logic, so it cannot provide any "magic" here. Instead, we must rely on the application's ability to recover from a crash.

What does a snapshot have to do with a crash, you may ask? Well, a snapshot of a volume or file system contains all of the persistent (i.e. the information that has been written to disk) information about a file system, but none of the transient information (i.e. residing only in memory). It is in this way is identical to the contents of a file system or volume that has crashed. (The difference being that even if a snapshot volume contains of several plexes, these plexes will not need to be resynchronized, which they do in case of a crash.) Most enterprise applications do provide for safe crash recovery, and for these, using snapshots should not be an issue. However, you must still be aware that recovery procedures must be applied when using a snapshot that was taken from a live file system.

A database using a raw device as storage without an intermediate file system layer optimizes performance by caching data in a sometimes large memory cache. Those data are flushed ("checkpointed") to the raw device from time to time (asynchronous I/O). To avoid loss of new data created by the last write transactions before a system crash, the database writes transactions which modify data nearly synchronously in a symbolic manner to a log device (called the redo-log). A database software that fulfills enterprise needs even in case of a crash must replay all synchronously stored transactions to the asynchronously flushed database structure starting from the point of the last database checkpoint.

Now assume a snapshot taken from an online database: the database structure and the transaction log do not carry the same timestamp, indicating that recovery is needed before opening the database. Here, too, the database must apply its (crash) recovery procedure to roll the redo log forward, thus integrating the most recent changes into the database.

To sum up: As long as the snapshot mechanism does not provide full application awareness including application recovery strategies, it cannot create a consistent snapshot of the data set of a running application. To actually get a consistent point in time copy, you must cleanly stop the application and, if based on a file system, unmount it before taking the snapshot. This limitation is valid under all circumstances: whether using software or hardware volume management, because they both suffer from the split between transient information in the kernel and persistent information on disk.

One way to overcome this limitation is to integrate the kernel buffer cache and application memory into the snapshot layer. This can only be done in a virtualized environment, in which the snapshot software can – at least theoretically – cooperate with the virtualization software to flush the relevant memory pages into the snapshot when it is taken and therefore maintain a higher level of data integrity. But storage management for virtualized hosts is only evolving now, and there is not much experience available yet.

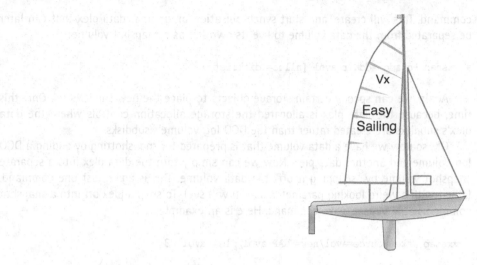

9.2 PHYSICAL RAW DEVICE SNAPSHOTS

9.2.1 OVERVIEW

A physical snapshot requires an extra copy of the volume data or, in terms of VxVM objects, an extra synchronized plex within the volume. Like all complete plex synchronization processes, this means a lot of I/O with system and application performance drawbacks and a certain amount of time (current hardware does around 1 GB per minute). Repeating that for every backup every day sounds rather wasteful, and it is.

In order to overcome both the complexities of creating new mirrors and separating them from their originals, then creating new volume objects

By the time VxVM 4.0 was being developed many new snapshot types and features had been developed and required elegant integration into the VxVM command structure. One of the most important older snapshot features (introduced in VxVM 3.2), the DCO ("data change object") with its data change log volume to dramatically improve snapback performance (explanation will follow), was made the default for all volume-based snapshots. Therefore, creation of another volume data copy for snapshot purposes should be prepared with an associated DCO log volume to get the full snapshot feature set. This is done using the **vxsnap prepare** command:

```
# vxsnap -g adg prepare avol [alloc=<disklist>]
```

We have now added a DCO log volume to our data volume. If we specified the alloc parameter with a list of storage objects (disks, controllers, enclosures, etc.), VxVM will have used only those storage objects to place the new DCO log volume's subdisks on.

In addition, VxVM has set some important internal variables to the appropriate values (e.g. the "fastresync" flag was set to "on"). But a new plex, a new instance of the data, has not been created yet. To create it, we issue another simple command, the **vxsnap addmir** command. This will create, and start synchronisation of, another data plex that can later be separated from the data volume to live its own life as a snapshot volume:

```
# vxsnap -g adg addmir avol [alloc=<disklist>]
```

Again, we can specify certain storage objects to place the new subdisks on. Only this time, because the data plex is allocated the storage allocation controls where the data plex's subdisks are created rather than the DCO log volume's subdisks.

OK, so now we have a data volume that is prepared for snapshotting by adding a DCO log Volume and another data plex. Now we can simply turn the data plex into a separate snapshot volume by "snapping it off" the data volume. This is again just one command, (albeit with a weird looking parameter, as you will see). To snap a plex off into a snapshot volume use the vxsnap make command. Here is an example:

```
# vxsnap make source=avol/new=SNAP-avol/plex=avol-03
```

This creates a volume which is separate from the source volume (source=avol), gives it the new name SNAP-avol (new=SNAP-avol) using the data plex avol-03 (plex=avol-03). You can now use that new volume, the SNAP-avol. It contains an exact copy of the data volume at the very moment the vxsnap make command was run. Be aware that file system and application data recovery is required which is equivalent to the recovery after a system crash (see introduction).

At any time you can refresh the contents of the snapshot volume using the vxsnap refresh command. The most common use for refreshing is to update a snapshot just before it is backed up. Here's an example for refreshing:

```
# vxsnap refresh SNAP-avol source=avol
```

All data blocks that have been changed in either the snapshot volume SNAP-avol or the original volume avol will be read from avol and copied into the appropriate regions in SNAP-avol by running the vxsnap refresh command.

Because data is copied to the target SNAP-avol at block level (i.e. into the raw device), it cannot be done while SNAP-avol is mounted, of course. Your file system device driver will say "thank you for not totally confusing me".

9.2.2   A Look at What Goes on Inside

In order to understand snapshots we need to reiterate what happens when we add another data plex to a mirrored volume. We assume you know what a mirrored volume looks like in the vxprint output, and start with the added mirror. Here's what you get:

```
# vxassist -g adg [-b] mirror avol [layout=<layout>] [<storage-attributes>]
# vxprint -rtg adg avol
[...]
v  avol        -            ENABLED ACTIVE  2097152 SELECT   -        fsgen
pl avol-01     avol         ENABLED ACTIVE  2097152 CONCAT   -        RW
sd adg01-01    avol-01      adg01   0       2097152 0        c1t1d0   ENA
```

238

```
pl avol-02       avol        ENABLED  ACTIVE  2097152  CONCAT   -        RW
sd adg02-01      avol-02     adg02    0       2097152  0        c1t1d1   ENA
pl avol-03       avol        ENABLED  ACTIVE  2097152  CONCAT   -        RW
sd adg03-01      avol-03     adg03    0       2097152  0        c1t1d2   ENA
```

Pretty simple and pretty obvious: a third plex was added, along with its subdisk, and that's it. Theoretically, we could now use the appropriate low-level commands for creating an empty volume object, and for disassociating the third plex from the original volume and attaching it into the newly created one. We would thus obtain a new volume initialized with the data contents of the original volume at the time that we disassociated the third plex. But doing so requires a lot of know-how about creating and handling low-level objects. So a long time ago Veritas created an easy to use front-end for creating snappable plexes. We could actually use this now deprecated form of snapshot commands which are subcommands to **vxassist**. For completeness, this legacy version will be covered in its own section later in this chapter. But because its interface and objects were developed over a long time the concepts are less easy to grasp than they are with the new approach which uses the new **vxsnap** command. So let us now jump way ahead in the development of VxVM and right into the most advanced snapshot mechanism in Volume Manager.

Let's first look at what happens when we prepare a volume for snapshotting:

```
# vxsnap prepare avol
# vxprint -rLtg adg avol
[...]
v  avol          -           ENABLED  ACTIVE  2097152  SELECT   -        fsgen
pl avol-01       avol        ENABLED  ACTIVE  2097152  CONCAT   -        RW
sd adg01-01      avol-01     adg01    0       2097152  0        c1t1d0   ENA
pl avol-02       avol        ENABLED  ACTIVE  2097152  CONCAT   -        RW
sd adg02-01      avol-02     adg02    0       2097152  0        c1t1d1   ENA
dc avol_dco      avol        avol_dcl

v  avol_dcl      -           ENABLED  ACTIVE  544      SELECT   -        gen
pl avol_dcl-01   avol_dcl    ENABLED  ACTIVE  544      CONCAT   -        RW
sd adg03-01      avol_dcl-01 adg03    0       544      0        c1t1d2   ENA
pl avol_dcl-02   avol_dcl    ENABLED  ACTIVE  544      CONCAT   -        RW
sd adg01-02      avol_dcl-02 adg01    2097152 544      0        c1t1d0   ENA
```

This command added some new VxVM objects with funny names. In particular, a tiny volume was created, with the name avol_dcl. The name DCL stands for "Data Change Log". It is a log that keeps track of changes to a volume. However it does not store the actual data but just sets the appropriate bit in a multi-column bitmap corresponding to the region in the data volume that incurred a change. Because the volume needs to update the DCL bitmap when it writes, the volume object must contain information pointing to the DCL volume. This pointer is the "dc" object that was added to the volume (last line of the avol output).

This sounds rather confusing so let's draw the output into an image that is probably easier to understand. We will skip the plex internal structures, i.e. the subdisks. Their grouping within the plex is irrelevant for nearly all snapshot features.

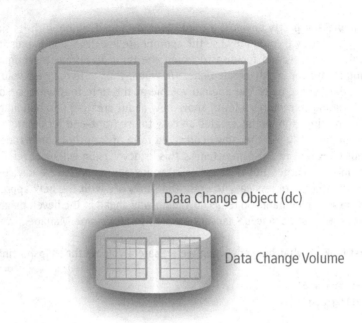

Data Change Object (dc)

Data Change Volume

Figure 9-3:   Snapshot prepared application volume with Data Change Log
(DCL) volume linked by a Data Change Object (DCO)

OK, again: the application data volume (top) is linked to a very small volume (bottom) with two plexes. You will not find a device driver for the small volume, it only serves for VxVM internal purposes and does not contain any application data. Actually it contains a mirrored multi-column bitmap, which among other things logs regions of the top-level volume affected by write I/Os. Because each bit position in the multi-column bitmap corresponds to a large region in the data volume the plex is drawn as a grid. We will explain further details of the DCO in the "Full Battleship" and the "Technical Deep Dive" part.

We still need to add another plex to get a volume data instance for the snapshot. The command **vxsnap** provides a keyword to add a mirror to both the data volume (top) and DC log volume (bottom). We used that in the introduction of this chapter and will now look at what objects are created by it:

```
# vxsnap -g adg addmir avol [alloc=<disklist>]
# vxprint -rLtg adg avol
[...]
v  avol        -           ENABLED  ACTIVE  2097152  SELECT   -       fsgen
pl avol-01     avol        ENABLED  ACTIVE  2097152  CONCAT   -       RW
sd adg01-01    avol-01     adg01    0       2097152  0        c1t1d0  ENA
```

pl avol-02	avol	ENABLED	ACTIVE	2097152	CONCAT	-	RW
sd adg02-01	avol-02	adg02	0	2097152	0	c1t1d1	ENA
pl avol-03	**avol**	**ENABLED**	**SNAPDONE**	**2097152**	**CONCAT**	**-**	**WO**
sd adg03-02	**avol-03**	**adg03**	**544**	**2097152**	**0**	**c1t1d2**	**ENA**
dc avol_dco	avol	avol_dcl					
v avol_dcl	-	ENABLED	ACTIVE	544	SELECT	-	gen
pl avol_dcl-01	avol_dcl	ENABLED	ACTIVE	544	CONCAT	-	RW
sd adg03-01	avol_dcl-01	adg03	0	544	0	c1t1d2	ENA
pl avol_dcl-02	avol_dcl	ENABLED	ACTIVE	544	CONCAT	-	RW
sd adg01-02	avol_dcl-02	adg01	2097152	544	0	c1t1d0	ENA
pl avol_dcl-03	**avol_dcl**	**DISABLED**	**DCOSNP**	**544**	**CONCAT**	**-**	**RW**
sd adg02-02	**avol_dcl-03**	**adg02**	**2097152**	**544**	**0**	**c1t1d1**	**ENA**

Application and DC log volume simply acquired another plex. Furthermore, note the difference in the application state (SNAPDONE) and in the access mode of the new top-level volume plex (WO = write-only) compared to the standard vxassist mirror command above. SNAPDONE only means, that the plex is marked for snapshot, its write-only access does not modify the regular read policy of the volume. The corresponding DC log volume plex is in DISABLED kernel state (no I/O possible, explanation see below in the latter sections of this chapter) and DCOSNP state, which marks the plex in the same manner as the SNAPDONE state of the top-level volume plex for snapshot purposes.

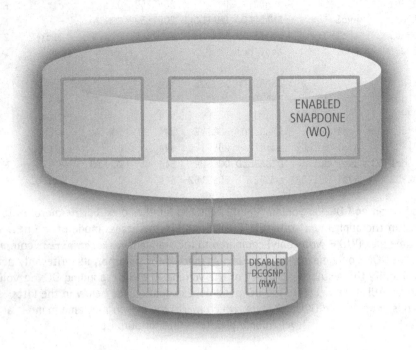

Figure 9-4:   Snapshot Prepared Application Volume with Data Change Log
Volume and Third Mirror

Currently the snapshot plex is still a full member of the volume except for read access
from the plex being prohibited – the snapshot plex remains WO, or write-only. But its data
changes synchronously with the other plexes. In other words: This plex is still live, it is not
yet a snapshot but is only prepared to become a snapshot. To actually create the snapshot,
to split it from the data volume, we need to enter a somewhat weird-looking command (we
will explain the strange slash-separated parameter syntax later):

```
# vxsnap -g adg make source=avol/new=SNAP-avol/plex=avol-03
# vxprint -rLtg adg
[...]
v  SNAP-avol      -              ENABLED  ACTIVE  2097152  ROUND    -        fsgen
pl avol-03        SNAP-avol      ENABLED  ACTIVE  2097152  CONCAT   -        RW
sd adg03-02       avol-03        adg03    544     2097152  0        c1t1d2   ENA
dc SNAP-avol_dco  SNAP-avol      SNAP-avol_dcl

v  SNAP-avol_dcl -               ENABLED  ACTIVE  544      ROUND    -        gen
pl avol_dcl-03   SNAP-avol_dcl   ENABLED  ACTIVE  544      CONCAT   -        RW
sd adg02-02      avol_dcl-03     adg02    2097152 544      0        c1t1d1   ENA
sp avol_snp      SNAP-avol       SNAP-avol_dco
```

```
v  avol          -              ENABLED  ACTIVE   2097152  SELECT   -       fsgen
pl avol-01       avol           ENABLED  ACTIVE   2097152  CONCAT   -       RW
sd adg01-01      avol-01        adg01    0        2097152  0        c1t1d0  ENA
pl avol-02       avol           ENABLED  ACTIVE   2097152  CONCAT   -       RW
sd adg02-01      avol-02        adg02    0        2097152  0        c1t1d1  ENA
dc avol_dco      avol           avol_dcl
v  avol_dcl      -              ENABLED  ACTIVE   544      SELECT   -       gen
pl avol_dcl-01   avol_dcl       ENABLED  ACTIVE   544      CONCAT   -       RW
sd adg03-01      avol_dcl-01    adg03    0        544      0        c1t1d2  ENA
pl avol_dcl-02   avol_dcl       ENABLED  ACTIVE   544      CONCAT   -       RW
sd adg01-02      avol_dcl-02    adg01    2097152  544      0        c1t1d0  ENA
sp SNAP-avol_snp avol           avol_dco
```

We already know that an easy understanding of snapshots at a glance is quite difficult. But once again, drawing an image based on the disturbing ASCII command output does help indeed. What happened when we split the snapshot from the data volume was this:

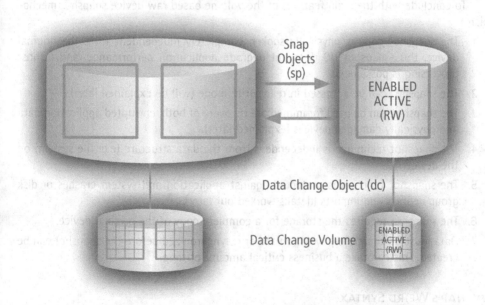

Figure 9-5: Application Volume with Split Snapshot Volume

Both plexes, the data plex (top) and the DC log volume plex formerly marked as SNAPDONE and DCOSNP respectively, have been broken off from their original volumes. They both changed their state to ACTIVE. Additionally the data plex changed to read-write access mode (RW) and the DC log plex changed its kernel state to ENABLED. Each was wrapped into a volume object. This was done to add application access to the snapshot volume (there are now device drivers for SNAP-avol in the /dev/vx/[r]dsk/adg directory) or to form a DC log volume. The DC log volume is linked to the snapshot data volume by a new DC object called SNAP-avol_dco (<snapvol>_dco in general) in the same manner we already mentioned for the running application volume. And finally, both data volumes are cross-linked by snap objects (type "sp" in the first column of the vxprint output) to enable the snapback procedure: the snapshot volume together with its associated DC log volume turns back into a synchronized member of the running application volume for further snapshot tasks (see the "Full Battleship" section below).

Note that without specifying storage attributes the snapshot volume and its associated DC log use subdisks placed on two different disks (here adg02 and adg03) and that the remaining original volume uses some of these disks as well (adg02 and adg03). This makes offhost snapshots impossible, as will be explained in the "Full Battleship" section.

The snapshot volume can be used just like any standard application volume: it can be mounted, accessed by another instance of the application, and so on. Its associated DC log volume ensures that write access to the snap volume is tracked and considered when snapping it back to the original volume or when refreshing the snapshot (any region that was modified in either the snapshot or the data volume needs be resynchronized). But snapping back and refreshing snapshots will be covered in the "Full Battleship" section.

To conclude with the main features of the volume based raw device snapshot mechanism:

1. The snapshot copy is physically spoken completely independent from the original device, thus snapshot I/O does not degrade application performance, and offhost processing is possible.

2. The snapshot can be accessed in read-write mode (will be explained later).

3. The snapshot can be used for immediate recovery of both, corrupted application data and physically damaged devices (explained later).

4. The snapshot technique is independent from the data structure (e.g. file system) on the device.

5. The snapshot function is protected against application and system crashes or disk group deports and imports (details worked out later).

6. The snapshot requires the storage for a complete copy of the original device.

7. Data must be completely synchronized or resynchronized before the snapshot can be created. This can take a business critical amount of time.

VXSNAP'S WEIRD SYNTAX

We promised earlier that we would explain the funny syntax on the vxsnap command line. Remember we had to cope with commands like this:

```
# vxsnap make source=avol/new=SNAP-avol/plex=avol-03
```

You may have thought "what were the developers smoking?" (or even: "I want some of the same stuff"!). But that would not be fair. They were actually being very smart people.

You see, creating a snapshot of a volume is easy, and would not require such funny slash-separated 3-tuples. However, what if you need to create snapshots of a great number of volumes, and they all need to be consistent with each other? You cannot rely on many snapshot commands simply executing in rapid succession and hope that there will be no inconsistencies. That would be totally inacceptable from an enterprise perspective.

Veritas' solution to this problem is to make the vxsnap command accept multiple snapshot volume source and destination tuples (triples in this case). Then, when the command is executed, they all snap at precisely the same point in time. In this case, consistency is guaranteed rather than approximated. While the cost of this approach is merely an atypical parameter format, its benefit is immeasurable.

9.2.3 A LOGICAL FILE SYSTEM SNAPSHOT

Another snapshot technique with a mostly inverted set of features compared to the above mentioned procedure is worth being explained in the Easy Sailing section: the legacy VxFS snapshot. It belongs to an older concept of snapshots and is not generally used in Veritas installations any more because VxFS offers vastly superior approaches today. However, most other common snapshots use a very similar concept. E.g. Solaris UFS snapshots or MS-Windows file system snapshots work on the same basis as the legacy snapshot file systems discussed here. They all share the huge drawback that they are not crash-proof, i.e. if the system holding the snapshot incurs a fault and crashes, the snapshot is lost and a new snapshot must be taken. While this does not sound too bad, keep in mind that this also means there is no way of ever getting the exact state of the file system back that we had at the time the snapshot had been initialized. This may well be a show-stopper for an enterprise evaluating snapshot mechanisms!

The technique is not only bound to the file system driver code, it is also a so-called logical snapshot, that is, unchanged data remains stored on the original device and is accessible by both the original device driver and the snapshot driver. Data that has been written, however, is first copied to the snapshot and subsequently overwritten on the original device. The snapshot device itself does not contain a complete file system, but just references: to the original data for all unchanged regions and to its own data store for the blocks that have been saved from the original before they were overwritten.

The physical snapshot device must provide storage capacity only for the originals of modified data (10% per day are sufficient in most cases).

As a data store for the snapshot file system you can use any device appropriate to serve as a base for VxFS (such as logical volumes of other software manufacturers, partitions, USB sticks, even RAM disks). Nevertheless, for our convenience in a Storage Foundation book, we choose Veritas volumes in the following explanation and demonstration.

First, we create the original device and file system, mount the latter and place a scratch file on it:

```
# vxassist make avol 1g layout=mirror init=active
# mkfs -F vxfs /dev/vx/rdsk/adg/avol
    version 7 layout
    2097152 sectors, 1048576 blocks of size 1024, log size 16384 blocks
```

```
    largefiles supported
# mount -F vxfs /dev/vx/dsk/adg/avol /mnt
# mkfile 10m /mnt/file0.10m
```

In order to create a VxFS snapshot, we need a considerably smaller cache device (we choose 10% of the original device, less than 5% are not supported). By mounting it with the special option -o snapof=<original-blockdevice>|<original-mountpoint>, we are telling the VxFS device driver to initialize the appropriate data structures and establish the snapshot; we do not need to place a VxFS on it before.

```
# vxassist make cacheavol 100m layout=mirror init=active
# mkdir /mnt_snap
```

Create the snapshot by using the original block device:

```
# mount -F vxfs -o snapof=/dev/vx/dsk/adg/avol \
  /dev/vx/dsk/adg/cacheavol /mnt_snap
```

Or, by using the original mount point (the result is identical):

```
# mount -F vxfs -o snapof=/mnt /dev/vx/dsk/adg/cacheavol /mnt_snap
# df -k /mnt*
Filesystem              kbytes   used   avail capacity  Mounted on
/dev/vx/dsk/adg/avol 1048576    27989 956808    3%      /mnt
/dev/vx/dsk/adg/cacheavol
                       1048576   27989 956801    3%      /mnt_snap
# ls -lA /mnt*
/mnt:
total 20480
-rw------T   1 root     root     10485760 Sep  6 18:04 file0.10m
drwxr-xr-x   2 root     root           96 Sep  6 17:57 lost+found

/mnt_snap:
total 20480
-rw------T   1 root     root     10485760 Sep  6 18:04 file0.10m
drwxr-xr-x   2 root     root           96 Sep  6 17:57 lost+found
```

As you can see, the original file system and its associated snapshot exactly *look* like two independent file systems on the surface. Do they also *behave* like independent file systems? Let's play a little bit:

```
# mkfile 10m /mnt/file1.10m
# df -k /mnt*
Filesystem              kbytes   used   avail capacity  Mounted on
/dev/vx/dsk/adg/avol 1048576    38229 947207    4%      /mnt
/dev/vx/dsk/adg/cacheavol
                       1048576   27989 956801    3%      /mnt_snap
```

```
# ls -lA /mnt*
/mnt:
total 40960
-rw------T   1 root     root        10485760 Sep  6 18:04 file0.10m
-rw------T   1 root     root        10485760 Sep  6 18:07 file1.10m
drwxr-xr-x   2 root     root              96 Sep  6 17:57 lost+found

/mnt_snap:
total 20480
-rw------T   1 root     root        10485760 Sep  6 18:04 file0.10m
drwxr-xr-x   2 root     root              96 Sep  6 17:57 lost+found
# rm /mnt/file0.10m
# df -k /mnt*
Filesystem             kbytes    used    avail capacity Mounted on
/dev/vx/dsk/adg/avol 1048576    27989  956808    3%     /mnt
/dev/vx/dsk/adg/cacheavol
                     1048576    27989  956801    3%     /mnt_snap
# ls -lA /mnt*
/mnt:
total 20480
-rw------T   1 root     root        10485760 Sep  6 18:07 file1.10m
drwxr-xr-x   2 root     root              96 Sep  6 17:57 lost+found

/mnt_snap:
total 20480
-rw------T   1 root     root        10485760 Sep  6 18:04 file0.10m
drwxr-xr-x   2 root     root              96 Sep  6 17:57 lost+found
# rm /mnt_snap/file0.10m
rm: /mnt_snap/file0.10m: override protection 600 (yes/no)? yes
rm: /mnt_snap/file0.10m not removed: Read-only file system
# rm -f /mnt_snap/file0.10m
# ls -lA /mnt_snap
total 2048
-rw------T   1 root     root        10485760 Sep  6 18:04 file0.10m
drwxr-xr-x   2 root     root              96 Sep  6 17:57 lost+found
```

Ok, as long as the snapshot file system is accessed in read mode, it seems to behave like an independent file system (we will see another exception below). Write access is blocked (the override question is misleading, the "force" option when removing a file always suppresses STDERR).

Once again, we conclude with the main features of the VxFS snapshot. Compared with the former conclusion to the physical raw device snapshot, the ordinals do correspond.

1. The logical snapshot copy is physically dependent on the original file system, thus degrading application performance: snapshot read I/Os on unchanged data are read from the original file system, and write I/Os on still unmodified data on the original file system force a copy-on-first-write. Offhost processing is not possible.

247

2. The logical snapshot can only be accessed in read-only mode.

3. The logical snapshot can be used for immediate recovery only of corrupted application data, not in case of physically damaged devices (explained later).

4. The logical snapshot method is bound to VxFS.

5. The logical snapshot function is destroyed after an unmount of the snapshot file system, even more in case of a system crash.

6. The logical snapshot requires, compared to the original device, only a small portion of storage.

7. No preparatory data synchronization is necessary (instead copy-on-first-write after snapshot creation), the logical snapshot is available immediately.

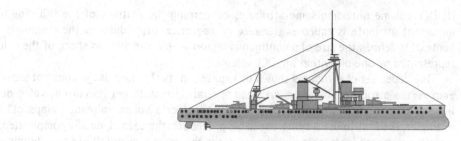

The Full Battleship

9.3 Features of and Improvements on the Raw Device Snapshot

9.3.1 Snapshot Region Logging by the Data Change Log

In the Easy Sailing section, we just described the structure of a volume prepared for a raw device snapshot (especially the Data Change Object "DCO" and the Data Change Log Volume "DCL"). But we did not explain, why we need all these strange objects to perform a snapshot operation. Actually, the `vxsnap make` command would fail without those additional objects. But, on the other side, the "Technical Deep Dive" section will indeed show a quite simple procedure to create a snapshot based only on a current data plex within the volume, thus without any further objects, logs, and so on, neither as VxVM objects nor as kernel structures. So why all this complicated DC stuff?

An intelligent snapshot mechanism should provide an optimized framework to serve tasks more elaborate than simply creating a frozen copy, using it once and then deleting or forgetting it completely. Some examples should illustrate that:

A snapshot could be used regularly, e.g. on a daily basis for backup purposes. Indeed, we could delete today's snapshot after having it used and recreate it completely from scratch tomorrow. But that would require full data synchronization every time the snapshot is created. Two major disadvantages readily come to mind: (1) the snapshot is never available immediately, and (2) we have an awful amount of unnecessary synchronization I/O degrading our system performance every time.

To approach the latter problem: why is synchronisation unnecessary? We could, physically spoken, skip an overwhelming portion of the synchronization, because most of our volume data did not change in the period between the previous and the current snapshot (the actual amount, of course, depends on the I/O behavior of the application). Currently, after having taken the previous snapshot, we do not have an appropriate object to log data changes. If the volume kept track of such changes, VxVM would know which regions to resynchronize and which to keep unmodified when "refreshing" the snapshot with the current data set.

This strongly desired log structure is represented by the Data Change Object (DCO) with its associated Data Change Log volume (DCL). The DCO links the application volume with its DCL volume providing some attributes concerning the features of the DCL. The most important attribute is called `regionsize` or `regionsz`, depending on the command line context. It defines the size of a contiguous region within the address space of the volume represented by one bit within the DCL volume.

The coded set of attributes shown by `vxprint` in its standard usage does not show the `regionsize` attribute. Therefore, we need special options to get its current value defining the bitmap structure of a snapshot "prepared" or a volume already "snapshot". Two examples, the first to use a comprehensible procedure, the second, deadly complicated, for scripting purposes (note, that `vxprint -e` needs the volume record ID `rid` to determine the associated DCO parent volume, not its name):

```
# vxprint -rLtg adg
[...]
v  avol          -             ENABLED  ACTIVE  2097152  SELECT   -       fsgen
pl avol-01       avol          ENABLED  ACTIVE  2097152  CONCAT   -       RW
sd adg01-01      avol-01       adg01    0       2097152  0        c1t1d0  ENA
pl avol-02       avol          ENABLED  ACTIVE  2097152  CONCAT   -       RW
sd adg02-01      avol-02       adg02    0       2097152  0        c1t1d1  ENA
dc avol_dco      avol          avol_dcl

v  avol_dcl      -             ENABLED  ACTIVE  544      SELECT   -       gen
pl avol_dcl-01   avol_dcl      ENABLED  ACTIVE  544      CONCAT   -       RW
sd adg03-01      avol_dcl-01   adg03    0       544      0        c1t1d2  ENA
pl avol_dcl-02   avol_dcl      ENABLED  ACTIVE  544      CONCAT   -       RW
sd adg01-02      avol_dcl-02   adg01    2097152 544      0        c1t1d0  ENA
# vxprint -g adg -F %regionsz avol_dco
128
# vxprint -g adg -cF %regionsz -e dco_parent_vol=$(vxprint -g adg -F %rid avol)
128
```

The number 128 stands, as usual, for 128 sectors, that is 64 kB. So, one bit within the DCL bitmap represents 64 kB within its data volume (as we have seen in the commands above, this volume is also called DCO parent volume, while the DCL volume is never called DCO child volume). If any amount of data within such a region is modified, its corresponding bit is set, marking that region's need for resynchronization. Given our example parent volume with its size of 1 GB (which comprises $16{,}384 = 2^{14}$ regions of 64 kB), we need 16,384 bits or 2,048 bytes or 2 kB space to form the region bitmap. But surprisingly, the bitmap volume is much larger in size (544 sectors = 272 kB). Well, one reason is, that the DCL volume contains a multi-function bitmap of 33 levels providing not only improved snapshot characteristics (see the "Technical Deep Dive" part). Furthermore, we need some "global", region independent attribute data. There may be still further explanations, but they are unknown to us, they are not officially documented.

If, for any reason, the region size must be different from the default, you can specify it. We mention the procedure to achieve it not only in order to introduce a new keyword of `vxsnap`, but also to show an interesting error message concerning the multi-function bitmap (explained later). The "restore" example below demonstrates that, under special conditions, the resynchronization I/O size depends on the region size. And, what is more, we urgently need it when creating full sized instant snapshots (see below).

```
# vxsnap -g adg unprepare avol
VxVM vxassist ERROR V-5-1-6169  Volume avol has drl attach to it, use -f option
to remove drl
# vxsnap -g adg -f unprepare avol
# vxprint -rtg adg
[...]
v  avol        -          ENABLED  ACTIVE  2097152  SELECT   -       fsgen
pl avol-01     avol       ENABLED  ACTIVE  2097152  CONCAT   -       RW
sd adg01-01    avol-01    adg01    0       2097152  0        c1t1d0  ENA
pl avol-02     avol       ENABLED  ACTIVE  2097152  CONCAT   -       RW
sd adg02-01    avol-02    adg02    0       2097152  0        c1t1d1  ENA
# vxsnap -g adg prepare avol regionsize=32
# vxprint -rLtg adg
[...]
v  avol        -          ENABLED  ACTIVE  2097152  SELECT   -       fsgen
pl avol-01     avol       ENABLED  ACTIVE  2097152  CONCAT   -       RW
sd adg01-01    avol-01    adg01    0       2097152  0        c1t1d0  ENA
pl avol-02     avol       ENABLED  ACTIVE  2097152  CONCAT   -       RW
sd adg02-01    avol-02    adg02    0       2097152  0        c1t1d1  ENA
dc avol_dco    avol       avol_dcl

v  avol_dcl    -          ENABLED  ACTIVE  1120     SELECT   -       gen
pl avol_dcl-01 avol_dcl   ENABLED  ACTIVE  1120     CONCAT   -       RW
sd adg03-01    avol_dcl-01 adg03   0       1120     0        c1t1d2  ENA
pl avol_dcl-02 avol_dcl   ENABLED  ACTIVE  1120     CONCAT   -       RW
sd adg01-02    avol_dcl-02 adg01   2097152 1120     0        c1t1d0  ENA
# vxprint -g adg -cF %regionsz -e dco_parent_vol=$(vxprint -g adg -F %rid avol)
32
```

Note the increased size of the DCL volume, because every 16 kB region is now mapped! Unlike our example, you should consider to increase the region size to get larger "restore" I/O sizes. Note also, that the flexible architecture of the bitmap is too "difficult" for the legacy vxdco command, use vxsnap instead.

To avoid too many confusing details now, we come back to our main question (DRL attributes and log version will follow): How can I make use of this logging feature, which should help to dramatically reduce the amount of data synchronization in case of a snapshot refresh? I only need to use another new keyword of vxsnap. The following example assumes a snapshot "prepared" volume (vxsnap prepare and vxsnap addmir already issued) and is surrounded by vxtrace and vxstat commands to demonstrate the effect:

```
# vxsnap -g adg make source=avol/newvol=SNAP-avol/plex=avol-03
# vxtrace -g adg -d /tmp/vxtrace.dump -o dev &
[1]     19003
# dd if=/dev/zero of=/dev/vx/rdsk/adg/avol bs=1024k count=4
```

```
4+0 records in
4+0 records out
# kill %1
[1] + Terminated              vxtrace -g adg -d /tmp/vxtrace.dump -o dev &
# vxtrace -g adg -f /tmp/vxtrace.dump -o dev
11 START write vdev avol block 0 len 2048 concurrency 1 pid 19037
11 END write vdev avol op 11 block 0 len 2048 time 2
12 START write vdev avol block 2048 len 2048 concurrency 1 pid 19037
12 END write vdev avol op 12 block 2048 len 2048 time 1
13 START write vdev avol block 4096 len 2048 concurrency 1 pid 19037
13 END write vdev avol op 13 block 4096 len 2048 time 1
14 START write vdev avol block 6144 len 2048 concurrency 1 pid 19037
14 END write vdev avol op 14 block 6144 len 2048 time 1
# vxtrace -g adg -d /tmp/vxtrace.dump -o all &
[1]      19049
# vxstat -g adg -r
# vxsnap -g adg reattach SNAP-avol source=avol
# kill %1
[1] + Terminated              vxtrace -g adg -d /tmp/vxtrace.dump -o all &
# vxtrace -g adg -f /tmp/vxtrace.dump -o all | grep atomic
78 START atomic_copy vol avol op 79 block 0 len 2048 nsrc 32 ndest 1
78 END atomic_copy vol avol op 79 block 0 len 2048 time 2
86 START atomic_copy vol avol op 87 block 2048 len 2048 nsrc 32 ndest 1
86 END atomic_copy vol avol op 87 block 2048 len 2048 time 1
94 START atomic_copy vol avol op 95 block 4096 len 2048 nsrc 32 ndest 1
94 END atomic_copy vol avol op 95 block 4096 len 2048 time 1
102 START atomic_copy vol avol op 103 block 6144 len 2048 nsrc 32 ndest 1
102 END atomic_copy vol avol op 103 block 6144 len 2048 time 2
# vxstat -g adg -f ab
```

		ATOMIC COPIES			READ-WRITEBACK	
TYP NAME	OPS	BLOCKS	AVG(ms)	OPS	BLOCKS	AVG(ms)
vol avol	4	8192	12.0	0	0	0.0
vol avol_dcl	0	0	0.0	0	0	0.0

Indeed, it works! Instead of a full resynchronization, only those volume blocks are resynchronized which were previously overwritten by the dd command. It is, by the way, completely accidental that the I/O size of the dd command is identical to that of the resynchronization thread: 2,048 sectors = 1,024 kB = 1 MB. This is the Atomic Copy default, a snap "reattach" is indeed a plex attach, vxtask list would show the I/O type ATCOPY within the operation PLXSNAP. We simply have chosen 1 MB for dd to get corresponding numbers in both vxtrace outputs.

So we have solved one major disadvantage of a physical snapshot: Only data modified since the snapshot was taken are rewritten to the reattached snapshot plex. Not only is the amount of synchronization I/O dramatically reduced together with a lower system load. Furthermore, the plex marked for snapshot purposes becomes available for the next snapshot quite a lot faster. A few pages later, we will learn another procedure to really immediately bring the snapshot to the current data state (at least it looks and behaves so).

But now, we will first turn to another feature of the raw device snapshot.

9.3.2 Reverting the Resynchronization Direction

It should not happen, but it could happen that, while the snapshot still exists, the original device becomes unusable, either by hardware failures or by corrupted (application) data: lost files or database tables, invalid values, patches of the sort "hot destroy" instead of "hot fix". Note that volume redundancy does not protect against the latter scenario! Our best copy of volume data is most likely provided by the snapshot. Of course, in case of a disk outage, we need to recover disks and disk group first. Under normal conditions, the synchronization is directed by VxVM from the ENABLED/ACTIVE plexes (not by the volume layer) to the snapshot plex, which will become a member of the original volume once again. In this special case, we need a reversed synchonization direction: the original plexes with I/O fail or damaged data enter the STALE state (that's why the application access must be stopped first), the "snapbacked" plex forms the single current volume address space (at this stage, the application could already be restarted!), and finally, the synchronization thread is started from the volume based on the latter plex to the stale ones.

```
# vxsnap -g adg make source=avol/new=SNAP-avol/plex=avol-03
# dd if=/dev/zero of=/dev/vx/rdsk/adg/avol bs=1024k count=4
4+0 records in
4+0 records out
# vxstat -g adg -r
# vxsnap -g adg restore avol source=SNAP-avol destroy=yes
# vxstat -g adg -vp
```

		OPERATIONS		BLOCKS		AVG TIME(ms)	
TYP	NAME	READ	WRITE	READ	WRITE	READ	WRITE
vol	avol	0	0	0	0	0.0	0.0
pl	avol-01	0	64	0	8192	0.0	8.0
pl	avol-02	0	64	0	8192	0.0	7.7
pl	avol-03	65	0	8208	0	2.2	0.0
vol	avol_dcl	0	0	0	0	0.0	0.0
pl	avol_dcl-01	18	29	258	434	0.0	1.0
pl	avol_dcl-02	0	29	0	434	0.0	1.0
pl	avol_dcl-03	6	5	96	80	1.7	8.0

The testing scenario resembles the former one (we skipped vxtrace, its output would be too long). Five remarks:

1. The source keyword in the latter vxsnap command does not indicate the original volume, but the snapshot volume, thus specifying the synchronization/"restore" direction.

2. Physical synchronization may be omitted by adding syncing=no, the application volume would be restored "logically" (see logical snapshots below for further details).

3. Without destroy=yes (or with destroy=no), the snapshot volume would remain a separate volume (this is the reverted equivalent to vxsnap refresh explained

253

below).

4. The I/O sizes are smaller compared to a `reattach` resynchronization: 8,192 sectors = 4,096 kB in 64 I/Os correspond an I/O size of 64 kB, which is our default DCO region size. `vxtask list` would show the I/O type SNAPSYNC within the operation SNAPSYNC. We have smaller granularity for resynchronization, but the main I/O strategy remains identical.

5. Don't ask us, why the source plex was read one I/O in addition, we do not know the answer.

9.3.3 THE SNAP OBJECTS

Another new object type related to snapshots needs further investigation, the snap object ("sp") linking the snapshot volume to its original volume and vice-versa. Why do we need them? The first observation: In case of the keywords `reattach`, `restore`, and `refresh`, the command `vxsnap` would fail without the `source` volume keyword and a specified (target) volume. The second observation, seemingly contradictory: We will demonstrate a procedure to instantly create a snapshot relation between previously independent volumes a few pages later. To conclude, the snap objects mark the volumes as members of a snapshot interconnection (called "chain"), thus prohibiting their inadvertently snap `unprepare` or volume destruction:

```
# vxsnap -g adg unprepare SNAP-avol
VxVM vxsnap ERROR V-5-1-6170   Volume SNAP-avol is in snapshot chain
# vxassist -g adg remove volume SNAP-avol
VxVM vxassist ERROR V-5-1-10127 deleting volume SNAP-avol:
       Record is associated
```

Warning: The snap objects do not protect against the `vxedit -rf rm` command, in spite of the manual page to `vxsnap dis`! The snapshot volume would be destroyed together with all snap objects, leaving the original volume in the snap "prepared" state (and vice-versa).

But the most important function of the snap objects is to indicate, that the intelligent DC log is ready for use in case of snapshot `reattach`, `restore`, and `refresh`. Without snap objects, it is possible to create or recreate a snapshot relation between the two data volumes (full sized instant snapshot), but any synchronization task would mean 100 percent synchronization.

How does the snap object identify its source and its target volume? The `vxprint -t` command does not show any appropriate attributes, only the location of the `sp` object under the DCL volume, and the naming convention indicates source and target (which is not a must, as we know). Other options (`-1, -A, -a, -m`) print two snap object attributes: GUIDs unmistakably identifying the source (attribute name "vol_guid") and the target volume ("snapshot_vol_guid"). The `-F` option allows to specify a desired output format, as given in the following example:

```
# vxprint -g adg -cF 'snapobject %name: source=%vol_guid '\
  'target=%snapshot_vol_guid'
object SNAP-avol_dco: source=- target=-
object avol_dco: source=- target=-
object SNAP-avol_snp: source={71840bae-1dd2-11b2-88f6-0003ba07fc88}
target={78b99146-1dd2-11b2-88ed-0003ba07fc88}
object avol_snp: source={78b99146-1dd2-11b2-88ed-0003ba07fc88} target={71840bae-
1dd2-11b2-88f6-0003ba07fc88}
```

Note: The first two lines of the output belong to the data change objects linking the data volumes to their DCL volume. The option -c cannot differentiate between snap objects and DC objects. Note also, that the literal expression "snapobject" at the beginning of the argument to the -F option was shortened to "object" as a result of an internal programming error of vxprint.

Well, the identification by GUIDs indeed is unique, but it is quite unreadable for us. The Shell with its powerful capabilities (here: loops, conditionals, command substitution) allows us to generate a quite unreadable expression, but the output is of the sort we like to see:

```
# printf '%-15s %-15s %s\n' SNAP_OBJECT SOURCE TARGET; \
  vxprint -g adg -cF '%type %name %vol_guid %snapshot_vol_guid' |
  while read Type Name VGuid SVGuid; do
  [[ $Type == sp ]] || continue
  printf '%-15s %-15s %s\n' $Name \
  $(vxprint -g adg -vne v_guid=$VGuid) \
  $(vxprint -g adg -vne v_guid=$SVGuid)
  done
SNAP_OBJECT      SOURCE         TARGET
SNAP-avol_snp    avol           SNAP-avol
avol_snp         SNAP-avol      avol
```

Fortunately, vxsnap itself provides a powerful keyword to print snapshot information. We show two examples:

```
# vxsnap -g adg print
NAME    SNAPOBJECT      TYPE    PARENT    SNAPSHOT    %DIRTY    %VALID

avol       --           volume  --        --          --        100.00
        SNAP-avol_snp   volume  --        SNAP-avol   0.00      --

SNAP-avol avol_snp      volume  avol      --          0.00      100.00
```

The relation of the snap objects to the source and target volumes is printed together with "dirty" and "valid" percentage (explained later).

```
# vxsnap -g adg -n print
NAME        DG        OBJTYPE SNAPTYPE PARENT    PARENTDG   SNAPDATE
```

```
avol        adg        vol      -        -        -        - -
SNAP-avol   adg        vol      mirbrk   avol     adg      2008/09/14 08:54
```

This command does not show the names of the snap objects, but, besides the relation of original and snapshot volume, the snapshot type ("mirror break", we will learn another type later) and, quite important, the snapshot date, i.e. the date the snapshot plex was dissociated from the original volume.

The keyword list of vxsnap produces nearly the same output and may be skipped for further investigation.

9.3.4 CLEARING THE SNAPSHOT RELATION

Sometimes you could decide to never again bring back the snapshot volume to its original location, e.g. you want to go on with your application in the test location for an undefined period. It would simplify the administration to cut off the snapshot interconnection:

```
# vxprint -rLtg adg
[...]
v  SNAP-avol     -              ENABLED  ACTIVE  2097152  ROUND    -        fsgen
pl avol-03       SNAP-avol      ENABLED  ACTIVE  2097152  CONCAT   -        RW
sd adg03-02      avol-03        adg03    544     2097152  0        c1t1d2   ENA
dc SNAP-avol_dco SNAP-avol      SNAP-avol_dcl

v  SNAP-avol_dcl -              ENABLED  ACTIVE  544      ROUND    -        gen
pl avol_dcl-03   SNAP-avol_dcl  ENABLED  ACTIVE  544      CONCAT   -        RW
sd adg02-02      avol_dcl-03    adg02    2097152 544      0        c1t1d1   ENA
sp avol_snp      SNAP-avol      SNAP-avol_dco


v  avol          -              ENABLED  ACTIVE  2097152  SELECT   -        fsgen
pl avol-01       avol           ENABLED  ACTIVE  2097152  CONCAT   -        RW
sd adg01-01      avol-01        adg01    0       2097152  0        c1t1d0   ENA
pl avol-02       avol           ENABLED  ACTIVE  2097152  CONCAT   -        RW
sd adg02-01      avol-02        adg02    0       2097152  0        c1t1d1   ENA
dc avol_dco      avol           avol_dcl

v  avol_dcl      -              ENABLED  ACTIVE  544      SELECT   -        gen
pl avol_dcl-01   avol_dcl       ENABLED  ACTIVE  544      CONCAT   -        RW
sd adg03-01      avol_dcl-01    adg03    0       544      0        c1t1d2   ENA
pl avol_dcl-02   avol_dcl       ENABLED  ACTIVE  544      CONCAT   -        RW
sd adg01-02      avol_dcl-02    adg01    2097152 544      0        c1t1d0   ENA
sp SNAP-avol_snp avol           avol_dco

# vxsnap -g adg dis SNAP-avol
# vxprint -rLtg adg
[...]
```

```
v  SNAP-avol       -             ENABLED  ACTIVE  2097152  ROUND   -        fsgen
pl avol-03         SNAP-avol     ENABLED  ACTIVE  2097152  CONCAT  -        RW
sd adg03-02        avol-03       adg03    544     2097152  0       c1t1d2   ENA
dc SNAP-avol_dco   SNAP-avol     SNAP-avol_dcl

v  SNAP-avol_dcl   -             ENABLED  ACTIVE  544       ROUND   -        gen
pl avol_dcl-03     SNAP-avol_dcl ENABLED  ACTIVE  544       CONCAT  -        RW
sd adg02-02        avol_dcl-03   adg02    2097152 544       0       c1t1d1   ENA

v  avol            -             ENABLED  ACTIVE  2097152  SELECT  -        fsgen
pl avol-01         avol          ENABLED  ACTIVE  2097152  CONCAT  -        RW
sd adg01-01        avol-01       adg01    0       2097152  0       c1t1d0   ENA
pl avol-02         avol          ENABLED  ACTIVE  2097152  CONCAT  -        RW
sd adg02-01        avol-02       adg02    0       2097152  0       c1t1d1   ENA
dc avol_dco        avol          avol_dcl

v  avol_dcl        -             ENABLED  ACTIVE  544       SELECT  -        gen
pl avol_dcl-01     avol_dcl      ENABLED  ACTIVE  544       CONCAT  -        RW
sd adg03-01        avol_dcl-01   adg03    0       544       0       c1t1d2   ENA
pl avol_dcl-02     avol_dcl      ENABLED  ACTIVE  544       CONCAT  -        RW
sd adg01-02        avol_dcl-02   adg01    2097152 544       0       c1t1d0   ENA
```

The snap objects are removed. From now on, VxVM handles both volumes as completely distinct volumes, even though they are still snap "prepared". A somewhat softer version is performed by vxsnap split: In case of a still running synchronization thread of a full sized instant snapshot (see below), it would fail. This keyword is designed to temporarily remove the snap objects only for a fully synchronized snapshot and to recreate them at any time by way of building a logical snapshot (see below).

9.3.5 DELETING THE SNAPSHOT

Combined with our knowledge about volume destruction, we are now able to "cleanly" remove a snapshot (don't forget to stop application access and/or to unmount the corresponding file system as the first step):

```
# vxsnap -g adg split SNAP-avol
# vxassist -g adg remove volume SNAP-avol
```

The procedure for impatient and courageous guys never committing mistakes:

```
# vxedit -g adg -rf rm SNAP-avol
```

9.3.6 OFFHOST PROCESSING

A physical snapshot is a frozen, but nevertheless complete copy of the volume address space. As already mentioned in the introduction to snapshots, we could want to transfer the access to this copy to another host, e.g. for the following purposes: offhost backup, exhaustive reporting with several data warehouse like full table scans, separated testing environment, and so on.

But alas! VxVM regulates the access to its volumes on a per disk group base. Unfortunately, the original volume and its snapshot volume are kept in the same disk group. We must conclude, that either offhost processing is impossible or we need the expensive Cluster Volume Manager license to enable parallel access to disk groups or the disk group must be split. The latter is indeed implemented.

The Disk Group Split and Join feature (DGSJ) was introduced in VxVM 3.2 and got an improved administration by the vxsnap command. Splitting a disk group into two completely independent disk groups requires some intelligent planning of storage allocation of the volumes. So we usually need to specify the storage attributes when preparing the volume for snapshots and creating the snapshot related objects.

A standard volume is not bound to build its address spaces (plexes) from specific storage, the subdisk is a arbitrarily configurable instance between the physical and the virtual layer, in other words, its virtual position within the plex is completely independent from its physical position on the disk. Nevertheless, vxassist has a reasonable built-in limitation to serve redundancy and performance needs: You cannot stripe or mirror over subdisks on the same disk as long as the subdisks are part of the top level or the same sublevel volume.

When splitting a complex snapshot structure into two different disk groups, we do not want to destroy structures we want to keep alive and to go on working properly (the original volume should remain online). We do not want, as an example, to destroy its twofold redundancy (two data plexes). Since it is impossible and indeed not suitable for integrity needs to keep the original access of host A to mirror 1 and to switch the access to mirror 2 to host B, while the volume fully remains in use, VxVM does not allow to rupture a volume by splitting the disk group. Therefore, all disks used by a volume must either remain in the original disk group or completely split off into the new disk group.

The DCL volume of a snapshot "prepared" application volume is an integral part of its DCO parent volume, associated by the DC object. The disk group split must not destroy this logging volume as well, and it must not cut off its logging relation to the parent volume. The same is true for the snapshot side of our volume structure: The snapshot volume and its DCL volume if carrying redundancy (which is not the default) need to be kept connected.

To sum up: The set of disks used to build the application volume and its DCL volume on the "left" side (see image below) and the set of the snapshot volume and its DCL volume on the "right" side need to be strictly exclusive. Furthermore, all other volumes or comparable associations (replicated volume groups, volume sets, DCO logs, cache subdisks), if there are any within the same disk group, must conform to that rule. Otherwise, our attempt to split the disk group will fail! The next example (this time with the subdisks drawn) shows a properly configured scenario: All subdisks of the original volume and its DCL volume reside on disks adg01 and adg02, while the snapshot part only uses disk adg03.

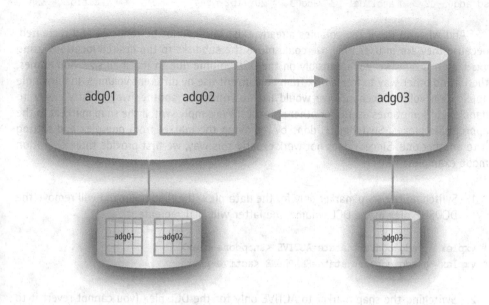

Figure 9-6: Application and snapshot volume ready for disk group split

But what can be done to achieve this layout? Make use of the storage attributes when creating volume and snapshot objects:

```
# vxassist -g adg make avol 1g layout=mirror nmirror=2 init=active \
  alloc=adg01,adg02
# vxsnap -g adg prepare avol alloc=adg01,adg02
# vxsnap -g adg addmir avol alloc=adg03
# vxprint -rLtg adg
[…]
v  avol          -              ENABLED  ACTIVE   2097152  SELECT   -       fsgen
pl avol-01       avol           ENABLED  ACTIVE   2097152  CONCAT   -       RW
sd adg01-01      avol-01        adg01    0        2097152  0        c1t1d0  ENA
pl avol-02       avol           ENABLED  ACTIVE   2097152  CONCAT   -       RW
sd adg02-01      avol-02        adg02    0        2097152  0        c1t1d1  ENA
pl avol-03       avol           ENABLED  SNAPDONE 2097152  CONCAT   -       WO
sd adg03-01      avol-03        adg03    0        2097152  0        c1t1d2  ENA
dc avol_dco      avol           avol_dcl

v  avol_dcl      -              ENABLED  ACTIVE   544      SELECT   -       gen
pl avol_dcl-01   avol_dcl       ENABLED  ACTIVE   544      CONCAT   -       RW
sd adg01-02      avol_dcl-01    adg01    2097152  544      0        c1t1d0  ENA
pl avol_dcl-02   avol_dcl       ENABLED  ACTIVE   544      CONCAT   -       RW
sd adg02-02      avol_dcl-02    adg02    2097152  544      0        c1t1d1  ENA
```

```
pl avol_dcl-03   avol_dcl      DISABLED DCOSNP   544          CONCAT    -        RW
sd adg03-02      avol_dcl-03   adg03    2097152  544          0         c1t1d2   ENA
```

And what to do, if the volumes already exist and cannot be removed and recreated, because they are in use? Well, we could move the subdisks to the desired locations using **vxsd mv** or **vxassist move**, sensibly on the DCL volume due to its small size. Sometimes, there is no other way to free a disk from concurrent use by different volumes. In our single application volume scenario, we would like to introduce another way, mostly easier to handle and sometimes useful for other purposes: We simply switch the snap markers to the appropriate plexes. Switching is done by removing the marker from one plex and setting it to another one. Since it does not work exactly this way, we first provide three operation mode examples:

1. Switching the snap marker only for the data plex (the first command will remove the DCOSNP plex in the DCL volume, the latter will NOT recreate it):

```
# vxplex -g adg convert state=ACTIVE <snapdone-plex>
# vxplex -g adg convert state=SNAPDONE <active-plex>
```

2. Switching the snap marker to ACTIVE only for the DCL plex (you cannot revert it to DCOSNP):

```
# vxplex -g adg convert state=ACTIVE <dcosnp-plex>
```

3. Switching the snap markers for both, the data and the DCL plex (the first command will remove the DCOSNP plex in the DCL volume):

```
# vxplex -g adg -o dcoplex=<dcosnp-plex> convert state=ACTIVE <snapdone-plex>
# vxplex -g adg -o dcoplex=<active-plex> convert state=SNAPDONE <active-plex>
```

Due to the removal of DCOSNP plexes when converting the appropriate data plex to the active state, we conclude that we must recreate the lost DCL plex before switching both plexes to serve as snapshot plexes:

```
# vxplex -g adg convert state=ACTIVE <snapdone-plex>
# vxassist -g adg mirror <dcl-volume> [alloc=<disk>]
# vxplex -g adg -o dcoplex=<active-plex> convert state=SNAPDONE <active-plex>
```

Having successfully prepared our subdisk usage, we perform the disk group split. There is no risk in executing the following command, because it will fail instead of destroying related object associations or making volumes in use inaccessible by moving them into a different disk group:

```
# vxsnap -g adg make source=avol/new=SNAP-avol/plex=avol-03
# vxdg split adg offdg SNAP-avol
# vxdisk list
```

```
[...]
c1t1d0s2      auto:cdsdisk      adg01        adg         online
c1t1d1s2      auto:cdsdisk      adg02        adg         online
c1t1d2s2      auto:cdsdisk      adg03        offdg       online
# vxprint -rLtg adg
[...]
v  avol         -              ENABLED  ACTIVE  2097152  SELECT   -        fsgen
pl avol-01      avol           ENABLED  ACTIVE  2097152  CONCAT   -        RW
sd adg01-01     avol-01        adg01    0       2097152  0        c1t1d0   ENA
pl avol-02      avol           ENABLED  ACTIVE  2097152  CONCAT   -        RW
sd adg02-01     avol-02        adg02    0       2097152  0        c1t1d1   ENA
dc avol_dco     avol           avol_dcl

v  avol_dcl     -              ENABLED  ACTIVE  544      SELECT   -        gen
pl avol_dcl-01  avol_dcl       ENABLED  ACTIVE  544      CONCAT   -        RW
sd adg01-02     avol_dcl-01    adg01    2097152  544     0        c1t1d0   ENA
pl avol_dcl-02  avol_dcl       ENABLED  ACTIVE  544      CONCAT   -        RW
sd adg02-02     avol_dcl-02    adg02    2097152  544     0        c1t1d1   ENA
sp SNAP-avol_snp avol          avol_dco
# vxprint -rLtg offdg
[...]
v  SNAP-avol    -              DISABLED ACTIVE  2097152  ROUND    -        fsgen
pl avol-03      SNAP-avol      DISABLED ACTIVE  2097152  CONCAT   -        RW
sd adg03-01     avol-03        adg03    0       2097152  0        c1t1d2   ENA
dc SNAP-avol_dco SNAP-avol     SNAP-avol_dcl

v  SNAP-avol_dcl -             DISABLED ACTIVE  544      ROUND    -        gen
pl avol_dcl-03  SNAP-avol_dcl  DISABLED ACTIVE  544      CONCAT   -        RW
sd adg03-02     avol_dcl-03    adg03    2097152  544     0        c1t1d2   ENA
sp avol_snp     SNAP-avol      SNAP-avol_dco
```

Now, the new disk group containing the snapshot volume and its DCL volume is ready for offhost processing. We are able to deport it and import it on another host, start the volumes, and attend our offhost duties. In many cases, it is quite reasonable to revert this procedure to be prepared for the next snapshot. First, we must stop our offhost processing, then deport the disk group and import it once again on the original host. Below are the steps required to join the already imported offhost disk group with the application disk group, start the snapshot volume and its DCL volume affected by the volume move (option -m), and reattach them to their original volumes (a refresh or a restore operation would only modify the keyword of the last command):

```
# vxdg join offdg adg
# vxrecover -g adg -m
# vxsnap -g adg reattach SNAP-avol source=avol
```

9.3.7   FULL SIZED VOLUME BASED INSTANT SNAPSHOTS

Let's turn to another functionality of the multi-layered DCL bitmap! We already mentioned, that the amount of time needed to synchronize a new snapshot plex or to bring an existing snapshot volume to the current state of application data is somewhat harmful. Sometimes, we immediately need the snapshot.

One layer within the DCL bitmap of the snapshot volume provides pointer functionality: If the bit is set, its correspondent region data are physically stored in the snapshot volume itself, whether these data are the original snapshot data or data modified by write access to the snapshot volume. If the bit is cleared, its correspondent region data are read from the original device, because data did not change since the snapshot. This kind of procedure to simulate a physical snapshot is called "logical snapshot".

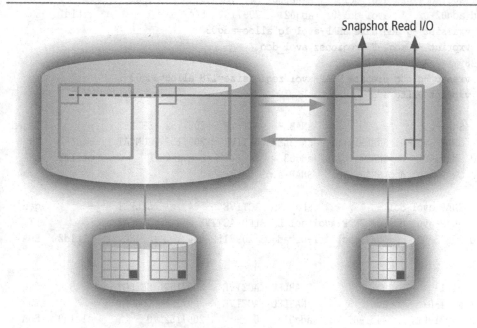

Snapshot Read I/O

Figure 9-7:   Read access to a full sized "logical" snapshot

Such a snapshot is indeed immediately ready for use. We only need to specify an appropriate volume as a snapshot for the application volume, VxVM will clear all bits within the "logical snapshot" bitmap, thus providing a simulated copy of the application volume accessed by another volume driver. We will now explain the mode of operation together with the necessary configuration step by step. Let's start at the very beginning with the creation of the application volume and the volume to become its logical snapshot. Note that the size of both top-level volumes and the region size of both bitmaps are identical.

```
# vxassist -g adg make avol 1g layout=mirror init=active alloc=adg01,adg02
# vxsnap -g adg prepare avol alloc=adg01,adg02
# vxprint -rLtg adg
[...]
```

v avol	–		ENABLED	ACTIVE	2097152	SELECT	–	fsgen
pl avol-01	avol		ENABLED	ACTIVE	2097152	CONCAT	–	RW
sd adg01-01	avol-01	adg01	0	2097152	0		c1t1d0	ENA
pl avol-02	avol		ENABLED	ACTIVE	2097152	CONCAT	–	RW
sd adg02-01	avol-02	adg02	0	2097152	0		c1t1d1	ENA
dc avol_dco	avol	avol_dcl						
v avol_dcl	–		ENABLED	ACTIVE	544	SELECT	–	gen
pl avol_dcl-01	avol_dcl		ENABLED	ACTIVE	544	CONCAT	–	RW
sd adg01-02	avol_dcl-01	adg01	2097152	544	0		c1t1d0	ENA

```
pl avol_dcl-02   avol_dcl     ENABLED  ACTIVE   544      CONCAT    -         RW
sd adg02-02      avol_dcl-02  adg02    2097152  544      0         c1t1d1    ENA
# vxassist -g adg make SNAP-avol 1g alloc=adg03
# vxprint -g adg -F %regionsz avol_dco
128
# vxsnap -g adg prepare SNAP-avol regionsize=128 alloc=adg03
# vxprint -rLtg adg
[...]
v  SNAP-avol      -           ENABLED  ACTIVE   2097152  SELECT    -         fsgen
pl SNAP-avol-01 SNAP-avol     ENABLED  ACTIVE   2097152  CONCAT    -         RW
sd adg03-01      SNAP-avol-01 adg03    0        2097152  0         c1t1d2    ENA
dc SNAP-avol_dco SNAP-avol    SNAP-avol_dcl


v  SNAP-avol_dcl -            ENABLED  ACTIVE   544      SELECT    -         gen
pl SNAP-avol_dcl-01 SNAP-avol_dcl ENABLED ACTIVE 544    CONCAT    -         RW
sd adg03-02      SNAP-avol_dcl-01 adg03 2097152 544     0         c1t1d2    ENA


v  avol           -           ENABLED  ACTIVE   2097152  SELECT    -         fsgen
pl avol-01        avol        ENABLED  ACTIVE   2097152  CONCAT    -         RW
sd adg01-01      avol-01      adg01    0        2097152  0         c1t1d0    ENA
pl avol-02        avol        ENABLED  ACTIVE   2097152  CONCAT    -         RW
sd adg02-01      avol-02      adg02    0        2097152  0         c1t1d1    ENA
dc avol_dco       avol        avol_dcl


v  avol_dcl       -           ENABLED  ACTIVE   544      SELECT    -         gen
pl avol_dcl-01    avol_dcl    ENABLED  ACTIVE   544      CONCAT    -         RW
sd adg01-02      avol_dcl-01  adg01    2097152  544      0         c1t1d0    ENA
pl avol_dcl-02    avol_dcl    ENABLED  ACTIVE   544      CONCAT    -         RW
sd adg02-02      avol_dcl-02  adg02    2097152  544      0         c1t1d1    ENA
```

The current content of the disk group exactly looks like an application volume with its split or dissociated snapshot volume (the snap objects are missing). But remember: Until now, our volumes never had a snapshot relation. And keep in mind: Creating the volume designed to serve as snapshot took only a few seconds (unless you are not familiar with the procedure).

The next step is to tell VxVM that the latter volume should serve as a logical snapshot to the application volume. Quite easy with the **vxsnap** command:

```
# vxsnap -g adg make source=avol/snap=SNAP-avol sync=no
# vxprint -rLtg adg
...
v  SNAP-avol      -           ENABLED  ACTIVE   2097152  SELECT    -         fsgen
pl SNAP-avol-01 SNAP-avol     ENABLED  ACTIVE   2097152  CONCAT    -         RW
sd adg03-01      SNAP-avol-01 adg03    0        2097152  0         c1t1d2    ENA
dc SNAP-avol_dco SNAP-avol    SNAP-avol_dcl
```

```
v  SNAP-avol_dcl -            ENABLED  ACTIVE    544     SELECT    -       gen
pl SNAP-avol_dcl-01 SNAP-avol_dcl ENABLED ACTIVE 544     CONCAT    -       RW
sd adg03-02       SNAP-avol_dcl-01 adg03 2097152 544     0         c1t1d2  ENA
sp avol_snp       SNAP-avol    SNAP-avol_dco


v  avol          -            ENABLED  ACTIVE  2097152   SELECT    -       fsgen
pl avol-01       avol         ENABLED  ACTIVE  2097152   CONCAT    -       RW
sd adg01-01      avol-01      adg01    0       2097152   0         c1t1d0  ENA
pl avol-02       avol         ENABLED  ACTIVE  2097152   CONCAT    -       RW
sd adg02-01      avol-02      adg02    0       2097152   0         c1t1d1  ENA
dc avol_dco      avol         avol_dcl

v  avol_dcl      -            ENABLED  ACTIVE    544     SELECT    -       gen
pl avol_dcl-01   avol_dcl     ENABLED  ACTIVE    544     CONCAT    -       RW
sd adg01-02      avol_dcl-01  adg01    2097152   544     0         c1t1d0  ENA
pl avol_dcl-02   avol_dcl     ENABLED  ACTIVE    544     CONCAT    -       RW
sd adg02-02      avol_dcl-02  adg02    2097152   544     0         c1t1d1  ENA
sp SNAP-avol_snp avol         avol_dco
```

We already recognize the snap objects linking the snapshot volume to its application volume and vice-versa. Currently, assuming no application write I/Os, the snapshot bitmap of SNAP-avol_dcl marks all snapshot regions as "invalid", i.e. all data must be read from the application volume.

The command vxsnap provides a useful keyword to print the amount of "valid", i.e. to the snapshot volume already synchronized regions:

```
# vxsnap -g adg print
NAME      SNAPOBJECT      TYPE     PARENT     SNAPSHOT     %DIRTY    %VALID

avol        --            volume   --         --           --       100.00
            SNAP-avol_snp volume   --         SNAP-avol    0.00      --

SNAP-avol avol_snp        volume   avol       --           0.00      0.00
```

The last word (column %VALID) in the last line (object name SNAP-avol) shows, that no data were already stored on the snapshot volume (0.00%). But what becomes of data overwritten by write access of the application? The snapshot mechanism must store the original data set to the snapshot volume before it is physically overwritten by the application for the first time ("copy on first write"). Furthermore, the corresponding bit in the DCL bitmap needs to be set to indicate that the snapshot is prohibited to read those region data from the application volume.

Indeed, vxsnap prints out, that some portions of the snapshot volume (depending on the application I/O size) are now "valid", i.e. physically stored within the snapshot volume. We overwrite the first 100 MB of our volume:

```
# dd if=/dev/zero of=/dev/vx/rdsk/adg/avol bs=1024k count=100
100+0 records in
100+0 records out
# vxsnap -g adg print
NAME     SNAPOBJECT     TYPE     PARENT    SNAPSHOT    %DIRTY    %VALID

avol     --             volume   --        --          --        100.00
         SNAP-avol_snp  volume   --        SNAP-avol   9.77      --

SNAP-avol avol_snp      volume   avol      --          9.77      9.77
```

Don't forget: 100 MB is less than 10% of 1 GB, because 1 GB consists of 1,024 MB! 9.77% of the original volume is already copied to the snapshot volume, and both volumes differ in 9.77% of data (column %DIRTY).

We could want to convert the logical snapshot into a physical one, e.g. to enable offhost processing or to save copy-on-first-write I/Os at a later, busy period by writing application volume data to the snapshot volume right now. We could, of course, show real patience until all regions of the application volume are overwritten by new data. But there are two ways to start immediate snapshot synchronization.

1. At any time, we can start data transfer to the snapshot volume, enabling, if desired, the "background" operation mode (option -b) and a performance throttle (specified in milliseconds). We may also pause and resume it with the throttle started by, or completely terminate it.

```
# vxsnap -g adg -b [-o slow=<#>] syncstart SNAP-avol
# vxtask list
TASKID  PTID TYPE/STATE    PCT    PROGRESS
  172        SNAPSYNC/R 10.06% 0/2097152/210944 SNAPSYNC SNAP-avol adg
# vxsnap -g adg syncpause SNAP-avol
# vxtask list
TASKID  PTID TYPE/STATE    PCT    PROGRESS
  172        SNAPSYNC/P 11.23% 0/2097152/235520 SNAPSYNC SNAP-avol adg
# vxsnap -g adg print
NAME     SNAPOBJECT     TYPE     PARENT    SNAPSHOT    %DIRTY    %VALID

avol     --             volume   --        --          --        100.00
         SNAP-avol_snp  volume   --        SNAP-avol   9.77      --

SNAP-avol avol_snp      volume   avol      --          9.77      11.33
# vxsnap -g adg syncresume SNAP-avol
# vxtask list
TASKID  PTID TYPE/STATE    PCT    PROGRESS
  172        SNAPSYNC/R 11.52% 0/2097152/241664 SNAPSYNC SNAP-avol adg
# vxsnap -g adg syncstop SNAP-avol
# vxsnap -g adg print
```

```
NAME     SNAPOBJECT    TYPE     PARENT    SNAPSHOT    %DIRTY    %VALID

avol     --            volume   --        --          --        100.00
         SNAP-avol_snp volume   --        SNAP-avol   9.77      --

SNAP-avol avol_snp     volume   avol      --          9.77      13.38
```
vxsnap -g adg syncresume SNAP-avol
VxVM vxsnap ERROR V-5-1-6680 No instant operation is running on the volume SNAP-avol

2. When creating the snapshot relation between the two volumes, we may simply omit the keyword sync or write sync=yes. This will immediately start a synchronization thread on all volume regions:

vxsnap -g adg make source=avol/snap=SNAP-avol [sync=yes]

A fully synchronized snapshot volume does not only look and behave like a physical snapshot, it is actually a physical snapshot, and there is no difference in the result compared to the legacy snapshot mechanism: all snapshot I/Os are taken from the snapshot device, offhost processing is possible, and so on.

Another remark concerning full sized instant snapshots: The volume intended to become the instant snapshot of an application volume may not reside within the same disk group. When establishing the snapshot relation, we may specify within the slash separated tuple of the vxsnap command the keyword snapdg:

vxsnap -g adg make source=avol/snap=SNAP-avol/snapdg=offdg

9.3.8 SNAPSHOT REFRESH

Now, with the knowledge of logical snapshot relations based on the multi-functional bitmap of the DCL volume, we will easily understand another feature of the DCO based raw device snapshots, whether in complete or partial physical state: the snapshot refresh. "Refreshing" the snapshot, that is updating the data set represented by the snapshot to the current content of the application volume, simply means converting the snapshot DCO bitmap from its current state (most probably a mixture of physical and logical pointer bits or already indicating a fully synchronized snapshot) to a plain logical bitmap.

At any time, independent from the procedure which created the snapshot volume, but nevertheless only without current access to it, a snapshot volume can be refreshed. The refresh operation may invoke background synchronization at the same time (default behavior), but this is, compared to the logical snapshot creation, just as well optional.

vxsnap -g adg refresh SNAP-avol [sync=no]

9.3.9 SPACE OPTIMIZED VOLUME BASED INSTANT SNAPSHOTS

Consider you do not want or need a physical snapshot at all, and your snapshot will be used only for a few hours (e.g. for backup purposes). Another physical instance of the volume address space, as required by the volume snapshot mechanisms hitherto explained, could evoke inconvenient questions about wasting storage. And those questions should be taken seriously, because they point to an undeniable weakness of physical snapshots: Data remaining unchanged during the period of the snapshot are stored twice (application and snapshot volume, if physical snapshot) or waste space on the snapshot volume (logical snapshot). For logical snapshots, it would be sufficient to provide storage only for the original data, before they are overwritten by the application. Data unchanged remain stored on the application volume, while the snapshot bitmap simply continue to point to them.

Maybe you remember the construct of the VxFS based logical snapshot presented in the "Easy Sailing" section. Indeed, we created a snapshot device containing a bitmap of exactly that functioning and providing the storage required to save the original data, before they were overwritten. We mentioned, that for many temporary purposes 10% of the application size would be sufficient to serve as a snapshot device.

The VxVM based space optimized snapshot uses a somewhat different architecture in order to support a shared cache, i.e. a cache providing dynamic storage for more than one application volume. Thus, several application volumes can store their original data in one storage device to benefit from dynamic storage requirements: an application requests for snapshot purposes more storage, another application less than expected.

But what is our snapshot device now? We talked about application and cache volumes, not about snapshot volumes. Well, the snapshot is indeed not a physical device anymore except for the small storage needed to build the already known DCO bitmap, marking whether the snapshot data are physically to be read from the application volume or from the cache volume. The snapshot volume is still a regular volume as well as its plex, but the subdisk is a virtual one (called "subcache"), not defined on a disk device or a subvolume (other subdisks are still not drawn in the following picture).

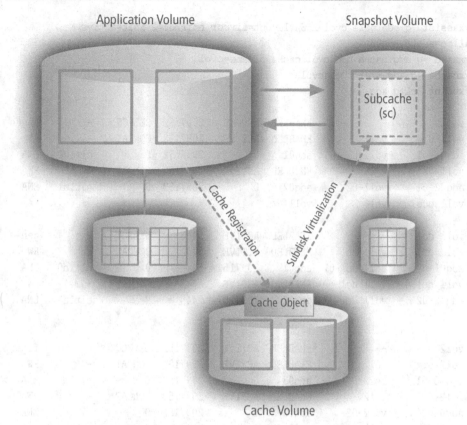

Figure 9-8: Space optimized snapshot with cache volume and subcache

Further details of space optimized snapshots with a shared cache volume are best demonstrated by the procedure to create them. We choose two application volumes in the simplest plex layout, vol1 and vol2 respectively.

```
# vxassist -g adg make vol1 1g layout=mirror nmirror=2 init=active \
  alloc=adg01,adg02
# vxassist -g adg make vol2 1g layout=mirror nmirror=2 init=active \
  alloc=adg03,adg04
# vxsnap -g adg prepare vol1 alloc=adg01,adg02
# vxsnap -g adg prepare vol2 alloc=adg03,adg04
```

Our cache volume will be mirrored to provide the same redundancy for the snapshots as for the application volumes. Its size of 256 MB allows an average of more than 10% of modified original data for both application volumes. Finally, we need a new object type called "cache object" serving as a cache volume registration instance for the snapshots and as a so-called in-core bitmap on used regions in the cache volume. For recovery purposes, the cache object can be started and stopped.

```
# vxassist -g adg make cvol 256m layout=mirror nmirror=2 init=active \
  alloc=adg05,adg06
# vxmake -g adg cache cobjcvol cachevolname=cvol
# vxcache -g adg start cobjcvol
# vxprint -rLtg adg
[...]
v  vol1         -             ENABLED  ACTIVE   2097152  SELECT    -       fsgen
pl vol1-01      vol1          ENABLED  ACTIVE   2097152  CONCAT    -       RW
sd adg01-01     vol1-01       adg01    0        2097152  0         c1t1d0  ENA
pl vol1-02      vol1          ENABLED  ACTIVE   2097152  CONCAT    -       RW
sd adg02-01     vol1-02       adg02    0        2097152  0         c1t1d1  ENA
dc vol1_dco     vol1          vol1_dcl

v  vol1_dcl     -             ENABLED  ACTIVE   544      SELECT    -       gen
pl vol1_dcl-01  vol1_dcl      ENABLED  ACTIVE   544      CONCAT    -       RW
sd adg01-02     vol1_dcl-01   adg01    2097152  544      0         c1t1d0  ENA
pl vol1_dcl-02  vol1_dcl      ENABLED  ACTIVE   544      CONCAT    -       RW
sd adg02-02     vol1_dcl-02   adg02    2097152  544      0         c1t1d1  ENA


v  vol2         -             ENABLED  ACTIVE   2097152  SELECT    -       fsgen
pl vol2-01      vol2          ENABLED  ACTIVE   2097152  CONCAT    -       RW
sd adg03-01     vol2-01       adg03    0        2097152  0         c1t1d2  ENA
pl vol2-02      vol2          ENABLED  ACTIVE   2097152  CONCAT    -       RW
sd adg04-01     vol2-02       adg04    0        2097152  0         c1t1d3  ENA
dc vol2_dco     vol2          vol2_dcl

v  vol2_dcl     -             ENABLED  ACTIVE   544      SELECT    -       gen
pl vol2_dcl-01  vol2_dcl      ENABLED  ACTIVE   544      CONCAT    -       RW
sd adg03-02     vol2_dcl-01   adg03    2097152  544      0         c1t1d2  ENA
pl vol2_dcl-02  vol2_dcl      ENABLED  ACTIVE   544      CONCAT    -       RW
sd adg04-02     vol2_dcl-02   adg04    2097152  544      0         c1t1d3  ENA


co cobjcvol     cvol          ENABLED  ACTIVE

v  cvol         cobjcvol      ENABLED  ACTIVE   524288   SELECT    -       fsgen
pl cvol-01      cvol          ENABLED  ACTIVE   524288   CONCAT    -       RW
sd adg05-01     cvol-01       adg05    0        524288   0         c1t1d4  ENA
pl cvol-02      cvol          ENABLED  ACTIVE   524288   CONCAT    -       RW
sd adg06-01     cvol-02       adg06    0        524288   0         c1t1d5  ENA
```

Well, life is not always as easy as one could desire it! But it will get even more complicated, because we still have no snapshots.

```
# vxsnap -g adg make source=vol1/new=SNAP-vol1/cache=cobjcvol
```

```
# vxsnap -g adg make source=vol2/new=SNAP-vol2/cache=cobjcvol
# vxprint -rLtg adg
[…]
v  SNAP-vol1     -          ENABLED  ACTIVE   2097152  SELECT    -      fsgen
pl SNAP-vol1-P01 SNAP-vol1  ENABLED  ACTIVE   2097152  CONCAT    -      RW
sc SNAP-vol1-S01 SNAP-vol1-P01 cobjcvol 0     2097152  0         -      ENA
dc SNAP-vol1_dco SNAP-vol1  SNAP-vol1_dcl

v  SNAP-vol1_dcl -          ENABLED  ACTIVE   544      SELECT    -      gen
pl SNAP-vol1_dcl-01 SNAP-vol1_dcl ENABLED ACTIVE 544   CONCAT    -      RW
sd adg07-01      SNAP-vol1_dcl-01 adg07 0      544      0         c1t1d6 ENA
sp vol1_snp      SNAP-vol1  SNAP-vol1_dco

v  SNAP-vol2     -          ENABLED  ACTIVE   2097152  SELECT    -      fsgen
pl SNAP-vol2-P01 SNAP-vol2  ENABLED  ACTIVE   2097152  CONCAT    -      RW
sc SNAP-vol2-S01 SNAP-vol2-P01 cobjcvol 0     2097152  0         -      ENA
dc SNAP-vol2_dco SNAP-vol2  SNAP-vol2_dcl

v  SNAP-vol2_dcl -          ENABLED  ACTIVE   544      SELECT    -      gen
pl SNAP-vol2_dcl-01 SNAP-vol2_dcl ENABLED ACTIVE 544   CONCAT    -      RW
sd adg08-01      SNAP-vol2_dcl-01 adg08 0      544      0         c1t1d7 ENA
sp vol2_snp      SNAP-vol2  SNAP-vol2_dco

v  vol1          -          ENABLED  ACTIVE   2097152  SELECT    -      fsgen
pl vol1-01       vol1       ENABLED  ACTIVE   2097152  CONCAT    -      RW
sd adg01-01      vol1-01    adg01    0        2097152  0         c1t1d0 ENA
pl vol1-02       vol1       ENABLED  ACTIVE   2097152  CONCAT    -      RW
sd adg02-01      vol1-02    adg02    0        2097152  0         c1t1d1 ENA
dc vol1_dco      vol1       vol1_dcl

v  vol1_dcl      -          ENABLED  ACTIVE   544      SELECT    -      gen
pl vol1_dcl-01   vol1_dcl   ENABLED  ACTIVE   544      CONCAT    -      RW
sd adg01-02      vol1_dcl-01 adg01   2097152  544      0         c1t1d0 ENA
pl vol1_dcl-02   vol1_dcl   ENABLED  ACTIVE   544      CONCAT    -      RW
sd adg02-02      vol1_dcl-02 adg02   2097152  544      0         c1t1d1 ENA
sp SNAP-vol1_snp vol1       vol1_dco

v  vol2          -          ENABLED  ACTIVE   2097152  SELECT    -      fsgen
pl vol2-01       vol2       ENABLED  ACTIVE   2097152  CONCAT    -      RW
sd adg03-01      vol2-01    adg03    0        2097152  0         c1t1d2 ENA
pl vol2-02       vol2       ENABLED  ACTIVE   2097152  CONCAT    -      RW
sd adg04-01      vol2-02    adg04    0        2097152  0         c1t1d3 ENA
dc vol2_dco      vol2       vol2_dcl
```

```
v   vol2_dcl      -               ENABLED  ACTIVE  544      SELECT    -       gen
pl  vol2_dcl-01   vol2_dcl        ENABLED  ACTIVE  544      CONCAT    -       RW
sd  adg03-02      vol2_dcl-01     adg03    2097152 544      0         c1t1d2  ENA
pl  vol2_dcl-02   vol2_dcl        ENABLED  ACTIVE  544      CONCAT    -       RW
sd  adg04-02      vol2_dcl-02     adg04    2097152 544      0         c1t1d3  ENA
sp  SNAP-vol2_snp vol2            vol2_dco

co  cobjcvol      cvol            ENABLED  ACTIVE

v   cvol          cobjcvol        ENABLED  ACTIVE  524288   SELECT    -       fsgen
pl  cvol-01       cvol            ENABLED  ACTIVE  524288   CONCAT    -       RW
sd  adg05-01      cvol-01         adg05    0       524288   0         c1t1d4  ENA
pl  cvol-02       cvol            ENABLED  ACTIVE  524288   CONCAT    -       RW
sd  adg06-01      cvol-02         adg06    0       524288   0         c1t1d5  ENA
```

The result looks terrible, but don't give up! Some little drawing will do no harm:

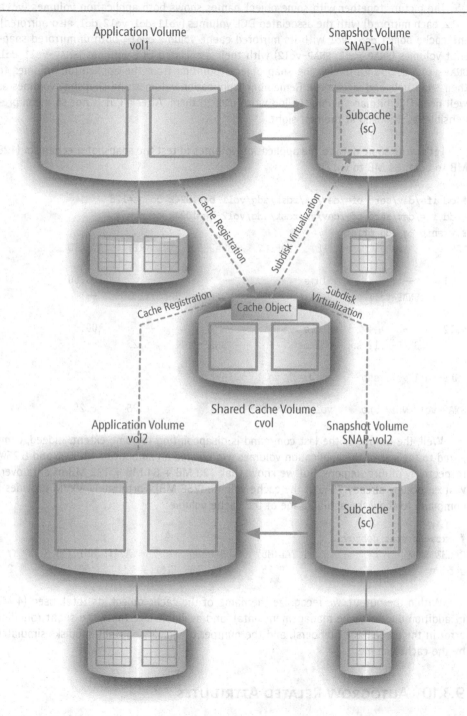

Figure 9-9:   Space optimized snapshots of two volumes with shared cache

The picture together with some object names shows both application volumes (vol1, vol2, each mirrored) with the associated DCL volumes (vol1_dcl, vol2_dcl, also mirrored), the cache object cobjcvol with its mirrored cache volume cvol, both unmirrored snapshot volumes (SNAP-vol1, SNAP-vol2) with their associated DCL volumes (SNAP-vol1_dcl, SNAP-vol2_dcl), and, finally, the snap objects pointing from the application volumes to their snapshots and vice-versa. Remember: application volumes and snapshot volumes as well need DCL bitmap volumes to log write I/Os to them. After all, it is not so incomprehensible, as it looked at the first sight.

Let's write some data to the application volumes to test the snapshot mechanism (128 MB to vol1, 64 MB to vol2):

```
# dd if=/dev/zero of=/dev/vx/rdsk/adg/vol1 bs=1024k count=128
# dd if=/dev/zero of=/dev/vx/rdsk/adg/vol2 bs=1024k count=64
# vxsnap -g adg print
NAME        SNAPOBJECT      TYPE     PARENT    SNAPSHOT      %DIRTY    %VALID

vol1        --              volume   --        --            --        100.00
            SNAP-vol1_snp   volume   --        SNAP-vol1     12.50     --

vol2        --              volume   --        --            --        100.00
            SNAP-vol2_snp   volume   --        SNAP-vol2     6.25      --

SNAP-vol1 vol1_snp          volume   vol1      --            12.50     12.50

SNAP-vol2 vol2_snp          volume   vol2      --            6.25      6.25
```

Well, the output of the last command is disappointing to some extent. Indeed, compared to the size of the application volumes, we created an amount of 12.50% and 6.25% respectively of dirty regions. But we know, that 128 MB + 64 MB = 192 MB of data overwritten occupy already 75% of the cache volume (256 MB). Fortunately, VxVM provides a command to show the actual usage of the cache volume:

```
# vxcache stat cobjcvol
CACHE NAME                TOTAL(Mb)    USED(Mb) (%)    AVAIL(Mb) (%)    SDCNT
cobjcvol                        256     196 (76)          60 (23)         2
```

Within the output, we recognize the name of the cache object, its total, used (4 MB in addition due to cache management data), and available size (note the slight rounding error in the percentage numbers), and the number of virtual snapshot subdisks simulated by the cache volume.

9.3.10 AUTOGROW RELATED ATTRIBUTES

A detailed analysis of the cache object attributes reveals some further interesting features of the space optimized snapshot (excerpts):

```
# vxprint -g adg -m cobjcvol
cache cobjcvol
[...]
        autogrow=off
[...]
        hwmark=90
        autogrowby=104848
        max_autogrow=1048576
[...]
```

Currently, an attribute called autogrow seems to be turned off (you may specify autogrow=on, when creating the cache object). Another attribute called hwmark could mean a high water mark, obviously specified in percent unit. Reaching or exceeding the high water mark of the cache object could trigger an automated growth of its cache volume, probably by 104,848 sectors (about 51 MB, which is approximately 20% of the original cache volume size) defined by the attribute autogrowby. In case of subsequent cache limit events, the attribute max_autogrow seems to set a final limit to the cache volume size. Let's activate and test our assumptions by overwriting further 40 MB:

```
# vxcache -g adg set autogrow=on cobjcvol
# vxcache -g adg set max_autogrow=400m cobjcvol
# vxprint -g adg -F '%name %cachevol_len %autogrow %max_autogrow' cobjcvol
cobjcvol 524288 on 819200
# dd if=/dev/zero of=/dev/vx/rdsk/adg/vol2 bs=1024k count=40 oseek=64
```

After a few seconds, the cache volume has grown:

```
# vxcache -g adg stat cobjcvol
CACHE NAME                  TOTAL(Mb)     USED(Mb) (%)       AVAIL(Mb) (%)    SDCNT
cobjcvol                          307      236 (76)              71 (23)          2
# vxprint -rtg adg cvol
[...]
v  cvol       cobjcvol    ENABLED ACTIVE  629136  SELECT    -         fsgen
pl cvol-01    cvol        ENABLED ACTIVE  629136  CONCAT    -         RW
sd adg05-01   cvol-01     adg05   0       629136  0         c1t1d4    ENA
pl cvol-02    cvol        ENABLED ACTIVE  629136  CONCAT    -         RW
sd adg06-01   cvol-02     adg06   0       629136  0         c1t1d5    ENA
```

Since the cache volume is mirrored, we expect, that VxVM issued a read-writeback synchronization thread for the additional volume size. We undertake to check for synchronization I/Os when triggering once again an autogrow of the cache volume:

```
# dd if=/dev/zero of=/dev/vx/rdsk/adg/vol2 bs=1024k count=64 oseek=104
# while :; do vxtask list | tail +2; done
...
42015       RDWRBACK/R 50.79% 629136/733984/682384 RESYNC cvol adg
```

```
...
^C
# vxcache -g adg stat cobjcvol
CACHE NAME                    TOTAL(Mb)    USED(Mb) (%)      AVAIL(Mb) (%)    SDCNT
cobjcvol                            358     300 (83)              58 (16)         2
# vxprint -rtg adg cvol
[...]
v  cvol        cobjcvol   ENABLED  ACTIVE  733984  SELECT   -              fsgen
pl cvol-01     cvol       ENABLED  ACTIVE  733984  CONCAT   -              RW
sd adg05-01    cvol-01    adg05    0       733984  0        c1t1d4         ENA
pl cvol-02     cvol       ENABLED  ACTIVE  733984  CONCAT   -              RW
sd adg06-01    cvol-02    adg06    0       733984  0        c1t1d5         ENA
```

It worked once again! Furthermore, we could verify the predicted read-writeback synchronization. And finally, root@localhost already got two e-mails of the following sort:

```
[...]
Subject: Volume Manager cache grow notification on host haensel
[...]
Got a grow event notification for cache-volume cvol associated to cache-object
cobjcvol in disk-group adg
```

Another try! But remember: Our cache volume has a size of about 358 MB. The next autogrow event will try to add another 51 MB to it, which will exceed the defined maximum size of the cache volume (400 MB).

```
# dd if=/dev/zero of=/dev/vx/rdsk/adg/vol2 bs=1024k count=64 oseek=168
# vxcache -g adg stat cobjcvol
CACHE NAME                    TOTAL(Mb)    USED(Mb) (%)      AVAIL(Mb) (%)    SDCNT
cobjcvol                            358     236 (65)             122 (34)         1
```

Oops! No resize operation did happen! The amount of used cache volume space was even reduced! And, what is more, the number of virtual subdisks simulated by the cache object was decremented. This looks suspiciously like a damaged snapshot to vol2:

```
# vxprint -rLtg SNAP-vol2
[...]
v  SNAP-vol2      -                   ENABLED  ACTIVE  2097152  SELECT   -         fsgen
pl SNAP-vol2-P01  SNAP-vol2           ENABLED  ACTIVE  2097152  CONCAT   -         RW
sc SNAP-vol2-S01  SNAP-vol2-P01 cobjcvol 0     2097152  0        -         ENA
dc SNAP-vol2_dco  SNAP-vol2           SNAP-vol2_dcl

v  SNAP-vol2_dcl  -                   ENABLED  ACTIVE  544      SELECT   -         gen
pl SNAP-vol2_dcl-01 SNAP-vol2_dcl ENABLED ACTIVE 544            CONCAT   -         RW
sd adg08-01       SNAP-vol2_dcl-01 adg08 0       544      0        c1t1d7    ENA
sp vol2_snp       SNAP-vol2           SNAP-vol2_dco
```

No, this snapshot seems to work properly. What about SNAP-vol1?

```
# vxprint -rLtg adg SNAP-vol1
VxVM vxprint ERROR V-5-1-924 Record SNAP-vol1 not found
```

O my god! The "wrong" snapshot was destroyed! So, the first conclusion we draw from our observations, is to always set the max_autogrow attribute to an integer multiple of the autogrowby value plus the initial size of the cache volume. Another conclusion is not to rely too much on the autogrow features of the space optimized snapshots: A final cache overflow will destroy some of them. Furthermore, not tested by our investigations above, multiple fast I/Os writing on the application or snapshot volumes may be faster than the autogrow mechanism leading to destroyed or disabled snapshots. Consider this when defining the hwmark and autogrowby attribute values.

Note: VxVM 4.x did not destroy the snapshots, but disabled them. Nevertheless, the effect was the same: You could reuse the snapshots only by deleting and recreating them.

If you fear a soon cache overflow or your cache volume occupies too much storage, you may manually resize the cache volume. The vxcache command provides appropriate keywords for those operations: growcacheby, growcacheto, shrinkcacheby, and shrinkcacheto.

Who tells VxVM, that the cache volume has reached or exceeded the high water mark threshold? How is cache volume resizing performed? During the boot process, a script named vxcached is started into background, which itself invokes vxnotify with the option -C (cache events):

```
# ptree $(pgrep -xu0 vxcached)
2626  /sbin/sh - /usr/lib/vxvm/bin/vxcached root
  3583  /sbin/sh - /usr/lib/vxvm/bin/vxcached root
    3584  vxnotify -C -w 15
```

We recognize a process architecture similar to the vxrelocd/vxsparecheck and vxconfigbackupd processes explained in the troubleshooting chapter (see page 372). vxnotify is informed by the kernel about the cache event and generates standard output like the following:

```
grow on cachevolume cvol rid 0.8240 for cache cobjcvol rid 0.8254 dg adg dgid
1220261661.45.haensel
```

vxcached captures the output and invokes a command growing the cache volume by the defined amount of space, if possible. If necessary, you may create your own cache event handling with a self-written script comparable to vxcached - without Veritas support, of course.

9.3.11 CASCADING SNAPSHOTS

The full sized instant and the space optimized volume snapshots provide another useful feature compared to the exclusively physical legacy full sized snapshot. Assume you want to create multiple snapshots on the same application device, e.g. hourly on a database volume each day for database recovery strategies against logical database errors such as inadvertently dropped tables. At 11:15 pm your database writes new data to a volume region still unchanged since mid-night. As you may remember, the legacy full-sized snapshot mechanism needs to copy the original data set to ALL existing snapshot volumes, before the new data set can be stored on the application volume. In our case, the database write I/O will have to wait for 24 (0:00 am to 11:00 pm) copy-on-first-writes - a performance drawback intolerable in enterprise environments!

In contrast, the instant snapshot mechanisms (full sized and space optimized) may maintain a cascading relationship by using the keyword `infrontof`: The original data set is copied only once to the latest snapshot device (full sized) or to the cache volume (space optimized), and the DCL volume bitmaps of the snapshots reflect the new location of these data - independent from the number of existing snapshots. We demonstrate the effect for a space optimized snapshot, but narrow a little bit the number of snapshots created at an hourly base:

```
# vxassist -g adg make vol 1g layout=mirror nmirror=2 init=active
# vxsnap -g adg prepare vol
# vxassist -g adg make cvol 256m layout=mirror nmirror=2 init=active
# vxmake -g adg cache cobjcvol cachevolname=cvol autogrow=on
# vxcache -g adg start cobjcvol
# vxsnap -g adg make source=vol/new=SP01-vol/cache=cobjcvol
# vxsnap -g adg make source=vol/new=SP02-vol/\
  infrontof=SP01-vol/cache=cobjcvol
# vxsnap -g adg make source=vol/new=SP03-vol/\
  infrontof=SP02-vol/cache=cobjcvol
# vxsnap -g adg make source=vol/new=SP04-vol/\
  infrontof=SP03-vol/cache=cobjcvol
# vxcache -g adg stat
CACHE NAME                   TOTAL(Mb)    USED(Mb) (%)     AVAIL(Mb) (%)    SDCNT
cobjcvol                         256         4 (1)           252 (98)        4
# vxsnap -g adg -n print
NAME        DG         OBJTYPE SNAPTYPE PARENT    PARENTDG   SNAPDATE
vol         adg        vol     -        -         -          - -
SP01-vol    adg        vol     spaceopt vol       adg        2008/09/21 09:00
SP02-vol    adg        vol     spaceopt vol       adg        2008/09/21 10:00
SP03-vol    adg        vol     spaceopt vol       adg        2008/09/21 11:00
SP04-vol    adg        vol     spaceopt vol       adg        2008/09/21 12:00
# vxprint -g adg -cF '%{assoc:-15} %creation_time' \
  -e 'sp_vol_name~/^SP0[1-4]-vol$/'
SP01-vol       Tue Sep 21 09:00:00 2008
SP02-vol       Tue Sep 21 10:00:00 2008
```

```
SP03-vol        Tue Sep 21 11:00:00 2008
SP04-vol        Tue Sep 21 12:00:00 2008
# dd if=/dev/zero of=/dev/vx/rdsk/adg/vol bs=1024k count=100
# vxcache -g adg stat
CACHE NAME             TOTAL(Mb)    USED(Mb) (%)    AVAIL(Mb) (%)   SDCNT
cobjcvol                     256     104 (40)            152 (59)       4
```

9.3.12   A FINAL EXAMPLE FOR VOLUME SNAPSHOTS

For all those of our readers still not satisfied by the complexity of snapshot structures, we provide the output of a vxprint command. Please decode! Note: This is a realistic scenario! If most of the data centers do not use advanced VxVM volume architectures, then it does probably not mean, that complex volumes are unnecessary, but that the administrators need (better) Storage Foundation courses.

```
v  SNAP-vol1     -            ENABLED  ACTIVE  419430400 SELECT   -        fsgen
pl SNAP-vol1-P01 SNAP-vol1    ENABLED  ACTIVE  419430400 CONCAT   -        RW
sc SNAP-vol1-S01 SNAP-vol1-P01 cobjcvol 0      419430400 0        -        ENA
dc SNAP-vol1_dco SNAP-vol1    SNAP-vol1_dcl

v  SNAP-vol1_dcl -            ENABLED  ACTIVE  7488      SELECT   -        gen
pl SNAP-vol1_dcl-01 SNAP-vol1_dcl ENABLED ACTIVE 7488   CONCAT   -        RW
sd adg05-01      SNAP-vol1_dcl-01 adg05 87607552 7488   0        c1t1d4   ENA
sp vol1_snp      SNAP-vol1    SNAP-vol1_dco

v  SNAP-vol2     -            ENABLED  ACTIVE  419430400 SELECT   -        fsgen
pl SNAP-vol2-P01 SNAP-vol2    ENABLED  ACTIVE  419430400 CONCAT   -        RW
sc SNAP-vol2-S01 SNAP-vol2-P01 cobjcvol 0      419430400 0        -        ENA
dc SNAP-vol2_dco SNAP-vol2    SNAP-vol2_dcl

v  SNAP-vol2_dcl -            ENABLED  ACTIVE  7488      SELECT   -        gen
pl SNAP-vol2_dcl-01 SNAP-vol2_dcl ENABLED ACTIVE 7488   CONCAT   -        RW
sd adg07-01      SNAP-vol2_dcl-01 adg07 87607552 7488   0        c1t1d6   ENA
sp vol2_snp      SNAP-vol2    SNAP-vol2_dco

v  vol1          -            ENABLED  ACTIVE  419430400 SELECT   vol1-03  fsgen
pl vol1-03       vol1         ENABLED  ACTIVE  419430400 STRIPE   2/512    RW

sv vol1-S01      vol1-03      vol1-L01 1       122107648 0/0      2/2      ENA
v2 vol1-L01      -            ENABLED  ACTIVE  122107648 SELECT   -        fsgen
p2 vol1-P01      vol1-L01     ENABLED  ACTIVE  122107648 CONCAT   -        RW
s2 adg01-02      vol1-P01     adg01    0       122107648 0        c1t1d0   ENA
p2 vol1-P02      vol1-L01     ENABLED  ACTIVE  122107648 CONCAT   -        RW
s2 adg03-02      vol1-P02     adg03    0       122107648 0        c1t1d2   ENA
```

```
sv vol1-S02      vol1-03       vol1-L02 1       87607552 0/122107648 2/2    ENA
v2 vol1-L02      -             ENABLED  ACTIVE  87607552 SELECT       -      fsgen
p2 vol1-P03      vol1-L02      ENABLED  ACTIVE  87607552 CONCAT       -      RW
s2 adg05-02      vol1-P03      adg05    0       87607552 0            c1t1d4 ENA
p2 vol1-P04      vol1-L02      ENABLED  ACTIVE  87607552 CONCAT       -      RW
s2 adg07-02      vol1-P04      adg07    0       87607552 0            c1t1d6 ENA

sv vol1-S03      vol1-03       vol1-L03 1       122107648 1/0         2/2    ENA
v2 vol1-L03      -             ENABLED  ACTIVE  122107648 SELECT      -      fsgen
p2 vol1-P05      vol1-L03      ENABLED  ACTIVE  122107648 CONCAT      -      RW
s2 adg02-02      vol1-P05      adg02    0       122107648 0           c1t1d1 ENA
p2 vol1-P06      vol1-L03      ENABLED  ACTIVE  122107648 CONCAT      -      RW
s2 adg04-02      vol1-P06      adg04    0       122107648 0           c1t1d3 ENA

sv vol1-S04      vol1-03       vol1-L04 1       87607552 1/122107648 2/2    ENA
v2 vol1-L04      -             ENABLED  ACTIVE  87607552 SELECT       -      fsgen
p2 vol1-P07      vol1-L04      ENABLED  ACTIVE  87607552 CONCAT       -      RW
s2 adg06-02      vol1-P07      adg06    0       87607552 0            c1t1d5 ENA
p2 vol1-P08      vol1-L04      ENABLED  ACTIVE  87607552 CONCAT       -      RW
s2 adg08-02      vol1-P08      adg08    0       87607552 0            c1t1d7 ENA
dc vol1_dco      vol1          vol1_dcl

v  vol1_dcl      -             ENABLED  ACTIVE  7488     SELECT       -      gen
pl vol1_dcl-01   vol1_dcl      ENABLED  ACTIVE  7488     CONCAT       -      RW
sd adg06-01      vol1_dcl-01   adg06    87607552 7488    0            c1t1d5 ENA
pl vol1_dcl-02   vol1_dcl      ENABLED  ACTIVE  7488     CONCAT       -      RW
sd adg08-01      vol1_dcl-02   adg08    87607552 7488    0            c1t1d7 ENA
sp SNAP-vol1_snp vol1          vol1_dco

v  vol2          -             ENABLED  ACTIVE  419430400 SELECT      vol2-03 fsgen
pl vol2-03       vol2          ENABLED  ACTIVE  419430400 STRIPE      2/512   RW

sv vol2-S01      vol2-03       vol2-L01 1       122107648 0/0         2/2    ENA
v2 vol2-L01      -             ENABLED  ACTIVE  122107648 SELECT      -      fsgen
p2 vol2-P01      vol2-L01      ENABLED  ACTIVE  122107648 CONCAT      -      RW
s2 adg09-02      vol2-P01      adg09    0       122107648 0           c1t1d8 ENA
p2 vol2-P02      vol2-L01      ENABLED  ACTIVE  122107648 CONCAT      -      RW
s2 adg11-02      vol2-P02      adg11    0       122107648 0           c1t1d10 ENA

sv vol2-S02      vol2-03       vol2-L02 1       87607552 0/122107648 2/2    ENA
v2 vol2-L02      -             ENABLED  ACTIVE  87607552 SELECT       -      fsgen
p2 vol2-P03      vol2-L02      ENABLED  ACTIVE  87607552 CONCAT       -      RW
s2 adg13-02      vol2-P03      adg13    0       87607552 0            c1t1d12 ENA
p2 vol2-P04      vol2-L02      ENABLED  ACTIVE  87607552 CONCAT       -      RW
s2 adg15-02      vol2-P04      adg15    0       87607552 0            c1t1d14 ENA
```

```
sv vol2-S03      vol2-03      vol2-L03 1    122107648 1/0           2/2      ENA
v2 vol2-L03      -            ENABLED  ACTIVE  122107648 SELECT      -        fsgen
p2 vol2-P05      vol2-L03     ENABLED  ACTIVE  122107648 CONCAT      -        RW
s2 adg10-02      vol2-P05     adg10    0      122107648 0           c1t1d9   ENA
p2 vol2-P06      vol2-L03     ENABLED  ACTIVE  122107648 CONCAT      -        RW
s2 adg12-02      vol2-P06     adg12    0      122107648 0           c1t1d11  ENA

sv vol2-S04      vol2-03      vol2-L04 1    87607552 1/122107648 2/2      ENA
v2 vol2-L04      -            ENABLED  ACTIVE  87607552 SELECT       -        fsgen
p2 vol2-P07      vol2-L04     ENABLED  ACTIVE  87607552 CONCAT       -        RW
s2 adg14-02      vol2-P07     adg14    0      87607552 0            c1t1d13  ENA
p2 vol2-P08      vol2-L04     ENABLED  ACTIVE  87607552 CONCAT       -        RW
s2 adg16-02      vol2-P08     adg16    0      87607552 0            c1t1d15  ENA
dc vol2_dco      vol2         vol2_dcl

v  vol2_dcl      -            ENABLED  ACTIVE  7488      SELECT       -        gen
pl vol2_dcl-01   vol2_dcl     ENABLED  ACTIVE  7488      CONCAT       -        RW
sd adg14-01      vol2_dcl-01  adg14    87607552 7488     0           c1t1d13  ENA
pl vol2_dcl-02   vol2_dcl     ENABLED  ACTIVE  7488      CONCAT       -        RW
sd adg16-01      vol2_dcl-02  adg16    87607552 7488     0           .c1t1d15 ENA
sp SNAP-vol2_snp vol2         vol2_dco

co cobjcvol      cvol         ENABLED  ACTIVE

v  cvol          cobjcvol     ENABLED  ACTIVE  209715200 SELECT      cvol-03  fsgen
pl cvol-03       cvol         ENABLED  ACTIVE  209715200 STRIPE      2/128    RW

sv cvol-S01      cvol-03      cvol-L01 1    104857600 0/0          2/2      ENA
v2 cvol-L01      -            ENABLED  ACTIVE  104857600 SELECT      -        fsgen
p2 cvol-P01      cvol-L01     ENABLED  ACTIVE  104857600 CONCAT      -        RW
s2 adg17-02      cvol-P01     adg17    0      104857600 0           c1t1d16  ENA
p2 cvol-P02      cvol-L01     ENABLED  ACTIVE  104857600 CONCAT      -        RW
s2 adg19-02      cvol-P02     adg19    0      104857600 0           c1t1d18  ENA

sv cvol-S02      cvol-03      cvol-L02 1    104857600 1/0          2/2      ENA
v2 cvol-L02      -            ENABLED  ACTIVE  104857600 SELECT      -        fsgen
p2 cvol-P03      cvol-L02     ENABLED  ACTIVE  104857600 CONCAT      -        RW
s2 adg18-02      cvol-P03     adg18    0      104857600 0           c1t1d17  ENA
p2 cvol-P04      cvol-L02     ENABLED  ACTIVE  104857600 CONCAT      -        RW
s2 adg20-02      cvol-P04     adg20    0      104857600 0           c1t1d19  ENA
```

9.4 VERITAS FILE SYSTEM BASED SNAPSHOTS

9.4.1 CACHE OVERFLOW ON A TRADITIONAL SNAPSHOT

The "Easy Sailing" section already described a snapshot mechanism based on VxFS, providing a completely logical snapshot with a mountable snapshot device storing only the originals of data overwritten by the application. We still didn't explain the snapshot behavior when exceeding the capacity of the snapshot device. Do we have something comparable to the autogrow feature of the volume based space optimized snapshot?

To get an answer, we will create a file system containing four files at 5 MB and an appropriate snapshot device (10% in size of the original file system). We choose the simplest volume layouts to indicate that we do not deal with volume based raw device snapshots and their plex break-off:

```
# vxassist -g adg make vol 100m
# mkfs -F vxfs /dev/vx/rdsk/adg/vol
# mount -F vxfs /dev/vx/dsk/adg/vol /mnt
# for i in 1 2 3 4; do mkfile 5m /mnt/file$i; done
# vxassist -g adg make snapvol 10m
# mount -F vxfs -o snapof=/mnt /dev/vx/dsk/adg/snapvol /mnt_snap
# ls -lA /mnt*
/mnt:
total 40960
-rw------T  1 root     root      5242880 Sep 21 08:19 file1
-rw------T  1 root     root      5242880 Sep 21 08:19 file2
-rw------T  1 root     root      5242880 Sep 21 08:19 file3
-rw------T  1 root     root      5242880 Sep 21 08:19 file4
drwxr-xr-x  2 root     root           96 Sep 21 08:18 lost+found

/mnt_snap:
total 40960
-rw------T  1 root     root      5242880 Sep 21 08:19 file1
-rw------T  1 root     root      5242880 Sep 21 08:19 file2
-rw------T  1 root     root      5242880 Sep 21 08:19 file3
-rw------T  1 root     root      5242880 Sep 21 08:19 file4
drwxr-xr-x  2 root     root           96 Sep 21 08:18 lost+found
# df -k /mnt*
Filesystem            kbytes    used  avail capacity  Mounted on
/dev/vx/dsk/adg/vol   102400   22645  74777    24%    /mnt
/dev/vx/dsk/adg/snapvol
                      102400   22645  74771    24%    /mnt_snap
```

Currently, the original and the snapshot file system contain exactly the same files, in other words, the bitmap of the snapshot device only points to the data set of the original file system. On first thought, we expect a cache overflow after removing two files from the original file system:

```
# rm /mnt/file1 /mnt/file2
# ls -lA /mnt*
/mnt:
total 20480
-rw------T  1 root    root    5242880 Sep 21 08:19 file3
-rw------T  1 root    root    5242880 Sep 21 08:19 file4
drwxr-xr-x  2 root    root         96 Sep 21 08:18 lost+found

/mnt_snap:
total 40960
-rw------T  1 root    root    5242880 Sep 21 08:19 file1
-rw------T  1 root    root    5242880 Sep 21 08:19 file2
-rw------T  1 root    root    5242880 Sep 21 08:19 file3
-rw------T  1 root    root    5242880 Sep 21 08:19 file4
drwxr-xr-x  2 root    root         96 Sep 21 08:18 lost+found
# df -k /mnt*
Filesystem           kbytes    used   avail capacity  Mounted on
/dev/vx/dsk/adg/vol  102400   12405   84377     13%   /mnt
/dev/vx/dsk/adg/snapvol
                     102400   22645   74771     24%   /mnt_snap
# od -cAd /mnt_snap/file1
0000000 \0 \0 \0 \0 \0 \0 \0 \0 \0 \0 \0 \0 \0 \0 \0 \0
*
5242880
# od -cAd /mnt_snap/file2
0000000 \0 \0 \0 \0 \0 \0 \0 \0 \0 \0 \0 \0 \0 \0 \0 \0
*
5242880
```

Hmm! Nothing happened except for a proper handling by the snapshot still providing the file contents of the files removed on the original file system (tested by an od read). We enter into an impatient testing instead of a calm deliberation:

```
# rm /mnt/file?
# ls -lA /mnt*
/mnt:
total 0
drwxr-xr-x  2 root    root         96 Sep 21 08:18 lost+found

/mnt_snap:
total 40960
-rw------T  1 root    root    5242880 Sep 21 08:19 file1
-rw------T  1 root    root    5242880 Sep 21 08:19 file2
-rw------T  1 root    root    5242880 Sep 21 08:19 file3
```

```
-rw------T   1 root     root     5242880 Sep 21 08:19 file4
drwxr-xr-x   2 root     root          96 Sep 21 08:18 lost+found
# df -k /mnt*
Filesystem            kbytes    used   avail capacity  Mounted on
/dev/vx/dsk/adg/vol   102400    2165   93978     3%    /mnt
/dev/vx/dsk/adg/snapvol
                      102400   22645   74771    24%    /mnt_snap
# od -cAd /mnt_snap/file?
0000000  \0  \0  \0  \0  \0  \0  \0  \0  \0  \0  \0  \0  \0  \0  \0  \0
*
20971520
```

What is this? Is it some kind of wizardry? No, because VxFS (as other file systems) did not completely remove the file. Some file system basics: How is a file stored within the file system? First, the directory file for the directory containing our file provides a mapping between the file name and the inode number, all this occupying only a few bytes. Since the directory file is updated by this operation, its inode reflects the new modification time, and potentially a new block is assigned for it. Secondly, an inode is allocated (in VxFS as part of an inode structural file, default size 256 bytes, configurable to 512 bytes) storing all the file attributes (such as file type, modification time, owner, permissions) and the required address-length-pairs (VxFS) to denote the physical location of the stored file contents. Thirdly and finally, we need storage for the data blocks ("extents" in VxFS) whose size summed up correspond to the file size (rounded up to the next block multiple).

What happens, if a file is removed from the file system? The entry mapping file name and inode number is cleared (VxFS) within the directory file, and the modification time of the directory file is updated. Furthermore, the inode, being now invalid, is removed from the inode structural file (VxFS). But the predominant amount of storage, the data blocks covering the file contents remain unchanged on the device as long as no new data are written to the file system. That's why our removal of all four files only copied a few metadata blocks to the snapshot device.

Furnished with the appropriate file system knowledge, we expect that overwriting one file on the original file system will not exceed the limit of the snapshot storage. But overwriting the second file will ... Well, be in for a surprise!

```
# mkfile 5m /mnt/file1
# ls -lA /mnt*
/mnt:
total 10254
-rw------T   1 root     root     5242880 Sep 21 09:18 file1
drwxr-xr-x   2 root     root          96 Sep 21 08:18 lost+found

/mnt_snap:
total 40960
-rw------T   1 root     root     5242880 Sep 21 08:19 file1
-rw------T   1 root     root     5242880 Sep 21 08:19 file2
-rw------T   1 root     root     5242880 Sep 21 08:19 file3
-rw------T   1 root     root     5242880 Sep 21 08:19 file4
```

```
drwxr-xr-x   2 root      root           96 Sep 21 08:18 lost+found
# df -k /mnt*
Filesystem              kbytes    used   avail capacity Mounted on
/dev/vx/dsk/adg/vol     102400    7285   89178     8%   /mnt
/dev/vx/dsk/adg/snapvol
                        102400   22645   74771    24%   /mnt_snap
# mkfile 5m /mnt/file2
# ls -lA /mnt*
/mnt:
total 20480
-rw------T   1 root      root      5242880 Sep 21 09:18 file1
-rw------T   1 root      root      5242880 Sep 21 09:20 file2
drwxr-xr-x   2 root      root           96 Sep 21 08:18 lost+found

/mnt_snap:
total 40960
-rw------T   1 root      root      5242880 Sep 21 08:19 file1
-rw------T   1 root      root      5242880 Sep 21 08:19 file2
-rw------T   1 root      root      5242880 Sep 21 08:19 file3
-rw------T   1 root      root      5242880 Sep 21 08:19 file4
drwxr-xr-x   2 root      root           96 Sep 21 08:18 lost+found
# df -k /mnt*
Filesystem              kbytes    used   avail capacity Mounted on
/dev/vx/dsk/adg/vol     102400   12405   84377    13%   /mnt
/dev/vx/dsk/adg/snapvol
                        102400   22645   74771    24%   /mnt_snap
```

Did we unfoundedly gloat with our file system knowledge? No, the piece of information provided by the command output was stored still within the file system kernel cache. But the system console shows a warning message, and an od command (or other read accesses) is unable to read the file content (which produces another console message):

```
Sep 21 09:20:12 haensel vxfs: WARNING: msgcnt 1 mesg 028: V-2-28: vx_snap_alloc
- /dev/vx/dsk/adg/snapvol snapshot file system out of space
```

```
# od -cAd /mnt_snap/file2
0000000
```

```
Sep 21 09:20:55 haensel vxfs: WARNING: msgcnt 2 mesg 032: V-2-32: vx_disable - /
dev/vx/dsk/adg/snapvol snapshot file system disabled
```

To sum up: A physical overflow of the snapshot device will disable the snapshot file system making all snapped data inaccessible. There is no way to recover the snapshot, and, what is more, there is no way to show the current quota of the snapshot device while the snapshot is still enabled. So, it is a good idea to choose a somewhat oversized snapshot device and not to rely for too long a period on its proper functioning. But don't forget the main advantage of this kind of snapshot: It is cheap in storage and license costs.

Two final remarks: A file system based access to the snapshot via its mount point (such as ls, find, tar) does not show any particularity, the snapshot behaves like a regular mounted file system. A standard raw device access to the snapshot storage (e.g. by dd) only gets the physical snapshot storage device data, because the pointing bitmap is not understood. If you want to perform a valid backup of your snapshot file system close to raw device access, you must use the vxdump tool (and for restore purposes the corresponding vxrestore command).

Refreshing a VxFS snapshot (even a disabled one) is quite easy: Just unmount the snapshot and mount it once again. You may restore the file system content of the application file system by simply copying the required files from the snapshot mount to the application mount. If the amount of copied files will exceed the capacity of the snapshot device (the snapshot will handle those copy operations as overwritten or new files on its original file system), you must copy your files to a temporary staging file system. To delete a snapshot: Unmount it and remove the snapshot device.

9.4.2 VxFS Storage Checkpoints

General Concept

Let's turn to a snapshot concept really deserving to be called an intelligent mechanism suitable for enterprise needs! To understand its capabilities and advantages (and only a few weaknesses), we recall the flexible layout of VxFS (in the following example on a 128 MB volume with a 10 MB file on VxFS version 7 layout), as shown by the ncheck command:

```
# ncheck -F vxfs -o sector= /dev/vx/rdsk/adg/vol
/dev/vx/rdsk/adg/vol:

sectors(204800)         blocks(0)
------------------      ------------------
0/0-0/204799            0/0-0/102400

fileset    fset      match match devid/
name       indx inode indx  inode sectors        name
---------- ---- ----- ----  ----- -------------  -------------------
STRUCTURAL    1     3   -       35 0/18-0/21      <fileset_header>
STRUCTURAL    1     4   1        - 0/22-0/29      <inode_alloc_unit>
STRUCTURAL    1     5   1       37 0/4640-0/4655  <inode_list>
STRUCTURAL    1     5   1       37 0/48-0/63      <inode_list>
STRUCTURAL    1     5   1       37 0/4624-0/4639  <inode_list>
STRUCTURAL    1     5   1       37 0/32-0/47      <inode_list>
STRUCTURAL    1     6   -        - 0/30-0/31      <current_usage_tbl>
STRUCTURAL    1     7   -       39 0/64-0/65      <object_loc_tbl>
STRUCTURAL    1     8   -       40 0/80-0/1103    <device_config>
STRUCTURAL    1     9   -       41 0/1104-0/3151  <intent_log>
STRUCTURAL    1    11   -        - 0/66-0/67      <fs_allocation_policy>
```

STRUCTURAL	1	32	–	–	0/68–0/69	\<history_log\>
STRUCTURAL	1	33	–	–	0/4614–0/4615	\<device_label\>
STRUCTURAL	1	33	–	–	0/0–0/17	\<device_label\>
STRUCTURAL	1	35	–	3	0/4608–0/4611	\<fileset_header\>
STRUCTURAL	1	37	1	5	0/4640–0/4655	\<inode_list\>
STRUCTURAL	1	37	1	5	0/48–0/63	\<inode_list\>
STRUCTURAL	1	37	1	5	0/4624–0/4639	\<inode_list\>
STRUCTURAL	1	37	1	5	0/32–0/47	\<inode_list\>
STRUCTURAL	1	39	–	7	0/4612–0/4613	\<object_loc_tbl\>
STRUCTURAL	1	40	–	8	0/4656–0/5679	\<device_config\>
STRUCTURAL	1	41	–	9	0/1104–0/3151	\<intent_log\>
STRUCTURAL	1	64	999	–	0/70–0/77	\<inode_alloc_unit\>
STRUCTURAL	1	65	999	97	0/3152–0/3167	\<inode_list\>
STRUCTURAL	1	69	999	–	0/3168–0/3183	\<bsd_quota\>
STRUCTURAL	1	70	999	–	0/3184–0/3199	\<bsd_quota\>
STRUCTURAL	1	71	–	–	0/78–0/79	\<state_alloc_bitmap\>
STRUCTURAL	1	72	–	–	0/3200–0/3201	\<extent_au_summary\>
STRUCTURAL	1	73	–	105	0/3264–0/3279	\<extent_map\>
STRUCTURAL	1	73	–	105	0/3232–0/3263	\<extent_map\>
STRUCTURAL	1	73	–	105	0/3216–0/3231	\<extent_map\>
STRUCTURAL	1	97	999	65	0/3152–0/3167	\<inode_list\>
STRUCTURAL	1	105	–	73	0/3264–0/3279	\<extent_map\>
STRUCTURAL	1	105	–	73	0/3232–0/3263	\<extent_map\>
STRUCTURAL	1	105	–	73	0/3216–0/3231	\<extent_map\>
UNNAMED	999	4	–	–	0/16384–0/36863	/file.10m
–	–	–	–	–	0/3202–0/3215	\<free\>
–	–	–	–	–	0/3280–0/4607	\<free\>
–	–	–	–	–	0/4616–0/4623	\<free\>
–	–	–	–	–	0/5680–0/16383	\<free\>
–	–	–	–	–	0/36864–0/204799	\<free\>

The first column reveals two file system instances to the raw device. First, the STRUCTURAL file set carrying index 1 (column 2) accesses the "files" storing general file system metadata such as the intent log, two object location tables to store the current position of most metadata files, extent maps, and so on (last column; for redundancy purposes, those metadata are addressed mostly by two inodes, see column 3 and 5). Furthermore, the STRUCTURAL file set contains metadata for its own file set (match index 1 in column 4) and for the current file system as visible by the virtual file system of the operating system and in use by an application (match index 999). Secondly, we recognize the standard file system for application purposes, called UNNAMED and carrying file set index 999, and, in our example, the physical location of a 10 MB file (column 6; 0 before the slash denotes the volume counter within a volume set, the numbers after the slash indicate start and end sectors). Free space on the file system device is listed at the end.

Please recall the required procedure of other snapshot mechanisms when overwriting an existing file or data set: The original file or data set must be copied to a snapshot container outside of the application device (snapshot device, cache device), before the new file or data set can be written to the application device. We have a noticeable performance drawback by additional I/Os.

The VxFS snapshot mechanism called "Storage Checkpoint" does not need a separate snapshot container, because it uses free space within the same device for snapshot purposes. To distinguish between the active file system and a snapshot file system, VxFS simply adds another file system instance to the device (besides STRUCTURAL and UNNAMED) arbitrarily named (we will choose "CP" and a time stamp) and with a partially own set of metadata. As long as the file system remains unchanged, both file system instances' metadata point to the same file contents.

```
# fsckptadm create CP$(date +%H%M) /mnt
# mount -F vxfs -o remount /dev/vx/dsk/adg/vol /mnt
# ncheck -F vxfs -o sector= /dev/vx/rdsk/adg/vol
/dev/vx/rdsk/adg/vol:


sectors(204800)          blocks(0)
-----------------        -----------------
0/0-0/204799             0/0-0/102400


fileset      fset       match  match devid/
name         indx inode indx  inode sectors         name
----------   ---- ----- ----- ----- -------------   -------------------
STRUCTURAL    1      3    -       35 0/3280-0/3295   <fileset_header>
STRUCTURAL    1      3    -       35 0/18-0/21       <fileset_header>
STRUCTURAL    1      4    1       -  0/22-0/29       <inode_alloc_unit>
STRUCTURAL    1      5    1       37 0/4640-0/4655   <inode_list>
STRUCTURAL    1      5    1       37 0/48-0/63       <inode_list>
STRUCTURAL    1      5    1       37 0/4624-0/4639   <inode_list>
STRUCTURAL    1      5    1       37 0/32-0/47       <inode_list>
STRUCTURAL    1      6    -       -  0/30-0/31       <current_usage_tbl>
STRUCTURAL    1      7    -       39 0/64-0/65       <object_loc_tbl>
STRUCTURAL    1      8    -       40 0/80-0/1103     <device_config>
STRUCTURAL    1      9    -       41 0/1104-0/3151   <intent_log>
STRUCTURAL    1     11    -       -  0/66-0/67       <fs_allocation_policy>
STRUCTURAL    1     32    -       -  0/68-0/69       <history_log>
STRUCTURAL    1     33    -       -  0/4614-0/4615   <device_label>
STRUCTURAL    1     33    -       -  0/0-0/17        <device_label>
STRUCTURAL    1     35    -       3  0/196608-0/196623 <fileset_header>
STRUCTURAL    1     35    -       3  0/4608-0/4611   <fileset_header>
STRUCTURAL    1     37    1       5  0/4640-0/4655   <inode_list>
STRUCTURAL    1     37    1       5  0/48-0/63       <inode_list>
STRUCTURAL    1     37    1       5  0/4624-0/4639   <inode_list>
STRUCTURAL    1     37    1       5  0/32-0/47       <inode_list>
STRUCTURAL    1     39    -       7  0/4612-0/4613   <object_loc_tbl>
STRUCTURAL    1     40    -       8  0/4656-0/5679   <device_config>
STRUCTURAL    1     41    -       9  0/1104-0/3151   <intent_log>
STRUCTURAL    1     64   999      -  0/70-0/77       <inode_alloc_unit>
STRUCTURAL    1     65   999      97 0/3152-0/3167   <inode_list>
```

```
STRUCTURAL    1    69   999    -  0/3168-0/3183 <bsd_quota>
STRUCTURAL    1    70   999    -  0/3184-0/3199 <bsd_quota>
STRUCTURAL    1    71    -     -  0/78-0/79      <state_alloc_bitmap>
STRUCTURAL    1    72    -     -  0/3200-0/3201 <extent_au_summary>
STRUCTURAL    1    73    -   105  0/3264-0/3279 <extent_map>
STRUCTURAL    1    73    -   105  0/3232-0/3263 <extent_map>
STRUCTURAL    1    73    -   105  0/3216-0/3231 <extent_map>
STRUCTURAL    1    74  1000    -  0/3208-0/3215 <inode_alloc_unit>
STRUCTURAL    1    75  1000   76  0/5680-0/5695 <inode_list>
STRUCTURAL    1    76  1000   75  0/5680-0/5695 <inode_list>
STRUCTURAL    1    81  1000    -  0/3296-0/3311 <bsd_quota>
STRUCTURAL    1    82  1000    -  0/3312-0/3327 <bsd_quota>
STRUCTURAL    1    97   999   65  0/3152-0/3167 <inode_list>
STRUCTURAL    1   105    -    73  0/3264-0/3279 <extent_map>
STRUCTURAL    1   105    -    73  0/3232-0/3263 <extent_map>
STRUCTURAL    1   105    -    73  0/3216-0/3231 <extent_map>
UNNAMED     999     4    -     -  0/16384-0/36863 /file
   -          -     -    -     -  0/3202-0/3207 <free>
   -          -     -    -     -  0/3328-0/4607 <free>
   -          -     -    -     -  0/4616-0/4623 <free>
   -          -     -    -     -  0/5696-0/16383 <free>
   -          -     -    -     -  0/36864-0/196607 <free>
   -          -     -    -     -  0/196624-0/204799 <free>
```

Note the new file set match index 1000 in the fourth column of the ncheck output providing a separate inode allocation unit, an inode list file addressed by two inodes, and two BSD quota files. The first column does not list the new checkpoint, as it still does not differ from the active file system. The command fsckptadm to create the snapshot will be explained in more detail, of course. Please be aware, that ncheck operates on the raw device, while fsckptadm defines the storage checkpoint based on the mount point, i.e. by using the block device driver. In order to immediately demonstrate the effect of file system modifications by ncheck, the file system caches need to be flushed to the raw device, which is best performed by a remount (keeps read caches valid by flushing all dirty blocks).

Since we did not create another snapshot device, we must use the application block device driver to mount the storage checkpoint by specifying the storage checkpoint instance of the file system. But unlike the legacy VxFS snapshot, the time the checkpoint was created defines its time stamp, not the time it was mounted. The storage checkpoint may not be mounted to work as a snapshot.

```
# fsckptadm list /mnt
/mnt
CP1203:
        ctime                = Wed Sep 21 12:03:11 2008
        mtime                = Wed Sep 21 12:03:11 2008
        flags                = largefiles
# mkdir /mnt_CP1203
# mount -F vxfs -o ckpt=CP1203 /dev/vx/dsk/adg/vol:CP1203 /mnt_CP1203
```

```
# ls -lA /mnt*
/mnt:
total 20480
-rw-------   1 root     root     10485760 Sep 21 10:19 file
drwxr-xr-x   2 root     root           96 Sep 21 10:17 lost+found

/mnt_CP1203:
total 0
-rw-------   1 root     root     10485760 Sep 21 10:19 file
drwxr-xr-x   2 root     root           96 Sep 21 10:17 lost+found
# df -k /mnt*
Filesystem              kbytes    used   avail capacity  Mounted on
/dev/vx/dsk/adg/vol     102400   12449   84336    13%    /mnt
/dev/vx/dsk/adg/vol:CP1203
                        102400   12449   84336    13%    /mnt_CP1203
```

A snapshot is intended to provide a frozen image in spite of write I/Os. Let's overwrite our file! We do not use the mkfile command immediately on our file system, because it shows some strange behavior when applied to a VxFS file system (zero device space reserved, but not actually written).

```
# mkfile 10m /tmp/file
# cp /tmp/file /mnt
# mount -F vxfs -o remount /dev/vx/dsk/adg/vol /mnt
# ncheck -F vxfs -o sector= /dev/vx/rdsk/adg/vol
...
UNNAMED     999     4    -    - 0/36864-0/40959 /file
UNNAMED     999     4    -    - 0/49152-0/65535 /file
CP1203     1000     4    -    - 0/16384-0/36863 /file
...
# ls -lA /mnt*
/mnt:
total 20480
-rw-------   1 root     root     10485760 Sep 21 12:55 file
drwxr-xr-x   2 root     root           96 Sep 21 10:17 lost+found

/mnt_CP1203:
total 20480
-rw-------   1 root     root     10485760 Sep 21 10:19 file
drwxr-xr-x   2 root     root           96 Sep 21 10:17 lost+found
# df -k /mnt*
Filesystem              kbytes    used   avail capacity  Mounted on
/dev/vx/dsk/adg/vol     102400   22689   74736    24%    /mnt
/dev/vx/dsk/adg/vol:CP1203
                        102400   22689   74736    24%    /mnt_CP1203
```

The storage used by the original file (sectors 16384-36863, assigned to UNNAMED, see the previous ncheck output) is now assigned to the storage checkpoint CP1203 only, i.e. the metadata set of CP1203 keeps its information on that file showing its former content and attributes. The "overwriting" new file got a previously free storage location (in our case fragmented into two pieces due to the internal extent organization of VxFS) with own attributes (visible at the different modification time stamp in the ls output).

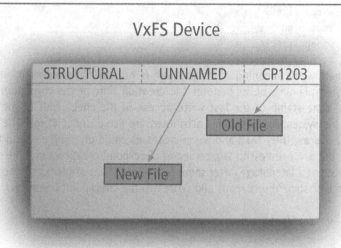

VxFS Device

Figure 9-10: No "Copy on First Write" using VxFS Storage Checkpoints

Unlike the snapshot mechanisms we hitherto described in this chapter, the VxFS storage checkpoint does NOT perform a copy-on-first-write I/O! The application does NOT suffer from remarkable performance drawback! We will demonstrate some reasonable exceptions from that general rule in the "Technical Deep Dive" section. But in spite of some official Veritas/Symantec documentation, a copy-on-first-write is not the general I/O rule (one of the extremely rare situations a company sells its products with deteriorating information).

Storage Checkpoint Administration

Our example above already used the fsckptadm command to create a storage checkpoint. To see some statistical details of the active file system and the storage checkpoint, you may add the option -v ("verbose"):

```
# fsckptadm -v create CP$(date +%H%M) /mnt
CP1503:
        ctime                   = Wed Sep 21 15:03:26 2008
        mtime                   = Wed Sep 21 15:03:26 2008
        flags                   = largefiles
        # of inodes             = 32
```

```
              # of blocks         =  0
              # of reads          =  0
              # of writes         =  0
              # of pushes         =  0
              # of pulls          =  0
              # of moves          =  0
              # of move alls      =  0
              # of merge alls     =  0
              # of logged pushes  =  0
              # of enospc retries =  0
              # of overlay bmaps  =  0
```

Unfortunately, the meaning of the output is not officially reported, and only few entries are self-explaining. ctime denotes the creation time of the checkpoint, mtime the "modification" time stamp of the last write access to the checkpoint (if mounted read-write). Some file system or checkpoint attributes are listed under flags. The counters to inodes, (data) blocks, (file) read and write accesses could give some useful hints on file system usage, but are, needless to say, zeroed at checkpoint creation time. The same output may be produced at a later stage, after some overwritten files or blocks on the UNNAMED file system instance or some direct reads and writes to the checkpoint instance:

```
# fsckptadm -v list /mnt
/mnt
CP1203:
              ctime               =  Wed Sep 21 12:03:11 2008
              mtime               =  Wed Sep 21 15:54:26 2008
              flags               =  largefiles
              # of inodes         =  32
              # of blocks         =  10240
              # of reads          =  2
              # of writes         =  1
              # of pushes         =  0
              # of pulls          =  0
              # of moves          =  0
              # of move alls      =  0
              # of merge alls     =  0
              # of logged pushes  =  0
              # of enospc retries =  0
              # of overlay bmaps  =  0
```

Adding the option -1 to the last mentioned command includes statistics to the UNNAMED file system instance. Omitting all options provides a short overview of existing storage checkpoints together with time stamps and flags (use fsckptadm info to display only one checkpoint):

```
# fsckptadm list /mnt
/mnt
CP1503:
```

```
        ctime                   =  Wed Sep 21 15:03:26 2008
        mtime                   =  Wed Sep 21 15:03:26 2008
        flags                   =  largefiles
CP1203:
        ctime                   =  Wed Sep 21 12:03:11 2008
        mtime                   =  Wed Sep 21 15:54:26 2008
        flags                   =  largefiles, mounted
```

If the cache volume of a space optimized volume snapshot gets out of space (autogrow disabled or maximum size for autogrow reached), snapshot volumes become disabled or are completely deleted. If copy-on-first-write operations overflow the cache device for the legacy VxFS snapshot, the snapshot will be disabled. In both cases, the mentioned snapshot behavior is not configurable. VxFS storage checkpoints provide a configurable flag called removable. If the file system device holding the active file system and the storage check-points as well runs out of space, you may decide what should happen: Should a checkpoint be removed to free space in favor of the running application (flag removable set), or should the checkpoint be kept, while application write I/Os are prohibited (removable cleared)? You may specify a removable checkpoint by adding the option -r when creating it. But at any time you may toggle the removable flag value by issuing a fsckptadm set|clear command, as shown in the following, somewhat disappointing example (file system 100 MB in size):

```
# mount -F vxfs /dev/vx/dsk/adg/vol /mnt
# mkfile 20m /tmp/file
# cp /tmp/file /mnt/file0
# cp /tmp/file /mnt/file1
# cp /tmp/file /mnt/file2
# fsckptadm create Ckpt /mnt
# mkdir /mnt_ckpt
# mount -F vxfs -o ckpt=Ckpt /dev/vx/dsk/adg/vol:Ckpt /mnt_ckpt
# df -k /mnt*
Filesystem              kbytes     used   avail capacity Mounted on
/dev/vx/dsk/adg/vol     102400    63649   36336    64%   /mnt
/dev/vx/dsk/adg/vol:Ckpt
                        102400    63649   36336    64%   /mnt_ckpt
# cp /tmp/file /mnt/file0
# df -k /mnt*
Filesystem              kbytes     used   avail capacity Mounted on
/dev/vx/dsk/adg/vol     102400    84129   17136    84%   /mnt
/dev/vx/dsk/adg/vol:Ckpt
                        102400    84129   17136    84%   /mnt_ckpt
# cp /tmp/file /mnt/file1
cp: /mnt/file1: No space left on device
# fsckptadm list /mnt
/mnt
Ckpt:
        ctime                   =  Thu Sep 21 08:44:56 2008
```

```
         mtime                    = Thu Sep 21 08:44:56 2008
         flags                    = largefiles, mounted
# fsckptadm set remove Ckpt /mnt
# fsckptadm list /mnt
/mnt
Ckpt:
         ctime                    = Thu Sep 21 08:44:56 2008
         mtime                    = Thu Sep 21 08:44:56 2008
         flags                    = largefiles, removable, mounted
# cp /tmp/file /mnt/file1
cp: /mnt/file1: No space left on device
```

Rats! Why is the checkpoint not removed in favor of the running application? Well, the checkpoint is still in use, because it is mounted. Our hope is, that we only need to unmount it in order to make it actually removable. Next try:

```
# umount /mnt_ckpt
# cp /tmp/file /mnt/file1
cp: /mnt/file1: No space left on device
```

Wow! That looks bad! We consult the manual page to fsckptadm and note an imprecise expression:

```
Under some conditions, when the file system runs out of space, removable Storage
Checkpoints are deleted.
```

Consulting the VxFS Administrator's Guide with its vague allusions to that topic, we get the impression, that database I/Os keeping the preallocated space for the database file at the same position by overwriting only some blocks within the file will produce an ENOSPC event ("Error: No space"). Let's start once again at the very beginning with database like I/O using Perl (the Shell is unable to write into an existing file without changing the file size):

```
# umount /mnt
# mkfs -F vxfs /dev/vx/rdsk/adg/vol
# mount -F vxfs /dev/vx/dsk/adg/vol /mnt
# mkfile 80m /tmp/file
# cp /tmp/file /mnt
# df -k /mnt
Filesystem              kbytes    used   avail capacity  Mounted on
/dev/vx/dsk/adg/vol     102400   84085   17178    84%    /mnt
# fsckptadm -r create Ckpt /mnt
# fsckptadm list /mnt
/mnt
Ckpt:
         ctime                    = Thu Sep 21 09:23:21 2008
         mtime                    = Thu Sep 21 09:23:21 2008
```

```
flags                    = largefiles, removable
```

The following Perl statement will overwrite a region of 10 MB at the beginning of the database file (for details see the comments at the end of each line). Since our file system device still holds about 17 MB free space, we do not expect a removal of the snapshot.

```
# perl -e '
  $m10=1024*1024*10;                 # define 10 MB
  $Block="x" x $m10;                 # a block 10 MB in size
  open(FH,"+< /mnt/file") || die;    # open read-write access by keeping the file
  sysseek(FH,0,0);                   # set file pointer to beginning of file
  syswrite(FH,$Block,$m10,0);        # write 10 MB block
  close(FH);'                        # close file
# df -k /mnt
Filesystem          kbytes    used   avail capacity  Mounted on
/dev/vx/dsk/adg/vol 102400   94377    7529     93%   /mnt
# ls -l /mnt
total 163840
-rw-------   1 root     root    83886080 Sep 21 09:36 file
drwxr-xr-x   2 root     root          96 Sep 21 09:17 lost+found
# fsckptadm list /mnt
/mnt
Ckpt:
        ctime                = Thu Sep 21 09:23:21 2008
        mtime                = Thu Sep 21 09:23:21 2008
        flags                = largefiles, removable
```

Correct, the file system usage increased by approximately 10 MB. Now the final blow! The next 10 MB region will be overwritten, thus blasting the space still available within the file system.

```
# perl -e '
  $m10=1024*1024*10;
  $Block="x" x $m10;
  open(FH,"+< /mnt/file") || die;
  sysseek(FH,$m10,0);                # set file pointer to 10 MB offset
  syswrite(FH,$Block,$m10,0);
  close(FH);'
# df -k /mnt
Filesystem          kbytes    used   avail capacity  Mounted on
/dev/vx/dsk/adg/vol 102400   84101   17163     84%   /mnt
# ls -l /mnt
total 163840
-rw-------   1 root     root    83886080 Sep 21 09:40 file
drwxr-xr-x   2 root     root          96 Sep 21 09:17 lost+found
# fsckptadm list /mnt
/mnt
```

```
# fsckptadm -lv list /mnt
/mnt
UNNAMED:
        ctime              =  Thu Sep 21 09:17:57 2008
        mtime              =  Thu Sep 21 09:19:02 2008
        flags              =  largefiles, mounted,
        # of inodes        =  32
        # of blocks        =  84085
        # of reads         =  0
        # of writes        =  15
        # of pushes        =  292
        # of pulls         =  0
        # of moves         =  0
        # of move alls     =  0
        # of merge alls    =  0
        # of logged pushes =  1
        # of enospc retries =  1
        # of overlay bmaps =  0
```

Finally we got it! We already noticed that the Perl script needed more time to execute compared to the previous one due to checkpoint deletion. The file system space held by the storage checkpoint was freed, the checkpoint removed, and the detailed output to the active file system indeed displays an enospc ("Error: No space") event evoking the checkpoint removal.

The sequence of removal in case of multiple checkpoints is determined by their age ("first in, first out") and the priority of nodata storage checkpoints (see next paragraph) over data checkpoints.

Further flags of storage checkpoints are of less interest, so we will refer to them only in few words. A checkpoint may be marked as non-mountable (flag nomount), either by creating it (option -u) or by setting it afterwards (fsckptadm set nomount …), thus prohibiting undesired access by non-root users (a root user may always clear the nomount flag).

A nodata checkpoint provides a snapshot for the file system metadata (such as file attributes, extent addresses), but not for file contents (option -n when creating, fsckptadm set nodata … later). Issuing an ncheck command reveals, that only the metadata set is created for the snapshot even by modified file contents. The snapped file system metadata may serve, to mention an example, as a source to decide which files to save by an incremental backup. Naturally, a nodata storage checkpoint can never be converted to a data checkpoint.

As an intelligent snapshot mechanism, multiple VxFS storage checkpoints do not produce an overwhelming amount of additional I/Os. If a file is completely replaced by a new version, only the UNNAMED file system instance redirects its pointer to the new file version, while all existing checkpoints simply remain unchanged. If a VxFS checkpointed file system indeed performs a copy-on-first-write (e.g. by a database I/O, see the "Technical Deep Dive" section), the current file system instance keeps its file data block addresses, and all checkpoints redirect their addresses to the saved file block.

You cannot refresh a storage checkpoint to the current data set of the active file system by a single step. Instead, create a new storage checkpoint and, if you need to free space on the device or do not want to keep previous storage checkpoints, simply remove them.

Recovering a file system by a storage checkpoint may accomplished by three ways:

1. Mount the appropriate checkpoint to a temporary mount point (if it is not already mounted) and copy only those files to the application mount point you want to recover. A complete file system recovery using this procedure is space consuming, because the current files of the application mount are kept within the device for the still existing checkpoints. Destroy all unnecessary checkpoints to get more space.

2. Unmount the regular file system instance for the application (probably UNNAMED) and mount the desired checkpoint at the application mount point. Then restart (and recover) your application. All checkpoints created after the currently mounted one lose their snapshot functionality. Therefore, they should be removed. Unfortunately the checkpoint based file system instance remains a checkpoint, so we need to mount it by specifying its checkpoint name (and accordingly to modify entries in /etc/vfstab or in cluster resource configurations, and so on).

3. Therefore, a complete file system recovery by reactivating a storage checkpoint should also link the default file system instance to the checkpoint, not to UNNAMED anymore. VxFS provides an executable to do so:

```
# fsckptadm list /mnt
/mnt
CP1200:
        ctime               =  Sun Sep 28 12:00:00 2008
        mtime               =  Sun Sep 28 12:00:00 2008
        flags               =  largefiles
CP1100:
        ctime               =  Sun Sep 28 11:00:00 2008
        mtime               =  Sun Sep 28 11:00:00 2008
        flags               =  largefiles
CP1000:
        ctime               =  Sun Sep 28 10:00:00 2008
        mtime               =  Sun Sep 28 10:00:00 2008
        flags               =  largefiles
CP0900:
        ctime               =  Sun Sep 28 09:00:00 2008
        mtime               =  Sun Sep 28 09:00:00 2008
        flags               =  largefiles
# umount -f /mnt
# fsckpt_restore -l /dev/vx/dsk/adg/vol
/dev/vx/dsk/adg/vol:

UNNAMED:
        ctime               =  Sun Sep 28 08:53:10 2008
```

```
         mtime                  = Sun Sep 28 08:53:10 2008
         flags                  = largefiles, file system root

CP1200:
         ctime                  = Sun Sep 28 12:00:00 2008
         mtime                  = Sun Sep 28 12:00:00 2008
         flags                  = largefiles

CP1100:
         ctime                  = Sun Sep 28 11:00:00 2008
         mtime                  = Sun Sep 28 11:00:00 2008
         flags                  = largefiles

CP1000:
         ctime                  = Sun Sep 28 10:00:00 2008
         mtime                  = Sun Sep 28 10:00:00 2008
         flags                  = largefiles

CP0900:
         ctime                  = Sun Sep 28 09:00:00 2008
         mtime                  = Sun Sep 28 09:00:00 2008
         flags                  = largefiles


Select storage checkpoint for restore operation
 or <Control/D> (EOF) to exit
 or <Return> to list storage checkpoints: CP1000
CP1000:
         ctime                  = Sun Sep 28 10:00:00 2008
         mtime                  = Sun Sep 28 10:00:00 2008
         flags                  = largefiles

UX:vxfs fsckpt_restore: WARNING: V-3-24640: Any file system changes or storage
checkpoints
made after Sun Sep 28 10:00:00 2008 will be lost.

Restore the file system from storage checkpoint CP1000 ? (ynq) y
(Yes)
UX:vxfs fsckpt_restore: INFO: V-3-23760: File system restored from CP1000
# mount -F vxfs /dev/vx/dsk/adg/vol /mnt
# fsckptadm -l list /mnt
/mnt
CP1000:
         ctime                  = Sun Sep 28 10:00:00 2008
         mtime                  = Sun Sep 28 12:36:19 2008
         flags                  = largefiles, mounted,
CP0900:
```

```
ctime              = Sun Sep 28 09:00:00 2008
mtime              = Sun Sep 28 09:00:00 2008
flags              = largefiles
```

Technical Deep Dive

9.5 CREATING A FULL SIZED VOLUME SNAPSHOT USING LOW-LEVEL COMMANDS

In order to create a snapshot without data change object (DCO) and data change log volume (DCL) we may issue some basic VxVM commands. This kind of snapshot, however, does not provide several advanced features of the standard snapshots created by the vxsnap command: no fast mirror resynchronization, no instant availability or instant refresh of the snapshot, and no space optimizing strategies. Our basic snapshot procedure is a simple plex break-off and, when reattaching it to its original volume, a simple plex attach operation. Our example will be supplemented with some vxstat commands to verify procedure and amount of synchronization.

Step 1   We create the application volume containing two mirrors, place a file system on it, and mount it to simulate application access. The mirrors are completely synchronized by a read-writeback thread.

```
# vxstat -g adg -r
# vxassist -g adg make vol 1g layout=mirror nmirror=2
# vxstat -g adg -f ab vol
                    ATOMIC COPIES            READ-WRITEBACK
TYP NAME          OPS    BLOCKS AVG(ms)   OPS    BLOCKS AVG(ms)
vol vol             0         0  0.0     1024  2097152  15.5
# mkfs -F vxfs /dev/vx/rdsk/adg/vol
# mount -F vxfs /dev/vx/dsk/adg/vol /mnt
```

Step 2   We attach another plex intended to become our snapshot plex. Since the new plex still does not contain valid volume data, VxVM starts an atomic copy synchronization thread. We must await complete synchronization, until the plex may be used for snapshot purposes.

```
# vxstat -g adg -r
# vxassist -g adg mirror vol
# vxstat -g adg -f ab vol
                    ATOMIC COPIES            READ-WRITEBACK
TYP NAME          OPS    BLOCKS AVG(ms)   OPS    BLOCKS AVG(ms)
vol vol          1024  2097152  12.9        0         0  0.0
```

Step 3   A frozen copy of volume data might be achieved by offlining one plex. But an offlined plex is twofold unavailable: its offline state prevents VxVM from reading and writing to the plex, and there is no device driver to this plex enabling application access. So, we dissociate the plex from the volume immediately stopping application I/O to it by the volume driver. Note the addition of the -V option to the plex dissociating command. It shows the basic `vxplex` command used for the volume usage type `fsgen` without actually dissociating the plex. We will come back to the meaning of the usage type.

```
# vxprint -rtg adg
[...]
v  vol          -            ENABLED ACTIVE 2097152 SELECT   -        fsgen
pl vol-01       vol          ENABLED ACTIVE 2097152 CONCAT   -        RW
sd adg01-01     vol-01       adg01   0      2097152 0        c1t1d0   ENA
pl vol-02       vol          ENABLED ACTIVE 2097152 CONCAT   -        RW
sd adg02-01     vol-02       adg02   0      2097152 0        c1t1d1   ENA
pl vol-03       vol          ENABLED ACTIVE 2097152 CONCAT   -        RW
sd adg03-01     vol-03       adg03   0      2097152 0        c1t1d2   ENA
# vxplex -g adg -V dis vol-03
/usr/lib/vxvm/type/fsgen/vxplex -U fsgen -g adg -g adg -- dis vol-03
# vxplex -g adg dis vol-03
# vxprint -rtg adg
[...]
pl vol-03       -            DISABLED IOFAIL 2097152 CONCAT   -        RW
sd adg03-01     vol-03       adg03   0      2097152 0        c1t1d2   ENA

v  vol          -            ENABLED ACTIVE 2097152 SELECT   -        fsgen
pl vol-01       vol          ENABLED ACTIVE 2097152 CONCAT   -        RW
sd adg01-01     vol-01       adg01   0      2097152 0        c1t1d0   ENA
pl vol-02       vol          ENABLED ACTIVE 2097152 CONCAT   -        RW
sd adg02-01     vol-02       adg02   0      2097152 0        c1t1d1   ENA
```

Step 4   A dissociated plex is still unavailable to an application due to its missing device driver. Only volumes provide a driver. Furthermore, a dissociated plex is forced to enter the kernel DISABLED state. In order to enable data availability, we add an empty volume to the dissociated plex and start both, plex and volume as well.

```
# vxmake -g adg vol SNAP-vol plex=vol-03 usetype=fsgen
# vxvol -g adg start SNAP-vol
# vxprint -rtg adg
[...]
v  SNAP-vol     -            ENABLED ACTIVE 2097152 ROUND    -        fsgen
pl vol-03       SNAP-vol     ENABLED ACTIVE 2097152 CONCAT   -        RW
sd adg03-01     vol-03       adg03   0      2097152 0        c1t1d2   ENA

v  vol          -            ENABLED ACTIVE 2097152 SELECT   -        fsgen
pl vol-01       vol          ENABLED ACTIVE 2097152 CONCAT   -        RW
sd adg01-01     vol-01       adg01   0      2097152 0        c1t1d0   ENA
```

```
pl vol-02       vol          ENABLED ACTIVE  2097152 CONCAT   -      RW
sd adg02-01     vol-02       adg02   0       2097152 0        c1t1d1 ENA
```

Step 5   We dissociated the plex while the associated volume was mounted. In real life, you normally create a snapshot on a running application. Consequently, the data set presented by a snapshot volume is inconsistent from the application's point of view. In our example, the volume usetype fsgen forced the execution of a special vxplex command (see option -V above) triggering the file system layer to flush dirty kernel memory pages to the volume before dissociating it. Nevertheless, we expect our file system data set being inconsistent at least for one reason: the file system is marked as ACTIVE by the main super block simply due to its mounted state. So, we issue a file system check command, which will run really fast by replaying the file system log. However, our example working on Storage Foundation 5.0 MP1 does not need a file system check. Note that most software and patch versions of SF automatically issue a file system check after snapshot creation or plex dissociation.

```
# fsck -F vxfs -y /dev/vx/rdsk/adg/SNAP-vol
file system is clean - log replay is not required
```

Step 6   The snapshot volume may be mounted now and, for instance, used by backup tools. Afterwards, you could want to delete the snapshot volume. Our example demonstrates the steps necessary to reattach the snapshot to its original volume. First, we stop the snapshot volume and dissociate its plex once again, but this time from its snapshot volume. The empty volume should be deleted to prevent error messages from inadvertent volume access (as long as the volume exists as a standard volume, there is a driver on it).

```
# mkdir /mnt_snap
# mount -F vxfs /dev/vx/dsk/adg/SNAP-vol /mnt_snap
# df -k /mnt*
Filesystem          kbytes    used   avail capacity Mounted on
/dev/vx/dsk/adg/vol 1048576   17749  966408    2%   /mnt
/dev/vx/dsk/adg/SNAP-vol
                    1048576   17749  966408    2%   /mnt_snap
[...]
# umount /mnt_snap
# vxvol -g adg stop SNAP-vol
# vxplex -g adg dis vol-03
# vxedit -g adg rm SNAP-vol
# vxprint -rtg adg
[...]
pl vol-03       -            DISABLED -       2097152 CONCAT   -      RW
sd adg03-01     vol-03       adg03   0       2097152 0        c1t1d2 ENA

v  vol          -            ENABLED ACTIVE  2097152 SELECT   -      fsgen
pl vol-01       vol          ENABLED ACTIVE  2097152 CONCAT   -      RW
sd adg01-01     vol-01       adg01   0       2097152 0        c1t1d0 ENA
```

```
pl vol-02        vol          ENABLED ACTIVE  2097152 CONCAT    -         RW
sd adg02-01      vol-02       adg02   0       2097152 0         c1t1d1    ENA
```

Step 7   Reattaching the plex to its original volume means incrementing the number of data mirrors within the volume. Since our "orphaned" plex contains stale application data (to an amount unknown to VxVM), a full atomic copy synchronization thread is inevitable.

```
# vxstat -g adg -r
# vxplex -g adg att vol vol-03
# vxstat -g adg -f ab vol
                   ATOMIC COPIES            READ-WRITEBACK
TYP NAME           OPS    BLOCKS AVG(ms)    OPS    BLOCKS AVG(ms)
vol vol            1024   2097152 12.7      0      0      0.0
# vxprint -rtg adg
[…]
v  vol          -           ENABLED ACTIVE  2097152 SELECT    -         fsgen
pl vol-01       vol         ENABLED ACTIVE  2097152 CONCAT    -         RW
sd adg01-01     vol-01      adg01   0       2097152 0         c1t1d0    ENA
pl vol-02       vol         ENABLED ACTIVE  2097152 CONCAT    -         RW
sd adg02-01     vol-02      adg02   0       2097152 0         c1t1d1    ENA
pl vol-03       vol         ENABLED ACTIVE  2097152 CONCAT    -         RW
sd adg03-01     vol-03      adg03   0       2097152 0         c1t1d2    ENA
```

9.6 LEGACY SNAPSHOT COMMANDS

The powerful vxsnap command was introduced in VxVM 4.0 to simplify administration of former snapshot mechanisms and especially to manage the new snapshot concepts: full sized instant snapshot and space optimized instant snapshot with shared cache volume. But vxsnap did not and still does not cover all VxVM 3.x snapshot techniques. Especially the kernel based fast mirror resynchronization was dropped from the vxsnap capabilities in favor to an exclusively DCO based snapshot architecture. Therefore, it is still worth to explain pre-vxsnap snapshot techniques and their command line interface.

9.6.1 FULL SIZED SNAPSHOT WITHOUT FMR

In the previous section, we already introduced the basic snapshot procedure of a so-called third mirror break-off. We recall that the snapshot was not instantly available, that it needed full resynchronization when reattaching it to its original volume (no fast mirror resynchronization), that it took a 100% volume size portion of storage, and that an immediate refresh by keeping the separate snapshot volume was impossible.

In VxVM 3.0, a new vxassist subtool was implemented to serve as an easy to handle interface to that snapshot procedure.

1. Adding a mirror-plex for snapshot purposes (a simple vxassist mirror command, see

step 2 above; we assume the twofold mirrored application volume already created), is replaced by **vxassist snapstart**. In order to verify the amount of synchronization I/Os, we reset the kernel I/O counters of VxVM and display atomic copy I/Os, as usual:

```
# vxstat -g adg -r
# vxassist -g adg snapstart vol
# vxstat -g adg -f a vol
                          ATOMIC COPIES
TYP NAME                  OPS    BLOCKS AVG(ms)
vol vol                   1024  2097152 12.7
# vxprint -rtg adg
[...]
v  vol        -           ENABLED ACTIVE   2097152 SELECT   -        fsgen
pl vol-01     vol         ENABLED ACTIVE   2097152 CONCAT   -        RW
sd adg01-01   vol-01      adg01   0        2097152 0        c1t1d0   ENA
pl vol-02     vol         ENABLED ACTIVE   2097152 CONCAT   -        RW
sd adg02-01   vol-02      adg02   0        2097152 0        c1t1d1   ENA
pl vol-03     vol         ENABLED SNAPDONE 2097152 CONCAT   -        WO
sd adg03-01   vol-03      adg03   0        2097152 0        c1t1d2   ENA
```

Note two small differences to the basic mirror tool: The new plex is marked for snapshot purposes by its application state SNAPDONE to tell the next step (creating a snapshot) which plex to dissociate. Furthermore, its mode is restricted to WO which stands for write-only: New volume data will keep the snapshot prepared plex up-to-date, but this plex, in most cases only a temporary member of the volume, will not modify the regular volume read policy.

2. Steps 3 to 4 (plex dissociation, volume frame, volume start), in most VxVM versions also step 5 (automatic file system check) of the previous chapter are replaced by:

```
# vxassist -g adg snapshot vol
# vxprint -rtg adg
[...]
v  SNAP-vol   -           ENABLED ACTIVE   2097152 ROUND    -        fsgen
pl vol-03     SNAP-vol    ENABLED ACTIVE   2097152 CONCAT   -        RW
sd adg03-01   vol-03      adg03   0        2097152 0        c1t1d2   ENA

v  vol        -           ENABLED ACTIVE   2097152 SELECT   -        fsgen
pl vol-01     vol         ENABLED ACTIVE   2097152 CONCAT   -        RW
sd adg01-01   vol-01      adg01   0        2097152 0        c1t1d0   ENA
pl vol-02     vol         ENABLED ACTIVE   2097152 CONCAT   -        RW
sd adg02-01   vol-02      adg02   0        2097152 0        c1t1d1   ENA
```

If you do not agree with the snapshot volume name automatically created by VxVM, you may specify it at snapshot creation:

```
# vxassist -g adg snapshot vol svol
```

3. Having terminated our duties with the snapshot volume, we might decide to reattach the snapshot plex to its original volume (see steps 6 and 7 above):

```
# vxstat -g adg -r
# vxassist -g adg snapback SNAP-vol
# vxstat -g adg -f a vol
                     ATOMIC COPIES
TYP NAME              OPS    BLOCKS AVG(ms)
vol vol              1024   2097152   12.8
# vxprint -rtg adg
[...]
v  vol          -          ENABLED  ACTIVE   2097152 SELECT    -        fsgen
pl vol-01       vol        ENABLED  ACTIVE   2097152 CONCAT    -        RW
sd adg01-01     vol-01     adg01    0        2097152 0         c1t1d0   ENA
pl vol-02       vol        ENABLED  ACTIVE   2097152 CONCAT    -        RW
sd adg02-01     vol-02     adg02    0        2097152 0         c1t1d1   ENA
pl vol-03       vol        ENABLED  SNAPDONE 2097152 CONCAT    -        WO
sd adg03-01     vol-03     adg03    0        2097152 0         c1t1d2   ENA
```

The command recreates the volume layout as it was at the end of step 1. Even the plex state is SNAPDONE again, and read access to it is prohibited. We did not need to specify the source volume. Obviously, somewhere, the snapshot relation between application volume and its snapshot volume was kept. But where? No snap objects are shown by vxprint, even by displaying all attributes (options -a or -m). The relation was stored in the kernel memory of VxVM. Thus, a system reboot or a disk group deport would have destroyed the snapshot relation.

4. Step 3 could be replaced by other procedures, which we will mention in few words. If you want to redirect the resynchronization, that is, from the snapshot plex to the original volume (don't forget to terminate application access), add the appropriate option:

```
# vxassist -g adg -o resyncfromreplica snapback SNAP-vol
```

After a system reboot or a disk group deport and re-import, the snapshot volume looks like and is indeed a volume completely independent from its former source volume. Advertently clearing the snapshot relation between both volumes does not require, of course, disk group deport and import, simply issue:

```
# vxassist -g adg snapclear vol [SNAP-vol]
```

Removing a snapshot volume does not differ from deleting a standard volume, in spite of the snapshot relation. Use one of the following commands:

```
# vxedit -g adg -rf rm SNAP-vol
# vxassist -g adg remove volume SNAP-vol
```

9.6.2 FULL SIZED SNAPSHOT WITH KERNEL BASED FMR

The simple snapshot mechanism lacks a very important feature. Even though in many cases only a small percentage of data has changed between the original and the snapshot volume (either by writing to the original volume or to the snapshot volume), all volume data are synchronized when reattaching the snapshot plex. The advanced snapshot techniques explained in the main parts of this chapter use a DCL volume linked to the application volume by a DC object to track changed regions in a bitmap. In VxVM 3.1, another way to log modified regions of the volumes (original and snapshot) was introduced: a bitmap within the kernel memory. Well, we already know, that memory based region tracking is lost in case of a system reboot or disk group deport. But, not to forget an advantage, a kernel memory based bitmap does not degrade the performance of an application volume.

Either kernel or DCL volume based bitmap: We must tell the volume that we want to activate fast mirror resynchronization (FMR). The volume attribute `fastresync` must be set before dissociating the snapshot plex from its volume. For an already existing volume, enter:

```
# vxprint -g adg -F %fastresync vol
off
# vxvol -g adg set fastresync=on vol
# vxprint -g adg -F %fastresync vol
on
```

To set the `fastresync` attribute at volume creation time, issue:

```
# vxassist -g adg make vol 1g layout=mirror nmirror=2 fastresync=on
```

The following example, once again, demonstrates the effect of the kernel FMR bitmap. We modify application AND snapshot volume by 10 MB, but at non-overlapping regions. Thus, we expect synchronization of only 20 MB totally.

```
# vxassist -g adg make vol 1g layout=mirror nmirror=2 fastresync=on \
    init=active
# vxassist -g adg snapstart vol
# vxassist -g adg snapshot vol
# dd if=/dev/zero of=/dev/vx/rdsk/adg/vol bs=1024k count=10
# dd if=/dev/zero of=/dev/vx/rdsk/adg/SNAP-vol bs=1024k count=10 oseek=10
# vxstat -g adg -r
# vxassist -g adg snapback SNAP-vol
# vxstat -g adg -f a vol
                      ATOMIC COPIES
```

```
TYP NAME              OPS     BLOCKS AVG(ms)
vol vol                20     40960   13.0
```

9.6.3 Full Sized Snapshot with DCL Volume Based FMR Version 0

The DCO structure is not an invention of VxVM 4.0, though this software version extended the DCO capabilities. Its basic task in VxVM 3.2 was to allow for fast mirror resynchronization in case of a snapback operation by persistently storing the required region bitmap in a DCL volume, not in the kernel memory, thus enabling offhost processing combined with the simultaneously introduced "Disk Group Split and Join" (DGSJ) feature. Adding DCO capabilities to a volume was a three-steps procedure with unique sequence: First, add the DCO structure, then enable FMR on the volume, and finally create the snapshot plex (or convert an existing plex to a snapshot plex). See the commands in detail:

```
# vxassist -g adg addlog vol logtype=dco
# vxvol -g adg set fastresync=on vol
# vxassist -g adg snapstart vol
# vxprint -rLtg adg
[...]
v  vol           -          ENABLED  ACTIVE   2097152  SELECT    -        fsgen
pl vol-01        vol        ENABLED  ACTIVE   2097152  CONCAT    -        RW
sd adg01-01      vol-01     adg01    0        2097152  0         c1t1d0   ENA
pl vol-02        vol        ENABLED  ACTIVE   2097152  CONCAT    -        RW
sd adg02-01      vol-02     adg02    0        2097152  0         c1t1d1   ENA
pl vol-03        vol        ENABLED  SNAPDONE 2097152  CONCAT    -        WO
sd adg03-01      vol-03     adg03    0        2097152  0         c1t1d2   ENA
dc vol_dco       vol        vol_dcl

v  vol_dcl       -          ENABLED  ACTIVE   144      SELECT    -        gen
pl vol_dcl-01    vol_dcl    ENABLED  ACTIVE   144      CONCAT    -        RW
sd adg01-02      vol_dcl-01 adg01    2097152  144      0         c1t1d0   ENA
pl vol_dcl-02    vol_dcl    ENABLED  ACTIVE   144      CONCAT    -        RW
sd adg02-02      vol_dcl-02 adg02    2097152  144      0         c1t1d1   ENA
pl vol_dcl-03    vol_dcl    DISABLED DCOSNP   144      CONCAT    -        RW
sd adg03-02      vol_dcl-03 adg03    2097152  144      0         c1t1d2   ENA
```

Replace the last command, if you want to mark an existing plex for snapshot purposes, by the following:

```
# vxplex -g adg -o dcoplex=vol_dcl-03 convert state=SNAPDONE vol-03
```

If you start from scratch, you may specify the first two snapshot related steps at volume creation time:

```
# vxassist -g adg make vol 1g layout=mirror,log nmirror=2 fastresync=on \
```

```
logtype=dco
```

The snapshot and snapback commands are identical to the earlier snapshot techniques. Note the unusual small size of the DCL volume compared to the advanced vxsnap created DCL volume. This makes a difference to be explained.

9.7   DCO VERSION 0 AND VERSION 20

The data change object linking the DCL volume to its application volume provides some interesting details. Issue the following command first on a legacy DC object created by vxassist addlog, then on a vxsnap built DC object:

```
# vxassist -g adg make vol00 1g layout=mirror,log nmirror=2 fastresync=on \
  logtype=dco init=active
# vxassist -g adg make vol20 1g layout=mirror,log nmirror=2 init=active
# vxsnap -g adg prepare vol20
# vxprint -g adg -m vol00_dco > /tmp/dco00
# vxprint -g adg -m vol20_dco > /tmp/dco20
# sdiff -w 80 /tmp/dco*
dco vol00_dco                          | dco vol20_dco
[...]
        parent_vol=vol00               |         parent_vol=vol20
        log_vol=vol00_dcl              |         log_vol=vol20_dcl
        comment="DCO for vol00"        |         comment="DCO for vol20"
[...]
        p_flag_move=off                          p_flag_move=off
        badlog=off                               badlog=off
[...]
        sp_num=0                                 sp_num=0
        regionsz=0                     |         regionsz=128
        version=0                      |         version=20
        drl=off                        |         drl=on
        sequentialdrl=off                        sequentialdrl=off
        drllogging=off                 |         drllogging=on
        snap=                                    snap=
```

Besides the object names and the record IDs skipped in the output above, we notice three major differences: the version number (0 and 20), the configurable region size and the ability to serve as dirty region log in version 20.

Let's start by examining the last feature. As we already know, a DRL is intended to track region changes in a mirrored volume for a certain amount of time in order to speed up resynchronization after a system crash. We will, by all means, just simulate a system crash. But nevertheless, be sure to carry out the following procedure in a test environment and to unmount all non-OS file systems except for our test volumes beforehand. Console access is a prerequisite.

```
# mkfs -F vxfs /dev/vx/rdsk/adg/vol00
# mkfs -F vxfs /dev/vx/rdsk/adg/vol20
# mkdir /mnt00 /mnt20
# mount -F vxfs /dev/vx/dsk/adg/vol00 /mnt00
# mount -F vxfs /dev/vx/dsk/adg/vol20 /mnt20
# vxprint -g adg -F '%name %devopen' vol00 vol20
vol00 on
vol20 on
# uadmin 5 0
panic[cpu513]/thread=300046b4b20: forced crash dump initiated at user request
[...]
dumping to /dev/dsk/c0t2d0s1, offset 215220224, content: kernel
[...]
ok boot -s
[...]
Requesting System Maintenance Mode
SINGLE USER MODE

Root password for system maintenance (control-d to bypass): password
# vxprint -rLtg adg
[...]
```

v vol00	-	ENABLED	NEEDSYNC	2097152	SELECT	-		fsgen
pl vol00-01	vol00	ENABLED	ACTIVE	2097152	CONCAT	-		RW
sd adg01-01	vol00-01	adg01	0	2097152	0		c1t1d0	ENA
pl vol00-02	vol00	ENABLED	ACTIVE	2097152	CONCAT	-		RW
sd adg02-01	vol00-02	adg02	0	2097152	0		c1t1d1	ENA
dc vol00_dco	vol00	vol00_dcl						
v vol00_dcl	-	ENABLED	NEEDSYNC	144	SELECT	-		gen
pl vol00_dcl-01	vol00_dcl	ENABLED	ACTIVE	144	CONCAT	-		RW
sd adg01-02	vol00_dcl-01	adg01	2097152	144	0		c1t1d0	ENA
pl vol00_dcl-02	vol00_dcl	ENABLED	ACTIVE	144	CONCAT	-		RW
sd adg02-02	vol00_dcl-02	adg02	2097152	144	0		c1t1d1	ENA
v vol20	-	ENABLED	NEEDSYNC	2097152	SELECT	-		fsgen
pl vol20-01	vol20	ENABLED	ACTIVE	2097152	CONCAT	-		RW
sd adg01-03	vol20-01	adg01	2097296	2097152	0		c1t1d0	ENA
pl vol20-02	vol20	ENABLED	ACTIVE	2097152	CONCAT	-		RW
sd adg02-03	vol20-02	adg02	2097296	2097152	0		c1t1d1	ENA
dc vol20_dco	vol20	vol20_dcl						
v vol20_dcl	-	ENABLED	NEEDSYNC	544	SELECT	-		gen
pl vol20_dcl-01	vol20_dcl	ENABLED	ACTIVE	544	CONCAT	-		RW
sd adg01-04	vol20_dcl-01	adg01	4194448	544	0		c1t1d0	ENA
pl vol20_dcl-02	vol20_dcl	ENABLED	ACTIVE	544	CONCAT	-		RW

```
sd adg02-04     vol20_dcl-02 adg02     4194448 544       0           c1t1d1     ENA
# vxprint -g adg -F '%name %devopen' vol00 vol120
vol00 off
vol20 off
# vxstat -g adg -f ab
                   ATOMIC COPIES              READ-WRITEBACK
TYP NAME           OPS    BLOCKS AVG(ms)      OPS      BLOCKS AVG(ms)
vol vol00          0         0    0.0         0           0    0.0
vol vol00_dcl      0         0    0.0         1         144   10.0
vol vol20          0         0    0.0         0           0    0.0
vol vol20_dcl      0         0    0.0         1         544   10.0
# vxstat -g adg -r
# exit
svc.startd: Returning to milestone all.
[...]
```

Please be patient until the boot process at the end of the legacy run-level 2 (vxvm-recover) has started the volume recovery of the OS volumes, before it turns to application volumes. During the early stage of the boot process, only the DCL volumes were synchronized.

```
# vxstat -g adg -f ab
                   ATOMIC COPIES              READ-WRITEBACK
TYP NAME           OPS    BLOCKS AVG(ms)      OPS      BLOCKS AVG(ms)
vol vol00          0         0    0.0      16384     2097152    1.3
vol vol00_dcl      0         0    0.0          2         144    5.0
vol vol20          0         0    0.0          0           0    0.0
vol vol20_dcl      0         0    0.0          9         592    0.0
```

Indeed! Volume vol20 furnished with a DC object of version 20 did not synchronize the data volume because we had not written data to it immediately before the system crash (in case of I/O just a very small portion of the volume would have been synchronized). On the other side, the DC object of version 0 obviously does not provide dirty region logging, it has been completely resynchronized. Adding the legacy DRL plex to the application volume would cover this task.

We cannot answer the question probably arising why the DCL volumes were synchronized twice, the first time during the single-user mode (vxvm-startup2), the second time during the general volume resynchronization (vxvm-recover). Twofold synchronization is harmless to data consistency and, given the small size of the DCL volumes, means a system load you do not need to bother about.

Do you remember that a data plex attached by the vxsnap addmir command got the state pair ENABLED/SNAPDONE, while the attached DCL plex got DISABLED/DCOSNP as long as the snapshot is not performed? Well, the data plex must remain ENABLED, otherwise it would not be kept up-to-date. But the DCL plex attached for snapshot purposes may not be updated for dirty region log or temporary plex detach tasks, because we already have two active DCL plexes providing sufficient redundancy. Therefore, the DCL plex designed to be broken off together with the snapshot data plex got the DISABLED state to avoid unnecessary DCL plex I/O.

DC objects of version 0 or 20 just track changes to a volume in case of a snapshot plex break-off depending on the software version and the license you installed. An enterprise license implements another feature we all were waiting a long time for: optimized synchronization in case of temporary disk outage still keeping the volume enabled due to healthy data plexes. Assume a Dual data center scenario with volumes neatly mirrored over both sites. Furthermore, assume a temporary power failure at one site. The applications will continue to produce new data, but only on the remaining site. After powering back the failed site, the mirrors just differ to a certain amount of data (maybe 5%). The (fully licensed) DC object kept track of write changes to the volumes during the plexes' detach and will resynchronize just the affected regions. Regarding the technical behavior, a DC object version 0 differs only slightly from that of version 20.

```
# dd if=/dev/rdsk/c1t1d1s2 of=/var/tmp/c1t1d1s2 bs=128k iseek=1 count=8
# dd if=/dev/zero of=/dev/rdsk/c1t1d1s2 bs=128k oseek=1 count=8
# vxconfigd -k
# vxdisk -g adg list
DEVICE        TYPE         DISK       GROUP     STATUS
c1t1d0s2      auto:cdsdisk adg01      adg       online
-             -            adg02      adg       failed was:c1t1d1s2
# vxprint -rLtg adg
[...]
v  vol00       -            ENABLED  ACTIVE   2097152 SELECT    -        fsgen
pl vol00-01    vol00        ENABLED  ACTIVE   2097152 CONCAT    -        RW
sd adg01-01    vol00-01     adg01    0        2097152 0         c1t1d0   ENA
pl vol00-02    vol00        DISABLED NODEVICE 2097152 CONCAT    -        RW
sd adg02-01    vol00-02     adg02    0        2097152 0         -        NDEV
dc vol00_dco   vol00        vol00_dcl

v  vol00_dcl   -            ENABLED  ACTIVE   144     SELECT    -        gen
pl vol00_dcl-01 vol00_dcl   ENABLED  ACTIVE   144     CONCAT    -        RW
sd adg01-02    vol00_dcl-01 adg01    2097152  144     0         c1t1d0   ENA
pl vol00_dcl-02 vol00_dcl   DISABLED NODEVICE 144     CONCAT    -        RW
sd adg02-02    vol00_dcl-02 adg02    2097152  144     0         -        NDEV

v  vol20       -            ENABLED  ACTIVE   2097152 SELECT    -        fsgen
pl vol20-01    vol20        ENABLED  ACTIVE   2097152 CONCAT    -        RW
sd adg01-03    vol20-01     adg01    2097296  2097152 0         c1t1d0   ENA
pl vol20-02    vol20        DISABLED NODEVICE 2097152 CONCAT    -        RW
sd adg02-03    vol20-02     adg02    2097296  2097152 0         -        NDEV
dc vol20_dco   vol20        vol20_dcl

v  vol20_dcl   -            ENABLED  ACTIVE   544     SELECT    -        gen
pl vol20_dcl-01 vol20_dcl   ENABLED  ACTIVE   544     CONCAT    -        RW
sd adg01-04    vol20_dcl-01 adg01    4194448  544     0         c1t1d0   ENA
```

```
pl vol20_dcl-02 vol20_dcl    DISABLED NODEVICE 544       CONCAT    -      RW
sd adg02-04     vol20_dcl-02 adg02    4194448 544       0         -      NDEV
# dd if=/dev/zero of=/dev/vx/rdsk/adg/vol00 bs=1024k count=10
# dd if=/dev/zero of=/dev/vx/rdsk/adg/vol20 bs=1024k count=10
# dd if=/var/tmp/c1t1d1s2 of=/dev/rdsk/c1t1d1s2 bs=128k oseek=1
# vxdisk scandisks
# vxdg -g adg -k adddisk adg02=c1t1d1
# vxstat -g adg -r
# vxrecover -g adg
# vxstat -g adg -f ab
```

		ATOMIC COPIES			READ-WRITEBACK		
TYP	NAME	OPS	BLOCKS	AVG(ms)	OPS	BLOCKS	AVG(ms)
vol	vol00	11	22528	23.6	0	0	0.0
vol	vol00_dcl	1	144	0.0	0	0	0.0
vol	vol20	10	20480	19.0	0	0	0.0
vol	vol20_dcl	1	544	10.0	0	0	0.0

Tracking changes of volume data when a mirror is temporarily unavailable is not only useful in case of temporary disk outage. In order to keep a frozen volume data set, you do not need to go back to the somewhat oversized snapshot functionality. Just set one plex within the volume to OFFLINE state. Look at the following procedure to resynchronize the offlined plex to the current volume data set in case you want to continue with it. Only changed regions are synchronized.

```
# vxmend -g adg off vol00-02 vol20-02
# dd if=/dev/zero of=/dev/vx/rdsk/adg/vol00 bs=1024k count=10
# dd if=/dev/zero of=/dev/vx/rdsk/adg/vol20 bs=1024k count=10
# vxstat -g adg -r
# vxmend -g adg on vol00-02 vol20-02
# vxrecover -g adg
# vxstat -g adg -f ab
```

		ATOMIC COPIES			READ-WRITEBACK		
TYP	NAME	OPS	BLOCKS	AVG(ms)	OPS	BLOCKS	AVG(ms)
vol	vol00	11	22528	20.9	0	0	0.0
vol	vol00_dcl	0	0	0.0	0	0	0.0
vol	vol20	10	20480	20.0	0	0	0.0
vol	vol20_dcl	0	0	0.0	0	0	0.0

If you need to fall back to the frozen application data set:

```
# vxmend -g adg off vol00-02 vol20-02
# dd if=/dev/zero of=/dev/vx/rdsk/adg/vol00 bs=1024k count=10
# dd if=/dev/zero of=/dev/vx/rdsk/adg/vol20 bs=1024k count=10
# vxvol -g adg stop vol00 vol20
# vxmend -g adg on vol00-02 vol20-02
# vxmend -g adg fix stale vol00-01 vol20-01
# vxmend -g adg fix clean vol00-02 vol20-02
```

```
# vxstat -g adg -r
# vxrecover -g adg -s
# vxstat -g adg -f ab
                     ATOMIC COPIES              READ-WRITEBACK
TYP NAME            OPS    BLOCKS AVG(ms)    OPS    BLOCKS AVG(ms)
vol vol00            11    22528    20.9      0        0    0.0
vol vol00_dcl         0        0     0.0      0        0    0.0
vol vol20            10    20480    17.0      0        0    0.0
vol vol20_dcl         0        0     0.0      0        0    0.0
```

9.8 VxFS Storage Checkpoint Behavior

One of the most remarkable strengths of a VxFS storage checkpoint is its capability to avoid copy-on-first-writes in favor of just a slightly modified metadata set. We already mentioned that under specific circumstances VxFS switches to copy-on-first-writes, and we mentioned as well reasonable causes for that behavior. Let's test and discuss that topic!

We need four different types of write I/O operations onto a file system:

1. A file to be deleted (Delete.1k)
2. A file to be replaced by (new) content (Replace.1k)
3. A file to be enlarged (Append.1k5)
4. A file to be written by databases (DBIO.10m; the file remains at the same position keeping the same size, but some blocks within it are replaced)

```
# vxassist -g adg make vol 128m
# mkfs -F vxfs /dev/vx/rdsk/adg/vol
# mount -F vxfs /dev/vx/dsk/adg/vol /mnt
# cd /tmp
# mkfile 1k Delete.1k
# mkfile 1k Replace.1k
# mkfile 3b Append.1k5
# mkfile 10m DBIO.10m
# cp Delete.1k Replace.1k Append.1k5 DBIO.10m /mnt
# ls -l /mnt
total 20488
-rw-------   1 root     root     10485760 Sep 21 10:43 DBIO.10m
-rw-------   1 root     root         1536 Sep 21 10:43 Append.1k5
-rw-------   1 root     root         1024 Sep 21 10:43 Delete.1k
-rw-------   1 root     root         1024 Sep 21 10:43 Replace.1k
drwxr-xr-x   2 root     root           96 Sep 21 10:42 lost+found
# mount -F vxfs -o remount /dev/vx/dsk/adg/vol /mnt
# ncheck -F vxfs -o sector= /dev/vx/rdsk/adg/vol
[...]
UNNAMED     999       4       -       - 0/3202-0/3203 /Delete.1k
UNNAMED     999       5       -       - 0/3204-0/3205 /Replace.1k
```

```
UNNAMED    999      6     -      - 0/3208-0/3211 /Append.1k5
UNNAMED    999      7     -      - 0/16384-0/36863 /DBIO.10m
[...]
# fsckptadm create CKPT /mnt
# rm /mnt/Delete.1k
# cp /tmp/Replace.1k /mnt
# cat /tmp/Append.1k5 >> /mnt/Append.1k5
# perl -e '
  $Block="x" x 8192;
  open(FH,"+< /mnt/DBIO.10m") || die;
  sysseek(FH,81920,0);
  syswrite(FH,$Block,8192,0);
  close(FH);'
# mount -F vxfs -o remount /dev/vx/dsk/adg/vol /mnt
# ncheck -F vxfs -o sector= /dev/vx/rdsk/adg/vol
[...]
UNNAMED    999      5     -      - 0/5696-0/5697 /Replace.1k
UNNAMED    999      6     -      - 0/5698-0/5699 /Append.1k5
UNNAMED    999      6     -      - 0/3208-0/3211 /Append.1k5
UNNAMED    999      7     -      - 0/16384-0/36863 /DBIO.10m
CKPT       1000     4     -      - 0/3202-0/3203 /Delete.1k
CKPT       1000     5     -      - 0/3204-0/3205 /Replace.1k
CKPT       1000     6     -      - 0/3214-0/3215 /Append.1k5
CKPT       1000     7     -      - 0/5712-0/5727 /DBIO.10m
[...]
# mount -F vxfs -o ckpt=CKPT /dev/vx/dsk/adg/vol:CKPT /mnt_ckpt
# ls -l /mnt*
/mnt:
total 20488
-rw-------  1 root     root     10485760 Sep 21 10:50 DBIO.10m
-rw-------  1 root     root         3072 Sep 21 10:50 Append.1k5
-rw-------  1 root     root         1024 Sep 21 10:50 Replace.1k
drwxr-xr-x  2 root     root           96 Sep 21 10:42 lost+found

/mnt_ckpt:
total 22
-rw-------  1 root     root     10485760 Sep 21 10:43 DBIO.10m
-rw-------  1 root     root         1536 Sep 21 10:43 Append.1k5
-rw-------  1 root     root         1024 Sep 21 10:43 Delete.1k
-rw-------  1 root     root         1024 Sep 21 10:43 Replace.1k
drwxr-xr-x  2 root     root           96 Sep 21 10:42 lost+found
```

Examining the output of the ncheck and ls commands (especially the sector numbers and the time stamps), we conclude:

1. The deleted file content of Delete.1k remains at the same location within the file system (3202-3203), but is now addressed only by the checkpoint metadata. No copy-on-first-write!

2. The original data set of the overwritten, replaced file Replace.1k remains as well at the same location within the file system (3204-3205, 10:43), but visible only to the checkpoint after being overwritten. The new data blocks of the new file version (5696-5697, 10:50) visible to the active file system did not overwrite the previous version. No copy-on-first-write!

3. The blocks used to store the two versions of the file Append.1k5 display a somewhat tricky, but quite intelligent behavior. Recall that, except for very large file systems, the default block size of VxFS is 1 kB. So, storing 1.5 kB of the original file Append.1k5 allocated two file system blocks at 1 kB size each (sector numbers 3208-3211).

Figure 9-11: VxFS blocks of Append.1k5 before appending data

Appending another 1.5 kB to this file enlarges the same file (inode number 6 remains unchanged) to a size of 3 kB. The two file system blocks of the original file (sectors 3208-3211, the last sector was previously unused) are still assigned to the active file system, so the first 512 bytes of the appended data are stored conveniently in the unused sector of the second 1 kB block. For the last 1 kB of the appended data a new file system block at a quite distant location (sectors 5698-5699) was allocated by the UNNAMED instance.

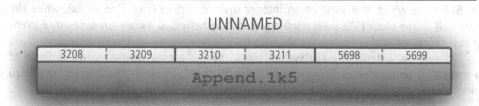

Figure 9-12: UNNAMED VxFS blocks of Append.1k5 with appended data

The content of the second file system block of Append.1k5 in its original state was copied to another location (sectors 3214-3215) and mapped by the checkpoint metadata, while the first block completely unmodified remains visible through the active and the checkpoint file system at the same time (not shown by the ncheck output).

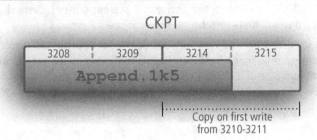

Figure 9-13: CKPT VxFS blocks of Append.1k5 (data appended in UNNAMED)

The command fsckptadm provides an interface to track block changes and displays block allocations by the file system instances:

```
# fsckptadm blockinfo /mnt/Append.1k5 Ckpt /mnt
/mnt/Append.1k5:         <offset, len, flag>
                <0k, 1k, >
                <1k, 0k, CHANGED>
                <1k, 0k, EXTENDED>
                <2k, 1k, EXTENDED>
# fsckptadm blockinfo /mnt_ckpt/Append.1k5 Ckpt /mnt
/mnt_ckpt/Append.1k5:    <offset, len, flag>
                <0k, 1k, >
                <1k, 0k, CHANGED>
```

It is indeed quite difficult to generate a satisfactory output even by executing fsckptadm blockinfo. The second file system block (offset of 1k) was actually extended by 512 bytes which is in case of an integer division indeed 0 kB (len of 0k), while the first half of the block (512 B rounded down to 0 kB) effected a copy-on-first-write event (<1k, 0k, CHANGED>).

To sum up: Extending a file system block invokes a copy-on-first-write in favor of a preferably unfragmented active file (in spite of the fragmented allocation of the third block).

4.   Based on our experience with the latter file, we assume a comparable block allocation policy in case of database-like I/O: The old block will be copied to another location, before the new data will be written to the original block position, thus keeping the active database file unfragmented. Our assumption is proved correct by a detailed analysis of the output of the ncheck command above and the following fsckptadm command:

```
# fsckptadm blockinfo /mnt/DBIO.10m Ckpt /mnt
/mnt/DBIO.10m:  <offset, len, flag>
```

```
                <0k, 80k, >
                <80k, 8k, CHANGED>
                <88k, 10152k, >
# fsckptadm blockinfo /mnt_ckpt/DBIO.10m Ckpt /mnt
/mnt_ckpt/DBIO.10m:     <offset, len, flag>
                <0k, 80k, >
                <80k, 8k, CHANGED>
                <88k, 10152k, >
```

Figure 9-14: VxFS block allocation in case of database I/O

CHAPTER 10: ENCAPSULATION AND ROOT MIRRORING

by Dr. Albrecht Scriba

10.1 INTRODUCTION AND OVERVIEW

Within the previous chapters of this book, we always created volumes based on freshly initialized disks. So from the application's point of view, the content of the volumes was uninitialized. Of course, there was some kind of data on the disks (any sequence of bits), but we didn't bother to restore them to an application usable state. Instead we created file systems after volume creation, initialized a starter database, and so on.

Now we turn to a somewhat different procedure to create volumes on already existing application data, so we can move raw device control to VxVM in order to apply all the nice features of an advanced volume management: adding redundancy, resizing, relayouting for performance reasons, online migration to another storage array, etc.

This procedure is called encapsulation, and you can hear a lot of strange myths about it. But the basic steps of this procedure are surprisingly simple, as we will see in this introductory chapter. Only two details need further investigation. They are presented in the "Technical Deep Dive" section: subdisk alignment and the infamous "B0" Ghost subdisk (see page 330) that often appears on encapsulated disks.

V. Herminghaus and A. Sriba, *Storage Management in Data Centers*,
DOI: 10.1007/978-3-540-85023-6_10, © Springer-Verlag Berlin Heidelberg 2009

So why did we call the basic steps surprisingly simple? Because all kinds of volume management have one thing in common, as shown in chapter 1: They all store application data in extents, i.e. in an ordered list of contiguous disk regions (e.g. logical partitions of AIX). Encapsulation basically places VxVM subdisks (just another kind of extent) exactly over the preexisting extents containing application data and orders these subdisks in exactly the same manner within a VxVM plex, as they were ordered in the former volume management. Adding a volume layer to this plex leads to an application driver showing the same data as before.

The very simplest way to store application data is a Solaris partition, so we only have one extent on one disk. This chapter focuses on the procedure of encapsulating a Solaris partition, although it might be adapted to more complex data structures of other volume managers.

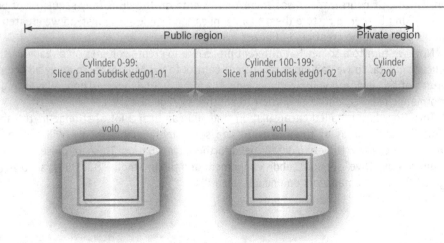

Figure 10-1:   Encapsulation technique (slightly simplified)

Just to clear up whatever misunderstandings may remain: When an application (usually the file system) does I/O to a device there is always some kind of mechanism that maps the block number or extent specification to the physical layer of the device. For a Solaris partition, this function is almost trivial: it simply adds the offset of the partition start to the block number to get to the physical block. It needs meta information from the VTOC in order to do that. If we create a virtual object in VxVM that translates the logical block numbers of the virtual object to the same physical block numbers, then we can access the data by either of the two means: via partitioning and via VxVM. We could even add a third volume management product and add meta info for that, too, like Sun LVM (aka SDS). Of course we must not access the data in an uncoordinated way or risk losing data integrity. But again: In principle, all you need is meta data for the current device driver that points to the same extents (or maps the extents in the same way) as the original data and we can encapsulate whatever we want.

Placing a subdisk over a Solaris partition requires, as we already know, two preceding steps. We must prepare the disk for VxVM use (creating private and public region and initializing the former with a basic data structure), and we must build a disk group out of this disk or add the disk to an existing disk group. In other words: You cannot define VxVM objects without a disk group containing at least one active configuration copy within the private region.

Here is a commented list of actions that need to be performed in order to add a VxVM volume interface to already existing application data. Currently, we will not discuss the individual command lines. This is left to the "Technical Deep Dive" section of this chapter. Consider the following list as a look behind the scenes. You do not necessarily have to understand all the steps if you just want to encapsulate a few disks. There is a simple command for that, which is discussed right after this list. But you may eventually require this look behind the scenes if you want to really understand encapsulation, if you run into problems with encapsulating, or if you wish to encapsulate in a non-standard way (e.g. not all of the partitions of a disk).

10.2 THE SECRETS OF ENCAPSULATION

1. In addition to the existing partitions (the ones to be encapsulated) we create the well known VxVM partitions. For the cdsdisk layout a slice with tag 15 is put over the whole disk . For the sliced layout, a slice with tag 15 is put over an unused disk cylinder anywhere on the disk for the private region and a slice bearing tag 14 over the remainder of or over the whole disk (see below) as the public region. So it is obvious, that you cannot encapsulate a disk without some free space to put the private region on. Furthermore, you need one (for cdsdisk) or two (for sliced) unused partitions in order to keep all applications running during these preparatory steps. Otherwise you would need to stop at least some applications using some partitions on that disk, to remember offset and length of these partitions and to remove them. Finally, a cdsdisk layout cannot be used under the already mentioned restrictions: disks not supporting SCSI mode sense (such as IDE) and OS or EFI disks. In addition, since the offset of the private region of a CDS disk must be 256 sectors, we cannot encapsulate a partition located in that region.

2. We initialize the private region with the appropriate basic data set depending on the VxVM partition layout we created in step 1 (cdsdisk or sliced). Steps 1 and 2 resemble the usual procedure of disk initialization using vxdisksetup.

3. We create a new disk group out of this initialized disk or add the disk to an existing disk group. Note that there is no difference to the standard way of creating or adding to disk groups.

4. We define subdisks with the corresponding offset and length over the partitions we want to encapsulate, associate them with plexes, create volumes for the plexes and attach the plexes into the volumes, then start the volumes in order to enable I/O. Now we have an active volume driver for each encapsulated partition. Since vxassist, the easy to handle default top-down tool for volume creation, is unable to specify the exact offset of the subdisks, we have to resort to using low-level vxmake commands.

5. During all these steps applications can remain online until we want to switch to the freshly created volume drivers for I/O. Unfortunately, due to OS restrictions, we cannot replace the legacy drivers with the volume drivers while the application is running. So we must stop the applications and restart them using the volume drivers this time. You may adapt the vfstab as well or specify the new raw device drivers for your database.

6. In case you do not need the legacy partitions anymore, you may remove them from the disk's VTOC.

7. Now freedom awaits you! Your disks, disk groups, and volumes created by encapsulation of partitions behave exactly the same as standard disks, disk groups, and volumes. You may convert to CDS disks and a CDS disk group, add new disk members, create redundancy to the volumes, resize or relayout them, add logs, and so on — all that without interrupting running applications anymore.

Fortunately, VxVM provides a script called vxencap that performs all these steps in collaboration with the run level script /etc/rcS.d/S86vxvm-reconfig (Solaris 9) or by restarting the svc:/system/vxvm/vxvm-reconfig FMRI in Solaris 10. Here is the standard procedure for application and OS disks together with some comments:

```
# vxencap -g <DG> [-c] <dmname>=c#t#d#
```

This command collects data from the parameters (disk access, disk media, and disk group name; for optional layout parameters see the "Full Battleship" part) and from the disk itself (disk's VTOC) and stores them together with the new VTOC and a command summary in ASCII files under /etc/vx/reconfig.d/disk.d/c#t#d#. The -c option is used to create a new disk group, otherwise the disk is added to an already existing disk group. The script defaults to creating cdsdisk layout (and a CDS disk group), if possible and if not instructed otherwise by further parameters. In case you encapsulate an OS disk of Solaris 9, the logging mount option of some OS partitions in the last field of the vfstab will be changed to nologging (see the "Full Battleship" part).

Be aware that the vxencap command does not change the partition table of the disk yet. This job is done by the additional init-scripts supplied by VxVM. Nothing happens to the disk 's VTOC before you go on to the next step:

```
# init 6          # reboot the system
```

During the next boot, the run level script /etc/rcS.d/S86vxvm-reconfig (Solaris 9) is invoked during the boot process. In Solaris 10, this is integrated into the service framework as the FMRI svc:/system/vxvm/vxvm-reconfig. It reads the disk configuration files created above and performs the necessary tasks to bring all data partitions under VxVM control by encapsulating them. Unfortunately, the disk group is always marked as boot disk group, even in case of a simple application disk. In the latter case, you should clear this entry by issuing the vxdctl bootdg command with the appropriate parameter: either the correct boot disk group or the reserved word nodg if there is no boot disk group yet (i.e. if your root disk is not yet encapsulated).

Since the Solaris OpenBoot PROM only recognizes partitions, encapsulating an OS disk will, of course, not remove those partitions that are required during the early boot process. But an OBP alias for the OS disk is created called vx-<dmname>. Note that the OBP boot-device list is not updated. Instead of a reboot, you may stop all applications using this disk if they are not required by the OS (unfortunately, an umount / command will not work, even with the -f option), execute the run level script manually with the start parameter, and restart your applications. If you compare the output of this script with the seven steps mentioned above, you can easily map them. Here's a walk-through of encapsulating a Solaris disk without rebooting. All partitions of the disk have been unmounted before we start:

```
# vxencap -g edg -c edg01=c2t4d3
  The c2t4d3 disk has been configured for encapsulation.
# /etc/rcS.d/S86vxvm-reconfig start
  VxVM vxvm-reconfig INFO V-5-2-324 The Volume Manager is now reconfiguring
(partition phase)...                                            (step 1)
  VxVM vxvm-reconfig INFO V-5-2-499 Volume Manager: Partitioning c2t4d3 as an
encapsulated disk.                                              (step 1)
  VxVM vxvm-reconfig INFO V-5-2-323 The Volume Manager is now reconfiguring
(initialization phase)...                                       (step 2)
  VxVM vxvm-reconfig INFO V-5-2-497 Volume Manager: Adding edg01 (c2t4d3) as an
encapsulated disk.                                              (step 3)
VxVM vxcap-vol INFO V-5-2-89 Adding volumes for c2t4d3...       (step 4)
Starting new volumes...                                 (step 4)
VxVM vxcap-vol INFO V-5-2-444 Updating /etc/vfstab...    (step 5)
Remove encapsulated partitions...                              (step 6)
```

10.3 ROOT DISK ENCAPSULATION

Encapsulating the root disk is performed in a very similar way to encapsulating a normal data disk. However, it is different in that the target disk group normally does not exist yet, therefore it needs to be created on-the-fly by the vxencap command. This is done by supplying the parameter for "create disk group "-c -g <dgname>" to vxencap.

So the complete command chain for encapsulating the root disk is this:

```
# vxencap -c -g osdg -c rootdisk=c0t0d0
 The c0t0d0 disk has been configured for encapsulation.
# init 6
```

As you can see, after successful encapsulation (including the reboot that is necessary to switch the access path from the standard **/dev/dsk/c#t#d#s#** devices to volume paths like **/dev/vx/dsk/rootvol**) the / file system is now mounted from a volume manager volume:

```
# df -k /
Filesystem              kbytes    used    avail capacity  Mounted on
/dev/vx/dsk/bootdg/rootvol
                        6196278 3534270 2600046    58%    /
```

The volume manager path to all boot file systems has automatically been persisted into the **/etc/vfstab** file:

```
# grep rootvol /etc/vfstab
/dev/vx/dsk/bootdg/rootvol  /dev/vx/rdsk/bootdg/rootvol  /  ufs  1  no  logging
#NOTE: volume rootvol () encapsulated partition c0t0d0s0
```

10.4 ROOT DISK MIRRORING

Encapsulation seems to be an interesting thing from a technical point of view. But until now, no convincing advantages of OS disks under VxVM control are implemented. The usual counterpart of OS disk encapsulation, the root disk mirroring, is still missing.

Against several misunderstandings, we emphasize that root disk mirroring is NOT based on a different technique compared to regular volume mirroring. The OS mirror is NOT a physical copy of the encapsulated OS disk, therefore, it may be placed on completely different disk hardware. Once again: The physical position of the subdisks is independent from their virtual position within the plex. The only restrictions implemented in the **vxassist** command are reasonable: no striping in a plex or mirroring in a volume based on one disk device.

The regular mirror procedure (**vxassist mirror**) keeps plex layout attributes, while the plex internal subdisk concatenation is ignored. We may conclude that size and position of private and public region may not correspond on both disks, that the physical position of the mirror subdisks are very probably not identical to those on the original disk, and that the concatenation of the strange ghost subdisk (more on that in the technical deep dive beginning on page 330) and the main subdisk within a plex is not repeated on the mirror disk.

Nevertheless, mirrors of OS volumes differ in one **additional** feature: In order to boot from the disk providing the mirrored subdisks, they need partitions defined at exactly the same position. You may call this a reversed encapsulation: While encapsulation defines subdisks over partitions on the original disk, reverse encapsulation defines partitions over subdisks on the mirror disk.

Implementing an OS mirror basically does not differ from the regular volume mirroring: We need another disk device (due to boot capabilities this disk must use the sliced format), add it to the boot disk group and mirror the volumes. However, if you just run vxassist mirror on all the boot volumes, then the OBP device aliases are not updated to enable booting from the mirror disk, and the VTOC on the target disk will not be updated with the slice information pertaining to the newly created subdisks. I.e. the VTOC will not contain slices for those file systems which are required during the boot phase, and so the new boot mirror will not be actually bootable. This is because the step that we called reverse encapsulation is never performed by vxassist.

You can execute reverse encapsulation by calling the script vxbootsetup -g <bootdg>. Or you can make use of the vxmirror script for mirroring the boot volumes. The vxmirror script will automatically call vxbootsetup after mirroring all boot volumes. It also creates an OpenBoot PROM device alias as a mnemonic to enable easy booting from the alternate disk. The following steps mirror the boot disk after it has been successfully encapsulated:

```
# vxdisksetup -i c0t2d0 format=sliced privlen=1m # prepare a boot mirror
# vxdg -g osdg adddisk osdg02=c0t2d0      # add it to the boot disk group
# vxmirror -g osdg osdg01        # mirror everything and reverse encapsulate
! vxassist -g osdg mirror rootvol
! vxassist -g osdg mirror swapvol
! vxassist -g osdg mirror var
! vxassist -g osdg mirror opt
! vxbootsetup -g osdg    # this script does reverse encapsulation and devaliases
```

If you look at the VTOCs of the two bootable disk mirrors now, you will see that they differ significantly. This should prove that boot disk mirroring is definitely not a physical copy of a the boot disk, but merely a normal volume-by-volume copy, plus the reverse encapsulation:

```
# prtvtoc -h /dev/rdsk/c0t0d0s2
      0      2    00    4198320   12586800   16785119
      1      3    01          0    4198320    4198319
      2      5    00          0   78156480   78156479
      3     14    01          0   78156480   78156479
      4     15    01   78148320       8160   78156479
      5      7    00   16785120    4198320   20983439
      6      0    00   20983440   12586800   33570239
# prtvtoc -h /dev/rdsk/c0t2d0s2
      0      2    00    4206480   12586800   16793279
      1      3    01       8160    4198320    4206479
      2      5    00          0   78156480   78156479
      3     14    01       8160   78148320   78156479
      4     15    01          0       8160       8159
```

```
5     7   00   16793280   4198320   20991599
6     0   00   20991600   12586800  33578399
```

You can verify that the root file system (and /usr, /var, and swap as well) now contain two plexes, i.e. they are mirrored and therefore failsafe:

```
# vxprint -rtg osdg rootvol
[...]
v  rootvol      -                    ENABLED  ACTIVE   4198320   ROUND    -        root
pl rootvol-01   rootvol              ENABLED  ACTIVE   4198320   CONCAT   -        RW
sd osdg01-B0    rootvol-01  osdg01   78148319 1                 0        c0t0d0   ENA
sd osdg01-01    rootvol-01  osdg01   0        4198319  1                 c0t0d0   ENA
pl rootvol-02   rootvol              ENABLED  ACTIVE   4198320   CONCAT   -        RW
sd osdg02-01    rootvol-02  osdg02   0        4198320  0                 c0t2d0   ENA
```

For our convenience, the vxbootsetup program (the final command called internally by vxmirror) has created device aliases in the Solaris Boot PROM so that we can boot from either one of the mirrors by addressing them symbolically (vx-odsg01 and vx-osdg02):

```
# eeprom nvramrc
nvramrc=devalias vx-osdg01 /pci@1f,0/ide@d/disk@0,0:a
devalias vx-osdg02 /pci@1f,0/ide@d/disk@2,0:a
```

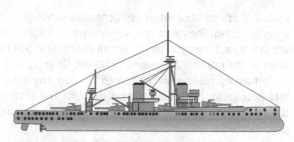

The Full Battleship

10.5 REMARKS TO VXENCAP AND OS MIRRORING

The script vxencap provides some built-in intelligence to choose the proper disk layout: If possible, it prepares for a cdsdisk, otherwise for a sliced layout. We recall the reasons that may prevent using cdsdisk layout: no SCSI mode sense support, OS or EFI disk, or a data partition to be encapsulated at the beginning of the disk. If you want to force a sliced layout, you can make use of the option -f:

```
# vxencap -g <diskgroup> [-c] -f sliced <dmname>=c#t#d#
```

Unlike the default of VxVM 5.x for a private region size of 32 MB, vxencap will create a default private region length of 1 MB (or rounded up to the next cylinder boundary, if sliced). Assuming that encapsulation is performed mostly on the OS disk with its simple data structures, this default is indeed reasonable. In case you want to specify a different private region size, just use the option -s:

```
# vxencap -g <diskgroup> [-c] -s <size> <dmname>=c#t#d#
```

In order to promote other than the built-in defaults, enter the desired key-value pairs into /etc/default/vxencap:

```
format=sliced
privlen=4096
```

Regarding the VxVM object names to be created by way of encapsulation, vxencap allows for specification only of the disk group and the disk media name. We may guess, and we guess quite correctly, that the subdisk names are derived from the disk media name (<dmname>-##) and the plex names from the volume names (<volname>-##), as usual. But what about the volume names? In case of an OS disk the root device is named rootvol and the swap device is named swapvol. Other partitions of an OS disk are named after the last part of the current mount directory. In case of a non-OS disk, the volumes to be created are named after the disk media name, the partition number, and the usual vol extension (<dmname><partition#>vol).

The root disk of Solaris 9 encapsulated by VxVM in conjunction with the logging option of ufs on the root device generates subsequent kernel panics, when rebooting after a system crash. The cause is a well-known and aging programming error. Two workarounds are available. Either you do not install the current Solaris patch 113073-14 (or 113073-13) in favor of the rather old version 113073-08. Or you accept the modifications of /etc/vfstab performed by vxencap which turned the logging options of the root and the swap device into nologging. No solution is satisfactory: The first one is not tolerated by Sun support, the second one discards the file system logging feature, thus noticeably delaying the boot process after a system crash.

An encapsulation procedure initialized by vxencap requires some prerequisites fulfilled, as already mentioned in the "Easy Sailing" part: At least one (cdsdisk layout) or two (sliced) unused partition numbers must be available, and at least one disk cylinder must not be part of an OS or application partition in order to form the private region. While the former restriction can only be ignored by way of an exhaustive low-level procedure (see the "Technical Deep Dive" part), the latter provides a special exception built into vxencap. An OS disk providing the root device contains mostly also the swap device. A swap device does not hold data required after a reboot except for the memory pages dumped in case of a kernel panic. Therefore, the required space to form the private region may be and indeed will be cut off from the swap device by vxencap, if all disk cylinders of the OS disk are in use.

Although the vxencap script does not bother for peculiar partition numbers, you should ensure that the root device is stored on partition 0 and the swap device on partition 1. Otherwise, when creating the OS mirror by the standard vxmirror command, the invoked vxbootsetup script will completely fail, for it is strictly bound to the mentioned partition numbers.

Any encapsulation via vxencap and the related VxVM reconfiguration script will try to set the VxVM bootdg attribute. Quite correct, if your first encapsulation task points to the root disk! But wrong in any other case! Then, you should clear the bootdg attribute (stored in /etc/vx/volboot) before encapsulating the OS disk. Note that the bootdg disk group name is a reserved name, because it is a symbolic link to the actual boot disk group name under /dev/vx/rdsk and /dev/vx/dsk, respectively.

```
# vxdg bootdg
edg
# vxdctl list | grep bootdg
bootdg:   edg
# grep bootdg /etc/vx/volboot
bootdg edg
# vxdctl bootdg nodg
```

We already mentioned another weakness of the reconfiguration script: The OpenBoot PROM attribute boot-device is not updated during encapsulation. Well, assuming the default device alias entry disk typically pointing to the device we encapsulated, we encounter no restrictions. But the mirror disk provided with partitions and an NVRAM device alias by vxbootsetup to boot from should be added to the boot-device list. Unfortunately, the task must be executed manually:

```
# eeprom boot-device
```

```
boot-device=disk net
# eeprom boot-device='vx-osdg01 vx-osdg02 disk net'
```

VxVM 5.0 "delights" us with another programming error in vxbootsetup: The device alias definitions stored in the OpenBoot PROM NVRAM are not concatenated line-by-line as it should be, but by spaces, thus invalidating all but the first entry. Once again, repair it manually in order to use the aliases.

```
# eeprom nvramrc
nvramrc=devalias vx-osdg01 /pci@1f,0/ide@d/disk@0,0:a devalias vx-osdg02 /
pci@1f,0/ide@d/disk@2,0:a
# eeprom nvramrc='devalias vx-osdg01 /pci@1f,0/ide@d/disk@0,0:a
  devalias vx-osdg02 /pci@1f,0/ide@d/disk@2,0:a'
# eeprom nvramrc
nvramrc=devalias vx-osdg01 /pci@1f,0/ide@d/disk@0,0:a
devalias vx-osdg02 /pci@1f,0/ide@d/disk@2,0:a
```

Sometimes, you may read or hear the recommendation to mirror the OS disk by the script vxrootmir. We do not recommend so, because vxrootmir <mirror-dmname> just mirrors rootvol and provides the mirrored disk with an appropriate partition and an OpenBoot PROM device alias by invoking vxbootsetup. No other OS volumes are mirrored!

Technical Deep Dive

10.6 THE GHOST SUBDISK

Encapsulating a disk means placing volumes together with their related plexes and subdisks over partitions. So we expect a simple volume layout containing one plex each and just one subdisk within the latter exactly corresponding to the partitions. Nevertheless, in most cases we discover one strange volume whose plex contains two subdisks, one of them only one sector in size.

```
# vxprint -rtg osdg rootvol
[...]
v  rootvol       -           ENABLED  ACTIVE  815176  ROUND     -        root
pl rootvol-01    rootvol     ENABLED  ACTIVE  815176  CONCAT    -        RW
sd osdg01-B0     rootvol-01  osdg01   815175  1       0         c0t0d0   ENA
sd osdg01-01     rootvol-01  osdg01   0       815175  1         c0t0d0   ENA
pl rootvol-02    rootvol     ENABLED  ACTIVE  815176  CONCAT    -        RW
sd osdg02-01     rootvol-02  osdg02   0       815176  0         c0t2d0   ENA
```

This small subdisk, sometimes called "Ghost subdisk", is indeed cloak-and-dagger at first sight, but quite easy to understand at second thought as an unavoidable protection against disk failure for VxVM disks.

The volume table of contents of the disk (VTOC) which is located at the very first sector of the disk, stores the partition table and some disk attributes. It is strictly necessary for normal disk I/O operations, for the device drivers need partition information to calculate I/O offsets. A damaged VTOC requires immediate recovery by re-labeling the disk.

```
# prtvtoc -h /dev/rdsk/c4t6d0s2
       2     5     01        0   35368272   35368271
       7    15     01        0   35368272   35368271
# dd if=/dev/zero of=/dev/rdsk/c4t6d0s2 bs=512 count=1
# prtvtoc -h /dev/rdsk/c4t6d0s2
prtvtoc: /dev/rdsk/c4t6d0s2: Unable to read Disk geometry
# format c4t6d0
[...]
format> label
Ready to label disk, continue? yes

format> quit
# prtvtoc -h /dev/rdsk/c4t6d0s2
       0     2     00        0     263872     263871
       1     3     01   263872     263872     527743
       2     5     01        0   35368272   35368271
```

```
       6      4    00       527744  34840528  35368271
```

As the example above demonstrated, the VTOC may be overwritten by standard device drivers. We have chosen the backup partition (slice 2) covering the whole disk which is not a device for regular I/O operations. Nevertheless, even a regular data partition may contain the VTOC. And indeed, most formatted disks provide a partition starting at cylinder 0, thus including the VTOC into the partition space. Therefore, the block device drivers for partitions skip the first 16 sectors of their raw device partition, the main super block being the first file system object is always placed at sector 16 of the raw device. Why 16 sectors, not just one? Well, not only the VTOC needs protection, but also a possible boot block stored at sector 1 to 15 of the root partition.

```
# fstyp -v /dev/rdsk/c4t6d0s0
ufs
magic   11954   format  dynamic time    Sat Oct  4 08:24:30 2008
sblkno  16      cblkno  24      iblkno  32      dblkno  2240
[...]
```

All the same, even the swap device driver skips the first 16 sectors (although a boot block is of no use on a swap device).

```
# swap -l
swapfile            dev   swaplo blocks  free
/dev/dsk/c0t0d0s1   32,1      16 2097632 2097632
```

Even a disk under VxVM control must not overwrite the VTOC. The cdsdisk layout of a VxVM disk always skips the first 256 sectors of a disk, thus protecting not only the Solaris VTOC, but also other OS specific structures of other operating systems.

```
# vxdisk list c4t1d0 | grep ^private:
private:   slice=2 offset=256 len=2048 disk_offset=0
```

A freshly initialized VxVM disk of sliced layout even skips the first cylinder of a disk by starting the private region at cylinder 1 and defining the public region on the remainder of the disk. What is more, the active private region skips the first sector of the private region as partition for a reason we will explain later.

```
# prtvtoc -h /dev/rdsk/c4t3d0s2
       2      5    01          0  35368272  35368271
       3     15    01       4712      4712      9423
       4     14    01       9424  35358848  35368271
# vxdisk list c4t3d0 | grep ^private:
private:   slice=3 offset=1 len=4455 disk_offset=4712
```

Unlike the cdsdisk layout, the start position of the private region of the sliced layout is not fixed. In fact, the private region may be placed at ANY position on the disk, not only at the beginning (after first cylinder, default) or the end of the disk (vxdisksetup -ie c#t#d#;

see the next topic of the current chapter). Consequently, the public region may cover the first cylinder together with the VTOC. Just an example of a (small) sliced disk whose private region is located at the end of the disk (not created by `vxdisksetup -ie` ...):

```
# prtvtoc /dev/rdsk/c4t8d0s2
[...]
*    4712 sectors/cylinder
*     176 cylinders
*     174 accessible cylinders
[...]
*                          First    Sector   Last
* Partition  Tag  Flags   Sector    Count   Sector  Mount Directory
       2      5    01          0   819888   819887
# fmthard -d 3:15:01:$((819888-4712)):4712 /dev/rdsk/c4t8d0s2
# fmthard -d 4:14:01:0:$((819888-4712)) /dev/rdsk/c4t8d0s2
# vxdisk -f init c4t6d0 format=sliced
# vxdisk list
[...]
c4t6d0s2    auto:sliced    -              -          online
# prtvtoc -h /dev/rdsk/c4t8d0s2
       2      5    01          0   819888  819887
       3     15    01     815176     4712  819887
       4     14    01          0   815176  815175
```

Red alert! A subdisk placed over the VTOC but arranged at a plex offset greater than 0 by way of subdisk concatenation may receive block or swap device I/O, thus overwriting the VTOC and making disk and volume unusable (VxVM 4.x, VxVM 5.0 keeps partition information in the kernel until the next reboot). The following picture uses the sector and cylinder numbers of the command output above. Note that it does not show an actual configuration possibility of VxVM, for VxVM does not allow a subdisk to be placed over the VTOC by a technique still to be explained.

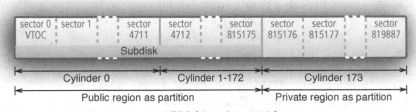

Figure 10-2:   A subdisk covering the VTOC (virtual example)

Now assume two disks initialized by VxVM in the layout above and the subdisks of each disk concatenated within a plex.

Figure 10-3:   A VxVM volume built on subdisks concatenated within the plex and the location of the VTOCs covered by the subdisks (virtual example)

Red alert, indeed! The VTOC being part of the second subdisk is located in the middle of the virtual address space provided by the plex. Even a block or a swap device driver skipping the first 16 sectors of the device (now a volume device!) may overwrite the VTOC of the second disk.

Therefore, any virtual volume manager providing concatenate or stripe capabilities MUST protect the VTOC, for it is not protected by the device drivers anymore. VxVM has implemented a quite simple solution: The start sector of the public region as subdisk container (not as partition) is moved one sector rearwards, thus starting immediately after the VTOC.

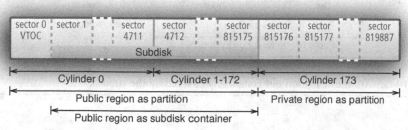

Figure 10-4:   Protecting the VTOC by moving the public region as subdisk container one sector rearwards

Note that the subdisk offsets of the disk group configuration are calculated against the public region as subdisk container. Therefore, the subdisk drawn in the figure above has an offset of 0 sectors. Some commands to verify the disk layout and the subdisk position:

```
# vxdisk list c4t8d0
[...]
public:    slice=4 offset=1 len=815175 disk_offset=0
private:   slice=3 offset=1 len=4711 disk_offset=815176
[...]
# vxdg init adg adg01=c4t8d0 cds=off
# vxdg -g adg set align=1
# vxdg -g adg free
DISK          DEVICE      TAG          OFFSET     LENGTH     FLAGS
adg01         c4t8d0s2    c4t8d0       0          815175     -
# vxmake -g adg sd adg01-01 disk=adg01 offset=0 len=815175
# vxprint -stg adg
SD NAME        PLEX         DISK     DISKOFFS LENGTH   [COL/]OFF DEVICE   MODE
[...]
sd adg01-01    -            adg01    0        815175   -         c4t8d0   ENA
```

We immediately recognize a disadvantage of this solution: The public region and the subdisk is one sector smaller than before. Well, you might believe that we easily could squander one sector. No, there is indeed a realistic scenario where we urgently need this sector. Assume an OS disk completely in use except for one cylinder we kept for the private region (or cut of from the swap partition by VxVM tools during encapsulation). The following figure just shows the OS root partition, for multiple partitions do not modify the basic problem:

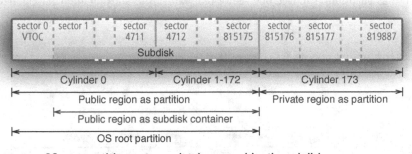

Figure 10-5:   OS root partition not completely covered by the subdisk

The root volume based on the subdisk is one sector smaller than the root partition. However, one sector less in size is not the main problem. Look at the data at the beginning of the root device **as partition**:

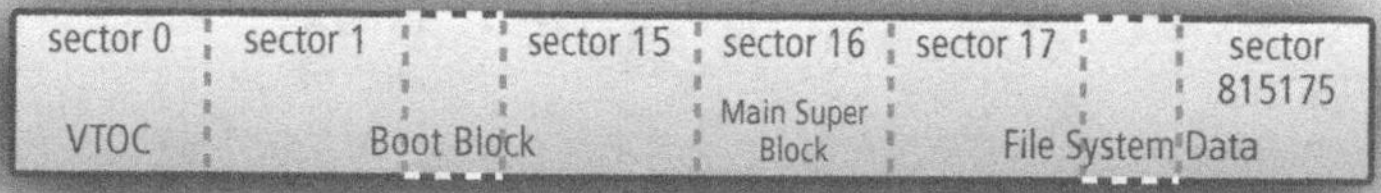

sector 0	sector 1			sector 15	sector 16	sector 17		sector 815175
VTOC		Boot Block			Main Super Block		File System Data	

Figure 10-6: File system structure of the root device as partition

Now we compare it to the data at the beginning of the root device **as volume** based on the subdisk starting at disk offset 1 (which is offset 0 within the public region as subdisk container):

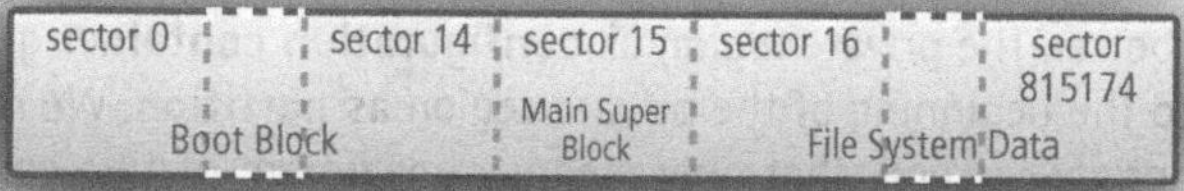

sector 0		sector 14	sector 15	sector 16		sector 815174
	Boot Block		Main Super Block		File System Data	

Figure 10-7: File system structure of the root device as volume

The OpenBoot PROM accesses the boot device as partition, so the missing VTOC and the wrong boot block position within the root volume are ignored. During kernel initialization, the root device is mapped by vxio as a kernel memory volume exactly on the root partition (including the VTOC), so the file system provides proper structures. But the remount of the root device as volume based on the disk group configuration stored within the private region of the OS disk during the single user mode/milestone will detect a corrupt file system: Sector 16 of rootvol does not contain the main super block!

Well, the main super block kept its correct position on the root partition. We simply need to adjust the offsets within the plex of rootvol by moving them one sector rearwards. That may be easily accomplished by the capabilities of a logical volume management with completely flexible subdisk architecture: Concatenate the main subdisk of rootvol to a subdisk just one sector in size, to the "Ghost subdisk"!

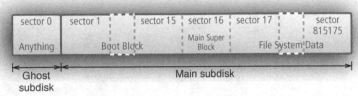

Figure 10-8: File system structure of the root device as volume with "Ghost subdisk"

Finally the main super block is located at the correct volume device offset. The Ghost subdisk is placed at the plex offset 0. But where to place the Ghost subdisk physically? A logical volume management discerns between the physical and the logical position of its building blocks. We might initialize another disk for the disk group in order to store the Ghost subdisk. What a ridiculous waste of space! A new disk for a subdisk of just 1 sector!

VxVM can do better. The private region **as configuration container** gets an offset of 1 sector compared to the beginning of the private region **as partition**. We may easily forego one sector of the private region, that only means a maximum of two configurable VxVM objects less than before (approx. 3000 objects in our example). But you cannot define a subdisk outside of the public region. No trouble whatsoever! We extend the public region partition to the boundaries of the whole disk, thus covering the private region partition as well. In order to prohibit subdisks within the configuration part of the private region, we limit the end of the public region as subdisk container to the first sector of the private region as partition.

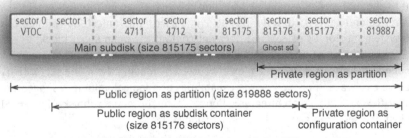

Figure 10-9: Extended public region and the position of the Ghost subdisk

The same disk configuration by command output:

```
# vxdisk list c4t8d0
[...]
```

```
public:    slice=3 offset=1 len=815176 disk_offset=0
private:   slice=4 offset=1 len=4171 disk_offset=815176
[...]
```

Given the usual drivers performing I/O (block or swap device), the Ghost subdisk will not be affected by any I/O, for they skip the first 16 sectors of the device. Therefore, the Ghost subdisk is NOT a performance drawback, although some people promoting a cheaper but less intelligent volume management try to make you believe so. It does not look really pretty, maybe. If you care for beauty, then install your Solaris system on a disk keeping the first (two) cylinders unused by OS partitions. Or you should mirror the volumes created by encapsulation (we assume c0t0d0s2 and its disk media name osdg01) to a freshly initialized sliced VxVM disk (osdg02). That disk layout always skips the first cylinder and creates the private region and public region partitions mutually exclusive on the remaining disk (see OS mirror section above, p.324-326). Then, re-initialize and re-mirror the original OS disk by the following list of commands:

```
# vxplex -g bootdg -o rm dis $(
  vxprint -g bootdg -pne 'pl_sd.sd_dmname="osdg01"')
# vxdg -g bootdg rmdisk osdg01
# vxdisksetup -i c0t0d0 format=sliced privlen=1m
# vxdg -g bootdg adddisk osdg01=c0t0d0
# vxmirror -g bootdg osdg02 osdg01
```

10.7 MANUAL ENCAPSULATION WALKTHROUGH

10.7.1 ASSUMPTIONS AND PREREQUISITES

Two purposes are connected with the following section: to help an understanding of the basic encapsulation procedure and to show some kind of "worst case" scenario where the standard command line interfaces will fail. What does "worst case" exactly mean?

1. The vxencap script needs at least one (cdsdisk layout) or two (sliced) unused partitions in order to create the VxVM partition (cdsdisk) or the private region and public region partitions (sliced). But unfortunately, all partitions are already in use and cannot be foregone.

2. Any encapsulation procedure needs a small amount of unused disk space in order to create the private region out of it and to store the new VxVM objects. But there is no free space on the disk to become the private region.

3. Encapsulation enables volume sizes beyond disk limits, data redundancy, performance tuning, and the flexibility of online volume management. Our example will deal only with data mirroring, for new worries will await us (further resize and relayout operations are plain sailing and therefore not discussed).

4. For cross platform compatibility (and another reason to be explained later), we wish to convert the file systems of type ufs on our partitions into vxfs.

5. As long as the first disk cylinder is in use by a partition holding application data, any encapsulation procedure will protect the VTOC by replacing sector 0 by the Ghost subdisk to recreate the proper device offsets (see previous section). The private region cannot be placed at the fixed disk offset of 256 sectors of the cdsdisk layout. Thus, a sliced layout must be created without the capabilities of "Cross Platform data Sharing". Both the Ghost subdisk colliding with the CDS disk group subdisk alignment of 8 kB and the wrong position of the private region hinder us to easily activate CDS features.

6. Veritas software is designed to aid high availability. But two file system based OS limitations force a temporary application interruption: It is impossible to replace the partition drivers by their corresponding volume drivers and to modify the file system layout from ufs to vxfs, while the application is running on the device. All we can do is to try to stop and restart the applications as quickly as possible. That calls suspiciously for a script running the commands in uninterrupted sequence.

Just look at the following command outputs to determine the current state of the partition based "applications" (the file systems each holding a large file are mounted):

```
# prtvtoc /dev/rdsk/c4t1d0s2
[...]
*     4712 sectors/cylinder
*     7508 cylinders
*     7506 accessible cylinders
```

```
[...]
*                         First    Sector    Last
* Partition  Tag  Flags   Sector    Count    Sector  Mount Directory
        0     0   00           0  5051264   5051263  /mnt0
        1     0   00     5051264  5051264  10102527  /mnt1
        2     5   01           0 35368272  35368271
        3     0   00    10102528  5051264  15153791  /mnt3
        4     0   00    15153792  5051264  20205055  /mnt4
        5     0   00    20205056  5051264  25256319  /mnt5
        6     0   00    25256320  5051264  30307583  /mnt6
        7     0   00    30307584  5060688  35368271  /mnt7
# df -k /mnt?
Filesystem            kbytes     used   avail capacity Mounted on
/dev/dsk/c4t1d0s0    2474263  2098193  326585    87%   /mnt0
/dev/dsk/c4t1d0s1    2474263  2098193  326585    87%   /mnt1
/dev/dsk/c4t1d0s3    2474263  2098193  326585    87%   /mnt3
/dev/dsk/c4t1d0s4    2474263  2098193  326585    87%   /mnt4
/dev/dsk/c4t1d0s5    2474263  2098193  326585    87%   /mnt5
/dev/dsk/c4t1d0s6    2474263  2098193  326585    87%   /mnt6
/dev/dsk/c4t1d0s7    2478975  2098193  331203    87%   /mnt7
# for i in 0 1 3 4 5 6 7; do fstyp /dev/rdsk/c4t1d0s$i; done | uniq
ufs
```

10.7.2 BASIC CONSIDERATIONS

Our desperate try to use the standard vxencap script and following the clean-up:

```
# vxencap -g edg -c edg01=c4t1d0
  VxVM vxencap ERROR V-5-2-213
It is not possible to encapsulate c4t1d0, for the following reason:
    <VxVM vxslicer ERROR V-5-1-754 Not enough free partitions.>
# rm -r /dev/vx/reconfig.d/disk.d/c4t1d0
```

Well, that did not work! Some thoughts and remarks on the list of difficulties will clear the way we need to walk on. Since our "worst case" assumption does not allow for a removal of any application data, we may shrink a device only at its end to free a small amount of space for the private region. This implies that we cannot shrink the first partition at its beginning in order to enable a cdsdisk layout, and that we must convert ufs, which cannot be shrunken, to vxfs at least on one partition at the very beginning. We choose slice 5 (for an imaginary reason) to be stopped early in order to convert the file system to vxfs and to shrink it by one cylinder.

Furthermore, the inevitable sliced layout requires two unused partition numbers. Partition 5, already suffering early application shutdown, will serve as the private region (even though located in the middle of the disk), partition 7 (once again for an imaginary reason) will define the public region and must be freed from application access as well.

10.7.3 STORING THE DISK LAYOUT

Since our procedure removes two partitions from the VTOC before the correspondent subdisks are created, storing the offset and the length of the partitions is required (except for the backup slice, of course). By the way, we will determine the size of a disk cylinder and of the whole disk in order to create the private and the public region in the proper size. Finally, we will convert the partition offsets into subdisk offsets (decremented by 1 due to the VTOC protection) and, for the first slice (slice 0, VTOC protection) and slice 5 (one cylinder split to become the private region), the partition lengths into subdisk lengths. Here is our first code fragment:

```
Disk=c4t1d0
File=/tmp/$Disk.$$

prtvtoc /dev/rdsk/${Disk}s2 |
nawk '
    $3=="sectors/cylinder" {print "SecPerCyl",$2; SecPerCyl=$2}
    $1~/^[0134567]$/ {
        if ($1==5) {print "OffsetPrivReg",$6-SecPerCyl+1; $5-=SecPerCyl}
        if ($4==0) {print "FirstPart",$1;$5--} else {$4--}
        print $1,$4,$5
    }
    $1==2 {print "SecOfDisk",$5}
' > $File
```

10.7.4 DEFINING PRIVATE AND PUBLIC REGION

Nothing happened to the disk and to the applications, because our script collected data in a non-intrusive manner. The next step requires application stop for partition 5: The file system needs to be unmounted in order to convert ufs to vxfs in order to shrink the file system by the size of one cylinder. Conversion of ufs to vxfs just inactivates the former ufs metadata by addressing the blocks holding file content by vxfs metadata. So, a file system check is required to free the device from invalid ufs structures (a full check without log replay, for there are still no valid log data). Finally, the current vxfs file system is shrunken by the size of one cylinder which requires a temporary mount.

```
NewSize=$(nawk '$1==5 {print $3}' $File)
umount /mnt5
vxfsconvert -y /dev/rdsk/${Disk}s5
fsck -F vxfs -o full,nolog -y /dev/rdsk/${Disk}s5
mount -F vxfs /dev/dsk/${Disk}s5 /mnt5
fsadm -F vxfs -b $NewSize -r /dev/rdsk/${Disk}s5 /mnt5
umount /mnt5
```

Defining subdisks, plexes, and volumes requires a disk initialized for VxVM (private and public region) as a disk group member. The previous step created disk space one cylinder in size and not used by the file systems. In order to initialize the disk for VxVM, we still need two unused partition numbers: The file system of partition 5 is unmounted, and partitions 5 and 7 are removed from the VTOC.

```
umount /mnt7
fmthard -d 5:0:0:0:0 /dev/rdsk/${Disk}s2
fmthard -d 7:0:0:0:0 /dev/rdsk/${Disk}s2
```

We redefine partitions 5 and 7 to become private and public region. The private region, formerly the last cylinder of slice 5, is located in the middle of the disk. Therefore, slice 7 as the public region must cover the whole disk in order to cover all application partitions. As we already know, VxVM does not worry about a private region being part of the public region. Disk initialization for VxVM is completed by writing a basic structure into the private region.

```
SecPerCyl=$(nawk '$1=="SecPerCyl" {print $2}' $File)
SecOfDisk=$(nawk '$1=="SecOfDisk" {print $2}' $File)
OffsetPrivReg=$(nawk '$1=="OffsetPrivReg" {print $2}' $File)
fmthard -d 5:15:01:$OffsetPrivReg:$SecPerCyl /dev/rdsk/${Disk}s2
fmthard -d 7:14:01:0:$SecOfDisk /dev/rdsk/${Disk}s2
vxdisk -f init $Disk format=sliced privlen=1m
```

10.7.5 CREATING SUBDISKS, PLEXES, AND VOLUMES

We already overcame some difficult obstacles. Remember that still five of seven applications are running without interruption. The next steps define the typical VxVM objects to create the volume drivers on the disk spaces accessed by the partitions. But, of course, the disk must become a disk group member first. The following code part defines the default disk group for the script, initializes the disk group and creates the Ghost subdisk located at the first sector of the private region. The variable FirstPart stores the number of the partition starting at cylinder 0, because the Ghost subdisk is needed for offset alignment within the corresponding plex.

```
export VXVM_DEFAULTDG=edg
vxdg init edg edg01=$Disk cds=off
vxdg set align=1
# Ghost subdisk
vxmake sd edg01-B0 disk=edg01 offset=$((OffsetPrivReg-1)) len=1
FirstPart=$(nawk '$1=="FirstPart" {print $2}' $File)
```

Within a loop over all application partition numbers, the subdisks are placed over the partitions, and the plexes and finally the volumes are built out of them. The volumes are started, the still mounted file systems unmounted, the underlying partitions removed, the file systems converted to vxfs and checked, and finally remounted as vxfs based on the volume drivers.

```
for i in 0 1 3 4 5 6 7; do
    nawk '$1=='$i' {print $2,$3}' $File | read Offset Len
    vxmake sd edg01-0$i disk=edg01 offset=$Offset len=$Len
    if ((i==FirstPart)); then
        vxmake plex vol$i-01 sd=edg01-B0,edg01-0$i
    else
        vxmake plex vol$i-01 sd=edg01-0$i
    fi
    vxmake vol vol$i plex=vol$i-01 usetype=fsgen
    vxvol start vol$i
    if ((i!=5 && i!=7)); then
        umount /mnt$i
        fmthard -d $i:0:0:0:0 /dev/rdsk/${Disk}s2
    fi
    if ((i!=5)); then
        vxfsconvert -y /dev/vx/rdsk/edg/vol$i
        fsck -F vxfs -o full,nolog -y /dev/vx/rdsk/edg/vol$i
    fi
    mount -F vxfs /dev/vx/dsk/edg/vol$i /mnt$i
done
```

Wow, the worst part has completed! Our script has (successfully, we hope) executed the time-critical parts of the conversion. All applications are online once again and do not need to be stopped for the following volume and file system management tasks. Lean back for a few seconds and breathe deeply! Then, have a look at the complete script once again with some comments, output redirections, and further output displaying the time required to execute the steps (41 sec. totally, most applications stopped just for a few seconds).

```
# cat ./encap_advanced
#!/bin/ksh

Disk=c4t1d0
File=/tmp/$Disk.$$

# Store disk layout
echo $(date +%H:%M:%S): Storing disk layout
prtvtoc /dev/rdsk/${Disk}s2 |
nawk '
    $3=="sectors/cylinder" {print "SecPerCyl",$2; SecPerCyl=$2}
    $1~/^[0134567]$/ {
        if ($1==5) {print "OffsetPrivReg",$6-SecPerCyl+1; $5-=SecPerCyl}
        if ($4==0) {print "FirstPart",$1;$5--} else {$4--}
        print $1,$4,$5
    }
    $1==2 {print "SecOfDisk",$5}
' > $File
```

342

```
# Convert /mnt5 to VxFS, then shrink it to create space for private region
echo $(date +%H:%M:%S): Convert /mnt5 to VxFS and shrink
NewSize=$(nawk '$1==5 {print $3}' $File)
umount /mnt5
vxfsconvert -y /dev/rdsk/${Disk}s5 >/dev/null 2>&1
fsck -F vxfs -o full,nolog -y /dev/rdsk/${Disk}s5 >/dev/null
mount -F vxfs /dev/dsk/${Disk}s5 /mnt5
fsadm -F vxfs -b $NewSize -r /dev/rdsk/${Disk}s5 /mnt5 >/dev/null
umount /mnt5

# Delete partitions 5 and 7
echo $(date +%H:%M:%S): Delete partitions 5 and 7
umount /mnt7
fmthard -d 5:0:0:0:0 /dev/rdsk/${Disk}s2
fmthard -d 7:0:0:0:0 /dev/rdsk/${Disk}s2

# Initialize disk as VxVM disk
echo $(date +%H:%M:%S): Initialize disk as VxVM disk
SecPerCyl=$(nawk '$1=="SecPerCyl" {print $2}' $File)
SecOfDisk=$(nawk '$1=="SecOfDisk" {print $2}' $File)
OffsetPrivReg=$(nawk '$1=="OffsetPrivReg" {print $2}' $File)
fmthard -d 5:15:01:$OffsetPrivReg:$SecPerCyl /dev/rdsk/${Disk}s2
fmthard -d 7:14:01:0:$SecOfDisk /dev/rdsk/${Disk}s2
vxdisk -f init $Disk format=sliced privlen=1m

# Create disk group, build subdisks, plexes, volumes
echo $(date +%H:%M:%S): Create disk group
export VXVM_DEFAULTDG=edg
vxdg init edg edg01=$Disk cds=off
vxdg set align=1
# Ghost subdisk
vxmake sd edg01-B0 disk=edg01 offset=$((OffsetPrivReg-1)) len=1
FirstPart=$(nawk '$1=="FirstPart" {print $2}' $File)

for i in 0 1 3 4 5 6 7; do
    echo $(date +%H:%M:%S): Create volume vol$i
    nawk '$1=='$i' {print $2,$3}' $File | read Offset Len
    vxmake sd edg01-0$i disk=edg01 offset=$Offset len=$Len
    if ((i==FirstPart)); then
        vxmake plex vol$i-01 sd=edg01-B0,edg01-0$i
    else
        vxmake plex vol$i-01 sd=edg01-0$i
    fi
    vxmake vol vol$i plex=vol$i-01 usetype=fsgen
    vxvol start vol$i
    if ((i!=5 && i!=7)); then
```

```
        umount /mnt$i
        fmthard -d $i:0:0:0:0 /dev/rdsk/${Disk}s2
    fi
    if ((i!=5)); then
        echo $(date +%H:%M:%S): Convert vol$i to VxFS
        vxfsconvert -y /dev/vx/rdsk/edg/vol$i >/dev/null 2>&1
        fsck -F vxfs -o full,nolog -y /dev/vx/rdsk/edg/vol$i >/dev/null
    fi
    echo $(date +%H:%M:%S): Mount vol$i to /mnt$i
    mount -F vxfs /dev/vx/dsk/edg/vol$i /mnt$i
done
```

 # ./encap_advanced
```
16:05:11: Storing disk layout
16:05:11: Convert /mnt5 to VxFS and shrink
16:05:16: Delete partitions 5 and 7
16:05:16: Initialize disk as VxVM disk
16:05:18: Create disk group
16:05:20: Create volume vol0
16:05:22: Convert vol0 to VxFS
16:05:25: Mount vol0 to /mnt0
16:05:25: Create volume vol1
16:05:26: Convert vol1 to VxFS
16:05:34: Mount vol1 to /mnt1
[...]
16:05:48: Create volume vol7
16:05:49: Convert vol7 to VxFS
16:05:52: Mount vol7 to /mnt7
```

We check the results. Note that the private region as configuration container indeed covers just 1 MB of the private region as partition, as instructed by our initialization parameters.

 # vxdisk list c4t1d0
```
[...]
info:      format=sliced,privoffset=1,pubslice=7,privslice=5
[...]
public:    slice=7 offset=1 len=35368271 disk_offset=0
private:   slice=5 offset=1 len=2048 disk_offset=25251608
[...]
```
 # vxprint -rtg edg
```
[...]
dm edg01        c4t1d0s2      auto     2048      35368271 -

v  vol0         -             ENABLED  ACTIVE    5051264  ROUND      -          fsgen
pl vol0-01      vol0          ENABLED  ACTIVE    5051264  CONCAT     -          RW
sd edg01-B0     vol0-01       edg01    25251607 1         0          c4t1d0     ENA
```

```
sd edg01-00      vol0-01        edg01     0       5051263 1         c4t1d0   ENA

v  vol1          -              ENABLED   ACTIVE  5051264 ROUND     -        fsgen
pl vol1-01       vol1           ENABLED   ACTIVE  5051264 CONCAT    -        RW
sd edg01-01      vol1-01        edg01     5051263 5051264 0         c4t1d0   ENA
[...]
v  vol7          -              ENABLED   ACTIVE  5060688 ROUND     -        fsgen
pl vol7-01       vol7           ENABLED   ACTIVE  5060688 CONCAT    -        RW
sd edg01-07      vol7-01        edg01     30307583 5060688 0        c4t1d0   ENA
# df -k /mnt?
Filesystem              kbytes     used    avail capacity Mounted on
/dev/vx/dsk/edg/vol0 2525632 2098928    400042    84%     /mnt0
/dev/vx/dsk/edg/vol1 2525632 2098928    400042    84%     /mnt1
/dev/vx/dsk/edg/vol3 2525632 2098928    400042    84%     /mnt3
/dev/vx/dsk/edg/vol4 2525632 2098928    400042    84%     /mnt4
/dev/vx/dsk/edg/vol5 2523276 2098928    397833    85%     /mnt5
/dev/vx/dsk/edg/vol6 2525632 2098928    400042    84%     /mnt6
/dev/vx/dsk/edg/vol7 2530344 2098928    404460    84%     /mnt7
# for i in 0 1 3 4 5 6 7; do fstyp /dev/vx/rdsk/edg/vol$i; done | uniq
vxfs
```

10.7.6 MIRRORING AND PREPARING FOR CDS

Data redundancy still lacks. While planning volume mirroring, we keep in mind that we want to migrate to a CDS disk group. Therefore, we initialize the second disk of our disk group in the cdsdisk layout. As long as the cds disk group attribute is cleared, we may mix both disk layouts within a disk group. Our slight hope to easily convert disks and disk group by the standard vxcdsconvert command, so that CDS capabilities are activated, is (we might have expected it) immediately dashed.

```
# vxdisksetup -i c4t2d0 privlen=1m
# vxdg -g edg adddisk edg02=c4t2d0
# vxdisk -g edg list
DEVICE       TYPE          DISK      GROUP       STATUS
c4t1d0s2     auto:sliced   edg01     edg         online
c4t2d0s2     auto:cdsdisk  edg02     edg         online
# vxcdsconvert -g edg -o novolstop group evac_subdisks_ok=yes privlen=1m
VxVM vxcdsconvert ERROR V-5-2-2763 c4t1d0s2: Public and private regions overlap
VxVM vxcdsconvert ERROR V-5-2-3120 Conversion process aborted
```

Well, no flight in a luxurious airplane, instead a long exhausting way on foot? No, we still may make use of efficient VxVM scripts. But in order to achieve the desired result by not too long a list of commands, we must use our brains a little bit. A simple volume mirroring executed by vxmirror would produce a result we could not go on with (we assume the same disk and cylinder size for the mirror disk). Why? A requirement for the conversion to a CDS disk group is still not met: the subdisk alignment to 8 kB blocks. Neither all volume sizes nor all subdisk offsets nor all subdisk lengths on the mirror disk are or would be integer multiples of 8 kB:

```
# vxprint -g edg -vF '%name %len'|nawk '{printf "%s %.2f\n",$1,$2/16}'
vol0 315704.00
vol1 315704.00
vol3 315704.00
vol4 315704.00
vol5 315409.50
vol6 315704.00
vol7 316293.00
# vxprint -g edg -se 'sd_dmname="edg02"' -F '%name %offset %len' |
  nawk '{printf "%s %10.2f %10.2f\n",$1,$2/16,$3/16}'
edg02-01      150.50   315704.00
edg02-02   315854.50   315704.00
edg02-03   631558.50   315704.00
edg02-04   947262.50   315704.00
edg02-05  1262966.50   315409.50
edg02-06  1578376.00   315704.00
edg02-07  1894080.00   316293.00
```

Since the original disk has sliced layout and must be remirrored, we may ignore the subdisk offsets unsuitable to a CDS disk group. But the wrong volume length bothers us. What is the next integer multiple of the current volume length? How many sectors are missing? Nevertheless, adding the difference of the desired and the current volume size to the volume length in order to create an integer multiple of 8 kB fails:

```
# vxprint -g edg -F %len vol5
5046552
# echo $(((5046552/16+1)*16))
5046560
# echo $((5046560-5046552))
8
# vxresize -g edg -F vxfs -x vol5 +8 edg01
VxVM vxassist ERROR V-5-1-436 Cannot allocate space to grow volume to 5046560
blocks
VxVM vxresize ERROR V-5-1-4703 Problem running vxassist command for volume vol5,
in diskgroup edg
```

Is it indeed impossible to allocate just eight blocks on the original disk? We built the private region out of a partition one cylinder in size, i.e. 4712 sectors given our example. But we fixed the size of the private region as configuration container by 1 MB (= 2048 sectors), therefore 4712 - 2048 = 2664 sectors should be available for new subdisks (1 sector already in use by the Ghost subdisk). We remember that in most cases the "Cannot allocate space" error message is misleading: There is enough space, but layout restrictions would be violated. The current layout restriction is the default diskalign attribute of vxassist enforcing subdisk creation at cylinder boundaries. Once recognized as the source of our troubles, we simply turn it of and retry the resize operation:

```
# vxassist help showattrs
#Attributes:
 layout=nomirror,nostripe,nomirror-stripe,nostripe-mirror,nostripe-mirror-
col,nostripe-mirror-sd,
noconcat-mirror,nomirror-concat,span,nocontig,raid5log,noregionlog,diskalign,no
storage
[...]
# echo layout=nodiskalign > /etc/default/vxassist
# vxassist help showattrs
#Attributes:
 layout=nomirror,nostripe,nomirror-stripe,nostripe-mirror,nostripe-mirror-
col,nostripe-mirror-sd,
noconcat-mirror,nomirror-concat,span,nocontig,raid5log,noregionlog,nodiskalign,
nostorage
[...]
# vxresize -g edg -F vxfs -x vol5 +8 edg01
# vxmirror -g edg edg01
! vxassist -g edg mirror vol0
! vxassist -g edg mirror vol1
! vxassist -g edg mirror vol3
! vxassist -g edg mirror vol4
! vxassist -g edg mirror vol5
! vxassist -g edg mirror vol6
! vxassist -g edg mirror vol7
```

The nodiskalign attribute ensures that the mirror procedure of vxmirror (based on vxassist mirror commands) will not fit the subdisks at cylinder boundaries anymore, will place the first subdisk immediately after the private region of the mirror disk (having cdsdisk layout), and therefore will not run out of space. The mirror disk already fulfills all criteria to become part of a CDS disk group.

The original disk must be re-initialized as a CDS suitable disk and completely re-mirrored by the same procedure.

```
# vxplex -g edg -o rm dis $(vxprint -g edg -pne 'pl_sd.sd_dmname="edg01"')
# vxdg -g edg rmdisk edg01
# vxdisksetup -i c4t1d0 privlen=1m
# vxdg -g edg adddisk edg01=c4t1d0
# vxdisk -g edg list
DEVICE       TYPE          DISK        GROUP       STATUS
c4t1d0s2     auto:cdsdisk  edg01       edg         online
c4t2d0s2     auto:cdsdisk  edg02       edg         online
# vxprint -dtg edg
DM NAME          DEVICE      TYPE    PRIVLEN PUBLEN  STATE

dm edg01         c4t1d0s2    auto    2048    35365968 -
```

```
dm edg02        c4t2d0s2      auto    2048    35365968 -
# vxmirror -g edg edg02
! vxassist -g edg mirror vol0
! vxassist -g edg mirror vol1
! vxassist -g edg mirror vol3
! vxassist -g edg mirror vol4
! vxassist -g edg mirror vol5
! vxassist -g edg mirror vol6
! vxassist -g edg mirror vol7
```

10.7.7 CONVERTING TO CDS

Now the final steps! VxFS is already a cross platform compatible file system (except for Windows), but the disk group is still not completely prepared for CDS. The subdisk alignment needs to be changed to 8 kB, and the cds attribute of the disk group must be set. The former vxassist defaults are reset, a file system defragmentation may be useful, and appropriate /etc/vfstab entries should contain the volume drivers and vxfs.

```
# vxprint -Gg edg -F '%align %cds'
1 off
# vxdg -g edg set align=16
# vxdg -g edg set cds=on
# vxprint -Gg edg -F '%align %cds'
16 on
# rm /etc/default/vxassist
# for i in 0 1 3 4 5 6 7; do fsadm -F vxfs -de /mnt$i; done
# vi /etc/vfstab
[...]
/dev/vx/dsk/edg/vol0  /dev/vx/rdsk/edg/vol0  /mnt0  vxfs  2  yes  -
[...]
```

CHAPTER 11: TROUBLESHOOTING

by Dr. Albrecht Scriba

11.1 INTRODUCTION

Fixing VxVM related problems should never be a game of trial and error. If you are going to mess around in the depths of volume management you need to know what you are doing! For this reason we have decided to write this chapter as a training lesson more than a direct hands-on guide so that you do your training long before you actually need the skill. If you are not familiar with the procedures you should not start repairing serial split brain conditions or other advanced errors in large-scale production systems. So take your time and learn the troubleshooting techniques thoroughly first. There is enough material in this chapter to make you an expert if you care to read it and actually do the exercises. So sit down in front of your VxVM host, get yourself your favorite non-alcoholic beverage and let's begin:

In order to test several troubleshooting scenarios, we need procedures to simulate some kinds of disk outage, because we do not want to actually destroy disks – even if it may take all of your self control not to destroy all those infernal machines with an axe! First, we need to simulate a completely destroyed disk, then a disk temporarily unavailable, but still physically healthy, and finally a disk with some unusable regions on it.

There are several ways to tell VxVM, that a disk is unusable unexpectedly from VxVM's point of view. But note that we probably cannot power off the disk as long as we use disk LUNs provided by a storage array. Other ways have in common, that some relevant data structures are removed from the private region by OS provided tools which, of course, do not inform VxVM, that the disk is regularly unreachable.

Starting with VxVM 5.0, removing the VxVM partitions from a disk does not make the

V. Herminghaus and A. Sriba, *Storage Management in Data Centers*,
DOI: 10.1007/978-3-540-85023-6_11, © Springer-Verlag Berlin Heidelberg 2009

disk unusable for VxVM as long as VxVM still has usable disk data within the kernel. To tell VxVM to update or rebuild its kernel database, you must deport and import the corresponding disk group (which is not a realistic scenario) or restart or disable and re-enable vxconfigd (which breaks the communication to vxnotify). Nevertheless, we will choose the latter procedure, although it is not completely compatible with an actual disk failure.

Simulating a disk temporarily unreachable is performed by the usual steps alluded above and presented below to make a disk unavailable, followed by the reconstruction of the erased private region data. Unfortunately, we do not know a technique to simulate a disk only partially damaged (only some regions on it are not accessible anymore). To achieve this scenario, we would need a kernel layer concatenating real disks or array LUNs to a "disk" visible to the usual disk drivers, and we would make one of those basic disks or LUNs unavailable. Any suggestions are welcome!

To make a disk unusable for VxVM, use the following sequence of commands (you should write a script out of them). We will store the private region data to be removed in order to restore them later, if we want to simulate a temporary disk outage.

Sliced Disk

Get the slice number of the private region, store the first block of 128 kB of the private region data at an appropriate location, overwrite that disk space with zeros, and finally update the VxVM kernel database:

```
# Slice=$(prtvtoc -h /dev/rdsk/c#t#d#s2 | awk '$2==15 {print $1}')
# dd if=/dev/rdsk/c#t#d#s$Slice of=/var/tmp/c#t#d#s$Slice bs=128k count=1
# dd if=/dev/zero of=/dev/rdsk/c#t#d#s$Slice bs=128k count=1
# vxconfigd -k
```

CDS Disk

Nearly the same procedure, except for the different location of the private region (disk offset of 128 kB):

```
# dd if=/dev/rdsk/c#t#d#s2 of=/var/tmp/c#t#d#s2 bs=128k iseek=1 count=1
# dd if=/dev/zero of=/dev/rdsk/c#t#d#s2 bs=128k oseek=1 count=1
# vxconfigd -k
```

If you want to keep the PID of vxconfigd (for whatever reason), you may replace the last command for both disk layouts by:

```
# vxdctl disable
# vxdctl enable
```

In order to get a disk we "destroyed" by this procedure usable again for VxVM, we only need to write the stored private region data back to the appropriate slice.

Sliced Disk

Get the slice number of the private region (if you forgot it), and restore the first 128 kB of the private region:

```
# Slice=$(prtvtoc -h /dev/rdsk/c#t#d#s2 | awk '$2==15 {print $1}')
# dd if=/var/tmp/c#t#d#s$Slice of=/dev/rdsk/c#t#d#s$Slice bs=128k
```

CDS Disk
Restore the stored private region data to the appropriate disk offset:

```
# dd if=/var/tmp/c#t#d#s2 of=/dev/rdsk/c#t#d#s2 bs=128k oseek=1
```

During the boot process several VxVM daemons are started, mostly by the script /etc/rc2.d/S95vxvm-recover (Solaris 9) and /lib/svc/method/vxvm-recover (Solaris 10) respectively. Two of those daemons are of special interest in case of a disk becoming unexpectedly unavailable (for whatever reason): vxrelocd (default configuration) or vxsparecheck. Both daemons (they must not run at the same time) perform automated tasks to find subdisk or disk replacements for the damaged objects. We will discuss thoroughly their behavior in another part of this chapter. To get an understanding of what happens, if disks encounter problems, we should stop them to prevent VxVM from any automated configuration change.

```
# pkill -9 -xu0 'vxrelocd|vxsparecheck'
```

Having terminated your VxVM troubleshooting tests, you should start the appropriate daemon by issuing one of the following commands:

```
# nohup /usr/lib/vxvm/bin/vxrelocd root &
# nohup /usr/lib/vxvm/bin/vxsparecheck root &
```

Vx
Easy
Sailing

11.2 DISK OUTAGE

To test the following scenarios (disk persistently damaged or temporarily inaccessible), please create a disk group containing at least two disks and two volumes in it, each of size 1 GB, one volume (called vol1 here) without redundancy, another volume (vol2) with two plexes/mirrors:

```
# vxdisksetup -i c4t1d0
# vxdisksetup -i c4t2d0
# vxdg init adg adg01=c4t1d0 adg02=c4t2d0
# vxassist -g adg make vol2 1g nmirror=2 init=active alloc=adg01,adg02
# vxassist -g adg make vol1 1g alloc=adg01
```

Issuing I/O to a volume (partially) built on a failed disk will, as a first reaction of the system, show some console messages comparable to the following output example. The disk driver gives up after some retries, then the VxVM Dynamic Multipathing driver (vxdmp) disables all its paths to the disk driver (the example only shows one path) and successively, since not a single path but the underlying disk has failed, its DMP node to the disk. Finally, the plex I/O error is reported and the plex "detached" from the volume (still a volume member, but in kernel state DISABLED) due to the failed subdisk belonging to it.

```
Sep 21 18:54:06 sols scsi: WARNING: /pci@1f,0/pci@1/scsi@2/sd@1,0 (sd47):
Sep 21 18:54:06 sols    SCSI transport failed: reason 'incomplete': retrying
command
Sep 21 18:54:08 sols scsi: WARNING: /pci@1f,0/pci@1/scsi@2/sd@1,0 (sd47):
Sep 21 18:54:08 sols    disk not responding to selection
[…]
Sep 21 18:54:25 sols vxdmp: NOTICE: VxVM vxdmp V-5-0-112 disabled path 32/0x178
belonging to the dmpnode 210/0x30
Sep 21 18:54:25 sols vxdmp: NOTICE: VxVM vxdmp V-5-0-111 disabled dmpnode
```

```
210/0x30
Sep 21 18:54:25 sols vxio: WARNING: VxVM vxio V-5-0-151 error on Plex vol2-01
while writing volume vol2 offset 0 length 1
Sep 21 18:54:25 sols vxio: WARNING: VxVM vxio V-5-0-4 Plex vol2-01 detached from
volume vol2
Sep 21 18:54:25 sols vxio: WARNING: VxVM vxio V-5-0-386 adg01-01 Subdisk failed
in plex vol2-01 in vol vol2
```

As long as not strictly instructed to analyze private region access, VxVM keeps the former physical disk state (I/O failure does not automatically imply disk failure). A device scan or a reboot will change the device state to error (or online invalid, if you only simulate the disk outage).

```
# vxdisk list
[...]
c4t1d0s2      auto:cdsdisk   -           -          online
c4t2d0s2      auto:cdsdisk   adg02       adg        online
[...]
-             -              adg01       adg        failed was:c4t1d0s2
# vxdisk scandisks
# vxdisk list
[...]
c4t1d0s2      auto           -           -          error
c4t2d0s2      auto:cdsdisk   adg02       adg        online
[...]
-             -              adg01       adg        failed was:c4t1d0s2
```

What happens to the VxVM object states, if a disk becomes unavailable, but there are still other healthy disks within the disk group? Of course, the disk group configuration is not lost, because it is stored within multiple private regions (5 as default and if the disk group contains at least 5 disks). VxVM will immediately synchronize the disk group configuration to another disk with a previously inactive configuration, if the damaged disk had an active one. Therefore, the disk group membership of the damaged disk regarding its disk media name, its previous device access, its disk ID, and some other attributes are still known. On the other side, the disk having lost its device access looses its physical membership of the disk group too — in the words of the VxVM documentation: The disk is "detached" from the disk group, as shown by the command output above or the vxprint output below:

```
# vxprint -dtg adg
DM NAME       DEVICE       TYPE    PRIVLEN  PUBLEN    STATE

dm adg01      -            -       -        -         NODEVICE
dm adg02      c4t2d0s2     auto    2048     35365968  -
```

All subdisks located on the disk which has become unavailable (state NODEVICE), become unavailable as well (mode NODEVICE, abbreviated NDEV in the output of vxprint).

```
# vxprint -stg adg
SD NAME          PLEX        DISK        DISKOFFS LENGTH   [COL/]OFF DEVICE   MODE
[...]
sd adg01-01      vol2-01     adg01       0        2097152  0         -        NDEV
sd adg01-02      vol1-01     adg01       2097152  2097152  0         -        NDEV
sd adg02-01      vol2-02     adg02       0        2097152  0         c4t2d0   ENA
```

What is the effect of subdisks having no underlying physical substrate anymore to the virtual objects of volumes? The answer is quite simple and was already given by the console output: Any plex containing a damaged subdisk is completely cut off from any I/O (application or kernel initiated), even though there may be still other healthy subdisks in it. The application state of the plex enters the NODEVICE state, the kernel state becomes DISABLED, thus preventing the plex from any I/O. If this plex was the last healthy or the only plex within the volume, that is, the volume now has no working instance of its address space, the volume itself enters kernel state DISABLED (no I/O on the volume anymore) by keeping the previous application state (normally ACTIVE).

```
# vxprint -rtg adg
[...]
v  vol1         -           DISABLED ACTIVE   2097152 SELECT    -        fsgen
pl vol1-01      vol1        DISABLED NODEVICE 2097152 CONCAT    -        RW
sd adg01-02     vol1-01     adg01    2097152  2097152 0         -        NDEV

v  vol2         -           ENABLED  ACTIVE   2097152 SELECT    -        fsgen
pl vol2-01      vol2        ENABLED  ACTIVE   2097152 CONCAT    -        RW
sd adg01-01     vol2-01     adg01    0        2097152 0         c4t2d0   ENA
pl vol2-02      vol2        DISABLED NODEVICE 2097152 CONCAT    -        RW
sd adg02-01     vol2-02     adg02    0        2097152 0         -        NDEV
```

Having physically replaced the damaged disk or chosen another unused disk instead, there are several tools provided by VxVM to repair disk, disk group, subdisk, plex, and volume states. To our experience, best known by most VxVM administrators is the ASCII based interactive tool vxdiskadm (especially menus 4 "Remove a disk for replacement" and 5 "Replace a failed or removed disk"). But in many cases, it means breaking a fly on the wheel. Even for the mouse pushers and button pressers having the patience and the memory and processor resources to start the vea GUI there are menu items to repair VxVM object states. The command line interface provides some troubleshooting commands, sometimes with obviously overlapping capabilities, thus producing still more trouble in your head. Therefore, we strongly recommend the following list of low-level commands. They are easy to understand, they are straight-forward, they perform only the necessary steps, and they are capable to solve all kind of disk outage with only one small difference at the beginning.

11.2.1 DISK PERMANENTLY DAMAGED

Let's start with a completely and irreversibly damaged disk. In case you want to simulate that, look at the procedure and commands mentioned above. Do not forget to stop vxrelocd or vxsparecheck at first! Be sure to "destroy" the disk which is common to both volumes! Check the results by looking at the output of the vxdisk and vxprint commands.

    1.   The damaged disk must be replaced as the first step (in our virtual disk trouble-shooting scenario, we do not need to do anything).

    2.   Since VxVM does not send repeated test I/Os on a failed disk, nothing happens to the disk state for VxVM. In order to get the disk out of the currently mistaken error state, we initiate a device scan. People usually issue the command:

```
# vxdctl enable
```

VxVM will have a look at all disks visible to the OS. In large enterprise environments, this could take several minutes. However, the main purpose of this command is to bring vxconfigd in the fully enabled mode during the boot process, thus importing all disk groups except for the already imported boot disk group. To specify only a subset of disks visible to the OS you should use in our example:

```
# vxdisk scandisks device=c4t1d0
```

As a result, the disk becomes online invalid, i.e. the disk is physically visible by its VxVM device driver as a healthy disk, but there is no valid private region on it.

```
# vxdisk list
[...]
c4t1d0s2     auto:none       -              -             online invalid
c4t2d0s2     auto:cdsdisk    adg02          adg           online
[...]
-            -               adg01          adg           failed was:c4t1d0s2
```

    3.   The new disk must be initialized in the same manner as you would initialize any other disk for use by VxVM. The disk becomes completely online for VxVM, but is, of course, still not a disk group member.

```
# vxdisksetup -i c4t1d0 [...]
# vxdisk list
[...]
c4t1d0s2     auto:cdsdisk    -              -             online
c4t2d0s2     auto:cdsdisk    adg02          adg           online
[...]
-            -               adg01          adg           failed was:c4t1d0s2
```

4.   The next step is a little bit tricky to understand. We cannot add the disk to the disk group in the usual manner, because the disk media name (adg01 in our example) together with its associated attributes already exists within the disk group configuration:

```
# vxdg -g adg adddisk adg01=c4t1d0
VxVM vxdg ERROR V-5-1-559 Disk adg01: Name is already used
```

Choosing another disk media name does not help:

```
# vxdg -g adg adddisk adg03=c4t1d0
# vxdisk list
[…]
c4t1d0s2     auto:cdsdisk     adg03     adg          online
c4t2d0s2     auto:cdsdisk     adg02     adg          online
[…]
-            -                adg01     adg          failed was:c4t1d0s2
```

Now we have a disk group with three configured disk members, one of them still failed and detached from the disk group. Undo this stuff:

```
# vxdg -g adg rmdisk adg03
```

We need a procedure to add a new device access (which may be the same as the previous) to an already known disk group member by keeping (option -k) the configured disk attributes:

```
# vxdg -g adg -k adddisk adg01=c4t1d0
# vxdisk list
[…]
c4t1d0s2     auto:cdsdisk     adg01     adg          online
c4t2d0s2     auto:cdsdisk     adg02     adg          online
[…]
```

Finally we got it! The disk group is completely recovered. By adding the new disk to the disk group, all subdisks in NDEV state immediately become ENA (which stands for ENABLED). Since we do not have damaged subdisks within the plexes anymore, their application states NODEVICE are changed to RECOVER (IOFAIL if simulated): They have a physically healthy substrate, but during the disk outage they lost I/O and do not contain the current volume data. Therefore they remain in kernel state DISABLED.

```
# vxprint -rtg adg
[…]
v  vol1        -                 DISABLED ACTIVE   2097152 SELECT     -       fsgen
pl vol1-01     vol1              DISABLED RECOVER  2097152 CONCAT     -       RW
sd adg01-02    vol1-01           adg01    2097152  2097152 0          -       ENA

v  vol2        -                 ENABLED  ACTIVE   2097152 SELECT     -       fsgen
```

```
pl vol2-01      vol2         ENABLED  ACTIVE   2097152 CONCAT   -        RW
sd adg01-01     vol2-01      adg01    0        2097152 0        c4t2d0   ENA
pl vol2-02      vol2         DISABLED RECOVER  2097152 CONCAT   -        RW
sd adg02-01     vol2-02      adg02    0        2097152 0        -        ENA
```

5. Redundant volumes may have had a working plex during all the time of the disk outage (vol2 in our example). Plexes in DISABLED kernel state now can be resynchronized:

```
# vxrecover -g adg [-b] [vol2]
# vxprint -rtg adg
[...]
v  vol1          -            DISABLED ACTIVE   2097152 SELECT   -        fsgen
pl vol1-01       vol1         DISABLED RECOVER  2097152 CONCAT   -        RW
sd adg01-02      vol1-01      adg01    2097152  2097152 0        -        ENA

v  vol2          -            ENABLED  ACTIVE   2097152 SELECT   -        fsgen
pl vol2-01       vol2         ENABLED  ACTIVE   2097152 CONCAT   -        RW
sd adg01-01      vol2-01      adg01    0        2097152 0        c4t2d0   ENA
pl vol2-02       vol2         ENABLED  ACTIVE   2097152 CONCAT   -        RW
sd adg02-01      vol2-02      adg02    0        2097152 0        -        ENA
```

Skipping the volume names as parameters to vxrecover will synchronize all volumes within the disk group affected by the damaged disk, but still in kernel state ENABLED. The background option -b works as usual: Having started the kernel I/O threads to synchronize, the command returns. Please remember: The volume carries on to be usable by the application in a transactional manner during synchronization (here: atomic copy).

6. Volumes without a healthy plex, thus in kernel state DISABLED (in our example vol1) cannot be recovered using vxrecover, because they do not have current or valid plex data. For the same reason, they cannot be started regularly. Try it:

```
# vxvol -g adg start vol1
VxVM vxvol ERROR V-5-1-1198 Volume vol1 has no CLEAN or non-volatile ACTIVE
plexes
```

Otherwise, a normal reboot would start such volumes with their applications, even though the volumes do not provide any application data (we replaced the damaged disk). We must forcibly start those volumes, so we can restore application data from backups:

```
# vxvol -g adg -f start vol1
# vxprint -rtg adg vol1
[...]
v  vol1          -            ENABLED  ACTIVE   2097152 SELECT   -        fsgen
pl vol1-01       vol1         ENABLED  ACTIVE   2097152 CONCAT   -        RW
sd adg01-02      vol1-01      adg01    2097152  2097152 0        -        ENA
```

Just to provide an overview, we repeat the steps to recover from complete disk outage without extensive commentaries and misleading commands:

1. Replace the damaged disk.
2. Instruct VxVM to scan the disk access:
   ```
   # vxdisk scandisks device=c#t#d#
   ```
3. Disk recovery:
   ```
   # vxdisksetup -i c#t#d# […]
   ```
4. Disk group and subdisk recovery:
   ```
   # vxdg -g <diskgroup> -k adddisk <failed-dmname>=c#t#d#
   ```
5. Recovery of ENABLED volumes:
   ```
   # vxrecover -g <diskgroup> [-b] [<volumes>]
   ```
6. Start of DISABLED volumes:
   ```
   # vxvol -g <diskgroup> -f start <volumes>
   ```

11.2.2 DISK TEMPORARILY UNAVAILABLE

Having successfully repaired a damaged disk and the VxVM state changes, let's turn to a temporary disk outage, e.g. due to temporary power outage of a disk or a disk array (simulated by restoring the private region data).

Now the big surprise! To recover from temporary disk outage, we just need to modify step 1 and skip step 3:

1. Instead of replacing the disk, we must make the disk available again, e.g. by powering on the disk or the disk array. As already mentioned, VxVM does not monitor disk availability (it only monitors path availability according to your DMP configuration), so nothing happens to the VxVM disk and disk group states.

2. Initiate a test for device access to inform VxVM that the disk has come back.

```
# vxdisk scandisks device=c4t1d0
```

Now, initializing the disk by vxdisksetup (step 3 above) would be a bad idea. It would overwrite a still valid private region, possibly with a different size, thus maybe overwriting application data on the first subdisk or at least placing the subdisks at different physical disk offsets and, in consequence, spoiling still existing application data. Skip this step, by all means!

Steps 3 to 5 are completely identical to steps 4 to 6 of the former procedure. Unlike a damaged disk, a disk temporarily unavailable will provide the best possible application data when forcibly starting a disabled volume.

To sum up once again, but for temporary disk outage:

1. Make the disk available again.
2. Instruct VxVM to scan the disk access:

```
# vxdisk scandisks device=c#t#d#
```

3. Disk group and subdisk recovery:

```
# vxdg -g <diskgroup> -k adddisk <failed-dmname>=c#t#d#
```

4. Recovery of ENABLED volumes:

```
# vxrecover -g <diskgroup> [-b] [<volumes>]
```

5. Start of DISABLED volumes:

```
# vxvol -g <diskgroup> -f start <volumes>
```

11.2.3 REPLACING AN OS DISK

We still need to turn toward special problems when replacing a damaged OS disk. We assume that you have mirrored your OS volumes, so you still have a running system.

Why is it not sufficient to execute the already described procedure to replace a failed disk, if the new disk is intended to hold a mirror of the OS volumes? Well, during the first stage of the boot process, the Open Boot Prom reads the disk VTOC to identify the boot device partition carrying tag 2 and containing the root file system to be mounted later on /. The kernel root device (this is not necessarily identical to the boot device) may not be based upon a partition driver. But even in case your OS will be accessed by VxVM volumes, the root device /pseudo/vxio@0:0 specified in /etc/system needs a partition for the root file system to build a kernel RAM configured volume on it.

Therefore, if you are trying to replace a failed OS disk using the regular procedure, you will encounter at least one, probably even two problems. First, you cannot boot from the replaced disk because it has no partitions on it. Remember, mirroring volumes on a disk does not mean mirroring a disk's physical structure. So at least, we need to put appropriate partitions over the subdisks created by volume mirroring. Secondly, since partitions are always aligned to cylinder boundaries, offset and length of the original subdisks probably do not fit to different disk hardware.

To avoid any problems like that, it is useful to remove subdisks configured on the failed disk together with their associated plexes and to recreate the mirrors according to the cylinder specifications of the new disk. We do not spoil any redundancy because, due to the failed disk, we already lost volume redundancy. We only remove VxVM objects currently not having a physical disk substrate. The following is the commented procedure when replacing a failed OS disk:

1. Replace the damaged disk by a healthy one or select another free disk. Be sure to use a disk providing the required space to mirror all volumes of the still working OS disk.

2. Have VxVM scan the new device.

```
# vxdisk scandisks device=c#t#d#
```

3. Initialize the disk for VxVM use, that is, create a sliced disk layout which is required for OS disks. If necessary, limit the size of the private region to 1 MB, for example (VxVM 5.0 is built to create 32 MB as default).

```
# vxdisksetup -i c#t#d# format=sliced [privlen=1m]
```

4.   Add to the still known (we assume osdg02), but physically failed disk group member a new (and possibly different) device access:

```
# vxdg -g bootdg -k adddisk osdg02=c#t#d#
```

5.   So far so good, no big difference to the standard procedure! But now, remove all subdisks configured on the failed OS disk together with their associated plexes. Given the standard output of vxprint, this is hard work, even harder if scripted. But the early developers of VxVM were obviously passionate Unix guys. They designed vxprint as a powerful tool! An approach step by step:

List all plex names of the boot disk group:

```
# vxprint -g bootdg -pn
```

List all subdisks configured on disk osdg02:

```
# vxprint -g bootdg -se 'sd_dmname="osdg02"'
```

First combination: List all plex names having at least one associated subdisk on disk osdg02:

```
# vxprint -g bootdg -pne 'pl_sd.sd_dmname="osdg02"'
```

Now the final wizardry using Shell command substitution (poor who still does remove the plexes command by command):

```
# vxplex -g bootdg -o rm dis $(
  vxprint -g bootdg -pne 'pl_sd.sd_dmname="osdg02"')
```

6.   Instead of volume recovery we add a mirror to the OS volumes being still active on the other OS disk (we assume osdg01). The VxVM script vxmirror we execute takes care, that the new subdisks are aligned to disk cylinder boundaries, and builds appropriate partitions over these subdisks (for a detailed procedure with explanations see the "Technical Deep Dive" part). Fortunately, vxmirror prints out a log of issued commands to support our understanding of the procedure.

```
# vxmirror -g bootdg osdg01 osdg02
! vxassist -g bootdg mirror rootvol osdg02
! vxassist -g bootdg mirror swapvol osdg02
! vxassist -g bootdg mirror var osdg02
! vxassist -g bootdg mirror opt osdg02
! vxbootsetup -g bootdg osdg02
```

The script vxmirror, as shown by the listed commands, mirrors all volumes built of subdisks on osdg01 which are currently not redundant. The second disk specification osdg02 is optional and denotes the disk to use for the mirrors — mostly unnecessary because we mostly have only two disks within the boot disk group. Furthermore, by invoking vxbootsetup, it builds partitions on the new subdisks, writes a boot block on the root partition (obviously as a fallback, because the volume mirroring as a raw device procedure already did copy it), and creates, if missing, an alias entry in the OBP nvramrc (but not in boot-device).

Maybe you remember: This step is completely identical to the procedure to add a mirror to an encapsulated OS disk explained in chapter 10. The "Full Battleship" part will add some remarks on creating a partition based vfstab as a boot process troubleshooting prerequisite.

The summary of these steps:

1. Replace the failed OS disk.
2. Instruct VxVM to scan the disk access:
   ```
   # vxdisk scandisks device=c#t#d#
   ```
3. Disk recovery:
   ```
   # vxdisksetup -i c#t#d# format=sliced [...]
   ```
4. Disk group and subdisk recovery:
   ```
   # vxdg -g bootdg -k adddisk <failed-dmname>=c#t#d#
   ```
5. Remove all failed subdisks and their associated plexes:
   ```
   # vxplex -g bootdg -o rm dis $(
       vxprint -g bootdg -pne 'pl_sd.sd_dmname="<failed-dmname>"')
   ```
6. Add mirrors to the volumes and place partitions over the subdisks:
   ```
   # vxmirror -g bootdg <active-dmname> [<failed-dmname>]
   ```

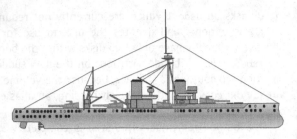

The Full Battleship

11.3 Disk Outage in Detail

11.3.1 A Complete Disk Array Temporarily Unavailable

Failure of a single disk, whether totally or temporarily, is a scenario rarely occurring in today's data centers, except maybe of an OS disk. Most data centers rely on intelligent disk arrays providing a configurable set of virtual LUNs based on the known RAID concepts. If just one physical disk of the array fails, the disk array administrator is notified to replace the failed disk, while the LUNs used by host applications remain fully accessible due to the RAID based redundancy.

A more widespread failure is the temporary outage of a complete disk array, e.g. by power failure of the disk array or of a site of a data center, or by loss of all paths to that array. Bringing back the accessibility of the array to its client hosts leads maybe to a terribly high number of LUNs detached from their disk groups (we assume the members of the disk group spread over more than one array, so the disk group is not completely unavailable; for the latter scenario see page 363). Of course, step number 3 explained above to recover these disks detached from their disk groups (vxdg -k adddisk …) will work properly, but that would mean an awful lot of commands to execute.

Well, fortunately, on Unix systems we have a powerful Shell. So it is quite easy to issue a loop on all failed disks currently detached from their disk group, but at the same time VxVM initialized by recovering their device access. To prevent unexpected results, we make sure, that those disks are really identical to the already configured disk group members and not freshly initialized disks with different physical properties. A simple way to check the identity may be achieved by comparing the disk IDs. As explained on page 91 of the Disk Group chapter each time a disk is initialized by VxVM, it is tagged by a unique disk ID comprising the initialization date in Unix time format, an internal counter, and the initializing VxVM host ID, separated by dots.

The following command lists the current disk ID associated with the physical device access:

```
# vxdisk -s list c4t1d0
[…]
diskid: 1213183912.30.sols
```

[...]

To show the disk ID associated with the disk media name as part of the disk group configuration, we use the vxprint command. Note that this command does not require physical disk access. Since the VxVM kernel module vxspec is the source of imported disk group information, we may execute it even against disks physically failed.

```
# vxprint -g adg -F %diskid adg01
1213183912.30.sols
```

To demonstrate the necessary steps to recover multiple disks, we provide a simple code fragment to recover all those disks currently detached due to a temporary failure by skipping freshly initialized disks:

```
# List all disks
vxdisk -q list |
# Filter detached disks, print DMName, DGroup, last DAName
nawk '$1=="-" {sub(/^was:/,"",$NF); print $3,$4,$NF}' |
while read DMName DGroup DAName; do
    # Get current disk ID
    CurrDiskID=$(vxdisk -s list $DAName | nawk '$1=="diskid:" {print $2; exit}')
    # Get disk ID configured in disk group
    DGConfDiskID=$(vxprint -g $DGroup -F %diskid $DMName)
    # Not identical? Next disk
    [[ $CurrDiskID != $DGConfDiskID ]] && continue
    # Add device access
    vxdg -g $DGroup-k adddisk $DMName=$DAName
done
```

Since this task should happen more often than a single disk failure, VxVM provides a script called vxreattach to recover a set of temporary failed disks. Its basic strategy looks like the code fragment above, but it is, of course, surrounded by a lot of check commands, not to forget the extensive copyright notes. Its usage is:

```
# vxreattach [-r] [-b] <daname> [<daname> ...]
```

Adding the option -r also recovers all plexes within enabled volumes, which were disabled (according to step 4 above). As usual, -b ("background") terminates the vxreattach command after having started the kernel threads to synchronize the stale plexes.

11.3.2   A Disk Group Temporarily Inaccessible

Our previous topic assumed that the disk group configuration is still not lost. What happens if all your disks holding the active disk group configuration become unavailable at once? You might consider this a scenario rarely occurring. But sometimes your disk group is built from disks of just one disk array. Are you ready to exclude a power failure of the disk array?

Even if you neatly spread your disks over more than one array, you cannot deny the possible risk to loose your disk group configuration. If one array fails temporarily, VxVM automatically switches all its active disk group configuration disk roles to the remaining array. If the first mentioned disk array comes back, all active configuration disks are kept at the latter array! Now that array suffers from a power failure or, even worse, gets damaged...

The current section deals with a temporary outage of the disk group configuration disks (persistent loss will be explained later). No physical substrate for storing VxVM objects, for logging object states, and for modifying attribute values is available. Volumes using these disks will get I/O failures on their subdisks, thus VxVM disables the affected plexes and volumes, if all of their plexes are disabled. You will see a lot of error messages on the console sent from the device drivers and the **vxdmp** and **vxio** kernel modules (compare page 352). Instead of our agitated expressions above, we may put oil on troubled waters given this scenario: As long as VxVM keeps disk group configuration data in the kernel, the disk group remains online in spite of some or all of its disks being inaccessible. There is, to calm you down a little bit more, an easy way to store the disk group configuration held by the kernel memory to still healthy, but currently inactive private regions. Simply make all disks of the disk group to active configuration and log disks:

```
# vxedit -g adg set nconfig=all adg
# vxedit -g adg set nlog=all adg
# vxdg list adg
[…]
copies:    nconfig=all nlog=all
config:    seqno=0.1457 permlen=1280 free=1273 templen=4 loglen=192
config disk c4t1d0s2 copy 1 len=1280 state=clean online
config disk c4t2d0s2 copy 1 len=1280 state=clean online
config disk c4t3d0s2 copy 1 len=1280 state=clean online
[…]
log disk c4t1d0s2 copy 1 len=192
log disk c4t2d0s2 copy 1 len=192
log disk c4t3d0s2 copy 1 len=192
[…]
```

Marking disks as active configuration disks will flush to them the disk group configuration stored in the kernel. If you discard your kernel disk group configuration, e.g. by restarting **vxconfigd** in order to re-read the non-existent physical disk group configuration, before flushing it to other disks, you will encounter problems:

```
# vxconfigd -k
VxVM vxconfigd ERROR V-5-1-583 Disk group adg: Reimport of disk group failed:
        Disk group has no valid configuration copies
# vxdisk -g adg list
VxVM vxdisk ERROR V-5-1-607 Diskgroup adg not found
# vxdisk list
DEVICE       TYPE          DISK        GROUP        STATUS
[…]
c4t1d0s2     auto:cdsdisk  adg01       adg          online dgdisabled
```

```
c4t2d0s2      auto:cdsdisk      adg02                adg              online dgdisabled
[...]
```

There is only one way to recover a `dgdisabled` disk group: Reattach the disks, so that at least one valid disk group configuration copy is accessible, and re-import (maybe forced) the disk group (which requires application stop, if not already stopped).

```
# vxdg deport adg
# vxdg [-f] import adg
# vxdisk -g adg list
DEVICE        TYPE              DISK          GROUP          STATUS
c4t1d0s2      auto:cdsdisk      adg01         adg            online
c4t2d0s2      auto:cdsdisk      adg02         adg            online
# vxrecover -g adg -s [-b]
```

11.3.3   A Partially Failed Disk ("Failing")

A scenario indeed rarely occurring is a partial disk failure, that is the disk is still visible, but some regions on it are damaged. Given virtual LUNs this should not happen. A disk whose public region is still accessible by VxVM, but nevertheless encountered I/O errors due to unreadable subdisks, is not detached from the disk group, but remains a disk group member. That disk is only marked as `failing` by VxVM (as shown in the output of `vxdisk` and `vxprint`):

```
# vxdisk -g adg list
DEVICE        TYPE              DISK          GROUP          STATUS
c4t1d0s2      auto:cdsdisk      adg01         adg            online failing
c4t2d0s2      auto:cdsdisk      adg02         adg            online
# vxprint -dtg adg
DM NAME       DEVICE            TYPE     PRIVLEN  PUBLEN    STATE

dm adg01      c4t1d0s2          auto     2048     35365968  FAILING
dm adg02      c4t2d0s2          auto     2048     35365968  -
```

The `failing` flag set by VxVM prohibits allocation of free space of this disk when creating new subdisks during volume creation, when searching for subdisk replacement by hot relocation, and so on.

If a disk gets partially damaged, VxVM sets the `failing` flag on it and marks affected subdisks as FAIL (`vxprint -t` output, column MODE). But this is not a one-to-one condition. If you see the `failing` flag on a disk, you cannot conclude that the disk must be partially damaged. In most cases, the cable connection to the disk is somewhat instable, that is, you can issue I/O in general, but sometimes an I/O request fails. Therefore, the first step is to determine, if the disk or the cabling to the disk is damaged.

If you determine, that you had cable problems, and you can fix it, you should remove the misleading `failing` flag (this is never done automatically by VxVM):

```
# vxedit -g adg set failing=off adg01
```

In case of a partially damaged disk, you should replace the disk as soon as possible. Maybe there are still other usable subdisks on that disk, whose data you want to move to another disk within the disk group. An easy way to do so is to execute:

```
# vxevac -g <diskgroup> <dmname-to-evac> [<dmname-as-replacement> ...]
```

vxevac is a Shell script invoking **vxassist move** commands on volumes with subdisks on the specified disk. Unfortunately, the script is designed to exit the evacuation process if a volume move fails. In our case of a failing disk, this will happen for the damaged subdisk. So you must move the other volumes manually:

```
# vxassist -g <diskgroup> move <volume> alloc=\!<dmname-to-evac>,\
  [<dmname-as-replacement>,...]
```

In either case, the damaged subdisk will remain on the failing disk. How can you replace that disk? Of course, you could simply perform a physical removal of the disk, thus producing a completely failed disk within VxVM. This would send e-mails, trigger SNMP consoles, and so on. That's why we should use a procedure telling VxVM that we indeed do want to remove the disk. This is a little bit tricky:

```
# vxdg -g adg rmdisk adg01
VxVM vxdg ERROR V-5-1-552 Disk adg01 is used by one or more subdisks.
        Use -k to remove device assignment.
```

Of course, we cannot remove a disk group member still in use by subdisks, even if these subdisks are physically unusable. But they are still known to the disk group configuration. We need to keep (-k) the disk group membership and the configured disk attributes by "detaching" the disk from the disk group, that is, to remove only the device assignment:

```
# vxdg -g adg -k rmdisk adg01
```

This disk now looks like a failed disk except for the object states: REMOVED instead of NODEVICE. Note that the `failing` flag is cleared by this procedure:

```
# vxdisk list
DEVICE          TYPE            DISK        GROUP        STATUS
[...]
c4t1d0s2        auto:cdsdisk    -           -            online
c4t2d0s2        auto:cdsdisk    adg02       adg          online
[...]
-               -               adg01       adg          removed was:c4t1d0s2
# vxprint -dtg adg
DM NAME         DEVICE          TYPE        PRIVLEN PUBLEN    STATE

dm adg01        -               -           -       -         REMOVED
```

```
dm adg02        c4t2d0s2       auto    2048      35365968 -
# vxprint -rtg adg
[...]
v  vol1         -              DISABLED ACTIVE   2097152   SELECT    -          fsgen
pl vol1-01      vol1           DISABLED REMOVED  2097152   CONCAT    -          RW
sd adg01-02     vol1-01        adg01    2097152  2097152   0         -          RMOV

v  vol2         -              ENABLED  ACTIVE   2097152   SELECT    -          fsgen
pl vol2-01      vol2           DISABLED REMOVED  2097152   CONCAT    -          RW
sd adg01-01     vol2-01        adg01    0        2097152   0         -          RMOV
pl vol2-02      vol2           ENABLED  ACTIVE   2097152   CONCAT    -          RW
sd adg02-01     vol2-02        adg02    0        2097152   0         c4t2d0     ENA
```

The steps to replace the removed disk correspond exactly to the steps to replace a failed disk, as described and explained on page 352 above. But maybe, in addition, you will want to move back the subdisks to their original disk media location afterwards:

```
# vxassist -g <diskgroup> move <volume> \!<dmname-as-replacement> <orig-dmname>
```

11.3.4 HOT RELOCATION

VxVM provides two mutually exclusive mechanisms handling disk failures by automatically searching for disk or subdisks replacement: vxrelocd or vxsparecheck. Our previous tests simulating disk outage were unrealistic to some extent, for we stopped the running instance of this process pair in order to understand the basic principles of disk recovery. It is time we demonstrate and explain how these mechanisms work. The default process starting with VxVM 3.0 is vxrelocd, so this is our first candidate.

The script vxrelocd, started into background by /etc/rc2.d/S95vxvm-recover (Solaris 9) or /lib/svc/method/vxvm-recover (Solaris 10), itself invokes vxnotify as a child process by capturing and evaluating STDOUT of the latter process for disk and plex detach messages (-f) awaiting 15 sec. (-w 15) after the last detach event before responding to the failure.

```
# ptree -a $(pgrep -xu0 vxrelocd)
1     /sbin/init -s
 2786  /sbin/sh - /usr/lib/vxvm/bin/vxrelocd root
  3747  /sbin/sh - /usr/lib/vxvm/bin/vxrelocd root
   3748  vxnotify -f -w 15
```

The following commands together with their output simulate a failed disk, demonstrate the behavior of hot relocation and explain the steps necessary to recreate the original configuration.

1.   We create a mirrored (vol2) and a non-redundant volume (vol1), both having in common a subdisk on disk adg01.

```
# vxassist -g adg make vol2 1g layout=mirror nmirror=2 init=active \
  alloc=adg01,adg02
# vxassist -g adg make vol1 1g alloc=adg01
# vxprint -rtg adg
[...]
dm adg01        c1t1d0s2      auto      2048      122171136 -
dm adg02        c1t1d1s2      auto      2048      122171136 -
dm adg03        c1t1d2s2      auto      2048      122171136 -

v  vol1         -             ENABLED   ACTIVE    2097152   SELECT    -         fsgen
pl vol1-01      vol1          ENABLED   ACTIVE    2097152   CONCAT    -         RW
sd adg01-02     vol1-01       adg01     2097152   2097152   0         c1t1d0    ENA

v  vol2         -             ENABLED   ACTIVE    2097152   SELECT    -         fsgen
pl vol2-01      vol2          ENABLED   ACTIVE    2097152   CONCAT    -         RW
sd adg01-01     vol2-01       adg01     0         2097152   0         c1t1d0    ENA
pl vol2-02      vol2          ENABLED   ACTIVE    2097152   CONCAT    -         RW
sd adg02-01     vol2-02       adg02     0         2097152   0         c1t1d1    ENA
```

2.   The disk failure is simulated by overwriting the private region and restarting vxconfigd. Some seconds later, we notice an atomic copy synchronization thread to resynchronize the plex of vol2 affected by the disk failure (for details see the "Technical Deep Dive" section).

```
# dd if=/dev/zero of=/dev/rdsk/c1t1d0s2 bs=128k oseek=1 count=1
# vxconfigd -k
# vxtask -g adg list
TASKID  PTID TYPE/STATE    PCT     PROGRESS
 50555 50555    ATCOPY/R 28.61% 0/2097152/600064 PLXATT vol2 vol2-01 adg
```

3.   As proved by the output of vxprint, vol1 has lost its single and last healthy plex, no automatic recovery is possible, the volume is DISABLED. During resynchronization of vol2, we already recognize that the failed plex vol2-01 got a new subdisk adg03-01 on another disk (adg03). After synchronization has completed, the plex is a full member of the volume, entering application state ENABLED and mode RW. Hot relocation has fulfilled its primary task.

Note that in case of a more complicated plex layout (concatenating and/or striping of subdisks) the whole affected plex becomes disabled due to the failed subdisk and must be synchronized completely. Replacement on a per-subdisk level by hot relocation does not imply resynchronization just on a per-subdisk base. Layering the volume subdisk by subdisk (if possible) or at least column by column would help to reduce synchronization I/O. On the other side, adding a DCL volume with its capability to track volume region changes does not avoid full plex synchronization — strange enough!

```
# vxprint -rtg adg
[...]
dm adg01        -             -         -         -         NODEVICE
```

```
dm adg02         c1t1d1s2      auto      2048      122171136 -
dm adg03         c1t1d2s2      auto      2048      122171136 -

v  vol1          -             DISABLED ACTIVE   2097152 SELECT   -        fsgen
pl vol1-01       vol1          DISABLED NODEVICE 2097152 CONCAT   -        RW
sd adg01-02      vol1-01       adg01     2097152 2097152 0        -        NDEV

v  vol2          -             ENABLED  ACTIVE   2097152 SELECT   -        fsgen
pl vol2-01       vol2          ENABLED  STALE    2097152 CONCAT   -        WO
sd adg03-01      vol2-01       adg03     0        2097152 0        c1t1d2   ENA
pl vol2-02       vol2          ENABLED  ACTIVE   2097152 CONCAT   -        RW
sd adg02-01      vol2-02       adg02     0        2097152 0        c1t1d1   ENA
# vxprint -rtg adg
[...]
dm adg01         -             -         -        -       NODEVICE
dm adg02         c1t1d1s2      auto      2048      122171136 -
dm adg03         c1t1d2s2      auto      2048      122171136 -

v  vol1          -             DISABLED ACTIVE   2097152 SELECT   -        fsgen
pl vol1-01       vol1          DISABLED NODEVICE 2097152 CONCAT   -        RW
sd adg01-02      vol1-01       adg01     2097152 2097152 0        -        NDEV

v  vol2          -             ENABLED  ACTIVE   2097152 SELECT   -        fsgen
pl vol2-01       vol2          ENABLED  ACTIVE   2097152 CONCAT   -        RW
sd adg03-01      vol2-01       adg03     0        2097152 0        c1t1d2   ENA
pl vol2-02       vol2          ENABLED  ACTIVE   2097152 CONCAT   -        RW
sd adg02-01      vol2-02       adg02     0        2097152 0        c1t1d1   ENA
```

4. vxrelocd was invoked with the parameter root, specifying a mail recipient, meaning root@localhost. You should extend the list of mail recipients according to your needs by editing /etc/rc2.d/S95vxvm-recover (Solaris 9) or /lib/svc/method/vxvm-recover (Solaris 10). During the process of hot relocation, several mails are sent (sorted in chronological order):

```
Subject: Volume Manager failures on host haensel
[...]
Failures have been detected by the VERITAS Volume Manager:

failed disks:
 adg01

failed plexes:
vol1-01
vol2-01

The Volume Manager will attempt to find spare disks, relocate failed
subdisks and then recover the data in the failed plexes.
```

Subject: Volume Manager failures on host haensel
[...]
Unable to relocate failed subdisk from plex vol1-01 because no
suitable mirror was found from which to recover data.

Subject: Volume Manager failures on host haensel
[...]
Attempting to relocate subdisk adg01-01 from plex vol2-01.
Dev_offset - length 2097152 dm_name adg01 da_name c1t1d0s2.
The available plex vol2-02 will be used recover the data.

Subject: Attempting VxVM relocation on host haensel
[...]
VERITAS Volume Manager is preparing to relocate for diskgroup adg.
Saving the current configuration in:
/etc/vx/saveconfig.d/adg.080928_095541.mpvsh

Subject: Attempting VxVM relocation on host haensel
[...]
Volume vol2 Subdisk adg01-01 relocated to adg03-01, but not yet recovered.

Subject: Volume Manager failures on host haensel
[...]
Recovery complete for volume vol2 in disk group adg.

   5.   Our final goal is still not reached. vol1 is further on unusable due to its DISABLED
kernel state. The failed disk adg01 should be reattached to the disk group. Although vol2
has regained its redundancy by implementing a previously free disk, we should move the
subdisk currently named adg03-01 back to its original location in order to completely
recover the former configuration. Since the latter task needs some further explanation, we
separate it (step 6) from the current section.

```
# vxdisksetup -i c1t1d0
# vxdg -g adg -k adddisk adg01=c1t1d0
# vxvol -g adg -f start vol1
# vxprint -rtg adg
[...]
dm adg01        c1t1d0s2      auto      2048      122171136 -
dm adg02        c1t1d1s2      auto      2048      122171136 -
dm adg03        c1t1d2s2      auto      2048      122171136 -

v  vol1         -             ENABLED   ACTIVE    2097152   SELECT    -         fsgen
pl vol1-01      vol1          ENABLED   ACTIVE    2097152   CONCAT    -         RW
sd adg01-02     vol1-01       adg01     2097152   2097152   0         c1t1d0    ENA

v  vol2         -             ENABLED   ACTIVE    2097152   SELECT    -         fsgen
```

pl vol2-01	vol2		ENABLED	ACTIVE	2097152	CONCAT	-		RW
sd adg03-01	vol2-01	adg03	0		2097152	0		c1t1d2	ENA
pl vol2-02	vol2		ENABLED	ACTIVE	2097152	CONCAT	-		RW
sd adg02-01	vol2-02	adg02	0		2097152	0		c1t1d1	ENA

6. Our final task: placing the "hot relocated" subdisk to its original disk. We already know several ways with specific advantages and disadvantages:

```
# vxmake -g adg sd adg01-01 disk=adg01 offset=0 len=1g
# vxsd -g adg -d mv adg03-01 adg01-01
# vxedit -g adg rm adg03-01
```

Advantage: Full control on the position of the subdisk
Disadvantage: Where do we know the original location and name of the subdisk? Furthermore: Some tricky work
Note: The option -d of the vxsd mv command discards the hot relocation information stored as subdisk attributes, see below.

```
# vxassist -g adg move vol2 alloc=\!adg03,adg01
```

Advantage: Not too much work, because on a per-volume base
Disadvantage: Once again, where do we know the original location and name of the subdisk? No control on the position of the subdisk on the target disk, subdisks of the volume intentionally placed on adg03 are moved as well

```
# vxevac -g adg adg03 adg01
```

Advantage: Just one simple command
Disadvantage: Once again, where do we know the original location and name of the subdisk? No control on the position of the subdisk on the target disk, all subdisks on adg03 are moved

Fortunately, a subdisk provides an attribute pair designed to bail us out, i.e. to support subdisk move tasks after hot relocation has taken place:

```
# vxprint -g adg -m adg03-01
[...]
        orig_dmname=adg01
        orig_dmoffset=0
# vxprint -g adg -F '%name %orig_dmname %orig_dmoffset' \
  -e 'sd_orig_dmname="adg01"'
adg03-01 adg01 0
```

The hot relocation process obviously stored the original disk media name and the public region offset of the subdisk on that disk. It did not save as subdisk attribute values the length of the original subdisk (in most cases identical to the current length, see note below) and its name (a VxVM object together with all attribute values holds 256 bytes within the

371

private region, storing the former subdisk name would waste space). But recall a mail sent by **vxrelocd** mentioning a configuration saving file under /etc/vx/saveconfig.d, where you can extract the missing information from.

In case of disk group members carrying sliced layout, we may encounter some rounding-up of the length of the subdisk to disk cylinder boundaries. Note that the **vxassist** default layout comprises diskalign:

```
# vxassist help showattrs
#Attributes:
 layout=nomirror,nostripe,nomirror-stripe,nostripe-mirror,
nostripe-mirror-col,nostripe-mirror-sd,
noconcat-mirror,nomirror-concat,span,nocontig,raid5log,noregionlog,diskalign,
nostorage
[…]
```

We provide a commented code fragment to relocate subdisks to their original location:

```
# We need current subdisk name, original disk media name and offset, and length
Fields='%name %orig_dmname %orig_dmoffset %len'
# Subdisk counter
((SdCount=0))

# Print subdisk attributes, if generated by hot relocation
vxprint -g adg -se 'sd_orig_dmname!=""' -F "$Fields" |
while read SdName SdDisk SdOffset SdLen; do
    # New subdisk name, based on original disk name + "UR" + counter
    UrSdName=${SdDisk}-UR-$((SdCount+=1))
    # Recreate original subdisk
    vxmake -g adg sd $UrSdName disk=$SdDisk offset=$SdOffset len=$SdLen ||
    continue
    # Move subdisk content and swap plex association, discard hot reloc info
    vxsd -g adg -d mv $SdName $UrSdName || continue
    # Remove hot relocation generated subdisk
    vxedit -g adg rm $SdName
done
```

A somewhat similar procedure (see the "Technical Deep Dive" section) was implemented into the VxVM script **vxunreloc**. While our code fragment relocated all subdisks to their original location, **vxunreloc** just relocates subdisks originating from one disk specified by a required command parameter. While we were bound to the exact subdisk positions, **vxunreloc** is able to round up to disk specific cylinder boundaries (option -f). Finally, **vxunreloc** allows for the specification of an alternate target disk (option -n).

```
# vxunreloc -g adg adg01
# vxtask -g adg list
TASKID  PTID TYPE/STATE    PCT   PROGRESS
```

```
   50568                  ATCOPY/R 20.80% 0/2097152/436224 SDMV adg03-01 adg01-UR-001 adg
# vxprint -rtg adg vol2
[...]
v  vol2          -           ENABLED   ACTIVE    2097152  SELECT    -         fsgen
pl %1            vol2        ENABLED   TEMPRM    2097152  CONCAT    -         WO
sd adg01-UR-001  %1          adg01     0         2097152  0         c1t1d0    ENA
pl vol2-01       vol2        ENABLED   ACTIVE    2097152  CONCAT    -         RW
sd adg03-01      vol2-01     adg03     0         2097152  0         c1t1d2    ENA
pl vol2-02       vol2        ENABLED   ACTIVE    2097152  CONCAT    -         RW
sd adg02-01      vol2-02     adg02     0         2097152  0         c1t1d1    ENA
```

After hot relocation has terminated, we could rename the subdisk:

```
# vxprint -rtg adg vol2
[...]
v  vol2          -           ENABLED   ACTIVE    2097152  SELECT    -         fsgen
pl vol2-01       vol2        ENABLED   ACTIVE    2097152  CONCAT    -         RW
sd adg01-UR-001  vol2-01     adg01     0         2097152  0         c1t1d0    ENA
pl vol2-02       vol2        ENABLED   ACTIVE    2097152  CONCAT    -         RW
sd adg02-01      vol2-02     adg02     0         2097152  0         c1t1d1    ENA
# vxedit -g adg rename adg01-UR-001 adg01-01
# vxprint -rtg adg vol2
[...]
v  vol2          -           ENABLED   ACTIVE    2097152  SELECT    -         fsgen
pl vol2-01       vol2        ENABLED   ACTIVE    2097152  CONCAT    -         RW
sd adg01-01      vol2-01     adg01     0         2097152  0         c1t1d0    ENA
pl vol2-02       vol2        ENABLED   ACTIVE    2097152  CONCAT    -         RW
sd adg02-01      vol2-02     adg02     0         2097152  0         c1t1d1    ENA
```

The hot relocation procedure does not need disks specified as spare disks, any space on any regular disk (see below) may serve as "spare parts inventory". But a disk marked as spare disk will have higher priority for the implemented subdisk selection policy spare=yes — but only if the volume move requires more than one disk (see "Technical Deep Dive"). If you need to restrict subdisk replacement only to spare disks, enter spare=only into /etc/default/vxassist (spare=no would exclude spare disks from hot relocation).

If you want to exclude a disk from the "spare parts inventory" by keeping the default selection policy spare=yes, e.g. in order not to degrade its performance, mark it as nohotuse. Obviously, spare and nohotuse are mutually exclusive. We recall the commands:

```
# vxedit -g adg set spare=on|off adg01
# vxedit -g adg set nohotuse=on|off adg01
```

At first sight, the vxrelocd procedure looks "finely granulated", avoiding any unnecessary I/O and being capable to spread multiple subdisks originating from one failed disk to several target disks in case we did not provide a spare disk of appropriate space. But at second thought, what would you like to do with a disk partially unusable? Of course, you would like to evacuate it as soon as possible. Evacuating means finding replacements for

ALL subdisks residing on the affected disk, not just for the failed subdisks. Then, you surely would want to replace it by a new one and finally to relocate all moved subdisks.

11.3.5 HOT SPARE

The legacy technique in VxVM 2.x, called "Hot spare", provided a procedure similar to what we described in the last phrase of the antecedent paragraph and may be still reactivated in lieu of hot relocation:

```
# pkill -9 -xu0 vxrelocd
# nohup /usr/lib/vxvm/bin/vxsparecheck root &
# vi /etc/rc2.d/S95vxvm-recover  (Solaris 9)
# vi /lib/svc/method/vxvm-recover  (Solaris 10)
[...]
# vxrelocd root &          (commented out)
[...]
vxsparecheck root &        (removed comment sign)
[...]
```

Hot spare works on a per-disk base: Each failed disk will be replaced by another disk holding appropriate space to cover all subdisks of the failed disk. Replacing disks must be marked as spare disks. For details, see the following example on our well-known volumes vol1 and vol2:

1.   We select a disk of the disk group to become a spare disk. Our tries to create a volume demonstrate, that a spare disk is excluded from the list of generically available disks as long as we do not explicitly allocate it by storage attributes.

```
# vxdisk -g adg list
DEVICE        TYPE           DISK        GROUP        STATUS
c1t1d0s2      auto:cdsdisk   adg01       adg          online
c1t1d1s2      auto:cdsdisk   adg02       adg          online
c1t1d2s2      auto:cdsdisk   adg03       adg          online
# vxedit -g adg set spare=on adg03
# vxdisk -g adg list
DEVICE        TYPE           DISK        GROUP        STATUS
c1t1d0s2      auto:cdsdisk   adg01       adg          online
c1t1d1s2      auto:cdsdisk   adg02       adg          online
c1t1d2s2      auto:cdsdisk   adg03       adg          online spare
# vxassist -g adg make demovol 1g layout=stripe ncol=3
VxVM vxassist ERROR V-5-1-435 Cannot allocate space for 2097152 block volume
# vxassist -g adg make demovol 1g layout=stripe ncol=3 alloc=adg01,adg02,adg03
# vxedit -g adg -rf rm demovol
# vxprint -rtg adg
[...]
dm adg01         c1t1d0s2      auto     2048       122171136 -
```

```
dm adg02      c1t1d1s2    auto    2048    122171136 -
dm adg03      c1t1d2s2    auto    2048    122171136 SPARE

v  vol1       -           ENABLED ACTIVE  2097152 SELECT  -          fsgen
pl vol1-01    vol1        ENABLED ACTIVE  2097152 CONCAT  -          RW
sd adg01-02   vol1-01     adg01   2097152 2097152 0       c1t1d0     ENA

v  vol2       -           ENABLED ACTIVE  2097152 SELECT  -          fsgen
pl vol2-01    vol2        ENABLED ACTIVE  2097152 CONCAT  -          RW
sd adg01-01   vol2-01     adg01   0       2097152 0       c1t1d0     ENA
pl vol2-02    vol2        ENABLED ACTIVE  2097152 CONCAT  -          RW
sd adg02-01   vol2-02     adg02   0       2097152 0       c1t1d1     ENA
```

2.   We "destroy" disk adg01 holding subdisks for both volumes in order to see how the vxsparecheck daemon handles a disk failure. The first effect of a failed disk is of course, independent on hot relocation or hot spare working or not, that it is detached from the disk group, that all affected plexes enter kernel state DISABLED, and that volumes loosing their last healthy plex become DISABLED as well. In addition to this basic procedure, vxsparecheck will immediately mark subdisks to be placed on the spare disk as RLOC (for "relocate", see the output of an additionally started vxnotify).

```
# dd if=/dev/zero of=/dev/rdsk/c1t1d0s2 bs=128k oseek=1 count=8
# vxconfigd -k
# vxnotify -f -w 15
[...]
detach disk c1t1d0s2 dm adg01 dg adg dgid 1223834080.19.haensel
detach plex vol2-01 volume vol2 dg adg dgid 1223834080.19.haensel
relocate subdisk adg01-01 plex vol2-01 volume vol2 dg adg dgid
1223834080.19.haensel
disabled vol vol1 rid 0.1155 dgid 1223834080.19.haensel adg
detach plex vol1-01 volume vol1 dg adg dgid 1223834080.19.haensel
[...]
# vxprint -rtg adg
[...]
dm adg01      -           -       -       -         NODEVICE
dm adg02      c1t1d1s2    auto    2048    122171136 -
dm adg03      c1t1d2s2    auto    2048    122171136 SPARE

v  vol1       -           DISABLED ACTIVE   2097152 SELECT  -         fsgen
pl vol1-01    vol1        DISABLED NODEVICE 2097152 CONCAT  -         RW
sd adg01-02   vol1-01     adg01    2097152  2097152 0       -         NDEV

v  vol2       -           ENABLED  ACTIVE   2097152 SELECT  -         fsgen
pl vol2-01    vol2        DISABLED NODEVICE 2097152 CONCAT  -         RW
sd adg01-01   vol2-01     adg01    0        2097152 0       -         RLOC
pl vol2-02    vol2        ENABLED  ACTIVE   2097152 CONCAT  -         RW
sd adg02-01   vol2-02     adg02    0        2097152 0       c1t1d1    ENA
```

3. The second action of vxsparecheck is, after the default waiting period of 15 seconds, to exclusively reserve the spare disk and to forcibly remove the failed disk (device access c1t1d0s2), both visible in command outputs only for few seconds. Then, vxsparecheck swaps the names of the spare disk and the removed disk: The disk media name adg01, previously belonging to c1t1d0s2, gets the new device access c1t1d2s2, while adg03 enters the REMOVED state. The subdisks, previously storing their data on c1t1d0s2, are now placed on c1t1d2s2. Since these subdisks get a physically healthy disk, the affected plexes change their application state from NODEVICE to RECOVER (IOFAIL, if simulated). The failed disk itself is then completely removed, even as a disk group member.

```
# vxprint -dtg adg
[...]
dm adg01      -          -       -      -          NODEVICE
dm adg02      c1t1d1s2   auto    2048   122171136  -
dm adg03      c1t1d2s2   auto    2048   122171136  RESERVED
# vxprint -dtg adg
[...]
dm adg01      c1t1d2s2   auto    2048   122171136  -
dm adg02      c1t1d1s2   auto    2048   122171136  -
dm adg03      -          -       -      -          REMOVED
# vxprint -rtg adg
[...]
dm adg01      c1t1d2s2   auto    2048   122171136  -
dm adg02      c1t1d1s2   auto    2048   122171136  -

v  vol1       -          DISABLED ACTIVE  2097152  SELECT   -        fsgen
pl vol1-01    vol1       DISABLED RECOVER 2097152  CONCAT   -        RW
sd adg01-02   vol1-01    adg01    2097152 2097152  0        c1t1d2   ENA

v  vol2       -          ENABLED  ACTIVE  2097152  SELECT   -        fsgen
pl vol2-01    vol2       DISABLED RECOVER 2097152  CONCAT   -        RW
sd adg01-01   vol2-01    adg01    0        2097152 0        c1t1d2   RLOC
pl vol2-02    vol2       ENABLED  ACTIVE  2097152  CONCAT   -        RW
sd adg02-01   vol2-02    adg02    0        2097152 0        c1t1d1   ENA
```

4. Finally, synchronization threads are started in order to bring the subdisks residing on the new device to the current volume states (if possible). The plex associated to an ongoing ENABLED volume enter into the STALE state and, after resynchronization, into ACTIVE. The non-redundant volume vol1 remains DISABLED.

```
# vxtask -g adg list
TASKID  PTID TYPE/STATE    PCT     PROGRESS
 50575        PARENT/R  0.00% 1/0(1) VXRECOVER adg01 adg
 50576 50576  ATCOPY/R 21.58% 0/2097152/452608 PLXATT vol2 vol2-01 adg
# vxprint -rtg adg
[...]
```

```
dm adg01        c1t1d2s2     auto      2048     122171136 -
dm adg02        c1t1d1s2     auto      2048     122171136 -

v  vol1         -            DISABLED  ACTIVE   2097152   SELECT    -          fsgen
pl vol1-01      vol1         DISABLED  RECOVER  2097152   CONCAT    -          RW
sd adg01-02     vol1-01      adg01     2097152  2097152   0         c1t1d2     ENA

v  vol2         -            ENABLED   ACTIVE   2097152   SELECT    -          fsgen
pl vol2-01      vol2         ENABLED   STALE    2097152   CONCAT    -          WO
sd adg01-01     vol2-01      adg01     0        2097152   0         c1t1d2     RLOC
pl vol2-02      vol2         ENABLED   ACTIVE   2097152   CONCAT    -          RW
sd adg02-01     vol2-02      adg02     0        2097152   0         c1t1d1     ENA
# vxprint -rtg adg
[...]
v  vol1         -            DISABLED  ACTIVE   2097152   SELECT    -          fsgen
pl vol1-01      vol1         DISABLED  RECOVER  2097152   CONCAT    -          RW
sd adg01-02     vol1-01      adg01     2097152  2097152   0         c1t1d2     ENA

v  vol2         -            ENABLED   ACTIVE   2097152   SELECT    -          fsgen
pl vol2-01      vol2         ENABLED   ACTIVE   2097152   CONCAT    -          RW
sd adg01-01     vol2-01      adg01     0        2097152   0         c1t1d2     ENA
pl vol2-02      vol2         ENABLED   ACTIVE   2097152   CONCAT    -          RW
sd adg02-01     vol2-02      adg02     0        2097152   0         c1t1d1     ENA
```

5.   Like vxrelocd, vxsparecheck was invoked with the parameter root (or with an extended list of mail recipients) and dispatched two mails during our failure and recovery example (sorted in chronological order):

Subject: Volume Manager failures on host haensel
[...]
VxVM vxsparecheck NOTICE V-5-2-191 Failures have been detected by the VERITAS Volume Manager:

failed disks:
 adg01

failed plexes:
 vol1-01
 vol2-01

failed subdisks:

failed volumes:
 vol1
VxVM vxsparecheck ERROR V-5-2-533
The Volume Manager will attempt to find hot-spare disks to replace any

failed disks and attempt to resyncrhonize the data in the failed plexes
from plexes on other disks.

VxVM vxsparecheck ERROR V-5-2-330
The data in the failed volumes listed above is no longer available. It
will need to be restored from backup.

Subject: Attempted VxVM recovery on host haensel
[...]
VxVM vxsparecheck INFO V-5-2-279
Replacement of disk adg01 in group adg with disk device
c1t1d2s2 has successfully completed and recovery is under way.

VxVM vxsparecheck ERROR V-5-2-373 The following volumes:

vol1

occupy space on the replaced disk, but have no other enabled mirrors
on other disks from which to perform recovery. These volumes must have
their data restored.
VxVM vxsparecheck INFO V-5-2-434
To restore the contents of any volumes listed above, the volume should
be started with the command:

        vxvol -f start <volume-name>

and the data restored from backup.

6. Unlike **vxunreloc** for **vxrelocd**, the final, manual recovery after disk replacement
is not supported by a VxVM script. So we "replace" and recover the "failed" disk and restore
the original configuration (if necessary): The subdisk replacement in **vol2** is moved back to
the previous device access. **vol1**, holding no reasonable application data, is best recovered
by forcibly deleting the subdisk and adding a new one located on the new disk (a subdisk
move would mean synchronization of unusable data, so why bother?).

```
# vxedit -g adg rename adg01 adg03
# vxdisksetup -i c1t1d0
# vxdg -g adg adddisk adg01=c1t1d0
# vxdisk -g adg list
DEVICE          TYPE            DISK        GROUP       STATUS
c1t1d0s2        auto:cdsdisk    adg01       adg         online
c1t1d1s2        auto:cdsdisk    adg02       adg         online
c1t1d2s2        auto:cdsdisk    adg03       adg         online
# vxassist -g adg -b move vol2 alloc=\!adg03,adg01
# vxtask -g adg list
TASKID  PTID TYPE/STATE    PCT    PROGRESS
```

```
  50581           ATCOPY/R 25.78% 0/2097152/540672 SDMV adg01-01 adg01-02 adg
# vxprint -rtg adg vol2
[...]
v vol2           -            ENABLED  ACTIVE   2097152  SELECT   -        fsgen
pl %2            vol2         ENABLED  TEMPRM   2097152  CONCAT   -        WO
sd adg01-02      %2           adg01    0        2097152  0        c1t1d0   ENA
pl vol2-01       vol2         ENABLED  ACTIVE   2097152  CONCAT   -        RW
sd adg01-01      vol2-01      adg03    0        2097152  0        c1t1d2   ENA
pl vol2-02       vol2         ENABLED  ACTIVE   2097152  CONCAT   -        RW
sd adg02-01      vol2-02      adg02    0        2097152  0        c1t1d1   ENA
# vxsd -g adg -f -o rm dis adg01-02
# vxprint -rtg adg vol1
[...]
v vol1           -            DISABLED ACTIVE   2097152  SELECT   -        fsgen
pl vol1-01       vol1         DISABLED(SPARSE) RECOVER 0 CONCAT   -        RW
# vxdg -g adg free adg01
DISK          DEVICE        TAG          OFFSET    LENGTH     FLAGS
adg01         c1t1d0s2      c1t1d0       2097152   120073984  -
# vxmake -g adg sd adg01-02 disk=adg01 offset=2097152 len=2097152
# vxsd -g adg assoc vol1-01 adg01-02
# vxprint -rtg adg vol1
[...]
v  vol1          -            DISABLED ACTIVE   2097152  SELECT   -        fsgen
pl vol1-01       vol1         DISABLED RECOVER  2097152  CONCAT   -        RW
sd adg01-02      vol1-01      adg01    2097152  2097152  0        c1t1d0   ENA
# vxvol -g adg -f start vol1
# vxedit -g adg set spare=on adg03
# vxprint -rtg adg
[...]
dm adg01         c1t1d0s2     auto     2048     122171136 -
dm adg02         c1t1d1s2     auto     2048     122171136 -
dm adg03         c1t1d2s2     auto     2048     122171136 SPARE

v  vol1          -            ENABLED  ACTIVE   2097152  SELECT   -        fsgen
pl vol1-01       vol1         ENABLED  ACTIVE   2097152  CONCAT   -        RW
sd adg01-03      vol1-01      adg01    2097152  2097152  0        c1t1d0   ENA

v  vol2          -            ENABLED  ACTIVE   2097152  SELECT   -        fsgen
pl vol2-01       vol2         ENABLED  ACTIVE   2097152  CONCAT   -        RW
sd adg01-02      vol2-01      adg01    0        2097152  0        c1t1d0   ENA
pl vol2-02       vol2         ENABLED  ACTIVE   2097152  CONCAT   -        RW
sd adg02-01      vol2-02      adg02    0        2097152  0        c1t1d1   ENA
```

11.4 SYNCHRONIZATION TASKS

11.4.1 OPTIMIZING RESYNCHRONIZATION

If a disk has failed and was replaced by a new one, the affected plexes do not contain reasonable application data, they must be completely synchronized. If a disk or a disk array is only inaccessible for a certain period and then comes back, those plexes contain stale application data. Depending on the duration of inaccessibility and the amount of application write I/Os, they are still physically synchronized in many or most regions of the volume.

Given a simple mirrored volume, VxVM does not know where the synchronization of regions may be skipped, so a complete synchronization is necessary. It would be a good idea to mark regions affected by write I/Os starting from the time when the plexes became disabled. After bringing online the temporarily failed disks by the procedure explained above, VxVM would need to synchronize only some regions of the plexes with a noticeable reduction of sync I/O.

A data change object (DCO) of version 20 together with its associated data change log volume (DCL) is capable not only to perform fast mirror synchronization of snapshots, not only to provide instant or space optimized snapshots, and not only to serve as a replacement to the former plex based Dirty region log. It also tracks the regions of write I/Os to a mirrored volume, if one or more of its plexes become unavailable. Let's test it!

1.   We create three mirrored volumes within a disk group consisting of two disks. The first volume (vol1) will keep the nologging layout, vol2 gets a DCO of version 0, while vol3 is supplied with a DCO of version 20. Note the different commands to create the different versions of a DCO. Also note the nice wizardry of vxprint to generate a formatted output of some specified attributes (option -F). Finally note that the DCL volume to DCO version 0 is smaller in size (144 sectors) than the volume to version 20 (544 sectors). The latter is designed to fulfill more tasks than the former (see chapter 9 on snapshots).

```
# vxassist -g adg make vol1 1g nmirror=2 init=active
# vxassist -g adg make vol2 1g nmirror=2 init=active
# vxassist -g adg addlog vol2 logtype=dco
```

The last two commands may be shortened to:

```
# vxassist -g adg make vol2 1g layout=mirror,log nmirror=2 logtype=dco \
  init=active
```

The third volume:

```
# vxassist -g adg make vol3 1g nmirror=2 init=active
# vxsnap -g adg prepare vol3
# vxprint -rLtg adg
```

```
[...]
V  NAME        RVG/VSET/CO KSTATE   STATE    LENGTH   READPOL    PREFPLEX UTYPE
PL NAME        VOLUME      KSTATE   STATE    LENGTH   LAYOUT     NCOL/WID MODE
SD NAME        PLEX        DISK     DISKOFFS LENGTH   [COL/]OFF  DEVICE   MODE
DC NAME        PARENTVOL   LOGVOL
[...]
v  vol1        -                    ENABLED ACTIVE  2097152  SELECT     -        fsgen
pl vol1-01     vol1                 ENABLED ACTIVE  2097152  CONCAT     -        RW
sd adg01-01    vol1-01     adg01    0       2097152 0        c4t1d0   ENA
pl vol1-02     vol1                 ENABLED ACTIVE  2097152  CONCAT     -        RW
sd adg02-01    vol1-02     adg02    0       2097152 0        c4t2d0   ENA


v  vol2        -                    ENABLED ACTIVE  2097152  SELECT     -        fsgen
pl vol2-01     vol2                 ENABLED ACTIVE  2097152  CONCAT     -        RW
sd adg01-02    vol2-01     adg01    2097152 2097152 0        c4t1d0   ENA
pl vol2-02     vol2                 ENABLED ACTIVE  2097152  CONCAT     -        RW
sd adg02-02    vol2-02     adg02    2097152 2097152 0        c4t2d0   ENA
dc vol2_dco    vol2        vol2_dcl

v  vol2_dcl    -                    ENABLED ACTIVE  144      SELECT     -        gen
pl vol2_dcl-01 vol2_dcl             ENABLED ACTIVE  144      CONCAT     -        RW
sd adg01-04    vol2_dcl-01 adg01    6291456 144     0        c4t1d0   ENA
pl vol2_dcl-02 vol2_dcl             ENABLED ACTIVE  144      CONCAT     -        RW
sd adg02-04    vol2_dcl-02 adg02    6291456 144     0        c4t2d0   ENA


v  vol3        -                    ENABLED ACTIVE  2097152  SELECT     -        fsgen
pl vol3-01     vol3                 ENABLED ACTIVE  2097152  CONCAT     -        RW
sd adg01-03    vol3-01     adg01    4194304 2097152 0        c4t1d0   ENA
pl vol3-02     vol3                 ENABLED ACTIVE  2097152  CONCAT     -        RW
sd adg02-03    vol3-02     adg02    4194304 2097152 0        c4t2d0   ENA
dc vol3_dco    vol3        vol3_dcl

v  vol3_dcl    -                    ENABLED ACTIVE  544      SELECT     -        gen
pl vol3_dcl-01 vol3_dcl             ENABLED ACTIVE  544      CONCAT     -        RW
sd adg01-05    vol3_dcl-01 adg01    6291600 544     0        c4t1d0   ENA
pl vol3_dcl-02 vol3_dcl             ENABLED ACTIVE  544      CONCAT     -        RW
sd adg02-05    vol3_dcl-02 adg02    6291600 544     0        c4t2d0   ENA
# F='%{name:-10} %{version:2} %{drl:-4} %{drllogging:-4}'
# vxprint -g adg -F "$F" vol2_dco vol3_dco
vol2_dco   0 off  off
vol3_dco  20 on   on
```

2. We make a disk of the disk group used by all volumes unavailable for VxVM, perform write I/O of 1 MB on each volume, and recover the temporarily failed disk and the disk group.

```
# dd if=/dev/rdsk/c4t1d0s2 of=/var/tmp/c4t1d0s2 bs=128k iseek=1 count=8
# dd if=/dev/zero of=/dev/rdsk/c4t1d0s2 bs=128k oseek=1 count=8
# vxconfigd -k
# vxdisk list
DEVICE        TYPE           DISK        GROUP       STATUS
[...]
c4t1d0s2      auto:cdsdisk   -           -           online invalid
c4t2d0s2      auto:cdsdisk   adg02       adg         online
[...]
-             -              adg01       adg         failed was:c4t1d0s2
# for i in 1 2 3; do
  dd if=/dev/zero of=/dev/vx/rdsk/adg/vol$i bs=128k count=8; done
# dd if=/var/tmp/c4t1d0s2 of=/dev/rdsk/c4t1d0s2 bs=128k oseek=1
# vxdisk scandisks device=c4t1d0
# vxdisk list
DEVICE        TYPE           DISK        GROUP       STATUS
[...]
c4t1d0s2      auto:cdsdisk   -           -           online
c4t2d0s2      auto:cdsdisk   adg02       adg         online
[...]
-             -              adg01       adg         failed was:c4t1d0s2
# vxdg -g adg -k adddisk adg01=c4t1d0
# vxdisk list
DEVICE        TYPE           DISK        GROUP       STATUS
[...]
c4t1d0s2      auto:cdsdisk   adg01       adg         online
c4t2d0s2      auto:cdsdisk   adg02       adg         online
[...]
```

3.   Before resynchronizing the volumes, we reset the I/O counters of VxVM for the disk group. We expect five synchronization tasks: three tasks for the three top-level volumes, and two tasks for the two mirrored DCL volumes. After resynchronization, we check for mirror sync I/Os, i.e. for I/O types "Atomic Copy" and "Read-Writeback". Since we had a failed disk producing one disabled plex within each volume, we do not expect Read-Writebacks, but you never know...

```
# vxstat -g adg -r
# vxrecover -bg adg
# vxtask list
TASKID  PTID  TYPE/STATE    PCT    PROGRESS
   364        PARENT/R    0.00%  5/0(1) VXRECOVER
   365   365  ATCOPY/R   00.98%  0/2097152/20480 PLXATT vol1 vol1-01 adg
# vxtask list
TASKID  PTID  TYPE/STATE    PCT    PROGRESS
   364        PARENT/R   20.00%  5/1(1) VXRECOVER
   369   369  ATCOPY/R   16.02%  0/2097152/335872 PLXATT vol2 vol2-01 adg
```

```
# vxstat -g adg -f ab
                        ATOMIC COPIES              READ-WRITEBACK
TYP NAME          OPS   BLOCKS AVG(ms)      OPS   BLOCKS AVG(ms)
vol vol1         1024  2097152    71.3        0        0    0.0
vol vol2         1024  2097152    61.8        0        0    0.0
vol vol2_dcl        1      144    20.0        0        0    0.0
vol vol3            1     2048    80.0        0        0    0.0
vol vol3_dcl        1      544    30.0        0        0    0.0
```

Indeed, the command output exactly provides the information we expected before: five synchronization tasks mentioned in the first output line of the two **vxtask list** command examples after the title. But the most important information lies in the output of **vxstat**: Without mirror logging or with a DCO version 0, the volume was resynchronized completely: 1024 I/O operations at 2048 sectors (= 1 MB) each, totally 1 GB. However, the third volume was synchronized just with 1 I/O at 1 MB (remember, we wrote 1 MB new data on each volume). The DCL volumes, due to their small size not furnished with another DCO structure, are synchronized completely.

11.4.2 CONTROLLING SYNCHRONIZATION BEHAVIOR

In most cases, VxVM selects the appropriate synchronization mechanisms to recreate full volume redundancy. If a plex is in a state known to specify stale or inaccessible data (such as NODEVICE, IOFAIL, RECOVER, STALE, OFFLINE), while there is at least one healthy plex (ACTIVE, CLEAN, under certain circumstances EMPTY and SNAPDONE) within the volume, then VxVM uses the "Atomic Copy" procedure, thus reading the volume based on the healthy plexes and writing these data to the bad plex. Application write I/Os are written to all plexes, read requests are just taken from the healthy plexes before or during resynchronization.

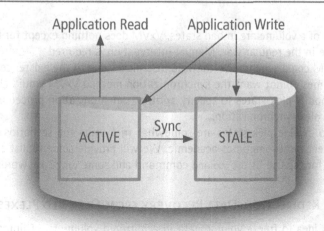

Figure 11-1: "Atomic Copy" Synchronization

If all plexes are in a healthy state, but VxVM knows, that there is need to synchronize (e.g. the devopen volume attribute is on, because the system crashed, while there was write I/O to the raw device, or the volume with its file system was mounted), VxVM does not spoil the still existing redundancy on nearly all parts of the volume (as some less intelligent volume manager software does by marking one data copy as bad). All healthy plexes remain healthy, for load balancing reasons the synchronization direction changes every 256 MB, and for performance reasons the round robin read policy remains in use. To provide a transactional raw device, VxVM immediately writes back every read I/O to the other plexes to ensure data integrity when reading those data blocks once again, but probably from the other plex. Therefore, this technique is called "Read-Writeback". The topic of Read-Writeback synchronisation is difficult to understand, and you want to refer to the additional coverage in the Volume chapter, page 132.

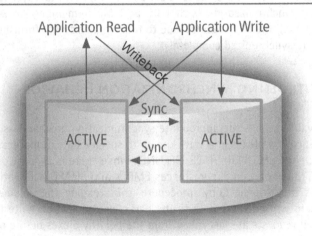

Figure 11-2: "Read-Writeback" Synchronization

If all plexes of a volume are in bad states, VxVM does nothing except for forbidding to start the volume in the regular way. Manual intervention is required.

Even if VxVM could synchronize the volume's plexes due to the existence of a healthy plex, we sometimes do not want the synchronization method VxVM would choose. So we need ways to modify plex states to specify another synchronization procedure or even to completely skip plex synchronization.

The ways to change plex states are somewhat tricky, and the scenarios making such modifications necessary sometimes academic. We will provide some realistic scenarios to show examples for the use of the vxmend command and some vxvol keywords.

ATOMIC COPY REDIRECTION: DATA RECOVERY FROM OFFLINED PLEXES

It is a good idea to freeze volume data in a mirrored volume by offlining a data plex when applying software upgrades or patches, modifying the application configuration, and so on. Upgrades and patches could make things even worse, a misconfigured application cannot be started. A data plex may be offlined at any time, independent from the volume state:

```
# vxprint -rtg adg vol
[...]
v  vol       -            ENABLED  ACTIVE   2097152  SELECT   -       fsgen
pl vol-01    vol          ENABLED  ACTIVE   2097152  CONCAT   -       RW
sd adg01-01  vol-01       adg01    0        2097152  0        c1t1d0  ENA
pl vol-02    vol          ENABLED  ACTIVE   2097152  CONCAT   -       RW
sd adg02-01  vol-02       adg02    0        2097152  0        c1t1d1  ENA
# vxmend -g adg off vol-02
# vxprint -rtg adg vol
[...]
v  vol       -            ENABLED  ACTIVE   2097152  SELECT   -       fsgen
pl vol-01    vol          ENABLED  ACTIVE   2097152  CONCAT   -       RW
sd adg01-01  vol-01       adg01    0        2097152  0        c1t1d0  ENA
pl vol-02    vol          DISABLED OFFLINE  2097152  CONCAT   -       RW
sd adg02-01  vol-02       adg02    0        2097152  0        c1t1d1  ENA
```

In case the upgraded, patched, or modified data work fine, we soon should synchronize the offlined plex according to the current volume data in order to establish data redundancy.

```
# vxmend -g adg on vol-02
# vxprint -rtg adg vol
[...]
v  vol       -            ENABLED  ACTIVE   2097152  SELECT   -       fsgen
pl vol-01    vol          ENABLED  ACTIVE   2097152  CONCAT   -       RW
sd adg01-01  vol-01       adg01    0        2097152  0        c1t1d0  ENA
pl vol-02    vol          DISABLED STALE    2097152  CONCAT   -       RW
sd adg02-01  vol-02       adg02    0        2097152  0        c1t1d1  ENA
```

Of course, the plex contains stale data and is therefore still disabled for any I/O. Atomic copy resynchronization is not started automatically, we issue volume recovery.

```
# vxrecover -g adg -b vol
# vxtask -g adg list
TASKID  PTID TYPE/STATE   PCT    PROGRESS
  251   251  ATCOPY/R 11.62% 0/2097152/243712 PLXATT vol vol-02 adg
```

During synchronization, the synchronized plex is available for application write I/Os (kernel state ENABLED), but blocked for read access (mode WO).

```
# vxprint -rtg adg vol
[...]
v  vol       -            ENABLED  ACTIVE   2097152  SELECT   -       fsgen
```

```
pl vol-01          vol               ENABLED ACTIVE   2097152 CONCAT    -        RW
sd adg01-01        vol-01    adg01   0        2097152 0        c1t1d0   ENA
pl vol-02          vol               ENABLED STALE    2097152 CONCAT    -        WO
sd adg02-01        vol-02    adg02   0        2097152 0        c1t1d1   ENA
```

If we crashed the application due to the "high enterprise quality" of a patch, our offlined plex provides most probably the most up-to-date application data. So we must switch the synchronization direction. It is impossible and indeed of no use to enable access to another data set (the offlined plex), while the volume is in use. This would spoil any transactional device characteristics. Consequently, we need to stop application and volume first. Our example unmounts the file system on the volume, but you may assume any other required application termination in order to free the raw device from I/O.

```
# umount /mnt
# vxvol -g adg stop vol
# vxprint -rtg adg vol
[…]
v  vol              -                 DISABLED CLEAN   2097152 SELECT    -        fsgen
pl vol-01          vol               DISABLED CLEAN   2097152 CONCAT    -        RW
sd adg01-01        vol-01    adg01   0        2097152 0        c1t1d0   ENA
pl vol-02          vol               DISABLED OFFLINE 2097152 CONCAT    -        RW
sd adg02-01        vol-02    adg02   0        2097152 0        c1t1d1   ENA
```

The corrupted data set (vol-01) is still marked as healthy by VxVM (CLEAN), the correct data set (vol-02) is still in OFFLINE state. We want to mark vol-01 as STALE and vol-02 as CLEAN or ACTIVE to force the desired synchronization direction.

```
# vxmend -g adg on vol-02
# vxprint -rtg adg vol
[…]
v  vol              -                 DISABLED CLEAN   2097152 SELECT    -        fsgen
pl vol-01          vol               DISABLED CLEAN   2097152 CONCAT    -        RW
sd adg01-01        vol-01    adg01   0        2097152 0        c1t1d0   ENA
pl vol-02          vol               DISABLED STALE   2097152 CONCAT    -        RW
sd adg02-01        vol-02    adg02   0        2097152 0        c1t1d1   ENA
# vxmend -g adg fix clean vol-02
VxVM vxmend ERROR V-5-1-1182 Volume vol contains plexes in the CLEAN state
```

VxVM does not like your attack to its knowledge of missing data integrity, because two clean plexes would mean a fully synchronized, healthy volume. The keyword active instead of clean would work, but then the volume would be marked as NEEDSYNC, thus evoking read-writeback synchronization. Our task needs another procedure.

```
# vxmend -g adg fix stale vol-01
# vxmend -g adg fix clean vol-02
# vxprint -rtg adg vol
[…]
```

v	vol	-	DISABLED	CLEAN	2097152	SELECT	-	fsgen
pl	vol-01	vol	**DISABLED**	**STALE**	2097152	CONCAT	-	RW
sd	adg01-01	vol-01	adg01	0	2097152	0	c1t1d0	ENA
pl	vol-02	vol	**DISABLED**	**CLEAN**	2097152	CONCAT	-	RW
sd	adg02-01	vol-02	adg02	0	2097152	0	c1t1d1	ENA

This works! The roles of good and stale plex are swapped. Now enable and resynchronize the volume in the correct direction. Both commands listed below are in this case absolutely identical. Finally, restart your application.

```
# vxvol -g adg [-o bg] start vol
# vxrecover -g adg [-b] -s vol
# mount -F <fstype> /dev/vx/dsk/adg/vol /mnt
```

ATOMIC COPY INSTEAD OF READ WRITEBACK: ONE PLEX IS FEW I/OS FARTHER THAN THE OTHER

We assume a total, but cascading power outage in a data center. The volume, mirrored across two LUN arrays, first looses on the physical layer one data plex and some seconds later the other one. Due to the timeouts of the stateless Fibre Channel protocol, both plexes keep their healthy ACTIVE state, but the latter contains more current data. After powering on the data center, VxVM would resynchronize the volume using the read-writeback method. If we cannot recover the volume data generated during the last seconds before the total power outage by application recovery strategies (e.g. the online redo logs of an Oracle database reside on the same LUN arrays), we can tell VxVM, that we do not have two healthy plexes, but just one. Since the boot process already starts resynchronization (`/etc/rc2.d/S95vxvm-recover` Solaris 9, `/lib/svc/method/vxvm-recover` Solaris 10), we must boot into the single user mode or milestone. Remember: `/etc/rcS.d/S35vxvm-startup1` for the OS disk group and `/etc/rcS.d/S85vxvm-startup2` (Solaris 9, same file names in Solaris 10 under `/lib/svc/method`) for other disk groups respectively just start volumes without synchronization, marking them as NEEDSYNC and thus forcing read writeback application I/Os (`vxrecover -s -n`).

```
ok boot -s
[...]
# vxprint -rtg adg vol
[...]
```

v	vol	-	ENABLED	**NEEDSYNC**	2097152	SELECT	-	fsgen
pl	vol-01	vol	ENABLED	ACTIVE	2097152	CONCAT	-	RW
sd	adg01-01	vol-01	adg01	0	2097152	0	c1t1d0	ENA
pl	vol-02	vol	ENABLED	ACTIVE	2097152	CONCAT	-	RW
sd	adg02-01	vol-02	adg02	0	2097152	0	c1t1d1	ENA

```
# vxmend -g adg off vol-02
# vxmend -g adg on vol-02
# vxprint -rtg adg vol
[...]
```

v	vol	-	ENABLED	NEEDSYNC	2097152	SELECT	-	fsgen

```
pl vol-01        vol              ENABLED  ACTIVE   2097152  CONCAT   -        RW
sd adg01-01      vol-01           adg01    0        2097152  0        c1t1d0   ENA
pl vol-02        vol              DISABLED STALE    2097152  CONCAT   -        RW
sd adg02-01      vol-02           adg02    0        2097152  0        c1t1d1   ENA
# exit
```

The continued boot process will now resynchronize the volume using the atomic copy method (/etc/rc2.d/S95vxvm-recover or /lib/svc/method/vxvm-recover):

```
vxrecover -b -o iosize=64k > /dev/null
```

FORCE ATOMIC COPY SYNCHRONIZATION: I/O ON DISKS OUTSIDE OF VxVM

As long as all disk I/Os are managed by the VxVM kernel, its integrity states are correct. But VxVM does not hinder the device drivers to accept I/Os issued outside of VxVM. It is quite easy to execute a dd command immediately on partition drivers, generating mirror inconsistency, where VxVM believes mirrors to be coherent. As soon as possible, we must mark the damaged plex as a bad plex. Probably you should stop the application to prevent it from decisions based on wrong data. But you are not forced by VxVM to stop the volume.

```
# vxmend -g adg off vol-02
# vxmend -g adg on vol-02
# vxprint -rtg adg vol
[...]
v  vol          -                ENABLED  NEEDSYNC 2097152  SELECT   -        fsgen
pl vol-01        vol              ENABLED  ACTIVE   2097152  CONCAT   -        RW
sd adg01-01      vol-01           adg01    0        2097152  0        c1t1d0   ENA
pl vol-02        vol              DISABLED STALE    2097152  CONCAT   -        RW
sd adg02-01      vol-02           adg02    0        2097152  0        c1t1d1   ENA
# vxrecover -g adg [-b] vol
```

One command less, but executable only against a stopped volume:

```
# vxmend -g adg fix stale vol-02
# vxprint -rtg adg vol
[...]
v  vol          -                DISABLED CLEAN    2097152  SELECT   -        fsgen
pl vol-01        vol              DISABLED CLEAN    2097152  CONCAT   -        RW
sd adg01-01      vol-01           adg01    0        2097152  0        c1t1d0   ENA
pl vol-02        vol              DISABLED STALE    2097152  CONCAT   -        RW
sd adg02-01      vol-02           adg02    0        2097152  0        c1t1d1   ENA
# vxrecover -g adg [-b] -s vol
```

We will discuss another example in a boot troubleshooting section (booting without VxVM).

FORCE READ-WRITEBACK SYNCHRONIZATION: SUSPICIOUS PLEX DATA

You fear differences in very small regions of your mirrors, because you forgot to disable disk track caching, and your data center suffered a power outage. Small data sets still not written physically to the disk platters but already committed to the volume layer (the devopen attribute is already set to off) could be dangerous for your application. Therefore, you decide to synchronize the mirrors, but you do not know, which mirror is good and which is bad (probably they are both affected by data loss). To keep redundancy, you prefer to choose the read-writeback method.

```
# vxprint -rtg adg vol
[...]
v  vol        -       ENABLED  ACTIVE  2097152  SELECT   -       fsgen
pl vol-01     vol     ENABLED  ACTIVE  2097152  CONCAT   -       RW
sd adg01-01   vol-01  adg01    0       2097152  0        c1t1d0  ENA
pl vol-02     vol     ENABLED  ACTIVE  2097152  CONCAT   -       RW
sd adg02-01   vol-02  adg02    0       2097152  0        c1t1d1  ENA
# vxrecover -g adg vol
```

The recovery command will not resynchronize the volume, because, according to VxVM, the volume is still synchronized. Otherwise, you would see the volume state NEEDSYNC. Since a read-writeback synchronization could change the current volume content (a data block was read from the first plex by the application, but is synchronized from the second plex by VxVM), the volume must be stopped.

```
# vxvol -g adg stop vol
# vxmend -g adg fix empty vol
# vxprint -rtg adg vol
[...]
v  vol        -       DISABLED  EMPTY  2097152  SELECT   -       fsgen
pl vol-01     vol     DISABLED  EMPTY  2097152  CONCAT   -       RW
sd adg01-01   vol-01  adg01    0       2097152  0        c1t1d0  ENA
pl vol-02     vol     DISABLED  EMPTY  2097152  CONCAT   -       RW
sd adg02-01   vol-02  adg02    0       2097152  0        c1t1d1  ENA
```

The volume now looks and behaves like a freshly created volume. No plex has priority over the other one, so VxVM will choose read-writeback synchronization.

```
# vxvol -g adg [-o bg] start avol
    or:
# vxrecover -g adg [-b] -s avol
# vxtask -g adg list
TASKID  PTID TYPE/STATE   PCT    PROGRESS
   176       RDWRBACK/R 69.73% 0/2097152/1462272 VOLSTART vol adg
```

Skip Synchronization: Volume Data Unusable

As already explained in the Volume chapter on page 120, you may create new mirrored volumes without synchronization either by a sequence of vxmake commands and finally by starting the DISABLED/EMPTY volume executing:

```
# vxvol -g adg init active vol
```

Or you may issue the vxassist command with a special parameter:

```
# vxassist -g adg make vol 1g layout=mirror init=active
```

In case VxVM tells you that the volume must be synchronized, but you are not interested in the volume data, because you want to restore the volume data from a backup image, you could believe it would be sufficient to mark the volume as DISABLED/EMPTY:

```
# vxprint -rtg adg vol
[...]
v  vol         -          ENABLED  NEEDSYNC 2097152 SELECT   -       fsgen
pl vol-01      vol        ENABLED  ACTIVE   2097152 CONCAT   -       RW
sd adg01-01    vol-01     adg01    0        2097152 0        c1t1d0  ENA
pl vol-02      vol        ENABLED  ACTIVE   2097152 CONCAT   -       RW
sd adg02-01    vol-02     adg02    0        2097152 0        c1t1d1  ENA
# vxvol -g adg stop vol
# vxprint -rtg adg vol
[...]
v  vol         -          DISABLED NEEDSYNC 2097152 SELECT   -       fsgen
pl vol-01      vol        DISABLED ACTIVE   2097152 CONCAT   -       RW
sd adg01-01    vol-01     adg01    0        2097152 0        c1t1d0  ENA
pl vol-02      vol        DISABLED ACTIVE   2097152 CONCAT   -       RW
sd adg02-01    vol-02     adg02    0        2097152 0        c1t1d1  ENA
# vxmend -g adg fix empty vol
VxVM vxmend ERROR V-5-1-1211 Volume vol has plexes in the ACTIVE state, use -o
force
# vxmend -g adg -o force fix empty vol
# vxprint -rtg adg vol
[...]
v  vol         -          DISABLED EMPTY    2097152 SELECT   -       fsgen
pl vol-01      vol        DISABLED EMPTY    2097152 CONCAT   -       RW
sd adg01-01    vol-01     adg01    0        2097152 0        c1t1d0  ENA
pl vol-02      vol        DISABLED EMPTY    2097152 CONCAT   -       RW
sd adg02-01    vol-02     adg02    0        2097152 0        c1t1d1  ENA
# vxvol -g adg init active vol
# vxprint -rtg adg vol
[...]
v  vol         -          ENABLED  NEEDSYNC 2097152 SELECT   -       fsgen
pl vol-01      vol        ENABLED  ACTIVE   2097152 CONCAT   -       RW
```

sd adg01-01	vol-01	adg01	0	2097152	0	c1t1d0	ENA
pl vol-02	vol	ENABLED	ACTIVE	2097152	CONCAT	-	RW
sd adg02-01	vol-02	adg02	0	2097152	0	c1t1d1	ENA

Oops! VxVM did not forget the need for synchronization. The volume looked like a freshly created volume, but only within the standard output of vxprint. A volume attribute kept the information for recovery: cdsrecover_seqno, set to a value not equal to 0 (mostly 1). Unfortunately, this attribute value cannot be reset to 0. We only know one way to dupe VxVM: Store the volume attributes recursively into a file, edit the value of cdsrecover_seqno, rebuild the volume and initialize it by skipping synchronization:

```
# vxprint -rmg adg vol > /tmp/vol
# vxedit -g adg -rf rm vol
# vi /tmp/vol
[...]
        cdsrecover_seqno=0
[...]
# vxmake -g adg -d /tmp/vol
# vxvol -g adg init active vol
# vxprint -rtg adg vol
[...]
```

v vol	-	**ENABLED**	**ACTIVE**	2097152	SELECT	-	fsgen
pl vol-01	vol	ENABLED	ACTIVE	2097152	CONCAT	-	RW
sd adg01-01	vol-01	adg01	0	2097152	0	c1t1d0	ENA
pl vol-02	vol	ENABLED	ACTIVE	2097152	CONCAT	-	RW
sd adg02-01	vol-02	adg02	0	2097152	0	c1t1d1	ENA

11.5 RESTORE OF LOST VxVM OBJECTS

11.5.1 VXPRINT AND VXMAKE CAPABILITIES

Often, the cause of trouble does not stem from the machines, but sits or stands before them. So we need to consider what to do, if we inadvertently removed objects from the VxVM configuration.

Fortunately, we can use a special output format of vxprint to store the disk group configuration in a manner to be read by vxmake in order to rebuild the objects. The following table shows in a comparison of the syntax, how both commands specify the appropriate VxVM objects:

VxVM Object Type	vxprint options	vxprint type abbreviations	vxmake type abbreviations
Volume	-v	v	vol
Plex	-p	pl	plex
Subdisk	-s	sd	sd
Subvolume	-s	sv	sd
Data Change Object	-c	dc	dco
Snap Object	-c	sp	-
Cache Object	-C	co	cache
Subcache	-s	sc	sd
Replicated Volume Group	-V	rv	rvg
Remote Link	-P	rl	rlink
Volume Set	-x	vt	vset

The vxprint command is able to store all disk group configuration data together with hardware related information, such as the current disk device access path. Unfortunately, the corresponding vxmake command cannot define disk and disk group attribute values (therefore not shown in the table above). So we take in mind two restrictions: First, we must initialize the required disks and create the disk group out of them with the well-known commands, before we can read the still missing disk group configuration into vxmake. Furthermore, we need to eliminate any disk and disk group information before sending the stored configuration to vxmake.

To begin with the latter task: To print all disk group configuration data, including the disk and disk group objects, vxprint provides two options: -a to print attribute-value pairs word by word, one terribly long line for each object. This output is useful for scripting purposes, because Unix provides many tools to split into lines and words (e.g. awk/nawk/gawk, the Shell itself), but rarely into separate paragraphs. The other option, -m, creates an output containing the same information, but differently formatted: attribute-value pairs line by line, grouped together to sometimes long paragraphs (only the first line to an object is not indented).

The output of vxprint -m is understood by vxmake. We still need to skip disk and disk group data by choosing appropriate options. This is much more comfortable than generating the whole output and then erasing the wrong lines by using an editor. Recalling the options table above, we enter the following command:

```
# vxprint -g <diskgroup> -m -vpscCVPx > <configfile>
```

11.5.2 RESTORE OF ALL VOLUMES IN A DISK GROUP

If necessary, we initialize disks and recreate the empty disk group manually. We must take care, that the position and length of the private region corresponds to the former settings. Otherwise, the subdisks would be recreated at a different position on the disks, thus providing unusable volume data and possibly failing in creating subdisks at a position outside of the physical disk, if the private region becomes larger than the former one. Then, we read the stored configuration into vxmake:

```
# vxmake -g <diskgroup> -d <configfile>
```

That is already nearly all! All disk group objects are recreated at exactly the same physical and virtual location and with the same attribute values. The single exception (we might expect this from our knowledge to the vxmake command): Volumes and plexes are still stopped in the state pair DISABLED/EMPTY. To start the volumes together with read-writeback mirror or RAID5 plex synchronization, simply issue:

```
# vxvol -g <diskgroup> startall
```

To skip synchronization (the disk group was cleanly deported, the volumes were stopped, or we do not care for any previous data):

```
# vxvol -g <diskgroup> init active <volume-list>
```

Some pages before, we demonstrated other ways to specify the synchronization method against the assumptions of VxVM. You may apply them as well.

11.5.3 RESTORE OF SOME VOLUMES IN A DISK GROUP

In case of a lost volume, while the disk group and other objects are still configured and alive, we must filter only those objects and attributes belonging to that volume from the stored configuration file. First the good news: vxprint is capable to read the disk group configuration not only from the kernel (the default), not only from the physical private region (/usr/lib/vxvm/diag.d/vxprivutil), but also from a configuration file in the vxprint -m output format. We only add the option -D together with the source. Currently only STDIN, specified with the minus sign, is implemented. Thanks to the Shell, we redirect STDIN to the configuration file (the following two commands are identical in result):

```
# vxprint -rLtg <diskgroup> -D - < <configfile>
# cat <configfile> | vxprint -rLtg <diskgroup> -D -
```

Of course, any other output formatting options besides -rLt used above are allowed, even -m. So, by specifying the volume name together with the "related" option -r, we finally get the desired filtered volume output to be piped into vxmake (instead of a configuration file, vxmake -d understands the minus sign as its argument, now reading from STDIN):

```
# vxprint -rmg <diskgroup> -D - <volume> < <configfile> |
  vxmake -g <diskgroup> -d -
```

We mentioned "good news", because there are, unfortunately, also bad news: This powerful filtering procedure currently does not work in VxVM 5.0 (VxVM 4.x is fine), it produces a core dump due to segmentation fault (jump into not included memory regions). As an acceptable work-around for VxVM 5.0, we propose to store the disk group configuration twice. First, the whole disk group configuration data (except for disks and disk group, of course):

```
# vxprint -g <diskgroup> -m -vpscCPVx > <configfile>.<diskgroup>
```

And, additionally, all volume configuration data, volume by volume, into different configuration files:

```
# for Volume in $(vxprint -g <diskgroup> -vne 'v_layered=off && v_islog=no'); do
  vxprint -rmg <diskgroup> $Volume > <configfile>.<diskgroup>.$Volume; done
```

To restore an inadvertently removed volume, use the volume specific configuration file without further filtering by the vxprint command:

```
# vxmake -g <diskgroup> -d <configfile>.<diskgroup>.<volume>
```

The manual page of vxmake also mentions another configuration format understood by vxmake. This format exactly corresponds to the command line options of vxmake, excluding the vxmake command itself and the disk group option -g with its argument. Since there is no easy way to store the current disk group configuration using this layout, we skip further details.

11.5.4 RESTORE OF THE ENTIRE DISK GROUP CONFIGURATION

The boot process (/etc/rc2.d/S95vxvm-recover or /lib/svc/method/vxvm-recover) starts another VxVM daemon of some interest for disk group disaster scenarios:

```
# ptree $(pgrep -xu0 vxconfigbackupd)
501   /sbin/sh - /usr/lib/vxvm/bin/vxconfigbackupd
  1323   /sbin/sh - /usr/lib/vxvm/bin/vxconfigbackupd
    1324   vxnotify
```

Comparable to the vxrelocd/vxnotify daemon pair, vxconfigbackupd is informed by vxnotify about every VxVM event, even about small configuration changes. See the following example: vxnotify is started on one terminal, while we execute a simple plex attach to a volume on another terminal.

```
# vxnotify
connected
[...]
# vxassist -g adg mirror vol
# vxnotify        (continued)
change dg adg dgid 1223834080.19.sols
change dg adg dgid 1223834080.19.sols
```

```
change dg adg dgid 1223834080.19.sols
^C
```

The first message belongs to the creation of a new plex together with its subdisk(s), the second indicates the begin, the last the end of plex synchronization.

Now, vxconfigbackupd captures the output of vxnotify and triggers in case of configuration change events a new backup of the new (!) configuration. You will find the backups under /etc/vx/cbr/bk:

```
# cd /etc/vx/cbr/bk
# ls -l
drwxr-xr-x  2 root     root      1536 Jun 12 12:25 adg.1213178377.21.sols
drwxr-xr-x  2 root     root      1536 Oct 12 21:14 adg.1223834080.19.sols
drwxr-xr-x  2 root     root      1536 Oct 12 10:08 osdg.1198162173.6.sols
```

Each subfolder is named after the name and the ID of the related disk group. Concerning the disk group adg, we recognize two versions. Remember: Only the disk group ID is unique. Obviously, the disk group adg was once unavailable and freshly created under the same name, but naturally not with the same disk group ID. The content of the latter adg folder is (given VxVM 5.0):

```
# cd adg.1223834080.19.sols
# ls -l
-rw-r--r--  1 root     root    655360 Oct 12 21:14 1223834080.19.sols.binconfig
-rw-r--r--  1 root     root      8035 Oct 12 21:14 1223834080.19.sols.cfgrec
-rw-r--r--  1 root     root      1695 Oct 12 21:14 1223834080.19.sols.dginfo
-rw-r--r--  1 root     root      3190 Oct 12 21:14 1223834080.19.sols.diskinfo
```

The first file with extension binconfig is nearly a physical copy of the disk and disk group configuration part of the private region. The next file (cfgrec) contains the output of vxprint -mg adg (including disk and disk group objects and attributes), the third (dginfo) some VxVM version and particularly disk group information, the last file (diskinfo) details to the disk group members.

Note the large size of the private region copy file. Our disk group example deals with private regions only 1 MB in size. In VxVM 5.0, the default size of the private region is 32 MB, so in enterprise environments providing many disk groups the binconfig files occupy large amounts of storage of the root file system. That's why only the last known configuration is stored by VxVM 5.0, while VxVM 4.x holds the last six versions as a source to recover former disk group configurations.

Well, that is a nice thing. We just prepare the disk group in order to get some experience on the procedure to recover a disk group. Unfortunately, a simple vxdg destroy command will also remove the backup of the disk group configuration (there are other ways to recreate a destroyed disk group, see below). So we temporarily rename the backup folder and make sure that no private region data exist anymore on the disks.

```
# cd /etc/vx/cbr/bk
# ls -d adg.*
```

```
adg.1213178377.21.sols  adg.1223834080.19.sols
# mv adg.1223834080.19.sols adg.1223834080.19.sols.renamed
# vxdg destroy adg
# mv adg.1223834080.19.sols.renamed adg.1223834080.19.sols
# vxdiskunsetup c4t1d0
# vxdiskunsetup c4t2d0
# dd if=/dev/zero of=/dev/rdsk/c4t1d0s2 bs=128k oseek=1 count=8
# dd if=/dev/zero of=/dev/rdsk/c4t2d0s2 bs=128k oseek=1 count=8
# /usr/lib/vxvm/diag.d/vxprivutil dumpconfig /dev/rdsk/c4t1d0s2
VxVM vxprivutil ERROR V-5-1-1735 scan operation failed:
        Format error in disk private region
# /usr/lib/vxvm/diag.d/vxprivutil dumpconfig /dev/rdsk/c4t2d0s2
VxVM vxprivutil ERROR V-5-1-1735 scan operation failed:
        Format error in disk private region
```

Are you convinced that neither in the kernel memory nor on the disks any usable disk group data are available? Our single hope lies in the configuration backup. Look at the following commands, how to (and how not to) reactivate the disk group (the option -p signifies "precommit").

```
# vxconfigrestore -p adg
VxVM vxconfigrestore ERROR V-5-2-3717 There are two backups that have the same
diskgroup name adg with different diskgroup id :
   1213178377.21.sols -- backup at Thu Jun 12 12:25:42 MEST 2008
   1223834080.19.sols -- backup at Sun Oct 12 21:14:26 MEST 2008

VxVM vxconfigrestore INFO V-5-2-3721 Use diskgroup_id to do the restoration.
# vxconfigrestore -p 1223834080.19.sols
Diskgroup 1223834080.19.sols configuration restoration started ......

Installing volume manager disk header for c4t1d0s2 ...
c4t1d0s2 disk format has been changed from cdsdisk to none.
Installing volume manager disk header for c4t2d0s2 ...
c4t2d0s2 disk format has been changed from cdsdisk to none.

1223834080.19.sols's diskgroup configuration is restored (in precommit state).
Diskgroup can be accessed in read only and can be examined using
vxprint in this state.

Run:
   vxconfigrestore -c 1223834080.19.sols ==> to commit the restoration.
   vxconfigrestore -d 1223834080.19.sols ==> to abort the restoration.
```

We notice that the disks of the disk group were initialized to some extent (whatever volume manager disk header means, see below; note also the erroneously inverted direction in the expression from cdsdisk to none). Commands exploring kernel information on the disk group work as usual, even modification of the configuration is possible, obviously unrestricted (including mirror synchronization):

```
# vxdisk -g adg list
DEVICE       TYPE          DISK       GROUP       STATUS
c4t1d0s2     auto:cdsdisk  adg01      adg         online
c4t2d0s2     auto:cdsdisk  adg02      adg         online
# vxprint -rtg adg
[...]
v  vol        -             ENABLED  ACTIVE  2097152  SELECT   -        fsgen
pl vol-01     vol           ENABLED  ACTIVE  2097152  CONCAT   -        RW
sd adg01-01   vol-01        adg01    0       2097152  0        c4t1d0   ENA
pl vol-02     vol           ENABLED  ACTIVE  2097152  CONCAT   -        RW
sd adg02-01   vol-02        adg02    0       2097152  0        c4t2d0   ENA
# vxassist -g adg -b make newvol 1g layout=mirror
# vxtask -g adg list
TASKID  PTID TYPE/STATE    PCT     PROGRESS
  177        RDWRBACK/R 44.43% 0/2097152/931840 VOLSTART newvol adg
```

So what do they mean with the expression Diskgroup can be accessed in read only in the output of vxconfigrestore? Well, read access to the volumes is possible, but write access is blocked. Therefore, you may analyze the content of the volumes in order to check the proper position of the subdisks.

```
# dd if=/dev/vx/rdsk/adg/vol of=/dev/null count=1
1+0 records in
1+0 records out
# dd if=/dev/zero of=/dev/vx/rdsk/adg/vol count=1
write: Permission denied
1+0 records in
1+0 records out
```

What became of the physical state of the disks? Well, the partitions for VxVM were recreated. In VxVM 4.x (our example), the private region got initialized, but just with the disk group and the disk media object on disks formerly being inactive configuration disks (c4t1d0s2). In addition, volume related objects are written to the private region of previously active config disks (c4t2d0s2). VxVM 5.0 does not write any disk group configuration on the disks at this stage, working just with the kernel configuration.

```
# prtvtoc -h /dev/rdsk/c4t1d0s2
      2     5    01      0 35368272  35368271
      7    15    01      0 35368272  35368271
# prtvtoc -h /dev/rdsk/c4t2d0s2
      2     5    01      0 35368272  35368271
      7    15    01      0 35368272  35368271
# /usr/lib/vxvm/diag.d/vxprivutil dumpconfig /dev/rdsk/c4t1d0s2 |
  awk '!/^[ #]/ && NF>0'
VxVM vxconfigdump ERROR V-5-1-624 Error (File block 16): Invalid magic number
```

```
dg    adg
dm    adg01
# /usr/lib/vxvm/diag.d/vxprivutil dumpconfig /dev/rdsk/c4t2d0s2 |
  awk '!/^[ #]/ && NF>0'
dg    adg
dm    adg01
dm    adg02
plex  vol1-01
dm    adg03
sd    adg02-01
sd    adg03-01
vol   vol1
plex  vol1-02
sd    adg01-02
```

As indicated by the output of the command **vxconfigrestore** -p, the disk group configuration must be committed (-c) or discarded (-d). Assuming a proper disk group configuration, we commit it. Redundant volumes are synchronized (even **newvol** once again) in order to ensure data integrity. Any requests to modify synchronization behavior may be achieved by modification of the plex states during the precommit stage (see the examples beginning on page 383).

```
# vxconfigrestore -c 1223834080.19.sols
Committing configuration restoration for diskgroup 1223834080.19.sols ....

1223834080.19.sols's diskgroup configuration restoration is committed.
# vxprint -rtg adg newvol
[...]
v  newvol        -              ENABLED  SYNC    2097152  SELECT   -      fsgen
pl newvol-01     newvol         ENABLED  ACTIVE  2097152  CONCAT   -      RW
sd adg01-01      newvol-01      adg01  0         2097152  0     c4t1d0    ENA
pl newvol-02     newvol         ENABLED  ACTIVE  2097152  CONCAT   -      RW
sd adg02-01      newvol-02      adg02  0         2097152  0     c4t2d0    ENA
# vxtask -g adg list
TASKID  PTID TYPE/STATE   PCT    PROGRESS
   179       RDWRBACK/R 89.06% 0/2097152/1867776 VOLSTART newvol adg
```

11.5.5 RESTORE OF A DESTROYED DISK GROUP

VxVM protects against most erroneous actions destroying volume data. Dissociating a plex (that is, an instance of the volume address space) from its volume will fail, if this plex was the last healthy plex in the volume (unless you specified **vxplex** -o force dis). All the same, you cannot dissociate a subdisk from its plex except by **vxsd** -o force dis. Removing a volume by VxVM interfaces is absolutely impossible as long as the volume attribute **devopen** is set to on (current I/O on raw device or file system mounted).

Nevertheless, it happens from time to time (hopefully not too often) that you destroyed

VxVM objects you wanted or should have wanted to keep. The former sections explained and demonstrated how to recreate them out of configuration files and how to restore a disk group, if their (active configuration) disks were destroyed. Our task now is to provide a way to recover from an inadvertently destroyed disk group configuration.

```
# vxdisk -g adg list
DEVICE      TYPE           DISK       GROUP      STATUS
c1t1d0s2    auto:cdsdisk   adg01      adg        online
c1t1d1s2    auto:cdsdisk   adg02      adg        online
# vxdg destroy adg
# vxdisk -o alldgs list
DEVICE      TYPE           DISK       GROUP      STATUS
[...]
c1t1d0s2    auto:cdsdisk   -          -          online
c1t1d1s2    auto:cdsdisk   -          -          online
[...]
```

Obviously, the disk group has gone, at least for the **vxdisk list** tool. Let's have a closer look to one of the disks formerly belonging to the destroyed disk group.

```
# vxdisk -s list c1t1d0
[...]
diskid:   1223448582.74.haensel
dgname:
dgid:     1223448150.61.haensel
hostid:
info:     format=cdsdisk,privoffset=256,pubslice=2,privslice=2
```

That looks more encouraging than we expected. The disk group name indeed was erased from the disk configuration stored in the private region together with the disk group ownership (field hostid), but the disk group ID providing a unique identification in case of disk group name collisions is still available. In order to determine the amount of disk group configuration data still present, we analyze the content of the private region (converted into a well arranged output format).

```
# /usr/lib/vxvm/diag.d/vxprivutil dumpconfig /dev/rdsk/c1t1d0s2 | vxprint -rtD -
v  vol        -            DISABLED ACTIVE   2097152  SELECT  -    fsgen
pl vol-01     vol          DISABLED ACTIVE   2097152  CONCAT  -    RW
sd adg01-01   vol-01       adg01    0        2097152  0       -    DIS
pl vol-02     vol          DISABLED ACTIVE   2097152  CONCAT  -    RW
sd adg02-01   vol-02       adg02    0        2097152  0       -    DIS
```

A full comparison of the unconverted output with the last disk group configuration stored by vxprint -m would reveal that none of these attributes has gone. Only those two attributes of the **disk configuration** mentioned above are lost: the disk group name and the disk group ownership. Well, that can easily be recreated by importing the disk group using the disk group ID. You do not need to specify the disk group name, for it is automatically taken from the **disk group configuration**.

```
# vxdg import 1223448150.61.haensel
# vxdisk -g adg list
DEVICE        TYPE          DISK      GROUP     STATUS
c1t1d0s2      auto:cdsdisk  adg01     adg       online
c1t1d1s2      auto:cdsdisk  adg02     adg       online
```

To sum up: Identify at least one disk formerly belonging to the destroyed disk group (the disk may not provide an active configuration copy of the disk group). Get the disk group ID from the disk configuration and import the disk group by its ID. That's all!

Did you shiver when reading about the task of disk identification in the previous paragraph? Indeed, this could be extremely complicated if you administer a large environment with numerous disks and if you do not remember the device access of at least one disk. Searching for other locations of stored disk group configuration files, we draw a blank. The disk group configuration copy created by **vxconfigbackupd** under /etc/vx/cbr/bk was removed as a result of the disk group destruction. Only **vxrelocd** and **vxsparecheck** provide an automated configuration backup under /etc/vx/saveconfig.d, which survives even disk group destruction. But very probably, you will not get a disk outage ready at hand to get the necessary backup file created in order to manage an inadvertent disk group destruction.

We provide a dirty procedure to map the disk group name to its disk group ID and to identify a disk formerly belonging to the destroyed disk group – dirty, for it is undocumented. A file named after the disk group in a subdirectory of /var, designed to store the temporary utility attribute values to tutil0, tutil1, and tutil2, has kept information on object names even of the destroyed disk group. The content is, however, somewhat coded, but fortunately, Unix provides valuable tools to filter printable characters:

```
# file /var/vxvm/tempdb/adg
/var/vxvm/tempdb/adg:   data
# strings -n 3 /var/vxvm/tempdb/adg | grep -v VBLK
VMDB
adg
1223448150.61.haensel
adg
adg01
adg02
adg01-01
adg02-01
vol
vol-01
vol-02
```

The line containing the disk group name is immediately followed by the specification of the disk group ID. Our task, the mapping of the disk group name to its ID, was successful.

As a procedure of last resort, you must analyze all available disks obviously not belonging to an active disk group. Check for the existence and value of the disk group ID stored in the disk configuration part of the private region and filter from the disk group configuration part the name of the disk group. We provide a short ksh script displaying device access name, disk group name, and disk group ID for all appropriate disks. The device access name may be helpful in case of multiple instances of a disk group name (same name, but different disk group IDs).

```
# List all disks being no disk group member and print device access
vxdisk -qo alldgs list | awk '$4=="-" {print $1}' |
while read daname; do
    # Get disk group ID, if any
    DGID=$(vxdisk -s list $daname | awk '$1=="dgid:" && NF==2 {print $2}')
    # Next disk, if no disk group ID
    [[ -z $DGID ]] && continue
    # Print device access
    printf '%-12s ' $daname
    # Dump disk group configuration of disk's private region
    /usr/lib/vxvm/diag.d/vxprivutil dumpconfig /dev/vx/rdmp/$daname |
    # Filter name and disk group ID from disk group object
    vxprint -D - -GF '%{name:-12} %dgid'
done
```

An example output of two destroyed disk groups:

```
c1t1d0s2    adg       1223278682.30.haensel
c1t1d1s2    adg       1223278682.30.haensel
c1t1d2s2    adg       1223278682.30.haensel
c1t1d3s2    adg       1223278682.30.haensel
c1t1d4s2    bdg       1223278792.32.haensel
c1t1d5s2    bdg       1223278792.32.haensel
```

11.5.6 SERIAL SPLIT BRAIN OF A DISK GROUP

In general, it is a good idea to mirror your volumes across two (or more) separated locations, for all volumes go on to provide data access in case of a data center outage. It is also a good idea to improve the availability of your applications by putting them under control of a clustering software (a "campus cluster").

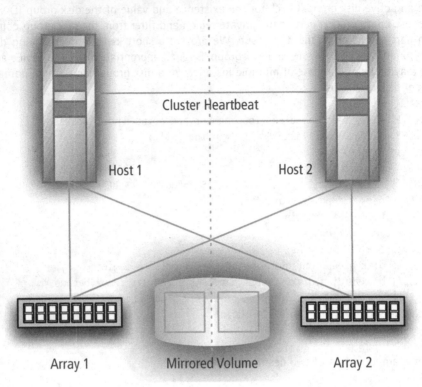

Figure 11-3: A Mirrored Volume in a Campus Cluster

Nevertheless, this architecture includes a new problem in case of a network partition: Each cluster host believes being the only surviving cluster node, thus starting all those applications that were (and still are) running on the other node. We enter the world of the dreaded cluster split brain. Loss of application data consistency is now a matter of seconds.

However, our current topic is not application data consistency. As long as no disk group configuration changes are performed, the disk group remains consistent across all nodes. But what happens if both nodes modify the disk group? Then, no modified version can be considered the current one by VxVM, administrator intervention is required. The VxVM documentation calls this scenario a "Serial Split Brain" (SSB). Our example below will simulate it by a sequential removal of the private region content from both disks of a disk group.

1.   The disk group configuration contains a simple volume mirrored across both disks of the disk group.

```
# vxprint -rtg adg
[...]
```

```
dm adg01       c4t1d0s2      auto      2048     35365968  -
dm adg02       c4t2d0s2      auto      2048     35365968  -

v  vol         -             ENABLED   ACTIVE   2097152   SELECT    -         fsgen
pl vol-01      vol           ENABLED   ACTIVE   2097152   CONCAT    -         RW
sd adg01-01    vol-01        adg01     0        2097152   0         c4t1d0    ENA
pl vol-02      vol           ENABLED   ACTIVE   2097152   CONCAT    -         RW
sd adg02-01    vol-02        adg02     0        2097152   0         c4t2d0    ENA
```

2. We store the private region content of the first disk and clear it afterwards. In order to inform the kernel on the damaged disk state, we deport and forcibly re-import the disk group. Finally, we modify the disk group configuration by adding a new volume.

```
# dd if=/dev/rdsk/c4t1d0s2 of=/var/tmp/c4t1d0s2 bs=128k iseek=1 count=8
# dd if=/dev/zero of=/dev/rdsk/c4t1d0s2 bs=128k oseek=1 count=8
# vxdg deport adg
# vxdg -f import adg
VxVM vxdg WARNING V-5-1-560 Disk adg01: Not found, last known location: c4t1d0s2
# vxassist -g adg make newvol 1g
```

3. The following commands simulate the view on the disk group from another cluster node: The disk group is deported, its previous configuration restored on the first disk, while the second disk's private region is temporarily overwritten. A forced re-import indeed shows the old configuration (unlike a real cluster scenario, the volume is DISABLED due to the re-import). Once again, we modify the disk group by adding a volume.

```
# vxdg deport adg
# dd if=/var/tmp/c4t1d0s2 of=/dev/rdsk/c4t1d0s2 bs=128k oseek=1
# dd if=/dev/rdsk/c4t2d0s2 of=/var/tmp/c4t2d0s2 bs=128k iseek=1 count=8
# dd if=/dev/zero of=/dev/rdsk/c4t2d0s2 bs=128k oseek=1 count=8
# vxdg -f import adg
VxVM vxdg WARNING V-5-1-560 Disk adg02: Not found, last known location: c4t2d0s2
# vxprint -rtg adg
[...]
```

```
dm adg01       c4t1d0s2      auto      2048     35365968  -
dm adg02       -             -         -        -         NODEVICE

v  vol         -             DISABLED  ACTIVE   2097152   SELECT    -         fsgen
pl vol-01      vol           DISABLED  ACTIVE   2097152   CONCAT    -         RW
sd adg01-01    vol-01        adg01     0        2097152   0         c4t1d0    ENA
pl vol-02      vol           DISABLED  NODEVICE 2097152   CONCAT    -         RW
sd adg02-01    vol-02        adg02     0        2097152   0         -         NDEV
# vxassist -g adg make newvol 1g
```

4. Any clean-up procedure should start by stopping the application and deporting the disk group in order to discard any locally stored data and configurations. Regarding the disk group configuration, our simulation needs to recreate the private region content

on the second disk. Currently, no configuration copy may be interpreted as a newer version compared to the other one. VxVM should not and indeed will not decide in favor of one copy, when detecting the "Serial Split Brain" by trying to import the disk group.

```
# vxdg deport adg
# dd if=/var/tmp/c4t2d0s2 of=/dev/rdsk/c4t2d0s2 bs=128k oseek=1
# vxdg import adg
VxVM vxdg ERROR V-5-1-587 Disk group adg: import failed: Serial Split Brain
detected. Run vxsplitlines
```

5.   We observe the recommendation of the last command output. **vxsplitlines** informs us about different configuration copies, where they are stored, how to access them in order to decide for one copy (**vxprivutil dumpconfig**), and how to restore the disk group based on our copy selection (**vxdg -o selectcp=1223115776.23.sols import**). The copy selection is based on the disk ID assigned by VxVM during disk initialization.

```
# vxsplitlines -g adg
   VxVM vxsplitlines NOTICE V-5-2-2708 There are 2 pools.
The Following are the disks in each pool. Each disk in the same pool
has config copies that are similar.
   VxVM vxsplitlines INFO V-5-2-2707 Pool 0.
c4t2d0s2 adg02
To see the configuration copy from this disk issue
/etc/vx/diag.d/vxprivutil dumpconfig /dev/vx/dmp/c4t2d0s2
To import the diskgroup with config copy from this
disk use the following command
/usr/sbin/vxdg -o selectcp=1223115776.23.sols import adg
The following are the disks whose ssb ids don't match in this config
copy
adg01

   VxVM vxsplitlines INFO V-5-2-2707 Pool 1.
c4t1d0s2 adg01
To see the configuration copy from this disk issue
/etc/vx/diag.d/vxprivutil dumpconfig /dev/vx/dmp/c4t1d0s2
To import the diskgroup with config copy from this
disk use the following command
/usr/sbin/vxdg -o selectcp=1223014683.15.sols import adg
The following are the disks whose ssb ids don't match in this config
copy
adg02
```

6.   We analyze the content of the private regions on the disks (using the DMP drivers). The default output format of **vxprivutil dumpconfig** is similar to the output generated by **vxprint -m** (except for comments on device blocks). Mostly, we do not need to check so many details of the disk group. Therefore, at least for demonstration purposes on commands working neatly together, we pipe the output into a reformatting **vxprint** com-

mand. Indeed, the subdisk location of newvol differs, as emphasized in the output.

```
# /etc/vx/diag.d/vxprivutil dumpconfig /dev/vx/dmp/c4t1d0s2 | vxprint -rtD -
Disk group: adg
[...]
v  vol          -              DISABLED ACTIVE  2097152 SELECT    -        fsgen
pl vol-01       vol            DISABLED ACTIVE  2097152 CONCAT    -        RW
sd adg01-01     vol-01         adg01    0       2097152 0         -        DIS
pl vol-02       vol            DISABLED ACTIVE  2097152 CONCAT    -        RW
sd adg02-01     vol-02         adg02    0       2097152 0         -        DIS

v  newvol       -              DISABLED ACTIVE  2097152 SELECT    -        fsgen
pl newvol-01    newvol         DISABLED ACTIVE  2097152 CONCAT    -        RW
sd adg01-02     newvol-01      adg01    2097152 2097152 0         -        DIS
# /etc/vx/diag.d/vxprivutil dumpconfig /dev/vx/dmp/c4t2d0s2 | vxprint -rtD -
Disk group: adg
[...]
v  vol          -              DISABLED ACTIVE  2097152 SELECT    -        fsgen
pl vol-01       vol            DISABLED ACTIVE  2097152 CONCAT    -        RW
sd adg01-01     vol-01         adg01    0       2097152 0         -        DIS
pl vol-02       vol            DISABLED ACTIVE  2097152 CONCAT    -        RW
sd adg02-01     vol-02         adg02    0       2097152 0         -        DIS

v  newvol       -              DISABLED ACTIVE  2097152 SELECT    -        fsgen
pl newvol-01    newvol         DISABLED ACTIVE  2097152 CONCAT    -        RW
sd adg02-02     newvol-01      adg02    2097152 2097152 0         -        DIS
```

7. Just to make sure, that the command output of vxsplitlines identified the disks properly, we compare it to the disk IDs. Then, we import the disk group based on our selected disk group configuration copy (newvol's subdisk on disk adg01).

```
# vxdisk -s list c4t1d0
[...]
diskid: 1223014683.15.sols
[...]
# vxdisk -s list c4t2d0
[...]
diskid: 1223115776.23.sols
[...]
# vxdg -o selectcp=1223014683.15.sols import adg
```

8. Being somewhat distrustful given our experience with software products for many years, we check for the result and perform a detailed comparison of the physical contents of the private region copies. Hooray, they are indeed identical regarding the disk group configuration!

```
# vxprint -rtg adg
```

```
[...]
dm adg01        c4t1d0s2      auto     2048     35365968 -
dm adg02        c4t2d0s2      auto     2048     35365968 -

v  vol          -             DISABLED ACTIVE   2097152 SELECT  -        fsgen
pl vol-01       vol           DISABLED ACTIVE   2097152 CONCAT  -        RW
sd adg01-01     vol-01        adg01    0        2097152 0       c4t1d0   ENA
pl vol-02       vol           DISABLED ACTIVE   2097152 CONCAT  -        RW
sd adg02-01     vol-02        adg02    0        2097152 0       c4t2d0   ENA

v  vola         -             DISABLED ACTIVE   2097152 SELECT  -        fsgen
pl vola-01      vola          DISABLED ACTIVE   2097152 CONCAT  -        RW
sd adg01-02     vola-01       adg01    2097152  2097152 0       c4t1d0   ENA
# /etc/vx/diag.d/vxprivutil dumpconfig /dev/vx/dmp/c4t1d0s2 > /tmp/c4t1
# /etc/vx/diag.d/vxprivutil dumpconfig /dev/vx/dmp/c4t2d0s2 > /tmp/c4t2
# diff /tmp/c4t[12]        (no output, i.e. no difference)
```

11.6 Booting without VxVM

A heavily corrupted VxVM installation could lead to an unbootable system. At least two steps within the boot process could fail.

1. Kernel initialization and configuration are based on the root device. The root device is the Open Boot Prom device providing access to the physical partition that holds the root file system. The root file system may not be a unique device, your system naturally provides in most cases two or more, because mostly you have mirrored your OS devices. But even one instance of the root file system may be accessed by different drivers.

By the Open Boot Prom disk driver:

```
/ssm@0,0/pci@18,700000/pci@1/scsi@2/disk@2,0:a
```

As a pseudo device, by the VxVM kernel module responsible for the conversion of application I/O requests into disk I/Os:

```
/pseudo/vxio@0:0
```

Without a `rootdev` entry in the `/etc/system` file, the boot device (such as `/ssm@0,0/pci@18,700000/pci@1/scsi@2/disk@2,0:a`) automatically serves as root device (by default, `/etc/system` under Solaris only contains comments). For the need to start VxVM step by step, already the root device must be redirected to the VxVM kernel module `vxio`. Therefore, a working boot process based on VxVM needs two active lines in the file `/etc/system`:

```
rootdev:/pseudo/vxio@0:0
set vxio:vol_rootdev_is_volume=1
```

The latter line sets a memory flag indicating to create a virtual volume on the root device (vol_rootdev_is_volume is a symbolic memory address name). If you like kernel panics in an early stage of the boot process, just feel free to corrupt any of these two lines. But if both lines are missing, the boot process chooses the boot device as the root device, thus building and configuring the kernel based on the standard disk driver.

2.   Even if the file /etc/system does not contain the required entries for a VxVM encapsulated OS disk, so that a partition based boot process is initiated, we must deal with another barrier: The file /etc/vfstab still contains volume drivers. Quite early in the single user mode/milestone, the required OS file systems /, /usr, and /var are mounted or remounted in read-write mode based on the entries in /etc/vfstab. But the volume drivers specified in this file will fail in case of a corrupted VxVM installation. Therefore, we need a file version containing partition drivers.

In order to be well prepared for the recovery of a completely corrupted VxVM installation, any bootable disk should contain a partition bootable and a volume bootable version of /etc/system and /etc/vfstab in addition to the active files. Quite simple for /etc/system:

```
# cp /etc/system /etc/system.vol
# cp /etc/system /etc/system.part
# vi /etc/system.part    (commented out by asterisk followed by space or completely erased)
[...]
* rootdev:/pseudo/vxio@0:0
* set vxio:vol_rootdev_is_volume=1
[...]
```

Creating a partition based /etc/vfstab for each bootable disk is a lot more complicated. We need a mapping of the mount points to the numbers of the partitions covering the subdisks of our OS volumes on our disks. Actually, we will settle for the volume names, assuming that they correspond to the default names (rootvol mounted on /, swapvol for the swap device, <volume> mounted on */<volume>). An approach step by step! The subdisk offsets are calculated against the beginning of the public region (do not be alarmed by the ghost subdisk osdg01-B0, we will take it in mind):

```
# vxprint -g bootdg -sF '%name %dm_offset'
osdg01-B0 78083039
osdg01-01 0
osdg01-02 4198319
[...]
```

On the other side, the partition offsets are calculated against the beginning of the disk.

```
# prtvtoc -h /dev/rdsk/c0t0d0s2
    0    2    00    4198320   12586800   16785119
    1    3    01          0    4198320    4198319
    2    5    00          0   78156480   78156479
```

[...]

Therefore, the subdisk offsets plus the offset of the public region on the disk will result in the partition offsets. Where do we get the public region offset from?

```
# vxdisk list c0t0d0s2 | nawk '$1=="public:"'
public:    slice=3 offset=1 len=78083040 disk_offset=0
```

In the output above, `disk_offset` specifies the offset of the public region **as partition** relative to the disk beginning, while `offset` denotes the offset of the public region **as subdisk container** relative to the beginning of the public region **as partition**. So, we must add `offset` and `disk_offset` to the subdisk offsets in order to get the subdisk offsets relative to the disk beginning which are, of course, identical to the partition offsets. We erase the key words together with their equal sign from the output above and add the resulting third to the fifth word to get the public region offset **as subdisk container** to the beginning of the disk:

```
# vxdisk list c0t0d0s2 |
  nawk '$1=="public:" {gsub(/[^ =]+=/,""); print $3+$5}'
1
```

Just one exception: If a partition starts at sector 0, it contains the VTOC at the beginning. To protect the VTOC, the public region starting at sector 0 **as partition** gets an `offset` of one sector **as subdisk container** (see the Encapsulation chapter, page 330). Our calculation above would produce a negative value (-1) for the corresponding subdisk. In that case, we modify the value to 0 and fix the miscalculation due to the ghost subdisk. Here is our script with some comments, but without error checking:

```
# vi map_vol_part
#!/bin/ksh
# c#t#d#s2 syntax is required
Disk=$1

# Get disk offset of public region as subdisk container
PubRegOffset=$(vxdisk list $Disk |
nawk '$1=="public:"{gsub(/[^ =]+=/,""); print $3+$5}')

prtvtoc -h /dev/rdsk/$Disk |
# Skip backup, private and public region partition
nawk '$2!=5 && $2!=14 && $2!=15 {print $1,$4}' |
while read Slice DiskOffset; do
    ((SubdiskOffset=DiskOffset-PubRegOffset))
    # Handle VTOC protection by ghost subdisk
    ((SubdiskOffset==-1)) && ((SubdiskOffset=0))
    # Get plexes to the corresponding subdisks on the disk
    # and print associated volume name
    Volume=$(vxprint -g bootdg -pF %assoc -e \
```

```
    "pl_sd.sd_dm_offset=$SubdiskOffset && pl_sd.sd_da_name=\"$Disk\"")
    printf '%-12s %s\n' $Volume $Slice
done
# chmod 744 map_vol_part
# ./map_vol_part c0t0d0s2
rootvol      0
swapvol      1
var          5
opt          6
# ./map_vol_part c0t2d0s2
rootvol      0
swapvol      1
opt          5
var          6
```

Finally, we got the data required to create vfstabs for each bootable disk. Look at the example based on Solaris 9 (Solaris 10 adds three more lines for /devices, ctfs, and objfs):

```
# vi /etc/vfstab.c0t0d0s2
```

#device	device	mount	FS	fsck	mount	mount
#to mount	to fsck	point	type	pass	at boot	options
fd	-	/dev/fd	fd	-	no	-
/proc	-	/proc	proc	-	no	-
swap	-	/tmp	tmpfs	-	yes	-
/dev/dsk/c0t0d0s0	/dev/rdsk/c0t0d0s0	/	ufs	1	no	logging
/dev/dsk/c0t0d0s1	-	-	swap	-	no	-
/dev/dsk/c0t0d0s5	/dev/rdsk/c0t0d0s5	/var	ufs	1	no	logging
/dev/dsk/c0t0d0s6	/dev/rdsk/c0t0d0s6	/opt	ufs	1	yes	logging

Be sure to create vfstabs for ALL your bootable disks in order to be prepared for an unexpected system-wide VxVM failure. Did you ever use the vi editor at an early stage of the single user mode/milestone without a /tmp device, thus only with single line editing capabilities? Well, then you will appreciate our hints:

```
# cp /etc/vfstab /etc/vfstab.vol
# vi /etc/vfstab.c0t0d0s2
[...]
# vi /etc/vfstab.c0t2d0s2
[...]
```

Since we are now prepared for the worst (a Solaris system without working VxVM), let's test the procedure to boot for once based on partitions. Our VxVM disaster simulation is created by renaming the basic kernel module vxio.

```
# mv /kernel/drv/sparcv9/vxio /kernel/drv/sparcv9/vxio.renamed
```

A regular reboot will fail due to the wrong files /etc/system and /etc/vfstab, as explained above. We could easily copy the proper files before rebooting, but this would not fit to an unexpected VxVM disaster. Therefore, without any system reconfiguration, we shut down our system to the Open Boot Prom.

```
# init 0          (or halt)
```

The Open Boot Prom provides a mechanism to boot from alternate devices and kernel configurations. That's exactly what we need: a kernel configuration based on a different /etc/system (still not part of the OBP device tree, therefore without leading slash below). Other requested parameter defaults simply require confirmation. Further on, we just enter the single user mode/milestone, skipping even the execution of its run-level scripts, for our basic VxVM kernel module is corrupted.

```
ok boot -ab
Boot device: /pci@1f,0/ide@d/disk@0,0:a  File and args: -ab
Enter filename [kernel/sparcv9/unix]: enter
Enter default directory for modules [/platform/SUNW,Sun-Blade-100/kernel /plat-
form/sun4u/kernel /kernel /usr/kernel]: enter
Name of system file [etc/system]: etc/system.part
SunOS Release 5.10 Version Generic_118833-36 64-bit
Copyright 1983-2006 Sun Microsystems, Inc.  All rights reserved.
Use is subject to license terms.
root file system type [ufs]: enter
Enter physical name of root device
[/pci@1f,0/ide@d/disk@0,0:a]: enter
[…]
Root password for system maintenance (control-d to bypass): password
```

In order to activate the partition based files /etc/system and /etc/vfstab, our root file system must be remounted to achieve read-write access. A proper key table alleviates this task. Since it is of no use to execute the VxVM run-level scripts during the following reboot, we create a touch file designed to skip them.

```
# loadkeys
# awk '$3=="/"' /etc/vfstab.c0t0d0s2
/dev/dsk/c0t0d0s0   /dev/rdsk/c0t0d0s0   /        ufs    1    no        logging
# mount -F ufs -o remount /dev/dsk/c0t0d0s0 /
# cp /etc/system.part /etc/system
# cp /etc/vfstab.c0t0d0s2 /etc/vfstab
# touch /etc/vx/reconfig.d/state.d/install-db
# reboot
```

Our system now boots without the need for interaction based on partitions of the disk c0t0d0s2 (our example). It is deadly important to keep in mind that our copy and touch actions, the succeeding boot process, and our VxVM repair modified the OS file systems only on c0t0d0s2, without the knowledge of VxVM. Therefore, the OS mirrors are now out of sync. But the last known states of the corresponding plexes stored within the private region are ACTIVE, signifying that the mirrors are coherent. By all means, before performing a volume based boot, we must tell VxVM that the plex mirrors on the other OS disk(s) are stale (see the repairing commands below). Otherwise, the default read policy SELECTED, which means ROUND ROBIN given our simple plex layouts, leads to inconsistent and unpredictable results, to a system unable to work properly.

```
# cp /etc/system.vol /etc/system
# cp /etc/vfstab.vol /etc/vfstab
# rm /etc/vx/reconfig.d/state.d/install-db
# mv /kernel/drv/sparcv9/vxio.renamed /kernel/drv/sparcv9/vxio
# vxconfigd -m boot
# PlexList=$(vxprint -g bootdg -pne 'pl_sd.sd_daname!="c0t0d0s2"')
# vxmend -g bootdg off $PlexList
# vxmend -g bootdg on $PlexList
# vxprint -rtg bootdg
[...]
v  rootvol      -           ENABLED  ACTIVE  12586800 ROUND   -        root
pl rootvol-01   rootvol     ENABLED  ACTIVE  12586800 CONCAT  -        RW
sd osdg01-02    rootvol-01  osdg01   4198319 12586800 0       c0t0d0   ENA
pl rootvol-02   rootvol     DISABLED STALE   12586800 CONCAT  -        RW
sd osdg02-03    rootvol-02  osdg02   29367840 12586800 0      c0t2d0   ENA
[...]
# reboot
```

The reboot process will be based upon volumes and start plex synchronization in the background. Fortunately and finally!

Technical Deep Dive

11.7 MORE THAN TWO OS MIRRORS: EMERGENCY DISK

Sometimes it may be desirable to supply OS or application volumes with a third mirror, e.g. to achieve even higher redundancy or an increased read performance due to the usual round robin read policy. But to mention the most important reason for a third plex (in a special state) within OS or application volumes, mirroring data does not protect against some awful data destroying errors. Some examples: You issue the dreaded `rm -r *` command within the wrong directory, the database did not survive a test run with imported data, an OS "patch" made our system unbootable, and so on.

We focus on the procedure to protect OS volumes by adding a third plex in order to form an emergency boot disk. The emergency disk must hold a bootable OS image which is not updated by every I/O, but only in intervals decided by the administrator (manually or automated). How can we create a third OS mirror? The answer seems quite simple: by the same way we did it for the second OS mirror. Indeed? Let's try it!

1.   We initialize a new disk and add it to the boot disk group:

```
# vxdisksetup -i c0t4d0 format=sliced privlen=1m
# vxdg -g osdg adddisk osdg03=c0t4d0
# vxdisk -g osdg list
DEVICE        TYPE          DISK        GROUP        STATUS
c0t2d0s2      auto:sliced   osdg01      osdg         online
c0t3d0s2      auto:sliced   osdg02      osdg         online
c0t4d0s2      auto:sliced   osdg03      osdg         online
```

2.   We try to add mirrors by the usual `vxmirror` command:

```
# vxmirror -g osdg osdg01 osdg03
VxVM vxmirror ERROR V-5-2-3604 No non-redundant volumes to mirror
```

Oops! The main purpose of `vxmirror` was (and still is) to mirror non-redundant volumes. Mirroring OS volumes is just a special subtask. But all our volumes are still mirrored. We need another procedure.

3.   We create the third mirrors using the `vxassist` command, thus avoiding the mirror check mechanisms of the `vxmirror` script. First, we need a list of OS volumes, but only of top-level volumes, not of subvolumes, DCL volumes, or cache volumes. Unfortunately, the development of attributes to the `-e` option of `vxprint` often lags behind the implementation of new object attributes: The volume attribute **layered**, introduced by VxVM 3.0 long

ago, was not activated for -e until VxVM 5.0 in the usual manner (v_layered). The attribute iscachevol, belonging to space optimized snapshots starting with VxVM 4.0, is still not implemented for -e. Therefore, make sure by an advanced volume analysis you only mirror the correct volumes. The first of the following commands, being compatible to VxVM 4.x, just skips DCL volumes (you won't expect subvolumes and snapshot cache volumes on OS disks, will you?), the second one subvolumes as well.

```
# vxprint -g osdg -vne 'v_isdcolog=off'
opt
rootvol
swapvol
var
# vxprint -g osdg -vne 'v_isdcolog=off && v_layered=off'
opt
rootvol
swapvol
var
```

4. Taking this output or a partially reduced list of volumes, we write a simple Shell loop to add another mirror to the volumes:

```
# for vol in $(vxprint -g osdg -vne 'v_isdcolog=off && v_layered=off'); do
  vxassist -g osdg mirror $vol osdg03; done
```

Mirroring rootvol carrying usage type root automatically creates a partition number 0 over the mirror subdisk and enters a new OBP alias definition for the new disk:

```
# prtvtoc -h /dev/rdsk/c0t4d0s2
    0     2    00   2110976  16812416  18923391
    2     5    00         0  35368272  35368271
    3    15    01         0      9424      9423
    4    14    01      9424  35358848  35368271
# eeprom nvramrc
devalias vx-osdg01 /ssm@0,0/pci@18,700000/pci@1/scsi@2/disk@2,0:a
devalias vx-osdg02 /ssm@0,0/pci@18,700000/pci@1/scsi@2/disk@3,0:a
devalias vx-osdg03 /ssm@0,0/pci@18,700000/pci@1/scsi@2/disk@4,0:a
```

5. We still need partitions over the remaining OS volumes and, in case of a damaged boot block within the rootvol, the installboot command to recreate it. These tasks are best performed by the vxbootsetup script. A hint for deep-sea divers: VxVM also provides some interesting low-level commands executed by vxbootsetup: vxpartadd, vxedvtoc, vxmksdpart, and vxeeprom.

```
# vxbootsetup -g osdg osdg03
# prtvtoc -h /dev/rdsk/c0t4d0s2
    0     2    00   2110976  16812416  18923391
    1     3    01      9424   2101552   2110975
```

```
2      5    00        0  35368272  35368271
3     15    01        0      9424      9423
4     14    01     9424  35358848  35368271
5      0    00  25218624   8392072  33610695
6      7    00  18923392   6295232  25218623
```

6. The OBP attribute `boot-device` should be extended by an entry for the new OS disk:

```
# eeprom boot-device
boot-device=vx-osdg01 vx-osdg02 disk net
# eeprom boot-device='vx-osdg01 vx-osdg02 vx-osdg03 disk net'
# eeprom boot-device
boot-device=vx-osdg01 vx-osdg02 vx-osdg03 disk net
```

Note: Whenever issuing a `vxbootsetup` command on an OS disk, make sure beforehand, `rootvol` already furnished with partition 0 by the `vxassist mirror` command still keeps this partition association, and partition 1 designed to become the swap partition is still unused. Otherwise the `vxbootsetup` command will fail.

7. Our preparatory tasks created a third mirror still as a current and active part of the OS volumes. Inadvertent commands would remove, destroy or invalidate data on all three mirrors. We need a frozen copy of the current data, but nevertheless capable to boot from and to recover the volume to the frozen data set. We already discussed thoroughly several techniques provided by VxVM to establish a snapshot of a volume in chapter 9. The current chapter demonstrates another way to handle a bootable snapshot based on a procedure specific to OS volumes: They provide two independent drivers accessing the same data set, the volume and the partition driver.

In order to minimize plex operations, our procedure simply offlines the plexes holding the frozen data set.

```
# vxprint -g osdg -pne 'pl_sd.sd_dmname="osdg03"'
opt-03
rootvol-03
swapvol-03
var-03
# vxmend -g osdg off $(vxprint -g osdg -pne 'pl_sd.sd_dmname="osdg03"')
# vxprint -g osdg -pthe 'pl_sd.sd_dmname="osdg03"'
PL NAME        VOLUME      KSTATE    STATE     LENGTH   LAYOUT     NCOL/WID MODE
SD NAME        PLEX        DISK      DISKOFFS  LENGTH   [COL/]OFF  DEVICE   MODE
SV NAME        PLEX        VOLNAME   NVOLLAYR  LENGTH   [COL/]OFF  AM/NM    MODE
SC NAME        PLEX        CACHE     DISKOFFS  LENGTH   [COL/]OFF  DEVICE   MODE

pl opt-03      opt         DISABLED OFFLINE  8392072   CONCAT     -        RW
sd osdg03-04   opt-03      osdg03    25209200 8392072  0          c0t4d0   ENA

pl rootvol-03  rootvol     DISABLED OFFLINE  16812416  CONCAT     -        RW
```

```
sd osdg03-02    rootvol-03    osdg03    2101552   16812416 0            c0t4d0   ENA

pl swapvol-03   swapvol       DISABLED OFFLINE   2101552  CONCAT   -     RW
sd osdg03-01    swapvol-03    osdg03    0         2101552  0            c0t4d0   ENA

pl var-03       var           DISABLED OFFLINE   6295232  CONCAT   -     RW
sd osdg03-03    var-03        osdg03    18913968  6295232  0            c0t4d0   ENA
```

8.   But how is it possible to boot from the emergency disk which provides the frozen
copies of the OS volumes? We already implemented some of the prerequisites by invoking vxbootsetup (step 5 above): We put partitions over the subdisks, we re-installed as
a fallback the boot block on the root partition, and we created an OBP alias. Obviously,
it is useless to perform a VxVM based boot, for the plexes determining the frozen data
set are offlined. But we still have the partition drivers to the emergency disk, obstinately
and unteachable ignoring any plex states. Booting from the emergency disk exclusively
by the partition drivers require a modified kernel configuration file /etc/system to skip
root volume mapping on the root partition during kernel initialization and, what is more,
/etc/vfstab containing partition, not volume drivers.

Our first step will map the subdisks to their corresponding partition numbers in order
to create the correct /etc/vfstab. The basics and the procedures were already explained
in the "Full Battleship" part beginning on page 352, so we simply refer to them. Our file
/etc/vfstab for the emergency disk will contain the following entries instead of the volume drivers:

```
/dev/dsk/c0t4d0s0    /dev/rdsk/c0t4d0s0    /       ufs    1    no     logging
/dev/dsk/c0t4d0s1    -                     -       swap   -    no     -
/dev/dsk/c0t4d0s5    /dev/rdsk/c0t4d0s5    /opt    ufs    1    yes    logging
/dev/dsk/c0t4d0s6    /dev/rdsk/c0t4d0s6    /var    ufs    1    no     logging
```

9.   We offlined the emergency plexes while the OS was running, naturally. A file system check is required before mounting them. Then, we are able to modify /etc/system and
/etc/vfstab only on the emergency partition. As described in the section about booting
without VxVM beginning on page 406, we copy the versions of these files which allow a
partition boot to the active location.

```
# fsck -y /dev/rdsk/c0t4d0s0
** /dev/rdsk/c0t4d0s0
** Last Mounted on /
** Phase 1 - Check Blocks and Sizes
** Phase 2 - Check Pathnames
** Phase 3a - Check Connectivity
** Phase 3b - Verify Shadows/ACLs
** Phase 4 - Check Reference Counts
** Phase 5 - Check Cylinder Groups
211337 files, 5712887 used, 2541378 free (92722 frags, 306082 blocks, 1.1% frag-
mentation)
# fsck -y /dev/rdsk/c0t4d0s5
```

```
** /dev/rdsk/c0t4d0s5
** Last Mounted on /opt
[…]
# fsck -y /dev/rdsk/c0t4d0s6
** /dev/rdsk/c0t4d0s6
** Last Mounted on /var
[…]
# mount /dev/dsk/c0t4d0s0 /mnt
# cd /mnt/etc
# cp system.part system
# cp vfstab.c0t4d0s2 vfstab
# cd /
# umount /mnt
```

10.   Assume the current OS does not work anymore or has lost critical files. Therefore, we must boot from the emergency disk based on partitions. Nevertheless, the system startup procedure will start VxVM daemons as well. Quite correct, for we want to synchronize the damaged parts of the OS volumes from the offlined emergency plexes! Since our system afterwards should run on volumes, not on partitions, we reboot just to the single user mode/milestone based on partitions to swap the role of the data sets. The current section uses /sbin/sh syntax in order to conform to boot process recommendations.

```
# reboot vx-osdg03 -s
[…]
Rebooting with command: boot vx-osdg03 -s
[…]
Booting to milestone "milestone/single-user:default".
[…]
VxVM sysboot INFO V-5-2-3409 starting in boot mode...
[…]
VxVM sysboot INFO V-5-2-3390 Starting restore daemon...
Requesting System Maintenance Mode
SINGLE USER MODE

Root password for system maintenance (control-d to bypass): password
# df -k / /var
Filesystem            kbytes     used    avail capacity  Mounted on
/dev/dsk/c0t4d0s0    8262473  5729317  2450532    71%    /
/dev/dsk/c0t4d0s6    3099238  1269603  1767651    42%    /var
# vxprint -rtg osdg rootvol
[…]
v  rootvol     -              ENABLED  ACTIVE   16812416 ROUND    -       root
pl rootvol-01  rootvol        ENABLED  ACTIVE   16812416 CONCAT   -       RW
sd osdg01-02   rootvol-01     osdg01   2101551  16812416 0        c0t2d0  ENA
pl rootvol-02  rootvol        ENABLED  ACTIVE   16812416 CONCAT   -       RW
sd osdg02-02   rootvol-02     osdg02   2101552  16812416 0        c0t3d0  ENA
pl rootvol-03  rootvol        DISABLED OFFLINE  16812416 CONCAT   -       RW
```

416

```
sd osdg03-02    rootvol-03    osdg03    2101552 16812416 0         c0t4d0    ENA
# vxvol -g osdg stopall
# vxprint -rtg osdg rootvol
[...]
v  rootvol      -             DISABLED CLEAN   16812416 ROUND    -         root
pl rootvol-01   rootvol       DISABLED CLEAN   16812416 CONCAT   -         RW
sd osdg01-02    rootvol-01    osdg01    2101551 16812416 0         c0t2d0    ENA
pl rootvol-02   rootvol       DISABLED CLEAN   16812416 CONCAT   -         RW
sd osdg02-02    rootvol-02    osdg02    2101552 16812416 0         c0t3d0    ENA
pl rootvol-03   rootvol       DISABLED OFFLINE 16812416 CONCAT   -         RW
sd osdg03-02    rootvol-03    osdg03    2101552 16812416 0         c0t4d0    ENA
# vxprint -g osdg -pne 'pl_sd.sd_dmname~/^osdg0[12]$/'
opt-01
opt-02
rootvol-01
rootvol-02
swapvol-01
swapvol-02
var-01
var-02
# vxmend -g osdg -o force off `
  vxprint -g osdg -pne 'pl_sd.sd_dmname~/^osdg0[12]$/'`
# vxmend -g osdg on `
  vxprint -g osdg -pne 'pl_sd.sd_dmname="osdg03"'`
# vxprint -rtg osdg rootvol
[...]
v  rootvol      -             DISABLED CLEAN   16812416 ROUND    -         root
pl rootvol-01   rootvol       DISABLED OFFLINE 16812416 CONCAT   -         RW
sd osdg01-02    rootvol-01    osdg01    2101551 16812416 0         c0t2d0    ENA
pl rootvol-02   rootvol       DISABLED OFFLINE 16812416 CONCAT   -         RW
sd osdg02-02    rootvol-02    osdg02    2101552 16812416 0         c0t3d0    ENA
pl rootvol-03   rootvol       DISABLED STALE   16812416 CONCAT   -         RW
sd osdg03-02    rootvol-03    osdg03    2101552 16812416 0         c0t4d0    ENA
# vxmend -g osdg fix clean `
  vxprint -g osdg -pne 'pl_sd.sd_dmname="osdg03"'`
# vxprint -rtg osdg rootvol
[...]
v  rootvol      -             DISABLED CLEAN   16812416 ROUND    -         root
pl rootvol-01   rootvol       DISABLED OFFLINE 16812416 CONCAT   -         RW
sd osdg01-02    rootvol-01    osdg01    2101551 16812416 0         c0t2d0    ENA
pl rootvol-02   rootvol       DISABLED OFFLINE 16812416 CONCAT   -         RW
sd osdg02-02    rootvol-02    osdg02    2101552 16812416 0         c0t3d0    ENA
pl rootvol-03   rootvol       DISABLED CLEAN   16812416 CONCAT   -         RW
sd osdg03-02    rootvol-03    osdg03    2101552 16812416 0         c0t4d0    ENA
# cd /etc
# cp vfstab.vol vfstab
# cp system.vol system
```

```
# reboot vx-osdg03
```

11.   The system boots once again from the emergency disk, but based on volumes this time. Maybe you need to restore some files from the still not resynchronized damaged boot disks (that's why we kept their OFFLINE state). Simply use the partition drivers to access them. Then, you should synchronize the volumes to achieve redundancy. Counting four volumes, we expect four synchronization threads, sequentially executed. Surprisingly, `vxtask list` (without disk group specification) lists eight tasks. An extract of the disk group configuration during synchronization (in our example to the `opt` volume) indeed shows, that each stale plex is resynchronized by a particular thread — for whatever reason.

```
# fsck -y /dev/rdsk/c0t2d0s0
** /dev/rdsk/c0t2d0s0
** Last Mounted on /
[...]
# mount /dev/dsk/c0t2d0s0 /mnt
# cp /mnt/<path>/<file> /<path>
# umount /mnt
# vxmend -g osdg on `
  vxprint -g osdg -pne 'pl_sd.sd_dmname~/^osdg0[12]$/'`
# vxprint -rtg osdg rootvol
```

v	rootvol	-	ENABLED	ACTIVE	16812416	ROUND	-	root
pl	rootvol-01	rootvol	**DISABLED STALE**		16812416	CONCAT	-	RW
sd	osdg01-02	rootvol-01	osdg01	2101551	16812416	0	c0t2d0	ENA
pl	rootvol-02	rootvol	**DISABLED STALE**		16812416	CONCAT	-	RW
sd	osdg02-02	rootvol-02	osdg02	2101552	16812416	0	c0t3d0	ENA
pl	rootvol-03	rootvol	ENABLED	ACTIVE	16812416	CONCAT	-	RW
sd	osdg03-02	rootvol-03	osdg03	2101552	16812416	0	c0t4d0	ENA

```
# vxrecover -g osdg -b
# vxtask list
```

TASKID	PTID	TYPE/STATE	PCT	PROGRESS

VxVM vxtask WARNING V-5-1-2497 Unable to get disk group record: Record not in disk group

| 161 | | PARENT/R | 0.00% | **8**/0(1) VXRECOVER 539720.0 |
| 162 | 162 | ATCOPY/R | 03.90% | 0/8392072/327680 PLXATT 0.1052 0.1051 0.1 |

```
# vxtask -g osdg list
```

TASKID	PTID	TYPE/STATE	PCT	PROGRESS
162	162	ATCOPY/R	05.76%	0/8392072/483328 PLXATT opt opt-01 osdg

```
# vxprint -rtg osdg opt
```

v	opt	-	ENABLED	ACTIVE	8392072	ROUND	-	fsgen
pl	opt-01	opt	**ENABLED STALE**		8392072	CONCAT	-	WO
sd	osdg01-04	opt-01	osdg01	18913967	8392072	0	c0t2d0	ENA
pl	opt-02	opt	DISABLED	STALE	8392072	CONCAT	-	RW
sd	osdg02-03	opt-02	osdg02	18913968	8392072	0	c0t3d0	ENA
pl	opt-03	opt	ENABLED	ACTIVE	8392072	CONCAT	-	RW
sd	osdg03-04	opt-03	osdg03	25209200	8392072	0	c0t4d0	ENA

12. As the final step, the plexes containing subdisks on the emergency disk should be offlined, file system checked, and prepared for the next case of emergency — hopefully not too soon. The gap is closed.

```
# vxmend -g osdg off `vxprint -g osdg -pne 'pl_sd.sd_dmname="osdg03"'`
# fsck -y /dev/rdsk/c0t4d0s0
# fsck -y /dev/rdsk/c0t4d0s5
# fsck -y /dev/rdsk/c0t4d0s6
# mount /dev/dsk/c0t4d0s0 /mnt
# cd /mnt/etc
# cp system.part system
# cp vfstab.c0t4d0s2 vfstab
# cd /
# umount /mnt
```

You will surely agree, that we need to execute a lot of complicated commands. Why not write Shell scripts to make life easier and even to automate recovery? We present three scripts, the first called EmergencyDisk_Prepare to prepare the emergency disk (steps 11 and 12/7, 8 and 9), the second (EmergencyDisk_Restore) to boot the system from the emergency disk based on volumes in order to recover them (step 10), and finally a run level script (NOT_S99EmergencyDisk_Restore) to automate the latter task, typically disabled, but temporarily enabled by the first script.

Script EmergencyDisk_Prepare

```
#!/sbin/sh
echo Recovering OS disks. Please wait ...
vxmend -g osdg on `vxprint -g osdg -pne 'pl_sd.sd_dmname~/^osdg0[12]$/'`
vxrecover -g osdg || exit 1
echo FS checking partitions of emergency disk c0t4d0. Please wait ...
vxmend -g osdg off `vxprint -g osdg -pne 'pl_sd.sd_dmname="osdg03"'`
fsck -y /dev/rdsk/c0t4d0s0
fsck -y /dev/rdsk/c0t4d0s5
fsck -y /dev/rdsk/c0t4d0s6
mount /dev/dsk/c0t4d0s0 /mnt
cd /mnt/etc
cp system.part system
cp vfstab.c0t4d0s2 vfstab
cp rcS.d/NOT_S99EmergencyDisk_Restore rcS.d/S99EmergencyDisk_Restore
cd /
umount /mnt
echo The disk c0t4d0 is ready for emergency use.
exit 0
```

Script EmergencyDisk_Restore

```
#!/sbin/sh
vxvol -g osdg stopall
vxmend -g osdg -o force off `
vxprint -g osdg -pne 'pl_sd.sd_dmname~/^osdg0[12]$/'`
vxmend -g osdg on `vxprint -g osdg -pne 'pl_sd.sd_dmname="osdg03"'`
vxmend -g osdg fix clean `vxprint -g osdg -pne 'pl_sd.sd_dmname="osdg03"'`
cd /etc
cp vfstab.vol vfstab
cp system.vol system
mv rcS.d/S99EmergencyDisk_Restore rcS.d/NOT_S99EmergencyDisk_Restore
reboot vx-osdg03
```

Script **NOT_S99EmergencyDisk_Restore**

```
#!/sbin/sh
echo Stopping all volumes of disk group osdg
vxvol -g osdg stopall || exit 1
echo Offlining all plexes of disks osdg01, osdg02 ...
vxmend -g osdg -o force off `
vxprint -g osdg -pne 'pl_sd.sd_dmname~/^osdg0[12]$/'` || exit 2
echo Onlining all plexes of emergency disk osdg03 ...
vxmend -g osdg on `vxprint -g osdg -pne 'pl_sd.sd_dmname="osdg03"'` || exit 2
vxmend -g osdg fix clean `vxprint -g osdg -pne 'pl_sd.sd_dmname="osdg03"'` ||
exit 2
echo Creating /etc/vfstab and /etc/system for encapsulated OS disks
cd /etc
cp vfstab.vol vfstab
cp system.vol system
mv rcS.d/S99EmergencyDisk_Restore rcS.d/NOT_S99EmergencyDisk_Restore
echo Rebooting using encapsulated disk osdg03
reboot vx-osdg03
```

11.8 Hot Relocation Troubles

11.8.1 Plex Synchronization Skipped

In all software versions of VxVM we know, except for the unpatched version of VxVM 5.0, **vxrelocd** shows a strange failure handling under specific conditions. Within a diskgroup containing three disks we create three volumes: vol1 unmirrored, vol2 holding two, vol3 three data plexes. All volumes use a subdisk on the common disk adg01. We will make this disk unavailable to VxVM in order to analyze the failure handling of **vxrelocd**.

```
# vxassist -g adg make vol3 1g layout=mirror nmirror=3 init=active
# vxassist -g adg make vol2 1g layout=mirror nmirror=2 init=active \
```

```
      alloc=adg01,adg02
# vxassist -g adg make vol1 1g alloc=adg01
# vxprint -rtg adg
[...]
dm adg01       c1t1d0s2     auto     2048     122171136 -
dm adg02       c1t1d1s2     auto     2048     122171136 -
dm adg03       c1t1d2s2     auto     2048     122171136 -

v  vol1        -            ENABLED  ACTIVE   2097152   SELECT    -        fsgen
pl vol1-01     vol1         ENABLED  ACTIVE   2097152   CONCAT    -        RW
sd adg01-03    vol1-01      adg01    4194304  2097152   0         c1t1d0   ENA

v  vol2        -            ENABLED  ACTIVE   2097152   SELECT    -        fsgen
pl vol2-01     vol2         ENABLED  ACTIVE   2097152   CONCAT    -        RW
sd adg01-02    vol2-01      adg01    2097152  2097152   0         c1t1d0   ENA
pl vol2-02     vol2         ENABLED  ACTIVE   2097152   CONCAT    -        RW
sd adg02-02    vol2-02      adg02    2097152  2097152   0         c1t1d1   ENA

v  vol3        -            ENABLED  ACTIVE   2097152   SELECT    -        fsgen
pl vol3-01     vol3         ENABLED  ACTIVE   2097152   CONCAT    -        RW
sd adg01-01    vol3-01      adg01    0        2097152   0         c1t1d0   ENA
pl vol3-02     vol3         ENABLED  ACTIVE   2097152   CONCAT    -        RW
sd adg02-01    vol3-02      adg02    0        2097152   0         c1t1d1   ENA
pl vol3-03     vol3         ENABLED  ACTIVE   2097152   CONCAT    -        RW
sd adg03-01    vol3-03      adg03    0        2097152   0         c1t1d2   ENA
# dd if=/dev/zero of=/dev/rdsk/c1t1d0s2 bs=128k oseek=1 count=1
# vxconfigd -k
```

From a previous section of this chapter, we already know the default behavior of VxVM and especially of vxrelocd: All plexes affected by failed subdisks on the failed disk enter kernel state DISABLED and application state NODEVICE. As long as there are still other healthy plexes within a volume, the volume keeps its state pair ENABLED/ACTIVE, thus providing continued access. After some seconds, vxrelocd searches for subdisk replacement. A DISABLED volume (vol1 in our example) cannot relocate the failed subdisk, because it has no valid plex anymore to synchronize from. It is therefore skipped by vxrelocd. An ENABLED volume (vol2) will get a replacement subdisk (step 1) to become a synchronized member of the volume (step 2). But what happens, if vxrelocd cannot find the required space to relocate the failed subdisk (vol3, because we only have three disks within the disk group)? Well, the answer is quite simple: No subdisk relocation is performed.

Unfortunately, vxrelocd does not behave like this. Look at the following result created by vxrelocd in our example.

```
# vxprint -rtg adg
[...]
dm adg01       -            -        -        -         NODEVICE
dm adg02       c1t1d1s2     auto     2048     122171136 -
dm adg03       c1t1d2s2     auto     2048     122171136 -
```

v vol1	-	**DISABLED ACTIVE**		2097152	SELECT	-	fsgen
pl vol1-01	vol1	**DISABLED NODEVICE**		2097152	CONCAT	-	RW
sd adg01-03	vol1-01	adg01	4194304	2097152	0	-	**NDEV**
v vol2	-	ENABLED ACTIVE		2097152	SELECT	-	fsgen
pl vol2-01	vol2	**DISABLED IOFAIL**		2097152	CONCAT	-	RW
sd **adg03-02**	vol2-01	**adg03**	2097152	2097152	0	**c1t1d2**	**ENA**
pl vol2-02	vol2	ENABLED ACTIVE		2097152	CONCAT	-	RW
sd adg02-02	vol2-02	adg02	2097152	2097152	0	c1t1d1	ENA
v vol3	-	ENABLED ACTIVE		2097152	SELECT	-	fsgen
pl vol3-01	vol3	**DISABLED NODEVICE**		2097152	CONCAT	-	RW
sd adg01-01	vol3-01	adg01	0	2097152	0	-	**NDEV**
pl vol3-02	vol3	ENABLED ACTIVE		2097152	CONCAT	-	RW
sd adg02-01	vol3-02	adg02	0	2097152	0	c1t1d1	ENA
pl vol3-03	vol3	ENABLED ACTIVE		2097152	CONCAT	-	RW
sd adg03-01	vol3-03	adg03	0	2097152	0	c1t1d2	ENA

vol1 is indeed DISABLED, vol3 could not find another disk for subdisk relocation, so the affected plex remained in state DISABLED/NODEVICE. Although vol2, as expected, got the subdisk relocated to the third disk (adg03), vxrelocd skipped the plex synchronization, leaving the plex in the DISABLED/IOFAIL state (DISABLED/RECOVER in case of a complete disk failure).

The mails sent by vxrelocd give no further hints on the reason for the incomplete subdisk relocation. Some excerpts:

Subject: Volume Manager failures on host haensel
[...]
Failures have been detected by the VERITAS Volume Manager:

failed disks:
 adg01

failed plexes:
vol1-01
vol2-01
vol3-01

The Volume Manager will attempt to find spare disks, relocate failed subdisks and then recover the data in the failed plexes.

Subject: Volume Manager failures on host haensel
[...]
Attempting to relocate subdisk **adg01-02** from plex **vol2-01**.
Dev_offset - length 2097152 dm_name adg01 da_name c1t1d0s2.
The available plex **vol2-02** will be used **recover the data.**

Subject: Volume Manager failures on host haensel
[…]
Attempting to relocate subdisk **adg01-01** from plex **vol3-01**.
Dev_offset - length 2097152 dm_name adg01 da_name c1t1d0s2.
The available plex vol3-02 **vol3-03** will be used **recover the data.**

[…]
Subject: Attempting VxVM relocation on host haensel
[…]
Relocation was not successful for subdisks on disk adg01 in
volume **vol2** in disk group adg. No replacement was made and the
disk is still unusable.
[…]
Subject: Attempting VxVM relocation on host haensel
[…]
Volume **vol2** Subdisk adg01-02 **relocated** to adg03-02,
but **not yet recovered.**
[…]
Subject: Attempting VxVM relocation on host haensel
[…]
Relocation was not successful for subdisks on disk adg01 in
volume **vol3** in disk group adg. No replacement was made and the
disk is still unusable.
[…]

Due to a misplaced break condition in a loop, the recovery synchronization of volume
vol2 is not started, for vol3 (!) could not find a subdisk replacement. In order to complete
the recovery procedure, just execute the appropriate recovery command manually:

```
# vxrecover -g adg -b vol2
# vxtask -g adg list
TASKID  PTID TYPE/STATE   PCT    PROGRESS
   164   164     ATCOPY/R 32.23% 0/2097152/675840 PLXATT vol2 vol2-01 adg
# vxprint -rtg adg vol2
[…]
v  vol2        -          ENABLED  ACTIVE  2097152  SELECT   -        fsgen
pl vol2-01     vol2       ENABLED  ACTIVE  2097152  CONCAT   -        RW
sd adg03-02    vol2-01    adg03    2097152 2097152  0        c1t1d2   ENA
pl vol2-02     vol2       ENABLED  ACTIVE  2097152  CONCAT   -        RW
sd adg02-02    vol2-02    adg02    2097152 2097152  0        c1t1d1   ENA
```

11.8.2 UNRELOCATION OF SPLIT SUBDISKS

Hot relocation may not always find appropriate disk space to execute a one-to-one subdisk replacement. Will the hot relocation procedure fail, if a failed subdisk cannot be recreated on one target disk? Or will the subdisk be split into smaller fragments spread over multiple disks? Since this is a somewhat realistic scenario, we should examine VxVM's behavior. Within a disk group containing four disks at approx. 17 GB in size, we create a mirrored volume of 16 GB on the first two disks, while a mirrored dummy volume of 8 GB covers the last two disks. So, if one disk of the regular volume fails, the subdisk on it cannot be replaced by just one subdisk.

```
# vxassist -g adg make vol 16g layout=mirror alloc=adg01,adg02 init=active
# vxassist -g adg make dummy 8g layout=mirror alloc=adg03,adg04 init=active
# vxprint -rtg adg
[...]
dm adg01      c4t1d0s2      auto    2048    35365968 -
dm adg02      c4t2d0s2      auto    2048    35365968 -
dm adg03      c4t3d0s2      auto    2048    35365968 -
dm adg04      c4t4d0s2      auto    2048    35365968 -

v  dummy      -             ENABLED ACTIVE  16777216 SELECT    -         fsgen
pl dummy-01   dummy         ENABLED ACTIVE  16777216 CONCAT    -         RW
sd adg03-01   dummy-01      adg03   0       16777216 0         c4t3d0    ENA
pl dummy-02   dummy         ENABLED ACTIVE  16777216 CONCAT    -         RW
sd adg04-01   dummy-02      adg04   0       16777216 0         c4t4d0    ENA

v  vol        -             ENABLED ACTIVE  33554432 SELECT    -         fsgen
pl vol-01     vol           ENABLED ACTIVE  33554432 CONCAT    -         RW
sd adg01-01   vol-01        adg01   0       33554432 0         c4t1d0    ENA
pl vol-02     vol           ENABLED ACTIVE  33554432 CONCAT    -         RW
sd adg02-01   vol-02        adg02   0       33554432 0         c4t2d0    ENA
# vxdg -g adg free
DISK         DEVICE        TAG         OFFSET    LENGTH    FLAGS
adg01        c4t1d0s2      c4t1d0      33554432  1811536   -
adg02        c4t2d0s2      c4t2d0      33554432  1811536   -
adg03        c4t3d0s2      c4t3d0      16777216  18588752  -
adg04        c4t4d0s2      c4t4d0      16777216  18588752  -
```

Disk **adg01** is powered off and some I/O issued on the regular volume. Hot relocation detects the need for subdisk relocation. We turned on Shell debugging within the **vxrelocd** script to analyze its behavior:

```
+ vxassist -r -g adg move vol !adg01 adg02
+ vxassist -r -g adg move vol !adg01 adg03
+ vxassist -r -g adg move vol !adg01 adg04
+ vxassist -r -g adg move vol spare=yes !adg01
```

The script vxrelocd tried to find an appropriate disk as subdisk container by executing vxassist move commands. The first command failed, because disk adg02 was already in use by the other volume mirror. The next two commands failed, because disks adg03 and adg04 each could not provide the required free space. The fourth command succeeded, for only disk adg01 was excluded from the storage allocation, thus enabling multiple target disks. spare=yes assigned a higher priority to spare disks (which we did not define), the option -r included spare disks in the space calculation for the subdisk relocation.

Indeed, the failed subdisk is relocated to two split subdisks. That is good news. These subdisks are synchronized in the known way:

```
# vxprint -rtg adg vol
[...]
v  vol         -              ENABLED  ACTIVE  33554432  SELECT             -        fsgen
pl vol-01      vol            ENABLED  STALE   33554432  CONCAT             -        WO
sd adg03-02    vol-01         adg03    16777216 18588752 0        c4t3d0    ENA
sd adg04-02    vol-01         adg04    16777216 14965680 18588752 c4t4d0    ENA
pl vol-02      vol            ENABLED  ACTIVE  33554432  CONCAT             -        RW
sd adg02-01    vol-02         adg02    0        33554432 0        c4t2d0    ENA
# vxtask -g adg list
TASKID  PTID TYPE/STATE     PCT    PROGRESS
   165   165     ATCOPY/R 07.15% 0/33554432/2398208 PLXATT vol vol-01 adg
```

Well, so far so good! But what about those subdisk attributes of the two relocated subdisks storing the original disk media name and the original subdisk offset?

```
# vxprint -g adg -sF '%name %orig_dmname %orig_dmoffset' -e \
  'sd_orig_dmname!=""'
adg03-02 adg01 0
adg04-02 adg01 18588752
```

That looks quite encouraging! The correct offsets were calculated and stored. We expect a proper unrelocation with just one harmless disadvantage: Both subdisks will be unrelocated, but not joined into one subdisk. In order to analyze the procedure, we turn on Shell debugging once again.

```
# vxunreloc -g adg adg01
```

The interesting part of the debugging output together with the content of the subdisk creation template file:

```
+ vxmake -g adg -d /tmp/ur-mksd2869
+ vxsd -g adg -o rm -d mv adg03-02 adg01-UR-001
+ vxsd -g adg -o rm -d mv adg04-02 adg01-UR-002
# cat /tmp/ur-mksd2869
sd adg01-UR-001 disk=adg01 offset=0 len=18588752 comment=UNRELOC
sd adg01-UR-002 disk=adg01 offset=18588752 len=14965680 comment=UNRELOC
```

OK, great! We still expect two separated subdisks on the original disk, but no! vxunreloc was able to determine, that both subdisks being physically contiguous are also contiguous within the plex. They are automatically joined. Just the name of the original subdisk is lost.

11.9 PLEX STATES OVERVIEW

It is sometimes useful to know what all the plex states mean that are output from vxprint or vxinfo. Here is a list of plex states and their meaning, taken from the man page:

ACTIVE . . . . Either the volume is started and the plex is enabled, or the volume was not stopped cleanly and the plex was valid when the volume was stopped.

CLEAN . . . . The plex contains valid data and the volume was stopped cleanly.

DCOSNP . . . . A data change object (DCO) plex that is attached to a volume, and which can be used by a snapshot plex to create a DCO volume during a snapshot operation.

EMPTY . . . . The plex is part of a volume that has not yet been initialized.

IOFAIL . . . . The plex was detached because of an uncorrectable I/O failure on one of the subdisks in the plex.

LOG . . . . A dirty region logging (DRL) or RAID-5 log plex.

NODAREC . . . . No physical disk was found for one of the subdisks in the plex. This implies either that the physical disk failed, making it unrecognizable, or that the physical disk is no longer attached through a known access path.

NODEVICE . . . . A physical device could not be found corresponding to the disk ID in the disk media record for one of the subdisks associated with the plex. The plex cannot be used until this condition is fixed, or the affected subdisk is dissociated.

OFFLINE . . . . The plex was disabled using the vxmend off operation.

REMOVED . . . . A physical disk used by one of the subdisks in the plex was removed through administrative action with vxdg -k rmdisk.

SNAPATT . . . . The plex is being attached as part of a backup operation by the vxassist snapstart operation. When the attach is complete, the condition changes to SNAPDONE. A system reboot or manual starting of the volume removes the plex and all of its subdisks.

SNAPDIS. . . . . A vxassist snapstart operation completed the process of attaching the plex. It is a candidate for selection by the vxplex snapshot operation. A system reboot or manual starting of the volume dissociates the plex.

SNAPDONE . . . . A vxassist snapstart operation completed the process of attaching the plex. It is a candidate for selection by the vxassist snapshot operation. A system reboot or manual starting of the volume removes the plex and all of its subdisks.

SNAPTMP . . . . The plex is being attached as part of a backup operation by the vxplex snapstart operation. When the attach is complete, the condition changes to SNAPDIS. A system reboot or manual starting of the volume dissociates the plex.

STALE . . . . The plex does not contain valid data, either as a result of a disk replacement affecting one of the subdisks in the plex, or as a result of an administrative action on the plex such as vxplex det.

TEMP. . . . . The plex is associated temporarily as part of a current operation, such as vxplex cp or vxplex att. A system reboot or manual starting of a volume dissociates the plex.

TEMPRM. . . . . The plex was created for temporary use by a current operation. A system reboot or manual starting of a volume removes the plex.

TEMPRMSD . . . . The plex and its subdisks were created for temporary use by a current operation. A system reboot or manual starting of the volume removes the plex and all of its subdisks.

Another Kind of File System ;)

CHAPTER 12: FILE SYSTEMS

by Volker Herminghaus

Since you are reading a book about volume management for highly available UNIX systems in data centers we would like to assume that you have some basic understanding of what a file system is used for. We will spare both your time and ours describing the basic goals of a file system. But there are some essential differences between the various types of file systems that are very useful to point out. So let us begin with a short overview of the various file system types that have developed over time, and how their strengths increased. Yes, increased, not changed. As a general rule, file systems have indeed gotten a lot better over time without losing any important features relative to older implementations. Different from other aspects of computer technology one can safely say that so far, file system development has been a one-way road towards improvement, not heavily traded-off bloatware development as so many other parts of operating systems. At least if we ignore the non-sequential access methods of some older file systems. But those can be easily emulated on a higher level, and their omission from file system code probably improved performance rather than diminishing it.

12.1 BLOCK BASED FILE SYSTEMS

Most common file systems are based on allocating single individual blocks from the underlying partition or volume to store user data as well as file system metadata. There is always some higher-level data (the metadata mentioned above) that bundles these blocks together to the notion of a sequential file and stores meta information about the file and the total file system. This metadata has been stored in many different forms, including very arcane ones, over the course of time. As one of the most bizarre ones known to the current

V. Herminghaus and A. Sriba, *Storage Management in Data Centers*,
DOI: 10.1007/978-3-540-85023-6_12, © Springer-Verlag Berlin Heidelberg 2009

instance of humanity we would like to point out the "file system" of the Commodore 64 floppy disk (really!).

12.1.1   JUST FOR FUN: COMMODORE 64'S RUDIMENTARY FILE ACCESS

It was organized into a single directory (of limited length). The directory was stored in a fixed location. Each directory entry had a name and a starting block for the file. If a file was deleted, the first character of the name was overwritten by a special character to indicate the file's "deleted" state. There was no centralized information about the blocks that a file would consist of. Instead, the first block was pointed to by the directory entry, and the consecutive blocks were pointed to by the last byte of the previous block. In effect, this resulted in a linked list of blocks that could only be read sequentially. Even when a process (or should I say **"the program"**, as this was a single-tasking system) wanted to access the end of the file the system still had to read through all of the file's blocks in order to find its way to the end – after all, it had to read the whole linked list!

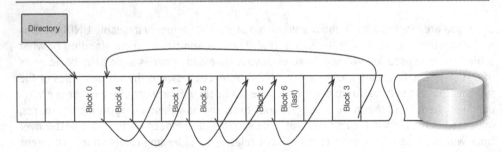

Figure 12-1:   The extremely basic Commodore 64 file system mixed meta data (the linked list of block numbers) with user data. Seeking required reading all blocks up to the end point. This was because mass storage can only be read in blocks rather than directly addressed, and in order to retrieve the pointer to the next block, the whole data block had to be transferred.

12.1.2   FAT – NOT A BIG IMPROVEMENT

A little better, although not much, was – and still is – the file system used by MS-DOS and, later, Windows "operating systems". It is called FAT (for File Allocation Table) file system and has a central root directory that allows for subdirectories. Files are still deleted by invalidating the first character of the file name. And the starting block is still stored in the file's directory entry. But one of the very few things that are better in this file system than in the Commodore 64's is that there now **is** a central location that holds a complete linked list of blocks for a file (the file allocation table). The FAT data structure works basically as an array of 12, 16, or 32-bit values in which each index is identical to the corresponding data block number in the data area of the file system. The first array element in the FAT corresponds to the first data block in the data portion of the file system, the one-hundredth element corresponds to the one-hundredth data block, etc. The values in the array are either NULL (in which case no further block follows) or the number of the next block in the file. In other words, there is still a linked list of blocks per file, but the list has been moved outside of the data portion of the file system, and into a separate data structure, which can be read independently without reading all of the file. Seeking in a file is therefore not awfully slow but merely pretty slow. Of course, the "great visionary" Bill Gates has provided enough lock-ins to make the FAT file system woefully inadequate for serious computing today and yesterday. For instance, the number of addressable blocks is limited and therefore the only way to scale the file system size up is to increase the size of the allocated units (called "clusters"). This is very wasteful because even for tiny files the file system must allocate at least one allocation unit. While most serious file systems have minimum allocation units of 1 KB, FAT file systems of a total size of merely 2 GB already require at least 32 KB allocation units. Apart from this, traversing linked lists really is not fast unless you are handling very few objects, i.e. blocks. This is not the case today, and neither FAT's feature set nor its performance can in any way compete with even the most primitive versions of e.g. UNIX file systems.

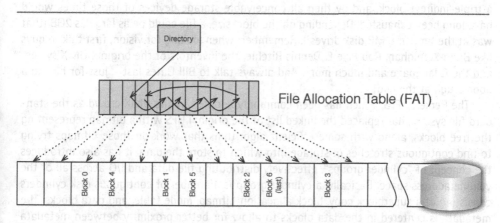

Figure 12-2: FAT file system moves the linkage information into a separate data structure, away from the user data, so it can be processed more quickly – somewhat.

Apart from its wastefulness FAT is extremely limited when it comes to file naming. FAT file names are inherently limited to an 8.3 pattern, and the extension to that naming pattern is incompatible with many file sharing protocols or shared media, and implemented in a very inefficient, hackish way. Ownership, group and other permissions are not supported, access times are not recorded, and support for multiple names referencing the same data is limited at best. In short, it is a very ancient, crufty file system that has survived solely because the majority of its users don't know better and are used to malfunctioning operating systems, so basically nobody ever bothered to fix it.

12.1.3 UFS – Finally Something Decent

What is known these days as UFS, or UNIX File System, is actually not the original AT&T System V UFS but the much more modern Berkeley FFS (Fast File System). The original UFS used a **"super block"** at a fixed location for finding the rest of the metadata and for maintaining file system global values such as clean/dirty state, size and degree to which the file system is full. It used a linked list for managing free blocks, and it invented the notion of an "inode", or **information node**, that holds all metadata pertaining to the file. The inode contained user and group ID of the file's owner, the numbers of the first ten blocks of the file, read and access time stamps as well as a time stamp for the last change to the inode, permission information, size, and a whole lot more. If the file was longer than the portion that can be addressed by the block numbers in the inode, then the next block number in the inode would not be the eleventh block of the file, but it would contain a so-called "indirect block", i.e. a block full of block numbers of file data blocks. Thus a file could be enlarged by a lot of blocks with just one extra block of metadata (the block containing the additional data block numbers, the indirect block). If that did still not suffice, then the next block number in the inode would be a double-indirect block containing the addresses of indirect blocks which in turn contained data block numbers. Number thirteen would be a triple-indirect block, and by then all conceivable storage devices of those times would have long been exhausted. Depending on the blocksize, a file could be as large as 2GB (that was at the time of 5 MB disk drives!). Remember: when looking for vision, first talk to guys like Brian Kernighan, Rob Pike & Dennis Ritchie, the inventors of the original UNIX system and the C language and much more. And always talk to Bill Gates last – just for having a good laugh at the end!

The Berkeley FFS, which has been commonly adopted by the UNIX crowd as the standard file system, has replaced the linked list of the original UFS with a bitmap representing the free blocks, along with some efficient algorithms that work on those bitmaps trying to find contiguous stretches of storage into which to store the data. It has also introduces the concept of "cylinder groups", effectively distributing file data and I/O across all of the volume address space. Basically, a cylinder group is a number of contiguous disk cylinders consisting of a superblock copy, block allocation bitmap, inode table, and data blocks. The metadata is centered in the data blocks to allow for better proximity between metadata and user data.

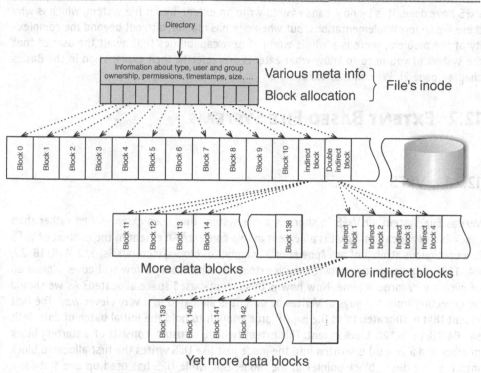

Figure 12-3: UFS uses inodes to concentrate meta information as well as
block allocation information into one place. Linked lists pointing
to data blocks are superseded by direct, indirect, double indirect
and triple indirect block lists.

Allocation of space for new files is done by first selecting a cylinder group (of which
there are usually many – newfs tells you the number of cylinder groups and the location of
the superblock copies when you create a UFS file system), and then allocating blocks in a
preferably contiguous fashion from that cylinder group. Multi-user I/O will therefore typically be distributed across several cylinder groups; a similar effect to striping on a volume
level. This makes sure that the disk or volume is used in a balanced way, especially with
respect to the usage of the (fixed) inodes for the data around the inode table.

Berkeley FFS is a pretty good file system, but it is still far from a really good one. For
one thing, block-based addressing requires a relatively large amount of metadata – one
block number per block. The fixed locations and sizes of UFS's metadata make it wasteful
and inflexible in extreme cases. File systems with very few very large files are a bad case
because a large number of inodes is reserved in vain. Likewise, the opposite case is bad, too.
File systems with lots of small files will eventually run out of inodes even if there is plenty
of space still left in the data portion of the file system. And lastly, advanced features like
point-in-time-copies, shrinking of file systems, or reorganizing the files ("defragmenting")
is not efficiently possible.

All of those advanced features, and many more advantages, can be done easily when one switches from block-addressing to extent-addressing. This is what the developers of VxFS have done. It is by no means easy to write an extent-based file system, which is why there are so few implementations. But when one has managed to get beyond the complexity of the problem, there is a whole world of new capabilities that await the user of that file system (if you need to know what extents are, refer to their explanation in the Basics chapter, page 2). Welcome to VxFS!

12.2 EXTENT BASED FILE SYSTEMS

12.2.1   VxFS

Veritas File System, or VxFS in short, is a file system that uses extent-based rather than block-based allocation. What is an extent in this context? An extent in the context of VxFS is a contiguous stretch of any "power of 2" number of blocks/sectors/KBs: 1, 2, 4, 8, 16, 32, 64, 128, ... up to multi-gigabyte length extents of which only a few will cover almost all of even a very large volume. Now how is this extent-based space allocated? As we should be expecting from the guys at Veritas by now, it is allocated in a very clever way: The first extent that is allocated to as file is just large enough to hold the initial batch of data, let's say 64 KB, i.e. a 128-block extent. This extent (which, as usual, consists of a starting block number and a length) is written into the inode just like UFS writes the first allocated block into the first direct block pointer in the inode. But while UFS has used up one slot for a single 8 KB block, VxFS has used it for 64 KB - a fourth of the metadata (an extent consists of two values – starting block and length – while a block number only consists of one). Now when the file is grown beyond the 64 KB previously allocated, the next extent is allocated. This extent will not be 64 KB, but rather it will be twice that amount: 128 KB, or 256 blocks. The rationale behind this is that when a file is growing it may grow very large. We do not know how large, but the more it grows, the higher the probability that it will grow even larger. So every time the file size exceeds its allocation, the file size basically doubles because the size of the new extent is equal to twice the current size of the file (minus the initial extent size, to be precise). And with every new extent the degree of contiguousness increases, and the amount of metadata per block rapidly decreases.

While this may sound extremely wasteful, it is really not wasteful at all. Just wait for another one or two pages...

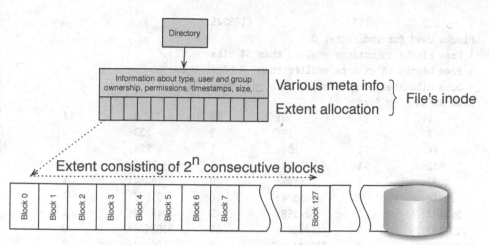

Figure 12-4: VxFS also uses inodes, but instead of pointing to individual blocks, it points to extents, which can be multi-megabytes in length. indirect and double indirect blocks are used, too. but are only seldom needed, because most file use far less than the ten extents that can be stored in the VxFS inode directly (VxFS allocation vastly prefers contiguousness over scattered allocation). An extent is a 32-bit block number plus a 16-bit block count, with the blocks in a file system being tunable to between 1 KB and 8 KB in length.

How Extents are Found

Extents are held in a free extent list, which is sorted by length and which can therefore be very rapidly searched and manipulated. In fact, you can look at the cree extent list of any VxFS file system by calling the file system administration tool, `fsadm`, with the appropriate options. The option "-E" lists extent information. Here is an example of what a freshly created and slightly filled 6 GB volume lists as the extent report:

```
# df -h -F vxfs
Filesystem          size  used  avail capacity  Mounted on
/dev/vx/dsk/adg/avol 6.0G  106M  5.5G    2%      /vxfs_mnt
```

Note that the net capacity of the volume is equal to the volume size: the full 6 GB are usable! In the case of UFS, a lot of the volume's capacity is filled with fixed-location metadata like inode tables, bitmaps, super block backups, and other cylinder group info.

```
# fsadm -E /vxfs_mnt
Extent Fragmentation Report
      Total     Average     Average     Total
      Files     File Blks   # Extents   Free Blks
```

503	177		1	6183245		

blocks used for indirects: 0
% Free blocks in extents smaller than 64 blks: 0.01
% Free blocks in extents smaller than 8 blks: 0.00
% blks allocated to extents 64 blks or larger: 91.01
Free Extents By Size

1:	21	2:	28	4:	16
8:	26	16:	3	32:	0
64:	1	128:	1	256:	1
512:	1	1024:	1	2048:	0
4096:	1	8192:	0	16384:	1
32768:	0	65536:	0	131072:	1
262144:	1	524288:	1	1048576:	1
2097152:	2	4194304:	0	8388608:	0
16777216:	0	33554432:	0	67108864:	0
134217728:	0	268435456:	0	536870912:	0
1073741824:	0	2147483648:	0		

The pyramid-shaped columns of number above are actually the whole free space information for the file system: you see that there are 21 free extents of size 1, 28 of size 2, 16 of size 4, and so on, until finally most of the empty volume space is contained in 2 free extents of size 2097152. The maximum extent size is 2 TB!

EFFICIENCY OF VxFS ALLOCATION

You may wonder what happens in the following scenario: A file keeps growing and therefore larger and larger extents are being appended to it. But then, just a small portion is written into the most recently allocated (and therefor largest) extent, and then the file is closed and stops growing. What happens to the remaining, empty space in that last extent? There are several possible scenarios that one may think of:

1. The remaining space is simply wasted and remains allocated "just in case" it will eventually be grown again.

This would be a very poor design, as we can never guarantee that the file will actually grow. If it does not, the space would be permanently wasted. Because we cannot guarantee eventual growth of the file, there would have to be some kind of timeout mechanism that would free the extent after some time, or when space is urgently needed. But it would be very hard to do this right, and it may never be done right.

2. The used part of the extent is re-allocated to a new, smaller extent and its contents are copied to there. After the copying process has finished, the long extent is freed.

That would certainly be possible, but it has a number of disadvantages. The first one is: do we really want to copy half a terabyte, just because we allocated another terabyte and only filled half of it? This takes several hours of permanent read/write I/O! The second one is: if there are so few extents free in a VxFS file system (see the example above), and we fill them ideally, when and how are we ever to get new, smaller extents? This is answered by the third possibility, which is how VxFS actually goes about in the case sketched above

3. The remaining part of the large extent is cut into smaller extents, and those are added to the free list.

Once you understand VxFS's allocation its elegance becomes obvious. Let's say we have allocated a 2 GB extent but only used 14 MB of it when we close the file. VxFS now chunks the 2 GB extent newly by splitting it into new extents of appropriate sizes:

The part of the extent that was actually used (fourteen MB) is split into an eight MB and a four MB and a two MB extent. The data is not moved, instead the 2 GB extent is simply split into several smaller extents, all being contiguous inside the original 2 GB extent. Eight plus four plus two is fourteen, so all the data can be held in just these three extents. Now there is 2 GB minus 14 MB left in the previously allocated 2 GB extent. This space is also simply rearranged into smaller extents of 16, 32, 64, 128 MB and so on, until the "unused half" of the original extent, 1 GB, is reached. All these extents are added to the free extent list and can subsequently be used for new files or for growing existing files.

VxFS actually manages by far the best trade-off between allocation size and amount of storage space wasted. It does not waste more than one KB per file, and at the same time, a single allocation unit can still be (currently) one TB in size. And if you used the appropriate tools provided by Veritas for this purpose, you could even pre-allocate one TB of contiguous space for your (data base) file and end up with just this one single extent descriptor in the inode, for a file of one TB!

We have prepared two little examples for you. The first example shows the relative outcomes for UFS versus VxFS on newly created file systems. In these cases, VxFS seems to have an advantage only on small volumes, while it seems to allocate much more space than UFS does on larger volumes. But the second example proves the opposite is right, and VxFS is actually much more efficient in handling space; it just doesn't show it as long as the file system is nearly empty. So let's look at the first example. We have prepared a number of volumes of various sizes and put a UFS on them, then we took the same volumes and put a VxFS on them. We ran df -h on both sets and will look at the results. First, the UFS file systems:

Filesystem	size	used	avail	capacity	Mounted on
/dev/vx/dsk/adg/100mvol	93M	1.0M	83M	2%	/ufs100m
/dev/vx/dsk/adg/1gvol	961M	1.0M	903M	1%	/ufs1g
/dev/vx/dsk/adg/10gvol	9.8G	10M	9.7G	1%	/ufs10g
/dev/vx/dsk/adg/50gvol	49G	50M	49G	1%	/ufs50g
/dev/vx/dsk/adg/500gvol	492G	64M	487G	1%	/ufs500g

Compare this to the VxFS file systems:

Filesystem	size	used	avail	capacity	Mounted on
/dev/vx/dsk/adg/100mvol	100M	2.1M	92M	3%	/vxfs100m
/dev/vx/dsk/adg/1gvol	1.0G	17M	944M	2%	/vxfs1g
/dev/vx/dsk/adg/10gvol	10G	20M	9.4G	1%	/vxfs10g
/dev/vx/dsk/adg/50gvol	50G	78M	47G	1%	/vxfs50g
/dev/vx/dsk/adg/500gvol	500G	191M	469G	1%	/vxfs500g

The first thing that jumps at you is that you see the actual volume size (e.g. 100 MB for the first volume) displayed in the file system size column. But that is just for VxFS! UFS shows a volume size of a mere 93 MB. And now look at the avail column. UFS shows just 83 MB versus VxFS showing 92 MB. So we have three questions to answer:

1. Why does UFS not show the full size of the volume, while VxFS does?

2. What took the additional 10 MB away from the UFS?

3. What took the 8 MB away from the VxFS?

The answer to question 1. is rather interesting: UFS dedicates a well defined set of blocks per file system to metadata such as inodes, bitmaps etc. That metadata is located at fixed locations in the file system and cannot be relocated. It takes up a significant portion of the volume and is not available for user data, only for meta data. In the given case, it is 7% of the total volume size, which reduces the available size to 93 MB out of 100 MB volume size (that ratio improves with increasing volume size as you can see from the 500 GB volume: 492 GB is the reported size, so 8 GB are wasted – a mere 1.5% instead of 7%). The ratio of meta data to user data can be tuned by manually supplying the appropriate parameters to mkfs when making the file system (e.g. mkfs -o nbpi=4096 … ->.4 KB of user data are expected per inode instead of the default 2 KB).

The answer to question 2. is probably well-known: UFS reserves some amount of the space (10% for small volumes, less for large volumes) for the root user. The default is ((64 MBytes/volume size)*100), rounded down to the nearest integer and limited between 1% and 10%, inclusively. This space can not be allocated by other users. This reservation is intended to prevent a non-priviledged user from filling up the / or /var file system, which might render the system unusable. Because UFS reserves some space for the root user only, the super-user could then still log in and clean up; there is still some working space left over for him in the / or /var file system. So this space is not really lost, it is merely reserved and can only be used by root. It could also be tuned to a minimum by manual intervention or by supplying the appropriate parameters to newfs or mkfs when making the file system (e.g. mkfs -o free=99 … -> only one percent is reserved).

The answer to question 3 is more interesting: VxFS writes the free extent records into a relatively large area called an extent_map. This extent_map is actually a file that is not visible to the user (except by using the ncheck utility – see the chapter about Point-In-Time Copies to learn more about ncheck for VxFS). It is a meta-data file. Now why does the extent_map take up 8 MB? This sounds like a lot! What VxFS seems to be doing is create all whole lot of, maybe even all, permutations of the free extents. For instance, if you had a file system with 16 MB free, you could create just one free extent record for that space. But you could also create two eight MB ones, or four four MB ones, or one eight and two four MB ones and so on until you have enough extents of every conceivable size ready to allocate as soon as one is requested. It goes without saying that this size grows more quickly than linear with growing volume size, because twice as much free space can be recombined in many more than two times the number of ways.

That is just one reason why the ratio of available space to volume size improves for UFS relative to VxFS with increasing volume size. For instance, the 500 GB UFS file system seems to have much more space available (487 GB) than the VxFS one (469 GB). But you will see that, as the file system fills up, the amount of blocks used for the extent_map decreases rapidly, until the extent map finally takes up almost no space at all when the volume is completely full. You will see, as a result, that a VxFS can still be filled to exactly the size of the volume (500 GB) minus the amount of used space (191 MB), while UFS can only be filled to the reported size (492 GB), so in the given example it wastes 8192 MB, while VxFS's overhead is just 191 MB!

The other reason why the df report for VxFS shows much less space available than one would derive from subtracting the used value from the size value is that VxFS pre-allocates lots of inodes when the file system is created. Each inode takes up 256 bytes (by default; it can be tuned to 512 bytes but there is no good reason to do so). These pre-allocated inodes are hidden from the usage because they are not really active. On the other hand, they are subtracted from the size in the output of the available column because that is a more realistic value in case you fill the file system with small files. The difference between UFS and VxFS here lies in the fact that UFS cannot claim the inodes back, while VxFS can. UFS therefore wastes lots of space for inodes that may never get used, while VxFS keeps all this dynamic and allocates only the amount of storage for meta data that it actually needs.

The second example will prove that. We have created a 1 GB volume for UFS and a 1 GB volume for VxFS. We will mount the two file systems and then fill them with data. The UFS will be filled by the non-priviledged user `luser` until the file system reports an overflow. Then, the root user will fill up the rest. We will then do the same for VxFS.

```
# newfs /dev/vx/rdsk/adg/1gvol
newfs: construct a new file system /dev/vx/rdsk/adg/1gvol: (y/n)? y
[...UFS file system is created...]
# mount /dev/vx/dsk/adg/1gvol /ufs1g
# df -h /ufs1g
Filesystem                    size   used  avail capacity Mounted on
/dev/vx/dsk/adg/1gvol  961M   1.0M   903M     1%   /ufs1g
```

File system has been created and mounted, 961 MB are free for data, 903 MB of which is free for non-priviledged users. UFS has wasted 39 MB on meta-data at fixed locations. We will now switch to the `luser` account and fill up as much of the file system as we can.

```
# su - luser
luser $ dd if=/dev/zero of=/ufs1g/USERDATA bs=1024k
dd: unexpected short write, wrote 344064 bytes, expected 1048576
903+0 records in
903+0 records out
luser $ exit
# df -h /ufs1g
Filesystem                    size   used  avail capacity Mounted on
/dev/vx/dsk/adg/1gvol  961M   904M    0K   100%   /ufs1g
```

The `luser` could only write 903 MB plus 344064 bytes (see error message form dd).

```
# dd if=/dev/zero of=/ufs1g/ROOTDATA bs=1024k
dd: unexpected short write, wrote 663552 bytes, expected 1048576
58+0 records in
58+0 records out
# df -h /ufs1g
Filesystem                    size   used  avail capacity Mounted on
/dev/vx/dsk/adg/1gvol  961M   961M    0K   100%   /ufs1g
```

Another 58 MB plus 663552 bytes could be used by root.

```
# umount /ufs1g
```

```
# mkfs -F vxfs /dev/vx/rdsk/adg/1gvol
[...VxFS file system is created...]
# mount -Fvxfs /dev/vx/dsk/adg/1gvol /vxfs1g
# df -h /vxfs1g
Filesystem                    size  used  avail capacity  Mounted on
/dev/vx/dsk/adg/1gvol         1.0G  17M   944M  2%         /vxfs1g
# su - luser
luser $ dd if=/dev/zero of=/vxfs1g/USERDATA bs=1024k
dd: unexpected short write, wrote 691200 bytes, expected 1048576
1007+0 records in
1007+0 records out
luser $ exit
# df -h /vxfs1g
Filesystem                    size  used  avail capacity  Mounted on
/dev/vx/dsk/adg/1gvol         1.0G  1.0G  0K    100%       /vxfs1g
```

In the case where a VxFS is sitting on top of the volume, the luser can fill the volume up with 1007 MB plus 691200 bytes of data – much more than even root was able to in the case of UFS! Exactly the 17 MB that were reported used by the VxFS could not be allocated, every byte of the rest could. But how did we get from 944 MB available space up to 1007 MB? The trick is that, while we are filling up the volume, we are allocating free extents by the thousands. VxFS is allocating them from the extent_map file, which takes up a lot of space in an empty file system, as we explained in the first example. The meta data for all permutations of these free extents are of course invalid once we have allocated the space that they point to, so these entries are then freed, which makes the extent_map considerable shorter. It turns out that the more the file system fills up the more meta data is freed from the extent_map, and thus the more free space becomes available for user data. Clever idea, is it not?

Now the question that any critical UNIX administrator must ask is: Why does VxFS not reserve any space for the root user? Is that not dangerous?

The answer is: No! If it were dangerous, don't you think the appropriate mechanism would have been implemented in VxFS. The explanation is that VxFS (on Solaris, at least), can not be used for any of the boot file systems, like /, /var, /usr, or /opt. And because it cannot be used for any of these file systems, there is no danger that a luser fills up the "VxFS root-FS" and the system gets stuck. There is simply no possibility to create something like a "VxFS root-FS".

But the smaller amount of meta data compared to UFS is not the primary advantage. It is just "yet another nice thing" about VxFS. The **really** nice things that are enabled by using extents instead of blocks (thereby limiting the complexity of handling contiguous allocation and reducing the amount of metadata) are discussed in the following section.

12.3 ADVANCED FILE SYSTEM OPERATIONS

ON-THE-FLY FILE SYSTEM OPTIMIZATION

Yes, you can optimize a VxFS just like you could optimize old FAT file systems (which needed it a lot more, due to its very poor allocation algorithms). The difference is that you can do so while the file system is active and undergoing user I/O. It is actually a very good idea to optimize your file systems (especially database table space files) daily, e.g. just before you start backing them up. The utility is the same fsadm that we used above to check the free extent list: fsadm. This time, the parameter is not -E, but -e. While -E simply outputs the report about extents and about possible extent optimization, -e actually causes the fsadm command to execute the optimization. If the file system had been in use for a long time and especially if it had run almost full for some time, you may see a significant advantage in file system performance after optimization compared to before. Here is an example of the (very simple) syntax

```
# fsadm -e /vxfs_mnt
```

There is also an optimization feature for the directories. During directory optimization, the most recently used files are moved to the beginning of the directory, some empty directory slots are created to speed up file creation, and small directories will be moved into their inode in order to save disk seeks. Several other directory optimizations are performed but due to extensive operating system caching strategies as well as the fact that enterprise-critical applications typically store their data in databases instead of flat file systems, these may not dramatically improve your performance. For completeness (and because directory optimization certainly does not hurt) we give you the necessary options for directory optimizations: They are -D for the report and -d for the actual optimization.

If you wonder if it is a good idea to do extent and directory optimization on the most critical file systems on a routine basis then the easy answer is: yes! Do it daily, just before you back up the file system, for example. If you do it routinely, there will be very little to optimize every day, and so the command will not take a long time to run. If you want a number: one minute per 20 GB-30 GB of file system data is a good average value for file system optimization (extents and directories) using a typical file system on 2008 hardware.

Sample command to optimize extents and directories:

```
# fsadm -de /vxfs_mnt
```

STORAGE CHECKPOINTS

Being able to remember the file system state at a particular point in time (see also the chapter about point-in-time copies) is a very nice thing, especially if the overhead in terms of storage space, processing time, and I/O latency is minimal. The VxFS file system provides a point-in-time scheme that satisfies all of these needs, as well as supplying the point-in-time copies as read-write full file systems which can be used recursively to create a whole tree of point-in-time copies. These point-in-time copies are called **storage checkpoints**. Being a feature of VxFS rather than VxVM, they have nothing whatsoever to do with the underlying volume or partition, i.e. you can use storage checkpoint on a partition as well as a SunVM metadevice or a VxVM volume. The only prerequisite is that the file system is of type VxFS, because only the VxFS driver knows how to handle them.

All of the storage checkpoints of a file system can be active at the same time, can be read from and written to, and can again be used as the basis of more point-in-time copies. It does much of what a source code control system is destined to do: keeping track of different instances of data that derive from the same ancestor. And like a source code control system, you can even consolidate your file system to a preferred instance, for instance if you want to reduce complexity or free storage space. Other features that are available with storage checkpoints are the ability to automatically discard them if the volume (or partition) fills up and many other things which are more rarely used. All of this can be done on the fly, provided the main (or original) file system is mounted.

In order to reduce redundancy we would like to point you to their in-depth description in the Point-In-Time-Copies chapter beginning on page 282.

FILE SYSTEM CONVERSION FROM UFS

Using the relatively simple command vxfsconvert the user is able to convert a UFS file system into a VxFS file system. The process takes about as long as an fsck run and it is not harmful if the system crashes or faults in the meantime, i.e. the whole process is transactional. What vxfsconvert does is read the UFS meta data (much like fsck does), gather them, allocate new VxFS meta data, and write that new meta data into free blocks of the UFS file system. When the whole file system has been processed and all VxFS meta data has been written into blocks that UFS considers free, the user is asked whether to commit the transaction. If the reply is positive, the vxfsconvert command then writes a new superblock onto the file system. This superblock points to the VxFS meta data rather than the UFS meta data. From the VxFS meta data point of view, the same files are referenced as were references from the UFS file system. Those blocks that contained UFS meta data, allocated or not, are marked free in the VxFS meta data, so they can be overwritten when the file system is mounted read-write.

Before the file system can be mounted, you must first do a full fsck on the new VxFS file system, i.e. fsck -F vxfs -o full $RAWDEVICE. This is because VxFS is a rather complicated file system and the vxfsconvert command does not need to duplicate things that fsck_vxfs implements anyway. We therefore pass the rest of the work to fsck_vxfs, which cleans up the file system for us. It does complain a lot, but all the complaints can be safely ignored. It is advisable to specify the -y flag to fsck to have fsck run continuously rather than stopping to ask for every file.

Here is a full run of converting a UFS on Solaris 10 into VxFS. The file system is almost completely full with data from a previous benchmark run:

```
# ls -l /ufs100m
total 48
drwxr-xr-x  18 root     root         512 Aug 23 19:38 0
drwxr-xr-x  18 root     root         512 Aug 23 19:38 1
drwxr-xr-x  18 root     root         512 Aug 23 19:40 10
```

```
drwxr-xr-x  18 root       root             512 Aug 23 19:41 11
drwxr-xr-x  18 root       root             512 Aug 23 19:41 12
drwxr-xr-x  18 root       root             512 Aug 23 19:41 13
drwxr-xr-x  18 root       root             512 Aug 23 19:41 14
drwxr-xr-x  18 root       root             512 Aug 23 19:42 15
drwxr-xr-x  18 root       root             512 Aug 23 19:38 2
drwxr-xr-x  18 root       root             512 Aug 23 19:38 3
drwxr-xr-x  18 root       root             512 Aug 23 19:39 4
drwxr-xr-x  18 root       root             512 Aug 23 19:39 5
drwxr-xr-x  18 root       root             512 Aug 23 19:39 6
drwxr-xr-x  18 root       root             512 Aug 23 19:40 7
drwxr-xr-x  18 root       root             512 Aug 23 19:40 8
drwxr-xr-x  18 root       root             512 Aug 23 19:40 9
drwx------   2 root       root            8192 Aug 23 19:29 lost+found
```

Because the file system is full we need a little more space for the conversion. It is sometimes tricky to add a whole lot to a file system in one go. If it does not work, split it into several increments. The increments may get larger very quickly. Note that growing in increments is only necessary with file systems that have almost no free space left!

```
# vxresize ufs100mvol +1m
# vxresize ufs100mvol +4m
# vxresize ufs100mvol +25m
# umount /ufs100m
```

Here we actually convert the UFS file system to a VxFS one. We'll measure the time it takes. Remember there are about 50.000 files in the file system, plus the machine is currently heavily loaded.

```
# time vxfsconvert /dev/vx/rdsk/adg/ufs100mvol
UX:vxfs vxfsconvert: INFO: V-3-21842: Do you wish to commit to conversion? (ynq)
y
```

If we reply "n" then nothing happens. The superblock is not updated, and we can mount the UFS again. But we chose "y", so the superblock is updated.

```
UX:vxfs vxfsconvert: INFO: V-3-21852:  CONVERSION WAS SUCCESSFUL

real    1m15.96s
user    0m2.86s
sys     0m1.22s
```

Now we need the VxFS-savvy `fsck` program to clean up behind our conversion:

```
# fsck -F vxfs -y -o full /dev/vx/rdsk/adg/ufs100mvol
super-block indicates that intent logging was disabled
cannot perform log replay
```

```
pass0 - checking structural files
pass1 - checking inode sanity and blocks
pass2 - checking directory linkage
pass3 - checking reference counts
pass4 - checking resource maps
fileset 1 au 0 imap incorrect - fix (ynq)y
fileset 1 au 0 iemap incorrect - fix (ynq)y
fileset 999 au 0 imap incorrect - fix (ynq)y
fileset 999 au 0 iemap incorrect - fix (ynq)y
[...]
fileset 999 au 5 iemap incorrect - fix (ynq)y
fileset 999 au 6 imap incorrect - fix (ynq)y
fileset 999 au 6 iemap incorrect - fix (ynq)y
no CUT entry for fileset 1, fix? (ynq)y
no CUT entry for fileset 999, fix? (ynq)y
au 0 emap incorrect - fix? (ynq)y
au 0 summary incorrect - fix? (ynq)y
au 0 state file incorrect - fix? (ynq)y
au 1 emap incorrect - fix? (ynq)y
[...]
au 3 summary incorrect - fix? (ynq)y
au 4 state file incorrect - fix? (ynq)y
au 4 emap incorrect - fix? (ynq)y
au 4 summary incorrect - fix? (ynq)y
au 4 state file incorrect - fix? (ynq)y
fileset 1 iau 0 summary incorrect - fix? (ynq)y
fileset 999 iau 0 summary incorrect - fix? (ynq)y
[...]
fileset 999 iau 5 summary incorrect - fix? (ynq)y
free block count incorrect 0 expected 30955 fix? (ynq)y
free extent vector incorrect fix? (ynq)y
OK to clear log? (ynq)y
flush fileset headers? (ynq)y
set state to CLEAN? (ynq)y
```

Once the file system has been checked we can now mount it using `mount -F vxfs …`:

```
# mount -F vxfs /dev/vx/dsk/adg/ufs100mvol /mnt
# df -h /mnt
/dev/vx/dsk/adg/ufs100mvol  130M  100M  30M  77%  /mnt
```

As you can see we now have a 130 MB volume which is filled with 100 MB (hey, we told you it was full, didn't we? That's why we added another 30 MB before the conversion). The remaining 30 MB are free for user data (unlike UFS, which would have taken a large bite out of that for its own statically allocated meta data(..

Suggested reading: If you want to know more about file systems, and especially clustered file systems, "Shared Data Clusters" by Dilip M. Ranade (lead technical engineer for Veritas cluster file systems) is a great book.

12.3.1 SUMMARY

This chapter gave an introduction into file systems based on an overview of the development of file systems and especially their allocation mechanisms. It shows that the use of extent-based allocation is superior to block-based allocation because of the smaller overhead per block, less compute-intensive algorithms and more direct access to the resulting disk blocks for any I/O. Also, VxFS uses the available space almost ideally, unlike UFS, which always allocates fixed amounts of metadata for some assumed worst case scenarios (like having very few, very large files, or having very many very little files). VxFS allocates its metadata dynamically and is therefore much more flexible and space-efficient.

Some of the features of VxFS were outlined, especially growing and shrinking file systems online, optimizing existing file systems, and using storage checkpoints. Both rely heavily on extent-based allocation and especially storage checkpoints would be very hard to implement efficiently with any block-based allocation scheme.

CHAPTER 13: TUNING STORAGE FOUNDATION

by Volker Herminghaus

13.1 BASICS ABOUT TUNING STORAGE FOUNDATION

Having read the chapter about SAN storage, Moore's law and the advancements in disk performance your expectations about **performance** tuning Storage Foundation should be low. After all, optimizing a resource that is aggressively used by hundreds of different hosts for thousands of different volumes, all accessing the same overloaded mechanically limited disk hardware at the same time is almost impossible because many optimizations that improve our application performance decrease everybody else's. Fortunately, VxVM and VxFS are extensively self-tuning. It is not usually necessary to tweak individual volumes or file systems to get very good performance out of them because they know some of the features of the underlying level and use them as best they can, usually without degrading aggregate performance. For instance, VxVM knows about your storage array's sweet spots because it identifies the type of LUN using its extensive array support libraries (ASLs). VxFS in turn knows about the layout of the VxVM volume and adapts its optimization parameters (parallelity, I/O-size etc.) to the volume layout as much as possible.

However it is still possible to base one's volume layouts on wrong assumptions which might lead to very poor performance. This is the part where we can help. We therefore limit this chapter to two areas that would not be considered **performance** tuning in the classical sense, but that certainly classify as **tuning** in the sense of adapting the product to best suit your requirements as well as to prevent anything that would actually hurt performance. The main points for the Easy Sailing part are:

V. Herminghaus and A. Sriba, *Storage Management in Data Centers*,
DOI: 10.1007/978-3-540-85023-6_13, © Springer-Verlag Berlin Heidelberg 2009

- Using reasonable volume parameters
- Setting these as defaults

As you can see, this is a rather short introduction into VxVM and VxFS tuning. Much more about performance tuning in general, benchmarking, and the limits of optimization can be found in this chapter's Technical Deep Dive section beginning on page 468.

13.1.1 TUNING VxVM BY USING REASONABLE PARAMETERS

Remember what we said in the chapter about SAN storage arrays? Storage arrays are typically used by a massive amount of hosts at the same time. Very often hundreds and sometimes thousands of machines access the same storage array. Most arrays have a very large buffer cache, so they can buffer any writes coming in to the array. These writes will be received at very high speed by the storage array, so the host is freed from these write I/Os rather rapidly. One could say that any kind of write I/O is probably the best case for accessing a storage array, since no disk seek time must be waited for by the requesting machine. The limiting factor for write I/O are the latency of the array. This latency is in turn defined by two parameters:

1) The basic latency of the unloaded array. This one given by the array hardware processing capabilities

2) The amount of load on the array's front end controllers that insert the writes into the write queue and onto the back-end controllers that distribute the writes to the individual disks onto which the data is ultimately persisted.

We obviously cannot change the basic hardware features of the array (at least not by software tuning ;), so we'll have to concentrate on the second point: the load on the array's front end and back end controllers. How can we influence that parameter? The simple, and rather obvious, point here is to reduce the absolute number of I/Os as much as possible. If the array's controller only has to deal with 1,000 I/Os per second instead of 5,000 I/Os per second, the algorithms internal to the array will have less objects to handle, will have shorter queues to process, and subsequently will work more efficiently. This increased efficiency results in shorter latency from the storage array and therefore can increase performance for our host **without** hurting other participants.

How to Reduce the Number of I/Os?

The obvious point, and actually the point where the most performance could be gained, is: modify the application to read and write more wisely. Unfortunately, most application developers couldn't care less about storage; they are too far removed from the storage hardware. The application developers usually rely on the database staff and it is the database staff who the application developers will typically resort to when performance problems arise. But database people tend to be technically a little on the weak side, and from our experience many of them will still fall for the same ancient myths that had already been proved wrong ten years ago.

For instance, it used to be very hard to rid a typical Oracle DBA of the idea that using a stripe size identical to Oracle's block size (usually 8 KB) is a brilliant idea. It is indeed a terrible idea, as it creates a massive overload of extraneous I/O without improving any other area of the storage hierarchy. But do not be surprised if your DBA dispels this as a myth, citing some obscure Oracle document he received fifteen years ago.

So basically we are stuck with having to do the whole tuning ourselves: the application developers only talk to the guys with the antiquated ideas about storage systems, so we must make the best out of the situation.

How can we make the best out of the situation? We can, first of all, **not** stripe out volumes unless we expect highly localized high-speed traffic to our volumes. This is not normally the case. Striping will lead to extraneous I/O whenever a stripe column boundary is crossed. This will cause additional overhead in the storage array controllers. The only advantage we might get is increased load balancing across several physical disks. But this may not be an advantage at all. The disks that we are transferring load to are only partially used by our volume. the rest of their capacity is shared with other hosts using the same storage array. They have allocated their LUNs on the same physical disks as we have. If we stripe heavily, then we will split single large I/Os into more small I/Os, resulting in more load on the storage array's controllers. But apart from this we might hit this one unlucky disk that happens to be massively overloaded with scattered read requests (which can not be ameliorated by caching). This would drag down out performance to abysmal levels, even if the rest of the volume actually did gain something from striping (which it usually does not).

Up to five years ago we would have recommended you choose physical disk spindles inside the storage array for your application, create LUNs from them, and use them wisely. It was at that time possible to actually tune storage arrays to your application. Because of the extreme consequences of Moore's law in recent years it has become next to impossible to successfully implement this nowadays. The best you can do now is to restrain yourself to do only very limited striping (or preferably use concatenation instead) in order not to generate additional I/Os on the storage array controllers..

On the other hand we should not overdo it. If you choose to do all your I/O on a single LUN then the host resident request queue for this LUN (which looks to your host system like a physical disk) may grow very large, which hampers performance on the host side. It is not generally a clever idea to increase the maximum queue size on the host, by the way: The algorithms used for queues work very well on short queue length, but processing time may grow rapidly with increasing queue lengths. In this case it is better to distribute the I/O onto several LUNs.

Not striping, but still distributing load across several LUNs to keeps queue lengths short may seem like an oxymoron, but actually it isn't: If you have control over the creation of the LUNs you can create several LUNs in such a way that they are on physically contiguous space. If you concatenate these LUNs (each of which may be many GBs in size), then you can have the best of both worlds: short queues on the host (at least for random I/O), and no additional load on the front and back end controllers in the storage array.

13.1.2 UNDERSTANDING AND MODIFYING VxVM DEFAULTS

Defaults for various VxVM commands are stored (in Solaris) in the /etc/defaults direc-tory, under the same name as the VxVM utility that the defaults pertain to. For instance, you could create a file /etc/defaults/vxdg to set the default type of Disk group (e.g. cds or not cds), or a file /etc/default/vxassist to set the defaults for volume and log char-acteristics.

IDENTIFYING VXASSIST DEFAULTS

You can check which defaults vxassist will use by issuing the command vxassist help showattrs (show attributes) On a system with an empty defaults file you will get an output that looks similar to this:

```
# vxassist help showattrs
#Attributes:
layout=nomirror,nostripe,nomirror-stripe,nostripe-mirror,
 nostripe-mirror-col,nostripe-mirror-sd,noconcat-mirror,nomirror-concat,
 span,nocontig,raid5log,noregionlog,diskalign,nostorage
mirrors=2 columns=0 regionlogs=1 raid5logs=1 dcmlogs=0 dcologs 0
autogrow=no destroy=no sync=no
min_columns=2 max_columns=8
regionloglen=0 regionlogmaplen=0 raid5loglen=0 dcmloglen=0 logtype=region
stripe_stripeunitsize=128 raid5_stripeunitsize=32
stripe-mirror-col-trigger-pt=2097152 stripe-mirror-col-split-trigger-pt=2097152
usetype=fsgen diskgroup= comment="" fstype=
sal_user=
user=0 group=0 mode=0600
probe_granularity=2048
mirrorgroups (in the end)
 alloc=
 wantalloc=vendor:confine
 mirror=
 wantmirror=
 mirrorconfine=
 wantmirrorconfine=protection
 stripe=
 wantstripe=
 tmpalloc=
```

What you see in the layout line is that `vxassist` will use no mirroring (`nomirror`), no striping (`nostripe`), and no combination of any mirroring or striping, and that it will allow the spanning of disks (`span`), will align subdisks to cylinder boundaries (`diskalign`), etc.

The next line shows that if you specify a mirrored layout on the command line (i.e. if you create a mirrored volume) then this volume will have by default 2 mirrors (`mirrors=2`).

Two lines further down you see

```
min_columns=2 max_columns=8
```

This refers to the boundaries of the stripe column default. Let's say you specify a striped layout (although you should think twice about doing it - remember what we said about reducing scattered reads!) but you do not specify a number of columns. In that case VxVM picks the default as follows:

It divides the number of disks in the Disk group by two to allow for later mirroring the volume. Then, from the result it picks the highest number of columns possible that is within the limits given by `min_columns` and `max_columns`. If we were using a Disk group with six disks and we gave the following command:

```
vxassist make avol 1g layout=stripe
```

(i.e. no mirroring), it would create a three-column stripe. If our Disk group had fourteen disks, then using the same command it would create a seven-column stripe. And if there were many more disks in the Disk group, like thirty or forty, it would still never exceed eight, because that is the value of `max_columns`.

CHANGING VXASSIST DEFAULTS

We can put our own default into a file and make vxassist use those defaults. The simplest way is to edit (or create) the file `/etc/default/vxassist`, which `vxassist` will use automatically unless you specify otherwise. If you like different sets of defaults for different tasks you could create several files and pass them to vxassist using the `-d $DEFAULTSFILE` parameter. In that case, vxassist will ignore `/etc/defaults/vxassist` and just read the default file that you passed it.

FORMAT OF THE VXASSIST DEFAULTS FILE

The defaults file for vxassist looks like a collection of command line parameters to vxassist. In principle, you could create a space-separated or newline-separated list of your favorite options. But the reality is more tricky, and there are important differences, which concern mirroring and striping: even if you set `nmirror=3` and `ncol=5` in the defaults file, these values will not be activated just because they are in the defaults file.

Only if the `vxassist` command actually receives the parameter appropriate for mirroring will the new default for `nmirror` be used. I.e. in the case given above, the volume will be a three-way mirror. And only if the parameter relevant for striping is used on the command line will the number of columns from the defaults file be applied.

So setting the `nmirror` attribute does not lead to mirroring, and setting the `ncol` attribute does not lead to striping. But there actually are ways to turn mirroring on by default.

One is to add "`mirror=yes`" to the defaults file. This will lead to all volumes, regardless of what is specified on the command line, being mirrored the default number of times (dependent on the rest of the file or the default that was compiled into `vxassist`).

While `mirror=yes` turns the default on for mirroring, there is no such parameter for striping. You cannot specify `stripe=yes` to coerce striping by default. You **can**, however, specify a default layout, using the "`layout=...`" parameter just like you used to one the command line. So with a defaults file like this:

```
# cat /etc/default/vxassist
columns=2
nmirror=3
```

You will get a concat volume unless you specify mirroring. If you do specify mirroring (`layout=mirror`) on the command line you will get a three-way mirror (because you changed the default value for the number of mirrors). But the volume will not be striped unless you also specify striping on the command line (`layout=stripe`, `layout=stripe-mirror` or similar). If you do specify striping, then the number of columns will default to two as given in the defaults file. If you add `mirror=yes` to the default file the volume will be mirrored. If you add layout=mirror instead, the volume will be mirrored, too. But if you add `layout=stripe-mirror`, it will be striped, but not mirrored. In that case you need an additional line adding `mirror=yes` to actually create striped and mirrored volumes be default. If this seems non-linear and counter-intuitive to you, then rest assured that you are not the only one who thinks so. But we cannot change the software, just explain it.

After you wrote your defaults file for `vxassist`, the output of the `vxassist showattrs` command will vary to reflect what you put into the defaults file. For instance, with a defaults file like this:

```
# cat /etc/default/vxassist
layout=stripe-mirror
mirror=yes
columns=2
nmirror=3
```

the output of `vxassist help showattrs` will change to resemble the new defaults:

```
# vxassist help showattrs
#Attributes:
 layout=mirror,nostripe,nomirror-stripe,stripe-mirror,
 nostripe-mirror-col,nostripe-mirror-sd, noconcat-mirror,nomirror-concat,
 span,nocontig,raid5log,noregionlog,diskalign,nostorage
 mirrors=3 columns=2 regionlogs=1 raid5logs=1 dcmlogs=0 dcologs 0
 autogrow=no destroy=no sync=no
 min_columns=2 max_columns=8
 regionloglen=0 regionlogmaplen=0 raid5loglen=0 dcmloglen=0 logtype=region
 stripe_stripeunitsize=128 raid5_stripeunitsize=32
 stripe-mirror-col-trigger-pt=2097152 stripe-mirror-col-split-trigger-pt=2097152
 usetype=fsgen diskgroup= comment="" fstype=
```

```
sal_user=
user=0 group=0 mode=0600
probe_granularity=2048
mirrorgroups (in the end)
 alloc=
 wantalloc=vendor:confine
 mirror=
 wantmirror=
 mirrorconfine=
 wantmirrorconfine=protection
 stripe=
 wantstripe=
 tmpalloc=
```

13.1.3   Tuning VxFS

Tuning Extent Allocation

Tuning a VxFS file system can be done on two levels: One is making sure the extents that are allocated for the files are as contiguous as possible, i.e. files do not consist of hundreds of little, non-sequential snippets, but rather of a single, large block. The VxFS file system is very good at allocating contiguously when a file is written, as has been discussed in the appropriate section on page 436 of the file system chapter. But during the lifetime of a file system extents are constantly being rewritten, new extents allocated, old extents freed and so on. The result is that files end up consisting of little snippets after all. This happens to both UFS and VxFS file systems. It is worse if the file system is nearly full, because then the system is less free to find appropriate extents (or blocks) for the files and must resort to allocating e.g. several small extents far away from the existing file rather than a single large extent close by.

The standard UFS offers no way of handling this slow but certain deterioration of file system contiguousness (and therefore deterioration of performance) except copying the files away, creating a new file system, and copying the files back. This is usually unacceptable due to the downtime involved. The VxFS does have utilities that do extent (and directory) reallocation on the fly, on a active file system. In fact it is highly recommended to perform a reallocation run at regular intervals, like daily, weekly, or at least monthly. The total cost in I/O load is not very high, but application performance will not degrade, as it would otherwise. In one real example from 2006 a file system for Oracle table spaces had an average(!) number of several hundred extents allocated per file. That was reduced to an average of one(!) extent per file during three successive runs of optimization, each of which took only a few minutes. File system performance for sequential I/O was increased by a factor of ten. This is an extreme case, but because so few people know the tools for VxFS optimization we suspect that there several Petabyte of storage out there which have become extremely scattered and would indeed profit a lot from a regular optimization. Refer to the file system chapter for more information about the `fsadm` command and how it can be used to optimize your file systems.

TUNING FILE SYSTEM PARAMETERS

VxFS defaults are dynamically created when the file system is started by reading (if applicable) the layout of the underlying volume and adapting several internal values to it (e.g. the maximum I/O size). But these values can be influenced by creating an entry in the file /etc/vxfstunetab. In this file, each line defines the VxFS tunables for one volume. You can read the initial value with vxtunefs $RAWDEVICE, then change their format to match the vxfstunetab file format (which unfortunately does not match at all), and then changing the values of the individual tunables for that file system. The next time the file system is mounted, these values will be applied.

Let's look at the tuning parameters for a newly created VxFS file system:

```
# vxassist -g adg make avol 1g
# mkfs -F vxfs /dev/vx/rdsk/adg/avol
    version 7 layout
    2097152 sectors, 1048576 blocks of size 1024, log size 16384 blocks
    largefiles supported
# mount -Fvxfs /dev/vx/dsk/adg/avol /mnt
# vxtunefs /mnt
Filesystem i/o parameters for /mnt
read_pref_io = 65536
read_nstream = 1
read_unit_io = 65536
write_pref_io = 65536
write_nstream = 1
write_unit_io = 65536
pref_strength = 10
buf_breakup_size = 1048576
discovered_direct_iosz = 262144
max_direct_iosz = 1048576
default_indir_size = 8192
qio_cache_enable = 0
write_throttle = 0
max_diskq = 1048576
initial_extent_size = 8
max_seqio_extent_size = 2048
max_buf_data_size = 8192
hsm_write_prealloc = 0
read_ahead = 1
inode_aging_size = 0
inode_aging_count = 0
fcl_maxalloc = 32537600
fcl_keeptime = 0
fcl_winterval = 3600
```

```
fcl_ointerval = 0
oltp_load = 0
```

The parameters reported by vxtunefs are actually derived from the volume layout. The VxFS specific mount command probes the underlying volume parameters and uses them to set the tunable parameters to something reasonable. Therefore it is seldom necessary to tune a VxFS file system for optimum performance with the underlying VxVM volume. At least this used to be the case if you were using physical disks rather than LUNs. You may find that some tuning may still be in order to adapt for application-specific I/O behavior or other special cases, even if the VxFS file system resides in a VxVM volume. If it does not reside in a VxVM volume but in a plain partition or a volume created by some other volume management product, then tuning is definitely a reasonable option. This is also true if you are using LUNs as the basis for your VxVM (or other) volumes, because the physical properties of LUNs allow much greater I/O sizes as well as greater parallelity than plain disks do.. Let's look at some volume layouts, their respective tunefs-parameters and how they change dependent on the volume layout.

First, we create four volumes: a concat volume, a stripe with 5 columns and a stripesize of 2048 blocks (or 1024k or 1 MB), a three-way mirror, and a stripe-mirror with three columns and two mirrors. We make VxFS file systems on them and mount them right away into directories with names corresponding to the volume layouts:

```
# mkdir /concat /stripe5col /mirror3way /stripemirror
# vxassist make concatvol 1g layout=concat
# mkfs -F vxfs /dev/vx/rdsk/adg/concatvol
    version 7 layout
    2097152 sectors, 1048576 blocks of size 1024, log size 16384 blocks
    largefiles supported
# mount -F vxfs /dev/vx/dsk/adg/concatvol /concat
# vxassist make stripe5colvol 1g layout=stripe ncol=5 stwid=1024k
# mkfs -F vxfs /dev/vx/rdsk/adg/stripe5colvol
    version 7 layout
    2097152 sectors, 1048576 blocks of size 1024, log size 16384 blocks
    largefiles supported
# mount -F vxfs /dev/vx/dsk/adg/stripe5colvol
# vxassist make mirror3wayvol 1g layout=mirror nmirror=3 init=active
# mkfs -F vxfs /dev/vx/rdsk/adg/mirror3wayvol
    version 7 layout
    2097152 sectors, 1048576 blocks of size 1024, log size 16384 blocks
    largefiles supported
# mount -F vxfs /dev/vx/dsk/adg/mirror3wayvol /mirror3way
# vxassist make stripemirrorvol 1g layout=stripe-mirror init=active
# mkfs -F vxfs /dev/vx/rdsk/adg/stripemirrorvol
    version 7 layout
    2097152 sectors, 1048576 blocks of size 1024, log size 16384 blocks
    largefiles supported
# mount -F vxfs /dev/vx/dsk/adg/stripemirrorvol  /stripemirror
```

Next, we dump the `vxtunefs` output for each file system into a file in /var/tmp, and then `diff` it with respect to the plain concat volume. Finally, we run the result over `cat -n` in order to get line numbers for convenient referencing:

```
# for MOUNTPOINT in /concat /stripe5col /mirror3way /stripemirror; do
  vxtunefs $MOUNTPOINT >/var/tmp/$MOUNTPOINT.tuna
done
```

First, let's look at the differences between the concat volume and the five column stripe we just created:

```
# diff /var/tmp/concat.tuna /var/tmp/stripe5col.tuna | cat -n
     1  1,8c1,8
     2  < Filesystem i/o parameters for /concat
     3  < read_pref_io = 65536
     4  < read_nstream = 1
     5  < read_unit_io = 65536
     6  < write_pref_io = 65536
     7  < write_nstream = 1
     8  < write_unit_io = 65536
     9  < pref_strength = 10
    10  ---
    11  > Filesystem i/o parameters for /stripe5col
    12  > read_pref_io = 1048576
    13  > read_nstream = 5
    14  > read_unit_io = 1048576
    15  > write_pref_io = 1048576
    16  > write_nstream = 5
    17  > write_unit_io = 1048576
    18  > pref_strength = 20
    19  15c15
    20  < max_diskq = 1048576
    21  ---
    22  > max_diskq = 83886080
```

What we see is that several parameters have changed. In particular, the preferred read-I/O and write-I/O size (lines 3, 6, 12, and 15) have adapted to reflect the stripe unit size of the striped volume. In addition, the number of read and write I/O streams (lines 4, 7, 13, and 16) has increased from one (which it is for the concat volume) to five (for the five column stripe). This reflects the fact that VxFS sees many more disks in the underlying storage and assumes it can put an I/O on each of the disks in parallel. Remember this assumption for the later part of the chapter. It will be the basis for some optimization for SAN storage.

Apart from the I/O parallelity parameters, the size of the disk queue generated per file has increased enormously (from 1MB to 80 MB). This result is arrived at by granting sixteen I/Os of the preferred I/O size (`read_pref_io` or `write_pref_io`) to every write stream (`write_nstream`). The concat volume has a preferred I/O size of 65536 (64KB) and only one write stream. sixteen times 64K is 1MB, so this is the maximum disk queue value for VxFS (the maximum number of bytes per file that reside in pages which are eligible for flushing to disk).

The five-way stripe, due to its large stripe unit size of 1 MB, gets the better end of it: five write streams (due to the five columns) multiplied by 1 MB multiplied by 16 yields the comparatively whopping 80 MB of queue size. Only after this size is exceeded does VxFS throttle write I/O to this file system; much later than in the case of the concat volume.

Now, let's check the differences between the concat volume and the three-way mirrored volume:

```
# diff /var/tmp/concat.tuna /var/tmp/mirror3way.tuna | cat -n
     1  1c1
     2  < Filesystem i/o parameters for /concat
     3  ---
     4  > Filesystem i/o parameters for /mirror3way
     5  3c3
     6  < read_nstream = 1
     7  ---
     8  > read_nstream = 3
```

As you see, not much has changed compared to the concat volume. Only the number of read streams has increased (lines 6 and 8) to reflect the number of plexes that can be read (three), so maximum read parallelization has increased. The stripe was better than that in this respect. It used five parallel read streams. So let's see what we get when we compare the concat volume with the stripe-mirror:

```
# diff /var/tmp/concat.tuna /var/tmp/stripemirror.tuna | cat -n
     1  1c1
     2  < Filesystem i/o parameters for /concat
     3  ---
     4  > Filesystem i/o parameters for /stripemirror
     5  3c3
     6  < read_nstream = 1
     7  ---
     8  > read_nstream = 3
     9  6c6
    10  < write_nstream = 1
    11  ---
    12  > write_nstream = 3
    13  8c8
    14  < pref_strength = 10
    15  ---
    16  > pref_strength = 20
    17  15c15
    18  < max_diskq = 1048576
    19  ---
    20  > max_diskq = 3145728
```

Again, the number of read streams has increased (lines 8 and 12) because this volume has three plexes instead of one. But because we stuck to the default stripe unit size of 64 KB (we did not specify "stwid=..." this time) the maximum disk queue has not increased dramatically; it is merely three times the value of the concat, which comes from the fact that there are now three columns that can be written to independently.

VxFS Tunable Parameters and How to Set Them

So, looking at the automatically generated VxFS tunables you might get the impression that striping a volume is not too bad after all. On the other hand, this book has been telling you over and over that striping in current data center setups at least tends to be counterproductive for performance. Who is right? Well, VxFS would be right and striping would be good if we are using physical disks. But if we are using SAN storage then VxFS is not right because then the parameters that the VxFS-specific mount command calculates are based on virtual objects (LUNs) rather than physical objects (disks). Virtual objects do not have the same limits as physical objects have (they were, after all, created specifically to overcome the limitations of their physical counterparts).

Using vxtunefs to Optimize Your SAN Storage

So the way to get the best of both world, to combine the enhanced features of virtual disks aka LUNs with the best volume layout (concat) without limiting the file system to ridiculously low values of disk queuing of parallelity is to tune your file systems to your SAN storage instead of some assumed physical disks.

You can do so by creating a file named /etc/vx/tunefstab that contains the tunable parameters for every file system of your host system. This file contains all the deviations from the default that you wish to impose on your file systems. If, like most data centers today, you are using basically one kind of storage array, and especially of you are using only one kind of LUN, then you can tweak the tunefstab file pretty easily: create a volume that resembles, on the VxVM level, the specifications of your LUNs.

E.g. if your LUNs are 6-way striped with a 512 KB stripe unit size, and you are mirroring all volumes (two plexes per volume) using VxVM, then you could create a sample volume that exposes all the underlying physical features to VxFS: just create a volume with two plexes, each of which is a 6-way stripe with 512 KB stripe unit size. Then, put a VxFS on it, mount it and run vxtunefs on the mount point.

The vxtunefs command will diligently create the necessary defaults to make the best out of a two-way mirror with underlying 6-column stripes with 512 KB stripe unit size, and output them to your terminal. Your job now is to catch that output, put it into /etc/vx/tunefstab for each volume that uses this particular SAN storage type and re-mount the volumes so the new values take effect. You will have to tweak the output format quite a bit to make a valid /etc/vx/tunefstab entry out of the vxtunefs output, but we will show you how to do it shortly.

ORGANIZATION OF THE /ETC/VX/TUNEFSTAB FILE

The file /etc/vx/tunefstab contains tuning information for all file systems, so in cluster systems it is a very good idea to replicate the file across all nodes in order to make sure that the relevant tuning parameters are accessible wherever a service group my go online.

The file is organized line by line, with each line containing either nothing, a comment, or the description of a single file system.

The following is a sample tunefstab for three of the four volumes we used. It also sets the system-wide default parameters for all **vxfs** file systems that have no specific entry in the tunefstab:

```
# cat /etc/vx/tunefstab
# Set some reasonable read/write defaults that match our SAN box
# These take precedence over the values derived from the volume
# layout which are found by mount_vxfs. Note that this does not
# seem to work any more as of Storage Foundation 5.0.
system_default  read_pref_io=1048576,write_pref_io=1048576,read_nstream=8

# Now fine-tune individual file systems
# This takes precedence over the values defined in system_default
/dev/vx/dsk/adg/stripemirror    max_diskq=83886080,write_nstream=8
/dev/vx/dsk/adg/stripe5col      max_diskq=3145728,write_pref_io=2097152

# The following entries will all be used, even if they are on
# different lines
/dev/vx/dsk/adg/concatvol       max_diskq=3145728,write_nstream=16
/dev/vx/dsk/adg/concatvol       read_nstream=16
```

The manual page for the /etc/vx/tunefstab file mentions an entry called **system_default**, which supposedly sets the values for all **vxfs** file systems. We have used this entry in the example above. But it seems like this entry does not work any more in Storage Foundation 5.0, as all tests performed on our hardware failed to produce any results using this setting.

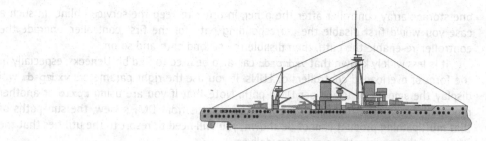

The Full Battleship

13.2 TOOLS FOR PERFORMANCE TUNING VxVM ON SAN STORAGE

VxWORK

A swiss company called **inƐtwork AG** has created a tool to ease administration and to improve performance on SAN storage by balancing the load as much as possible across all controllers in both the host and the storage array. It also recognizes and optimizes the paths to physical disks inside the array. Unless there are too many hosts attached to a single storage array this appears to be a very reasonably approach to optimization, because in many cases volumes under perform dramatically simply because of unfavorable mapping from volume blocks to hardware disk blocks. This problem can be fully remedied by using VxWork. In cases where there are too many hosts attached to a storage array it is not sure that there is a noticeable advantage, but it may be worth a try. Their web address is http://www.inwork.ch. Note that this is an independent third-party product and is not in any way related to Symantec.

TRACING AND BENCHMARKING VxVM VOLUMES

In addition to the commercial tool mentioned above there are several tools delivered with Storage Foundation that can help you find bottlenecks and possibly remove them. These tools come with the support package (VRTSspt). Two of them – vxdmpadm and vxtrace – are installed in /usr/sbin, but the benchmark program – vxbench – is installed in /opt/VRTSspt/FS/VxBench/vxbench_$RELEASE, where $RELEASE corresponds to the release number of the Solaris operating system, e.g. /opt/VRTSspt/FS/VxBench/vxbench_10. So how do these tools work, and what are the relevant command usages for performance tuning?

VXDMPADM

The vxdmpadm command controls the dynamic multipathing layer of VxVM. It is often used for inquiring path status, and in preparation of scheduled maintenance on paths. For instance, if there was a firmware upgrade due on the storage array then this is done on one storage array controller after the other, in order to keep the service online. In such a case you would first disable the corresponding path for the first controller, upgrade the controller, re-enable the path, then disable the second path and so on.

It is less widely known that vxdmpadm can also be used to find bottlenecks, especially in the form of overloaded controllers or LUNs. If you use the right parameters vxdmpadm will display the amount of usage per DMP path. Note that if you are using mpxio or another multipathing product that hides the individual paths from DMP's view, the sub-paths of that multipathing product cannot be shown; you will need to resort to the utilities that the vendor of that multipathing software delivers.

If you are using DMP then you can control gathering performance statistics and subsequently read out the statistics and display them by using simple vxdmpadm commands. The procedure – in short – is this:

```
# vxdmpadm iostat start # Automatically done at boot time
# vxdmpadm iostat show all      # Display all statistics
# vxdmpadm iostat reset # Set counters to zero
# vxdmpadm iostat show all interval=5 count=10   # more options
# vxdmpadm iostat stop  # Stop gathering statistics
```

It is good to know that gathering performance statistics is not CPU-intensive. You can leave it on without worrying about the overhead.

Here is a sample output of the command that shows the statistics:

```
# vxdmpadm iostat show all
```

			cpu usage = 52748us	per cpu memory = 32768b		
	OPERATIONS		KBYTES		AVG TIME(ms)	
PATHNAME	READS	WRITES	READS	WRITES	READS	WRITES
c1t1d1s2	2614	255	291	31	81.501718	42.064516
c2t17d1s2	2172	4983	271	587	82.704797	25.589438
c1t1d6s2	7109	2736	711	272	71.101266	18.393382
c2t17d6s2	5370	7162	663	810	70.126697	23.766667
c1t1d2s2	8452	2977	2257	235	19.428002	16.476596
c2t17d2s2	3824	5218	391	2443	62.506394	4.887843
c1t1d3s2	7767	7502	806	824	61.972705	21.253641
c2t17d3s2	6344	2308	765	249	58.785621	18.859438
c1t1d4s2	7116	7178	802	818	62.201995	21.117359
c2t17d4s2	6122	2028	765	253	59.546405	18.169960
c1t1d7s2	3990	4272	2149	3086	17.217310	3.563837
c1t1d9s2	2662	229	296	28	55.266892	43.071429

VXTRACE

A nice utility was developed for VxVM to follow I/Os from the Volume to the LUN and see what actually gets sent to the storage array. This tool is called vxtrace and will become your good friend especially when trying to find out exactly what kind of I/O pattern your application creates. This is often the entry point for optimization efforts. It goes without saying that in order to optimize, you first need to know what to optimize for. Does the application create mostly read or mostly write I/O? Are the I/Os large or small, consecutive or random? Do they address the whole volume or are they mostly limited to hot spots? You can find all that out using vxtrace on a mounted file system.

The following are a few walkthroughs of **vxtrace** on a volume while using vxbench (see below) to put database-like I/O onto a file in the file system residing on that volume.

```
# vxtrace -o dev,disk -g adg mirrorvol
1091 START read vdev mirrorvol block 3904352 len 16 concurrency 1 pid 24980
1092 START read disk c1t1d7s2 op 1091 block 3970144 len 16
1092 END read disk c1t1d7s2 op 1091 block 3970144 len 16 time 0
1091 END read vdev mirrorvol op 1091 block 3904352 len 16 time 1
1093 START read vdev mirrorvol block 34640160 len 16 concurrency 1 pid 24980
1094 START read disk c1t1d7s2 op 1093 block 34705952 len 16
1094 END read disk c1t1d7s2 op 1093 block 34705952 len 16 time 0
1093 END read vdev mirrorvol op 1093 block 34640160 len 16 time 0
1095 START read vdev mirrorvol block 23138688 len 16 concurrency 1 pid 24980
1096 START read disk c1t1d7s2 op 1095 block 23204480 len 16
1096 END read disk c1t1d7s2 op 1095 block 23204480 len 16 time 0
1095 END read vdev mirrorvol op 1095 block 23138688 len 16 time 1
1097 START read vdev mirrorvol block 61058832 len 16 concurrency 1 pid 24980
1098 START read disk c1t1d7s2 op 1097 block 61124624 len 16
1098 END read disk c1t1d7s2 op 1097 block 61124624 len 16 time 0
1097 END read vdev mirrorvol op 1097 block 61058832 len 16 time 0
1099 START read vdev mirrorvol block 11335712 len 16 concurrency 1 pid 24980
1100 START read disk c1t1d2s2 op 1099 block 44955936 len 16
1100 END read disk c1t1d2s2 op 1099 block 44955936 len 16 time 1
1099 END read vdev mirrorvol op 1099 block 11335712 len 16 time 1
1101 START read vdev mirrorvol block 71050496 len 16 concurrency 1 pid 24980
1102 START read disk c1t1d8s2 op 1101 block 25451776 len 16
1102 END read disk c1t1d8s2 op 1101 block 25451776 len 16 time 1
1101 END read vdev mirrorvol op 1101 block 71050496 len 16 time 1
```

And so on; you get the point: Every I/O is tagged (in the left most column) by an identifier that makes it easy to correlate the I/O START to the I/O END. Each I/O to or from a "**vdev**" (virtual device) is converted to an I/O to or from a "**disk**" (physical device, or what the computer thinks is a physical device). The length field always says "**len 16**", which means all I/Os in the (admittedly tiny) time frame we observed were 8KB in size (16 blocks). As you can see from the block numbers they are not sequential at all. In that particular case, nothing can be gained from tuning the I/O size to some large value (all I/Os are small anyway) or from making the files more contiguous (the I/Os access the file in a random fashion anyway, so that would not help).

Here is another example from a mirror-stripe that shows how striping can have a massively negative effect on volume I/O behavior if it is not used wisely:
```
# vxtrace -o dev,disk -g adg mirror-stripevol
1147 START read vdev mirror-stripevol block 43008 len 2048 concurrency 1 pid 25646
```

```
1148 START read disk c1t1d4s2 op 1147 block 89552896 len 64
1149 START read disk c1t1d5s2 op 1147 block 89552896 len 64
1150 START read disk c1t1d6s2 op 1147 block 89552896 len 64
1151 START read disk c1t1d2s2 op 1147 block 79293376 len 64
1152 START read disk c1t1d3s2 op 1147 block 89552960 len 64
1153 START read disk c1t1d4s2 op 1147 block 89552960 len 64
1154 START read disk c1t1d5s2 op 1147 block 89552960 len 64
1155 START read disk c1t1d6s2 op 1147 block 89552960 len 64
1156 START read disk c1t1d2s2 op 1147 block 79293440 len 64
1157 START read disk c1t1d3s2 op 1147 block 89553024 len 64
1158 START read disk c1t1d4s2 op 1147 block 89553024 len 64
1159 START read disk c1t1d5s2 op 1147 block 89553024 len 64
1160 START read disk c1t1d6s2 op 1147 block 89553024 len 64
1148 END read disk c1t1d4s2 op 1147 block 89552896 len 64 time 0
1161 START read disk c1t1d2s2 op 1147 block 79293504 len 64
1149 END read disk c1t1d5s2 op 1147 block 89552896 len 64 time 0
1162 START read disk c1t1d3s2 op 1147 block 89553088 len 64
1163 START read disk c1t1d4s2 op 1147 block 89553088 len 64
1164 START read disk c1t1d5s2 op 1147 block 89553088 len 64
1165 START read disk c1t1d6s2 op 1147 block 89553088 len 64
1166 START read disk c1t1d2s2 op 1147 block 79293568 len 64
1167 START read disk c1t1d3s2 op 1147 block 89553152 len 64
1150 END read disk c1t1d6s2 op 1147 block 89552896 len 64 time 0
1168 START read disk c1t1d4s2 op 1147 block 89553152 len 64
1169 START read disk c1t1d5s2 op 1147 block 89553152 len 64
1151 END read disk c1t1d2s2 op 1147 block 79293376 len 64 time 0
1170 START read disk c1t1d6s2 op 1147 block 89553152 len 64
1171 START read disk c1t1d2s2 op 1147 block 79293632 len 64
1172 START read disk c1t1d3s2 op 1147 block 89553216 len 64
1173 START read disk c1t1d4s2 op 1147 block 89553216 len 64
1174 START read disk c1t1d5s2 op 1147 block 89553216 len 64
1175 START read disk c1t1d6s2 op 1147 block 89553216 len 64
1152 END read disk c1t1d3s2 op 1147 block 89552960 len 64 time 0
1176 START read disk c1t1d2s2 op 1147 block 79293696 len 64
1177 START read disk c1t1d3s2 op 1147 block 89553280 len 64
1178 START read disk c1t1d4s2 op 1147 block 89553280 len 64
1179 START read disk c1t1d5s2 op 1147 block 89553280 len 64
1157 END read disk c1t1d3s2 op 1147 block 89553024 len 64 time 0
1156 END read disk c1t1d2s2 op 1147 block 79293440 len 64 time 0
1159 END read disk c1t1d5s2 op 1147 block 89553024 len 64 time 0
1158 END read disk c1t1d4s2 op 1147 block 89553024 len 64 time 0
1154 END read disk c1t1d5s2 op 1147 block 89552960 len 64 time 0
1153 END read disk c1t1d4s2 op 1147 block 89552960 len 64 time 0
1160 END read disk c1t1d6s2 op 1147 block 89553024 len 64 time 0
1155 END read disk c1t1d6s2 op 1147 block 89552960 len 64 time 0
1166 END read disk c1t1d2s2 op 1147 block 79293568 len 64 time 0
1167 END read disk c1t1d3s2 op 1147 block 89553152 len 64 time 0
```

```
1168 END read disk c1t1d4s2 op 1147 block 89553152 len 64 time 0
1170 END read disk c1t1d6s2 op 1147 block 89553152 len 64 time 0
1162 END read disk c1t1d3s2 op 1147 block 89553088 len 64 time 0
1161 END read disk c1t1d2s2 op 1147 block 79293504 len 64 time 0
1169 END read disk c1t1d5s2 op 1147 block 89553152 len 64 time 0
1174 END read disk c1t1d5s2 op 1147 block 89553216 len 64 time 0
1163 END read disk c1t1d4s2 op 1147 block 89553088 len 64 time 0
1175 END read disk c1t1d6s2 op 1147 block 89553216 len 64 time 0
1176 END read disk c1t1d2s2 op 1147 block 79293696 len 64 time 0
1177 END read disk c1t1d3s2 op 1147 block 89553280 len 64 time 0
1178 END read disk c1t1d4s2 op 1147 block 89553280 len 64 time 0
1179 END read disk c1t1d5s2 op 1147 block 89553280 len 64 time 0
1165 END read disk c1t1d6s2 op 1147 block 89553088 len 64 time 1
1172 END read disk c1t1d3s2 op 1147 block 89553216 len 64 time 6
1164 END read disk c1t1d5s2 op 1147 block 89553088 len 64 time 6
1171 END read disk c1t1d2s2 op 1147 block 79293632 len 64 time 7
1173 END read disk c1t1d4s2 op 1147 block 89553216 len 64 time 7
1147 END read vdev mirror-stripevol op 1147 block 43008 len 2048 time 7
```

The first and the last line of output are the START and END lines for the volume I/O number 1147, which is 1MB (2048 blocks). As you can see this single I/O is split up into lots of 32K (64 blocks) I/Os because the underlying volume is striped with a stripe unit size which is much smaller than the application's I/O size. It is obvious that this has a negative effect on the overall performance of the storage array. The storage array has to handle many more individual I/Os, cannot efficiently use its read-ahead cache etc. There might be an advantage if the storage array was dedicated to our host, because we are reading from several spindles in parallel. But first of all, storage arrays nowadays are usually shared by a massive number of hosts. And second, it is not at all certain that there actually would be any noticeable performance increase due to striping due to the increased read latency and the high speed of sequential access. Keep all the relevant parameters in mind when optimizing your storage!

That said, a realistic cycle of performance tuning a live application volume in a data center is the following:

1. Make sure any reasonable optimization can be done at all. This is usually **not** the case if several hundred servers are attached to the same storage array, as any optimization that works to the benefit of your server will work against the other servers.

2. Thoroughly optimize the file system first using (possibly several runs of) fsadm -de $MOUNTPOINT. Doing the following steps on a file system that is not optimized leads to bogus results, as I/Os that would normally be large and sequential will get split into smaller random I/Os.

3. Run vxprint to find the current volume layout

4. Run a cycle of vxdmpadm iostat reset / vxdmpadm iostat show all to find any obviously overloaded controllers or LUNs

5. Run the command vxtrace -o dev,disk -g $DG $VOLNAME on the volume or vxtrace -o dev,disk -g $DG $DISKNAME on an overloaded target several times during various operating cycles of the application, like during normal operation, backup,

database export, etc.

6. Identify the I/O pattern of the application.

7. Relayout the volume to match the I/O pattern of the application and ideally the I/O requirements of the storage array. For this, you need to know the internal organization of your storage array's LUNs. For example, a LUN may consist of a slice out of a RAID-5 group. The RAID-5 group may consist of eight disks and use a stripe size of 64 KB or 512 KB.

If performance is still lacking, there is probably not much you can do, at least from a Volume Manager perspective. Most likely your SAN or storage array is overloaded (this is all too common nowadays) or the data access code in the application is not optimal (also very common).

So we are not expecting you to experience any multi-digit performance gains by optimizing VxVM volumes and VxFS file systems. It happens, but is not very common. You still need to do it, though, because in many cases the persons responsible for the SAN infrastructure, the SAN and volume storage, the database, and the application that uses the database will quarrel about whose fault the perceived performance problem is. If you have optimized your volumes and file systems (and maybe gained 5 percent), not only can you seriously claim that from your side the optimum is reached, but you might even claim that you have been keeping the volumes in good shape all the time: only little could be gained. Now the issue lies with the other departments and you are outside of the firing line.

VXBENCH

If you have analyzed the application's I/O pattern then you can simulate this I/O pattern in a reliable, repeatable way using vxbench. This little program resides – as mentioned above – inside /opt/VRTSspt/FS/VxBench and there are several versions of it: one for each version of the Solaris OS. The one for Solaris 10, for instance, has the path /opt/VRTSspt/FS/VxBench/vxbench_10. It takes a number of parameters, most notably a workload parameter -w, which determines the type of I/O: read or write, sequential or random, memory-mapped or normal, asynchronous or synchronous etc. The parameter -i specifies the sub-options to the workload, like the size of each I/O, how many threads to use, how many I/Os to make etc. There is a great lot of options and it is probably best if you call vxbench -h yourself to get some help. We will tell you just what you need to know in addition to what you can see from the help text because there are some things in vxbench which are not obvious.

1. The most important thing is that vxbench does not create files. Files must exist or the program fails. But if you use existing files be careful not to specify any workload that does write I/O or you will lose data! If you want to check just the volume speed you can specify the raw device to skip the file system code path, but again, be careful if you specify writing workloads, as this may corrupt an existing file system on that device.

2. If your files are small then vxbench will likely read beyond the end of the file and terminate with an error. It sounds like a stupid oversight, but that is the way it has been for years , so there is probably a good (if not particularly obvious) reason to it. You can (and sometimes must) limit the maximum offset in a file that is accessed by vxbench to something significantly smaller than the file size. In particular, if you

are doing hundreds of one MB I/Os in a sequential workload, then it is better to stay hundreds of MBs away from the end of the file.

3. To simulate database I/O, you need to specify a synchronous open-type. That causes vxbench to open the file in synchronous mode, like databases usually do. The flag is vxbench -o dsync or vxbench -o sync. You can somewhat emulate the I/O behavior of Veritas Storage Foundation Database Edition for Oracle on database files by additionally mounting the volume in the following way:

```
# mount -F vxfs -o convosync=direct,mincache=direct,nodatainlog,delaylog \
        /dev/vx/dsk/$DG/$VOLNAME /$MOUNTPOINT
```

This will convert all synchronous I/O to direct I/O, which is unbuffered and therefore does not taint the operating system's buffer cache. It will also turn down the use of the file system's intent log in favor of the database's own transaction log.

One thing that should be obvious but may need to be mentioned: In order to exclude side effects due to caching on the side of the operating system, you must run all benchmarks on a freshly mounted file system (unless, of course, you are benchmarking a raw device). Unmounting the file system every time and remounting it before every test can be a tedious task, so we suggest a smarter way: Before you run the benchmark, change your working directory to the mount point that you want to test. If your current working directory is inside the mount point, then that file system cannot be unmounted. But the system does not know that. So if you now enter the umount command, the system will flush all the buffers that relate to the file system you are trying to unmount. Then, after all the buffers have been flushed and invalidated, the umount system call will fail. You are left with a file system that has nothing buffered in the system's cache without having to actually remount it.

And if you redirect stderr to /dev/null, you don't even get the error message. Here's an example of the command:

```
# cd $MOUNTPOINT # Make umount fail if tried on $MOUNTPOINT
# umount $MOUNTPOINT 2>/dev/null # Flush all buffers: no caching side effects
# vxbench -w rand_read -i iocount=50,iosize=8,maxfilesize=35g /stripe/DATAFILE
```

Technical Deep Dive

13.3 Performance Tuning

13.3.1 Overview and Disclaimer

One of the most prominent marketing features for all kinds of computer equipment and software is a vast array of mutually interdependent figures collectively called "performance". This ominous feature is usually measured by some software suite in what is called a "benchmark". Both words, performance as well as benchmark, are not well defined at all, mostly because performance and everything related to it is such a multi-faceted issue. This chapter will highlight performance from various perspectives. It will help you define what kind of performance you actually need, how to measure it and possible ways to increase it or, more likely, to prevent doing something that stands in the way of good performance. Be warned that it is not reliable possible to guide anyone towards achieving high performance in their particular setup. Too many variables influence each other. But anybody looking for ways to optimize their system's performance will find lots of useful information in this chapter, and with a little bit of luck, it may hint you towards the bottleneck that has so far throttled your system's throughput.

13.3.2 Identifying Performance and Performance Requirements

Since tuning reminds many of cars and motorbikes let's imagine that we are not running a data center but a car racing team. We do so not for the sake of a demoralizing the reader (running race cars is more fun than running computers) but also, as you will see, because it turns out the two fields are very comparable in surprisingly many fields.

In the following pages we will help you identify your exact needs. This question is harder to answer than you may think. Once you have found out what the goal is, you can use your technical, managerial, and social skills reach that goal. So here's the analogy:

A car racing team and a data center operation are similar in several ways because both

1. Use leading edge hardware and personnel.

> *It is very hard to win a car race with an old vehicle and an untrained or unmotivated team, just as it is hard to get decent and reliable performance from old computer systems and an untrained or unmotivated team.*

2. Employ extremely complex setups with multiple interdependencies. Only if all

of the parameters are set correctly will the computer – or the car – be competitive. Unfortunately, in race car setup as well as in computer setup, it is not at all easy to find the reason for poor performance, as there are so many possibilities and they are so intimately intertwined. **There is never a magic bullet to make any complex setup fast! But there are dozens of areas that can make it slow!**

> *Some parameters that are interdependent in race cars: Tire pressure, tire rubber mixture and construction, spring rate, damper rate, strut, toe-in, down force, weight, grip, engine power, track layout, tarmac type, temperature, average cornering speed etc.*

> *Some parameters that are interdependent in data center applications: Memory, CPU cores, degree of parallelization, latency, queue lengths, IOPS, I/O sizes, throughput, number of users, response times, etc.*

3. Must cope with certain budget restrictions, which may be alleviated by over performing

> *A race team gets money from the sponsors and from winning races. A successful team gets more prize money and attracts more sponsors and high-end staff. A data center has a limited budget, but if the operations run particularly well, the company can expand and pass more money towards the data center. Unfortunately, in the current global economic climate this often is not the case. Many managers take the short-sighted approach of demanding ever increasing shareholder value, thereby disgusting their staff and leading to eventual meltdown. We hope and trust it is a matter of time until this is fixed.*

4. Are multi-layered, with each layer not necessarily pursuing the same goal

> *While the race car driver may just want to arrive first and have fun doing so, the team management usually pursues longer-term goals: to ultimately win the championship in order to attract more sponsors; the sponsors, in turn, would prefer the team to display excellent craftsmanship and fairness in order to better convey their message. And the team owner may not be looking at just this year's championship, but may have much longer-term goals. In a data center, the typical administrator wants to shut up the machine as much as possible so he can do more interesting things or handle more machines. The application owners want their application to run at optimum speed and do not care about the others. The SAN admin wants everybody to use the same kind and size of LUN to reduce the complexity. The network and security people would*

like to install fingerprint and retina scanners in every network node and forward packets only after thorough inspection concerning all conceivable security holes discovered since 1975. The data center manager wants the whole thing as cheaply as possible and often couldn't care less about current technological and physical limits, especially when these get in the way of reducing cost.

5. Are confronted with sudden unexpected developments so they must be able to react to quickly and with great flexibility.

A race can be turned upside-down by a yellow-phase, a sudden onset of rain, a technical defect, driver errors and so on. A data center must cope with unexpectedly high user demand, technical defects and outages, administrator errors etc.

Even with all the similarities, there is also one big difference between a race car team and data center staff: races are only held at certain times, while data center applications are usually 24/365 due to the ubiquity of internet applications.

So here is the question: What is performance? What kind of performance do we wish to attain? This is usually connected to another question: Who are we optimizing for? The administrator? The manager? The SAN group? The network and security group? (Hint: the application owner is a good, but often forgotten, candidate in the real world, although the other candidates are just as valid). This is the first question that we need to clarify, lest we optimize for something impressive yet irrelevant. It sounds trivial, but in fact it is very often overlooked.

So think about the following things that you might be trying to reach. Each of them is a completely different, yet valid, aspect of performance:

Shortest time to execute a given task

That's obvious. It's like winning the race. But it may be prohibitively costly or very hard to administer.

Lightest system load to execute a given task

Sounds good, too. But it does not help if the machine is idling anyway, or it may cause too long a response time.

Largest number of users served

This goes into the cost-saving direction, with a bittersweet note that response time may be underrepresented

Lowest overall cost solution

The full emphasis on cost-saving

Shortest response time to the user

What the users want (but they don't want to pay a lot for it).

Now think about the following factors that might contribute to improving overall "performance":

CPU clock

> *Costs money*

Number of CPU cores

> *Costs money, especially license fees*

Parallelity of the problem set

> *Can't help it much...*

Parallelity of the implementation (software)

> *Requires really smart developers*

I/O operations per second of the machine

> *Costs money*

Size of the I/Os

> *Requires at least some degree of data locality in the application, ideally sequential access*

Latency of I/O

> *Requires money or smart solution to reduce*

On a more hardware-oriented technical level, the following aspects:

Protocols used

> *Can't usually help it much*

Long-range latencies

> *Requires smart solution or additional bunker site close by that holds just the logs and replicates asynchronously from there to the remote site*

Error rates and recovery mechanisms

> *Can't usually help it much; they are defined by the transport medium's physical properties and the protocol used...*

Timeout values

> *Can tweak them somewhat, but usually not much*

And on a more global level, these:

Number of systems connected to a storage array

> *Costs money to reduce*

Frame rate for SAN switches

Costs money to increase

Distance of the remote disaster recovery site

Can't usually help it much...

As you see, there are many parameters and optimization goals possible, so there can not be one performance tuning guide that does it all right. One could argue that in the context of this book at least, it should be clear that what is needed is a performance tuning guide to accelerate I/Os, right? It turns out that even this apparently simple goal is actually manifold: The first problem that springs to mind is the use of shared SAN resources. If user A makes his volumes run faster, then user B typically gets less performance. Storage arrays are usually saturated with I/O requests, and the more some egotistic application owner or admin optimizes his "own" LUNs, the more I/Os per second are loaded onto the shared disk spindles. But that is only part of the problem: User A will also tend to increase the volume's latency, because in most cases administrators will try to increase the striping factor in order to gain performance. Increasing the striping factor distributes the load across more LUNs, but also increases read latency and CPU and channel overhead. It will also degrade overall performance of the storage array instead of improving it because disk heads have to move more (because load is distributed across more targets) and the storage array's read-ahead cache is not used as efficiently. So in short: one cannot even say that "speeding up the volumes" is a good thing.

Alternatively, you may want to think about using storage checkpoints to speed up your backups. Storage checkpoints have been extensively covered in the chapter about point-in-time copies. They can speed up backups by allowing you, in combination with Oracle's RMAN (Recovery MANager) utility, to feed just those blocks into RMAN that have been updated since the last backup. But this feature is not part of the base license, so it may cost a lot of money to do implement a solution based on storage checkpoints. Finally, even if you manage to increase I/O throughput without degrading everybody else's you may not have an I/O-bound problem, but a memory-bound problem. In that case, it would be so much more worthwhile to just add memory to the system.

But the real problem comes when you look at how complex the I/O subsystem alone has become. It is next to impossible to know all the limiting factors in the chain from the application down to the disk hardware, but here's at least a list of some of the more important ones:

» OS queue length and buffer sizes

» OS I/O parallelity

» HBA frame buffers

» Buffer credits HBA <-> intermediate nodes <-> storage array

» Fabric speed and error rates

» Storage array (SA) front end controller HBA buffers

» SA back end controller queue length

» SA disk queue length and on-disk controller hardware

» SA disk rotational speed

» SA disk type (S-ATA tends to be slow in mixed read-write operation)

The bottom line is that optimization is best done as high up as possible: the people who write the software have control over the amount, frequency, and locality of data they read. If they fail to deliver a smart approach to a problem, the next layer is usually the database staff. More often than not, database staff think differently from systems staff, so it may be hard to talk to them. (Systems people – at least the good ones – tend to rely on strict logic and prefer to understand exactly what is going on. Database people are usually very happy that their database gives them some kind of table or view for everything they want to know, and they often do not question the origin of the values in these tables, not their exact meaning). Operating systems and their staff is stuck at the low end of the food chain, and is often accused, but rarely guilty, of delivering under performing I/O systems. So what we can at least do here is provide you with a set of argumentative guidelines so that you can redirect the tuning efforts to where they belong: higher up the food chain, towards the database and application.

13.3.3 COMPARATIVE BENCHMARKS OF VARIOUS VOLUME LAYOUTS

Just to give you a rough idea of how much or how little performance can be gained by varying the volume layout versus varying the access pattern we have done a series of benchmarks using vxbench on the test bed graciously provided by the fine people of Sun microsystems in Langen, Germany. The machine was a 16-core SPARC LDOM which was redundantly connected to a Hitachi 9980 storage array. The benchmarks were done on varying volumes, each created to the same size (100g) and with a vxfs file system on it. Only default parameters were used, the number of stripe columns (ncol) is 5. The volume layout is shown in the left most column. The kind of access is given in the next column: read and write (which are sequential), and rand_read and rand_write (random). The next column is the size of the individual I/Os in KBytes. It is not the blocksize of the file system or volume! The columns labeled PARLL contains the parallelity, i.e. the number of threads concurrently accessing the volume. The speed is output in the next column, and is given in MB/sec. The columns for time, sys, and user stand are given in seconds and are equivalent to the values output by the UNIX time command.

Two runs were executed, with different sort orders. This first run is ordered by layout, then I/O size, then access type. The second one is ordered by layout, then access type, then I/O size.

We urge you to look at how excruciatingly low the throughput in small random reads is. It is often below one MB/sec. Don't forget that this is the way that most data base accesses are one! Retrieving data from any table that is significantly larger than the physical machine memory almost always requires at least one, but usually several, random reads (the database needs to read several nodes of the index tables first before it knows which block or blocks the data resides on).

CONCAT

#	Layout	Access	BKSZ	PARLL	Speed	Time	Sys	User
	concat	write	8	32	23.91	0.082	0.02	0.00

concat	rand_write	8	32	17.86	0.109	0.02	0.00
concat	read	8	32	25.94	0.075	0.02	0.00
concat	rand_read	8	32	1.58	1.240	0.02	0.00
concat	write	64	32	96.16	0.162	0.02	0.00
concat	rand_write	64	32	78.81	0.198	0.02	0.00
concat	read	64	32	101.05	0.155	0.02	0.00
concat	rand_read	64	32	8.88	1.760	0.02	0.00
concat	write	512	32	142.06	0.880	0.02	0.00
concat	rand_write	512	32	138.93	0.900	0.02	0.00
concat	read	512	32	139.06	0.899	0.02	0.00
concat	rand_read	512	32	23.22	5.384	0.02	0.00
concat	write	1024	32	147.19	1.698	0.03	0.00
concat	rand_write	1024	32	146.47	1.707	0.03	0.00
concat	read	1024	32	140.43	1.780	0.02	0.00
concat	rand_read	1024	32	26.90	9.294	0.03	0.00

STRIPE

#	Layout	Access	BKSZ	PARLL	Speed	Time	Sys	User
	stripe	write	8	32	23.19	0.084	0.02	0.00
	stripe	rand_write	8	32	17.56	0.111	0.02	0.00
	stripe	read	8	32	26.46	0.074	0.02	0.00
	stripe	rand_read	8	32	1.08	1.817	0.02	0.00
	stripe	write	64	32	95.42	0.164	0.02	0.00
	stripe	rand_write	64	32	80.59	0.194	0.02	0.00
	stripe	read	64	32	95.01	0.164	0.02	0.00
	stripe	rand_read	64	32	7.11	2.197	0.02	0.00
	stripe	write	512	32	198.63	0.629	0.09	0.00
	stripe	rand_write	512	32	193.25	0.647	0.08	0.00
	stripe	read	512	32	229.04	0.546	0.09	0.00
	stripe	rand_read	512	32	28.22	4.430	0.09	0.00
	stripe	write	1024	32	220.81	1.132	0.16	0.00
	stripe	rand_write	1024	32	207.11	1.207	0.17	0.00
	stripe	read	1024	32	243.37	1.027	0.15	0.00
	stripe	rand_read	1024	32	29.16	8.574	0.14	0.00

MIRROR

#	Layout	Access	BKSZ	PARLL	Speed	Time	Sys	User
	mirror	write	8	32	21.58	0.091	0.03	0.00
	mirror	rand_write	8	32	14.76	0.132	0.04	0.00
	mirror	read	8	32	24.61	0.079	0.02	0.00
	mirror	rand_read	8	32	1.09	1.792	0.02	0.00
	mirror	write	64	32	83.64	0.187	0.04	0.00
	mirror	rand_write	64	32	72.51	0.215	0.04	0.00
	mirror	read	64	32	98.67	0.158	0.02	0.00
	mirror	rand_read	64	32	8.28	1.888	0.02	0.00

mirror	write	512	32	138.48	0.903	0.04	0.00
mirror	rand_write	512	32	133.18	0.939	0.05	0.00
mirror	read	512	32	138.95	0.900	0.02	0.00
mirror	rand_read	512	32	20.69	6.042	0.03	0.00
mirror	write	1024	32	144.94	1.725	0.04	0.00
mirror	rand_write	1024	32	142.19	1.758	0.05	0.00
mirror	read	1024	32	143.12	1.747	0.03	0.00
mirror	rand_read	1024	32	27.01	9.254	0.03	0.00

STRIPE-MIRROR

# Layout	Access	BKSZ	PARLL	Speed	Time	Sys	User
stripe-mirror	write	8	32	16.68	0.117	0.04	0.00
stripe-mirror	rand_write	8	32	10.69	0.183	0.04	0.00
stripe-mirror	read	8	32	22.63	0.086	0.02	0.00
stripe-mirror	rand_read	8	32	1.03	1.900	0.02	0.00
stripe-mirror	write	64	32	57.56	0.271	0.04	0.00
stripe-mirror	rand_write	64	32	72.70	0.215	0.04	0.00
stripe-mirror	read	64	32	94.23	0.166	0.02	0.00
stripe-mirror	rand_read	64	32	7.54	2.071	0.02	0.00
stripe-mirror	write	512	32	95.19	1.313	0.17	0.00
stripe-mirror	rand_write	512	32	92.51	1.351	0.18	0.00
stripe-mirror	read	512	32	221.67	0.564	0.09	0.00
stripe-mirror	rand_read	512	32	26.50	4.717	0.10	0.00
stripe-mirror	write	1024	32	111.04	2.251	0.34	0.00
stripe-mirror	rand_write	1024	32	112.10	2.230	0.34	0.00
stripe-mirror	read	1024	32	244.69	1.022	0.15	0.00
stripe-mirror	rand_read	1024	32	26.73	9.354	0.18	0.00

This is the output of the second run, this time ordered by access type rather than I/O size to make it more easy to compare the influence of the relative I/O sizes.

CONCAT

# Layout	Access	BKSZ	PARLL	Speed	Time	Sys	User
concat	write	8	32	24.68	0.079	0.02	0.00
concat	write	64	32	98.58	0.159	0.02	0.00
concat	write	512	32	144.78	0.863	0.02	0.00
concat	write	1024	32	146.85	1.702	0.03	0.00
concat	rand_write	8	32	17.88	0.109	0.02	0.00
concat	rand_write	64	32	79.23	0.197	0.02	0.00
concat	rand_write	512	32	137.94	0.906	0.03	0.00
concat	rand_write	1024	32	145.59	1.717	0.03	0.00
concat	read	8	32	25.89	0.075	0.02	0.00
concat	read	64	32	93.67	0.167	0.02	0.00
concat	read	512	32	135.17	0.925	0.02	0.00
concat	read	1024	32	140.03	1.785	0.02	0.00

concat	rand_read	8	32	0.44	4.467	0.02	0.00
concat	rand_read	64	32	2.79	5.595	0.02	0.00
concat	rand_read	512	32	14.34	8.714	0.02	0.00
concat	rand_read	1024	32	34.88	7.168	0.03	0.00

STRIPE

#	Layout	Access	BKSZ	PARLL	Speed	Time	Sys	User
	stripe	write	8	32	22.66	0.086	0.02	0.00
	stripe	write	64	32	94.09	0.166	0.02	0.00
	stripe	write	512	32	209.06	0.598	0.08	0.00
	stripe	write	1024	32	221.14	1.131	0.15	0.00
	stripe	rand_write	8	32	17.71	0.110	0.02	0.00
	stripe	rand_write	64	32	81.39	0.192	0.02	0.00
	stripe	rand_write	512	32	189.98	0.658	0.09	0.00
	stripe	rand_write	1024	32	202.33	1.236	0.17	0.00
	stripe	read	8	32	26.00	0.075	0.02	0.00
	stripe	read	64	32	97.31	0.161	0.01	0.00
	stripe	read	512	32	223.65	0.559	0.08	0.00
	stripe	read	1024	32	234.69	1.065	0.16	0.00
	stripe	rand_read	8	32	0.62	3.147	0.02	0.00
	stripe	rand_read	64	32	4.51	3.465	0.02	0.00
	stripe	rand_read	512	32	23.95	5.220	0.09	0.00
	stripe	rand_read	1024	32	44.35	5.637	0.16	0.00

MIRROR

#	Layout	Access	BKSZ	PARLL	Speed	Time	Sys	User
	mirror	write	8	32	10.92	0.179	0.04	0.00
	mirror	write	64	32	79.78	0.196	0.03	0.00
	mirror	write	512	32	130.31	0.959	0.04	0.00
	mirror	write	1024	32	138.40	1.806	0.05	0.00
	mirror	rand_write	8	32	14.81	0.132	0.04	0.00
	mirror	rand_write	64	32	60.45	0.258	0.04	0.00
	mirror	rand_write	512	32	132.12	0.946	0.05	0.00
	mirror	rand_write	1024	32	141.07	1.772	0.05	0.00
	mirror	read	8	32	24.12	0.081	0.02	0.00
	mirror	read	64	32	91.07	0.172	0.02	0.00
	mirror	read	512	32	136.33	0.917	0.02	0.00
	mirror	read	1024	32	140.23	1.783	0.03	0.00
	mirror	rand_read	8	32	0.49	3.976	0.02	0.00
	mirror	rand_read	64	32	4.27	3.660	0.02	0.00
	mirror	rand_read	512	32	20.06	6.231	0.03	0.00
	mirror	rand_read	1024	32	29.22	8.556	0.03	0.00

STRIPE-MIRROR

# Layout	Access	BKSZ	PARLL	Speed	Time	Sys	User
stripe-mirror	write	8	32	16.07	0.122	0.04	0.00
stripe-mirror	write	64	32	78.11	0.200	0.04	0.00
stripe-mirror	write	512	32	93.56	1.336	0.17	0.00
stripe-mirror	write	1024	32	112.78	2.217	0.33	0.00
stripe-mirror	rand_write	8	32	8.86	0.220	0.04	0.00
stripe-mirror	rand_write	64	32	68.97	0.227	0.04	0.00
stripe-mirror	rand_write	512	32	97.46	1.283	0.18	0.00
stripe-mirror	rand_write	1024	32	102.66	2.435	0.34	0.00
stripe-mirror	read	8	32	22.21	0.088	0.02	0.00
stripe-mirror	read	64	32	90.14	0.173	0.02	0.00
stripe-mirror	read	512	32	207.29	0.603	0.10	0.00
stripe-mirror	read	1024	32	203.92	1.226	0.18	0.00
stripe-mirror	rand_read	8	32	0.89	2.200	0.03	0.00
stripe-mirror	rand_read	64	32	4.79	3.263	0.02	0.00
stripe-mirror	rand_read	512	32	20.92	5.975	0.10	0.00
stripe-mirror	rand_read	1024	32	31.98	7.818	0.18	0.00

13.3.4 SUMMARY

We hope to have given a reasonable overview over the various tuning possibilities that come with Storage Foundation. We have to admit that there were times when it was much more fun to optimize volumes: Raw disks have such a charming amount of intricacies: you could run into any limit: queue size on disk and in the controller, cache size on disk and in the controller and in the OS, cache entry size on disk versus I/O size on the SCSI bus, hot spots and so on. Tuning a data center machine was like the fine art of preparing a race car: If the setup was completely optimal you had a chance of winning the race. But if any of a (large) number of parameters was wrong – let alone several – there was no way you could have gotten decent performance.

With SAN storage that fine art was lost. Everyone just allocated storage from the box, and the box did all the thinking. Physics suddenly seemed irrelevant.

But now the discrepancy between disk head speed, disk transfer rate, and disk size has grown so much out of proportion (and is still continuing to do so), that physics has come back big time. So let's all be a little reasonable and keep in mind that no storage array can speed up random reads as long as it uses rotating disks for backing store.

The number of disks times the number of transactions per second is the upper limit to all I/O activity on your storage array, and that number hasn't kept up remotely with Moore's law. In addition, we are probably not the only ones using the storage array, so if we optimize the volumes to maximize our own performance, it is very likely that performance for everybody else is deteriorating. The others will then try to optimize their volumes to gain performance, and eventually everybody's performance becomes lousy.

If you have performance problems, it is most likely that you are simply expecting too much from your storage array. To modify an old proverb: "It's the disk drives, stupid!"

CHAPTER 14: MISCELLANEOUS

by Volker Herminghaus

14.1 DISK FLAGS

There are several auxiliary flags that VxVM uses to maintain a disk's status or preferential use. All of them can be set and reset by the administrator, and some are maintained automatically. This section will discuss the flags, show you their intended (and unintended) uses, and how to set and reset the flags.

If you look at the following output, you will see some unusual states noted on the right-hand side, as well as two "broken" disk media, as you know them from the trouble-shooting chapter. In fact, the latter two disks (adg01 and adg06) were simply offlined while deported, then the disk group was re-imported and thus the error triggered.

```
# vxdisk list
DEVICE       TYPE          DISK      GROUP    STATUS
[...]
c0t2d0s2     auto          -         -        offline
c0t3d0s2     auto:cdsdisk  adg02     adg      online reserved
c0t4d0s2     auto:cdsdisk  adg03     adg      online failing
c0t10d0s2    auto:cdsdisk  adg04     adg      online nohotuse
c0t11d0s2    auto:cdsdisk  adg05     adg      online spare
c0t12d0s2    auto          -         -        offline
-            -             adg01     adg      removed was:c0t2d0s2
-            -             adg06     adg      failed was:c0t12d0s2
```

V. Herminghaus and A. Sriba, *Storage Management in Data Centers,*
DOI: 10.1007/978-3-540-85023-6_14, © Springer-Verlag Berlin Heidelberg 2009

OK, let's sum up what we see, then make some sense of it and find out how these flags are set and reset. The following flags are set on one or more of the disks:

`offline, online, reserved, failing, nohotuse, spare, removed, failed`

Let's go through them and discuss them one by one:

OFFLINE/ONLINE

This flag is set by the administrator and used as a general software ON/OFF-switch for the disk medium. The administrator can simulate switching off a disk drive using this flag. The command to offline a disk is the following:

```
# vxdisk offline $ACCESSNAME
```

Remember the accessname is the name in the left most column of the `vxdisk list` output. Example:

```
# vxdisk offline c0t2d0
```

You can reverse the effect of this command by the using the opposing command to online the disk again:

```
# vxdisk online $ACCESSNAME
```

Example:

```
# vxdisk online c0t2d0
```

As long as a disk is in the offline state, it behaves just like a disk that is physically offline. I.e. the private region contents cannot be read and therefore the output of vxdisk list $ACCESSNAME is greatly reduced. Compare the outputs of the same command: vxdisk list c0t12d0, on an online and an offline disk:

```
# vxdisk online c0t12d0
# vxdisk list c0t12d0s2
Device:    c0t12d0s2
devicetag: c0t12d0
type:      auto
hostid:
disk:      name= id=1211724452.55.infra0
group:     name=adg id=1211817259.120.infra0
info:      format=cdsdisk,privoffset=256,pubslice=2,privslice=2
flags:     online ready private autoconfig
pubpaths:  block=/dev/vx/dmp/c0t12d0s2 char=/dev/vx/rdmp/c0t12d0s2
guid:      {ea26335e-1dd1-11b2-8dfd-080020c28592}
```

```
udid:       IBM%5FDNES-318350Y%5FDISKS%5F%20%20%20%20%20%20%20%20AKFQ6556
site:       -
version:    3.1
iosize:     min=512 (bytes) max=2048 (blocks)
public:     slice=2 offset=2304 len=35834496 disk_offset=0
private:    slice=2 offset=256 len=2048 disk_offset=0
update:     time=1216851961 seqno=0.52
ssb:        actual_seqno=0.1
headers:    0 240
configs:    count=1 len=1280
logs:       count=1 len=192
Defined regions:
 config   priv 000048-000239[000192]: copy=01 offset=000000 enabled
 config   priv 000256-001343[001088]: copy=01 offset=000192 enabled
 log      priv 001344-001535[000192]: copy=01 offset=000000 enabled
 lockrgn  priv 001536-001679[000144]: part=00 offset=000000
Multipathing information:
numpaths:   1
c0t12d0s2             state=enabled

# vxdisk offline c0t12d0s2
# vxdisk list c0t12d0s2
Device:     c0t12d0s2
devicetag:  c0t12d0
type:       auto
flags:      offline private autoconfig
pubpaths:   block=/dev/vx/dmp/c0t12d0s2 char=/dev/vx/rdmp/c0t12d0s2
guid:       {ea26335e-1dd1-11b2-8dfd-080020c28592}
udid:       IBM%5FDNES-318350Y%5FDISKS%5F%20%20%20%20%20%20%20%20AKFQ6556
site:       -
Multipathing information:
numpaths:   1
c0t12d0s2             state=enabled
```

What you see is that all the information that is obtained by reading the private region of the disk is lost when the disk is offlined. In effect, the offlined disk looks much like a disk that is physically accessible, but does not have a private region. So this is how you turn disks on and off in software (after all, now they are virtualized disks, so you should be able to, shouldn't you?).

RESERVED

The disk with the accessname c0t3d0s2 (adg02) carries the flag **reserved**. This flag is set by the administrator to keep VxVM from automatically allocating any storage from those disks that carry the flag. The command to set the **reserved** flag, or indeed any of the flags **reserved, failing, nohotuse,** or **spare,** is the following:

```
# vxedit -g $DG set $FLAG=on $Disk
```

Example:

```
# vxedit -g adg set reserved=on adg02
```

The result of setting the reserved flag is that if you do not specify this particular disk when creating, mirroring, or expanding volumes or when doing other actions that allocate storage (like moving a volume around, evacuating a disk or relayouting a volume), then it will not be used for storage allocation. However, as soon as you specify the disk using the "alloc=..." parameter it is again eligible for storage allocation.

SPARE

The disk with the accessname c0t11d0s2 (adg05) carries the flag spare. This flag is used to keep VxVM from automatically allocating any storage from those disks that carry the flag, just like the reserved flag we just discussed.

The difference between reserved and spare is that a disk flagged as spare will be preferred by VxVM's hot relocation functionality: Subdisks on a failed disks will be relocated to free disk space automatically. This process prefers disks flagged as spare, and excludes those marked with the nohotuse or reserved flag. Disks marked as spare will not be used for storage allocation unless they are specified using the "alloc=..." parameter.

As you will see below, the spare disk does not even show up in the free region list obtained by the vxdg free command. Remember the list of disks in the disk group looks like this:

```
# vxdisk list
DEVICE        TYPE           DISK      GROUP      STATUS
[...]
c0t2d0s2      auto           -         -          offline
c0t3d0s2      auto:cdsdisk   adg02     adg        online reserved
c0t4d0s2      auto:cdsdisk   adg03     adg        online failing
c0t10d0s2     auto:cdsdisk   adg04     adg        online nohotuse
c0t11d0s2     auto:cdsdisk   adg05     adg        online spare
c0t12d0s2     auto           -         -          offline
-             -        adg01     adg        removed was:c0t2d0s2
-             -        adg06     adg        failed was:c0t12d0s2
```

Not let's get the list of free extents (or regions):

```
# vxdg free
GROUP       DISK        DEVICE        TAG        OFFSET     LENGTH      FLAGS
adg         adg02       c0t3d0s2      c0t3d0     0          17702192    r
adg         adg04       c0t10d0s2     c0t10d0    0          17679776    n
```

Not let's get the list of free extents including the spare disk. We do so by passing the -a (all) switch to the vxdg free command.

```
# vxdg -a free
GROUP        DISK      DEVICE      TAG       OFFSET    LENGTH     FLAGS
adg          adg02     c0t3d0s2    c0t3d0    0         17702192   r
adg          adg04     c0t10d0s2   c0t10d0   0         17679776   n
adg          adg05     c0t11d0s2   c0t11d0   0         8378496    s
```

As you can see, specifying the -a flag allows the free region from the spare disk to show up. In theory, the same would happen if you specified the -r switch to vxassist. This is supposed (and documented in the vxassist man page) to override the spare flag and therefore allow allocation of free space on spare disks. However, it does not work in version 5.0 (Solaris) as the following example, based on the same set of disks and flags, shows:

```
# vxassist maxsize # Will use only adg04 as all others are flagged
Maximum volume size: 17678336 (8632Mb)
# vxassist -r maxsize # Will also use only adg04, which is a bug!
Maximum volume size: 17678336 (8632Mb)
```

The above shows that neither the spare (adg05) disk nor the reserved (adg02) disk has been added to the eligible storage pool by using the -r flag. The workaround for this bug is to explicitly specify the disk by name for vxassist allocation. This will override the spare flag and well as the reserved flag (but not the failing flag), yielding the desired result:

```
# vxassist -r maxsize alloc=adg04,adg02
Maximum volume size: 35381248 (17276Mb)
```

Passing specific disks on the command line overrides the flags previously set by the administrator. It does not, however, override another flag, which is usually set by the VxVM kernel (although it could be set manually, too): the failing flag

FAILING

If I/O to a subdisk leads to an unrecoverable read- or write-error, then the VxVM kernel automatically sets the failing-flag for the VM disk that the subdisk resides on. This flag by itself does not trigger any action on behalf of VxVM (but the underlying I/O error does trigger the relocation process unless the default has been changed), and it can indeed be set or reset by the administrator at will using the following command:

```
# vxedit -g $DG set failing=on $Disk
```

Example:

```
# vxedit -g adg set failing=on adg03
```

A failing disk will continue to be used as long as there are subdisks on it. The relocation process does try to move all subdisks away from a failing disk, but it may fail to allocate sufficient alternative storage. In that case, and while the relocation is in progress, I/O is still done to as well as from the failing disk.

The failing-flag can only be reset by specifying `failing=off` instead of `failing=on`. Because the VxVM flags are persisted onto the private region, the usual attempts by less experienced administrators (rebooting, running `vxdctl enable`, etc) do not bear fruit.

A disk that carries the `failing`-flag is not used for new subdisk allocation or subdisk extension by VxVM. There is also no way to force `vxassist` to allocate subdisk space from a disk marked as failing. It is possible using `vxmake sd`, but that is not of general interest, since the manual allocation of individual subdisks is not widely used and skips all reasonable tests (like excluding the use of failing disks :-).

If you are certain that a disk is erroneously labeled `failing`, then you can reset the flag using the command outlined above and use it. In the days of SAN-based LUNs seeing failing disks has become a rather seldom event. Disks are either present and reliable, or missing and accordingly appear as `failed` disks in the `vxdisk list` output.

FAILED

Volume Manager marks disks failed when the private region cannot be accessed. This is in contrast to failing disks, which is the state of a disk when only subdisk data cannot be accessed. Failure of I/O to the private region is more critical because VxVM cannot persist any meta data onto a disk in that case.

Because user data is meaningless without meta data pointing to it, the loss of the private region is considered a final blow to the disk, and it is therefore considered completely unusable. It does not appear in the main portion of the `vxdisk list` output any more, where all imported disk media are usually displayed next to their access names. Instead, it is listed as a record with no associated access record at the end of the `vxdisk list` output (see `adg06 in the last line` below).

```
# vxdisk list
DEVICE        TYPE           DISK      GROUP       STATUS
[...]
c0t2d0s2      auto           -         -           offline
c0t3d0s2      auto:cdsdisk   adg02     adg         online reserved
c0t4d0s2      auto:cdsdisk   adg03     adg         online failing
c0t10d0s2     auto:cdsdisk   adg04     adg         online nohotuse
c0t11d0s2     auto:cdsdisk   adg05     adg         online spare
c0t12d0s2     auto           -         -           offline
-             -              adg01     adg         removed was:c0t2d0s2
-             -              adg06     adg         failed was:c0t12d0s2
```

NOHOTUSE

A disk is never flagged nohotuse automatically, by VxVM itself. This option is meant exclusively for the administrator in order to exclude disks from serving as a target for hot relocation. If you want to prevent hot relocation altogether it is not the best solution to flag all of the disks nohotuse. Rather, it is preferable to keep the relocation daemon from starting up in the boot process. This saves computer resources and serves the same purpose.

REMOVED

This last flag is set by VxVM when a disk is removed from a Disk group even if there are still subdisks allocated from its public region. Information about these subdisks must not get lost when the disk is removed, and so the Disk group keeps the disk record inside the disk group, but flags the disk as removed in the private region data base.

```
# vxdisk list
DEVICE        TYPE            DISK       GROUP      STATUS
[...]
c0t2d0s2      auto            -          -          offline
c0t3d0s2      auto:cdsdisk    adg02      adg        online reserved
c0t4d0s2      auto:cdsdisk    adg03      adg        online failing
c0t10d0s2     auto:cdsdisk    adg04      adg        online nohotuse
c0t11d0s2     auto:cdsdisk    adg05      adg        online spare
c0t12d0s2     auto            -          -          offline
-             -            adg01      adg        removed was:c0t2d0s2
-             -            adg06      adg        failed was:c0t12d0s2
```

14.1.1 SUMMARY

In this chapter we talked about states that can be flagged on a disk, like being reserved for, or excluded from hot relocation, becoming defective, being defective, or being removed from the disk group. We also learned that you can switch a disk on and off in software. But the flags themselves are only part of the game: It's how the VxVM state machine operates on them that makes understanding them worthwhile. For instance, you could temporarily exclude a number of disks from allocation simply by setting their failing or reserved flag, then resetting it later, after the allocation has been done.

As is the case with many UNIX software systems, VxVM is a very universal tool set that can be used as intended. But its mechanisms can also be used in ways the inventors may not have thought of. As long as you stay within reasonable limits, everything should still work fine.

CHAPTER 15: STORAGE FOUNDATION SOFTWARE STACK

by Volker Herminghaus

15.1 SOFTWARE OVERVIEW

Veritas Volume Manager operates in both user space and kernel space: User mode programs like vxassist interact with other user space programs like vxconfigd to create, modify, and delete volumes and other virtual objects. This is done during preparation of the volumes (i.e. creating them or starting them after importing a disk group) as well as during maintenance on the volumes (like resizing them or handling snapshots) or diagnosis (like running the vxprint and vxdisk list commands). In a running system where all necessary volumes have been started the only parts of VxVM actually needed are the device drivers that map volume regions to physical disk regions by applying the plex mapping table to I/O request (vxio) and for multiplexing disk paths (vxdmp). Of course it would be a very radical approach to try it, and full functionality could not be guaranteed, but it is in fact possible to run a UNIX machine using VxVM volumes without a single Volume Manager process running. It would not be possible to do any kind of maintenance on the volumes, like starting or stopping them, or importing or deporting a disk group, but those volumes that have already been started would be running perfectly well. This was a deliberate design decision by the developers because it eliminates a possible single point of failure: If a user process was necessary to enable volume I/O, then a system might be rendered unusable if this process crashed or was stopped by the user. Device drivers, unlike user processes, cannot be killed or unconfigured "against their will". Having the system be independent from user space processes for the bulk of the work (user I/O) was therefore a wise thing to do.

V. Herminghaus and A. Sriba, *Storage Management in Data Centers*,
DOI: 10.1007/978-3-540-85023-6_15, © Springer-Verlag Berlin Heidelberg 2009

15.1.1 STRUCTURE OF STORAGE FOUNDATION COMPONENTS

The graphic depiction shown below outlines the main components of storage foundation and their interaction. It serves as the basis for understanding the more complex environment of a full storage foundation installation. Depicting all the interdependencies would require a much larger canvas, and it is not really necessary to understand every aspect of the software stack; one can do a lot of useful work with just the basics.

The upper part of the diagram shows the user level programs, while the lower part shows the kernel level drivers, devices, and memory regions. The black arrows identify user-I/O and the grey arrows stand for control or metadata I/O. For instance, reading the diagram top down from the left we can see that a vxassist command to create a new volume contacts vxconfigd, which in turn contacts the config device. The config device is implemented by the vxspec device driver. The config device creates a new volume with its associated I/O mapping, stores it in the kernel memory region reserved for such information (the **volume mapping** cloud), and persists it to the private regions of the affected disk group via the vxdmp driver. The vxdmp driver alternates between all the available sd paths that are visible to vxdmp. Those paths are routed via fibre-channel (fc) drivers to their ultimate goal, the LUN. The information about the paths is gathered upon enabling the vxconfigd. This takes place automatically at boot time.

On the way back, I/O errors that become visible to vxio because they cannot be remedied by the vxdmp driver will be reported back to the vxspec driver, which passes them on to the vcevent device for notification to all connected vxnotify clients

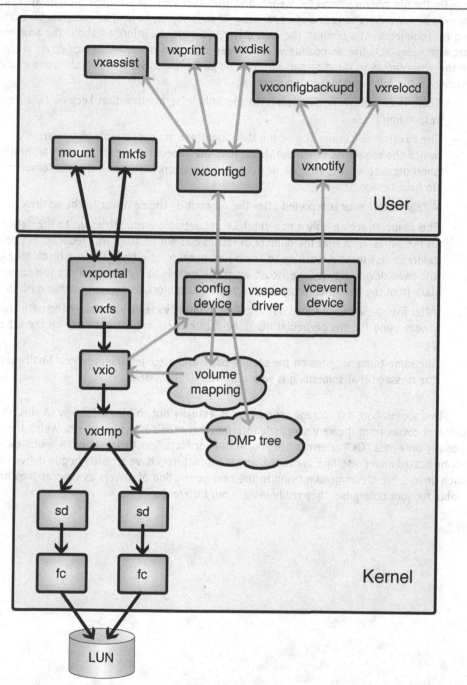

Figure 15-1:   Storage Foundation's main components and their mutual rela-
tionships

On the file system side, mkfs, mount, and any other user I/O is routed via the vxportal or vxfs device drivers to vxio and on to vxdmp. It follows that as long as vxdmp is still waiting for completion of a request, the vxio driver will never be informed about the problem because vxdmp acts like an opaque wall between vxio and the lower device driver layers. In the setup shown in the diagram, with two sd paths routed via two fc paths, one might encounter the following a common problem:

- There is an underlying problem with the SAN infrastructure that keeps a LUN from responding
- The fc driver will typically give the LUN about one minute to reply to a request, after which the request is timed out. Note that the timeout can not be made arbitrarily short because we are, after all, dealing with a network here, and networks sometimes do have benign delays.
- A "non-fatal" error is reported after the timeout by the fc driver to the sd driver
- The sd driver, seeing only a non-fatal, i.e. recoverable error, retries up to the default of five times. Note that the number of retries can not be arbitrarily reduced. We certainly do not want a machine to crash just because of a bad CRC in a block on e.g. the swap device, do we? We would want the system to try hard and get the correct data from the disk, then possibly revector the bad block to prevent further mishap.
- After five retries, each timed out after one minute, vxdmp will consider the path that it was using for this particular I/O to be faulted and will retry the I/O on the other path.
- The same thing happens on the second path, and after ten minutes vxio finally gets the message that something is wrong in the I/O subsystem.

This sounds bad, but storage foundation is actually not to blame for any of this. The problem comes from the very simplistic interface between fc and sd drivers, which traditionally only pass "OK" or errors like "non-fatal" or "fatal" to their parent. A much more sophisticated driver interface is needed, and manufacturers have recently begun delivering such drivers. We recommend moving to the new generation of drivers as soon as they are viable for your enterprise. They really make a big difference.

Technical Deep Dive

15.2 KERNEL SPACE DRIVERS

Veritas Volume Manager operates in both user space and kernel space: User mode programs are run to create, modify, and delete virtual objects, which are used by kernel drivers as replacements for physical disk media. The glue between user space programs and kernel space device drivers is the ioctl system call interface, via which the user mode programs can communicate their requests to the device drivers and thus effect changes to kernel mode variables.

Several device drivers are added to the system when installing storage foundation. We will discuss these drivers below. You can find them by searching for the string "^vx" in the /etc/name_to_major file which maps the device drivers' major numbers to their respective names. You can also run the modinfo command and search for " vx" in its output.

Finding all device drivers in a fully installed Storage Foundation 5.0 on Solaris 10 SPARC will get you a similar output to the following:

```
# grep vx /etc/name_to_major
vxportal 267
vxdmp 269
vxio 270
vxspec 271
vxfen 274

# modinfo|grep " vx"
 26  12b2b78  37f28 269   1  vxdmp (VxVM 5.0-2006-05-11a: DMP Drive)
 28  7c002000 337840 270   1  vxio (VxVM 5.0-2006-05-11a I/O driver)
 30  12e6ce0    d48 271   1  vxspec (VxVM 5.0-2006-05-11a control/st)
156  7bffce58    c30 267   1  vxportal (VxFS 5.0_REV-5.0A55_sol portal )
157  7b200000 1ba6d0  20   1  vxfs (VxFS 5.0_REV-5.0A55_sol SunOS 5)

# ls -lL /dev/vx|grep "^c"
crw-------  1 root   sys      271,      6 Aug  2 16:12 clust
crw-------  1 root   sys      271,      0 Aug  2 16:10 config
crw-r-----  1 root   sys      269, 262143 Aug  2 16:12 dmpconfig
crw-------  1 root   sys      271,      3 Aug  2 16:12 info
crw-------  1 root   sys      271,      2 Aug  2 16:18 iod
crw-------  1 root   sys      271,      7 Aug  2 16:18 netiod
crw-------  1 root   sys      271,      4 Aug  2 16:18 task
crw-------  1 root   sys      271,      5 Aug  2 16:18 taskmon
crw-------  1 root   sys      271,      1 Aug  2 16:18 trace
crw-------  1 root   sys      271,      8 Aug  2 16:18 vcevent
```

As you can see, most of the device files in the /dev/vx directory are instances of the vxspec device driver, which in our case has the major number 271. The only other driver is called dmpconfig, and it has the same major number as the vxdmp driver (269).

Let's look at the individual drivers one by one:

VXPORTAL

The vxportal device driver is used by vxfs file system utilities such as mkfs, mount, and fsadm, by the storage checkpoint administration utilities fsckptadm and fsckpt_restore and the quota utilities vxquotaon and vxquotaoff. Some commands may need to issue an ioctl to the VxFS modules even if no VxFS file systems are currently mounted. This attempt would fail because the vxfs device driver would not be active. For these cases the vxportal driver supplies the required interface to talk to the vxfs modules regardless of actual file systems being mounted.

VXDMP

The vxdmp driver has been discussed before and we would like to keep redundancy limited to volumes. Suffice it to say that the /dev/vx/dmpconfig device file is used to send ioctls to the vxdmp device driver to get and set operating modes etc. The individual devices reside in the /dev/vx/dmp and /dev/vx/rdmp directories and are (of course) also instances of the vxdmp device driver.

VXFEN

This driver is used by the Veritas Cluster Server in order to ensure that data is unharmed in split-brain situations (split-brain is a situation in which members of a cluster are unaware of the other members' existence and erroneously take over their services, leading to unco-ordinated write I/O on the shared storage. Because this corrupts data as well as metadata, even disk group private regions, it is generally considered a Very Bad Thing™ and VCS goes to great lengths to avoid this situation). It is not normally used in plain Volume Manger setups without clustering, and is not further discussed here. We are planning a new book about Veritas Cluster Server which will discuss this topic in detail.

VXSPEC

This device driver has multiple instances which all do quite different tasks, as you can see from the multiple instances of its major number (271) in the output of the ls command above. These instances are:

CLUST (VXCLUST)

This instance is used for clustered Volume Manager setups. It is used by vxconfigd, vxclust, vxdctl and vxdg.

CONFIG (VXCONFIG)

This device file is used for creating and modifying virtual objects. It was designed to be used solely by the vxconfigd process and can only ever be opened by one process at a time. The configuration daemon, vxconfigd, downloads volume configuration and address mapping into the kernel, and creates, deletes, and modifies virtual objects via this device.

INFO (VXINFO)

This device gathers and clears performance statistics for volume, plex, subdisk, and disk media objects from the kernel. It is used by very many of the VxVM utilities.

IOD (VXIOD)

This device is used to control the number and the behavior of the vxiod daemons. These daemons are discussed elsewhere in this book. They are mostly used for increasing the degree to which I/O can be done asynchronously.

NETIOD (VXNETIOD)

This device is used by /usr/sbin/vxnetd in Veritas Volume Replicator (VVR) setups.

TASK (VXTASK) / TASKMON (VXTASKMON)

These device files are used to create and query kernel level tasks in VxVM.

TRACE (VXTRACE)

This device is used by /usr/sbin/vxtrace to read all pre- and post-volume mapping I/Os, error records etc. from the kernel. It is not used by any other process.

VCEVENT (VXVCEVENT)

This instance of vxspec delivers events to the process that opens the device and reads from it. The most common user of this device file is the vxnotify command, which in turn is used by the relocation daemon (vxrelocd) to relocate subdisks from failed disks to free storage. In order to find failed disks vxrelocd spawns a vxnotify program which opens the /dev/vx/vcevent driver file. As soon as the Volume Manager kernel notices any configuration change, the vcevent driver passes that event to the listening process which can then act on the data supplied with the event in whichever way it deems appropriate. For instance, the vxnotify program will output the formatted data on its stdout channel.

Other clients for the vcevent device file are the vxcvol and vxibc commands, which are used in Veritas Volume Replicator (VVR) setups and are not discussed here.

VXIO

This is probably the most important driver of VxVM, since it is this driver that does the actual volume I/O mapping function. It reads the volume configuration that `vxconfigd` has previously downloaded into the kernel using the `vxconfig` device, and uses it to map the volume regions to their physical disk region counterparts. This driver uses the `vxdmp` driver to actually do read and write I/Os instead of the plain `sd` drivers. In addition, the `vxio` driver supports `ioctls` to inquire the process-ID of the configuration daemon `vxconfigd`, to detach a plex from a volume, to obtain an information record about a volume and to initiate `atomic copy` and `verify read` or `verify write` commands.

All volume block and character devices use the `vxio` driver and therefore the major number of all files addressed by /dev/vx/*dsk/*/* show up as (in our case) 270.

15.3 USER SPACE PROCESSES

Finding all Veritas Volume Manager processes in a running system is easy if you use the `ptools` located in /usr/proc/bin: For instance, the `pgrep` command searches the process table much more efficiently and much more precisely than any of the clumsy command chains that look like this:

```
ps -ef | grep -v grep | grep "vx" | awk '{ print $1 }'
```

The latter is a truly horrible, yet nearly ubiquitous construct, which will not only fail to find any process that happens to have the string "grep" anywhere in its command line, but it also spawns three extra processes (two `grep` and one `awk`). This is especially nasty if you recall that `awk` does in fact a much better job at `grep`'ing than `grep` does, so the two `grep` commands are really just overhead. But the biggest performance hog is the `ps` command, which uses the ancient approach of scanning the kernel's internal process table structure instead of resorting to the modern and fast /proc file system. We have found the disgusting contraption shown above in so many places that we cannot restrain ourselves from taking the opportunity to show you a better way. If you never use this kind of command chain to find a process then please consider yourself complimented by the authors; you are one out of a thousand that does it right!

After this short rant, here's how you really get all Veritas Volume Manager processes. The example below is from our Solaris 10 SPARC host running SF5.0 after a default installation:

```
# pgrep -lf vx
52 vxconfigd -x syslog -m boot
1649 /sbin/sh - /usr/lib/vxvm/bin/vxconfigbackupd
1021 /sbin/sh - /usr/lib/vxvm/bin/vxrelocd root
204 /sbin/vxesd
851 /opt/VRTSsmf/bin/vxsmf.bin -p RootSMF -B
915 /sbin/sh - /usr/lib/vxvm/bin/vxrelocd root
928 /sbin/sh - /usr/lib/vxvm/bin/vxconfigbackupd
791 /opt/VRTSob/bin/vxsvc -r /etc/vx/isis/Registry -e
```

```
693 /opt/VRTSobc/pal33/bin/vxpal -a VAILAgent -x
797 /opt/VRTSobc/pal33/bin/vxpal -a StorageAgent -x
877 /opt/VRTSsmf/bin/vxsmf.bin -p ICS -c /etc/vx/VxSMF/VxSMF.cfg --parentversion
1.
1000 /sbin/sh - /usr/lib/vxvm/bin/vxcached root
1001 vxnotify -C -w 15
916 /sbin/sh - /usr/lib/vxvm/bin/vxcached root
1650 vxnotify
1022 vxnotify -f -w 15
```

Here's the more structured output from a `ptree` command:

```
# ptree | grep vx
52      vxconfigd -x syslog -m boot
204     /sbin/vxesd
693     /opt/VRTSobc/pal33/bin/vxpal -a VAILAgent -x
791     /opt/VRTSob/bin/vxsvc -r /etc/vx/isis/Registry -e
797     /opt/VRTSobc/pal33/bin/vxpal -a StorageAgent -x
851     /opt/VRTSsmf/bin/vxsmf.bin -p RootSMF -B
 877    /opt/VRTSsmf/bin/vxsmf.bin -p ICS -c /etc/vx/VxSMF/VxSMF.cfg --parentve
915     /sbin/sh - /usr/lib/vxvm/bin/vxrelocd root
 1021   /sbin/sh - /usr/lib/vxvm/bin/vxrelocd root
   1022 vxnotify -f -w 15
916     /sbin/sh - /usr/lib/vxvm/bin/vxcached root
 1000   /sbin/sh - /usr/lib/vxvm/bin/vxcached root
   1001 vxnotify -C -w 15
928     /sbin/sh - /usr/lib/vxvm/bin/vxconfigbackupd
 1649   /sbin/sh - /usr/lib/vxvm/bin/vxconfigbackupd
   1650 vxnotify
```

There are many VxVM processes running — sixteen altogether, usually even more (some of the agents failed to start on our system: `actionagent` and `gridnode`) — of which many are not really necessary. The important ones are highlighted above. Being the frugal sysadmin type, we should try to get rid of as many unnecessary processes as possible, for the obvious reasons. But we need to be sure we know what we are doing, so what exactly are all these processes doing?

15.4 REDUCING VxVM's FOOTPRINT

Let's take a look at all the processes in the output above and see what they do and if we could just get rid of them without affecting operations. Note that you may lose support from the vendor by doing so. Consider this a theoretical exploration rather than a hands-on guide; we obviously do not take responsibility for anyone messing with the VxVM processes on production machines!

15.4.1 Essential VxVM Processes

VXCONFIGD

Do not stop this process. If it is stopped you can not use any of the other vx* commands any more, since they all communicate with the VxVM kernel via this daemon. Note that I/O to those volumes which are already started is not affected, but configuration changes — even those of the simplest kind — cannot be initiated any more.

VXESD

This process (called the event source daemon) tracks events on the fibre-channel fabric and triggers updates to the vxdmp device tree in case of a fabric reconfiguration. It is probably wise to keep it running if you are allocating your storage from a SAN, but you can certainly turn it off if you use pure SCSI disks (but then: who does?). The event source daemon uses the Storage Networks Industry Association's (SNIA) HBA API to gather fabric topology information and to correlate LUN paths information with World Wide Names and array port IDs, so it is only useful if your array and/or HBA driver vendor supports this protocol.

VXRELOCD WITH VXNOTIFY

The relocation daemon, important for automatic restoration of the redundancy of volumes which encountered I/O errors. The relocation daemon is actually a shell script which spawns a vxnotify process with parameters that make vxnotify return only faults, and batch all events together that are not separated by at least a 15-second interval without any events. This vxnotify process connects to the vcevent driver (see above) to be informed whenever any kind of fault is incurred. It then passes the fault as plain text to the calling vxrelocd process, which operates on the output, finds the faulted disks and relocates the subdisks from redundant volumes if the corresponding regions are still readable from another plex. It also sends e-mail to the administrator during all stages of its recovery attempts. Some administrators prefer to turn hot relocation off because they want to keep full control over storage allocation at all times. This is best done by uncommenting the appropriate line in the boot script (/lib/svc/method/vxvm-recover in Solaris 10).

15.4.2 Unessential VxVM Processes

VXSVC

This is the server process for the vea GUI. It is based on the antique and arcane CORBA (common object request broker architecture) and frequently takes several minutes to shut down, resulting in excessive delays when a machine running it must be rebooted cleanly (i.e. using init 6 rather than reboot). Unless your admins rely on the vea GUI for maintenance it may be a good idea to shut this server process down. While the GUI does enable the novice user to handle VxVM tasks in a relatively simple fashion, it often comes as a negative surprise to most UNIX users that the vxsvc process uses a registry file (/etc/vx/ isis/Registry) that tries to emulate the much-hated Windows registry. Here are some lines from the beginning of the file:

```
KEY „HKEY_LOCAL_MACHINE" (
        KEY „Software" (
                KEY „VERITAS" (
[...]
                [REG_SZ] „DomainController" = "<aHostname>";
```

That's right: HKEY_LOCAL_MACHINE! DomainController! REG_SZ! It is not immediately obvious what kind of advantage the addition of a registry would bring to a UNIX machine. But that is not the only Windows-like thing that vxsvc brought to UNIX. Its developers also added a ".ini"-file to Storage Foundation. This is what it looks like on our host:

```
# cat /etc/vx/isis/types.ini
[ALLOWED_MERGE_FAILURE]
vrts_vail* = "";
[...]
```

A true ".ini"-file, with the original Windows-ini-file syntax! On UNIX. No comment.

To summarize, the vxsvc process brings a lot of Windows to your UNIX machine. Whether you will think twice about deploying it, or whether you will leap into the air overjoyed about having The Power Of Windows™ on your UNIX system is of course up to you.

Keep in mind, however, that without vxsvc the new feature called Intelligent Storage Provisioning (ISP) will not work, so if you actually need that you will have to accept vxsvc on your machine.

15.4.3 Potentially Undesirable VxVM Processes

VXSMF

Called the system management framework and very poorly documented, this process "is primarily intended for developers and technical support staff. Customers should use this utility only under the guidance of a technical support person" (from the man page). It starts the initial Symantec Service Management Framework root process and all subordinate processes that are configured for the root process. The system management framework is a layer of communication and action daemons designed to enable inquiries and actions from a central management workstation to and from all machines in a data center. For instance, one could use the central management workstation to get a quick overview of the Storage Foundation licensing situation. Another interesting feature is the ability to query all storage layers as to how much of the storage arrays' total available storage is actually used for file system data. And storage arrays may be easily migrated from the management workstation because all connections from hosts to storage arrays are known to the central management workstation and can be replicated on the target array, the volumes could be mirrored to the target array, then the old mirrors removed from the source array etc.

This sounds truly great, if it works. What's not so great about it is that in order to keep this communication infrastructure secure, a whole authentication and authorization infrastructure must be built and maintained, a lot of processes are running on each host, and a number of ports must be opened for the communication to take place. Because the whole framework is (as of mid-2008, at least) rather poorly documented, it is not easy to convince anyone to actually use this additional layer. If you are not using it, then it is probably a good idea to shut it down and disable it from starting upon reboot.

VXPAL WITH STORAGEAGENT, GRIDNODE, ACTIONAGENT, VAIlAGENT ETC.

This daemon runs or issues commands to Veritas Provider Access Layer agents ("pal" stands for Provider Access Layer). The Provider Access Layer controls access to the software bus that is used by the so-called "providers" to interoperate with remote management processes like the GUI or the system management workstation outlined above. You can find the list of providers using the following command:

```
# pkginfo|grep "VRTS[^ ]*pr"
application VRTSddlpr    VERITAS Device Discovery Layer Services Provider
application VRTSfspro    VxFS Management Services Provider by Symantec
DataStorage VRTSmapro   Veritas Storage Mapping Provider from Symantec
application VRTSvmpro    VxVM Management Services Provider by Symantec
application VRTSvrpro    VVR Management Services Provider by Symantec
```

VXCONFIGBACKUPD

The configuration backup daemon. It uses a vxnotify process, similar to the way that vxrelocd does, to track changes to configurations in disk groups. Upon receiving a notification of a change it dumps all of the configuration information for the disk group affected to a backup directory (/etc/vx/cbr/bk/$DGID).

Originally a good idea, this feature is of rather dubious value today, as the concept has been altered (as a workaround for a serious flaw) to the point of making it almost worthless. The idea was to provide a means of "going back in time" several versions if something bad happened to your disk group, like if you accidentally deleted the wrong volume. Using the configuration backup that was previously created by the vxconfigbackupd one could reapply the private region contents of an earlier state of the disk group when the volume still existed. For that reason, earlier versions of Storage Foundation (4.x) kept up to six generations of disk group configuration backups. That turned out to be a problem, because with the size of the configuration data being about 24MB (at the time of writing this), having a lot of disk groups on a system would fill up the root file system very rapidly. For instance, a system with 30 disk groups would hold 6 generations of 30 disk group configuration backup copies at 24MB each, totalling over 4GB! This is less of a problem now but is certainly was a few years ago. That was the flaw mentioned above.

So the number of generations was cut from six to one. That was the workaround.

The reason why it is almost useless is the following: Any configuration change is immediately passed to the vxconfigbackupd, which will immediately overwrite the sole existing backup of the configuration with the current configuration. I.e. the backup is overwritten at the same time as the data is. There are only to ways to actually use the configuration backup data: One is to recover the most recent version of the configuration backup from tape. But that may not be up to data enough to use it. The other way — and that is what the vendor now officially announces its purpose to be — is to use it as a backup solely in case of unintended physical damage to the private region database, not for error recovery.

How does the vxconfigbackupd create its configuration backup? When vxconfigbackupd determines that the configuration must be backup up it runs vxconfigbackup, which in turn executes a number of commands, like vxdisk list, vxdctl support, vxprivutil dumpconfig etc., and saves the output in flat files. These commands can take a nontrivial amount of time and resources to execute, and generate about 24MB of data. Because the whole process is done every time the configuration of a disk group changes it can be very wasteful to keep this daemon running. Some examples of when a configuration backup is triggered include: creating a volume, resizing a volume, starting a volume, stopping a volume, importing a disk group, deporting a disk group, adding a disk to or removing a disk from a disk group. Weighing the likelihood of the configuration backup being able to help you out versus the amount of overhead created by generating of the configuration backup is up of course to you.

VXCACHED

The cache daemon vxcached catches notifications about cache volumes that are close to being full, and resizes them automatically for those cache volumes where such behavior was configured. A cache volume is a volume destined to hold the original data for incremental snapshots of several volumes. Setting up a group of incremental snapshots to write into a single cache volume is rather complicated and does not offer a huge advantage over more conventional approaches so we have not discussed the use of shared cache snapshots in this book.

INDEX

C

E

F

M

P

Q

R

S

T

U

W